Encyclopedia of Heads of States and Governments,
1900 through 1945

Encyclopedia of
Heads of States
and Governments
1900 through 1945

HARRIS M. LENTZ III

A companion volume to the author's 1994 volume
*Heads of States and Governments: A Worldwide Encyclopedia
of Over 2,300 Leaders, 1945 through 1992*

McFarland & Company, Inc., Publishers
Jefferson, North Carolina, and London

British Library Cataloguing-in-Publication data are available

Library of Congress Cataloguing-in-Publication Data

Lentz, Harris M.
    Encyclopedia of heads of states and governments, 1900
through 1945 / Harris M. Lentz III.
        p.   cm.
    Includes bibliographical references and index.
    ISBN 0-7864-0500-7 (library binding : 50# alkaline paper) ∞
    1. Heads of state—Biography.   2. Statesmen—Biography.
3. Biography—20th century.   I. Title.
D412.L45   1999
920'.009'04—dc21   98-53751
                                                        CIP

Manufactured in the United States of America

McFarland & Company, Inc., Publishers
  Box 611, Jefferson, North Carolina 28640

To Carla D. Clark
with gratitude and affection

Acknowledgments

I would like to thank the many individuals and institutions that assisted with this work by supplying me with information, reading my material, and encouraging my completion of this project. Special thanks to Carla Clark, whose assistance and friendship made the book possible. Also, I would like to express gratitude to my mother, Helene Z. Lentz, and my friends Nina and Mark Heffington, Kent Nelson, Anne and Monty Taylor, Doy L. Daniels, Jr., Tony Pruitt, Bobby Mathews, Casey Jones, Bettie Dawson, Dale Warren, Ed and Mary Anne Kuisbert, Paul Geary, Joy Martin, George and Leona Alsup, Fred Davis, Rosa Burnett, Nikki and Jimmy Walker, Laura Hunt, Denise Tansil, Gary Holder, and the fine folks at J. Alexander's, James Gattas and the Fox & Hound. Also, thanks to the Embassy of Finland, the Swiss Consulate, the Embassy of Chile, the Embassy of the Dominican Republic, the Embassy of Romania, the Embassy of El Salvador, Cornell University, the Embassy of Peru, Memphis and Shelby County Public Libraries, State Technical Institute Library, and the University of Memphis Library.

Contents

Preface

The first half of the twentieth century was one of the most turbulent in human history. Two world wars and numerous smaller conflicts during this period did much to shape the political and geographical landscape of today. With this book I hope to shed some light on the nearly 1,200 leaders who governed their respective nations between January 1, 1900, and December 31, 1945. I hope the reader will gain a sense of the history of each country covered through the biographical sketches of each leader. Some of the figures found in this book have left an indelible mark on the country they governed and, in some cases, the world at large; others are scarcely remembered even in their own homeland. Some brought peace and prosperity to their lands; others brought ruination and disaster. Some governed for decades; others lasted scarcely a day in power.

I have included all countries that had independent governments during the period of time covered. Some nations (e.g., Montenegro, Serbia, Saxony) were annexed or incorporated into other countries. Other countries were created or granted their independence during this period (e.g., Poland, Yugoslavia, Panama). Colonial administrations are not covered in this book, but some countries largely ruled by colonial powers, but with a semiautonomous government (e.g., Egypt, Zanzibar, Vietnam) will be found here.

I have attempted to include all elected, appointed, hereditary, or proclaimed leaders of the countries included. Typically, a monarch, president, or military junta leader is considered the head of state; a prime minister, premier, or grand vizier is considered the head of government. I have also included interim presidents for most nations. These were typically individuals who held the office for a short time between terms of elected presidents. Their entries are often brief. Most "acting presidents" are not included, however; in many countries an acting president takes over whenever the head of state is unable to perform his duties—often including times when the president is simply traveling out of the country. These individuals have virtually no impact on the government. I have included only a handful of acting

1

presidents who took their office because of the physical incapacity of the president.

The countries are listed alphabetically by the English-language name by which they are most commonly known. Places mentioned within individual entries are located within the countries being discussed unless otherwise indicated. I have generally used the current name of cities and towns within an entry (e.g., St. Petersburg for Leningrad). The name of the country is followed by a brief geographical and historical description. The biographical entries then follow, with heads of state listed in chronological order by term of office. They are followed by heads of government. When an individual has served multiple terms of office, the biographical entry follows the earliest listed term. For subsequent terms of office the reader is referred to the leader's first entry.

The entries of the leaders give biographical information, including dates of birth and death, where possible. I have also tried to include pertinent information concerning political careers and important events that occurred during the person's term of office. In all cases I have attempted to use the most common spelling of names of individuals and locations, consulting *The New York Times*, the *Encyclopaedia Britannica*, the *Times of London* and various reference works concerning individual countries as primary sources for spelling and diacritical marks. I have also relied upon official government information from the individual countries in regard to this matter.

Whenever possible I have verified facts in at least two sources, though it was sometimes necessary to rely on biographical information from a single reliable source on the more obscure leaders. I consulted a myriad of sources in compiling this book, including newspapers, encyclopedias, histories, and biographies. My research also included contact with the embassies and governments of many of the countries listed in this work, and in some cases I directly contacted individual heads of state or members of their families to ascertain accurate biographical information. I have attempted to make this book as comprehensive and as easy to use as possible.

Bibliography

BOOKS

Afghanistan: A Country Study. Washington, D.C.: U.S. Government Printing Office, 1986.

Alexander, Robert J., ed. *Biographical Dictionary of Latin American and Caribbean Political Leaders.* New York: Greenwood Press, 1988.

Algeria: A Country Study. Washington, D.C.: U.S. Government Printing Office, 1986.

Alisky, Marvin. *Historical Dictionary of Peru.* Metuchen, NJ: Scarecrow, 1979.

Ameringer, Charles D. *Don Pepe: A Political Biography of Jose Figueres of Costa Rica.* Albuquerque, NM: University of New Mexico Press, 1978.

Amirsadeghi, Hossein. *Twentieth Century Iran.* New York: Holmes and Meier, 1977.

Andersson, Ingvar. *A History of Sweden.* London: Weidenfeld and Nicolson, 1956.

Archer, Jules. *The Dictators.* New York: Bantam, 1968.

Arvil, Pierre. *Politics in France.* Baltimore: Penguin, 1969.

The Australian Encyclopedia. Sydney: Grolier Society of Australia, 1983.

Ayany, Samuel G. *A History of Zanzibar.* Nairobi: East Africa Literature Bureau, 1970.

Ayling, S.E. *Portraits of Power.* New York: Barnes and Noble, 1961.

Azimi, Fakhreddin. *Iran: The Crisis of Democracy, 1941–1953.* New York: St. Martin's, 1989.

Banani, Amin. *The Modernization of Iran, 1921–1941.* Stanford, CA: Stanford University Press, 1961.

Barteau, Harry C. *Historical Dictionary of Luxembourg.* Lanham, MD: Scarecrow, 1996.

Bizzarro, Salvatore. *Historical Dictionary of Chile.* Metuchen, NJ: Scarecrow, 1972.

Bolloten, Burnett. *The Spanish Civil War.* Chapel Hill: University of North Carolina Press, 1995.

Boorman, Howard L., ed. *Biographical Dictionary of the Republic of China.* New York: Columbia University Press, 1967.

Brace, Richard M. *Morocco Algeria Tunisia.* Englewood Cliffs, NJ: Prentice-Hall, 1964.

Brown, Archie, ed. *The Soviet Union: A Biographical Dictionary.* New York: Macmillan, 1991.

Bruegel, J.W. *Czechoslovakia Before Munich.* London: Cambridge University Press, 1973.

Bullock, Alan, and R.B. Woodlings, eds. *Twentieth Century Culture.* New York: Harper & Row, 1983.

Burns, E. Bradford. *A History of Brazil.* New York: Columbia University Press, 1980.

Calder, Bruce J. *The Impact of Intervention*. Austin: University of Texas Press, 1984.
Cambridge History of Japan. 6 vols. New York: Cambridge University Press, 1988.
Cammaerts, Emile. *Albert of Belgium*. London: Ivor Nicholson & Watson Ltd., 1935.
Carr, Raymond. *Spain, 1808–1975*. Oxford: Clarendon Press, 1983.
Chapman, Charles E. *A History of the Cuban Republic*. New York: Octagon Books, 1969.
Collier, Simon, Harold Blakemore and Thomas E. Skidmore, eds. *The Cambridge Encyclopedia of Latin America and the Caribbean*. Cambridge: Cambridge University Press, 1985.
Columbia Encyclopedia. Morningside Heights, NJ: Columbia University Press, 1950.
Coutouvidis, John, and Jaime Reynolds. *Poland 1939–1947*. New York: Holmes & Meir, 1986.
Creedman, Theodore S. *Historical Dictionary of Costa Rica*. Metuchen, NJ: Scarecrow, 1977.
Davis, Robert H. *Historical Dictionary of Colombia*. Metuchen, NJ: Scarecrow, 1977.
Delpar, Helen, ed. *Encyclopedia of Latin America*. New York: McGraw-Hill, 1974.
Derry, T.K. *A History of Modern Norway 1814–1972*. Oxford: Clarendon Press, 1973.
Dunn, E. Elmwood, and Svend E. Holcoe. *Historical Dictionary of Liberia*. Metuchen, NJ: Scarecrow, 1985.
Dupree, Louis. *Afghanistan*. Princeton, NJ: Princeton University Press, 1973.
Edelman, Marc, and Joanne Kennen, eds. *The Costa Rica Reader*. New York: Grove Weidenfeld, 1989.
Egypt: A Country Study. Washington, DC: U.S. Government Printing Office, 1991.
Embree, Ainslie T., ed. *Encyclopedia of Asian History*. New York: Scribner's.
Encyclopaedia Britannica. Chicago: Encyclopaedia Britannica, various editions.
Encyclopedia of Asian History. New York: Scribner's, 1988.
Encyclopedia of the Modern Middle East. 4 vols. New York: Macmillan, 1996.
Eyck, Erich. *History of the Weimar Republic*. Cambridge, MA: Harvard University Press, 1963.
Ezergails, Andrew. *The 1917 Revolution in Latvia*. London: Columbia University Press, 1974.
Flemion, Philip F. *Historical Dictionary of El Salvador*. Metuchen, NJ: Scarecrow, 1972.
Fryxell, Anders. *History of Sweden*. London: Richard Bently, 1944.
Galdames, Louis. *A History of Chile*. New York: Russell & Russell, 1964.
Galindez, Jesus de. *The Era of Trujillo*. Tucson: University of Arizona Press, 1973.
Gjerset, Knut. *The History of Norwegian People*. New York: Arno Press, 1969.
Goldstein, Melvyn C. *A History of Modern Tibet, 1913–1951*. Berkeley: University of California Press, 1989.
Goldwert, Marvin. *Democracy, Militarism, and Nationalism in Argentina, 1930–1966*. Austin: University of Texas Press, 1972.
Gregorian, Vartan. *The Emergence of Modern Afghanistan*. Stanford, CA: Stanford University Press, 1972.
Griffiths, John C. *Modern Iceland*. New York: Frederick A. Praeger, 1969.
Hayes, Paul M. *Quisling*. New York: Newton Abbot, 1971.
Heath, Dwight B. *Historical Dictionary of Bolivia*. Metuchen, NJ: Scarecrow, 1972.
Hedrick, Basil C., and Anne Hedrick. *Historical Dictionary of Panama*. Metuchen, NJ: Scarecrow, 1970.
Heinl, Robert Debs, Jr., and Nancy Gordon Heinl. *Written in Blood: The Story of the Haitian People 1492–1971*. Boston: Houghton-Mifflin, 1978.
Held, Joseph. *The Columbia History of Eastern Europe in the Twentieth Century*. New York: Columbia University Press, 1991.

Hilton, Ronald, ed. *Who's Who in Latin America*. 2 vols. Stanford, CA: Stanford University Press, 1971.

Holborn, Hajo. *History of Modern Germany, 1840–1945*. New York: Alfred A. Knopf, 1969.

Holden, David, and Richard Johns. *The House of Saud*. New York: Holt, Rinehart and Winston, 1981.

Hoptner, J.B. *Yugoslavia in Crisis, 1934–1941*. New York: Columbia University Press, 1962.

Howarth, David. *The Desert King—A Life of Ibn Saud*. London: Collins, 1964.

Hutton, Patrick H., ed. *Historical Dictionary of the Third French Republic*. 2 vols. New York: Greenwood, 1994.

The International Who's Who. London: Europa, various editions.

Iran: A Country Study. Washington, D.C.: U.S. Government Printing Office, 1989.

Iraq: A Country Study. Washington, D.C.: U.S. Government Printing Office, 1990.

Jackson, Gabriel. *The Spanish Republic and the Civil War, 1931–1939*. Princeton, NJ: Princeton University Press, 1972.

Jackson, George, ed. *Dictionary of the Russian Revolution*. New York: Greenwood Press, 1989.

Jelavich, Barbara. *History of the Balkans*. 2 vols. Cambridge, MA: Cambridge University Press, 1983.

Jordan: A Country Study. Washington, DC: U.S. Government Printing Office, 1991.

Karnow, Stanley. *Vietnam: A History*. New York: Viking, 1983.

Khoury, Philip S. *Syria and the French Mandate*. Princeton, NJ: Princeton University Press, 1987.

Kinross, Lord. *Ataturk*. New York: William Morrow, 1965.

Knight, Alan. *The Mexican Revolution*. 2 vols. Cambridge: Cambridge University Press, 1986.

Kodansha Encyclopedia of Japan. New York: Harper & Row, 1983.

Kolinski, Charles J. *Historical Dictionary of Paraguay*. Metuchen, NJ: Scarecrow, 1973.

Komarnicki, Titus. *Rebirth of the Polish Republic*. London: William Heinemann Ltd., 1957.

Korbel, Josef. *Poland Between East and West*. Princeton, NJ: Princeton University Press, 1963.

Kousoulas, D. George. *Modern Greece: Profile of a Nation*. New York: Scribner's, 1974.

Langley, Lester D. *Central America: The Real Story*. New York: Crown, 1985.

Langville, Alan R. *Modern World Rulers: A Chronology*. Metuchen, NJ: Scarecrow, 1979.

Lauring, Palle. *A History of the Kingdom of Denmark*. Copenhagen: Host & Son, 1963.

Lentz, Harris M., III. *Assassinations and Executions: An Encyclopedia of Political Violence, 1865–1986*. Jefferson, NC: McFarland, 1988.

Levine, Robert M. *Historical Dictionary of Brazil*. Metuchen, NJ: Scarecrow, 1979.

Levy, Felice, comp. *Obituaries on File*. 2 vols. New York: Facts on File, 1979.

Lewis, Bernard. *The Emergence of Modern Turkey*. London: Oxford University Press, 1958.

Liebenow, J. Gus. *Liberia: The Quest for Democracy*. Bloomington: Indiana University Press, 1925.

Lipschutz, Mark R., and R. Kent Rasmussen. *Dictionary of African Historical Biography*. Chicago: Aldine, 1978.

Livermore, H.L. *A New History of Portugal*. Cambridge, MA: Cambridge University Press, 1966.

Loppa, Frank J. *Dictionary of Modern Italian History*. Westport, CT: Greenwood, 1985.

Loveman, Brian. *Chile—The Legacy of Hispanic Capitalism*. New York: Oxford University Press, 1979.

Luck, James Murray. *A History of Switzerland*. Palo Alto, CA: Sposs. 1985.

MacDonald, John. *The Eastern Europe Collection*. 2 vols. New York: Arno Press, 1971.

MacDonnell, John De Courcy. *King Leopold II*. New York: University Press, 1905.

McLauchlan, Gordon, ed. *New Zealand Encyclopedia*. Auckland: David Bateman Ltd., 1984.

McLintock, A.H., ed. *An Encyclopedia of New Zealand*. Wellington: Owen, 1966.

Mamatey, Victor S. and Radomir Luza. *A History of the Czechoslovak Republic, 1918–1948*. Princeton, NJ: Princeton University Press, 1973.

Mansor, Menahem, ed. *Political and Diplomatic History of the Arab World, 1900–1967*. 7 vols. Washington, DC: NCR/Microcard Editions, 1972.

Maude, George. *Historical Dictionary of Finland*. Lanham, MD: Scarecrow, 1995.

May, Author J. *The Passing of the Hapsburg Monarchy 1914–1918*. 2 vols. Philadelphia: University of Pennsylvania Press, 1968.

Meyer, Harvey K. *Historical Dictionary of Honduras*. Metuchen, NJ: Scarecrow, 1977.

_____. *Historical Dictionary of Nicaragua*. Metuchen, NJ: Scarecrow, 1972.

Moore, Richard E. *Historical Dictionary of Guatemala*. Metuchen, NJ: Scarecrow, 1973.

Newton, Gerald. *The Netherlands, 1795–1977*. London: Westview Press, 1978.

Nousiainen, Jaakko. *The Finnish Political System*. Cambridge, MA: Harvard University Press, 1971.

Oakley, Stewart. *The Story of Denmark*. London: Faber & Faber, 1972.

Olson, James S., ed. *Historical Dictionary of the Spanish Empire, 1402–1975*. New York: Greenwood, 1992.

Opello, Jr., Walter C. *Portugal: From Monarchy to Pluralist Democracy*. Boulder, CO: Westview Press, 1991.

Otetea, Andrei. *A Concise History of Poland*. London: Robert Hale, 1985.

Palmer, Alan. *The Facts on File Dictionary of 20th Century History*. New York: Facts on File, 1979.

Palomlenyi, Erving. *A History of Hungary*. Budapest: Zrinyi Printing House, 1975.

Perusse, Roland I. *Historical Dictionary of Haiti*. Metuchen, NJ: Scarecrow, 1977.

Petran, Tabitha. *Syria*. New York: Praeger, 1972.

Petrovich, Michael Boro. *A History of Modern Serbia*. 2 vols. New York: Harcourt Brace Jovanovich, 1976.

Plummer, Brenda Gayle. *Haiti and the Great Powers, 1902–1915*. Baton Rouge: Louisiana State University Press, 1988.

Pollo, Stefanaq, and Arben Puto. *The History of Albania*. London: Routledge & Kegan Paul, 1981.

Polonsky, Antony. *Politics in Independent Poland 1921–39*. Oxford: Clarendon Press, 1972.

Poullada, Leon B. *Reform and Rebellion in Afghanistan, 1919–1929*. London: Cornell University Press, 1973.

Prouty, Chris and Eugene Rosenfeld. *Historical Dictionary of Ethiopia and Eritrea*. Metuchen, NJ: Scarecrow, 1981.

Raun, Toivo U. *Estonia and the Estonians*. Stanford, CA: Hoover Institute, 1991.

Renwick, George. *Luxembourg*. New York: Charles Scribner's Sons, 1970.

Richmond, J.C.B. *Egypt 1798–1952*. London: Methuen, 1977.

Robertson, William Spence. *History of Latin American Nations*. New York: D. Appleton-Century, 1943.

Roos, Hans. *A History of Modern Poland*. New York: Alfred A. Knopf, 1966.

Rose, Leo E., and John T. Scholz. *Nepal Profile of a Himalayan Kingdom*. Boulder, CO: Westview, 1980.

Rudolph, Donna K., and G.A. Rudolph. *Historical Dictionary of Venezuela*. Metuchen, NJ: Scarecrow, 1971.

Ryder, A.J. *Twentieth Century Germany: From Bismark to Brandt*. New York: Columbia University Press, 1973.

Sabaliunas, Leonas. *Lithuania in Crisis, 1939–1940*. Bloomington: Indiana University Press, 1972.

Sedwick, Frank. *The Tragedy of Manuel Azana*. Colombus: Ohio State University Press, 1963.

Senn, Alfred Erich. *The Emergence of Modern Lithuania*. Connecticut: Greenwood, 1975.

Seton-Watson, R.W. *A History of the Czechs and Slovaks*. Hamden, CN: Arcon, 1965.

_____. *A History of the Roumanians*. Hamden, CN: Arcon, 1963.

Shimoni, Yaacov, and Evyatar Levine, eds. *Political Dictionary of the Middle East in the 20th Century*. New York: Quadrangle, 1974.

Shreshtha, Kusum. *Monarchy in Nepal*. Bombay: Popular Prakashan, 1984.

Simon, Reeva. *Iraq Between the Two World Wars*. New York: Columbia University Press, 1986.

Singleton, Fred. *Twentieth Century Yugoslavia*. New York: Columbia University Press, 1976.

Smith, Harold. *Historical Dictionary of Thailand*. Metuchen, NJ: Scarecrow, 1976.

Spuler, Bertold, C.G. Allen, and Neil Saunders. *Rulers and Governments of the World*. 3 vols. London and New York: Bowker, 1977.

Stewart, Donald E.J. *Historical Dictionary of Cuba*. Metuchen, NJ: Scarecrow, 1981.

Stewart, John. *African States and Rulers*. Jefferson, NC: McFarland, 1989.

Stomberg, Andrew A. *A History of Sweden*. New York: Macmillan, 1969.

Storry, Richard. *A History of Modern Japan*. Baltimore: Penguin, 1968.

Sykes, Sir Percy. *A History of Persia*. 2 vols. London: MacMillan, 1963.

Tenenbaum, Barbara A. ed. *Encyclopedia of Latin American History and Culture*. 5 vols. New York: Charles Scribner's Sons, 1996.

Thailand: A Country Study. Washington, D.C.: U.S. Government Printing Office, 1989.

Thomas, Hugh. *The Spanish Civil War*. New York: Harper and Row, 1961.

Tunny, Christopher. *A Biographical Dictionary of World War II*. New York: St. Martin's, 1972.

Turkey: A Country Study. Washington, D.C.: U.S. Government Printing Office, 1988.

Volgyes, Ivan. *Hungary in Revolution 1918–1919*. Lincoln: University of Nebraska Press, 1971.

von Ranke, Leopold. *The History of Servia and the Servian Revolution*. New York: Da Capo Press, 1973.

Walker, Thomas W. *Nicaragua: The Land of Sandino*. Boulder, CO: Westview Press, 1991.

Wallace, William V. *Czechoslovakia*. Boulder, CO: Westview Press, 1976.

Warren, Harris Gaylord. *Rebirth of the Paraguayan Republic*. Pittsburgh: University of Pittsburgh Press, 1985.

Webster's Biographical Dictionary. Springfield, MA: Merriam, various editions.

Weinstein, Martin. *Uruguay: The Politics of Failure*. Westport, CT: Greenwood, 1975.

Werlich, David P. *Peru: A Short History*. Carbondale and Edwardsville: Southern Illinois University Press, 1978.

Whatt, David K. *Thailand: A Short History*. New Haven, CT: Yale University Press, 1984.

Whitfield, Danny J. *Historical Dictionary of Vietnam*. Metuchen, NJ: Scarecrow, 1976.

Who's Who in the World. Chicago: Marquis Who's Who, various editions.

Wilbur, Donald Newton, ed. *The Nations of Asia*. New York: Hart, 1966.
Willis, Jean L. *Historical Dictionary of Uruguay*. Metuchen, NJ: Scarecrow, 1974.
Win, May Kyi, and Harold E. Smith. *Historical Dictionary of Thailand*. Lanham, MD: Scarecrow, 1995.
Wise, L.F., and E.W. Egan. *Kings, Rulers and Statesmen*. New York: Sterling, 1967.
Wright, Ione, and Lisa M. Nekhom. *Historical Dictionary of Argentina*. Metuchen, NJ: Scarecrow, 1978.
Wuorinen, John H. *A History of Finland*. New York: Columbia University Press, 1965.
Wyatt, David K. *Thailand: A Short History*. New Haven: Yale University Press, 1984.
Wynot, Jr., Edward D. *Polish Politics in Transition*. Athens: University of Georgia Press, 1974.
Young, A. Morgan. *Imperial Japan, 1926–1938*. Westport, CT: Greenwood Press, 1938.

PERIODICALS

Annual Register of World Events (London), 1900–1960.
Current Biography (New York), 1940–1946.
Encyclopaedia Britannica Book of the Year (Chicago), 1940–1960.
Facts on File (New York), 1940–1946.
Memphis Commercial Appeal, 1900–1945.
Memphis Press Scimitar, 1920–1945.
Times of London, 1900–1960.

Heads of States and Governments, 1940–1945

Afghanistan

Afghanistan is a landlocked country in southwestern Asia. It was granted independence from Great Britain in August 1919.

HEADS OF STATE

ABDURRAHMAN KHAN (Emir; July 22, 1880–October 3, 1901). Abdurrahman Khan was born in Kabul in 1844. He was the son of Afzal Khan and the grandson of Emir Dost Mohammed Khan. Dost Mohammed died in 1863 and was succeeded by his son, Sher Ali Khan. Abdurrahman Khan's father and uncle, Azam Khan, led a revolt against Sher Ali. Abdurrahman went into exile in Samarkand in 1870 following the failure of his father's revolt. The British and Afghans engaged in a war in 1878, and Sher Ali died soon after. His son, Yakub Khan, was sent into exile and Abdurrahman returned to Afghanistan in 1880. The British supported his claim to the throne as emir on July 22, 1880. Abdurrahman was successful in putting down several rebellions over the next decade and used ruthless methods to crush his enemies. He reached an agreement with Russia that established Afghanistan's northern borders in 1887, and its eastern borders were settled with the British in 1893. Abdurrahman also attempted to modernize Afghanistan, building a modern hospital and encouraging the growth of industry. He died in Kabul on October 1, 1901.

HABIBULLAH KHAN (King; October 3, 1901–February 20, 1919). Habibullah Khan was born in Tashkent on July 3, 1872. He was the son of Emir Abdurrahman Khan. He succeeded his father to the throne on October 3, 1901. He continued the modernization of Afghanistan begun by his father and established the Habibia School in 1904. He also introduced electricity and automobiles into the country and modernized medical facilities. He maintained peaceful relations with the British and the Russians and secured domestic stability within the country. Habibullah also maintained Afghanistan's neutrality during World War I. He was assassinated at his camp in Kalagosh in the Laghman Valley on February 20, 1919.

AMANOLLAH KHAN (King; February 20, 1919–January 14, 1929). Amanollah Khan was born on June 1, 1892. He was the third son of Habibullah Khan. He was serving as governor of Kabul when his father was assassinated on February 20, 1919. He arranged his succession to the throne with the support of the army, preempting an attempt by his uncle, Nasirullah Khan, to lead the country. Soon after taking power, he challenged the British colonial administration in a brief military campaign that resulted in Afghanistan gaining control of its own foreign policy. Amanollah initiated political reforms in the country and promoted a constitution. He alienated the fundamentalist Moslems by his attempts to westernize Afghanistan's culture. His tax policies also were unpopular with the farming community. Several rebellions beset his regime in 1928, and his government was unprepared to withstand the assaults. He was forced to abdicate in favor of his older brother, Inayatullah Khan, on January 14, 1929, and went into exile in Locarno, Italy. Amanollah died in a clinic in Zurich, Switzerland, clinic after a long illness on April 25, 1960.

INAYATULLAH KHAN (King; January 14, 1929–January 17, 1929). Inayatullah Khan was born on October 20, 1888. He was the eldest son of Emir Habibullah Khan. His younger brother, Amanollah Khan, succeeded to the Afghan throne following his father's assassination in February 1919. Inayatullah spent much of the next decade in seclusion. Amanollah was forced to abdicate in the face of widespread rebellion on January 14, 1929. Inayatullah succeeded to the throne. A major rebellion led by the brigand Bachai Saqqao continued, and Inayatullah was forced to flee the country on January 17, 1929. He joined his brother in exile in India. He subsequently went to Iran, where he lived in exile for many years before his death in Teheran on August 14, 1946.

HABIBOLLAH GHAZI (King; January 17, 1929–October 13, 1929). Bachai Saqqao was a member of the Pejatk tribe from the north of Kabul. He served in the Afghan army before taking to the hills as a brigand leader. Known as "the Water Boy of the North," he was the leader of a rebellion against Amanollah Khan in 1929, forcing the ouster of Amanollah and his brother Inayatullah. Bachai Saqqao claimed the throne on January 17, 1929, and took the name Habibollah Ghazi. Amanollah's cousin, Mohammed Nadir Shah, returned to Afghanistan to lead government troops against the usurper. They drove him from the capital on October 13, 1929. Bachai Saqqao was captured and executed on November 3, 1929.

MOHAMMED NADIR SHAH (King; October 16, 1929–November 8, 1933). Sardar Mohammed Nadir Shah was born in Deradun, in Northern India, on April 10, 1880. He rose from being a stable boy to a position in the Afghan army, attaining the rank of general. He served his cousin, Amanollah Khan, as Afghanistan's minister to France from 1924 until 1928. When Amanollah and his brother Inayatullah were ousted by the brigand leader Bachai Saqqao in

1929, Nadir Shah returned to Afghanistan and took command of the loyalist army. He defeated Bachai Saqqao after a long campaign and was awarded the throne on October 16, 1929. He put down several other revolts soon after. Nadir Shah instituted political reforms and introduced a new constitution that provided for an elected legislature in 1930. He was assassinated in Kabul in the palace courtyard while awarding school prizes on November 8, 1933.

MOHAMMED ZAHIR SHAH (King; November 8, 1933–July 17, 1973). Mohammed Zahir Shah was born in Kabul on October 30, 1914. His father, Mohammed Nadir Shah, had been proclaimed King of Afghanistan in October 1929, following the overthrow of King Amanollah and his brother Inayatullah the previous January. Zahir was educated in France and attended the Kabul Infantry School. In 1931 he married Princess Houmairah Begum. Mohammed Zahir Shah was minister of education when he succeeded his father after Nadir's assassination on November 8, 1933. The 19-year-old king, with the advice and support of his uncle and prime minister, Sardar Hashim Khan, continued his father's programs of modernization and reform. During the 1930s Zahir largely depended on the financial support of Germany for these projects, though Afghanistan remained neutral during World War II. Following Germany's defeat, the United States began providing financial assistance. Zahir survived a short-lived revolt led by followers of the former king Amanollah in 1945. Two years later Afghanistan began a long-standing dispute with Pakistan, following the latter country's independence from Great Britain. Zahir's brother-in-law and cousin, Mohammed Daud Khan, became prime minister and reduced the king's power to that of a figurehead in September 1953. Two years later the dispute with Pakistan accelerated when Daud demanded the creation of an independent state on the

Afghan-Pakistan border. Violent clashes resulted in the closure of the Khyber Pass for several months until diplomatic intervention by the Soviet Union and the Western powers succeeded in temporarily easing tensions between the two countries. During the 1950s and 1960s, Zahir managed to balance Afghanistan between the Soviet Union and the United States and gained financial aid from both world powers. In March 1963 Zahir dismissed his powerful brother-in-law as prime minister. The following year he approved Afghanistan's first written constitution, which allowed a limited parliamentary democracy. Afghanistan's border dispute with Pakistan was also eased when diplomatic relations were restored. Zahir's rule was threatened during the late 1960s by outbreaks of civil disorder arising from demands for an increase

in democratization. A drought also added to the country's financial woes. The king managed to remain in power until July 17, 1973. Zahir was in Italy for health reasons when he was ousted by his former prime minister, Mohammed Daud Khan, who eliminated the monarchy and proclaimed Afghanistan a republic. Following his ouster, Zahir lived modestly in exile near Rome. He continued to receive monthly financial support from the Afghanistan government until Daud's overthrow in 1978, when the former king was stripped of his citizenship. He made few public statements during his exile, though he was reportedly considered a possible compromise leader of his country during the insurrection against the Soviet-backed administrations that followed Daud. Zahir's citizenship was restored in 1991.

HEADS OF GOVERNMENT

SARDAR MOHAMMED HASHIM KHAN (Prime Minister; November 8, 1933–May 14, 1946). Sardar Mohammed Hashim Khan, the son of Muhammad Yusof Khan, was born in 1884. Hashim joined his brother, Mohammed Nadir Shah, in diplomatic exile in France in 1926. Hashim returned to Afghanistan with his brother in 1929 to raise an army to defeat the brigand chief Bachai Saggao, also known as Habibollah Ghazi, who had seized control of Afghanistan. Following their victory, Nadir Shah became king of Afghanistan, and Hashim was named a member of the

council of ministers. Following Nadir's assassination on November 8, 1933, Hashim was named prime minister. He was the virtual ruler of Afghanistan during the early years of the reign of his nephew, Mohammed Zahir Shah. Hashim was responsible for restoring the orthodox and conservative way of life that former King Amanollah's reformation had threatened. Hashim remained as prime minister and Zahir's chief advisor until his retirement for health reasons on May 14, 1946. Hashim died in Kabul on October 26, 1953.

Albania

Albania is a country in southeastern Europe. It became an independent principality from Turkey after the Balkan wars in 1912 and 1913. The government was unstable during World War I until an agreement was reached by Italy, Greece, and Yugoslavia in 1920. Albania was occupied by Italy between 1939 and 1944.

HEADS OF STATE

WILLIAM OF WIED (Head of State; February 21, 1914–September 3, 1914). William of Wied was born on March 26, 1876, the third son of William, Prince of Wied, of the Rhenish Prussian royal family. He married Princess Sophie of Schoenberg-Waldenburg in 1906. He was chosen by the U.S., France, Great Britain and Italy in 1913 to rule Albania in 1913 and accepted the throne from the Albanian delegation on February 21, 1914. He arrived in the country the following month and set up his government in Durrës, naming Turhan Pasha Premëti as his prime minister. His reign was marked from the start by internal opposition. William left Albania on September 3, 1914, after the outbreak of World War I. He retired to Germany, where he served in the war effort. After the war, he petitioned the peace conference for permission to resume the throne, but was ignored. He died in 1945.

ZOG I (President; February 1, 1925–September 1, 1928; King; September 1, 1928–April 12, 1939). Ahmed Zogu was born in Burgajet castle in Mati Province on October 8, 1895; the son of Albanian clan leader Djemal Pasha. Zogu was educated in Constantinople. He supported Albania's abortive independence movement in 1912 and was a supporter of the claims of Prince William of Wied to the Albanian throne. He fought with the Austrian Army during World War I and distinguished himself militarily. He was called upon to serve as minister of the in-

terior in January 1920. He retained that position until the following November. Zogu served as commander-in-chief of the Albanian armed forces from October until December 1921 and was instrumental in resisting Yugoslavian incursions against Albania. He was again named minister of the interior in December 1921 and succeeded Djafer Ypi as prime minister on December 3, 1922. He survived an assassination attempt in early 1924 and resigned his position on March 3, 1924. He remained a powerful influence on the government until June of that year, when supporters of Bishop Fan S. Noli forced Zogu and his allies from power. Zogu went into exile in Yugoslavia. He returned to Albania to oust Noli's government in December 1924, was elected president on February 1, 1925, and Albania was proclaimed a republic. Albania signed the Pact of Tirana with Italy in November 1926 which brought Albania into Italy's sphere of influence. He also ruthlessly suppressed a revolt by Catholic tribes in Dukagjini in November of 1926. Zogu brought education and economic reforms to the country and modernized schools, roads and the banking industry.

Zogu was proclaimed King Zog I by the Albanian National Assembly on September 1, 1928. His reign brought political stability to the country for nearly a decade. He married the Hungarian Countess Geraldine Apponyi in April 1938, and their son, Leka, was born on April 5, 1939. A few days after the birth of his son the Italian army began an invasion of Albania. Zog and his family went into exile in Greece on April 12, 1939. He subsequently went to England, where he remained during World War II. After the war a Communist people's republic was proclaimed in Albania, and Zog continued his exile in Cairo, Egypt. He remained there until the mid–1950s, when he settled in a villa in Cannes, France, on the French Riviera. Zog was hospitalized in Suresnes, France, near Paris, in early April 1961 with stomach ulcers and a liver ailment. He died there on April 9, 1961.

ENVER HOXHA (President; November 10, 1945–January 13, 1946). Enver Hoxha was born to a poor Muslim family in Gjirokaster, Albania, on October 16, 1908. He attended the French school at Korçë on a scholarship and went to France to study at Montpellier University in 1930. When he lost his scholarship the following year, he moved to Paris, where he became involved with the French Communist Party. While in Paris, Hoxha also wrote a series of articles about Albania for the Communist newspaper *L'Humanité*. Hoxha began working for the Albanian Consulate in Brussels, Belgium, in 1934, but he lost his position when it was learned that he had written articles critical of the government of King Zog I. Hoxha returned to Albania and accepted a teaching position at his old school in Korçë. He remained involved in Communist activities and was arrested for conspiracy in early 1939. He was released from prison prior to the Italian invasion of Albania on April 7, 1939. Hoxha then moved to Tirana, Albania's capital, where he engaged in anti-Fascist activities. Hoxha founded the Albanian Communist Party in 1941 and edited the party newspaper. He was sentenced to death in absentia by the Italian regime when his activities were exposed. Hoxha was also a leader of the National Liberation Front, a Communist Resistance group that fought against the Italian and German occupa-

tion forces. Hoxha was named prime minister and army commander in chief in the provisional government formed in October 1944. The following year Hoxha became Albania's first postwar president on November 10, 1945, in a government recognized by the Allied powers. The new government proclaimed Albania a people's democracy early the next year. At that time Hoxha relinquished the Communist Party leadership to General Koci Xoxe and the presidency to Omer Nisani. Hoxha began the arduous task of rebuilding his war-torn country. As foreign minister, minister of defense, and head of government, Hoxha agitated for war reparations from Italy and for Albania's entry into the United Nations. His attempts were rebuffed by the United States and Great Britain, which had earlier withdrawn official recognition of his government. Albania's support for the Communist guerrillas during the civil war in Greece in the late 1940s further aggravated relations with the West. Albania's friendly relationship with its other neighbor, Yugoslavia, also ended during the Stalin-Tito feud of 1948. Hoxha replaced Xoxe, a Tito supporter, as first secretary of the Communist Party—now called the Albania Party of Labor—on October 6, 1948. Hoxha resigned as prime minister on July 20, 1954, having given up the foreign ministry the previous year. He continued to rule Albania as leader of the Communist Party. Albania was finally allowed into the United Nations in 1955. The Albanian government was considered one of the most brutal and repressive in the world. All religious activities were outlawed, and Hoxha ruthlessly crushed all opposition. Albania maintained a good relationship with the Soviet Union until the death of Stalin in 1953. The relationship between the two countries rapidly deteriorated in the post–Stalin period, however, and all ties were broken in 1961. Hoxha's regime then became closely tied with the Chinese government, but this alliance also soured after the death of Chairman Mao Tse-tung in 1976. Hoxha, who was the author of nearly 40 books, suffered from ill health in the early 1980s. He relinquished most of his duties to President Ramiz Alia in 1984. Hoxha died in Tirana of heart failure brought on by a diabetic condition on April 11, 1985.

HEADS OF GOVERNMENT

TURHAN PASHA PREMËTI (Prime Minister; March 17, 1914–September 3, 1914). Turhan Pasha Premëti was a leading Turkish diplomat who served as ambassador to Russia from 1908 until 1913. He briefly served as Albania's prime minister and minister of foreign affairs in a cabinet formed under William of Wied from March to September 1914. He was active in pursuing international recognition for a legitimate government for Albania and was again called upon to serve as prime minister on December 28, 1918. He stepped down on March 27, 1920, retired to Rome, and died in Neuilly, France, in 1927.

ESSAD PASHA (Prime Minister; October 5, 1914–December 1914). Essad Toptani was born in Tirana in 1863. He became head of the powerful Toptani family after the murder of his brother, Ghani Bey. He was a leader of the Young Turk movement in the Ottoman Empire in 1908 and entered the Turkish parliament as a deputy for Albania. He was placed in charge of the Ottoman army, commanding the forces at Shkodër. He surrendered the area to Montenegrin troops in 1913. Toptani, who was known as Essad Pasha, was named minister of internal affairs and of war under William of Wied for several months in 1914, until he was arrested on charges of treason in May of that year. He was sent to Italy, but returned to Albania following William's departure. He raised an army that occupied Tirana and forced the senate to name him head of state on October 5, 1914. He continued to rule central Albania until February 24, 1916, when he accompanied the Serbs against Austria-Hungary in Salonika. He attended the peace conference after World War I in an attempt to represent Albania. He subsequently retired to Paris, where he was instrumental in an unsuccessful coup attempt against the Albanian government in 1920. Essad Pasha was shot to death in Paris on June 13, 1920, by Avni Rustemi, an Albanian student, while leaving the Hotel Continental.

TURHAN PASHA PREMËTI (Prime Minister; December 28, 1918–March 27, 1920). *See earlier entry under Heads of Government.*

SULEIMAN DELVINO (Prime Minister; March 27, 1920–November 20, 1920). Suleiman Delvino was chosen to head the Albanian government on March 27, 1920. He stepped down as prime minister on November 20, 1920. Delvino was a leader of the opposition during the early 1920s. He returned to the government as minister of foreign affairs under Prime Minister Fan S. Noli in June 1924. When the government collapsed the following December, Delvino became a leading critic of the administration of Ahmed Zogu. He was accused of participation in a revolt against Zogu in November 1926. He and other political prisoners and refugees were pardoned in September 1927.

ELIAS VRIONI (Prime Minister; December 11, 1920–October 17, 1921). Elias Vrioni was born in Berat in 1883. Vrioni was chosen as prime minister on December 11, 1920. He suffered from poor health, which forced him to resign on October 17, 1921. Vrioni again briefly headed the government from June 1 to June 17, 1924, when Bishop Fan S. Noli became prime minister. Vrioni was again named prime minister following the fall of Noli on December 24, 1924. His government made way for Ahmed Zogu on January 10, 1925. Vrioni died in Paris on March 7, 1932.

PANDELI EVANGELI (Prime Minister; October 17, 1921–December 7, 1921). Pandeli Evangeli was born in Korçë in 1859. He served as governor of Korçë in 1914. He was named a member of the Albanian delegation to Paris in 1920. He was a member of the Liberal Party and joined Elias Vrioni's cabinet as foreign minister in December 1920. He succeeded Vrioni as prime minister on October 17, 1921; but resigned shortly thereafter on December 7 over a disagreement with the regency council about a ministerial appointment. He again served in the government as foreign minister from September 1922 until March 1924. He subsequently served in the Albanian senate and became its president in September 1927. He was president of the constituent assembly when Ahmed Zogu was proclaimed Zog I, King of the Albanians, in September 1928. Evangeli again was Albania's prime minister from March 6, 1930, until October 15, 1935.

HASSAN PRISHTINA (Prime Minister; December 7, 1921–December 11, 1921). Hassan Prishtina was a leader of the insurrection against the Turkish administration of Albania in 1912. He was named to Turhan Premëti's first government as minister of public works in March 1914. He was active in insurrections against the Serbian occupation forces during World War I. Prishtina formed a cabinet as prime minister and minister of foreign affairs on December 7, 1921. He had the support of only a small section of the public, and was forced to resign four days later on December 11, 1921. He was subsequently

a leader of the Kossovo Committee and led an unsuccessful insurrection against the government of Ahmed Zogu in 1923. He supported the government of Bishop Fan S. Noli in late 1924. He again participated in a revolt against Ahmed Zogu after his return to power in 1925.

IDOMENI KOSTURIS (Interim Prime Minister; December 11, 1921–December 24, 1921). Idomeni Kosturis was appointed interim prime minister of Albania, preceding Hassan Prishtina on December 11, 1921. He stepped down when Djafer Ypi formed a government on December 24, 1921.

DJAFER YPI (Prime Minister; December 24, 1921–December 2, 1922). Djafer Ypi was a Bektashi Moslem and a leader in the Albanian nationalist movement. He was named to Elias Vrioni's government as minister of justice in December 1920. He was called upon to form a government as prime minister on December 24, 1921, and also became foreign minister the following February. He stepped down as foreign minister in September 1922 and resigned as prime minister on December 2, 1922. He was subsequently appointed to the Council of Regency. He was again named to the government as minister of education by Ahmed Zogu in 1927. Ypi died on November 19, 1940.

AHMED ZOGU (Prime Minister; December 3, 1922–March 3, 1924). *See earlier entry under Heads of State.*

SHEVKET VERLACI (Prime Minister; March 5, 1924–June 1, 1924). Shevket Verlaci was a leading landowner in Albania and the father-in-law of Ahmed Zogu. He was called upon by the Regency Council to form a government as prime minister on March 5, 1924, but resigned as prime minister on June 1, 1924, to lead the Albanian army. Insurgents in Kossovo forced Verlaci and his forces to flee from Tirana in July 1924.

He went into exile and was tried and sentenced to death in absentia by the government of Bishop Fan S. Noli. He returned to Albania when Ahmed Zogu took over the government in early 1925.

ELIAS VRIONI (Prime Minister; June 1, 1924–June 17, 1924). *See earlier entry under Heads of Government.*

FAN S. NOLI (Prime Minister; June 17, 1924–December 24, 1924). Fan Stylian Noli was born in Ibrik Tepe in eastern Thrace in 1882. He was raised in the United States and was ordained a priest by the Russian Metropolitan in New York City. He was proclaimed a bishop in the Albanian Orthodox Church in 1908. Noli attended Harvard University from 1908 until 1912, when he returned to Albania to participate in the independence movement. He was the leader of the delegation to Geneva that secured Albania's admission into the League of Nations after World War I. Noli served as foreign minister in the government of Djafer Ypi from December 1921 until his resignation in February 1922. He was a leader of the opposition to Ahmed Zogu and was called upon to head the government on June 17, 1924, when his supporters staged a coup against Zogu and his allies. Noli was forced from power on December 24, 1924, when Zogu reclaimed the government. Noli went into exile in Italy and was sentenced to death in absentia by the Albanian government. Noli came to the United States in 1932 and settled in Boston, Massachusetts, where he was regarded as a leading scholar and religious leader. He died in Fort Lauderdale, Florida, on March 13, 1965.

ELIAS VRIONI (Prime Minister; December 24, 1924–January 10, 1925). *See earlier entry under Heads of Government.*

AHMED ZOGU (Prime Minister; January 10, 1925–February 1, 1925). *See earlier entry under Heads of State.*

HIQMET DELVINO (Prime Minister; May 11, 1928–September 7, 1928). Hiqmet Delvino was named chairman of the council of ministers and minister of justice by King Zog on May 11, 1928. Delvino resigned as head of the government on September 7, 1928.

KOCTCHO KOTTA (Prime Minister; September 7, 1928–March 3, 1930). Koctcho Kotta was born in 1889. He was a supporter of Ahmed Zogu and served in Shevket Verlaci's government as minister of public works and agriculture in the spring of 1924. He returned to the government as minister of public works following Ahmed Zogu's assumption of the presidency in February 1925. Kotta was named to Hiqmet Delvino's cabinet as minister of the interior in May 1928 and succeeded Delvino as prime minister on September 7, 1928. He headed the government until March 3, 1930. He was again named prime minister on November 9, 1936, and served until the Italian occupation of Albania on April 12, 1939. Kotta died in 1949.

PANDELI EVANGELI (Prime Minister; March 6, 1930–October 15, 1935). *See earlier entry under Heads of Government.*

MEHDI FRASHËRI (Prime Minister; October 22, 1935–November 9, 1936). Mehdi Frashëri was born in 1872 and educated in Constantinople. He served in the Turkish government service, became governor of Palestine, and was an early figure in Albania's independence movement. He was minister of the interior in Turhan Pasha Premëti's government in 1914. He remained active in Albanian politics and was again named to the government as minister of public works and agriculture by Elias Vrioni in 1920. He served as Albania's ambassador to Greece from 1923 until 1926. He also represented Albania at the League of Nations in Geneva from the mid-1920s. He was named prime minister by King Zog on

October 22, 1935, and held that post until November 9, 1936. Frasheri was interned in Italy following the Italian invasion of Albania in 1939. He returned to Albania as senior regent after the armistice in 1943. Frashëri was accused of being a traitor by pro-communist forces in the country and escaped back to Italy in 1944. He remained in exile in Rome until his death on May 25, 1963.

KOCTCHO KOTTA (Prime Minister; November 9, 1936–April 12, 1939). *See earlier entry under Heads of Government.*

ENVER HOXHA (Prime Minister; October 1944–July 20, 1954). *See earlier entry under Heads of State.*

Argentina

Argentina is the second largest country in South America. It was granted independence from Spain on July 9, 1816.

HEADS OF STATE

JULIO ARGENTINO ROCA (President; October 12, 1880–October 12, 1886; and October 12, 1898–October 12, 1904). Julio Argentino Roca was born in Tucumán Province, Argentina, in 1843, to a leading military family. He was educated at the National College in Entre Ríos Province, but left school to serve in the military with his father in 1859. Roca was active in the military campaign against Angel Vicente Penaloza in the early 1860s and was a distinguished combatant in Argentina's war against Paraguay. He attained the rank of staff major during the fighting, and served as commander in chief in Argentina's battles against the Pampas Indians in the 1870s. His successes in that campaign captured much new territory for Argentina and made Roca a popular figure in the country. After his return to Buenos Aires he was elected president, succeeding Nicolás Avellaneda on October 12, 1880. His administration ushered in a new oligarchy that dominated Argentina for the next several decades. Roca completed his term of office on October 12, 1886, and was succeeded by his brother-in-law, Miguel Juarez Cel-

man. Roca remained involved in the government and was instrumental in the suppression of a revolt in 1890. Roca subsequently toured Europe, where he studied various governments. He returned to Argentina and was elected president again. He succeeded José Uriburu in office on October 12, 1898. During his second term in office, he resumed diplomatic relations with the Vatican, which had been broken 16 years earlier; and he also settled long-standing boundary disputes with Chile and Brazil. Argentina experienced economic prosperity under Roca's rule. He retained office until the completion of his term on October 12, 1904, when his chosen successor Manuel Quintana, took office. Roca subsequently served as Argentina's minister to Brazil and, later, to France. He died in Buenos Aires on October 20, 1914.

MANUEL QUINTANA (President; October 12, 1904–March 12, 1906). Manuel Quintana was born in Buenos Aires on October 19, 1835. He studied at the University of Buenos Aires and received a degree in law in 1858. He was elected to the provincial congress in 1860 and became a senator in 1870. He served as minister of the interior in Luis Sáenz Peña's government from 1892 until 1895. He was selected to succeed Julio Roca as president of Argentina on October 12, 1904. He successfully put down a rebellion by radicals in 1905. Quintana died in office on March 12, 1906.

JOSÉ FIGUEROA ALCORTA (President; March 12, 1906–October 12, 1910). José Figueroa Alcorta was born in Córdoba on November 20, 1860. He studied at the University of Córdoba and graduated with a degree in law in 1882. He was elected to the legislature in 1885 and served in the cabinet from 1889 until 1892. He was governor of Córdoba from 1895 until 1898 and subsequently served in the senate. He was elected vice president under Manuel Quintana in 1904. He succeeded him as president on March 12, 1906, following the death of Quintana. Figueroa Alcorta closed congress when it refused to consider his budget proposals in 1908. He relinquished the presidency when Roque Sáenz Peña, was elected on October 12, 1910. Figueroa Alcorta served as ambassador to Spain in 1912. He was appointed to the Supreme Court of Justice in 1915, a position he held until his death in Buenos Aires on December 27, 1931.

ROQUE SÁENZ PEÑA (President; October 12, 1910–August 9, 1914). Roque Sáenz Peña was born in Buenos Aires on March 19, 1851. He entered the University of Buenos Aires to study law in 1870, but soon left to fight with government forces during the revolution of 1874. He returned to complete his education and was elected to parliament in 1876. He gained a reputation as a forceful orator and was selected president of the chamber the following year. Sáenz Peña joined the Peruvian army to fight in the war against Chile in 1879. He was badly wounded during the fighting and was briefly held prisoner. Following his release, he entered Argentina's diplomatic corps. During the administration of Carlos Pellegrini in the 1880s he served in various diplomatic positions, including undersecretary of the ministry of foreign relations and minister to Uruguay. He was the candidate for the Modernistas Party in 1891, but withdrew from the race when the opposition promoted the candidacy of his father, Luis Sáenz Peña. The elder Sáenz Peña took office in October 1892; the younger remained in the senate, but he resigned later in the year following political differences with his father. He returned to Buenos Aires and resumed his role in the diplomatic corps after his father left office in January 1895. He also became a leading advocate of political reform, and, together with Emilio Mitre and Carlos Pellegrini, he was elected to the congress in 1906. Sáenz Peña was the Union Naçional party's presidential candidate in 1910 and was elected with little opposition. He took office on October 12, 1910, and soon began his campaign to reform the political system in Argentina. His reform law took effect in February 1912; it allowed secret and compulsory voting for all males over the age of eighteen and mandated the inclusion of minority groups in the chamber of deputies. Sáenz Peña was unable, however, to solve Argentina's growing economic and labor problems and poor health plagued the later years of his administration. He relinquished most of his duties to his vice president, Victoriano de la Plaza, in October 1913. He died in office in Buenos Aires on August 9, 1914.

VICTORIANO DE LA PLAZA (President; August 9, 1914–October 12, 1916). Victoriano de la Plaza was born on November 2, 1840. He assumed the duties of president on October 6, 1913, due to President Roque Sáenz Peña's poor health. He succeeded to the office when Sáenz Peña died on August 9, 1914. He retained office until October 12, 1916, when Hipólito Irigoyen was elected. Plaza died on October 2, 1919.

HIPÓLITO IRIGOYEN (President; October 12, 1916–October 12, 1922). Hipólito Irigoyen was born to a poor family on July 12, 1852. He became a schoolteacher and entered politics in 1878 to serve a term in the Buenos Aires provincial legislature. He was elected to the national chamber of deputies two years later. He became independently wealthy as a ranch owner and was instrumental in the organization of the Radical Party in the early 1890s. He often challenged his uncle, the founder of the Radical Party, Leandro Alem, for leadership and claimed the position following Alem's death in 1896. Irigoyen advocated a position of intransigence for the party and refused to participate in elections or governments pending electoral reform. Following the legislation in 1912 that guaranteed free elections in Argentina, Irigoyen became the Radical Party's candidate for president in 1916. He made no campaign speeches and seldom appeared in public but was nevertheless elected president and took office on October 12, 1916. His hard-line position against other political groups led to a coalition of opposition to his regime and led to a congress that often opposed his reform proposals. He led Argentina on a path of neutrality during World War I. His turbulent regime ended on October 12, 1922, following the inauguration of his chosen successor, Marcelo T. de Alvear. Irigoyen soon broke with Alvear, leading his faction of the Radical Party in opposition to the new administration. Irigoyen returned to the presidency on October 12, 1928, defeating a coalition of the Conservatives and Alvear's faction of the Radicals. His second administration was marred by growing economic and social problems, which were exacerbated by the economic crisis in 1929. His unwillingness to compromise and his inability to alleviate the crisis led to the aging president's ouster by General José Uriburu on September 6, 1930, in Argentina's first military coup in over 70 years. Still claiming to be the constitutional president of the Argentine Republic, Irigoyen died on July 3, 1933, of complications from a throat problem.

MARCELO T. DE ALVEAR (President; October 12, 1922–October 12, 1928). Marcelo Torcuato de Alvear was born to a leading family in Buenos Aires on October 4, 1868. He graduated from the University of Buenos Aires with a degree in law in 1889, and soon became involved in the Radical Civic Union. He was active in the organization's uprising in 1893 and went into exile in Europe following its failure. He remained abroad for several years before returning to Argentina and being elected to congress in 1912. He served in Hipólito Irigoyen's government as ambassador to France from 1916 until 1920. He subsequently represented Argentina at the League of Nations organizational meetings in Geneva, Switzerland. Alvear was selected by Irigoyen to be his successor as president and took office on October 12, 1922. He was instrumental in improving Argentina's economic prosperity and decreasing the national debt. New schools were constructed, and Argentina and Chile's boundary treaty was ratified during his term of office. He completed his term and stepped down after Irigoyen's reelection to the presidency on October 12, 1928. Alvear led a reorganization of the radical movement in 1930. He was forced to go into exile by the military regime later in the year. He returned the following year but was arrested and again sent into exile. He settled in Paris for two years before returning to Argentina in 1933. He became president of the Radical Party after Irigoyen's death. He was defeated in a fraud-tainted election for the presidency by Roberto Ortíz in 1937. Alvear died in Buenos Aires on March 23, 1942.

HIPÓLITO IRIGOYEN (President; October 12, 1928–September 6, 1930). *See earlier entry under Heads of State.*

JOSÉ FÉLIX URIBURU (President; September 6, 1930–February 20, 1932). José Félix Uriburo was born in Salta on July 20, 1868. He was the nephew of José E. Uriburu, who served as Argentina's president from 1895 until 1898. He attended the Military School at Buenos Aires and reached the rank of colonel. He became director of the War College in 1907. He served as military attaché in Germany and England in the years preceding World War I. Uriburu was promoted to general in 1921 and served as inspector general of the army from 1923 until 1926. Uriburu led the military coup that ousted President Hipólito Irigoyen on September 6, 1930. Uriburu became provisional president of the military government and ruled under a state of siege. His government attempted to crush the political opposition through press censorship and the arrest and exile of leading members of the Radical Party. He refused to accept the results of an election that gave victory to the Radical Party in April 1931. Public pressure mounted against his regime, and another election was held. Agustín Justo was elected president and Uriburu stepped down on February 20, 1932. He went to Europe for medical treatment soon after leaving office and died in a Paris hospital on April 29, 1932, following surgery for stomach ulcers.

AGUSTÍN P. JUSTO (President; February 20, 1932–February 20, 1938). José Agustín Pedro Justo was born in Concepción del Uruguay, Entre Ríos Province, on February 26, 1876. He graduated from the Military College of San Martin in 1892 and began a distinguished career in the army. He served as director of the military academy from 1915 until 1922. He was promoted to the rank of brigadier general and named minister of war in the government of Marcelo de Alvear in 1922. He opposed the election of Hipólito Irigoyen as president in 1928 and participated in the military coup that ousted Irigoyen in Sep-

tember 1930. Justo served as commander-in-chief of the army in the subsequent provisional government. He was elected to succeed José Félix Uriburu as president and took office on February 20, 1932. He was instrumental in the formation of a conservative coalition, the Concordancia. During his term of office his government established Argentina's central bank and initiated a national income tax. His government continued to rule in a repressive manner and engaged in electoral fraud to maintain control of the country. Justo completed his term on February 20, 1938, and turned the government over to his handpicked successor Roberto Ortíz. Justo supported the Allies during World War II and opposed President Ramon S. Castillo's policy of neutrality. He became an advisor to the Brazilian army in 1942 in preparation for that country's entry into the war effort. Justo died of a cerebral hemorrhage in Buenos Aires on January 11, 1943.

ROBERTO M. ORTÍZ (President; February 20, 1938–June 24, 1942). Roberto M. Ortíz was born in Buenos Aires on September 24, 1886. He received a degree in law from the University of Buenos Aires in 1909. He became active in politics as a member of the Civic Radical Party. He was elected to the Buenos Aires city council in 1919 and to the chamber of deputies in 1920. He was appointed minister of public works in the government of Marcelo de Alvear in 1925 and aided Alvear in his attempt to reorganize the Radical Party in 1931. Ortíz was named minister of finance by President Agustín Justo in 1935. He left the cabinet two years later to become the Concordancia's presidential candidate. In an election widely believed to be fraudulent, Ortíz defeated Marcelo de Alvear and took office on February 20, 1938. He largely continued the policies of his predecessor, though he made some attempts to restore public trust in the government. Ortíz maintained Argentina's policy of neutrality in the early years of World War II, though he personally favored the Allied cause. His health deteriorated during his term due to a severe diabetic condition. He was forced to delegate many of his duties to his vice president, Ramon Castillo, in July 1940 because his condition had rendered him nearly blind. He resigned from office on June 24, 1942, and died in Buenos Aires of bronchial pneumonia on July 15, 1942.

RAMON S. CASTILLO (President; June 24, 1942–June 5, 1943). Ramon S. Castillo was born in Catamarca on November 20, 1873. He received a degree in law from the University of Buenos Aires and became a criminal judge in 1895. He held various judicial appointments before becoming professor of law at the National University in 1910. He was elected to the senate in 1932 and served in the cabinet as minister of justice and public instruction in 1936. He was minister of the interior from 1936 until 1937 and was elected vice president under Roberto Ortíz in 1938. He became acting president in July 1940 due to Ortíz's poor health. Castillo succeeded to the presidency on June 24, 1942, when Ortiz resigned from office. He continued Argentina's policy of neutrality during World War II. His reliance on the support of Fascist and pro–Axis forces in the country caused discontent. This culminated in the election of the extreme conservative, Robustiano Patron Costas, as his chosen successor in 1943. However, a revolution ensued, and Castillo was overthrown by a military coup led by General Arturo Rawson on June 5, 1943. He died in Buenos Aires on October 12, 1944.

ARTURO RAWSON (President; June 5, 1943–June 7, 1943). Arturo Rawson was born in Santiago del Estero on June 4, 1885. He was the grandson of a United States naval surgeon who began a medical practice in Argentina in 1817. Rawson graduated from the Military College in 1907 and subsequently served as a teacher there. He led a military coup against the government of President Ramon S. Castillo on June 5, 1943. Rawson served as provisional president for two days but stepped down on June 7, 1943, when the ruling military junta selected Pedro Pablo Ramírez to head the government. Rawson subsequently served as ambassador to Brazil. He was an opponent of the government of Edelmiro Farrell in 1945 and was briefly arrested for his activities against the government. He was arrested again in September 1951 for his support of General José Benjamin Menendez's revolt against the government of Juan D. Perón. He was released soon after and died of a heart attack in Buenos Aires on October 8, 1952.

PEDRO PABLO RAMÍREZ (President; June 7, 1943–March 9, 1944). Pedro Pablo Ramírez was born in La Paz, Entre Riós, on January 30, 1884. He received a military education at the War College and fought with the German army during World War I. Ramírez supported the right-wing coup led by General José Uriburu in 1930 and was named to the general staff. He also served as military attaché to Italy in 1930. He became minister of war in Ramon Castillo's government in 1942 and participated in the military coup that ousted Castillo on June 5, 1943. He succeeded General Arturo Rawson as president of the provisional government on June 7, 1943. His regime abolished political parties and placed restrictions on the press. Communists were driven underground and minorities, particularly Jews, were suppressed. His attempt to negotiate a supply of arms from Nazi Germany increased pressure on his government by the United States. Ramírez was persuaded to break off diplomatic relations with Germany and Japan in January 1944. His pro-Axis supporters called for his resignation, and he stepped down in favor of his vice president,

Edelmiro Farrell, on March 9, 1944. He retired from political activity and died of cancer in Buenos Aires on June 11, 1962.

EDELMIRO J. FARRELL (President; March 9, 1944–June 4, 1946). Edelmiro Julian Farrell was born in Avellaneda on August 12, 1887. He began a career in the military and held the rank of general when he supported the military coup that ousted Ramon D. Castillo as president on June 5, 1943. Farrell served as minister of war in Pedro Pablo Ramírez's administration and was later named vice president. When Ramírez was forced from office by supporters of Colonel Juan Perón, Farrell, a Perón ally, assumed the presidency on March 9, 1944. The Allied powers were concerned over Argentina's pro–Axis leanings during World War II. In 1945 Farrell, under pressure from the United States, declared war on Germany and Japan. Farrell remained president until June 4, 1946, when Perón was sworn into office. Upon leaving the presidency Farrell retired from military and public life. He died of a heart attack at the age of 93 in Buenos Aires on October 31, 1980.

Australia

Australia is a continent lying between the Pacific and Indian oceans. The six Australian colonies of New South Wales, Victoria, Queensland, South Australia, Western Australia, and Tasmania were unified into an autonomous federation within the British Commonwealth on January 1, 1901; the Northern Territory was added to the federation in 1911.

HEADS OF STATE

EARL OF HOPETOUN (Governor-General; January 1, 1901–July 17, 1902). John Adrian Louis Hope was born in Hopetoun, Scotland, on September 25, 1860. He was educated at Eton and Sandhurst. He graduated in 1879 and entered the House of Lords as the 7th Earl of Hopetoun in 1883, where he served as Conservative whip. He became a lord-in-waiting to Queen Victoria two years later. Lord Hopetoun was appointed governor of Victoria, Australia, in 1889. He was a popular governor, but stepped down in March 1895 to return to England as paymaster-general in Lord Salisbury's government. He held that position until he became lord chamberlain in 1898. Lord Hopetoun was appointed the first governor-general of Australia in October of 1900. He took office on January 1, 1901, when Australia achieved commonwealth status. He asked Edmund Barton to form a government as prime minister when Sir William Lyne, the previous premier, was unable to put a cabinet together. Lord Hopetoun's term was cut short when he resigned on July 17, 1902, over a dispute about insufficient funding for his position. He returned to England and was named Marquis of Linlithgow in October 1902. He briefly served as secretary for Scotland in 1905 before failing health forced his retirement. He died in Pau, France, on February 29, 1908.

HALLAM, BARON TENNYSON (Governor-General; July 17, 1902–January 21, 1904). Hallam, Baron Tennyson, was born in Twickenham, England, on October 11, 1852. He was the eldest son of the eminent Victorian poet, Alfred, Lord Tennyson. Hallam was educated at Marlborough College and Trinity College, Cambridge, where he studied law. He served for a number of years as his father's private secretary. He published an authorized memoir of his father, *Alfred, Lord Tennyson: a Memoir*, in 1897. He was appointed governor of South Australia in 1899 and became acting governor-general of Australia following the resignation of Lord Hopetoun on July 17, 1902. He secured the position of governor-general on January 9, 1903; and served until January 21, 1904, when he returned to England. He published an edition of his father's complete works in 1908 and edited a book of reminiscences, *Tennyson and His Friends*, in 1912. Lord Tennyson was appointed deputy governor of the Isle of Wight in 1913. He died there at his home in Freshwater on December 2, 1928.

BARON NORTHCOTE (Governor-General; January 21, 1904–September 9, 1908). Henry Stafford Northcote was born in London on November 18, 1846, the second son of Sir Henry Stafford Northcote, 1st Earl of Iddesleigh. The younger Northcote was educated at Eton and Merton College, Oxford, before becoming a clerk in the foreign office. He served as private secretary for his father at a mission in Washington to arrange the Alabama treaty in 1871. He accompanied Lord Salisbury to the Constantinople conference in 1876 and 1877 and again served under his father when he was chancellor of the exchequer from 1877 until 1880. Northcote was elected to Parliament as a Conservative from Exeter in 1880. He served as financial secretary to the war office from 1885 until 1886. He was appointed governor of Bombay in 1899 and was raised to the peerage as Baron Northcote in January 1900. He did much to

provide relief to Bombay during the plague and famine he found there, and saved the famous breed of Gujarati cattle from extinction by establishing a cattle farm. He was subsequently appointed governor-general of Australia and took office on January 21, 1904. He arrived at a period of political instability and was helpful in establishing a stable government under Alfred Deakin in July 1905. Northcote completed his term on September 9, 1908, and returned to England to take his seat in the House of Lords. He died at Eastwell Park, Ashford, Kent, on September 29, 1911.

EARL OF DUDLEY (Governor-General; September 9, 1908–December 21, 1909). William Humble Ward was born in London on May 25, 1867; and was educated at Eton. He succeeded his father to become the 2nd Earl of Dudley in 1885. He entered the House of Lords as a Conservative and served as parliamentary secretary to the board of trade from 1895 until 1902. Dudley was appointed lord-lieutenant of Ireland in 1902 and served until the Conservative ministry fell in 1905. He was named governor-general of Australia on September 9, 1908. He had a strained relationship with the Labor government of Andrew Fisher and retired to England on December 21, 1909. Dudley commanded the Worcestershire Yeomanry in Egypt and Gallipoli during World War I in 1915. Musical comedy star Gertie Millar became his second wife in 1924, and the couple subsequently established their home in France. Dudley died of cancer in a London hospital on June 29, 1932.

VISCOUNT CHELMSFORD (Governor-General; December 21, 1909–January 27, 1910). Frederic John Napier Tresigar was born at Belgrave, London, on August 12, 1868. He was educated at Winchester and graduated from Magdalen College, Oxford, in 1891. He succeeded his father to the title of

Viscount Chelmsford in 1905 and was subsequently appointed governor of Queensland, Australia. He was named governor of New South Wales in 1909. He briefly served as acting governor-general of Australia from December 21, 1909, until January 27, 1910, following the resignation of Lord Dudley. Lord Chelmsford remained as governor of New South Wales until 1913. He was appointed viceroy of India in 1916. He helped introduce the Montagu-Chelmsford reforms that gave India limited home rule in 1918. He was also faced with Mahatma Gandhi's first passive resistance campaign and with handling the Amritsar problem, when the local British commander, General Dyer, fired on a crowd of unarmed rioters, killing nearly four hundred in April 1919. Lord Chelmsford completed his term and returned to England in 1921. He served as agent general in London for New South Wales from 1926 until October 1927. He died suddenly of a heart attack in London on April 1, 1933.

BARON DENMAN (Governor-General; July 31, 1911–May 18, 1914). Thomas Denman was born in London on November 16, 1874. He was educated at Sandhurst and entered the Royal Scots as a lieutenant. He succeeded his great-uncle to the title of 3rd Baron Denman in 1894. He was wounded in action during the South African War in 1901. He served in the House of Lords as a Liberal and was chief government whip from 1907 until 1911 when he was appointed governor-general of Australia on July 31. During his term of office the federal capital was inaugurated at Canberra. Denman's support of Australia's right to complete control of her navy displeased the colonial office. Further disputes with the colonial office and the Australian government of Joseph Cook led to Denman's resignation on May 18, 1914. He returned to England and commanded a Yeomanry regiment during World War I

in 1914 and 1915. He was chief Liberal whip in the House of Lords from 1919 until 1924. Denman died in Hove, Sussex, England, on June 24, 1954.

VISCOUNT NOVAR (Governor-General; May 18, 1914–October 6, 1920). Ronald Crauford Munro-Ferguson was born in Kirkcaldy, Scotland, on March 6, 1860. He was educated at Sandhurst and joined the Grenadier Guards in 1880. He was elected to Parliament as a Liberal in 1884. He became private secretary for the foreign minister, Lord Roseberry, in 1886. Munro-Ferguson was a lord of the treasury from 1894 until 1895 and was named to the privy council in 1910. He was appointed governor-general of Australia on May 18, 1914. He developed a good working relationship with the leadership of the major political parties and continued to serve throughout World War I. He was interested in forestry and encouraged greater use for Australian timber. His term of office was scheduled to end in 1919, but was extended for a year in order to allow him to receive the Prince of Wales on his visit to Australia. Munro-Ferguson stepped down on October 6, 1920, and returned to England. He was subsequently raised to the peerage as Viscount Novar of Raith. He served as secretary for Scotland from 1922 until 1924. He died at his home near Kirkcaldy, Scotland, on March 30, 1934.

BARON FORSTER (Governor-General; October 6, 1920–October 8, 1925). Henry William Forster was born in Lewisham, Kent, on January 31, 1866. He was educated at Eton and New College, Oxford. He was elected to Parliament as a Conservative member from Sevenoaks in 1892. He served as junior lord of the treasury from 1902 until 1905 and was opposition whip to the Liberal government in 1911. He served as financial secretary to the war office from 1915 until 1919. He was raised to the peerage as Baron Forster of Lepe in December 1919 and was subsequently appointed governor-general of Australia on October 6, 1920. He was a popular figure in the country and completed his term of office on October 8, 1925. Lord Forster returned to England and retired from public life. He died in London on January 15, 1936.

BARON STONEHAVEN (Governor-General; October 8, 1925–October 2, 1930). John Lawrence Baird was born on June 27, 1874. He was educated at Eton and Christ Church, Oxford. He joined the diplomatic service in 1896 and was posted to Vienna. Over the next twelve years he was stationed in Cairo, Abyssinia, Paris, and Buenos Aires. He returned to England and was elected a Unionist member from Rugby in 1910. He served as Andrew Bonar Law's private secretary when he led the opposition from 1911 until 1914. He served as a member of the intelligence corps in France at the outbreak of World War I in 1914. He returned to London in 1916 to become a parliamentary member of the air board. He was named to the cabinet as minister of transport and commissioner of works in 1924. He was created Baron Stonehaven of Ury in 1925 and was then appointed governor-general of Australia on October 8, 1925. He completed his term on October 2, 1930, and returned to England to serve as chairman of the Conservative Party from 1930 until 1936. He was created Viscount Stonehaven in 1938. He died of a heart attack at his home in Stonehaven, Kincardineshire, England, on August 20, 1941.

BARON SOMERS (Governor-General; October 3, 1930–January 22, 1931). Arthur Herbert Tennyson Somers Cocks was born in Freshwater, Isle of Wight, on March 20, 1887. He succeeded his great-uncle to the title of Lord Somers in 1899. He was educated at New College, Oxford, and served as a lieutenant colonel in the First Life Guards. He served with distinction with a regiment in France during World War I from 1914 until 1918. He retired from the army in 1922 and served as lord-in-waiting to King George V from 1924 until 1926. He succeeded Lord Stradbroke as governor of Victoria in 1926. He briefly served as acting governor-general of Australia from October 3, 1930, until January 22, 1931. He then returned to England, where he pursued his interest in the Scout movement. He became Deputy Chief Scout in 1936 and succeeded Lord Baden-Powell as Chief Scout in January 1941. Lord Somers died at his home at Eastnor Castle, Herefordshire, England, on July 14, 1944.

SIR ISAAC ALFRED ISAACS (Governor-General; January 22, 1931–January 22, 1936). Isaac Alfred Isaacs was born on in Melbourne, Victoria, on August 6, 1855. He was educated as a lawyer and admitted to the Victoria bar in 1880. He served as a member of the Victoria legislative assembly from 1892 until 1901. He was elected to Australia's house of representatives in 1901 and served as attorney general from 1905 until 1906. He became a justice of the high court of Australia in 1906 and chief justice in 1930. Isaacs was appointed the first native-born governor-general of Australia by recommendation of Labor Prime Minister James H. Scullin on January 22, 1931. He completed his term on January 22, 1936. Isaacs died in Melbourne at the age of 92 on February 11, 1948.

LORD GOWRIE (Governor-General; January 23, 1936–January 29, 1945). Alexander G. A. Hore-Ruthven was born in Windsor on July 6, 1872. He was educated at Eton and entered the military. He commanded a camel corps in

Egypt against dervish tribesmen in the Sudan. He received the Victoria Cross for heroism during the campaign in 1898. He later served in Somaliland and became military secretary to the viceroy of Ireland in 1905, and military secretary to the governor-general of Australia in 1908. He served in France during World War I, and attained the rank of brigadier general. He served as governor of South Australia from 1928 until 1934 and was governor of New South Wales in 1935. Hore-Ruthven became governor-general of Australia on January 23, 1936. He represented the Crown in Australia during most of World War II, stepping down on January 29, 1945. He returned to England to serve as lieutenant governor of Windsor Castle and colonel of the Welsh Guards. He was created Earl of Gowrie in 1945. Lord Gowrie died in Sipton Moyne, Gloucester, on May 2, 1955.

PRINCE HENRY, DUKE OF GLOUCESTER (Governor General; January 30, 1945–January 30, 1947). Henry William Frederick Albert of the House of Hanover, later Windsor, was born on March 31, 1900, the third son of King George V and Queen Mary of Great Britain. Prince Henry entered Eton in 1913 and Sandhurst in 1918. He embarked on a career in the army and attained to the rank of major in the Tenth Royal Hussars. He was created Baron Culloden, Earl of Ulster, and Duke of Gloucester in 1928. He received a royal promotion to major general in 1936 following the death of his father and the abdication of his eldest brother, the Duke of Windsor. During World War II, Prince Henry served as a liaison with the British Expeditionary Forces. He was wounded in France near the end of the war. On November 16, 1943, he was appointed by his brother, King George VI, to the honorary position of governor-general of Australia, though he did not take office until January 30, 1945. He retired as the King's representative in Australia on January 30, 1947. Prince Henry was created a field marshal in 1955. He died at his home, Barnwell Manor, in Northamptonshire, on June 10, 1974.

HEADS OF GOVERNMENT

SIR EDMUND BARTON (Prime Minister; January 1, 1901–September 24, 1903). Edmund Barton was born in Glebe, Sydney, on January 8, 1849. He was educated at the University of Sydney and graduated in 1868. He was called to the New South Wales bar in 1871. He entered politics and was elected to the legislative assembly in 1879. He served as speaker of the assembly from 1883 until 1887 and served in Sir George Dibbs's cabinet as attorney general from January until March of 1889. He became the leader of the Federation movement after Sir Henry Parke's death in 1896. He led the delegation to London that presented the Commonwealth Constitution Bill to Parliament in 1900. Barton became Australia's first prime minister on January 1, 1901. He had difficulty leading the government, which was composed of leading statesmen from Australia's states. Barton was knighted in 1902. He resigned from office on September 24, 1903, and was subsequently appointed senior puisne judge of Australia's high court. He died in Meadlow, near Sydney, on January 7, 1920.

ALFRED DEAKIN (Prime Minister; September 24, 1903–April 27, 1904). Alfred Deakin was born in Collingwood, Melbourne, on August 3, 1856. He graduated from Melbourne University in 1877 and taught briefly before being called to the bar. He subsequently entered politics and was elected to the Victoria legislative assembly in 1880. He was a member of the radical wing of the Liberal Party. He was named to the cabinet as minister of public works and water supply in 1883. The coalition government collapsed in 1890, and Deakin returned to the practice of law. He entered the first federal cabinet as attorney general under Prime Minister Edmund Barton in 1901. He became prime minister on September 24, 1903, following Barton's resignation. His government fell on April 27, 1904, and Deakin led the opposition. He again became prime minister on July 5, 1905. Differences within the cabinet brought down the government on November 13, 1908. He headed a coalition government from June 22, 1909, until April 29, 1910, when he stepped down after being defeated in general elections. He continued to lead the Liberals until January 1913, when he retired due to failing health. Deakin served as chief of the Australian Commission to the Panama-Pacific Exposition in San Francisco in 1915. He died of meningo-encephalitis in Sydney on October 7, 1919.

JOHN CHRISTIAN WATSON (Prime Minister; April 27, 1904–August 18, 1904). John Christian Watson was born in Valparaiso, Chile, on April 9, 1867, and came to New Zealand as a child. He was educated in Oamaru, New Zealand, before moving to Australia as a young man. Watson headed the Labor Party in the Australian Parliament from 1901. He broke with Alfred Deakin's Liberal government in 1904 and forced Deakin to step down. Watson briefly headed the government as prime minister and treasurer from April 27, 1904, until August 18, 1904, when Sir George Reid formed a coalition government. Watson died in Melbourne on November 18, 1941.

SIR GEORGE HOUSTOUN REID (Prime Minister; August 18, 1904–July 5, 1905). Sir George Houstoun Reid was born in Johnston, Renfrewshire, Scotland, on February 22, 1848. He accompanied his family to Australia in 1852. He entered the state civil service in 1864 and became secretary to the attorney general in 1878. He was elected to Parliament for East Sydney in 1880 and served in the cabinet as minister of public instruction from 1883 until 1884. He became leader of the Free Trade Party in 1891. He became premier of New South Wales after the collapse of Sir George Dibbs' government in 1894. He retained office until 1899, when Sir William Lyne became head of the government. Reid became leader of the opposition after the Commonwealth was inaugurated in January 1901. He became prime minister of a coalition government with Alfred Deakin's Liberal Party on August 18, 1904. The government dissolved on July 5, 1905, and Reid returned to lead the opposition until 1908. He was appointed Australia's high commissioner to London in 1909, where he remained until 1915. Reid died in London after a long illness on September 12, 1918.

ALFRED DEAKIN (Prime Minister; July 5, 1905–November 13, 1908). *See earlier entry under Heads of Government.*

ANDREW FISHER (Prime Minister; November 13, 1908–June 2, 1909). Andrew Fisher was born in Crosshouse, Kilmarnock, Scotland, on August 29, 1862. He began working in the mines at the age of ten. He entered the miner's union and emigrated to Queensland in 1885. He initially worked for the railroad before organizing miners in the gold field. He was elected by the miners to represent them in the Queensland House of Assembly in 1893. He was defeated in the 1896 elections but returned to the Parliament in 1899. He was named to

Anderson Dawson's Labor government as minister of railways and public works. He was elected to the first federal Parliament of Australia in 1901 and served as minister of trade in Alfred Deakin's government in 1908. He succeeded Deakin as prime minister of a coalition government on November 13, 1908. He was defeated when his coalition was dissolved on June 2, 1909, but returned to head the government on April 29, 1910. His government founded the Commonwealth Bank and began the construction of Canberra as the federal capital. The Labor Party was defeated in elections in 1913, and Fisher was replaced as prime minister by a Liberal government under Joseph Cook on June 24, 1913. Fisher forced new elections the following year and Labor regained power. He again took office as prime minister on September 17, 1914. He supported England in its efforts during World War I, but the burden of leading the country during the war led to his resignation on October 27, 1915. He subsequently served as Australia's high commissioner in England, where he remained until 1921. He died of influenza in London on October 22, 1928.

ALFRED DEAKIN (Prime Minister; June 22, 1909–April 29, 1910). *See earlier entry under Heads of Government.*

ANDREW FISHER (Prime Minister; April 29, 1910–June 24, 1913). *See earlier entry under Heads of Government.*

JOSEPH COOK (Prime Minister; June 24, 1913–September 17, 1914). Joseph Cook was born in Silverdale, Staffordshire, England, on December 7, 1860. He emigrated to New South Wales in 1885, where he worked as a miner. He became secretary of the Miners Labor Union and was elected to the New South Wales legislative assembly in 1891. He became parliamentary leader of the Labor Party two years later. He was elected to the federal Parliament in 1901

as a member of the Free Trade Party. He succeeded George Reid as leader of the Free Trade Party in November of 1908, and was named minister of defense in Alfred Deakin's coalition government in 1909. The government fell the following year and Cook remained in opposition for the next three years. He became leader of the Liberal Party after Deakins' retirement in January 1913. He became prime minister on June 24, 1913. His government pledged Australia's support to the British government during the early days of World War I. The Labor Party regained control of the government, and Cook left office on September 17, 1914. Cook remained in the opposition to the Labor Party government of Andrew Fisher. He supported compulsory military conscription for the war effort and entered into a Nationalist coalition with Prime Minister William Hughes. Cook became deputy prime minister under Hughes in 1917, and he and Hughes represented Australia at the imperial war cabinet in June 1918. Cook served as treasurer from July 1920 until November 1921, when he resigned from parliament to serve as Australia's high commissioner to London. He returned to Australia in 1927 and retired from public life two years later. He subsequently became a leading real estate developer. Cook died in Sydney on July 30, 1947.

ANDREW FISHER (Prime Minister; September 17, 1914–October 27, 1915). *See earlier entry under Heads of Government.*

WILLIAM MORRIS HUGHES (Prime Minister; October 27, 1915–February 9, 1923). William Morris Hughes was born in Llandudno, Wales, on September 25, 1864. He was educated at St. Stephen's Church of England School in Westminster, London. Hughes emigrated to Australia in 1884. He worked at various jobs before joining the Socialist movement. He was elected to the

New South Wales legislative assembly in 1894. He was a founder of the Labor Party and a supporter of the federation of Australian colonies. He was elected to the federal House of Representatives in 1901. He served in Labor cabinets under John Watson in 1904 and Andrew Fisher in 1908, 1910 through 1913, and 1914 through 1915. He succeeded Fisher as prime minister when he retired on October 27, 1915. He led Australia during World War I. His support for mandatory military conscription led to a break in the Labor Party, and Hughes was expelled from the party in November 1916. He formed a coalition Nationalist Party and remained head of the government. He headed the Australian delegation to the Versailles peace conference after the war. His government fell on February 9, 1923. Hughes remained a leading political figure and served in Joseph Lyons' cabinet from 1932 until 1939. He was leader of the United Australia Party from 1941 until 1943. Hughes remained in parliament until his death from pneumonia and heart failure in Canberra on October 27, 1952.

STANLEY M. BRUCE (Prime Minister; February 9, 1923–October 22, 1929). Stanley Melbourne Bruce was born in St. Kilda, Victoria, on April 15, 1883. He was educated at Trinity College, Cambridge, and was called to the bar in 1906. He served in the Royal Fusiliers in Gallipoli and France during World War I. He returned to Australia in 1917 after being wounded in action. He was elected to the federal Parliament in 1918 as a member of the National Party. He was named Australia's representative to the League of Nations in 1921. He was treasurer in William Hughes' government in 1923 and became prime minister following Hughes' resignation on February 9, 1923. He also served in the government as foreign minister. Bruce led the country to economic recovery in the postwar era. He expanded railways and roads and created

the Commonwealth Council for Scientific and Industrial Research. His government fell on October 22, 1929, over a budgetary issue, and Bruce lost his seat in the Parliament. He returned to the government to serve as treasurer in Joseph Lyons's government in 1932. He was subsequently named high commissioner to London. He also represented Australia at the League of Nations from 1932 until 1939. He remained in England throughout World War II and served on the British war cabinet. He stepped down as high commissioner in 1945. He was created Viscount Bruce of Melbourne in 1947. He served as chairman of the World Food Council from 1947 until 1951. Bruce became chancellor of the Australian National University in 1951, and retained that post until his retirement in 1961. He returned to London and died at his home there on August 25, 1967.

JAMES HENRY SCULLIN (Prime Minister; October 22, 1929–January 6, 1932). James Henry Scullin was born in Ballarat, Victoria, on September 18, 1876. He worked as a sheep herder and in the gold mines as a young man. He joined the labor movement and formed a branch in Ballarat in 1903. Scullin was elected to the Parliament in 1910, but was defeated for reelection three years later. He subsequently served as editor of the Ballarat labor journal, *The Evening Echo*. Scullin returned to the Parliament in 1922. He became leader of the Labor Party in 1928 and headed the government as prime minister on October 22, 1929. He took office as Australia was undergoing the effects of the worldwide economic depression. Scullin was forced to institute harsh economic policies to prevent the nation from going into bankruptcy. The Labor Party was defeated in general elections in November of 1931, and Scullin was replaced as prime minister by Joseph Lyons on January 6, 1932. Scullin continued to lead the opposition until October 1935. He died in Melbourne on January 28, 1953, after a long illness.

JOSEPH ALOYSIUS LYONS (Prime Minister; January 6, 1932–April 7, 1939). Joseph Aloysius Lyons was born in Stanley, Tasmania, on September 15, 1879. He was educated at the Teachers' Training College in 1906. He became involved in politics and was elected to the Tasmanian House of assembly as a member of the Labor Party in 1909. He served as treasurer and minister of education and railway in the Tasmanian cabinet from 1914 until 1916. He served in the opposition until 1923, when he became premier of Tasmania. His government was defeated in 1928. Lyons was elected to the federal Parliament the following year and served as postmaster general and minister of works and railways in James Scullin's government. He resigned from the cabinet in January 1931 and became leader of the United Australia Party. He replaced Scullin as prime minister on January 6, 1932. He enacted measures to improve Australia's economic situation and reduce unemployment. He was returned to office after the elections of 1934 and 1937. Scullin retained office until his death in Sydney from heart failure on April 7, 1939.

SIR EARLE PAGE (Prime Minister; April 7, 1939–April 26, 1939). Earle Christmas Grafton Page was born in Grafton, New South Wales, on August 8, 1888. He was trained as a medical doctor at Sydney University and served as a surgeon in the Australian Army Medical Corps during World War I. He returned to Australia after the war and entered politics. He became a leader of the newly formed Country Party. He was instrumental in bringing down the government of William Hughes in February 1923. He served as deputy prime minister and treasurer in Stanley Bruce's subsequent government. While treasurer, Page formed the Australian Loan Council and served as its chairman until 1929.

He was again deputy prime minister and minister of commerce in Joseph Lyons' cabinet and succeeded to the office of prime minister when Lyons died in office on April 7, 1939. He resigned when the United Australia Party selected Robert Gordon Menzies to head the government on April 26, 1939. He remained leader of the Country Party until 1941. He served on John Curtin's war cabinet from 1942 to 1956. He was named minister of health in 1949 and remained in that position until he retired from the cabinet. Page remained in the Parliament until his defeat in general elections in December 1961. He died in Sydney on December 20, 1961.

ROBERT GORDON MENZIES (Prime Minister; April 26, 1939–August 29, 1941). Robert Gordon Menzies was born on December 20, 1894, in Jeparit in Victoria County. He was educated at Wesley College in Melbourne and received a law degree from the University of Melbourne. He began practicing law and was soon elected to the Victorian legislative council. From 1929 to 1934 Menzies served in the state assembly from Nunawading and was attorney general for Victoria from 1932 until 1934 when he was elected to Parliament representing Kooyong. He was appointed attorney general in the government of Prime Minister Joseph Lyons in 1935 and was named deputy leader of the United Australia Party the same year. In April 1939 Lyons died in office, and Menzies was selected to succeed him on April 26, 1939. The next year the United Australia Party won a one-seat majority in Parliament. As prime minister, Menzies declared war on Germany and began preparations to change Australia over to wartime production and economy. Menzies was forced to resign on August 29, 1941. He remained in the government of Arthur Fadden as minister of defense coordination until the Labor Party, under Joseph Curtin, came to power in October 1941. Following his term as prime minister, Menzies dissolved the coalition United Australia Party and formed the Liberal Party. On December 19, 1949, Menzies was again chosen as prime minister in a coalition government of the Liberal and Country Parties. A supporter of free enterprise, Menzies avidly pursued foreign investments and succeeded in vastly increasing Australia's industrialization. Menzies was also an anti-Communist who committed Australian troops to fight in the Korean War. He helped negotiate the ANZUS Treaty, which militarily allied Australia with New Zealand and the United States. In 1954 Australia joined SEATO. Menzies also was a supporter of the United States' policy in Vietnam. He was knighted by Queen Elizabeth II in March 1963. Menzies retired from office on January 25, 1966. He suffered a series of strokes beginning in 1968 and was confined to a wheelchair three years later. He died in Sydney on May 14, 1978.

SIR ARTHUR WILLIAM FADDEN (Prime Minister; August 29, 1941–October 7, 1941). Arthur William Fadden was born in Ingham, North Queensland, on August 13, 1895. He entered politics and was elected to the House of Assembly for Kennedy, Queensland, in 1932. He was elected to the House of Representatives in 1936, and served as a member of the Country Party. Fadden served as treasurer from 1940 until 1941. He briefly served as prime minister from August 29, 1941, until October 7, 1941, when John Joseph Curtin formed a government. He led the opposition from 1941 until 1943. Fadden returned to the government as deputy prime minister and treasurer in 1949 and served in this capacity until 1958. During this period he was acting prime minister several times when Prime Minister Robert Menzies was out of the country. Fadden also continued to lead the Country Party until his retirement from the Parliament in 1958. He died on April 22, 1973.

JOHN JOSEPH CURTIN (Prime Minister; October 7, 1941–July 5, 1945). John Joseph Curtin was born at Creswick, in Victoria, Australia, on January 8, 1885. Leaving home at an early age, he worked in various odd jobs before becoming affiliated with the Victoria Timber Workers Union in 1911. From 1917 to 1928 he was editor of the trade union paper *Westralian Worker*. Curtin was elected to parliament as a Labor member from Freemantle in 1928. He was defeated for reelection in 1931, but regained his seat in 1934. The following year he became leader of the opposition Labor Party. He served in that position until he was elected to succeed Arthur Fadden as prime minister and minister of defense on October 7, 1941. Shortly after his election, Japan bombed Pearl Harbor, and Curtin began preparations for a possible Japanese invasion of Australia. Curtin increased war production and worked closely with the United States and General Douglas MacArthur during the war. He suffered a heart attack in November 1944 and died of a heart ailment in Canberra on July 6, 1945.

FRANCIS M. FORDE (Prime Minister; July 6, 1945–July 13, 1945). Francis Michael Forde was born in Mitchell, Queensland, on July 18, 1890. He studied electrical engineering and taught school before entering Parliament as a Labor representative from Capricornia in 1922. He was first named to the cabinet in 1929 and served as minister for trade and customs from 1931 until 1932. Forde was deputy prime minister and minister for the army from 1941 to 1946. In April 1945 Forde led the Australian delegation to the United Nations Conference in San Francisco. He became acting prime minister of Australia on April 30, 1945, following the illness of John Curtin. Upon Curtin's death on July 6, 1945, Forde was appointed prime minister by the governor-general, the Duke of Gloucester, but served less than a week. He remained deputy prime minister in the government of Joseph Chifley until he lost reelection to his Parliament seat in 1946. From 1946 until 1953 Forde was Australian high commissioner to Canada. He returned to Australia and was again elected to Parliament in 1955, though he was narrowly defeated for reelection two years later. Forde then retired to a suburb of Brisbane, where he remained until his death on January 28, 1983.

JOSEPH B. CHIFLEY (Prime Minister; July 13, 1945–December 19, 1949). Joseph Benedict Chifley was born in Balthurst, New South Wales, on September 22, 1885. He worked with the New South Wales Railway and became a leader of the Federated Union of Locomotive Engineers. Chifley was elected to represent Macquarie in Parliament on the Labor Party ticket in 1928. The following year he was named minister of defense. He lost reelection in 1931 and was named a member of the Royal Commission on Monetary Banking Systems while out of office. Chifley returned to Parliament in 1940 and was appointed treasurer in the government of Prime Minister John Curtin in October 1941. He also served as acting prime minister when Deputy Prime Minister Francis M. Forde was out of the country during Curtin's illness. Curtin died on July 6, 1945, and Chifley defeated Forde for the leadership of the Labor Party on July 13, 1945. He was subsequently sworn in as prime minister. Chifley also remained treasurer in the new government. One of the major proposals of his government was the nationalization of Australian banks. Though the legislation authorizing this move was passed, it was declared unconstitutional. The Labor Party was defeated in the elections of 1949 and Chifley was replaced as prime minister by Robert Menzies. He remained party leader in opposition. He suffered a heart attack in 1950, and on June 13, 1951, he died suddenly in Canberra.

Austria

Austria is a landlocked country in central Europe, almost completely in the Alps. The Republic of Austria was proclaimed in November of 1918 after the breakup of the Austro-Hungarian Empire.

HEADS OF STATE

FRANZ JOSEF (Emperor; December 2, 1848–November 21, 1916). Franz Josef (Francis Joseph) was born at Schönbrunn Castle on August 18, 1830. He was the eldest son of Archduke Franz Karl and Princess Sophia of Bavaria. He became heir presumptive to the throne of his uncle, Ferdinand I. Franz Josef received military training and saw action in Italy in 1848. Ferdinand I abdicated on December 2, 1848, and Franz Josef was proclaimed emperor of Austria during a period of revolutionary fervor. An imperial charter incorporated Hungary with Austria in March 1849. He and his prime minister, Felix, Prince zu Schwarzenberg, used repressive measures against opponents of the regime. Franz Josef survived an assassination attempt in 1853. He married Elizabeth, the daughter of Maximilian, Duke of Bavaria, in April 1854. Austria engaged in a war against Sardinia and the French in 1859 (Italian War of 1859), which resulted in

Austria's loss of Lombardy. Austria also suffered defeat in the Austro-Prussian War in 1866 (Six Weeks War). The Austrian Empire subsequently became the Dual Monarchy of Austria-Hungary the following year. Austria occupied Bosnia-Herzegovina in 1878, which incurred the animosity of the Serbs. The Austro-German Alliance was formed in 1879, and Italy was included as part of the Triple Alliance in 1882. Austria's subsequent foreign policy was largely dominated by Germany. The Emperor agreed to the proposal of the Christian Social People's Party to introduce universal suffrage in the western half of the empire in 1906. The emperor's life was beset by numerous personal tragedies. His brother, Emperor Maximilian of Mexico, was overthrown and executed in Queretaro, on June 19, 1867. Franz Josef's only son, Archduke Rudolf, shot himself in an apparent suicide pact with his mistress at the hunting lodge of Mayerling on January 30, 1889. Franz Josef's wife, the Empress Elizabeth, was stabbed to death by an anarchist in Geneva on September 10, 1898. The Emperor's nephew, Francis Ferdinand, became heir to the throne. Francis Ferdinand and his wife were assassinated by Serbian nationalists at Sarajevo on June 28, 1914. This act led to war between Austria and Serbia, which soon involved most of Europe in World War I. Franz Josef's advanced age and failing health soon led to his death at Schönbrunn Castle on November 21, 1916.

KARL (Emperor; November 21, 1916–November 11, 1918). Karl Franz Josef was born at Persenbeug Castle in Lower Austria on August 17, 1887. He was the son of Archduke Otto and the grand-nephew of Emperor Franz Josef. Karl married Princess Zita of Bourbon-Parma in 1911. Karl became heir presumptive to the Austro-Hungarian throne following the assassination of the Archduke Francis Ferdinand on June 28, 1914. He commanded troops during World War I be-

fore succeeding to the throne upon the death of Emperor Franz Josef on November 21, 1916. His government made attempts to negotiate a peace settlement with Great Britain and France in 1917 without success. Following the defeat of Austria-Hungary on November 11, 1918, Karl withdrew from political affairs. He left Austria for Switzerland in March 1919 and was deposed by the Austrian parliament in April 1919. Karl made two abortive attempts to regain the Hungarian throne in 1921 and was subsequently banished from Hungary. He settled in exile in Madeira in October 1921. Karl died in Funchal, Madeira, on April 1, 1922.

MICHAEL HAINISCH (President; December 9, 1920–December 5, 1928). Michael Hainisch was born on August 15, 1858. He was educated at the Universities of Vienna, Leipzig, and Berlin, and received a doctorate in 1882. He was elected to Parliament in 1909. Hainisch was chosen by Parliament as a compromise candidate of the Pan-Germans and the Christian Socialists to become the first president of the Austrian Republic on December 9, 1920. Hainisch was a popular leader, despite the government's inability to solve the country's political and economic problems. He was re-elected by a large margin in 1924. Hainisch completed his second term of office and stepped down on December 5, 1928, but he remained a leading advocate of Austria's union with Germany. Hainisch retired to his country house in Gloggnitz, where he died on February 26, 1940.

WILHELM MIKLAS (President; December 5, 1928–March 13, 1938). Wilhelm Miklas was born in Krems on October 15, 1872. He was a philosophy professor at a preparatory school before his election to the Austrian Parliament during the reign of Emperor Franz Josef. Miklas was a member of the Christian Socialist Party and became president of the Parliament under the republic in 1923. He was chosen by Parliament to replace Michael Hainisch as president of the republic on December 5, 1928. He served as president for the next decade, but offered little interference in the conduct of the government. Miklas refused to dismiss Chancellor Kurt von Schuschnigg in March 1933 to allow the formation of a Nazi government under Arthur Seyss-Inquart, and he attempted to resist Austria's annexation by Adolf Hitler's Nazi Germany in 1938. Hitler ordered his troops to march into Austria, and Miklas was forced to resign on March 13, 1938, when he refused to sign the *Anschluss* agreement unifying Austria with Germany. Miklas retired from political affairs and remained inactive during World War II. He died in Vienna on March 15, 1956.

KARL RENNER (President; December 20, 1945–December 31, 1950). Karl Renner was born in Moravia on December 14, 1870. He studied law at the University of Vienna, where he joined the Social Democratic Party. He was elected to the national assembly in 1907, where he became a leader of the opposition to the Hapsburg monarchy. The Austro-Hungarian Empire was dissolved following the end of World War I, and Austria was proclaimed a republic on November 12, 1918. Renner served as chancellor and foreign minister of the first republic and signed the Treaty of St. Germain in 1919, which greatly reduced the status and power of Austria. Renner's coalition cabinet was dissolved on June 10, 1920, and he resigned as foreign minister in October of the same year.

Renner was elected to the national assembly in 1922, where he remained a member until 1934. He also served as assembly president from 1931 until 1933. Renner was subsequently jailed by the nationalist regime of Dr. Engelberg Dollfuss during a crackdown on Socialist elements in the government. Renner was released from prison a year later when it was ruled there was insufficient evidence to hold him for treason. He remained on the political sidelines during the abortive Nazi coup d'état and the assassination of Dollfuss and the subsequent unification of Austria with Hitler's Germany. Renner left Vienna during World War II and moved to Gloggnitz in Lower Austria. He participated in the anti–Nazi underground during this period. When Soviet forces occupied Austria in the spring of 1945, Renner was called upon to form a new government, which included a coalition of Social Democrats, Communists, and other small parties. The new government was approved and recognized by the Allied forces on April 29, 1945. Renner's government declared Austria's independence from Germany, and all Nazi laws were repealed. A general election was also called, and on November 28, 1945, Renner resigned as chancellor and was then selected by the new National Assembly to serve as federal president on December 20, 1945. As president, Renner worked for the removal of the occupation forces from Austria. He was denounced by the Communists in 1946 because of his support for democratic institutions. Renner remained president until his death in Vienna after a brief illness on December 31, 1950.

HEADS OF GOVERNMENT

HEINRICH VON WITTEK (Minister President; December 21, 1899–January 18, 1900). Heinrich von Wittek was born in Vienna on January 29, 1844. He served in the government as minister of railways before heading an interim government from December 21, 1899, until January 18, 1900. Wittek died in Vienna on April 10, 1930.

ERNST VON KOERBER (Minister President; January 19, 1900–December 27, 1904). Ernst von Koerber was born in Trient on November 6, 1850. He served in the Austrian civil service and headed several ministries during the late 1800s. He was called upon by the emperor to head the Austrian government on January 19, 1900. Koerber initiated numerous public works programs to help Austria recover from economic depression. He also attempted to negotiate a settlement of the dispute between German and Czech interests in Bohemia. The obstructionism of the Czechs in Parliament was a factor in Koerber's resignation on December 27, 1904. Koerber was named joint minister of finance for Austria-Hungary in February of 1915. He returned to office as minister president on October 21, 1916, following the assassination of Karl Stürgkh. Emperor Franz Josef died the following month; and Koerber came into conflict with his successor, Emperor Karl. The emperor's decree to make German the official language in Bohemia and disputes over financial issues led to Koerber's resignation on December 13, 1916. He retired from public life and died in Gutenbrunn on March 5, 1919.

KARL GAUTSCH VON FRANKENTHURN (Minister President; January 1, 1905–April 30, 1906). Karl Gautsch von Frankenthurn was born in Vienna on February 26, 1851. He began his career as a clerk in the department of finance. He subsequently became a teacher and director of the Theresianum Military Academy. He was named to Count Eduard von Taafe's government as minister of education in 1885. He was given the title of baron four years later. Gautsch stepped down with the government in November 1893. He returned to the military academy as director before joining Kasimir Badeni's government as minister of education in September of 1895. He succeeded Badeni as minister president on November 30, 1897. He remained head of the government until March 5, 1898. Gautsch again became minister president on January 1, 1905. He was instructed by the emperor to implement general suffrage in Austria. His system of compliance alienated the German and Polish minorities and resulted in his resignation on April 30, 1906. Gautsch was again named minister president on June 28, 1911, but his government collapsed on October 28, 1911, when he was unable to gain the support of the Czechs. Gautsch was inactive during World War I. He died at his home in Vienna on April 20, 1918.

KONRAD VON HOHENLOHE-SCHILLINGFÜRST (Minister President; May 2, 1906–May 28, 1906). Prince Konrad von Hohenlohe-Waldenburg-Schillingfürst was born in Vienna on December 16, 1863. He was the son of Prince Constantine von Hohenlohe-Schillingfürst. He was governor of Trieste for many years before joining Karl Gautsch von Frankenthurn's government as minister of the interior in 1905. He stepped down from the government in early 1906. Hohenlohe was called upon to succeed Gautsch as head of the government on March 2, 1906. He had resisted the appointment and resigned on May 28, 1906, over the issue of the Hungarian government being allowed to call its tariffs autonomous. Hohenlohe was sometimes referred to as the "Red Prince" because of his radical views and friendship with the Socialists. He died in Hiermarken while attending a hunt on December 21, 1918.

MAX WLADIMIR VON BECK (Minister President; June 2, 1906–November 7, 1908). Max Wladimir von Beck was born in Wahring on September 6, 1854. He was the tutor of Archduke Francis Ferdinand. He was chosen by Emperor Franz Josef to head a government composed of civil servants and members of Parliament on June 2, 1906. The archduke soon turned against Beck because of his government's support for modest electoral reforms. Beck opposed the annexation of Bosnia and tried to introduce political reforms in Bohemia, which gained the opposition of leading Czech politicians. Beck resigned on November 7, 1908. He died in Vienna on January 20, 1943.

RICHARD VON BIENERTH (Minister President; November 15, 1908–June 28, 1911). Richard von Bienerth was born in Verona on March 2, 1863. He was a civil servant and was called upon to replace Max von Beck as minister president on November 15, 1908. His nominally parliamentary regime was beset with difficulties and was unable to get substantive legislation passed. Bienerth dissolved the parliament in May 1911 to hold new elections. He resigned on June 28, 1911. He was granted the title Count Bienerth-Schmerling in 1915. Bienerth died in Vienna on June 3, 1918.

KARL GAUTSCH VON FRANKENSTHURN (Minister President; June 28, 1911–October 28, 1911). *See earlier entry under Heads of Government.*

KARL STÜRGKH (Minister President; November 3, 1911–October 21, 1916). Karl Stürgkh was born in Graz on October 30, 1859, to an impoverished noble family in Styria. He was educated at the University of Graz. Stürgkh entered the civil service in 1881 and was elected a deputy to the Reichsrath (parliament) ten years later. He served as a director in the ministry of public works in 1894. He served as Ernst von Koerber's parliamentary lieutenant from 1900 until 1904. He gained a reputation as an expert in educational matters and received the patronage of Rudolf Sieghart, a leading financier and newspaper pub-

lisher. Stürgkh headed the public works ministry in 1909 and was called upon to head the government on November 3, 1911. Stürgkh remained minister president of Austria following Archduke Francis Ferdinand's assassination on June 28, 1914, and the subsequent events leading to World War I. Stürgkh headed the government in the early years of the war and despite entreaties refused to convene Parliament. He remained minister president until October 21, 1916, when he was shot to death by the radical Socialist Friedrich Adler while having lunch at a Vienna hotel.

ERNST VON KOERBER (Minister President; October 21, 1916–December 13, 1916). *See earlier entry under Heads of Government.*

HEINRICH VON CLAM-MARTINIC (Minister President; December 20, 1916–June 23, 1917). Heinrich von Clam-Martinic was born in Vienna on January 1, 1873. He was from a noble Bohemian family and began his career as a federalist and Czech nationalist. He served in the upper chamber of the Austrian parliament and was minister of agriculture in the government of Ernst von Koerber in 1916. He was chosen to succeed von Koerber as minister president on December 20, 1916. He headed a government composed primarily of Germans and Poles. He called parliament into session in early 1917. Increased demands by the Poles for independence and the parliament's refusal to support Clam-Martinic's policies led to his resignation on June 23, 1917. He subsequently served as military governor of Montenegro until the collapse of the Hapsburg monarchy. Clam-Martinic died in Clam on March 7, 1932.

ERNST SEIDLER (Minister President; June 23, 1917–July 25, 1918). Ernst Ritter Seidler von Feuchtenegg was born in Schwechat on June 5, 1862. He had served as a tutor to Emperor

Karl in administrative law. He was an official at the ministry of agriculture when called upon to head an interim government on June 23, 1917. Seidler was unable to settle the disputes between the various nationalities in Austria as World War I continued. He tried to resign several times before the emperor accepted his resignation on July 25, 1918. He died in Vienna on January 23, 1931.

MAX, BARON HUSSAREK VON HEINLEIN (Minister President; July 25, 1918–October 17, 1918). Max Hussarek von Heinlein was born in Bratislava on May 3, 1865. He was the son of a field marshal and had served in the civil service. He was also a professor of law at the University of Vienna. He served as minister of education in the governments of Karl Stürgkh from 1911 until 1916 and Heinrich von Clam-Martinic in 1916 and 1917. He was chosen to head the government on July 25, 1918. Austria's war efforts were failing and various areas of the empire were clamoring for independence. With the support of the emperor, Hussarek proposed a federal Austria, which would grant home rule for Poland, the partition of Bohemia between Czech and German autonomous areas, and a Slav state. Nationalist leaders within Austria considered these concessions unacceptable and Hussarek stepped down on October 17, 1918. He died in Vienna on March 7, 1935.

HEINRICH LAMMASCH (Minister President; October 27, 1918–November 11, 1918). Heinrich Lammasch was born in Seitenstetten on December 21, 1853. He was a leading authority on international law and became professor at the University of Vienna in 1899. He also served as a member of the upper house of the Austrian Parliament. He was named to The Hague International Tribunal in 1900 and served on numerous international committees. Lammasch was a delegate to the second Hague Peace Conference in 1907, and was vice president of the Geneva convention committee. He was an advocate of the peace movement in 1918, and was chosen as Austria's minister president on October 27, 1918. His government conducted peace negotiations with the victorious Allied powers. He resigned following the abdication of Emperor Karl on November 11, 1918. Lammasch died in Salzburg, Austria, on January 6, 1920.

KARL RENNER (Chancellor; November 12, 1918–June 10, 1920). *See earlier entry under Heads of State.*

MICHAEL MAYR (Chancellor; June 10, 1920–June 21, 1921). Michael Mayr was born in Adlwang, Lower Austria, on April 10, 1864. He began his political career as a member of the Conservative Clerical Party before joining the Christian Socialists. Mayr was a professor of modern history at Innsbruck University for many years. He became secretary of state for constitutional reform following the separation of Austria and Hungary in 1918. Mayr was chosen to head the government as chancellor on June 10, 1920. He resigned on June 21, 1921. Mayr died the following year in Waldkirchen on May 22, 1922.

JOHANN SCHOBER (Chancellor; June 21, 1921–May 24, 1922). Johann Schober was born in Perg, Upper Austria, on November 14, 1874. He worked in the civil service in Vienna before joining the government police. He was appointed director of the Central Bureau of Police by Emperor Karl in 1914, continuing in that position after the transformation of Austria from an empire to a republic. He was called upon by Parliament to serve as chancellor on June 21, 1921. His government concluded a reconciliation treaty with Czechslovakia before Schober stepped down on May 24, 1922. He returned to his position with the police, where he introduced numerous reforms. He also became head of the international police commission in Vienna. Threats of violence from the Fascist Home Guards led parliament to recall Schober to head the government on September 26, 1929. He concluded a treaty with Italy and succeeded in negotiating the cancellation of war reparation payments in 1930. Schober resigned as chancellor on September 25, 1930. He subsequently served as vice-chancellor and minister of foreign affairs in Otto Ender's government. His attempts to establish a customs union between Austria and Germany in 1931 led to his resignation from the cabinet. Schober died of heart disease in Vienna on August 19, 1932.

IGNAZ SEIPEL (Chancellor; May 31, 1922–November 20, 1924). Ignaz Seipel was born in Vienna on July 19, 1876. Ordained a Catholic priest in 1899, he was professor of moral theology at the University of Salzburg for nearly a decade before accepting the same position at the University of Vienna. He was also the author of a book on the Austrian constitution and became an advisor to the Christian Socialist Party in 1917. He entered Heinrich Lammasch's cabinet as minister of social welfare in 1918. He was an opponent of the Communist regime of Bela Kun after the fall of the monarchy later in the year. Seipel served as an advisor to the governments of Michael Mayr and Johann Schober. He agreed to head the government as chancellor on May 31, 1922, following the resignation of Schober. Seipel was shot and seriously injured in an assassination attempt on June 1, 1924. The subsequent economic crisis and the threat of a railway strike led to his resignation on November 20, 1924. He again headed the government from October 20, 1926, until April 3, 1929, when rioting in Vienna forced his resignation. He subsequently served as foreign minister in the government of Karl Vaugoin. He remained a leading figure in the Christian Socialist Party until his death on August 2, 1932.

RUDOLF RAMEK (Chancellor; November 20, 1924–October 15, 1926). Rudolf Ramek was born in Teschen on April 12, 1881. He was elected to the chamber of deputies as a Christian Socialist from Salzburg after the establishment of the Austrian Republic. He formed a government as chancellor on November 20, 1924. His administration was beset with banking scandals that implicated leading members of the government, including the finance minister, Jakob Ahrer. Ramek's government was unable to improve Austria's economic problems, and he was replaced by Ignaz Seipel on October 15, 1926. He died in Vienna on July 7, 1941.

IGNAZ SEIPEL (Chancellor; October 20, 1926–April 3, 1929). *See earlier entry under Heads of Government.*

ERNST STEERUWITZ (Chancellor; April 30, 1929–September 25, 1929). Ernst Steeruwitz was born in Mies on September 23, 1874. He served as an officer in the Imperial Army until the monarchy was ousted at the end of World War I. He joined the Christian Socialist Party and was elected to Parliament in 1923. He succeeded Ignaz Seipel as chancellor on April 30, 1929. He also served in the government as foreign minister until his resignation on April 3, 1929. Steeruwitz subsequently retired from politics to concentrate on a business career. He died in Vienna after a long illness on October 19, 1952.

JOHANN SCHOBER (Chancellor; September 26, 1929–September 25, 1930). *See earlier entry under Heads of Government.*

KARL VAUGOIN (Chancellor; September 30, 1930–November 30, 1930). Karl Vaugoin was born in Vienna on July 8, 1873. He served in the Austrian army and was named minister of defense in 1920. He was instrumental in creating Austria's postwar army during the 1920s, serving as minister of the army and minister of war. He succeeded Johann Schober as chancellor on September 30, 1930. His government was short-lived, and he stepped down on November 30, 1930. He was president of the Austrian federal railway at the time of Germany's annexation of Austria in 1938. He returned from a vacation in Italy and was arrested by the Nazis. He was sent to Dachau concentration camp, where he remained during most of World War II. He lived in retirement after the war until his death in Krems on June 11, 1949.

OTTO ENDER (Chancellor; December 3, 1930–June 19, 1931). Otto Ender was born in Altach on December 24, 1875. He briefly served as chancellor of Austria from December 3, 1930, until June 19, 1931. He was named president of the Austrian Court of Accounts by Chancellor Engelberg Dollfuss in 1934 and helped to draft the new Austrian constitution that year. He retained that position until the *Anschluss* in 1938, when Germany annexed Austria. Ender was subsequently arrested by the Nazis and imprisoned at Dachau concentration camp during World War II. After Austria's independence was reestablished in 1945, Ender was considered a leading elder statesman. He retired from political affairs to head a Rhine shipping company and several auto-touring clubs. He died in Bregenz on June 25, 1960.

KARL BURESCH (Chancellor; June 21, 1931–May 6, 1932). Karl Buresch was born in Gross-Enzerdorf on October 12, 1878. He was educated at the University of Vienna and became a lawyer. He entered politics and was elected to the municipal council of Gross-Enzerdorf. He served as burgomaster there from 1916 until 1919, when he was elected to the national assembly as a member of the Christian Socialist Party. Buresch served as governor of Lower Austria from 1922 until 1931. He succeeded Otto Ender as chancellor on

June 21, 1931. His attempts to gain assistance from the League of Nations for Austria's financial difficulties drew criticism from his political opponents. He stepped down on January 27, 1932, but was invited to form a new government. He succeeded two days later and continued to head the government until May 6, 1932. He remained in the cabinet as minister of finance under Chancellor Engelberg Dollfuss. Buresch retained that position in Kurt von Schuschnigg's cabinet when Dollfuss was assassinated in 1934. He subsequently served as minister without portfolio in von Schuschnigg's government until his retirement in January 1936. Buresch died on September 16, 1936, at a Vienna sanatorium of complications from diabetes.

ENGELBERG DOLLFUSS (Chancellor; May 20, 1932–July 25, 1934). Engelberg Dollfuss was born in Kirnberg an der Mank in Lower Austria on October 4, 1892. He was educated at the universities of Vienna and Berlin, where he studied economics and law. He became active in politics, serving as secretary of the Lower Austrian Peasant Union. He directed the chamber of agriculture in Lower Austria from 1927, where he gained a reputation as an expert in agricultural matters. He served as president of the Austrian federal railways from 1930, and was named to the cabinet as minister of agriculture in March 1931. He was called on by the Clerical Christian Socialist Party to form a government as chancellor on May 20, 1932. He was attacked in the chamber by nationalist elements in July 1932 when he accepted a League of Nations loan agreement that required Austria to forgo a customs union with Germany. Dollfuss began to govern in an increasingly authoritarian manner. He formed the Patriotic Front in May 1933. He sought an alliance with Benito Mussolini's government in Italy and began to base Austria's government on the Fascist model. Dollfuss promoted a new constitution in May

1934, which established him as a virtual dictator. He ruthlessly suppressed and dissolved the Social Democratic Party before moving against the Nazi Party in May 1934. Civil violence erupted throughout the country. Dollfuss was assassinated in the chancellery in Vienna during an abortive Nazi coup attempt on July 25, 1934.

KURT VON SCHUSCHNIGG (Chancellor; July 30, 1934–March 11, 1938). Kurt von Schuschnigg was born in Riva on December 14, 1897. He entered politics and was elected to the chamber of deputies in 1927 as a member of the Christian Socialist Party. He served in Engelberg Dollfuss's cabinet as minister of justice and education from 1932 until he succeeded to the chancellorship on July 30, 1934, following the abortive Nazi coup that resulted in Dollfuss's murder. Von Schuschnigg signed an agreement with the German ambassador, Franz von Papen, in July 1936 that acknowledged Austria as a German state and guaranteed that Germany would respect Austria's sovereignty. Von Schuschnigg attempted to withstand further demands placed on his government by Adolf Hitler's Nazi regime in Germany. He tried to preserve Austria's independence and announced a plebiscite in March 1938 to determine the nation's future. Hitler responded by ordering the invasion of Austria. He demanded von Schuschnigg's resignation, and the chancellor complied on March 11, 1938. Hitler proceeded with the invasion and annexation of Austria. Von Schuschnigg was arrested by the Gestapo and remained imprisoned throughout World War II. After his release, he emigrated to the United States. He was a professor of political science at St. Louis University in Missouri for the next twenty years. Von Schuschnigg returned to Austria in 1967 to live in retirement. He died after a long illness in a rented room of a small house in Mutters, near Innsbruck, on November 18, 1977.

ARTHUR SEYSS-INQUART (Chancellor; March 12, 1938–April 30, 1939). Arthur Seyss-Inquart was born to a wealthy family in Stannern bei Iglau, Moravia, on July 22, 1892. He earned a degree in law at the University of Vienna and served in the Austrian army during World War I. After the war he settled in Vienna, where he practiced law. He was an early advocate of Austria's unification with Germany and became one of the first members of the Nazi Party in Austria. Chancellor Kurt von Schuschnigg was forced by Germany to appoint Nazis to his cabinet in February 1938, and Seyss-Inquart became minister of the interior and security. When Adolf Hitler ordered the invasion of Austria and forced von Schuschnigg's resignation on March 11, 1938, Seyss-Inquart became head of the government. He continued to serve as governor of Austria after the annexation by Germany until April 30, 1939. He was subsequently appointed vice-governor of Poland. Seyss-Inquart was named Reich Commissar for the German-occupied Netherlands in May 1940. He escaped to Germany following the liberation of The Netherlands in the spring of 1945. He was arrested by Canadian soldiers in May 1945. He was tried with other major war criminals before the International Military Tribunal in Nuremberg. Seyss-Inquart was charged for his role in the deportation of Dutch Jews and for the shooting of hostages. He was convicted of the "ruthless application of terrorism" on September 30, 1946, and sentenced to death. He was executed by hanging on October 16, 1946.

KARL RENNER (Chancellor; April 29, 1945–November 28, 1945). *See earlier entry under Heads of State*

LEOPOLD FIGL (Chancellor; November 28, 1945–April 2, 1953). Leopold Figl was born in Lower Austria in the town of Rust on October 2, 1902. He was trained as an agricultural engineer at the

Vienna Agricultural High School. He joined the Lower Austrian Peasants Union and rose to director in 1933. Figl opposed the *Anschluss* plebiscite, which united Austria and Germany. Following unification, Figl was arrested by the Nazi regime and imprisoned at the Dachau and Flossenburg concentration camps from 1938 to 1943. After his release he was active in the anti-Nazi underground until he was arrested again and sent to the Mauthausen concentration camp in 1944. Figl remained there until he was freed by the Soviet Red Army during the liberation of Austria in the spring of 1945. In May of that year he was appointed secretary of state in the cabinet of Dr. Karl Renner. On November 28, 1945, leading a coalition of the People's Party and Socialist Party, Figl succeeded Renner as federal chancellor of the independent Austrian Republic. With the assistance of the United States, Figl presided over the economic revival of Austria and remained chancellor following the October 1949 general elections. He withstood an attempt by the Communists to seize power during a general strike in 1951. Figl was forced by Socialist members of his coalition government to relinquish the chancellorship, and he was succeeded by Dr. Julius Raab on April 2, 1953. Figl was named foreign minister in the Raab government on November 23, 1953. As foreign minister, Figl signed the treaty with the Allied powers in Vienna on May 15, 1955, that officially recognized Austria's independence as a militarily neutral state. Figl resigned from the foreign ministry in 1959 to become the president of parliament, a position he held until 1962, when he returned to Lower Austria as governor. Dr. Figl died of cancer in Vienna on May 9, 1965.

Bavaria

Bavaria became independent from the Holy Roman Empire in 1806. It became an autonomous part of the German Empire in 1871. It became a republic and joined the Weimar Republic in 1918. In 1949, it joined the German Federal Republic (West Germany).

HEADS OF STATE

OTTO (King; June 13, 1886–November 13, 1913). Otto William Luitpold Adalbert Woldemar was born in Munich on April 27, 1848. He was the son of Maximilian II and Princess Marie of Prussia. Otto was declared an incurable lunatic in 1876 and was confined at Nymphenburg Castle and at Schleissheim. He became king of Bavaria on June 13, 1886, when his elder brother, King Ludwig II, who was also insane, drowned himself in Starnberg Lake. Otto was confined at Furstenreid Castle near Munich during his reign. He ruled under the regency of his uncle, Luitpold, until Luitpold's death in 1912. Otto was deposed the following year on November 13, 1913. He died at Furstenreid Castle on October 11, 1916.

LUITPOLD (Regent; June 1886–December 12, 1912). Luitpold Karl Josef Wilhelm Ludwig was born in Würzburg on March 12, 1821. He was the third son of King Ludwig I. He entered the military and fought with Austria against the Prussians in the Six Weeks War in 1866. Luitpold acted as regent during the later years of the reign of his insane nephew, Ludwig II. He also served as regent when his equally insane younger nephew Otto assumed the throne in June 1886. Luitpold was well regarded by the Bavarian people, and he introduced some electoral reforms in 1906. He continued to rule in his nephew's name until his death in Munich on December 12, 1912.

LUDWIG III (King; November 13, 1913–November 13, 1918). Ludwig Leopold Joseph Maria Aloys Alfred was born in Munich on January 7, 1845. He was the son of Prince Luitpold and suc-

ceeded his father as regent upon the latter's death on December 12, 1912. Ludwig deposed his insane cousin, King Otto, on November 13, 1913, and succeeded to the throne. Ludwig took very little part in the events of World War I. After the war the Bavarian revolution forced him from the throne on November 13, 1918. His wife, the Archduchess Marie-Therese of Austria-Este, died the day he was forced from power. Ludwig went into exile in Switzerland and Austria. He died at Sarvar Castle in Hungary on October 18, 1921.

Belgium

Belgium is a country located in northwestern Europe. It was granted independence from The Netherlands on October 4, 1830.

HEADS OF STATE

LEOPOLD II (King; December 10, 1865–December 17, 1909). Leopold was born at the Palace of Laeken in Brussels on April 9, 1835. He was the eldest son of King Leopold I and Louise of Orleans. The younger Leopold was created duke of Brabant in 1846. He entered the Belgian army as a young man and was stationed in Egypt, India, and China. He married Marie Henriette, daughter of the Austrian Archduke Joseph, in 1853. Leopold succeeded to the throne upon his father's death on December 10, 1865. He maintained Belgium's neutrality during the Franco-German War of 1870. He attempted to modernize Belgium's military during the remainder of his reign. Leopold engaged in the financial exploitation of the African Congo region and declared the formation of the Congo Free State with himself as absolute monarch in 1886. His exploitation of the territory led to much criticism in Belgium and internationally over the harsh

treatment of the natives. The Congo became a Belgian colony in 1908. Leopold died of an embolism at Laeken on December 17, 1909.

ALBERT (King; December 17, 1909–February 17, 1934). Albert was born in Brussels, Belgium, on April 8, 1875. He was the younger son of Philip, Count of Flanders, the brother of Leopold II, and Princess Marie of Hohenzollern. Albert's brother Bauduoin became heir presumptive to the Belgian throne following the death of Leopold II's only son, Prince Leopold, on January 22, 1869. Bauduoin died on January 23, 1891, placing Albert next in line of succession. He was trained by the military at the École Militaire and married Élisabeth, the daughter of Duke Charles Theodore of Bavaria, in October 1900. They had three children: Leopold in 1901, Charles in 1903, and Marie José in 1906. He succeeded his uncle, Leopold II, to the throne on December 23, 1909. He directed numerous legal and social reforms during the early years of his reign. Following the outbreak of hostilities with Germany in the early days of World War I, Albert commanded the Belgian forces. He accompanied his army on retreat to the Yser river following the fall of Antwerp and continued to lead his troops against the German invasion during the remainder of the war. He advocated the abolishment of Belgian neutrality after the conclusion of the war. Albert was killed at Marche-les-Dames, near Namur, after falling while rock climbing on February 17, 1934.

LEOPOLD III (King; February 17, 1934–July 16, 1951). Leopold was born in Brussels on November 3, 1901. He was the elder son of Albert I and Princess Elisabeth of Bavaria. Albert I ascended to the Belgian throne in 1909 and Leopold became Crown Prince. Leopold was allowed to join the Belgian army as a private during World War I. He was sent to Eton College in England after six months of fighting at the front lines. Following the war and the completion of Leopold's education, he accompanied his parents on state visits around the world. King Albert I was killed in a fall from a cliff while mountain climbing on February 17, 1934, and Leopold was proclaimed king six days later. Leopold's wife, Queen Astrid, whom he had married in 1926, was killed in an automobile accident in Switzerland in August 1935. Leopold was faced with a growing autonomy movement in the country and tried to pursue a policy of neutrality as World War II drew near. He withdrew

Belgium from the Locarno Pact with Great Britain and France in the hopes that he could maintain peace with Germany. His hopes were in vain, as the German army invaded Belgium on May 10, 1940. King Leopold led the Belgian army in fighting against the German invaders, but he was forced to surrender on May 28, 1940. He and his family were taken prisoner by the occupation forces. They were held in the palace of Laeken, where Leopold married Liliane Baels, a commoner, in 1942. The royal family was moved to Germany in March 1944 where they remained until their liberation by American troops the following May. Leopold's brother Charles had been appointed regent in Leopold's absence in 1944. Leopold did not return to Belgium following his release because of public criticism of his unconditional surrender to the Germans. He went to Switzerland instead. He remained there until a plebiscite was held in March 1950 to determine if Leopold could reclaim the throne. The vote narrowly approved Leopold's return to Belgium. He returned to Brussels on July 22, 1950, despite the continued opposition of the Walloon community. He was met with strikes, protests, and riots upon his return. In order to ease the tension his return caused, Leopold delegated much of his royal powers to his son, Baudouin, on August 11, 1950. He abdicated in favor of Baudouin on July 16, 1951, but continued to live at the royal palace, Laeken, until 1959. He remained a close advisor and confidant to his son. He died after a heart attack in Brussels on September 25, 1983.

HEADS OF GOVERNMENT

PAUL DE SMET DE NAEYER (Prime Minister; August 5, 1899–May 4, 1907). Paul de Smet de Naeyer was born on May 13, 1843. He was a leading po-

litical figure in Belgium, serving as prime minister from February 25, 1896, to January 23, 1899. Smet returned to head the government after a brief interval on August 4, 1899, and retained office until May 4, 1907. Smet also headed the ministry of finance during his administration. He subsequently served as minister of state. He died in Brussels on September 10, 1913.

JULES DE TROOZ (Prime Minister; May 4, 1907–December 31, 1907). Jules de Trooz was born in 1857. He served in Paul de Smet de Naeyer's government as minister of the interior. He succeeded Smet as prime minister on May 4, 1907, and died in office on December 31, 1907.

FRANZ SCHOLLAERT (Prime Minister; January 9, 1908–June 8, 1911). Franz Schollaert was born in 1851. He was elected to the chamber of deputies in 1888. He served in the cabinet as minister of education from 1895 until 1899. He served as vice president of the chamber in 1900 and became president the following year. He became minister of the interior in the government of Jules de Trooz and succeeded to the prime ministership on January 9, 1908, when de Trooz died in office. His administration passed the treaty annexing the Congo Free State. Schollaert remained prime minister until his government stepped down over a ministerial school bill on June 8, 1911. Schollaert died in Le Havre, France, on June 29, 1917.

CHARLES DE BROQUEVILLE (Prime Minister; June 14, 1911–June 3, 1918). Charles de Broqueville was born in 1860. He entered Parliament in 1892. He opposed the general conscription for the army in 1909. He was called upon by King Albert to head the government on June 14, 1911. Two years later he supported a defense bill calling for the reorganization of the army and for general conscription in the face of Germany's military expansion. He led Belgium throughout World War I and the German occupation, which forced the government to leave the country. He stepped

down on June 3, 1918. De Broqueville remained in the subsequent cabinet and was again named to head the government on October 18, 1932. He resigned on November 13, 1934. De Broqueville died on September 4, 1940.

GERHARD COOREMAN (Prime Minister; June 3, 1918–November 21, 1918). Gerhard Cooreman was born in 1852. He replaced Charles de Broqueville as head of the government on June 3, 1918. The government was still in exile at Le Havre during the German occupation. Cooreman stepped down on November 21, 1918, following the government's return to Belgium. He died on December 2, 1926.

LÉON DELACROIX (Prime Minister; November 22, 1918–October 31, 1920). Léon Delacroix was born in 1867. He attended Louvain University, where he received a degree in law. He began a law practice in 1889 and became president of the Cassation Court of Brussels in 1917. Delacroix became prime minister of Belgium on November 22, 1918, shortly after the armistice ending World War I. He also served in the government as minister of finance. He resigned on October 31, 1920, after the collapse of his three-party coalition. He was subsequently named as the Belgian government's representative to the Reparation Commission and served as a delegate to the committee organizing the Bank for International Settlements. He died of heart failure at a hotel in Baden-Baden, Germany, while attending a meeting on October 15, 1929.

HENRY CARTON DE WIART (Prime Minister; November 20, 1920–December 14, 1921). Count Henry Carton de Wiart was born in 1869. He was elected to the chamber of deputies in 1895 and served in the government as minister of justice from 1911 until 1918. He was the leader of the Catholic Party. Carton de Wiart succeeded Léon Delacroix as prime minister on November 20, 1920, and headed a government of national unity until December 14, 1921. He subsequently served as Belgium's representative to the League of Nations and the Inter-Parliamentary Union. He was influential in convincing King Leopold III not to abdicate following World War II. Carton de Wiart was appointed minister of justice in Gaston Eyskens' cabinet in August 1949. He was called upon to form a government in March 1950 but was unable to do so. He remained in Jean Duvieusart's cabinet as minister of justice until his death in Brussels on May 6, 1951.

GEORGES THEUNIS (Prime Minister; December 14, 1921–April 5, 1925). Georges Theunis was born in Montegnee, near Liege, in 1873. He attended the military academy and served in the army until 1897. He subsequently worked as an electrical engineer until the outbreak of World War I. He rejoined the army and was stationed in Paris and London. He participated in the Versailles Peace Conference. Theunis was called upon to form a government as prime minister on December 14, 1921. He was instrumental in repairing damage done to the country during the war. He stepped down from office on April 5, 1925. He headed the International Chamber of Commerce during the 1930s until again forming a government on November 19, 1934. His government was forced to resign on March 19, 1935, when inflation caused the devaluation of the Belgian franc. He was appointed ambassador to the United States shortly before World War II. He remained in the United States during the war as a leading spokesman for resisting the German occupation of his country. He returned to Belgium in 1945. Theunis died in Brussels on January 4, 1966.

ALOYS VAN DE VYVERE (Prime Minister; May 1, 1925–May 22, 1925). Aloys van de Vyvere was born in 1871.

He was a leading Catholic politician who formed a right-wing cabinet on May 1, 1925. His government was attacked by Liberals and was forced to resign on May 22, 1925.

PROSPER A. J. POULLET (Prime Minister; May 22, 1925–May 11, 1926). Prosper A. J. Poullet was born in 1868. He was a member of the Catholic Party and became prime minister of Belgium on May 22, 1925. His government attempted to improve the country's finances through tax increases and more social legislation. Poullet resigned on May 11, 1926. He served as minister of state and as minister of the interior in Charles de Broqueville's government from 1932 until 1934. He was a councillor in Paul Van Zeeland's government in 1935 until he was forced to resign due to poor health. Poullet died in Louvain on December 3, 1937.

HENRI JASPER (Prime Minister; May 20, 1926–May 21, 1931). Henri Jasper was born on July 28, 1870. He was educated at the University of Brussels. He practiced law and entered politics as a leader of the Catholic Party. He served in the government as minister of finance in 1918 and was elected to the chamber of deputies from Liege in 1919. He served in several cabinets as minister of the interior and foreign affairs in the 1920s. He formed a coalition government on May 20, 1926. He re-formed the cabinet with a coalition of Catholics and Liberals in November 1927 and presided over The Hague Reparation Conference in 1928. Jasper left office on May 21, 1931. He served as minister of finance in Charles de Broqueville's cabinet in 1931 and later served as foreign minister. Jasper retired from politics in 1936 and returned to the practice of law. He was called upon to form a government in February 1939 but died four days later on February 15, 1939, after surgery.

JULES RANKIN (Prime Minister; June 6, 1931–October 18, 1932). Jules Rankin was born in 1862. He was a leader of the Catholic Party and served in the cabinet as minister of justice in 1907. He formed a government as prime minister on June 6, 1931. He also served as minister of the interior. His government granted official recognition of the Flemish language. Conflicts between the Liberals and the Catholics over the language issue caused problems in the cabinet. The Liberals and Socialists called for the dissolution of parliament and new elections. Rankin stepped down on October 18, 1932, to prepare for new elections. He died on July 16, 1934.

CHARLES DE BROQUEVILLE (Prime Minister; October 18, 1932–November 13, 1934). *See earlier entry under Heads of Government.*

GEORGES THEUNIS (Prime Minister; November 19, 1934–March 19, 1935). *See earlier entry under Heads of Government.*

PAUL VAN ZEELAND (Prime Minister; March 25, 1935–October 25, 1937). Paul Van Zeeland was born in Soignies on November 11, 1893. He served with distinction in the Belgian army during World War I. He was educated at Louvain University, where he studied law, economics, and political science. He continued his education at Princeton University where he received a degree in economics. He returned to Belgium to teach at Louvain University. Van Zeeland was recognized as a leading economist and served as vice governor of the Belgian National Bank. King Leopold III called upon him to form a coalition government to deal with the growing economic crisis on March 25, 1935. He reformed the country's finances and devalued the Belgian franc, thus restoring the economic stability of the country. Van Zeeland, a Christian Democrat, narrowly defeated Léon Degrelle's Fas-

cist Rexist movement in the 1936 elections. His government was forced to resign on October 25, 1937, over a financial scandal involving the National Bank. Van Zeeland escaped from Belgium during the German occupation in 1940 and spent most of World War II in the United States. He returned to Belgium in 1944 to lead a commission for reparations. Van Zeeland was elected to the senate in 1946, was named minister of state in 1948, and was named foreign minister in Gaston Eyskens' cabinet in 1949. He retained that position under several successive cabinets until 1954. He was a supporter of King Leopold and opposed the king's decision to abdicate in 1951. Van Zeeland supported the Benelux concept and European unity. He became president of the Banque Belge d'Afrique after his retirement from politics. He died in Brussels on September 22, 1973.

PAUL ÉMILE JANSEN (Prime Minister; November 24, 1937–May 13, 1938). Paul Émile Jansen was born in Brussels in 1870. He received a law degree from the University of Brussels. Jansen was elected to the chamber of deputies in 1910, but was defeated for reelection two years later. He was returned to office in 1914. He served the Belgian government in London during the German occupation in World War I. He was instrumental in rebuilding the country in the postwar era. Jansen briefly served as minister of national defense in 1920 and was Belgium's delegate to the League of Nations from 1926 until 1929. He also served in the government as minister of justice from 1927 until 1931 and from 1932 until 1934. He was elected to the senate in 1935, but retired the following year to resume his law practice. Jansen returned to the government in 1937 to serve as minister of state. He was called upon to form a government after the resignation of Paul Van Zeeland, and finally succeeded in forming a cabinet composed of Liberals,

Socialists, and Catholics on November 24, 1937. He introduced such social reforms as unemployment and medical insurance and equality of the Flemish and French languages. He supported a strong national defense and a policy of neutrality. His government resigned over a budgetary problem on May 13, 1938. Jansen served as minister of foreign affairs from January until February 1939 and was named minister of justice in April 1939. He remained in the cabinet until Belgium was conquered by Germany in 1940. He escaped to Nice, France, where he was arrested by the Gestapo in 1943. He was imprisoned in Fresnes, France, and later in Weimar, Germany, where he died on July 4, 1944.

PAUL-HENRI SPAAK (Prime Minister; May 15, 1938–February 9, 1939). Paul-Henri Spaak was born in Schaerbeek on January 25, 1899. He came from a wealthy and politically active family. He was captured by the Germans during World War I and spent two years in a prison camp. He attended the Université Libre de Bruxelles after the war and received a degree in law. He joined the Socialist Party and led rallies and demonstrations during the 1920s. He was elected to the Belgian chamber of deputies in 1932 and became the leader of the Socialist Party's left wing. He was named minister of transport and communications in 1935 and became foreign minister in the cabinet of his uncle, Paul-Émile Jansen, the following year. Spaak became prime minister on May 15, 1938, and served until February 9, 1939. He was appointed foreign minister in September of that year. He escaped to London during the German occupation and served as foreign minister of the government-in-exile. He returned to Belgium after the liberation and was named deputy premier in February 1945. He headed the Belgian delegation to the United Nations Conference in San Francisco in April 1945 and helped draft the United Nations charter. He served as the

first president of the United Nations General Assembly in 1946. Spaak was asked to form a government on March 11, 1946, but resigned only a few weeks later, on March 20, 1946, when a vote of confidence resulted in a tie. He was named prime minister again on March 19, 1947. Spaak agreed to the formation of a customs union between Belgium, the Netherlands, and Luxembourg that became known as Benelux. The Social Christian Party secured an absolute majority in the elections in June 1949, and Spaak relinquished the prime ministership on June 28, 1949. He served as foreign minister in several subsequent cabinets and was instrumental in the creation of the European Common Market in March 1957. He resigned as foreign minister in May 1957 to serve as secretary-general of the North Atlantic Treaty Organization (NATO). He resigned from NATO in March 1961 and returned to serve Belgium as foreign minister the following month. He was a supporter of Britain's entry into the Common Market, and was highly critical of France's veto of the move in 1963. He was also instrumental in easing tensions between Belgium and its former African colony, the Congo. He retired as foreign minister in July 1966 and joined an industrial firm as an international adviser. Spaak became ill while vacationing in the Azores and returned to Brussels where he died of a kidney ailment on July 31, 1972.

HUBERT PIERLOT (Prime Minister; February 9, 1939–August 1, 1945). Hubert Pierlot was born in Cugnon on December 23, 1883. He studied law at the University of Louvair and became one of Belgium's most prominent lawyers. He served in the Belgian army during World War I and entered politics in 1919 as a member of the Catholic Party. He was elected to the senate in 1926 and was named minister of the interior in 1934. He was elected president of the Catholic Party in 1936 and became minister of agriculture. He was elected prime minister on February 9, 1939, also serving as foreign minister from April 1939 until January 1940. Following the German invasion of Belgium in 1940, Pierlot fled to France. He made his way to London where he set up a government-in-exile during the occupation. He returned to Brussels after the liberation in September 1944. He faced political problems when he tried to disband resistance groups that had fought during the occupation. He was forced to ban marches and public gatherings following a period of violent demonstrations. His government survived a general strike in December 1944. Pierlot resigned on February 7, 1945, after requesting more assistance from the Allied powers. He retired from active politics and was later made a count by the Belgian government. Pierlot died in Brussels on December 13, 1963.

ACHILLE VAN ACKER (Prime Minister; February 11, 1945–February 17, 1946). Achille Van Acker was born in Bruges on April 8, 1898. He served in the army during World War I and subsequently entered politics. He was elected to the Bruges city council in 1926 and entered Parliament as a Socialist member the following year. Van Acker remained in Belgium during the German occupation in 1940. He served as a resistance leader and helped to organize the Socialist Party. He was appointed minister of labor and social welfare following the liberation of Belgium in September 1944. Van Acker formed a coalition government on February 11, 1945, following the resignation of Prime Minister Hubert Pierlot. He began the task of rebuilding Belgium's damaged economy and reviving its coal production. Following parliamentary elections, Van Acker resigned as prime minister on February 17, 1946. The regent asked Christian-Social Party leader de Schrijver to form a cabinet, but he was unable to do so. Van Acker returned to office on March 31, 1946, when a government headed by Paul-Henri Spaak was unable to win a vote of confidence. Van Acker's next government was also short-lived and collapsed on July 9, 1946, over the question of prosecution of wealthy Belgians who were economic collaborators with Germany during the war. Van Acker again became prime minister on April 22, 1954. He retained the position until his Socialist-Liberal coalition was defeated by the Social Christian Party in the June 1958 elections. He was replaced by Gaston Eyskens on June 25, 1958. Van Acker was subsequently elected speaker of the lower house of Parliament. He retained that position until his retirement in 1974. He died of cancer in Bruges on July 10, 1975.

Bhutan

Bhutan is a protectorate of India in the Himalayan Mountains in southern Asia. A treaty was signed in 1910 giving Great Britain control over the foreign affairs of Bhutan without interference in its internal administration. In 1949 India assumed the role Great Britain formerly had held.

HEADS OF STATE

UGGYEN WANGCHUK (King; 1860s–August 21, 1926). Uggyen Wang-chuck was born in 1861 and succeeded his father as temporal rajah of Bhutan as an infant. Bhutan also had a spiritual leader who was believed to be the incarnation of a deity. Uggyen Wangchuck arranged the removal of the spiritual leader and claimed his authority as well. He was proclaimed the sole Maharajah of Bhutan in 1907. He signed an agreement with the British government in 1910 that provided for autonomous internal control, but stipulated that British advice would be followed in regard to foreign relations. He continued to rule Bhutan until his death on August 21, 1926.

JIGME WANGCHUK (King; Au-

gust 21, 1926–March 30, 1952). Jigme Wangchuck was born in 1902. He succeeded his father, Sir Uggyen Wangchuck, as *druk gyalpo*, or "dragon king," on August 21, 1926. Bhutan remained in almost complete isolation during his reign. Great Britain continued to control Bhutan's foreign relations during the first two decades of Jigme Wangchuck's rule. On August 8, 1949, the government of India replaced the British government as Bhutan's foreign advisor. Jigme Wangchuck remained Bhutan's leader until his death in Bomthang after a brief illness on March 30, 1952.

Bolivia

Bolivia is a country in central South America. It received its independence from Spain on August 6, 1825.

HEADS OF STATE

JOSÉ MANUEL PANDO (President; October 6, 1899–August 14, 1904). José Manuel Pando was born in Arica on December 25, 1848. He studied medicine in La Paz before joining the army in 1871 to oppose the dictatorship of Mariano Melgarejo. He served with distinction in the War of the Pacific (1879–1884) and attained the rank of lieutenant colonel. He was the commander of the victorious Liberal forces during the civil war of 1899. Pando became head of the ruling junta on October 6, 1899, following the resignation of President Sévero Fernández Alonso. Pando's government initiated many public works programs, for example, developing roads and railroads. He attempted to put down a Brazilian-sponsored separatist movement in the rubber-rich Acre region in the Amazon basin. Bolivia was forced to cede much of that region to Brazil with the Treaty of Petropolis in 1903. Pando completed his term of office on August

14, 1904, but remained active in politics and formed the Republican Party in 1914 after breaking with the Liberals. He was assassinated by political opponents on June 15, 1917.

ISMAEL MONTES (President; August 14, 1904–October 24, 1909). Ismael Montes was born in La Paz on October 5, 1861. He graduated from the University of San Andres in La Paz in 1876. After college, he entered the military and served in the war of the Pacific. He retired from the army as a captain in 1884 to continue his education. He became a lawyer in 1886 and soon became a district court judge in La Paz. He entered politics and was elected to the chamber of deputies as a Liberal in 1890. President Aniceto Arce arrested Montes and many other Liberal members of the chamber. He was sent into exile until an amnesty was proclaimed in 1894. He was subsequently reelected to the chamber of deputies. Montes fought with the Liberals during the civil war of 1899. He served as minister of war under President José Manuel Pando from 1901 to 1904. He was elected to succeed Pando as president and took office on August 14, 1904. His government supported vast public works programs that provided the country with new roads, railways, and a telegraph system through the use of foreign loans. Montes's term of office was extended by a year when the new president-elect died before assuming office. Montes relinquished the presidency to his hand-picked successor Eliodor Villazón, on October 24, 1909. He served as Bolivia's minister to France and England over the next several years. He returned to Bolivia and was again elected president, taking office on August 15, 1913. His second term of office was marred by domestic unrest brought on by an economic recession in 1914. His intransigent attitude split the Liberal Party that year, with dissidents forming the Republican Party. Montes completed his term and stepped down on August 16, 1917. He was subsequently appointed minister to France, where he remained until 1928. He was threatened with arrest by the government of Hernando Siles in 1929, but took refuge in the Chilean legation and went into exile. He remained in exile until Siles's ouster in June 1930. Montes was a candidate for vice president on a coalition ticket later in the year. He withdrew from the campaign under pressure from the ruling military junta. He was a founder of the Bolivian Central Bank in 1931 and a strong supporter of Bolivia's role in the Chaco War. He died in La Paz after a brief illness on December 18, 1933.

ELIODORO VILLAZÓN (President; October 24, 1909–August 15, 1913). Eliodoro Villazón was born in Sacaba, Cochabamba, on January 22, 1848. He became a lawyer and entered politics in 1871 when he was elected to the national assembly. He served as minister of finance in the government of Narciso Campero from 1880 until 1884. He subsequently represented Bolivia as a financial agent in Europe. He joined the Liberal Party upon his return to Bolivia. Villazón became foreign minister under José Manuel Pando after the Liberals came to power in 1899. He served as vice president under Ismael Montes from 1905 until his selection as president on December 24, 1909. He continued the public works programs of his predecessors and settled several boundary disputes during his term of office. He completed his term and stepped down on August 15, 1913. Villazón died in Cochabamba on September 12, 1940.

ISMAEL MONTES (President; August 15, 1913–August 16, 1917). *See earlier entry under Heads of State.*

JOSÉ GUTIÉRREZ GUERRA (President; August 16, 1917–July 12, 1920). José Gutiérrez Guerra was born in Sucre on September 5, 1869. He was elected to the presidency and succeeded Ismael Montes in office on August 16, 1917. Gutiérrez Guerra initially formed a coalition cabinet with members of the opposition Republican Party. The ruling Liberal Party was beset with internal differences and the Republicans seized the opportunity to oust Gutiérrez Guerra in a bloodless coup on July 12, 1920. Gutiérrez Guerra died on February 3, 1929.

JUAN BAUTISTA SAAVEDRA (President; July 12, 1920–September 4, 1925). Juan Bautista Saavedra Mallea was born in Sorata, La Paz Province, on August 30, 1870. He became a lawyer in 1896. Saavedra was recognized as a leading scholar on penal law and served in the Liberal government as minister of education. He broke with the Liberal Party in 1914 and joined the newly formed Republican Party. The Liberal government of José Gutiérrez Guerra was ousted in a bloodless coup by the

Republicans and Saavedra headed the interim ruling junta from July 12, 1920. The Republican national convention selected Saavedra over Daniel Salamanca to serve as president in January 1921. His government promoted social and labor legislation that legalized strikes and established an eight-hour work day. He also succeeded in increasing Bolivia's tin exports. In May 1925 José Gabino Villanueva was elected to succeed to the presidency. Saavedra refused to allow him to take office and had the election annulled. Saavedra extended his presidential term until September 4, 1925, when he turned over the office to senate president Felipe Guzmán. Saavedra subsequently served as Bolivia's minister to the League of Nations and various European countries. Saavedra was a critic of the government of Daniel Salamanca and its handling of the Chaco War. He was deported by Salamanca in February 1934 and went into exile in Santiago, Chile. Saavedra declined to return to serve as minister of defense in the government of Salamanca's successor, José Tejeda, in December 1934. However, he returned to Bolivia the following February and resumed the leadership of the Republican Socialist Party. He served on the Bolivian delegation to the Chaco peace conference in May 1935. Saavedra was again deported in June 1936 by President José David Toro. He died in Santiago, Chile, on March 1, 1939.

FELIPE GUZMÁN (President; September 4, 1925–January 10, 1926). Felipe Guzmán was born in 1879. He served as president of the Bolivian senate from the early 1920s until he was chosen by President Juan Bautista Saavedra to succeed to the presidency on September 4, 1925, after Saavedra had voided the election of José Gabino Villanueva. Guzmán's government oversaw a new election, and he relinquished office to Hernando Siles on January 10, 1926. Guzmán died in 1952.

HERNANDO SILES (President; January 10, 1926–June 25, 1930). Hernando Siles Reyes was born in Sucre in 1883. He received a degree in law from the University of Sucre in 1905. He served as a professor at the National Institute of Commerce in La Paz from 1911 until 1917 and was rector at San Francisco Xavier University in Sucre from 1917 until 1920. Siles was appointed minister to Mexico in 1920. He returned to Bolivia later in the year and was elected to the chamber of deputies. He served in Bautista Saavedra's cabinet as minister of education and minister of war in the early 1920s. Siles was elected president with the support of Saavedra in 1925, taking office on January 10, 1926. Siles broke with Saavedra and the Socialist Republican Party in January 1927 and formed the Nationalist Party. Bolivia engaged in a border dispute with Paraguay over the Chaco region in December of 1928. Bolivia's economy prospered during the early years of Siles's administration until the economic depression of 1929. The economic problems of Bolivia led to widespread popular discontent. Siles tried to engineer his own reelection by altering the constitution. He stepped down in May 1930 to allow his cabinet to head a provisional government while he ran for reelection. Antigovernment demonstrations erupted throughout the country, and a major revolt broke out in mid–June 1930. Siles was forced from power on June 25, 1930. A military junta took control of the government, and Siles went into exile. He was allowed to return to Bolivia four years later and held various diplomatic positions. Siles was killed in a plane crash while en route from Arequipa to Lima, Peru, on November 23, 1942.

CARLOS BLANCO GALINDO (President; June 25, 1930–March 5, 1931). Carlos Blanco Galindo was born in Cochabamba on March 12, 1882. He served in the Bolivian military and became the leader of the ruling military junta when Hernando Siles' government was deposed on June 25, 1930. Blanco Galindo served as acting president and prepared for new elections. During his short term of office, he granted autonomy to the universities and enacted habeas corpus laws. He stepped down on March 5, 1931, following the election of Daniel Salamanca. Blanco Galindo remained active in the military until his death in Cochabamba on October 2, 1953.

DANIEL SALAMANCA (President; March 5, 1931–November 27, 1934) Daniel Salamanca Urey was born in Cochabamba on July 8, 1868. He was educated at the University of San Simon, where he received a law degree. He joined the Liberal Party and was elected to the chamber of deputies in 1899. He was named to José Manuel Pando's government as minister of finance and industry in 1901. Salamanca was a founder of the Republican Party in 1914. He was an unsuccessful candidate for vice president in 1917 and was defeated by Bautista Saavedra for the presidency after the Republican coup in 1920. Salamanca subsequently retired from politics and returned to Cochabamba to teach at the university. He emerged from retirement to win the presidency as head of a Republican-Liberal coalition after the overthrow of the government of Hernando Siles. He took office on March 5, 1931, and instituted a policy of economic austerity and repression against his political opponents. Salamanca broke diplomatic relations with Paraguay, and a long series of border disputes in the Chaco region escalated into a war in July 1932. The war went badly for Bolivia, and Salamanca was deposed by the military while on a visit to Chaco headquarters in Villamontes on November 27, 1934. He retired to his home in Cochabamba to write his memoirs and died of a heart attack on July 17, 1935.

JOSÉ LUIS TEJADA SORZANO (President; November 27, 1934–May 17, 1936). José Luis Tejada Sorzano was born on January 12, 1882. He was educated as a lawyer and entered politics. He was elected to the chamber of deputies in 1914. He served in José Gutiérrez Guerra's cabinet as minister of finance from 1917 until 1920. He was elected vice president under Daniel Salamanca in 1931 and assumed the presidency when Salamanca was forced to resign on November 27, 1934. Tejada arranged a truce with Paraguay ending the Chaco War in June 1935. He received little support from the military and was ousted in a coup on May 17, 1936. He died on October 4, 1938.

JOSÉ DAVID TORO (President; May 17, 1936–July 13, 1937). José David Toro was born in Sucre on June 24, 1898. He entered the Bolivian military as a cadet and rose through the ranks to colonel. He served as chief of staff during the Chaco War. He and Germán Busch led the military coup that ousted President José Luis Tejada on May 17, 1936. Toro became head of the ruling military junta. He instituted a policy of military socialism, reforming the banking and tax systems. He nationalized the holdings of the Standard Oil Company and established the state-controlled Bolivian oil monopoly. Toro was ousted by his fellow junta member, Busch, on June 13, 1937. Toro remained politically active for the next decade. He died on July 25, 1977.

GERMÁN BUSCH (President; July 13, 1937–August 23, 1939). Germán Busch Becerra was born in Trinidad, El Beni, on March 23, 1903. He attended the military college and entered the army as a cadet. He became a colonel during the Chaco War. He was a leader of the military coup that ousted the government of José Luis Tejada in May 1936. Busch also ousted his fellow junta member, President José David Toro, on July 13,

1937. Busch adopted a new constitution and was elected constitutional president in May 1938. He continued the policy of military socialism, and encouraged the unionization of tin miners. Busch reportedly committed suicide at his home in La Paz on August 23, 1939, though some of his supporters claim that he was the victim of a political assassination.

CARLOS QUINTANILLA (President; August 23, 1939–April 15, 1940). Carlos Quintanilla was born in 1888. He served in the Bolivian military and was a commander during the Chaco War. He was army chief of staff under President Germán Busch and was selected to head the ruling military junta following Busch's death on August 23, 1939. Quintanilla reversed many of the social programs enacted during Busch's regime. He oversaw new elections and stepped down on April 15, 1940, following the selection of Enrique Peñaranda as president. Quintanilla died in 1964.

ENRIQUE PEÑARANDA (President; April 15, 1940–December 20, 1943). Enrique Peñaranda y del Castillo was born in Larecaja, La Paz Province, on November 17, 1891. He served in the Bolivian military, attaining the rank of colonel during the Chaco War. Peñaranda took a leave of absence from the military after Germán Busch's military coup in 1937. Peñaranda was named minister of defense in Carlos Quintanilla's government after Busch's death in August 1939. He was elected president of Bolivia and took office on April 15, 1940. Peñaranda supported a pro–United States foreign policy and broke relations with the Axis powers during World War II. He also initiated democratic reforms in the country. He was ousted in a military coup on December 20, 1943. He retired to Cochabamba and died there on June 8, 1969.

GUALBERTO VILLAROEL (President; December 20, 1943–July 21, 1946). Gualberto Villaroel Lopez was born in 1908. He joined the Bolivian army and fought against Paraguay in the Chaco War (1932–1935). Villaroel became president of Bolivia following a military coup on December 20, 1943. During his administration he implemented reforms that benefited the tin miners and the Bolivian Indians. His labor and land reform programs met with bitter opposition from the tin industry and land owners, and resulted in a rebellion against his regime. Villaroel survived an assassination attempt on March 12, 1945. The presidential palace in La Paz was attacked by a mob when a teachers' strike turned violent on July 21, 1946, and Villaroel was thrown from a balcony and lynched from a lamp post in the Plaza Murillo below.

Brazil

Brazil is the largest country in South America. It was granted independence from Portugal on September 7, 1822.

HEADS OF STATE

MANOEL DE CAMPOS SALLES (President; November 15, 1898–November 15, 1902). Manoel de Campos Salles was born in 1841. He was a successful São Paulo coffee planter before becoming president of Brazil on November 15,

1898. His administration was responsible for improving Brazil's financial affairs and restoring the country's credit through an increase in taxes. He completed his term of office on November 15, 1902. Campos Salles subsequently served as Brazil's minister to Argentina. He was chosen as a compromise candidate by Brazil's leading parties to stand for election to the presidency in 1914, but Campos Salles died on June 28, 1913, before the election took place.

FRANCISCO RODRIGUES ALVES (President; November 15, 1902–November 15, 1906). Francisco de Paula Rodrigues Alves was born on July 7, 1848. He received a law degree from the São Paulo Law School in 1870. He entered politics in 1889 as a member of the Republican Party and was active in the ouster of the monarchy. Rodrigues Alves subsequently assisted in the drafting of Brazil's constitution in 1891. He continued in politics, serving as a senator, minister of finance, and governor of São Paulo. He became president of Brazil on November 15, 1902. His administration engaged in numerous programs to modernize the country, and constructed the Municipal Theater, the National Library, and other public buildings in Rio de Janeiro. He was also instrumental in eradicating yellow fever by draining the swamps. Rodrigues Alves completed his term of office on November 15, 1906. He subsequently represented Brazil on various diplomatic missions and served another term as governor of São Paulo from 1912 until 1916. He was reelected to the presidency on November 15, 1918, but poor health prevented him from carrying out his duties. He died in Rio de Janeiro on January 16, 1919.

ALFONSO MOREIRA PENA (President; November 15, 1906–June 14, 1909). Alfonso Augusto Moreira Pena was born in Sánta Barbara, Minas Gerais, on November 30, 1847. He received a degree in law from the University of São Paulo. Pena entered politics in the 1870s and served as a provincial deputy in the empire from 1874 until 1878. He was elected a national deputy in 1879. He briefly served in the cabinet as minister of war from 1882 until 1883. He was minister of agriculture in 1883 and minister of justice in 1885. He also served on the committee that drafted Brazil's new constitution in 1891. The following year he returned to Minas Gerais, where he was governor until 1895. During this period he founded the city of Belo Horizonte to serve as capital of the state. Pena also served as president of the Bank of the Republic from 1894 until 1898. He was selected as vice president of Brazil in 1893 and was elected to succeed Francisco Rodrigues Alves as president, taking office on November 15, 1906. His government was instrumental in expanding Brazil's railway and telegraph systems and in reforming the currency exchange rate. Pena remained in office until his death following a bout of influenza on June 14, 1909.

NILO PEÇANHA (President; June 14, 1909–November 15, 1910). Nilo Procópio Peçanha was born in Rio de Janeiro on October 2, 1867. He served in the chamber of deputies before his selection as governor of the state of Rio de Janeiro in 1903. He served as vice president of Brazil under Alfonso Moreira Pena from November 1906 until he succeeded to the presidency upon Pena's death on June 14, 1909. Peçanha remained president until the election of Hermes Rodrigues da Fonseca, and stepped down on November 15, 1910. Peçanha continued to serve subsequent governments, as governor of Rio from 1914 until 1917 and as foreign minister from 1917 until 1918. He was instrumental in Brazil's decision to join with the Allies in World War I. He was elected to the Brazilian Senate in 1918 and was an unsuccessful candidate for the presidency in 1921 against Arturo da

Silva Bernardes. Peçanha died on May 31, 1924.

HERMES RODRIGUES DA FONSECA (President; November 15, 1910–November 15, 1914). Hermes Rodrigues da Fonseca was born on May 12, 1885. He was the nephew of Manoel Deodoro de Fonseca, the first president of the Brazilian Republic in 1889. The younger Fonseca entered into a career in the military and rose through the ranks. As minister of war in 1906, he embarked on a campaign to modernize the Brazilian army along European lines. His nomination to the presidency by the Republican Party led to a hotly contested election, with two provinces refusing to support his nomination. He defeated his civilian opponent, Rui Barbosa, in a controversial outcome and assumed the presidency on November 15, 1910. His regime survived two major naval revolts over the issue of capital punishment in the early months of his administration. His term of office ended on November 15, 1914, and Fonseca remained a major political and military figure in the country. He was serving as president of the Military Club in 1922 when he was arrested by the government for issuing orders to military officials without authority. He served six months in prison before the Supreme Court ordered his release. Soon after that, an abortive military uprising in his support took place on July 1, 1922. The revolt failed and Fonseca, whose health had failed during captivity, died on September 9, 1923.

WENCESLAU BRAZ PERIERA GOMES (President; November 15, 1914–November 15, 1918). Wenceslau Braz Periera Gomes was born in Itajuba, Minas Gerais, on February 26, 1868. Braz served in the Minas Gerais legislature and was governor of the state from 1908 to 1910. He was vice president under Hermes da Fonseca from 1910 until he was elected to succeed Fonseca as president and took office on Novem-

ber 15, 1914. His administration passed the Civil Code of 1917 and was instrumental in increasing domestic industrial production during World War I. His government was the only South American power to enter the war, when Braz joined the Allies and declared war on the Central Powers on October 27, 1917. After completing his term of office on November 15, 1918, Braz returned to his home town of Itajuba, where he led a private life away from political affairs. He died in Itajuba on May 15, 1966, at the age of 98.

FRANCISCO RODRIGUES ALVES (President; November 15, 1918–January 16, 1919). *See earlier entry under Heads of State.*

DELPHIM MOREIRA DA COSTA (President; January 16, 1919–April 12, 1919). Delphim Moreira da Costa Ribeiro was born in Minas Gerais on November 7, 1868. He attended the São Paulo School of Law and became active in politics in his home state. He served as governor of Minas Gerais from 1914 until 1918. Moreira was elected vice president under Francisco Rodrigues Alves in November 1918 and served as acting president due to Rodrigues Alves' poor health. He succeeded to the presidency when Rodriguez Alves died in office on January 16, 1919. Moreira's own health prevented him from actively leading the country, and many of his duties were carried out by Afranio de Melo Franco, his minister of the interior. He served as caretaker president until Epitácio da Silva Pessoa was elected by the legislature to complete Rodriguez Alves's term. Moreira resumed the position of vice president until his death the following year on July 1, 1920.

EPITÁCIO DA SILVA PESSOA (President; April 13, 1919–November 15, 1922). Epitácio da Silva Pessoa was born in Umbuzeiro, Paraíba State, on May 23, 1865. He graduated with a law degree from Recife Law Faculty in 1886. He served as minister of justice from 1898 until 1901 and was instrumental in drafting Brazil's new constitution. He served on the Brazilian Supreme Court from 1902 until 1912, when he was elected to the senate. He led the Brazilian delegation to the Versaille Peace Conference in 1919. He was selected by the legislature to complete Francisco Rodrigues Alves' term of office on April 13, 1919. His administration sought to improve Brazil's roads, railways, and educational system. He also instituted public works assistance for drought relief in the northeastern states. He completed his term on November 15, 1922, and was elected a member of the International Court of Justice at the Hague later in the year. He returned to Brazil to again serve in the senate in 1924. He was chosen to preside at the Pan-American Jurists' Committee in Rio de Janeiro in May 1927. He left his position and vacated his seat in the senate after the revolution in 1930. Two years later Pessoa was named by the United States to serve on the Permanent Commission of Arbitration between the United States and Great Britain. Pessoa died in Rio de Janeiro on February 13, 1942.

ARTURO DA SILVA BERNARDES (President; November 15, 1922–November 15, 1926). Arturo da Silva Bernardes was born in Vicosa, Minas Gerais, on August 8, 1875. He studied law in Ouro Preto and returned to Vicosa to practice law after his graduation. He entered politics in Minas Gerais in the early 1900s and served as mayor of Vicosa and is state deputy. He was elected to the federal legislature in 1909 and also became secretary of finance for Minas Gerais the following year. He held that position until 1914. He became governor of Minas Gerais in 1918. Bernardes was elected president of Brazil and took office on November 15, 1922. His government was besieged by revolutionists from the left and the right, and

most of his presidency was conducted under a state of siege. He initiated austerity programs to cut Brazil's budget deficit and increased the power of the executive branch. Brazil withdrew from the League of Nations in 1926. Bernardes completed his term of office on November 15, 1926. He was elected to the senate in 1929. He was involved in the unsuccessful revolt against the government of Getúlio Vargas in 1932 and went into exile in Portugal after its failure. He returned to Brazil in 1935 and was elected to the federal legislature. He lost his bid for reelection in 1937. Bernardes founded the Republican Party in 1945 and remained president of the party until his death from a heart attack at his home in Rio de Janeiro on March 23, 1955.

WASHINGTON LUIS (President; November 15, 1926–November 4, 1930). Washington Luis Pereira de Sousa was born in Rio de Janeiro on October 26, 1870. He moved to São Paulo in 1888, where he entered politics. He served as state deputy from 1904 until 1906 as a member of the Paulista Republican Party. He was subsequently state secretary of justice from 1906 until his selection as mayor of São Paulo in 1914. He retained office until 1919, and was selected as governor of São Paulo the following year. In 1924 he was elected to the senate. Luis became president of Brazil on November 15, 1926. The country suffered severely from the economic depression of 1929, and Brazil's coffee economy was seriously damaged. Luis supported Julio Prestes in the 1930 presidential election against Getúlio Vargas. A revolution took place in October 1930 that forced Luis from office on November 4, 1930, after a month-long civil war. Luis went into exile in Europe and the United States. He returned to Brazil in 1947 but did not resume his political activities. He died on August 4, 1957.

JULIO PRESTES (President-Elect; October 24, 1930–November 4, 1930).

Julio Prestes de Albuquerque was born in São Paulo on March 15, 1882. He was active in politics in São Paulo, serving in the state legislature and the national congress. He was elected governor of São Paulo in 1927 and was a close associate of President Washington Luis. He was supported by Luis as his successor in the elections of 1930, which violated the agreement with the state of Minas Gerais of alternating the presidency between Minas Gerais and São Paulo. Prestes defeated Getúlio Vargas in the election, though Brazil's economic crisis caused discontent with the government. Vargas supporters from the northeast and south besieged the capital and forced Luis from office before Prestes could assume the presidency. Prestes was sent into exile for several years and did not return to Brazil until the mid-1930s. He settled at his family's ranch in Itapetinnga, where he died on February 9, 1946.

GETÚLIO DORNELLES VARGAS (President; November 4, 1930–October 29, 1945). Getúlio Dornelles Vargas was born in São Borja, Rio Grande do Sul, on April 19, 1883. He was raised on his family's cattle ranch and was educated at the Rio Pardo Military Academy. He abandoned notions of a career in the military, however, and received a law degree from the University of Porto Alegre in 1907. Two years later he was elected to the Brazilian chamber of deputies for a single term, and he subsequently practiced law. Vargas returned to politics in 1919 when he was elected a state deputy. He was named minister of finance in the government of Washington Luis in 1926 and served until 1928, when he was elected president of the state of Rio Grande do Sul. He was defeated by Julio Prestes in his bid for the presidency of Brazil on the Liberal Alliance ticket in 1930. When the government refused to seat elected members of Vargas's party in the chamber of deputies, he led

an armed uprising against the government. President Luis and Prestes were ousted and sent into exile, and Vargas became leader of the ruling military junta on November 4, 1930. In 1934 he allowed a new progressive constitution to come into effect and was elected president in the subsequent election. Three years later Vargas announced his program *Estado Novo* (New state), suspended the constitution, and extended his term of office from four to six years. Vargas was a staunch supporter of the Allied cause during World War II and declared war on the Axis powers in August 1942. After the war, Vargas was faced with a serious economic recession in Brazil. He agreed to hold democratic elections without running as a candidate himself. The army was suspicious that Vargas might renege on his commitment and acted to ensure the election by deposing Vargas on October 29, 1945. He returned to his ranch in southern Brazil, where he formed the Brazil Labor Party and won election to a seat in the Brazilian Senate. He remained a powerful force in Brazil during the subsequent administration of Eurico Gaspar Dutra. He returned to the national scene as a candidate for president on October 3, 1950, and won by a large margin. He was sworn in for another term on January 31, 1951. Financial mismanagement and other scandals cost Vargas much of his popularity among the people, however. On August 4, 1954, Carlos Lacerda, a leading journalist and opponent of Vargas, was the target of an assassination attempt. Supporters of Vargas were implicated in the attack, and Vargas was pressured by the military to resign from the presidency. He gave in to the pressure on August 24, 1954, and turned his office over to Vice President João Café Filho. Shortly thereafter he returned to his room in the presidential palace and shot himself to death.

JOSÉ LINHARES (President; October 29, 1945–January 31, 1946). José

Linhares was born in Baturite, Ceara, on January 28, 1886. He attended medical school at the University of Brazil and received a bachelor of laws degree from the University of São Paulo in 1908. He began a law practice soon after and in 1913 became a criminal court judge in Rio de Janeiro. In 1931 Linhares was promoted to magistrate in the court of appeals of the federal district, and in 1937 he was appointed to the supreme court. He became the court's vice president in 1940. In accordance with the constitution, he succeeded Getúlio Vargas as president on October 29, 1945. Linhares proceeded with plans for democratic elections in December of that year and sought to ensure that the election was waged freely and fairly. He relinquished the presidency to the victor, Eurico Gaspar Dutra, on January 31, 1946. Linhares returned to his duties on the supreme court. He remained in this position until his retirement in 1956. He died of a heart attack in Rio de Janeiro, on July 26, 1957.

Bulgaria

Bulgaria is a country in southeastern Europe. It proclaimed its independence from the Ottoman Empire on September 22, 1908. The monarchy was abolished in 1946 and the country came under Communist control.

HEADS OF STATE

FERDINAND I (Prince; July 7, 1887–October 5, 1908; King, October 6, 1908–October 3, 1918). Ferdinand Maximilian Karl Leopold Maria was born in Vienna, Austria, on February 26, 1861. He was the youngest son of Prince Augustus of Saxe-Coburg-Gotha. He served in the Austrian army before his election as prince of Bulgaria on July 7, 1887, to succeed Prince Alexander. He assumed the throne on August 14, 1887, though Russia refused to accept his selection. He survived several assassination attempts and plots against his rule. Ferdinand married Princess Maria Luisa of Parma in April 1893. He settled his differences with Russia, and Czar Nicholas II was godfather to Ferdinand's first son, Boris, in 1896. Ferdinand's wife died in 1899, and he married Princess Eleanor of Reuss in 1908. Ferdinand proclaimed Bulgaria's independence from Turkey and became Bulgaria's king on October 6, 1908. He was a proponent of the Balkan League, consisting of Bulgaria, Greece, Serbia, and Montenegro. The league declared war on Turkey in October 1912 and won a military victory. An armistice proposed by the major powers was broken and Bulgaria resumed the fighting. Bulgaria soon found itself at war with its former allies Greece, Serbia, and Montenegro as well as with Turkey and Romania. Bulgaria was forced to surrender unconditionally and the Treaty of Bucharest took back all of the territory Bulgaria had acquired in its earlier victories. Ferdinand joined Bulgaria with Germany and the Central Powers during World War I in May 1915. After a series of victories against Serbia and Romania, Ferdinand's army was defeated by the Allies in Macedonia. Ferdinand was forced to accept an armistice in Salonika on September 30, 1918. He abdicated in favor of his son, Boris, on October 4, 1918. He left his palace in the middle of the night to go into exile in Coburg, Germany, where he remained until his death on September 10, 1948.

BORIS III (King; October 4, 1918–August 28, 1943). Boris Clement Robert Marie Pius Louis Stanislas Xavier was born in Sofia on January 30, 1894. He was the eldest son of King Ferdinand of Bulgaria and Princess Maria Luisa and was raised in the Orthodox church. He attended the military academy in Sofia and served in the Bulgarian army during the Balkan Wars and World War I. Ferdinand abdicated after Bulgaria's defeat in World War I, and Boris succeeded him to the throne on October 4, 1918. The Agrarian Party under Aleksandr Stambolski governed the country until Stambolski's ouster and murder in June 1923. The Agrarians and Communists attempted an armed revolt against the subsequent government of Alexander Tsankov and made several unsuccessful attempts on Boris's life in 1925. Boris dismissed Tsankov the following year. He married Princess Giovanni of Savoy, daughter of King Victor Emmanuel II of Italy, in 1930. A military coup in May 1934 took control of the government, but Boris kept the throne. He became more active in formulating foreign policy and attempted to maintain Bulgaria's neutrality in the early years of World War II. He was pressured by Germany to sign the Axis pact in March 1941, and Bulgaria declared war on Great Britain the following December. Boris refused to commit Bulgarian troops to the Russian campaign. Boris had an uncomfortable relationship with Adolf Hitler. He died on August 28, 1943, after a bitter argument with Hitler. Boris' death was reported to have been due to a heart attack, but other reports suggest the king may have been shot by an assassin or been poisoned.

SIMEON II (King; August 28, 1943–September 9, 1946). Simeon Borisov Saxe-Coburg-Gotha was born in 1937. He was the son of King Boris and Queen Joanna. He was proclaimed King Simeon II of Bulgaria following his father's death on August 28, 1943. Simeon ruled under a regency council headed by his uncle, Prince Cyril. Bulgaria was an ally of Germany during World War II, until the government was ousted by the anti–Fascist Fatherland Front in September 1944. Kimon Georgiev was installed as premier and many members of the old regime were arrested and executed. A referendum to proclaim Bulgaria a republic was passed on September 8, 1946, and King Simeon and his mother left the country to go into exile in Egypt the following week. Simeon attended Victoria College in Alexandria and the Valley Forge Military Academy in the United States. The royal family subsequently lived in exile in Spain. Simeon returned to Bulgaria in 1990 following the collapse of the Communist regime. Residency requirements prevented him from being a candidate in the 1992 presidential election.

CYRIL (Regent; August 28, 1943–September 9, 1944). Cyril (Kiril) was born in Sofia on November 17, 1895. He was the son of King Ferdinand of Bulgaria and the younger brother of King Boris III. He became regent following the death of King Boris on August 28, 1943, and the succession to the throne of his minor nephew, King Simeon. Cyril headed the regency council which also included Prime Minister Bogdan Filov and War Minister General Nikola Mihov. Cyril was ousted as regent by the anti–Fascist Fatherland Front government on September 9, 1944. He was arrested as a war criminal and was tried and executed with the rest of the regency council on February 1, 1945.

HEADS OF GOVERNMENT

TODOR IVANCHOV (Prime Minister; October 12, 1899–January 23, 1901). Todor Ivanchov (Ivantsev) was born in 1858. He was named to head the government by Prince Ferdinand on October 12, 1899. His government's economic policies were unpopular with the peasantry and nearly resulted in a revolt. Bulgaria also came close to war with Romania over the government's support of Macedonian nationalists. Ivanchov was dismissed from office on January 23, 1901. He died in 1905.

RACHO PETROV (Prime Minister; January 23, 1901–March 4, 1901). Racho Petrov was born in 1861. He was a general in the Bulgarian army. He was named to head the government on January 23, 1901, and was charged with the duty of holding new elections. Petrov was unable to form a personal political party to contest the election and allowed free elections to take place. He stepped down to allow the formation of a coalition government under Petko Karavelov on March 4, 1901. Petrov was again called upon by Prince Ferdinand to head the government from May 15, 1903, until November 14, 1906. He died on January 22, 1942.

PETKO KARAVELOV (Prime Minister; March 4, 1901–January 4, 1902). Petko Karavelov was born in Koprivshtitza in Eastern Rumelia in 1845. He was educated at Moscow University, where he studied philosophy and political economy. He returned to Bulgaria in 1877 and became a leader of the Liberal Party. He became prime minister in December 1880 but retired from office in July 1882, following Prince Alexander's coup. Karavelov worked as a teacher until the restoration of the constitution in 1884. He again headed the government from August 9, 1884. Following Prince Alexander's abdication, Karavelov served on the regency council, but retired in August 1886 over a disagreement with Stefan Stambolov. Karavelov was arrested and imprisoned following the Rutchuk revolt. He was released but was again arrested by order of Stambolov. He was sentenced to five years in prison. After his release he was elected to the chamber of deputies in 1895. He formed a coalition government with Stoyan Danev on March 4, 1901, following elections and served as prime minister from March 4, 1901, until his resignation on January 4, 1902, over a controversy concerning his proposal of a government tobacco monopoly. Karavelov died on February 7, 1903.

STOYAN DANEV (Prime Minister; January 4, 1902–March 27, 1903). Stoyan Danev was born on February 7, 1858. He was a leader of the Progressive Party. He participated in a coalition government formed by Petko Karavelov in March 1901. He became head of the government when Karavelov resigned on January 4, 1902. New elections were held giving Danev's party a majority in the Sobranye (parliament). During his term of office he signed a military treaty with Russia. Danev was forced to resign on March 27, 1903, over the issue of the appointment of a Serbian bishop in Uskub. He joined Ivan Gueshov's coalition government in 1911 to approve changes in the Bulgarian constitution. He again briefly headed the government from July 14, 1913, until July 15, 1913, during the Balkan War. Danev died on July 29, 1949.

RACHO PETROV (Prime Minister; May 15, 1903–November 14, 1906). *See earlier entry under Heads of Government.*

DIMITŬR PETKOV (Prime Minister; November 14, 1906–March 11, 1907). Dimitŭr Petkov was born in 1858. He was a leader of the pro-Austrian Stambulovist Party. He was called upon by King Ferdinand to head the government on November 14, 1906. His ministry was marked by widespread corruption and profiteering. Petkov was shot to death in Sofia on March 11, 1907.

PETŬR GUDEV (Prime Minister; March 16, 1907–January 29, 1908). Petŭr Gudev was born in 1863. He headed an interim government as prime minister from March 16, 1907, following the assassination of Dimitŭr Petkov until January 29, 1908, when Alexander Malinov formed a government. Gudev died in May 1932.

ALEXANDER MALINOV (Prime Minister; January 29, 1908–March 29, 1911). Alexander Malinov was born on April 20, 1867. He was educated at the University of Kiev in Russia, where he received a degree in law. He returned to Bulgaria in the late 1880s and entered politics. He was elected to the Sobranye in 1901 as a member of the Democratic Party. He became the party's leader in 1903 following the death of Petko Karavelov. Malinov was named to head the government on January 29, 1908. He held that position until March 1911. He was again called upon to be prime minister following Vasil Radoslavoff's resignation in June 1918. He stepped down in June 18, 1918, and signed the armistice with the Allies that ended Bulgaria's participation in World War I on September 26, 1918. Malinov resigned on November 28, 1918, in protest against the Romanian occupation of Dobrudja. Malinov was arrested when Aleksandr Stambolski's Agrarian government came to power in October 1919 and remained imprisoned until 1923. He again became prime minister on June 28, 1931, as the leader of a coalition government. He resigned soon after for reasons of health on

October 12, 1931. Malinov subsequently was elected president of the Sobranye. He served on the Bulgarian delegation to the World Economic Conference in London in 1933. Malinov died in Sofia on March 21, 1938, while addressing a crowd during a campaign rally.

IVAN GUESHOV (Prime Minister; March 29, 1911–June 30, 1913). Ivan Gueshov (Geshov) was born in Philippolis on February 20, 1849. He was educated at Victoria College in Manchester, England, and returned to Bulgaria in 1872. His criticism of Turkish rule in Bulgaria led to a death sentence in 1877, but his sentence was commuted to exile. He was pardoned and returned home in March 1878 following the signing of the Treaty of San Stephano. He served as president of the provincial assembly of Eastern Rumelia from 1878 until 1881 and became the governor of the Bank of Bulgaria in 1883. Gueshov served as a member of the cabinet formed after Prince Alexander's abdication in 1886. He resigned his position in opposition to Stefan Stambolov's pro-Austrian policies and retired from politics. He reentered the government in December 1894 to serve as minister of finance, but resigned three years later. Gueshov was elected president of the Sobranye in 1901 and became leader of the Nationalist Party. He was charged with forming a coalition government with Stoyan Danev on March 29, 1911, to approve a new constitution following Bulgaria's elevation to the status of kingdom. His government also approved the formation of the Balkan League with Serbia, Montenegro; and Greece and the subsequent war against Turkey. He stepped down on June 30, 1913, when Bulgaria engaged in battle with its former Allies. Gueshov was a leader of the opposition throughout World War I and opposed Bulgaria's alliance with Germany. He became president of the United Nationalist–Progressive Party in 1921. Gueshov died on March 11, 1924.

STOYAN DANEV (Prime Minister; July 14, 1913–July 15, 1913). *See earlier entry under Heads of Government.*

VASIL RADOSLAVOFF (Prime Minister; July 20, 1913–June 18, 1918). Vasil Radoslavoff was born in Lovtch on July 15, 1854. He was educated in Gabrovo, Prague, Vienna and Heidelberg. He entered politics in 1880 and was appointed minister of justice in 1884. He headed the government as prime minister from August 1886 until July 12, 1887. He served in Konstantin Stoilov's cabinet from 1894 and was minister of the interior from 1899 until 1901. He again became prime minister on July 20, 1913. Radoslavoff led his country into an alliance with Germany and the Central Powers during World War I, declaring war on Serbia in 1915. When the war went badly for Bulgaria, Radoslavoff resigned on June 18, 1918, and fled the country. He was tried in absentia for treason in 1923 and sentenced to life imprisonment for entering the war without parliamentary consent. He remained in exile in Germany and died in a Berlin hospital on October 21, 1929, shortly after having received permission to return to Bulgaria.

ALEXANDER MALINOV (Prime Minister; June 18, 1918–November 28, 1918). *See earlier entry under Heads of Government.*

TODOR TODOROV (Prime Minister; November 28, 1918–October 14, 1919). Todor Todorov was born in 1858. He was a leader of the National Party and served in the cabinet as minister of finance in 1913. Todorov led the postwar government as prime minister from November 28, 1918, until October 14, 1919. He died on August 5, 1924.

ALEKSANDR STAMBOLSKI (Prime Minister; October 14, 1919–June 9, 1923). Aleksandr Stambolski was born in Slavovitsa on March 1, 1879. He was educated at the Agricultural College in Halle, Germany. He returned to Bulgaria in 1897 and became a journalist, serving as editor of the Agrarian newspaper from 1902. He was elected to the Sobranye in 1908 and served as leader of the Agrarians. Stambolski opposed King Ferdinand's policies during the Balkan War and the king's proposed alliance with Germany and the Central Powers during World War I. Ferdinand ordered Stambolski's arrest in 1915, and he was court-martialed and sentenced to life imprisonment. Stambolski was released in September 1918 and raised an army of insurrectionists that forced Ferdinand's abdication. Stambolski supported the new king, Boris III, and joined the government as minister of public works in January 1919. He was named prime minister on October 14, 1919, and signed the Treaty of Neuilly in France the following year. He remained in power after his party was victorious in parliamentary elections in March 1920. His government complied with the terms of the peace treaty with the Allies and sought to improve relations with Yugoslavia. Stambolski was ousted by a military coup on June 9, 1923. He was at his native village of Slavovitsa when news of the coup reached him. He tried to flee the country but was found and shot to death by rebels when he resisted arrest on June 14, 1923.

ALEXANDER TSANKOV (Prime Minister; June 9, 1923–January 3, 1926). Alexander Tsankov (Aleksandur Zankov) was born in Oryakhovo on June 28, 1879. He attended Sofia University where he became an economics professor. He entered politics as leader of the National Concord in opposition to the government of Aleksandr Stambolski. Tsankov became head of a coalition government on June 9, 1923, following the ouster of Stambolski in a military coup. The following year Tsankov crushed a Communist rebellion. Bulgaria remained in a state of conflict, and an attempt was made on the life of King Boris in April 1924. A leading Bulgarian general was assassinated the following day. A bomb that killed over a hundred people and injured Tsankov was placed in a Sofia cathedral during the funeral. He proclaimed martial law and instituted harsh measures to crush the rebels. Tsankov was dismissed by King Boris and replaced by Andrei Liaptchev on January 3, 1926. Tsankov subsequently served as president of the Sobranye. He remained a leading political figure in Bulgaria. He was briefly arrested by the government of Petar Zlatev in 1935 for conspiring against the government. Tsankov was a leading supporter of Bulgaria's alliance with Germany during World War II. He escaped to Nazi Germany as the Russian army advanced on September 9, 1944, and was installed as head of a National Bulgarian government-in-exile. The Allied advance ended his government, and he surrendered to the United States army. He was interned for several months before being released. He subsequently went to Argentina in 1948. He lived in retirement in Buenos Aires, where he died on July 17, 1959.

ANDREI LIAPTCHEV (Prime Minister; January 3, 1926–June 28, 1931). Andrei Liaptchev (Lyapchev) was born in Resne, near Monastir, in Macedonia, on November 30, 1866. He was educated in Bulgaria and studied political economy in Zurich, Berlin, and Paris. He became active in politics as a member of the Democratic Party. He was named minister of finance in Alexander Malinov's party in 1908. Liaptchev fought with the Macedonian Legion during the Balkan War in 1912. He opposed Bulgaria's entry into World War I on the side of the Central Powers. He returned to the cabinet as minister of finance in 1918 and arranged the terms of Bulgaria's armistice after the war. He briefly served as minister of war in Malinov's cabinet after the abdication of King Ferdinand. He was an opponent of the government

of Aleksandr Stambolski and was imprisoned from 1922 until Stambolski's ouster the following year. He became the leader of the new Democratic Party in 1923 and succeeded Alexander Tsankov as prime minister on January 3, 1926. He restored stability to the country and attempted to modernize Bulgaria's economy. Liaptchev's Democratic Coalition was defeated in general elections in 1930 and he retired on June 28, 1931. He died of cancer in Sofia two years later on November 6, 1933.

ALEXANDER MALINOV (Prime Minister; June 28, 1931–October 12, 1931). *See earlier entry under Heads of Government.*

NIKOLA MUSHANOV (Prime Minister; October 12, 1931–May 19, 1934). Nikola Mushanov was born in Drnovo in 1872. He was elected to the Sobranye in 1902 and became the leader of the small Democratic Party. Mushanov was called upon to head the government as prime minister on October 12, 1931. He was ousted by Kimon Georgiev on May 19, 1934. Mushanov served as a leader of the opposition and was an opponent of Bulgaria's alliance with Germany during World War II. He remained in Bulgaria after the war and died there in July 1951.

KIMON GEORGIEV (Prime Minister; May 19, 1934–January 22, 1935). Kimon Georgiev was born in Pazardzhik in 1882. He attended military school and joined the Bulgarian army. He served in the infantry during World War I and was seriously wounded in action. In the 1920s he retired from the army and entered politics. Georgiev served in several governments in the late 1920s and early 1930s. He engineered the overthrow of the government and installed himself as premier on May 19, 1934. He served until January 22, 1935, and was briefly arrested by the subsequent administration. Georgiev was an opponent of the pro-Axis government that ruled Bulgaria during World War II and organized the Fatherland Front in opposition. He succeeded in ousting the council of regents on September 9, 1944, and became premier the following day. The new government arranged a surrender to the Allies. Georgiev was defeated in the elections of 1946 and left office as premier on November 23, 1946. He subsequently served as foreign minister in the Communist government of Georgi Dimitrov. Georgiev retired from politics in 1952 and lived in obscurity until his death in Sofia on September 28, 1969.

PETAR ZLATEV (Prime Minister; January 22, 1935–April 21, 1935). Petar Zlatev was born in 1881. He served in the Bulgarian army, rising to the rank of general. He served in Kimon Georgiev's cabinet as minister of war early in 1935 before ousting Georgiev as head of the government on January 22, 1935. He instituted repressive measures that brought about his removal on April 21, 1935. Zlatev died on July 24, 1948.

ANDREI TOSHEV (Prime Minister; April 21, 1935–November 23, 1935). Andrei Toshev was born in 1868. He was a close advisor to King Ferdinand and served as Bulgaria's ambassador to Austria during the Balkan Wars and World War I. He was chosen by King Boris to head the government as prime minister on April 21, 1935. He was a supporter of Bulgaria's alliance with Germany. Toshev stepped down on November 23, 1935, and died on January 10, 1944.

GEORGI KIOSSIEVANOV (Prime Minister; November 23, 1935–February 16, 1940). Georgi Kiossievanov was born in 1884. He held his first government position under Aleksandr Stambolski in 1923. He survived Stambolski's ouster and held various governmental and diplomatic positions in succeeding years. He served as foreign minister from early 1935 and was chosen by King Boris to

head the government on November 23, 1935. He was considered an ineffective leader and a tool of King Boris. He continued to head the government until his dismissal on February 16, 1940. Kiossievanov served as Bulgaria's ambassador to Switzerland during World War II. He died on July 27, 1960.

BOGDAN FILOV (Prime Minister; February 16, 1940–September 14, 1943). Bogdan Filov was born in Stara Zagora on March 28, 1883. He was a leading Bulgarian academician and became a member of the Bulgarian Academy of Science in 1929. He served as president of the academy from 1937 until 1940. He was chosen to head the government by King Boris on February 16, 1940. He signed the Vienna Agreement in March 1941 that brought Bulgaria into World War II on the side of Germany. After King Boris' death in August 1943, Filov became the leading political figure in the country. He arranged the appointment of a regency council consisting of himself, Prince Cyril, and General Nikola Mihov, the minister of war. He stepped down as prime minister on September 14, 1943, and named Dobri Bozhilov as his successor. He remained a strong supporter of Germany during the war. The regency council was ousted on September 9, 1944, when Kimon Georgiev's Fatherland Front formed a government. Filov was arrested and tried for war crimes. He was executed along with the rest of the regency council and numerous other members of the wartime government on February 1, 1945.

DOBRI BOZHILOV (Prime Minister; September 14, 1943–June 1, 1944). Dobri Bozhilov was born in 1884. He served as minister of finance from 1938. He was named by Bogdan Filov to succeed him as prime minister on September 14, 1943, but Filov continued to control the government, and Bozhilov stepped down on June 1, 1944. He was then named director of the National

Bank, where he remained until his removal in August 1944. Bozhilov was arrested following the establishment of the Fatherland Front government in September 1944. He was tried for war crimes and was executed on February 1, 1945.

IVAN BAGRIANOV (Prime Minister; June 1, 1944–September 2, 1944). Ivan Bagrianov was born in 1892. He was educated in Germany and commanded a German artillery unit during World War I. He was a close friend of King Boris and a leading member of the Agrarian Party. He served in various governments until his resignation in 1941. He was chosen to head the government on June 1, 1944. He was considered an acceptable candidate by both Germany and the Allies. He attempted to extract Bulgaria from the war by declaring neutrality, and Bulgaria withdrew from the conflict in August 1944. His proposal was unacceptable to the Allies, and Russian troops continued to advance. Bagrianov was forced to resign on September 2, 1944. He was arrested after the establishment of the Fatherland Front gov-

ernment later in the month. He was tried as a war criminal and executed on February 1, 1945.

KONSTANTIN MURAVIEV (Prime Minister; September 2, 1944–September 9, 1944). Konstantin Muraviev was born in 1893. He was a nephew of Aleksandr Stambolski and served in his government as minister of war from 1919 until 1923. Muraviev also served in the Agrarian coalition cabinet from 1931 until 1934. He was chosen to head the government on September 2, 1944, with the task of pulling Bulgaria out of World War II. He agreed with the Allies' demands that Bulgaria declare war on Germany. He was replaced by the Fatherland Front government under Kimon Georgiev on September 9, 1944, as the Russian army advanced. He was subsequently arrested and tried for war crimes. Muraviev was sentenced to life imprisonment. He died on January 31, 1965.

KIMON GEORGIEV (Prime Minister; September 10, 1944–October 27, 1946). *See earlier entry under Heads of Government.*

Canada

Canada is a country in the north of North America. The British North America Act of July 1867 is the Canadian Constitutions. Canada belongs to the Commonwealth of Nations and consists of ten provinces and two territories.

HEADS OF STATE

EARL OF MINTO (Governor-General; November 12, 1898–December 10, 1904). Gilbert John Murray Kynynmound Elliot was born in London on July 9, 1845. He was educated at Eton and Trinity College, Cambridge. He was commissioned into the Scots Guard in 1867 and saw action in the

Russo-Turkish War of 1877 while attached to the Turkish army. He also served in the Afghan campaign of 1879 and in the Egyptian War of 1882, where he was severely wounded at Magfar. He served as chief of the Canadian staff during Luis Riel's rebellion in the Canadian Northwest in 1885. He became the

4th Earl of Minto in 1891 and was appointed governor-general of Canada on November 12, 1898. Steps were taken toward further Canadian autonomy under Prime Minister Wilfrid Laurier during Lord Minto's term of office, which ended on December 10, 1904. He succeeded Earl Curzon as viceroy of India in 1905 and retained that position until 1910. He subsequently returned to Great Britain and died in Hawick, Scotland, on March 1, 1914.

EARL OF GREY (Governor-General; December 10, 1904–October 13, 1911). Earl Albert Henry George Grey was born at St. James' Palace in London, on November 28, 1851. He was educated at Harrow and received a degree in 1873 from Trinity College, Cambridge. He was elected to the British House of Commons from South Northumberland in 1880. He succeeded his uncle to the earldom, becoming the 4th Earl of Grey in 1894. He succeeded Dr. Jameson as administrator of Rhodesia in 1894, where he remained for three years. He subsequently served as director of the South African Chartered Company from 1898 until his appointment as governor-general of Canada on December 10, 1904. He was a popular figure with the Canadian people, and his term was extended twice before he stepped down on October 13, 1911. He returned to Great Britain, where he involved himself in social and agricultural reforms. He died on August 29, 1917, at Howick House, Northumberland, after a long illness.

ARTHUR, DUKE OF CONNAUGHT (Governor-General; October 13, 1911–November 11, 1916). Arthur William Patrick Albert was born in Buckingham Palace on May 1, 1850. He was the third son of Queen Victoria and Prince Albert. He entered the British army in 1868 and saw action in Canada during the Red River Rebellion and the Fenian raid in 1870. He returned to England to serve on the privy council the fol-

lowing year. He was created Duke of Connaught and Strathern and Earl of Sussex in April 1874. The Duke married Princess Louisa of Prussia in 1879. He continued to distinguish himself in the military, commanding a brigade in the Egyptian War of 1882. He rose to the rank of field marshal in 1902. He served as inspector-general of the armed forces from 1904 until 1907. He was appointed governor-general of Canada on October 13, 1911, where he remained during the early years of World War I until November 11, 1916. He subsequently returned to England. The Duke represented the Crown at the opening of the new legislature in New Delhi, India, in 1920. He remained a distinguished member of the British royal family until his death after a long illness at his country home at Bagshot Park, Surrey, on January 16, 1942.

DUKE OF DEVONSHIRE (Governor-General; November 11, 1916–August 11, 1921). Victor Christian William Cavendish was born in London on May 31, 1868. He was the eldest son of Lord Edward Cavendish. He was educated at Eton and Trinity College, Cambridge. He was elected to the House of Commons as a Liberal Unionist from West Derbyshire in 1891. He remained in the House of Commons until 1908, when he succeeded his uncle to become the 9th Duke of Devonshire. He served as civil lord of the admiralty from 1915 until 1916, when he succeeded the Duke of Connaught as governor-general of Canada. He took office on November 11, 1916, and completed his term on August 11, 1921, after which he returned to England. He retired from public affairs and died at Chatsworth House, Devonshire, England, on May 6, 1938.

VISCOUNT BYNG OF VIMY (Governor-General; August 11, 1921–October 2, 1926). Julian Hedworth George Byng was born in Barnet, England, on September 11, 1862. He was the seventh son of the 2nd Earl of Stratford. He attended Eton and was commissioned in the British army in 1883. He saw action in the Sudan in 1884 and served with distinction in the South African War between 1899 and 1902. He served as commandant of the Cavalry School from 1904 until 1905, and rose to the rank of major general in 1909. He was given command in Egypt in 1912. He commanded the 3rd Cavalry Division and, subsequently, the Cavalry Corps in the early years of World War I. He was placed in command of the Canadian Corps in 1916. He succeeded General Allenby as commander of the Third Army in 1917. He was created Baron Byng of Vimy and Thorpe-le-Soken for his service to the nation during the war. He retired from the army in November 1919. He was appointed governor-general of Canada, and took office on August 11, 1921. Lord Byng became involved in a constitutional controversy in 1926 when he refused Prime Minister W. L. Mackenzie King's call for a new election and invited Arthur Meighen to form a new government. Lord Byng completed his term on October 2, 1926. He returned to England and was appointed commissioner of police in metropolitan London in 1928. He held that position until 1934. He died of heart failure after abdominal surgery at Thorpe-le-Soken, Essex, England, on June 6, 1935.

VISCOUNT WILLINGDON (Governor-General; October 2, 1926–April 4, 1931). Freeman Freeman-Thomas was born in Ratton on September 12, 1886. He was educated at Eton and Trinity College, Cambridge, where he was renowned as a cricketer. He was elected to the British House of Commons in 1900 as a Liberal member from Hastings. He was defeated for reelection in 1906 but was returned in a by-election later in the year from Cornwall. He was raised to the peerage as 1st Baron of Ratton in 1910 and became lord-in-waiting

to King George V the following year. He was appointed governor of Bombay in 1913 and remained in that position throughout World War I. He returned to India to serve as governor of Madras in 1919. He returned to England in 1924 and was created First Viscount of Willingdon. He also led the Indian delegation at the League of Nations in 1924. He was appointed governor-general of Canada, serving from October 2, 1926, until April 4, 1931. He then succeeded Lord Halifax as Viceroy of India. Lord Willingdon temporarily crushed Mahatma Gandhi's civil disobedience movement, driving the Congress Party underground for several years. He returned to England in 1936. Lord Willingdon died in London of pneumonia on August 12, 1941.

EARL OF BESSBOROUGH (Governor-General; April 4, 1931–November 2, 1935). Vere Brabazon Ponsonby was born on October 27, 1880. He was educated at Harrow and Trinity College, Cambridge. He was called to the bar in 1903 and served on the London county council from 1907 until 1910. He was elected to the House of Commons as a Conservative from Cheltenham in 1910. He represented Dover in the House of Commons from 1913 until 1920. He spent much of that period serving in the army as a staff officer at Gallipoli and in France during World War I. He became a leading business executive during the 1920s and was chairman of the board of several major businesses. He also became the 9th Earl of Bessborough. He was appointed to succeed Lord Willingdon as governor-general of Canada on April 4, 1931. He hosted the Imperial Conference at Ottawa in July 1932. Lord Bessborough completed his term on November 2, 1935, and returned to England. He resumed his business ventures and became president of the Council of Foreign Bondholders. He became chairman of the League of Nations Loans Committee in 1937. Lord Bessborough died at his home in Hampshire, England, on March 10, 1956.

LORD TWEEDSMUIR (Governor-General; November 2, 1935–February 11, 1940).

John Buchan was born in Perth, Scotland, on August 26, 1875. He was educated at the University of Glasgow and Brasenose College, Oxford. He served as secretary to Lord Milner, high commissioner for South Africa, from 1901 until 1903. He subsequently gained notoriety for authoring such adventures stories as *Prester John* (1910), *The Thirty-Nine Steps* (1915), and *Greenmantle* (1916). He also wrote a 24-volume history of World War I and biographies of such historical figures as Augustus, Sir Walter Scott, Oliver Cromwell, and Julius Caesar. Buchan was elected to the Parliament for the Scottish Universities in 1927. He was raised to the peerage as Baron Tweedsmuir in 1935. He also became governor-general of Canada that year, taking office on November 2, 1935. Lord Tweedsmuir suffered a brain concussion as a result of a fall in the bathroom in Government House, Ottawa, and died five days later on February 11, 1940, at the Neurological Institute of the Royal Victoria Hospital in Montreal after three operations failed to relieve the pressure on his brain.

EARL OF ATHLONE (Governor-General; June 21, 1940–July 31, 1945).

Alexander Augustus Frederick William Alfred George was born at Kensington Palace on April 14, 1874. He was the son of the German Duke of Teck and Princess Mary. He was known as Prince Alexander and was educated at Eton and Sandhurst. He subsequently joined the cavalry and served in the Matabele War in Rhodesia in 1894. He was also active in the South African War and World War I. He turned down an appointment to serve as governor-general of Canada in 1914 in order to remain in the military. Prince Alexander took the family name of Cambridge and became known as the Earl of Athlone in July 1917, due to the unpopular German connections of his previous name and title. He served as governor-general of South Africa from January 21, 1924, until January 26, 1931. He was then named governor and constable of Windsor Castle. He was also selected as chancellor of London University that year. He was named to succeed Lord Tweedsmuir as governor-general of Canada on June 21, 1940. He retained that position until July 31, 1945, when he returned to England. He remained chancellor of London University until his retirement in 1955. The Earl of Athlone died on January 16, 1957, in Kensington Palace after a long illness.

HEADS OF GOVERNMENT

SIR WILFRID LAURIER (Prime Minister; July 11, 1896–October 6, 1911).

Sir Wilfrid Laurier was born in St. Lin, Quebec, on November 20, 1841. He graduated from McGill University in 1864 with a degree in law. He was elected to the Quebec legislature in 1871 and entered the Canadian House of Commons three years later. He was named to the cabinet as minister of inland revenue in 1877. He went into opposition the following year and became the leader of the Liberal Party in 1887. He replaced Sir Charles Tupper as prime minister on July 11, 1896. His government settled the Manitoba school difficulties and encouraged the development of Canada's natural resources. The last British troops were withdrawn from Canada during his administration and the Dominion gained the right to negotiate separate commercial treaties. He continued to lead the government until October 6, 1911, when his cabinet fell over the issue of trade reciprocity with the United States. He continued to lead the opposition to Robert Borden's Conservative government, but he gave the government his support after the start of World War I in 1914 although the Liberal Party had a bitter split over the issue of conscription into the national service during the war. Laurier continued to head the Liberal Party until his death in Ottawa on February 17, 1919.

ROBERT L. BORDEN (Prime Minister; October 10, 1911–July 10, 1920). Robert Laird Borden was born in Grand Pre, Nova Scotia, on June 26, 1854. He attended the Acacia Villa Seminary and worked as a teacher for several years before studying law. He joined a practice in Halifax in 1882. He entered politics as a Conservative in 1896 and was elected to the House of Commons. He succeeded Sir Charles Tupper as leader of the Conservative opposition in 1901. He was defeated for reelection in 1904, but was returned to the House of Commons in a by-election the following year. He came to national prominence as an opponent of Wilfrid Laurier's Liberal government's support of unilateral reciprocity in trade with the United States. The Conservatives were victorious in the elections of 1911 and Borden became prime minister on October 10, 1911. He continued to hold office throughout World War I and became the first overseas minister to attend a meeting of the British War Cabinet in July 1915. He served on the Imperial War Cabinet in 1917 and 1918. Borden formed a Unionist government composed of Conservatives and Liberals supporting compulsory military service in 1917. He headed the Canadian delegation to the Paris Peace Conference in 1919. Borden retired on July 10, 1920, due to poor health, and was succeeded as prime minister by Arthur Meighen. He retired from active politics and served as chancellor of Queen's University in Kingston from 1924 until 1930. Borden died of a heart attack at his home in Ottawa on June 10, 1937.

ARTHUR MEIGHEN (Prime Minister; July 10, 1920–December 29, 1921). Arthur Meighen was born in Anderson, Ontario, on June 16, 1874. He was educated at the University of Toronto and opened a law practice in Portage la Prairie, Manitoba. He became active in politics in 1908 and was elected to the House of Commons as a Conservative. He was named to Robert Borden's ministry as solicitor general in 1913 and served as secretary of state and minister of mines in 1917. He remained in the coalition Unionist government as minister of the interior from October 1917 until he succeeded Borden as prime minister and leader of the Conservatives on July 10, 1920. The Conservatives were defeated in elections the following year and Meighen relinquished office on December 29, 1921. He led the opposition to William MacKenzie King's Liberal government. He was again called upon to form a government by the governor-general, Lord Byng, on June 29, 1926. The government collapsed soon after and the Conservatives were defeated in general elections. Meighen was again succeeded as prime minister by Liberal leader William MacKenzie King on September 25, 1926. He subsequently retired from politics. He returned to lead the party in the senate under the Conservative government of Richard B. Bennett until 1935. He briefly headed the Conservatives in 1941, but permanently retired from politics when he failed to win a seat in the Parliament. Meighen died in Toronto on August 5, 1960.

WILLIAM LYON MACKENZIE KING (Prime Minister; December 29, 1921–June 29, 1926). William Lyon MacKenzie King was born in Kitchener, Ontario, on December 17, 1874. He attended the University of Toronto and Harvard, where he studied economics and political science. He returned to

Canada in 1900 to enter the civil service and became deputy minister of labor. He was named to the Liberal cabinet of Sir Wilfrid Laurier as minister of labor in 1909 and served until the defeat of the government in 1911. He worked in private industry until the death of Laurier in 1919. King was then elected leader of the Liberal Party and became prime minister on December 29, 1921, when the Party achieved victory. He remained in office with the support of the Progressive Party until June 29, 1926, when he lost a vote of confidence in the Parliament following revelations of corruption in the customs department. The governor-general, Lord Byng, refused King's request to call for new elections and Conservative leader Arthur Meighen formed a government. New parliamentary elections were called following the collapse of the successive Conservative government and the Liberal Party was again victorious. King again became prime minister on September 25, 1926. He promoted closer relations between Canada and the United States, and his government also reduced taxes and the national debt. His unwillingness to grant federal aid to the provinces brought about a defeat for the Liberal Party in the elections of 1930. He was replaced as prime minister by Conservative leader Richard Bennett on August 6, 1930. King remained leader of the opposition until he again formed a Liberal government on October 12, 1935. He was basically an isolationist and tried to avoid Canadian commitments in Europe. He sought to increase exports and to maintain Canada's autonomy. Canada declared war on the Axis Powers on September 10, 1939, shortly after the start of World War II. King called elections in 1940 and received a large majority. He sought to avoid initiating compulsory military service during the war, but was forced to do so in order to provide reinforcements. Canada also supplied food and munitions for the war effort. The Liberal Party remained in power following elections in 1945, and King led Canada back to a peacetime economy. He also supported Canada's involvement in such international organizations as the United Nations and the North Atlantic Treaty Organization. King resigned as prime minister on November 15, 1948, due to ill health. He died of pneumonia at his country home in Kingsmere, Quebec, on July 22, 1950.

ARTHUR MEIGHEN (Prime Minister; June 29, 1926–September 25, 1926). *See earlier entry under Heads of Government.*

WILLIAM LYON MACKENZIE KING (Prime Minister; September 25, 1926–August 6, 1930). *See earlier entry under Heads of Government.*

RICHARD BEDFORD BENNETT (Prime Minister; August 7, 1930–October 23, 1935). Richard Bedford Bennett was born in Hopewell Hill, New Brunswick, on July 3, 1870. He was educated at Dalhousie University in Halifax and began practicing law in 1893. He was elected to the legislative assembly of the Northwest Territories in 1897 and was elected to the House of Commons from Calgary as a Conservative in 1911. He served in the government as director general of national service in 1916 and became minister of justice in 1921. He succeeded Arthur Meighen as leader of the Conservatives in 1927 and formed a government as prime minister on August 7, 1930. He also served in the government as minister of finance and external affairs. His government was unable to improve the financial crisis brought on by the worldwide economic depression. The Conservative Party was badly defeated by the Liberals in the elections of 1935, and Bennett relinquished office to William MacKenzie King on October 23, 1935. He led the Conservative opposition until his retirement from politics in 1938. He settled in England the following year and was created First Viscount Bennett in 1941. He was found dead at his home in Mickleham, Surrey, England, on June 27, 1947.

WILLIAM LYON MACKENZIE KING (Prime Minister; October 23, 1935–November 15, 1948). *See earlier entry under Heads of Government.*

Chile

Chile is a country on the South Pacific coast of South America. It was granted independence from Spain on September 18, 1810.

HEADS OF STATE

FEDERICO ERRÁZURIZ EC-HAURREN (President; December 26, 1896–July 12, 1901). Federico Errázuriz Echaurren was born in Santiago on September 16, 1850. He was the son of Federico Errázuriz Zañartu, who served as Chile's president from 1871 until 1876. He was educated as a lawyer and began his political career in the final year of his father's administration when he was elected to the chamber of deputies. He was named to the cabinet in 1890 as minister of war. He was an opponent of President José Manuel Balmaceda Fernández and was involved in the civil war that broke out in 1891 following Balmaceda's assassination. Errázuriz was elected to the senate in 1894 and served in President Jorge Montt's cabinet as minister of justice and public instruction. He was the Liberal-Conservative coalition's candidate for president in 1896. He was successful in the campaign and took office on December 26, 1896. Errázuriz ruled in a conciliatory fashion, allowing supporters of the deposed president Balmaceda to join the government. He instituted reforms in education and health care and expanded public works projects. Errázuriz suffered from poor health during the final year of his term. He died on July 12, 1901.

ELIAS FERNANDEZ ALBANO (President; July 12, 1901–August 18,

1901). Elias Fernandez Albano was born in 1845. He was educated as a lawyer and entered politics in 1884 with his election to the chamber of deputies. He was named minister of the interior in the cabinet of President Federico Errázuriz Echaurren in 1896. He served as acting president following Errázuriz's death on July 12, 1901, until President German Riesco took office on August 18, 1901. He was again named to the position by President Pedro Montt in 1906. He succeeded to the presidency of Chile following Montt's death on August 16, 1910. Fernandez died in office of pneumonia on September 6, 1910.

GERMÁN RIESCO ERRÁZURIZ (President; August 18, 1901–September 18, 1906). Germán Riesco Errázuriz was born on May 18, 1854. He was a practicing lawyer before entering politics. He was elected to the senate in 1900. He was the Liberal coalition's candidate for president in 1901 and took office on August 18, 1901. During his administration the Transandine Railroad, connecting Santiago to Buenos Aires, was completed and the boundary dispute between Chile and Argentina was settled in 1902. His administration also began the construction of numerous public works projects. He completed his term of office and stepped down on September 18, 1906. Riesco returned to his law practice and remained active in politics until his death from a heart attack in Santiago on December 8, 1916.

PEDRO MONTT (President; September 18, 1906–August 16, 1910). Pedro Montt was born in Santiago on June 29, 1848. He was the son of Manuel Montt, who served as Chile's president from 1851 until 1861. The younger Montt was educated at the Instituto Nacional and was elected to the chamber of deputies in 1876. He became president of the chamber in 1885. Despite his opposition to the government of President José Balmaceda, Montt was appointed to the cabinet as minister of justice and public education in 1886. He was active in the revolution that deposed Balmaceda in 1891. He was subsequently sent to the United States as Chile's minister. He was defeated for the presidency of Chile in 1901 but was elected five years later on the National Union ticket and took office on September 18, 1906. Montt was instrumental in avoiding an armed conflict between Chile and Argentina, and he also instituted development of better sanitation and health facilities. He also completed the numerous public works projects begun by his predecessor, Germán Riesco. Montt suffered from poor health in his later years in office. He visited the United States in the summer of 1910 and died of a heart attack while vacationing in Bremen, Germany, on August 16, 1910.

ELIAS FERNANDEZ ALBANO (President; August 16, 1910–September 6, 1910). *See earlier entry under Heads of State.*

EMILIANO FIGUEROA LARRAÍN (President; September 6, 1910–September 18, 1911). Emiliano Figueroa Larraín was born in 1866. He was a practicing lawyer and a leading member of the Democratic Party. Figueroa Larraín became acting president of Chile following the death of Elias Fernandez Albano on September 6, 1910. He presided over the election that resulted in Ramon Barros Luco taking office on September 18, 1911. Figueroa Larraín remained active in politics and returned to the presidency on December 23, 1925, following the resignation of Arturo Alessandri Palma. Figueroa Larraín's second term was marked with political and civil disorder. He stepped down on May 4, 1927, to allow Carlos Ibáñez del Campo to take power. Figueroa Larraín died on May 16, 1931.

RAMON BARROS LUCO (President; September 18, 1911–December 23, 1915). Ramón Barros Luco was born in Santiago in 1835. He attended the National University and received a degree in law in 1858. He was elected to the chamber of deputies in 1861. He became president of the chamber in 1879 and held that position several times between 1888 and 1892. As president of the chamber he was a member of the revolutionary junta that deposed President José Balmaceda in 1891. Barros Luco became president of the senate in 1896. He briefly served as acting president during Germán Riesco's illness in 1903. He was a member of the council of state and was minister of the interior several times over the next few years. Barros Luco was chosen as Chile's president by the congress in 1910 when a deadlock was reached between the two leading candidates. He was sworn into office on September 18, 1911. Barros Luco had difficulty maintaining a stable government, with most of his cabinets lasting only a few weeks. He succeeded in implementing a number of public works programs during his term, and a commercial treaty was signed with Argentina and Brazil in 1915. He completed his term of office on December 23, 1915, and died in 1919.

JUAN LUIS SANFUENTES ANDONAEGUI (President; December 23, 1915–June 25, 1920). Juan Luis Sanfuentes Andonaegui was born in Santiago on December 27, 1858. He received a degree in law from the National University in 1879. He was elected to the chamber of deputies as a Liberal in 1888. He supported President José Balmaceda during the civil war of 1891 and temporarily abandoned politics after Balmaceda's defeat. He returned to politics in 1900 and founded the Liberal Democratic Party. He was subsequently elected to the senate. He served in President Germán Riesco's cabinet as minister of finance in 1903 and became president of the senate in 1906. He received his party's nomination for the presidency in 1915 and was elected by a narrow margin. He took office on December 23, 1915. His administration maintained Chile's neutrality during World War I. He was responsible for making elementary education compulsory and reducing the public debt. He stepped down from office on June 25, 1920. Sanfuentes retired to private life and died on July 27, 1930.

LUIS BARROS BORGOÑO (President; June 25, 1920–September 23, 1920). Luis Barros Borgoño was born on March 25, 1858. He received a degree in law from the National University in 1880. He became chief of staff at the foreign ministry in 1883. He held various ministerial positions over the next two decades. He was acting president between June 25, 1920, and September 23, 1920, following the resignation of Juan Luis Sanfuentes. He was the nominee of the Radical Union Party in the 1920 presidential election but was defeated by Arturo Alessandri y Palma. He was named minister of the interior in 1925 and returned to the presidency when Alessandri resigned on October 1, 1925. He retained office until December 23, 1925, when Emiliano Figueroa Larraín took office. Barros Borgoño died in 1943.

ARTURO ALESSANDRI Y PAL-MA (President; December 23, 1920–September 8, 1924). Arturo Alessandri y Palma was born near Linares, Chile, on December 20, 1868. His father was an Italian immigrant. He graduated with a law degree from the University of Chile in 1893. He was elected to the chamber of deputies in 1897. He served in several governments as minister of industry and minister of finance, and gained a reputation as a liberal. His concern for the working class earned him the title of "the Lion of Tarapaca." He was the liberal coalition candidate for president of Chile in 1920. He was elected and sworn into office on December 23, 1920. Alessandri was forced into exile by the military on September 8, 1924. He returned to Chile the following January and resumed the presidency on March 21, 1925. He was instrumental in rewriting the Chilean constitution to grant the president greater powers before leaving office on October 1, 1925. He again became president on December 24, 1932. His government shifted sharply to the right during this term of office, alienating many of his earlier followers. He was largely concerned with Chile's economic recovery from the depression during much of his term. He left office on December 24, 1938. Alessandri was again elected to the senate in 1946. He remained there until his death on August 24, 1950.

LUIS ALTAMIRANO (President; September 8, 1924–January 23, 1925). Luis Altamirano Talavera entered the Chilean army as a captain during the civil war of 1891. He rose through the ranks with commissions throughout Europe and South America. He was promoted to lieutenant general and was named minister of industry and public works in July 1923. Altamirano replaced Domingo Amunategui Solar as minister of the interior in September 1924. He became head of a military junta which replaced President Arturo Alessandri y Palma on September 8, 1924. He continued to head the government until he was ousted by a another military coup led by Carlos Ibáñez del Campo on January 23, 1925. Altamirano subsequently retired from politics. He died in Santiago on July 25, 1936.

CARLOS IBÁÑEZ DEL CAMPO

(President; January 23, 1925–March 21, 1925). Carlos Ibáñez del Campo was born in Linares, Chile, on November 3, 1877. He entered the military school in Santiago in 1894 and rose to the rank of lieutenant in 1903. That year he went to El Salvador, where he spent the next five years training the army. Ibáñez returned to Chile in 1908 with the rank of captain. In subsequent years he served as section chief of the ministry of war and director of the cavalry school. He was assigned to Paris as military attaché in 1924, but returned to Chile in September of that year to take part in a military rebellion. Ibáñez was also active in the coup d'etat in January of 1925 and was leader of the military junta that followed from January 23, 1925, until March 21, 1925, when ousted president Arturo Alessandri y Palma was recalled to office. He continued to serve in the government as minister of war and was appointed minister of the interior and vice president in the government of President Emiliano Figueroa Larraín in 1927. He succeeded as president when Figueroa resigned on May 4, 1927. Ibáñez's administration was plagued by severe economic problems which resulted in his overthrow on July 26, 1931. He went into exile in Argentina and remained there until 1937. Ibáñez then returned to Chile, where he ran unsuccessfully for president in 1938 and 1942. He was elected to the Chilean Senate in 1949. In 1952 Ibáñez again ran for president and gained a plurality of the popular vote. He was confirmed as president by the national congress. Ibáñez was an admirer of Argentina's Juan Péron and attempted to instill a sense of Chilean nationalism and anti-American sentiment in the country, but had little success. During his term of office, it was feared that Ibáñez would revert to a dictatorial style of government, but he ruled in a conciliatory fashion. He remained in office until his term expired on November 3, 1958. He died of throat cancer in Santiago on April 28, 1960.

ARTURO ALESSANDRI Y PALMA (President; March 21, 1925–October 1, 1925). *See earlier entry under Heads of State.*

LUIS BARROS BORGOÑO (President; October 1, 1925–December 23, 1925). *See earlier entry under Heads of State.*

EMILIANO FIGUEROA LARRAÍN (President; December 23, 1925–May 4, 1927). *See earlier entry under Heads of State.*

CARLOS IBÁÑEZ DEL CAMPO (President; May 4, 1927–July 26, 1931). *See earlier entry under Heads of State.*

PEDRO OPAZO LETELIER (President; July 26, 1931–July 27, 1931). Pedro Opazo Letelier was born in 1876. He served in Luis Barros Borgoño's cabinet in 1920. He represented Talca in the chamber of deputies from 1921 until 1924, when he was elected to the senate. He became president of the senate in May 1930. He became vice president of the republic in 1931 and succeeded to the presidency following Carlos Ibáñez del Campo's ouster on July 26, 1931. He was replaced by Juan Esteban Montero on the following day. He remained in Montero's government as minister of the interior. Opazo continued to serve in the senate until 1949.

JUAN ESTEBAN MONTERO (President; July 27, 1931–August 18, 1931). Juan Esteban Montero Rodríguez was born in 1878. He was a leading lawyer and professor at the National

University. He held his first position in government in 1931 when he was appointed minister of the interior in the government of Carlos Ibáñez del Campo. Ibáñez was forced to resign on July 27, 1931, and Montero became provisional president on the following day. He resigned from office to run for the presidency and was succeeded by Manuel Trucco on August 18, 1931. Montero received the nomination of the Conservative Party and was elected to the presidency. He again took office on November 15, 1931. Chile's political situation remained turbulent and Montero's government was beset with strikes and demonstrations. He proclaimed martial law before his ouster in a military coup led by Colonel Marmaduque Grove on June 4, 1932. Montero went into exile in Spain. He returned to Chile in March 1933. He retired from active politics and died in Santiago on February 25, 1948.

MANUEL TRUCCO FRANZANI (President; August 18, 1931–November 15, 1931). Manuel Trucco Franzani was born in 1874. He was educated as a civil engineer and teacher at the National University. He became director general of the State Railways in 1918. He was elected to the senate in 1926 and was appointed minister of the interior in August 1931. He became acting president on August 18, 1931, when Juan Esteban Montero stepped down from office. He cut the salary of government employees to help reduce Chile's budget deficit. Trucco relinquished office on November 15, 1931, when Montero was elected to the presidency. He subsequently served as ambassador to the United States from 1933 until 1939. Trucco died in Santiago on October 25, 1954.

JUAN ESTEBAN MONTERO (President; November 15, 1931–June 4, 1932). *See earlier entry under Heads of State.*

ARTURO PUGA OSORIO (President; June 4, 1932–June 12, 1932). Arturo Puga Osorio was a general in the Chilean army when he participated in the military junta that ousted President Juan Esteban Montero on June 4, 1932. He led the junta composed of Carlos Dávila Espinosa, Eugenio Matte Hurtado, and Marmaduque Grove Vallejo until he was replaced by Grove on June 12, 1932.

MARMADUQUE GROVE VALLEJO (President; June 12, 1932–June 17, 1932). Marmaduque Grove Vallejo was born in Copiapo on July 6, 1878. He graduated from the Escuela Militar in 1898 and entered the artillery as a second lieutenant. He became an instructor at the Escuela Militar in 1901 and was sent to Germany for further military training in 1905. He returned to Chile as a captain in 1910. He rose to the rank of major in 1924. He participated in the military junta that ousted President Arturo Alessandri y Palma in September 1924. He and Carlos Ibáñez del Campo led another coup that recalled Alessandri to office four months later. He was promoted to colonel in 1926 and was a founder of the Chilean air force. He became military attaché in London in 1928. He returned to Chile in 1930 and was involved in an unsuccessful coup against Ibáñez del Campo. He was sent into exile on Easter Island, but soon escaped to France. He returned to Chile to command the air force after Ibáñez del Campo's ouster in August 1931. He led a coup that established Chile as a Socialist Republic on June 4, 1932, and served as provisional president from June 12, 1932, until he was ousted by Carlos Dávila Espinosa on June 17, 1932. He was the candidate of the Socialist Alliance in the presidential election in November 1932 but was defeated by Alessandri. He was again briefly exiled to Easter Island. He was elected to the senate in 1933 and became the leader of the Socialist Party. He again ran for the presidency in 1938, but withdrew in favor of Pedro Aguirre Cerda. He split with the Socialist Party in 1943 over the issue of merging with the Communists. He remained in the senate until his retirement in 1949. Grove died on May 15, 1954.

CARLOS DÁVILA ESPINOZA
(President; June 17, 1932–September 13, 1932). Carlos Guillermo Dávila Espinoza was born in Los Angeles, Chile, on September 5, 1887. He studied law at the University of Chile and Columbia University. He began working as a journalist at the Santiago newspaper, *El Mercurio*, in 1914. He founded *La Nación* in 1917 and served as editor until 1927, when he was appointed ambassador to the United States. He returned to Chile in 1931 and founded the news magazine *Hoy* the following year. He participated in the ruling junta that ousted President Juan Esteban Montero on January 4, 1932. Dávila became head of the junta on June 17, 1932, and proclaimed himself provisional president on July 8, 1932. Dávila was ousted in another coup led by Bartolomé Blanche Espejo on September 13, 1932. Dávila settled in New York, where he continued to work as a journalist. He represented Chile at the Inter-American Financial and Economic Advisory Committee in 1939. He served as a member of the United Nations Council of Assistance and Rehabilitation from 1943 until 1946. He became secretary general of the Organization of American States in June 1954. He retained that position until his death at his residence at the Pan American Union in Washington, D.C., on October 19, 1955.

BARTOLOMÉ BLANCHE ESPEJO
(President; September 13, 1932–October 2, 1932). Bartolomé Blanche Espejo was born in 1879. He was a career military officer and joined with Carlos Ibáñez del Campo and Marmaduke Grove Vallejo in the military junta in 1924. He served as undersecretary of war

in Ibáñez del Campo's government from 1924 until 1925. He was director general of the police from 1925 until 1926 and minister of war from 1926 until 1931. Blanche led the coup on September 13, 1932, that ousted President Carlos Dávila Espinoza. He became interim president of Chile until October 2, 1932, when Supreme Court Chief Justice Abraham Oyandel Urrutia was persuaded to take the office and hold presidential elections. Blanche stepped down and returned to the military. He died in Santiago at the age of 91 on June 10, 1970.

ABRAHAM OYANDEL URRUTIA
(President; October 2, 1932–December 24, 1932). Abraham Oyandel Urrutia was born in 1874. He served as president of the Chilean supreme court and refused to accept the presidency of Chile after the ouster of Carlos Dávila Espinoza in September 1932. He was persuaded to restore constitutional rule and replaced coup leader Bartolomé Blanche Espejo as interim president on October 2, 1932. His government conducted presidential elections and Oyandel relinquished the office to Arturo Alessandri y Palma on December 24, 1932. Oyandel returned to serve on the supreme court. He died in Santiago on January 29, 1954.

ARTURO ALESSANDRI Y PALMA
(President; December 24, 1932–December 24, 1938). *See earlier entry under Heads of State.*

PEDRO AGUIRRE CERDA
(President; December 24, 1938–November 10, 1941). Pedro Aguirre Cerda was born in Pocuro, Aconcagua Province, on February 6, 1879. He attended the University of Chile, where he received degrees in education and law. He began practicing law in 1904 and subsequently taught law at the University of Chile. He went to Europe in 1910 to study administrative laws. He returned to Chile in 1915 and

was elected to the chamber of deputies as a member of the Radical Party. He was named to the cabinet as minister of education and justice in 1918. He became minister of the interior in 1920 and was elected to the senate the following year. Aguirre Cerda was the presidential candidate of the leftist Popular Front coalition in 1938. He narrowly defeated Conservative candidate Gustavo Ross and took office on December 24, 1938. He initiated economic reforms that were sidetracked by a devastating earthquake in January 1939. He remained a popular leader and established a minimum wage for workers, aided industrial development, and reformed the country's educational system. He retained office until his death at Moneda Palace in Santiago of an acute bronchial disorder on November 25, 1941.

GERONIMO MENDEZ ARANCIBIA (President; November 25, 1941–April 2, 1942). Geronimo Mendez Arancibia was born in 1884. He served as vice president under Pedro Aguirre Cerda. He became acting president during Aguirre Cerda's illness on November 10, 1941, and succeeded to the presidency when Aguirre Cerda died on November 25, 1941. Mendez stepped down on April 2, 1942, following the election of Juan Antonio Riós. He died in 1959.

JUAN ANTONIO RÍOS (President; April 2, 1942–June 27, 1946). Juan Antonio Riós Morales was born in Canete, Arauco Province, on November 10, 1888. He received a law degree from the University of Chile in 1914 and, in 1918, was elected alderman in Concep-

cion. He served as deputy mayor and police magistrate for Concepcion until 1921, when he was appointed consul general to Panama. In 1923 he was elected to the Chilean Parliament representing Arauco, Lebu, and Canete. He was elected to the senate in 1930 and served until congress was dissolved in 1932. He was then appointed minister of the interior in the government of President Arturo Alessandri y Palma. Shortly thereafter he was appointed minister of justice, a position he retained until March 1937. Pedro Aguirre Cerda was elected president in 1938 with the support of the Popular Front coalition. Riós' Radical Party withdrew from the coalition and relations between President Aguirre Cerda and Riós were strained. Aguirre Cerda died in November 1941 and Riós became a candidate for the presidency. On February 1, 1942, Riós defeated General Carlos Ibáñez del Campo and was sworn into office on April 2, 1942. His administration initially refused to sever diplomatic relations with the Axis powers, but diplomatic and economic pressures persuaded him to reverse his stance. This change of policy resulted in the inclusion of Chile as part of the United States Lend-Lease Program and helped Chile secure new loans for its troubled economy. In October 1945 Riós' entire Cabinet resigned in protest of his visit to the United States. Riós was also beset by a failing economy due to a decrease in the price of copper, and by labor strikes throughout the country. Riós' health failed early in 1946, and he gave up his presidential powers to Alfredo Duhalde Vázquez, the minister of the interior, on January 17, 1946. Riós died in Santiago on June 27, 1946.

China

China, the world's most populous country, is located in eastern Asia.

HEADS OF STATE

KUANG-HSU (Tsai-t'ien) (Emperor; January 13, 1875–November 14, 1908). Tsai-t'ien (Te-tsung) was born on August 14, 1871. He was the second son of Prince I-huan and the grandson of Emperor Hsuan-tsung. His cousin, Emperor Mu-tsung died on January 12, 1875, and his maternal aunt, the Dowager Empress Tz'u Hsi (Hsiao-ch'in), chose him as successor to the throne. He ascended the throne on February 25, 1875, with the Dowager Empresses Tz'u Hsi and Hsiao-chen as regents. The title Kuang Hsu was chosen to designate the years of his reign. Tsai-t'ien was proclaimed of age on February 7, 1887. He married a cousin on February 26, 1889, who became known as Empress Hsiao-ting. Dowager Empress Tz'u Hsi still retained considerable power at the court. Her use of funds designated for naval construction to build an imperial pleasure garden was instrumental in China's defeat by Japan in the war of 1895. Tsai-t'ien initiated a reform movement with the intention of removing Tz'u Hsi from power, but she anticipated the coup attempt and returned to Peking from her summer palace in September 1898. The emperor was confined on the palace grounds, and she acted in his name to crush the reform movement. The influence of court officials and foreign diplomats prevented Tsai-t'ien from being murdered or dethroned. The dowager empress resented foreign influence in China and sponsored an antiforeign movement known as the Boxer Rebellion in 1900. Foreign troops entered Peking to put down the uprising on August 14, 1900, and Tz'u Hsi fled the palace for a period, bringing the emperor with her. She continued to rule in his name and returned to Peking soon afterward. Tsai-t'ien remained a virtual prisoner until his death on November 14, 1908. It was considered likely that he had been poisoned. The dowager empress died the following day, but possibly predeceased, and his death was only announced first.

P'U-YI (Hsuan-tung) (Emperor, November 14, 1908–February 12, 1912). P'u-yi was born on February 7, 1906. He was the son of Tsai-feng, younger brother of Emperor Tsai-t'ien. It was arranged by the Dowager Empress Tz'u-Hsi before her death on November 15, 1908, that he would assume the throne the day after the death of the emperor. P'u-yi was three years old at the time of his ascension to the throne on January 22, 1909, and he took the reign name of Hsuan-tung. His father and the widow of Emperor Tsai-t'ien, Dowager Empress Hsiao-ting, were named as coregents. The Manchu dynasty ended on February 12, 1912, when the regents agreed to P'u-yi's abdication in the face of a republican uprising led by Sun Yat-sen. P'u-yi was permitted to remain in the Forbidden City in Peking. A coup led by General Chang Hsün briefly restored him to the throne on July 1, 1917, but republican forces crushed the rebellion and P'u-yi abdicated again on July 12, 1917. He was forced to leave the palace by General Feng Yu-hsiang in 1924. He took refuge in the Japanese diplomatic mission and subsequently lived in the Japanese settlement of Tientsin. He was sent to Manchuria when the Japanese took control of that area of China. He was installed as Emperor Kang Teh of the

Japanese puppet state of Manchukuo in March 1934. He was captured by the Russians after World War II and interned in Siberia until 1950. He was then handed over to the Communist regime in China. He was sent to a reeducation camp and spent a decade doing such labors as weeding the Peking Botanical Gardens. He was pardoned by the Supreme People's Court as having "repented and acknowledged his crimes against the Chinese People" in December 1959. He was granted citizenship in the People's Republic of China and lived quietly until his death of cancer in Peking on October 17, 1967.

SUN YAT-SEN (Provisional President; January 1, 1912–February 14, 1912). Sun Yat-sen was born in the village of Ts'uiheng in Kwangtung province on November 12, 1866. He began his education at the village school before joining his brother in Hawaii in 1879. He completed his education there, where he also became a Christian. He returned to his village in 1882 and went to Hong Kong the following year to train to be a doctor. He received his medical degree in 1892. He soon became involved in the movement to overthrow the Manchu dynasty. He took part in a rebellion in Canton following the Japanese defeat of China in the war of 1895. The revolt failed and Sun spent much of the next sixteen years as a fugitive. He traveled extensively, gaining support for his cause. The republican movement continued to grow and he allied himself with a number of other rebel groups. Sun merged these groups into the T'ung-meng-hui and became director. He initiated several unsuccessful uprisings in 1907 and 1908. Widespread revolts took place in 1911, and the Manchu regents gave the reins of government to Yuan Shih-k'ai in November 1911. Sun returned to China on December 25, 1911, and was proclaimed president of the provisional republican government by the provincial delegates in Nanking on January 1, 1912.

Conflicts still persisted, and there was a stalemate between the revolutionary forces and the imperial army under Yuan. Sun agreed to step down as president if Yuan would support the republic. Yuan agreed to the arrangement and the last Manchu Emperor, P'u-yi, abdicated on February 12, 1912. Sun resigned as president the following day, and Yuan was inaugurated as provisional president. Sun subsequently served the government as national director of railroad development. Sun's political organization evolved into the Kuomintang when it joined with several smaller parties. The Kuomintang dominated elections to the National Assembly in February 1913 and sought to limit Yuan's authority. Yuan attempted to ignore the will of the assembly, and Sun took part in the subsequent revolt against the Peking government. Yuan died in 1916. Sun continued to oppose the Peking government and established a rival government in Canton. He left Canton in May 1918 and made an usuccessful attempt to gain Japanese support for the constitutional movement. He continued to write and speak out in favor of his "Three Principles"— nationalism, democracy, and socialism. Sun returned to Canton in February 1923 and was established as the leader of a military government. Sun gained the support of the Soviet Union. Soviet military advisors trained and supplied arms to Sun's new army, and he reorganized the Kuomintang in 1924. He attempted to negotiate with the various warlords who controlled parts of China. He became ill in December 1924 and was diagnosed with cancer. Sun died in Peking on March 12, 1925.

YUAN SHIH-K'AI (President; February 15, 1912–June 6, 1916). Yuan Shih-k'ai was born at Hsiang Cheng in Honan on September 16, 1859. He entered into the military and became an aide to General Wu Chang-ching in 1879. He was placed in command of a Chinese garrison in Korea in 1884 and became the imperial resident there the following year. He remained in Korea until the start of the Sino-Japanese War in 1894. After the war he began to train the army in modern military methods. Yuan supported the Dowager Empress Tz'u Hsi in her antireformist counter coup against the emperor in 1898. He was subsequently named governor of Shantung Province and became governor general of Chihli in 1901. He became head of the foreign office in Peking in 1907, but was removed from his position following the death of the dowager empress in late 1908. Republican uprisings impelled the regents to recall Yuan in October 1911. He was named president of the council of ministers on November 1, 1911. Yuan was granted full powers to negotiate with the rebels. He arranged the abdication of the child emperor, P'u-yi, on February 12, 1912. As part of an agreement with nationalist leader Sun Yat-sen, Yuan became president of the provisional government of the Republic of China on February 15, 1912. The Kuomintang, Sun's republican party, clashed with Yuan and Sung Chiao-jen, a leading member of the Kuomintang, was assassinated, presumably by agents of Yuan, in March 1913. A second revolution against Yuan began the following summer. Yuan outlawed the Kuomintang and dismissed the parliament. He was officially elected president on October 6, 1913. For the next several years Yuan attempted to crush opposition to his government, as republicans and various warlords contested Yuan's power. He was forced to yield to many of Japan's demands on China in May 1915 when China could no longer count on protection from the European powers, then engaged in World War I. Yuan contrived to make himself the monarch of China in January 1916. Southern China rebelled against his ambitions and he soon renounced his plans. Yuan's military and political position deteriorated in the face of continued rebellion. He died soon after in Peking of uremia on June 6, 1916.

LI YUAN-HUNG (President; June 7, 1916–August 14, 1917). Li Yuan-hung was born in Huangp'i in 1864. He graduated from the Tientsin Naval Academy in 1889. He saw action during the Sino-Japanese War in 1894 and 1895. He subsequently served as an aide to Chang Chih-tung, the governor general of Hukwang. Li went to Japan on several occasions to learn modern military training, and he assisted Chang in building an army. He became commander and chief of the revolutionary army in Hupeh in October 1911. He was elected vice president of the provisional republican government under Sun Yat-sen in December 1911 and retained that position when Yuan Shih-k'ai became president in February 1912. Li remained at Hupeh, where he led his forces against the army of the Kuomintang nationalists when they rebelled against Yuan. He joined Yuan in Peking in December 1913 and headed the newly formed council of state in May 1914. Li assumed the presidency on June 7, 1916, following Yuan's death. He exercised little power, with Premier Tuan Ch'i-jui handling most of the affairs of government. Tuan's willingness to accept demands from Japan in regard to China's entry into World War I led to criticism in the National Assembly. Li dismissed Tuan on May 23, 1917, and named Li Ching-hsi as his replacement on May 28, 1917. General Chang Hsün led a military rebellion to restore the Manchu dynasty. Li recalled Tuan to the premiership on July 2, 1917. Li called for Feng Kuo-chang, the vice president, to assume the powers of the presidency on July 2, 1917, as he took refuge in the Japanese legation. After the Monarchists were put down, Li resigned the presidency on August 14, 1917, and went to Tientsin. He spent the next five years in retirement before being persuaded to resume the presidency on June 11, 1923. However, he was forced from office by supporters of Ts'ao K'un on June 13, 1923. Li went to Shanghai in September 1923 and then spent several months in Japan to recuperate from complications of diabetes. He returned to China and retired to his estate in Tsientsin, where he died on June 3, 1928.

FENG KUO-CHANG (President; August 14, 1917–October 10, 1918). Feng Kuo-chang was born in Chihli on January 7, 1859. His family's financial difficulties prevented Feng from completing his education. Feng entered the Anhwei army and was sent to the Peiyan Military Academy in Tientsin in 1885 for further training. He graduated five years later and served at Port Arthur. He saw action in the Sino-Japanese War from 1894 until 1895 and was sent to Japan as a military attaché after the war. He became an aide to Yuan Shih-k'ai and accompanied him to Shantung when Yuan became governor there in 1899. He assisted in the suppression of the Boxer Rebellion. He remained a leading advisor to Yuan and was placed in charge of a commission to reorganize the imperial army in 1903. He was instrumental in modernizing the military. When Yuan was given the command of the Imperial forces against the republican army in October 1911, Feng became commander of the First Army. Feng's troops retook the city of Hanyang from the rebels in November 1911. He returned to Peking at the end of the year and became chief of the military council in the president's office. He was promoted to full general in 1913 and continued to support Yuan when the republican Kuomintang again rebelled against the government. He was appointed military governor of Kiangsu Province in December 1913. Feng's relationship with Yuan became strained in 1915, and Feng refused to support Yuan's bid to become China's monarch. Feng began conspiring against Yuan with other military leaders in 1916; they called for Yuan to relinquish the presidency. Yuan died in June of that year, and Feng was named vice president under his successor as president, Li Yuan-hung. He became a rival of Premier Tuan Ch'i-jui

who held much of the power in the government. When General Chang Hsün began a rebellion to restore the Manchu dynasty in June 1917, Li stepped down from the presidency, and Feng assumed office on August 14, 1917. He went to Peking to assume his duties the following month. His rivalry with Tuan soon intensified. Tuan resigned as premier in November 1917, but with the support of Chang Tso-lin, Feng was forced to reappoint Tuan the following March. Feng agreed to step down as president following the completion of his term and, on October 10, 1918, relinquished the presidency to his elected successor Hsu Shih-ch'ang. Feng died of pneumonia in Peking on December 28, 1919.

HSU SHIH-CH'ANG (President; October 10, 1918–June 11, 1922). Hsu Shih-ch'ang was born in Honan Province on October 23, 1855. He entered the imperial bureaucracy in 1882 and became a close friend of Yuan Shih-k'ai. In 1896 Yuan named Hsu chief of staff in a newly formed military organization. Hsu accompanied Yuan on his subsequent assignments and became lieutenant general when Yuan reorganized the army in 1903. He became vice-chairman of the board of war in 1904 and acting chairman the following year. He subsequently served as president of the board of police and became a member of the grand council. After a special mission to Manchuria in 1907, Hsu was responsible for reorganization of the political and military structures there. He subsequently became governor general of Manchuria. He was recalled to Peking in 1909, where he continued to serve the imperial government. He withdrew from his positions to live in retirement in Tsingtao following the collapse of the Manchu dynasty in 1911. Yuan, who became president of China after the emperor's abdication, persuaded Hsu to return to Peking in May 1914 to serve as first minister. Hsu again retired when Yuan announced his intentions to establish himself as monarch. He returned to Peking in March 1916 when Yuan renounced his ambition. Hsu again stepped down the following month when he was unable to achieve a solution to the rebellions in southern China. Yuan died in June 1916, and Hsu served as executor of his estate. The following November, Hsu returned to Peking to try to arrange a truce in the rivalry between President Feng Kuo-chang and Premier Tuan Ch'i-jui. Both men agreed to step down and Hsu was chosen to replace Feng as president on October 10, 1918. He chose Ch'ien Neng-hsun to head the government as his premier. The continued influence of Tuan and his supporters made it impossible for Hsu to achieve a peace settlement between northern and southern China. Hsu was also forced to abandon his plan for China to sign the Treaty of Versailles in 1919. Hsu attempted to maintain some authority by playing his powerful rivals against each other. He was forced to step down on June 2, 1922, following the Chihli faction's defeat of Chang Tso-lin. He retired to Tientsin, and did not participate in politics again. He refused an offer from the Japanese to participate in the puppet regime in Manchukuo when Japan seized Manchuria in 1931. He continued to live in retirement until his death on June 6, 1939.

SUN YAT-SEN (President [Canton Government]; May 5, 1921–March 12, 1925). *See earlier entry under Heads of State.*

LI YUAN-HUNG (President; June 11, 1922–June 13, 1923). *See earlier entry under Heads of State.*

TS'AO K'UN (President; October 10, 1923–November 2, 1924). Ts'ao K'un was born in Tientsin on December 12, 1862. He worked as a peddler before joining the Anhwei army in 1882. He was trained at the Tientsin Military Academy and became an instructor there in

1890. He served in Korea and Manchuria during the Sino-Japanese War in 1894–95. He was assigned to Yuan Shih-k'ai's newly formed army after the war. He rose through the ranks and became commander of the 3rd Division in 1906. He supported Yuan's assumption of the presidency in 1912 and led troops against the antimonarchist revolt in 1916. He became military governor of Chihli in September 1916. He opposed General Chang Hsün's attempt to restore the Manchu dynasty in July 1917. Ts'ao's relationship with Anhwei faction leader Tuan Ch'i-jui deteriorated over the next several years. Ts'ao joined with Chang Tso-lin to oust Tuan's government in Peking and they defeated the Anhwei faction in July 1920. Ts'ao subsequently became inspector general of Chihli, Shantung, and Honan. Conflicts soon developed between Ts'ao's Chihli faction and Chang's Fengtien army. Ts'ao's troops, under the command of Wu P'ei-fu, defeated Chang's forces in April 1922. Ts'ao was elected president of China by the National Assembly and took office on October 10, 1923. Conflicts again arose between Ts'ao's supporters and Chang Tso-lin in September 1924. Wu P'ei-fu's subordinate, Feng Yu-hsiang, betrayed Ts'ao and Wu and ousted Wu from command. Ts'ao was forced to resign the presidency on November 2, 1924. Ts'ao was held under house arrest in Peking for the next two years. He subsequently went to Tientsin, where he lived in political retirement. He refused an offer by the Japanese to participate in the Manchukuo puppet government in 1937. Ts'ao died in Tientsin on May 17, 1938.

TUAN CH'I-JUI (President; November 24, 1924–April 20, 1926). Tuan Ch'i-jui was born in Hofei on March 6, 1865. He received military training from an early age and entered the Peiyang Military Academy in 1884. He was sent to Germany for further training in 1889 and served as an instructor at the Weihaiwei army base from 1891 until 1894.

He subsequently became a leading military aide to Yuan Shih-k'ai's newly formed army in 1895. He remained with Yuan for the next fifteen years, becoming commander of the Second Army in October 1911. Tuan became acting governor-general of Hupeh and Hunan the following month and was given command of the First Army. Tuan was named minister of war in March 1912 after Yuan assumed the presidency of China. Tuan refused to support Yuan's plans to become China's monarch and resigned from the government in May 1915. Yuan abandoned his plans and brought Tuan back into the government as premier and minister of war on April 22, 1916. Yuan died the following June, and Tuan assumed many of his powers when Li Yuan-hung took over the presidency. Tuan supported China's entry into World War I on the side of the Allies in 1917. The National Assembly agreed, but his opponents there forced his resignation on May 23, 1917. He subsequently withdrew to Tientsin. The following month he joined his forces with those of Ts'ao K'un's to oppose Chang Hsun's attempt to restore the Manchu dynasty. Chang was defeated, and Tuan returned to Peking as premier on July 14, 1917. Li Yuan-hung subsequently resigned the presidency. Tuan's government was opposed by nationalists under Sun Yat-sen in Canton, and a rival government was established in southern China. Tuan and the Anhwei faction favored a military solution to the rebellion while President Feng Kuo-chang's Chihli faction supported a peaceful reunification. Tuan was unsuccessful in his efforts to retake Hunan and Szechwan in the fall of 1917, and he resigned from the government. Tuan received support from other military leaders, and Feng was forced to name Tuan as commander of China's European expeditionary forces. Under continued pressure, Feng renamed Tuan premier on March 23, 1918. Tuan and Feng both agreed to resign from office on October 10, 1918,

though Tuan continued to exercise great influence in the government. Tuan's secret agreement to transfer German rights in Shantung to Japan after the war led to increased criticism of his regime. Ts'ao K'un allied himself with Chang Tso-lin to challenge Tuan's forces, and Tuan was forced from power in July 1920. He subsequently retired to Tientsin. He was recalled to Peking by Feng Yu-hsiang and Chang Tso-lin after Ts'ao K'un was ousted from the presidency, and Tuan became provisional president of China on November 24, 1924. He resigned from office on April 20, 1925, when Chang Tso-lin won a power struggle against Feng Yu-hsiang. Tuan again retired to Tientsin to study Buddhism. He opposed the Japanese seizure of Manchuria in 1931 and moved to Shanghai in January 1933. He died there three years later of gastric ulcers on November 2, 1936.

CHANG TSO-LIN (President; June 18, 1927–October 10, 1928). Chang Tso-lin was born to a peasant family in Haich'eng, Fengtien, in 1873. He entered the military while in his teens and saw action in the Sino-Japanese War in 1894–95. He returned to Fengtien after the war to organize a local militia. Chang's forces were allied with the Japanese in the Russo-Japanese War in 1904–05. He was granted increased military authority by Chao Erh-sun, the governor-general of Manchuria. He continued to rise in influence under the presidency of Yuan Shih-k'ai. To advance his position, he threatened to lead a Manchurian independence drive in 1915 and was named military governor of Fengtien to ensure his support of the Peking government. Chang supported Premier Tuan Ch'i-jui in his power struggle against President Feng Kuo-chang in 1918 and was rewarded with the post of inspector general of the Three Eastern Provinces in September 1918. He remained allied with Tuan until 1920, when he joined with the Chihli faction led by Ts'ao K'un to force Tuan from power. He subsequently broke with Ts'ao, and his forces were defeated in a battle with the Chihli faction in May 1922. He still maintained much of his power in Manchuria. He again challenged the Peking government in October 1924 and achieved victory with the assistance of defecting Chihli general Feng Yu-hsiang. He subsequently broke with Feng, who allied himself with other military leaders to challenge Chang's power. Chang received assistance from the Japanese to retain power. Military conflicts continued over the next several years with various factions fighting against Chang and each other. Chang claimed the title of president of the central government in Peking on June 18, 1927. The Nationalist army, now under Chiang Kai-shek, continued its advance on Peking. The Japanese pressured Chang to withdraw from Peking so as not to jeopardize Japanese interests in Manchuria. Chang abandoned Peking to go to Mukden in early June 1928. A bomb exploded under the private railway car he was traveling in while passing over a bridge on the morning of October 4, 1928. He died of his injuries on October 10, 1928.

CHIANG KAI-SHEK (President; October 10, 1928–December 27, 1931). Chiang Kai-shek was born in Chikow on October 31, 1886. He left home while in his teens to enter the newly formed Chinese National Military Academy in Paoting. He was sent for further training in Tokyo in 1907, where he attended the Imperial Military Staff College. Chiang also joined the Teng-men-hui, a revolutionary secret society, in 1907. Chiang deserted the Japanese army and returned to China following the overthrow of the Manchu dynasty in 1911. He served as a military leader in Sun Yat-sen's Republican government. He broke with Sun's successor, Yuan Shih-k'ai, leading an unsuccessful rebellion against him in 1913. Chiang then fled the country to Japan. He remained out of public life until 1918,

when he rejoined Sun Yat-sen in Canton. China was divided into areas controlled by warlords, who feuded among themselves. Sun wished to reunify China and formed the Nationalist Kuomintang for this purpose. Chiang became a major general in the southern armies in 1921. He went to the Soviet Union for several months in 1923 to study the Red Army and returned to China to establish a military academy near Canton. Chinese Communists joined with the Kuomintang, and the Soviet Union supplied military advisors and financial assistance. Chiang became leader of the Kuomintang and commander-in-chief of the revolutionary army following Sun Yatsen's death in 1925. Chiang married Soong Mei-ling, the daughter of the powerful Soong financial family, in 1927. He withstood attempts by the Communists to force him from power, but was forced into temporary retirement by the Kwangsi generals, Li Tsung-jen and Pai Tsung-hsi, in August 1927. He returned to power in January 1928 and launched an attack against the warlords, whom he defeated or neutralized. He captured Peking in 1928 and established a Nationalist government in Nanking with himself as president on October 10, 1928. Chiang retained the support of the Soviets until 1929, when he led a bloody assault against the Communists. The Communists withdrew to the north and established a rival government and army. Japan seized Manchuria in 1931, but Chiang continued his efforts to subdue the Communists before challenging Japan. Chiang also revived the Confucius cult in 1934 by launching the New Life Movement to give moral authority to his government. Chiang was captured by Chang Hseuh-liang, the former warlord of Manchuria, in Sian, in December 1936. He was held hostage for several weeks until his release was negotiated by Communist leader Chou En-lai. Chiang set aside the civil war with the Communists and entered to war with Japan in 1937. China fought alone until the bombing of

Pearl Harbor by the Japanese in December 1941, when it then gained the assistance of the Allied Powers during World War II. Chiang resumed the presidency on September 13, 1943, following the death of Lin Sen. He attended the Cairo Conference in 1943 where he met with United States President Franklin Roosevelt and British Prime Minister Winston Churchill. The Nationalists and the Communists fought their mutual enemy, the Japanese, until the surrender of Japan in 1945. The United States attempted to negotiate a compromise between the two rival parties, but Chiang was unwilling to form a coalition government with the Communists. The civil war resumed in 1946, and the Communists moved toward Chiang's stronghold in the south. Chiang's popularity had decreased in China due to rising inflation and an absence of promised reforms. His government was also rampant with corruption. The Communists captured Peking, and Chiang resigned as president on January 21, 1949. Chiang and the Nationalists fled from mainland China to the island of Formosa (now Taiwan). He reestablished the government on Formosa resumed the presidency on March 1, 1950. Chiang continued to receive financial and military assistance from the United States. He instituted land reforms and industrialized the island nation. He transformed the island into a prosperous exporting country. He excluded Taiwanese from the government and rejected native self-rule. Chiang's government continued to be recognized by the West as the legitimate government of China until 1971, when the People's Republic of China was admitted to the United Nations, claiming the seat held by China. The republican government suffered another blow in 1972 when American President Richard Nixon visited the People's Republic of China. Chiang suffered from pneumonia in July 1972. His health continued to fail until his death at the age of 87 from a heart attack in Taipei on April 5, 1975.

LIN SEN (President; December 27, 1931–August 11, 1943). Lin Sen was born in Minhsien, Fukien, in 1868. He graduated from the Anglo-Chinese college in Fochow in 1883 and began working for the Taipei Telegraph Office the following year. He remained there until 1895, when Taiwan was ceded to Japan. He subsequently became involved in the Chinese Nationalist movement to overthrow the Manchu dynasty. He was instrumental in gaining the support of Kiukiang for the Nationalists during the revolt in October 1911. He was elected to the senate in Peking after the establishment of the Nationalist government in 1912 and became its chairman. He left Peking to travel abroad after President Yuan Shih-k'ai broke with the Nationalist Kuomintang. Lin spent the next several years raising funds in the United States for the support of Sun Yat-sen's Nationalists. He returned to China after the death of Yuan in 1916. Parliament was reconvened until 1917, when Premier Tuan Ch'i-jui dissolved the assembly over the issue of China's entry into World War I. Lin went to Canton where the parliament reconvened itself and established a military government under Sun Yat-sen. Lin continued to serve as speaker of the senate and became governor of Fukien in November 1922. He became minister of construction in July 1923 after Sun had regained control of the Canton government. Lin became a member of the central executive committee of the Kuomintang in January 1924. He served on the state council of the Nationalist government after the death of Sun in March 1925. He spent the next several years directing nationalist activities in northern China. He became a member of the new state council with the Nationalist government reorganized in Nanking in October 1928. He was appointed president of the legislative Yuan by Chiang Kai-shek in February 1931. He supported impeachment proceedings against Chiang in April 1931 and an opposition government was formed.

The Japanese invasion of Manchuria restored unity to the Kuomintang and averted a civil war. Lin became chairman of the national government on December 27, 1931. The position was largely ceremonial with Chiang retaining most of the power of government and the military. Lin moved the capital to Chungking when the Japanese advanced on Nanking in November 1937. He opposed the Japanese puppet government of Manchukuo in Manchuria and denounced Wang Ching-wei's regime as traitorous in 1939. Lin suffered a serious stroke in May 1943. He remained China's head of state until his death in Chungking on August 1, 1943.

CHIANG KAI-SHEK (President; September 13, 1943–January 21, 1949). *See earlier entry under Heads of State.*

HEADS OF GOVERNMENT

JUNG-LU (Chief Grand Councilor; September 1898–April 11, 1903). Jung-lu was born on April 6, 1836, the son of a leading Chinese military officer who was killed in battle in 1852. Jung-lu entered the imperial bureaucracy after the death of his father. He became involved in the organization of a new army in 1861 and held high civil and military positions until he was forced to retire in 1879. He was recalled to active duty in 1887 and served the imperial court in various positions. He was president of the board of war after the Sino-Japanese War in 1895 and he was named governor-general of Chihli in June 1898. He was instrumental in putting down a rebellion against the dowager empress in September 1898. He was subsequently rewarded for his loyalty with the position of grand councilor and grand secretary and commanded the military forces of North China. He remained loyal to the dowager empress, though he feared the repercussions of the Boxer Rebellion in 1900. He fled Peking in August 1900 when Allied forces entered the city. He went to Sian where he continued to serve as head of the grand council. He returned to Peking in early 1902, but was largely inactive due to failing health. He died the following year on April 11, 1903.

I-K'UANG, PRINCE CH'ING (Chief Grand Councilor; April 1903– October 29, 1911). I-K'uang was born to a noble family in 1830. He became heir to his family's estates in 1850. He was named chief minister in the office of foreign affairs in 1884 and was also granted the title of Prince Ch'ing the same year. He fled to Hsuan-hua in 1900 when foreign troops invaded Peking during the Boxer Rebellion. He was ordered to return to Peking in August 1900 to negotiate a settlement with the invaders. I-K'uang was appointed chief grand councilor following the death of Jung-lu in April 1903. He was given the rank of premier in May 1911 but was forced to resign on October 29, 1911, as the Nationalist rebellion gained strength. He was named president of the privy council until the emperor abdicated the following month. I-K'uang retired to Tientsin where he died in 1916.

YUAN SHIH-K'AI (Premier; December 1911–February 14, 1912). *See earlier entry under Heads of State.*

T'ANG SHAO-YI (Premier; February 14, 1912–June 16, 1912). T'ang Shao-yi was born in Hsiangshan, Kwangtung, in 1860. In 1874 he was sent to the United States, where he attended Columbia University and New York University before being recalled to China in 1881. He worked as an assistant customs inspector in Korea, where he became associated with Yuan Shih-k'ai. T'ang served on Yuan's personal staff as deputy Chinese resident in Korea. He returned to China in 1896 and accompanied Yuan to Shantung when he was named governor there in 1899. He was appointed customs official in Tientsin in 1901 and was sent on a diplomatic mission to Tibet in 1904. He successfully negotiated an agreement with Great Britain that recognized China's interests in Tibet in 1906 but was forced to resign from his positions in Peking in 1907. He subsequently served as governor of Fengtien until mid-1909. He returned to prominence in Peking when Yuan Shih-k'ai became head of the government in December 1911. Yuan named T'ang premier on February 14, 1912, when he became president. Conflicts soon developed between Yuan and T'ang, and T'ang stepped down as premier on June 16, 1912. He retired from public life to enter business in Shanghai. He was an opponent of Yuan's plans to become emperor. T'ang returned to the government after Yuan's death in June 1916. He soon became allied with Sun Yat-sen's Kuomintang and opposed China's entry into World War I. He became minister of finance in Sun's Canton government in mid-1917 and remained part of the Canton government after Sun left in early 1919. He retired the following October to return to Hsiangshan, where he lived quietly. He again briefly headed the government from August 5, 1922, until September 19, 1922. He served on several commissions in the national government in the 1930s. He fled to the French concession in Shanghai after the start of the Sino-Japanese War in 1937. T'ang was assassinated by several axe-wielding men at his home in Shanghai on September 30, 1938. The identities and motives of his assailants were never discovered.

LU CHENG-HSIANG (Premier; June 29, 1912–September 21, 1912). Lu Cheng-hsiang was born in Shanghai in 1871. He was educated in French studies in Shanghai and Peking. He became an interpreter for Hsu Ching-ch'eng, China's minister to Russia, in 1892. He served as a chargé d'affaires at St. Petersburg several times over the next decade. He left Russia to become minister to the Netherlands in 1906 but returned to Russia as China's minister in 1911. Lu was named minister of foreign affairs after the abdication of the emperor in January 1912. He succeeded T'ang Shao-yi as premier on June 29, 1912, although he was opposed by Nationalists in the Parliament, who attempted to promote his impeachment. Lu resigned as foreign minister on September 18, 1912, and stepped down as premier three days later. He returned to head the foreign ministry in November 1912 following a crisis between China and Russia over Outer Mongolia. He resigned in September 1913 after the senate refused to ratify the treaty he had negotiated with Russia. He became a member of the state council in Peking in May 1914. He was renamed foreign minister in January 1915 and was forced to accept Japan's demands for concessions from China. Lu also served as secretary of state from June 1915 until March 1916. He stepped down as foreign minister after the death of Yuan Shih-k'ai in May 1916. He resumed the position of foreign minister in Tuan Ch'i-jui's government after China's entry into World War I in early 1917, and retained that office until December 1920. Lu was appointed minister to Switzerland in 1922 and represented China at the League of Nations. Lu, who had become a Christian while in Russia in 1911, entered St. André in Lophem-les-Brugers, Belgium, as a postulant in the Order of St. Benedict after the death of his wife in 1926. He took the name Pierre Celestin and was ordained in June 1935. He remained in Europe during the World War II and was instrumental in establishing diplomatic relations between China and the Vatican in 1943. Lu suffered from failing health in 1948 and died in Bruges, Belgium, on January 15, 1949.

CHAO PING-CHUN (Premier; September 21, 1912–March 1913). Chao Ping-chun was born in 1865. He succeeded Lu Cheng-hsiang as premier on September 21, 1912. He negotiated the Reorganization Loan Agreement before stepping down in April 1913. Chao died in February 1914.

HSIUNG HSI-LING (Premier; May 1913–February 1914). Hsiung Hsi-ling was born in Hunan in 1870. He was educated in Hunan and began working in the imperial bureaucracy in 1894. He remained in the government after the establishment of the republic in 1912 and was appointed minister of finance in T'ang Shao-yi's cabinet in March 1912. He stepped down together with the government three months later. He was named by President Yuan Shih-k'ai to head a government as premier in May 1913. He arrived in Peking the following August and formed a Progressive cabinet. Parliament was dissolved in June 1914, and Hsiung's cabinet stepped down the following month. He subsequently headed the national petroleum bureau. He returned to Hunan in 1915 as pacification commissioner. Hsiung was named to the political consultive board by Yuan's successor, Li Yuan-hung, in 1917. He was a leading supporter of federalism during the 1920s. He also gained a reputation for philanthropic work and served on the National Famine Relief Commission in 1929. He moved to Hong Kong in 1937 and died there shortly after the Japanese occupation in 1942.

SUN PAO-CH'I (Acting Premier; February 1914–May 1914). Sun Pao-ch'i was born in Hangchow on April 26, 1867. He received a classical education in China and entered the imperial bureaucracy in 1886. He was named minister to France in 1902. He returned to Peking to become chief secretary of the Grand Council in 1906. He was appointed minister to Germany the following year and returned to China to become governor of Shantung in 1909. He supported the Nationalist movement that overthrew the Manchu dynasty in February 1912. Sun became foreign minister in Hsiung Hsi-ling's cabinet in May 1913. He became acting premier in mid-February 1914 after Hsiung's resignation, serving until May 1914. He remained foreign minister until January 1915. He was appointed minister of finance in April 1916, but resigned two months later. He returned to office as director of the customs administration in 1917. He held various government positions until January 12, 1924, when Ts'ao K'un appointed him premier. His government established diplomatic relations with the Soviet Union. He resigned over a dispute with his finance minister, Wang K'o-min, on July 2, 1924. He temporarily abandoned politics to lead several industrial concerns and was named director of the Sino-French University in 1926. He supported Chang Tso-lin in December 1927 and again retired from politics after Chang's defeat in 1928. Sun's health began to fail in 1929, and he died on February 3, 1931 of a chronic intestinal disorder in Shanghai.

HSU SHIH-CH'ANG (Premier; May 1914–April 1916). *See earlier entry under Heads of State.*

TUAN CH'I-JUI (Premier, April 22, 1916–May 23, 1917). *See earlier entry under Heads of State.*

CHANG HSÜN (Premier; July 1, 1917–July 12, 1917). Chang Hsün was born to a poor family in Fengshin, Kiangsi Province, on December 14, 1854. He entered the army and saw action during the Sino-French War in Annam in 1884 and 1885 and also fought in the Sino-Japanese War from 1894 until 1895. He was subsequently selected by Yuan Shih-k'ai to be an officer in his newly created army. He fought against the rebels during the Boxer Rebellion in 1900. He was sent to Manchuria in 1906 as commander of forces in Fengtien and was made military commander of Kiangnan in 1911. He assumed command of the imperial armies in Nanking during the Nationalist rebellion in 1912. He held the positions of governor-general of Lian-Kiang and high commissioner of military affairs in southern China during the final months of the Manchu dynasty. He was promoted to general when Yuan Shih-k'ai assumed the presidency of the republican government in 1913. He remained a leading defender of the fallen dynasty. He led troops against the Kuomintang forces in Nanking when they rebelled against Yuan in September 1913. After the death of Yuan in June 1916, Chang began to plot the restoration of the Manchu dynasty. Chang led his troops into Peking and restored the child Emperor P'u-yi to the throne on July 1, 1917. Chang's coup met with much opposition, and the forces of Tuan Ch'i-jui and Feng Kuo-chang overwhelmed Chang's troops. Chang took refuge in the Dutch legation on July 12, 1917. He remained in the legation for over a year before he was pardoned by order of President Hsu Shih-ch'ang in October 1918. He retired to his home in Peking and moved to Tientsin in 1920. He remained in political retirement until his death there in September 1923.

TUAN CH'I-JUI (Premier; July 14, 1917–November 22, 1917). *See earlier entry under Heads of State.*

WANG SHIH-CHEN (Premier; September, 1917–March 23, 1918). Wang Shih-chen was born in Chengting, Chihli, in 1861. He was educated locally and entered the military in 1877. He was admitted to the military academy in 1885 and saw action in Korea during the Sino-Japanese War in 1894. He served under Yuan Shih-k'ai in his newly formed army in 1896. He rose through the ranks and became governor general of Hupeh and Hunan after the revolution in 1911. He served as minister of war before the es-

tablishment of the republic in 1912, when he retired to Chenting. He was recalled to Peking by President Yuan Shih-ka'i in 1914, became minister of war in 1915, and chief of the general staff the following year. He remained in the government after Yuan's death and was again named minister of war in June 1917. He was named to head the government as premier by President Feng Kuo-chang in September 1917 and also served as minister of war until his resignation on March 23, 1918. He was promoted to the rank of marshal in 1922 and headed the military reorganization committee. Wang remained a leading figure in the military until his death in Peking on July 1, 1930.

TUAN CH'I-JUI (Premier; March 23, 1918–October 10, 1918). *See earlier entry under Heads of State.*

CH'IEN NENG-HSUN (Premier; October 10, 1918–June 13, 1919). Ch'ien Neng-hsun was born in 1870. He served in the government as minister of the interior in 1913. He again held that position from 1917 until he succeeded Tuan Ch'i-jui as premier on October 10, 1918. He stepped down on June 13, 1919. Ch'ien died in 1924.

KUNG HSIN-CHAN (Premier; June 13, 1919–September 24, 1919). Kung Hsin-chan was named to head the government as premier on June 13, 1919. He retained office until September 24, 1919.

CHIN YÜN-P'ENG (Premier; September 24, 1919–July 2, 1920). Chin Yün-p'eng was born in Tsining, Shantung, in 1877. He attended the Peiyang Military Academy. He became a staff officer with the Third Imperial Army in 1911. He was promoted to lieutenant general and became a military advisor in the office of President Yuan Shih-k'ai the following year. He was named military governor of Shantung in 1913. Chin went to Peking in 1916 after the death of Yuan.

Chin was a supporter of Premier Tuan Ch'i-jui and became minister of war in the government of Ch'ien Neng-hsun in January 1919. He succeeded Ch'ien as premier on September 24, 1919. He resigned on July 2, 1920, after a conflict with Tuan's military subordinate, Hsu Shu-cheng. Tuan's regime was ousted by a military uprising led by Chang Tso-lin, Li Ch'un, and Ts'ao Kun. Chin returned to the post of premier and minister of war on August 9, 1920. He resigned on December 18, 1921, following a dispute within the cabinet over financial issues. Chin subsequently retired from politics to enter business. He went to Tientsin in 1926 and became a Buddhist monk in 1931. He is presumed to have died during World War II.

SA CHEN-PING (Premier; May 14, 1920–August 9, 1920). Sa Chen-ping was born in Minhou, Fukien, on March 30, 1859. He graduated from the Foochow Naval Academy in 1877 and continued his studies at the Royal Naval College in England. He returned to China in 1879 and entered the imperial navy. He commanded a cruiser during the Sino-Japanese War and was commander of the Kwangtung naval forces from 1903 until 1906. Sa rose to the rank of admiral in 1908 and became commander-in-chief of the imperial fleet in 1910. He opposed the nationalists during the revolution of 1911 and was forced to flee to Shanghai when the Ch'ing dynasty was overthrown. He was named president of the Woosung Maritime Academy by the republican government in 1912. He supported President Yuan Shih-k'ai and held several leading positions in the police and military during that administration. He retired from active duty after the death of Yuan in June 1916. Sa was recalled to duty to serve briefly as minister of the navy in June 1917. He again held that position in Chin Yun-peng's government in 1919. He succeeded Chin as acting premier from May 14, 1920, until August 9, 1920, following the over-

throw of Tuan Ch'i-jui. He subsequently returned to Fukien Province, where he served as governor from 1922 until 1927. He participated in an unsuccessful revolt in Fukien against the Nationalist government of Chiang Kai-shek in 1933. He subsequently retired from political affairs. Sa fled to Southeast Asia when the Sino-Japanese war broke out in July 1937. He returned to Fukien in 1945. He served as a member of the Chinese People's Political Consultative after the Communists took control of mainland China in 1949. Sa died two years later in Foochow on April 10, 1951.

CHIN YÜN-P'ENG (Premier; August 9, 1920–December 18, 1921). *See earlier entry under Heads of Government.*

LIANG SHIH-I (Premier; December 12, 1921–January 25, 1922). Liang Shih-i was born in Sanshui, Kwangtung Province, on May 5, 1869. He received a classical education in China. He served as director of the Feng-kang Academy in Sanshui for several years before going to Peking in 1902. He became closely associated with T'ang Shao-yi and joined his staff. Liang served as director general of railways from 1907 until 1911. He served in Yuan Shih-k'ai's government after the abdication of the monarchy. He served as acting minister of finance from 1913 until 1915. He was a proponent of China's entry into World War I on the side of the Allies. Liang's support of Yuan's attempt to become emperor led to an order for his arrest after Yuan's death in 1916. He fled to Hong Kong until the arrest order was rescinded in 1918. He returned to Peking to become chairman of the Bank of Communications and speaker of the National Assembly. President Hsu Shih-ch'ang named Liang premier on December 12, 1921. He was opposed by Wu P'ei-fu, who forced his resignation on January 25, 1922. This action precipitated the Chihli-Fengtien clash, and Liang fled to Japan under threat of arrest. He then went to Hong

Kong before embarking on a tour of Europe and the United States in 1924. He returned to Peking the following year and served as a financial advisor to Tuan Ch'i-jui. He went to Mukden to advise Chang Tso-lin after Tuan's ouster in April 1926. Liang served in the government when Chang took control of Peking in 1927. After Chang's ouster and assassination, Liang was again threatened with arrest. He retired to Hong Kong until the arrest order was rescinded in 1931. He subsequently advised the national government on financial matters until his death in Shanghai on April 9, 1933.

W. W. YEN (Premier; January 25, 1922–April 8, 1922). W.W. Yen (Yen Hui-ching) was born in Shanghai on April 2, 1877. He was educated in Shanghai and went to the United States in 1895. He attended the University of Virginia, where he graduated in 1900. He returned to China to teach at St. John's College until 1906. He served as editor of the *English and Chinese Standard Dictionary* in 1908. He also entered the diplomatic service. He became vice minister of foreign affairs in the Republican government in March 1912. The following year he was sent to represent China in Germany, Denmark, and Sweden. He remained in Denmark during World War I and returned to China in 1920. He was named foreign minister in August 1920. He served as acting premier from January 25, 1922, until April 8, 1922, and again from June 11, 1922, until August 5, 1922, when he was dropped from the cabinet. He continued to serve in the government and became minister of agriculture and commerce in the cabinet of his father-in-law, Sun Pao-ch'i, in January 1924. He again served as premier from September 13, 1924, until Feng Yu-hsiang's coup forced his resignation on October 31, 1924. Yen represented the government at a customs tariff conference in Peking in October 1925. He was again named premier on May 13, 1926

but was opposed by Chang Tso-lin, who forced his resignation on June 22, 1926. Yen retired to Tientsin, where he engaged in business activities. He was recalled by the government to serve as China's minister to the United States in September 1931. He also represented China at the League of Nations in Geneva, where he was instrumental in improving relations between China and the Soviet Union. He was named China's ambassador to Moscow in December 1932, but Soviet intervention in Sinkiang in 1934 damaged relations between the two countries, and Yen was recalled to China in October 1936. He largely retired from active service, though he served on several commissions during the Sino-Japanese War and World War II. He was sent by the National Government to meet with Communist leader Mao Tse-tung in February 1949. When the People's Republic of China was established the following October Yen became head of the Sino-Soviet Friendship Association in Shanghai. He died the following year in Shanghai on May 23, 1950.

CHOU TZU-CH'I (Premier; April 8, 1922–June 11, 1922). Chou Tzu-Ch'i was born in Canton in 1871. He received a classical education in China and attended Columbia University in the United States. After completing his studies, he worked as a secretary at the Chinese legation in Washington in 1896. He subsequently served in diplomatic positions in New York, Cuba, and San Francisco before being appointed first secretary at the Washington legation in 1904. He returned to China in 1908, where he served in the foreign ministry in Peking. He served on various diplomatic missions before the formation of the Republic in 1911. Chou was appointed vice minister of finance in Yuan Shih-k'ai's government. He was named military governor of Shantung in March 1912. He returned to Peking in August 1913 where he remained a leading member of the government. He left government service following Yuan's death in 1916. Chou's involvement in Yuan's attempt at establishing himself as emperor brought charges against Chou in July 1916. He fled into exile in Japan where he remained until the charges were dropped in February 1918. He returned to the government as director of the currency bureau in 1919. He was named minister of finance in August 1920 and, retained that position until May 1921. Chou was named acting premier on April 8, 1922. He relinquished his position on June 11, 1922. He subsequently retired from politics and traveled to the United States. He became interested in the film industry and returned to China to form the Peacock Motion Picture Corporation to produce and distribute films. He died in Shanghai on October 20, 1923, before he could carry out his plans.

W. W. YEN (Premier; June 11, 1922–August 5, 1922). *See earlier entry under Heads of Government.*

T'ANG SHAO-YI (Premier; August 5, 1922–September 19, 1922). *See earlier entry under Heads of Government.*

WANG CH'UNG-HUI (Premier; September 19, 1922–November 21, 1922). Wang Ch'ung-hui was born in Hong Kong in 1881. He was educated in Hong Kong and Tientsin, where he graduated from Peiyang University Law School in 1900. He received further legal training at Yale University in the United States from 1902 until 1905 and in Europe from 1905 until 1907. He returned to China in 1911 and became involved with Sun Yat-sen's nationalist movement. Wang served as foreign minister in the provisional government and became minister of justice in T'ang Shao-yi's cabinet in 1912. He resigned from the cabinet in July 1912 to teach at Futan University. Wang was named chief justice of the Chinese Supreme Court in 1920. He was named

as minister of justice in Liang Shih-i's government in December 1921, and he was appointed to the International Court of Justice at The Hague as a deputy judge in February 1922. He returned to the cabinet as justice minister in W. W. Yen's government in June 1922. Wang was named to head the government as premier on September 19, 1922. His government resigned on November 21, 1922. He subsequently returned to The Hague and also represented China at the League of Nations. He returned to China in 1925 and held several government positions. He joined Chiang Kai-shek's government in Nanking in March 1927, in which he was justice minister until mid–1928. He subsequently served in the state council and was instrumental in drafting the provisional constitution in 1931. Wang returned to the International Court of Justice as a full judge in 1931. He completed his term on the court and returned to China in 1936. He became minister of foreign affairs in March 1937 and signed the Sino-Soviet Non-Agression Pact the following August. Wang remained foreign minister until April 1941. He continued to serve in the government during World War II and accompanied the Chinese delegation to the United Nations Conference in San Francisco in 1945. He subsequently served on the state council and as president of the Judicial Yuan from June 1948. He accompanied Chiang Kai-shek's government to Formosa when the Communists gained control of mainland China in 1949. He continued to serve as president of the Judicial Yuan until his death in Taipei on March 15, 1958.

WANG TA-HSIEH (Premier; November 29, 1922–December 10, 1922). Wang Ta-hsieh served as an advisor to the government on foreign affairs during World War I. He became foreign minister in 1917. Wang briefly served as premier from November 29, 1922, until December 10, 1922.

WANG CHENG-T'ING (Premier; December 12, 1922–January 1923). Wang Cheng-t'ing (C. T. Wang) was born in Fenghua, Chekiang, on July 25, 1882. He was educated in China and Japan before going to the United States in 1907. He graduated from Yale University in 1910 and returned to China the following year. The imperial government was ousted in 1911, and Wang was called on by the provisional government to serve as an interpreter in the foreign ministry. He was named vice-minister of industry and commerce in the Republican government in March 1912 and became acting minister the following May. He stepped down from the cabinet in July 1912 and went to Shanghai. He returned to Peking the following year but again left the capital for Shanghai when the Kuomintang was outlawed in 1913. He returned to Peking to serve as vice-speaker of the senate after the death of President Yuan Shih-k'ai in June 1916. Wang went to Canton to join Sun Yat-sen's provisional government in June 1917. He represented the Canton government at the Paris Peace Conference at the end of World War I. He returned to China in February 1920 to work with a brokerage firm. He served on several diplomatic missions in the early 1920s and became minister of foreign affairs in November 1922. He served as acting premier from December 12, 1922, until mid–January 1923. He subsequently conducted a diplomatic mission to the Soviet Union. He returned to Peking in October 1924 to serve as foreign minister and finance minister in the provisional government. He stepped down the following month. He again served as foreign minister from December 1925 to March 1926. He returned to Shanghai where he became a leading business executive. He joined Chiang Kai-shek's national government in Nanking as foreign minister in June 1928. He retained that position until September 1931, when a student revolt forced his resignation. He was politically inactive for the next several years. Wang

was appointed ambassador to the United States in August 1936 and served until September 1938. He lived in Chungking during most of World War II. He served on the war crimes investigation commission after Japan's surrender in 1945. He remained in mainland China after the Communist takeover in 1949. He went to Hong Kong in 1952, where he worked with an insurance company. He died in Hong Kong on May 21, 1961.

CHANG SHAO-TSÊNG (Premier; January 1923–June 6, 1923). Chang Shao-tsêng was a leading Chinese military figure. He commanded a division of the Chinese Army in 1911 and supported the revolutionary movement that ousted the Manchu dynasty. He was named military governor of Shansi Province in 1912. Chang became military inspector general in 1916. He served as acting minister of war before becoming premier in January 1923. He stepped down on June 6, 1923, and fled to Tientsin when President Li Yuan-hung was forced from office. Chang was murdered in Tientsin on March 21, 1928.

KAO LING-WEI (Premier; June 13, 1923–January 12, 1924). Kao Ling-wei headed the government as premier from June 13, 1923, until January 12, 1924.

SUN PAO-CH'I (Premier; January 12, 1924–July 2, 1924). *See earlier entry under Heads of Government.*

V. K. WELLINGTON KOO (Premier; July 2, 1924–September 13, 1924). V. K. Wellington Koo (Ku Wei-chün) was born in Chiating, Kingsu, in 1887. He was educated at St. John's University and continued his studies in the United States. He received a degree in political science from Columbia University in 1912. He subsequently returned to China where he became a secretary in the presidential office. He was named councilor in the foreign ministry later in the year. He was sent to Mexico as China's minister in July 1915. Several months later he was named minister to the United States. He returned to China at the end of 1918 and accompanied the Chinese delegation to the Paris Peace Conference in January 1919. He refused to sign the Treaty of Versailles because of provisions that granted Japan rights to Shantung. He headed the Chinese delegation to the first League of Nations Assembly in November 1920 and also served as China's minister to Great Britain. He returned to China in 1922 and became minister of foreign affairs the following August. He resigned from the government when Wang Ch'unghui's cabinet fell later in the year. He again served as foreign minister in Sun Pao-ch'i's government from January 1924 until he replaced Sun as acting premier on July 2, 1924. He resigned on September 13, 1924, following Feng Yuhsiang's coup. He subsequently went to Tientsin, where he remained until May 1926. He returned to Peking to serve as minister of finance in W. W. Yen's government. He again became acting premier on October 1, 1926, and served until November 29, 1926. He remained in the government as foreign minister until his resignation in June 1927. Since he had been a prominent member of Chang Tso-lin's government, an arrest order for Koo was issued by the Nationalists after Chang's death in June 1928. Koo went to France and Canada before returning to China in 1929. He went to Mukden, where he served as an advisor to Chang Hsueh-liang. The arrest order was lifted by Chiang Kai-shek, and Koo returned to the national government following the Japanese occupation of Manchuria in September 1931. He served on several diplomatic missions over the next several years. He was named minister to France in 1932 and became ambassador in 1936. He also continued to represent China at the League of Nations. He was sent to London as ambassador in 1940 and remained there during most of World War II. He represented China at

the United Nations Conference in San Francisco and was a signatory of the United Nations Charter in June 1945. He became ambassador to the United States in May 1946. He remained in the United States after the Communist conquest of mainland China in 1949. He was elected to serve as a judge on the International Court of Justice in January 1957 and remained on the court until 1967, serving as the court's vice president during the last three years of his term. He returned to the United States to live in New York, and died at his home there on November 14, 1985.

W. W. YEN (Premier; September 13, 1924–October 31, 1924). *See earlier entry under Heads of Government.*

HUANG FU (Premier; November 2, 1924–November 1925). Huang Fu was born Huang Shao-lin in Paikuanchen, Chekiang Province, on March 8, 1880. He entered the Chekiang Military School under the name Huang Fu in 1904 and underwent further military study in Japan in 1908. He became chief of staff to Shanghai's military governor Ch'en Ch'i-mei in 1911, where he became a close associate of Chiang Kai-shek. He went into opposition against the government of President Yuan Shih-k'ai in 1912 and was forced to flee to Japan. He subsequently broke with Sun Yat-sen's revolutionary group. Huang moved to the United States in 1915. He returned to China to participate in a revolt against Yuan in 1916 and became military commander of Chekiang. He went to Tientsin in the fall of 1917 where he wrote several books. He traveled to the United States and Europe in 1921. He returned to Tientsin in 1922 and became acting foreign minister the following December. He resigned from the government in March 1923 but returned to serve as minister of education from September 1923 until January 1924, and again from September 1924. He collaborated with Feng Yu-hsiang in the coup that removed

Ts'ao Kun from power in October 1924, and Huang became acting premier on November 2, 1924. His cabinet was dissolved on November 24, 1925. He served on the customs tariff conference in October 1925. Huang became an advisor to Chiang Kai-shek in Nanking in January 1927 and mayor of Shanghai in July 1927. He was minister of foreign affairs in Chiang's government in February 1928 but resigned in May, after the Japanese attack on Shantung. He retired to Mokanshan and refused government appointments until September 1931, when he helped organize the New China Reconstruction Society. Huang was named minister of the interior in 1935. He resigned at the end of the year under criticism that he gave too many concessions to the Japanese. He returned to Mokanshan, but poor health forced his removal to a Shanghai hospital in August 1936. He died there of cancer of the liver on December 6, 1936.

HSU SHIH-YING (Premier; December 26, 1925–February 15, 1926). Hsu Shih-ying was born in Chinpu, Anhwei, in 1872. He received a classical education and entered the Imperial bureaucracy in Peking in May 1898. He worked with the board of punishments until 1905, when he helped organize the board of police affairs. Hsu was named to the high court in Mukden by Hsu Shih-ch'ang in April 1907. He traveled to the United States to study prisons and the judicial system in 1910. He became judicial commissioner in Shansi in November of the following year. He supported the establishment of the republic in 1912 and subsequently became chief justice of the supreme court. He was named minister of justice in Lu Cheng-hsiang's cabinet in July 1912. He stepped down in September 1913 and became governor of Fengtien two months later. He became governor of Fukien in May 1914. Hsu returned to the cabinet as minister of the interior in Tuan Ch'i-jui's cabinet in June 1916. He was named minister of communications the follow-

ing month. He left the government after a bribery scandal in 1917, but was acquitted of charges. He worked in the banking industry until September 1921 when he became governor of Anhwei. He resigned soon after and again briefly served as minister of justice in November 1922. He held several other positions in the government and became a leading aide to Tuan Ch'i-jui in 1924. Tuan named Hsu to head the government as premier on December 26, 1925. He resigned on February 15, 1926, as Tuan's government was threatened by the forces of Chang Tso-lin. Hsu went to Shanghai where he became involved with the autonomy movement. He served on several relief commissions in the late 1920s and early 1930s. He was appointed ambassador to Japan by the national government in 1936 and was unsuccessful in negotiating a solution to the Sino-Japanese War in 1937. He returned to China in January 1938. He continued to serve on relief agencies during World War II. He served as an advisor to the government in the late 1940s and went to Taiwan in 1950 after the Communist takeover of the mainland. He lived quietly in retirement and died in Taipei on October 13, 1964.

CHIA TEH-YAO (Premier; February 15, 1926–April 20, 1926). Chia Teh-yao served as minister of war under Hsu Shih-ying from December 1925 until he succeeded Hsu as acting premier on February 15, 1926. Chia stepped down from office on April 20, 1926.

HU WEI-TE (Premier; April 20, 1926–May 13, 1926). Hu Wei-te served the imperial government as minister to Russia in 1902. He was a supporter of the abdication of the Emperor in 1911. Hu briefly headed the government as acting premier from April 20, 1926, until May 13, 1926.

W. W. YEN (Premier; May 13, 1926–June 22, 1926). *See earlier entry under Heads of Government.*

TU HSI-KUEI (Premier; June 22, 1926–October 1, 1926). Tu Hsi-kuei was born in 1875. He served in the Chinese navy and eventually was promoted to the rank of admiral. He was named to the cabinet as minister of the navy in early 1926. He became premier on June 22, 1926, after Tuan Ch'i-jui's fall from power. He stepped down on October 1, 1926. Tu went on a world inspection tour with the navy in 1929 and 1930.

V. K. WELLINGTON KOO (Premier; October 1, 1926–November 29, 1926). *See earlier entry under Heads of Government.*

CHIANG KAI-SHEK (Premier; April 18, 1927–June 18, 1927). *See earlier entry under Heads of State.*

P'AN FU (Premier; June 18, 1927–October, 1928). P'an Fu was born in 1871. He was a leading supporter of Chang Tso-lin and was named to head the government as premier on June 18, 1927. He stepped down after Chang's fall from power in October 1928.

T'AN YEN-K'AI (Premier; October 10, 1928–September 22, 1930). T'an Yen-k'ai was born in Hangchow in 1879. He received a classical education in Hunan and became a teacher. T'an became president of the Hunan assembly in October 1909 and soon became governor of Hunan. T'an rebelled against the government of Yuan Shih-k'ai in October 1913, and when the revolt failed, he was removed from his position. He returned to Hunan as military and civil governor after Yuan's death in June 1916. He was ousted by Premier Tuan Ch'i-jui in December 1917. He returned to power in Hunan through military force in March 1922. T'an became minister of the interior in Sun Yat-sen's rebel nationalist government in Canton in February 1923. He subsequently served as minister of reconstruction from May until July 1923. T'an became a member of the government council in July 1925 after the death of Sun. T'an became president of the Executive Yuan, or premier, on October 10, 1928. He also served as acting president of the Nanking government while Chiang Kai-shek pursued military duties during the civil war. T'an retained his position until September 22, 1930, when he died in Nanking after suffering a stroke.

T. V. SOONG (Premier; September 22, 1930–November 1930). T. V. Soong was born Sung Tzu-wen in Shanghai in 1894. He was educated locally and in the United States. He received a degree in economics from Harvard University in 1915 and worked in the banking industry in the United States before returning to China in 1917. He served the nationalist government in Canton after his return and was named minister of finance in Kwangtung in 1926. Soong's three sisters had married China's most respected leaders: Sun Yat-sen, the father of the Chinese Republic; Chiang Kai-shek, the leader of the Nationalists; and H. H. Kung, a leading Chinese financier. Soong became minister of finance in Chiang's nationalist government in Nanking in 1928. He gained the support of leading Shanghai bankers for the Kuomintang. He served as acting president of the Executive Yuan at Nanking from September until November 1930 and from October 1932 until March 1933 while Wang Ching-wei was in Europe. Soong resigned his positions in the government in October 1933 over a disagreement with Chiang Kai-shek about military expenditures. He became chairman of the Bank of China in 1935. He was sent to the United States as China's special envoy to gain Western financial support for China during the Sino-Japanese war. Soong was appointed foreign minister in 1942, and he represented China at the United Nations organizing session in San Francisco in 1945. Soong also became acting president of the Legislative Yuan, or premier, on December 4, 1944. He resigned on March 1, 1947, after civil war had resumed between the nationalists and the Communists. He subsequently served as governor of Kwangtung Province. He resigned in March 1949 and fled to Hong Kong. He refused to join the nationalist government in Taiwan later in the year and went into exile in the United States. He settled in New York, where he remained until his death. Soong choked to death on April 25, 1971, when food lodged in his windpipe at a dinner party in San Francisco.

WANG CHING-WEI (Premier; July 13, 1930–October 10, 1930). Wang Ching-wei was born in Canton on May 4, 1883. He was educated in Canton and at the Tokyo Law College, where he received a degree in law in 1906. He became active in Sun Yat-sen's Nationalist movement. Wang was the leader of a conspiracy to assassinate the prince regent, Ts'ai-feng, in early 1910. The plot was foiled, and Wang was imprisoned until the nationalist revolt in October 1911. Wang subsequently went to Europe and remained in France during most of World War I. He returned to China in 1917 and rejoined Sun Yat-sen's movement in opposition to the Peking government. Wang was selected as chairman of the national government in Canton in July 1925, two months after the death of Sun. He emerged as one of the leading figures in the Kuomintang. His rivalry with nationalist military leader Chiang Kai-shek culminated with Chiang's crackdown on Communist elements in the Kuomintang. Wang, who was identified with the leftists, resigned in May 1926 and went to France. He returned to China in early 1927 and entered into a short-lived alliance with the Chinese Communist Party in Shanghai. He soon broke with the leftists and returned to France in December 1927. He subsequently headed the Kai-tsu-p'ai in opposition to Chiang's growing power. He and several other nationalist leaders attempted to form a rival government in Peking in July 1930, but their efforts collapsed the following October. Wang reconciled with Chiang in Nanking in late 1931 and was named president of the Executive Yuan, or premier, on January 28, 1932. Wang traveled to Europe from October 1932 until March 1933, leaving T. V. Soong to serve as acting president of the Executive Yuan in his absence. Wang maintained an uneasy alliance with Chiang for the next several years. He was badly injured in an assassination attempt at a Kuomintang central executive committee meeting in Nanking on November 1, 1935, and was forced to resign from office on December 1, 1935, when his injuries prevented him from carrying out his duties. He recuperated in Europe for a year before returning to China in December 1936. China became engaged in a war with Japan soon after his return. Wang was pessimistic about China's ability to withstand the Japanese assault and advocated a cessation of hostilities and a negotiated peace settlement. Wang was installed as leader of a puppet government in Japanese-controlled areas of China on March 30, 1940. Japan recognized Wang's government as the legitimate government of China, though hostilities continued between Japan and the nationalist forces of Chiang and the Communist army of Mao Tse-tung. Wang continued to head the government in Nanking during much of World War II. His government followed Japan's lead and declared war on Great Britain and the United States in January 1943. Wang's health began to fail in 1944, and he went to Japan for treatment. He died in Nagoya on November 10, 1944.

CHIANG KAI-SHEK (Premier; December 22, 1930–December 15, 1931). *See earlier entry under Heads of State.*

SUN FO (Premier; December 28, 1931–January 28, 1932). Sun Fo was born in Choy Hen, Kwangtung Province, in October 1891. He was the only son of

Sun Yat-sen, the leader of the Chinese Revolution. Sun Fo was attending school in Hawaii at the time of the overthrow of the Manchu regime. He briefly returned to China when his father became president of the Chinese Republic in January 1912. He then went to the United States to continue his education. He returned to China in August 1917 and assisted his father in the establishment of a provisional revolutionary government in Canton. Sun Fo became mayor of Canton in 1921, serving until the following year when the republican government was forced to abandon the city. Sun Fo returned to Canton as mayor in 1923, after his father allowed the Communists to join the Kuomintang government. Sun Yat-sen died in March 1925, and Sun Fo was named to the Kuomintang's central executive committee. He was appointed minister of communication in Chiang Kai-shek's Nationalist government in 1926. Sun Fo opposed Chiang's attack on the Communists later in the year and Chiang resigned as head of the government in August 1927. Sun Fo again joined the government as minister of finance. He resigned when Chiang returned to power in January 1928. He returned to the cabinet shortly thereafter to serve as minister of reconstruction. He served as minister of railways from 1928 until May 1931. He again broke with Chiang and joined with rebel forces in Canton. He attempted to negotiate a settlement between the rebels and Chiang's government in Nanking. Chiang again stepped down briefly, and Sun Fo became president of the Legislative Yuan on December 28, 1931. He continued to serve as premier until January 28, 1932. He was instrumental in arranging a truce between the nationalists and the Communists in 1937 so that both factions could fight the common enemy of Japan. Sun Fo remained in the nationalist government during the civil war that resumed after World War II. He was appointed premier on November 26, 1948, but re-

signed on March 12, 1949, as the Communists continued their advance through China. Sun Fo went into exile in France when the Nationalist government fled mainland China in 1949. He lived in the United States until October 1964, when he joined the nationalist government in Taiwan. He subsequently served as a senior advisor in the office of the president. Sun Fo died of a heart attack in Taipei at the age of eighty-one on September 13, 1973.

WANG CHING-WEI (Premier; January 28, 1932–December 1, 1935). *See earlier entry under Heads of Government.*

CHIANG KAI-SHEK (Premier; December 12, 1935–January 2, 1938). *See earlier entry under Heads of State.*

H. H. KUNG (Premier; January 2, 1938–November 20, 1939). H. H. Kung (K'ung Hsiang-hsi) was born in T'aiku on September 11, 1880, to a prominent family who claimed direct descendancy from Confucius. He was educated at an American Protestant school in T'aiku, where he converted to Christianity. Kung used his family's wealth and prestige to protect foreign missionaries in his area during the Boxer Rebellion in 1900. He was allowed to go to the United States in 1901 and continued his education at Oberlin College in Ohio. He received a degree in economics at Yale University in 1907. He returned to China the following year and joined Sun Yat-sen's revolutionary movement. He went to Tokyo in 1913 as secretary of the Chinese YMCA. He met Soong Ai-ling, eldest daughter of the prominent Soong family, and married her in 1914. His wife's younger sisters, Ching-ling and Mei-ling, married Sun Yat-sen and Chiang Kai-shek, respectively. He returned to China after the death of President Yuan Shih-k'ai in 1916. Two years later he embarked on a tour of England, France, and the United States. He returned to Shansi in 1919, where he conducted his family's business and continued to support Sun's nationalist movement. Sun died in March 1925, and Kung joined Chiang Kai-shek's national government in Canton in 1927. He became minister of industry and commerce the following year. He resigned from the government when Chiang temporarily stepped down in 1931. He headed a commission to tour European industries in 1932 and became governor of the Bank of China when he returned in April 1933. He succeeded his brother-in-law, T. V. Soong, as minister of finance in October 1933. He introduced numerous financial reforms, such as abandoning the silver standard in favor of paper currency. He succeeded Chiang Kai-shek as president of the Executive Yuan on January 2, 1938, during the Sino-Japanese War. Chiang resumed office on November 20, 1939, but Kung continued to serve as vice president and often acted in his stead until the autumn of 1944. He became acting president of the Executive Yuan in November 1944. He also continued to serve as finance minister until his retirement from politics in June 1945. He and his family went to the United States during the civil war in 1948 and remained there after the Communist takeover of the mainland the following year. Kung made several brief visits to Taiwan in the 1960s, but he continued to reside in the United States at his home in Locust Valley, Long Island, New York. He died of a heart ailment in a New York hospital on August 15, 1967.

CHIANG KAI-SHEK (Premier; November 20, 1939–December 4, 1944). *See earlier entry under Heads of State.*

T. V. SOONG (Premier; December 4, 1944–March 1, 1947). *See earlier entry under Heads of Government.*

Colombia

Colombia is a country on the northern coast of South America. It was granted independence from Spain on July 20, 1810.

HEADS OF STATE

MANUEL A. SANCLEMENTE (President; August 7, 1898–July 31, 1900). Manuel Antonio Sanclemente was born in 1814. He was a prominent Colombian lawyer and politician. He served in the government of Mariano Ospina Rodriguez as minister of war from 1857 to 1861. He remained a leading political figure and served as minister of government in Miguel Antonio Caro's administration in the 1890s. He succeeded Caro to the presidency on August 7, 1898. He initially deferred many of his duties to his vice president, José Manuel Marroquín, due to poor health. The nationalist Conservatives disapproved of Marroquín's conciliatory policies and attempted to use Sanclemente to counter his government. Sanclemente was officially deposed on July 31, 1900. He died two years later in 1902.

JOSÉ MANUEL MARROQUÍN (President; July 31, 1900–August 7, 1904). José Manuel Marroquín was born on August 6, 1827. He was a respected writer and poet, best known for his 1897 novel, *El Moro*. He became vice president under Manuel Sanclemente from August 7, 1898, and often served as acting president due to Sanclemente's poor health. Sanclemente resumed the presidency on November 3, 1898, when Marroquín's conciliatory policies during the War of a Thousand Days over Panama met with resistance from the nationalist Conservatives. Sanclemente was officially deposed on July 31, 1900, and Marroquín again became president. His administration witnessed the loss of Panama in a secession in 1903 that was sponsored by the United States. Marroquín stepped down on August 7, 1904. He died on September 19, 1908.

RAFAEL REYES PRIETO (President; August 7, 1904–July 8, 1909). Rafael Reyes Prieto was born to a prosperous family in Santa Rosa, Boyacá, on December 5, 1849. He engaged in several successful commercial ventures as a young man and explored the Putumayo region along the Amazon. He joined with the Conservative Party and was a prominent figure in the 1885 civil war. He was instrumental in the creation of Colombia's new constitution the following year. Reyes led the government forces in Santander against a liberal rebellion in 1895. Reyes subsequently broke with the ruling nationalist Conservatives in the 1890s. Another liberal revolt, the War of a Thousand Days, broke out in 1899. Reyes spent the next several years out of the country. He returned to Colombia and was chosen by the Conservatives as their presidential nominee in 1904. He was successful in a close election and took office on August 7, 1904. He formed a bipartisan cabinet and was successful in improving the country's economic conditions. He also sponsored reforms in public administration and reorganized the armed forces. Reyes' government became increasingly authoritarian, and he dissolved the Congress in 1905. Liberals and Conservatives joined together in a Republican Union to oppose Reyes. His negotiations with the United States resulted in an unpopular treaty over Panama's independence, and major demonstrations broke out in Bogotá in the summer of 1909. Reyes resigned from office on July 8, 1909, and left the country. He spent much of the next decade abroad. He eventually returned to Colombia and died in Bogotá on February 18, 1921.

JORGE HOLGUÍN (President; July 8, 1909–August 3, 1909). Jorge Holguín was born in Cali on October 30, 1848. He was from a politically prominent family. His uncle, Manuel María Mallarino, served as president of Colombia from 1855 until 1857, and his older brother, Carlos Holguín, was president from 1888 until 1892. Jorge Holguín joined the Conservatives and was active in the revolution of 1876. He served as minister of the treasury in Rafael Nunez's government in 1885. He was a member of the senate during the 1890s and served in the cabinets of Miguel Antonio Caro and Manuel Sanclemente. He was a leading supporter of Rafael Reyes and headed the commission that negotiated the Holguín-Avebury Convention in 1905 with Great Britain. The agreement with foreign investors revived Colombia's credit abroad. Holguín was designated Reyes's successor on July 8, 1909, when Reyes stepped down and left the country. He served as acting president until Ramon Gonzalez Valencia took office on August 3, 1909. He remained a prominent figure in Colombian politics and again became acting president following the resignation of Marco Fidel Suárez on November 11, 1921. He headed the government until August 7, 1922. Holguín died on March 2, 1928.

RAMON GONZALEZ VALENCIA (President; August 4, 1909–July 15, 1910). Ramon Gonzalez Valencia was born in 1854. He served in the Colombian military and was governor of Santander. He was vice president under Rafael Reyes from 1904 until his removal in 1905. He was chosen to replace Reyes as president on August 4, 1909. He retained office until the election of Carlos Restrepo on July 15, 1910. Gonzalez Valencia subsequently served as Colombia's ambassador to Venezuela. He died on October 3, 1928.

CARLOS RESTREPO (President; July 15, 1910–August 7, 1914). Carlos Eugenio Restrepo was born in Medellín on September 12, 1867. He was educated in the law and entered government service. He was active in the War of a Thousand Days from 1898 until 1901, when he became rector of the University of Antioquia. He subsequently taught constitutional law at the university. Restrepo was elected to congress as a Conservative in 1909. He was an opponent of the authoritarian government of Rafael Reyes. He was elected by congress to the presidency with the support of the Republican Union faction of the Conservatives and took office on July 15, 1910. He expanded Colombia's education and transportation systems while in office. He also oversaw negotiations for the Thomson-Urrutia Treaty with the United States, which granted Colombia $250,000,000 in a settlement of the Panama Canal issue. He completed his term on August 7, 1914. Restrepo was a supporter of Enrique Olaya Herrera for the presidency in 1930 and served as minister of the interior in his cabinet. He was named Colombia's ambassador to the Vatican in 1931, where he remained until 1934. Restrepo subsequently retired to Medellín, where he died on July 6, 1947.

JOSÉ VICENTE CONCHA (President; August 7, 1914–August 7, 1918). José Vicente Concha was born in Bogotá on April 21, 1867. He was a member of the historical faction of the Conservative Party and served as a secretary to President Miguel Antonio Caro in 1892. He subsequently served as governor of Cundinamarca and became an opponent of Caro. He was instrumental in the ouster of the Nationalist administration of Manuel Sanclemente in 1900. He served as minister of war in the subsequent cabinet of José Manuel Marroquín. He was a leading critic of the authoritarian regime of Rafael Reyes from 1904 until 1909. Concha was elected president in succession to Carlos Restrepo, taking office on August 7, 1914. During his administration Colombia was faced with an economic crisis, and he attempted to reorganize the country's finances. He maintained Colombia's neutrality during World War I, despite pressure from the United States to declare war on Germany. He completed his term on August 7, 1918. He remained a leading political figure and served in the Colombian senate. He was also a respected authority on constitutional law. He was appointed Colombia's ambassador to the Vatican by President Miguel Abadía Méndez in 1926. He died in Rome on December 9, 1929.

MARCO FIDEL SUÁREZ (President; August 7, 1918–November 11, 1921). Marco Fidel Suárez was born in Hatoviejo on April 23, 1855. He was educated at the seminary in Medellín, but left in 1877 before his ordination. He subsequently went to Antioquia and Bogotá, where he worked as a teacher. He entered politics in the early 1880s as a member of the nationalist wing of the Conservative Party. He was a supporter of President Manuel Sanclemente and opposed his ouster in July 1900. He spent the next decade in political retirement, reemerging in 1910. He successfully ran in the presidential election in 1917, defeating two other candidates in a campaign marked by allegations of fraud. He took office on August 7, 1918. His administration was beset by bitter opposition from the rival parties and controversy over the treaty to restore good relations between Colombia and the United States. Suárez was accused of financial misconduct in office in October 1921. He denied the charges but resigned under pressure on November 11, 1921. He then retired from political life to author his memoirs and died on April 3, 1927.

JORGE HOLGUÍN (President; November 11, 1921–August 7, 1922). *See earlier entry under Heads of State.*

PEDRO NEL OSPINA (President; August 7, 1922–August 7, 1926). Pedro Nel Ospina was born on September 18, 1858, at the presidential palace in Bogotá. He was the son of Mariano Ospina Rodríguez, Colombia's president from 1857 until 1861. He was raised in Guatemala and was educated at the University of California, where he received a degree in mining engineering. He returned to Colombia, where he entered the family coffee and mining businesses in Antioquia. He entered politics as a member of the historical wing of the Conservative Party and was elected to congress in 1892. He fought with distinction during the War of a Thousand Days and became minister of war in José Manuel Marroquín's government in 1901. He was involved in an unsuccessful plot against the government to restore ousted President Manuel Sanclemente and then went into exile. He traveled to Mexico, the United States, and Europe, learning about the textile industry. He returned to Colombia to establish a textile factory in 1906. Ospina resumed his political activities, defeated Benjamín Herrera for the presidency, and took office on August 7, 1922. The following year he embarked on an effort to reform Colombia's economic system. He adopted many of the reforms proposed by Edwin W. Kemmerer. The government established a central bank and created the office of national comptroller. His policies led to a growth in industry and railroads and stimulated public works projects. He completed his term of office on August 7, 1926. Ospina died on July 1, 1927.

MIGUEL ABADÍA MÉNDEZ (President; August 7, 1926–August 7, 1930). Miguel Abadía Méndez was born in La Vega de los Padres on June 5, 1867. He was educated at the College of the Holy Ghost, where he received a degree in law in 1889. He taught constitutional law and political economics at the National University. He entered politics as a member of the historical wing of the Conservative Party and served as a publicist for the party. He also edited several newspapers in Bogotá. He served in several Conservative cabinets near the turn of the century, heading the ministries of finance, education, and foreign affairs. He was an opponent of the dictatorship of Rafael Reyes and was imprisoned by the Reyes regime. He was freed in 1909 upon his election to congress. Abadía served as minister of the government in three Conservative administrations between 1918 and 1926. He was unopposed for the presidency in the 1926 elections and took office on August 7. His government borrowed heavily from abroad to initiate public works programs and stimulate industry. A subsequent economic crisis led to strikes by workers in the petroleum industry. Civil unrest increased following the harsh repression of the strike of the banana workers in December 1928. Abadía was forced to reorganize his cabinet, and the Conservative Party splintered as a result. Abadía was succeeded by the Liberal Party victor, Enrique Olaya Herrera, on August 7, 1930. Abadía's political career never recovered, and he suffered from severe mental illness near the end of his life. He died of pneumonia at his farm, Tegualda, near Bogotá, on May 15, 1947.

ENRIQUE OLAYA HERRERA (President; August 7, 1930–August 7, 1934). Enrique Olaya Herrera was born in Guateque, Boyaca, in 1881. He fought with the liberals in their unsuccessful rising, the War of a Thousand Days, from 1899 until 1903. He was an opponent of the government of General Rafael Reyes and was a founder of the Republican Union coalition that forced Reyes' ouster in 1909. He served several terms in the Colombian legislature and was the editor and publisher of several liberal newspapers. He served in Colombia's foreign service in several South American countries before being named minister to the United States by President Pedro Nel Ospina in 1922. He retained that position until 1929, when he returned to Colombia to contest the presidency. He headed a ticket of liberals and dissident conservatives known as the National Concentration. He was victorious in the election and took office on August 7, 1930. The worldwide economic depression continued to adversely affect Colombia. He attempted to govern in a conciliatory fashion, balancing the interests of the Liberals and Conservatives. He initiated moderate social reforms and land distribution. He also called upon the League of Nations to settle a border dispute with Peru. He completed his term of office and stepped down on August 7, 1934. He briefly served in the subsequent government of Alfonso López Pumarejo as foreign minister from February 1935 until he was sent as special ambassador to the Vatican in August of that year. He died two years later in a Rome hospital on February 18, 1937.

ALFONSO LÓPEZ PUMAREJO

(President; August 7, 1934–August 7, 1938). Alfonso López Pumarejo was born in San Bartolome de las Palmas (now Hondas) on January 31, 1886. He came from a wealthy family and was educated at private schools and then in England and the United States. He returned to Colombia in 1904, where he managed his father's businesses. López became active in the "republicanism" movement and founded the *El Liberal* newspaper in 1910. In 1915 he was elected to the assembly on the Liberal Party ticket. He also remained active in business affairs and became the Colombian head of the American Mercantile Bank in 1919. When Dr. Enrique Olaya Herrera, the Liberal Party candidate, was elected president of Colombia with López's support in 1930, López was named minister to London. In 1933 he

was appointed to the cabinet as foreign minister. In this position he was instrumental in settling a border dispute and preventing a war with Peru. The following year López announced his candidacy for president and was elected in February 1934 by an overwhelming majority. He took office on August 7, 1934, and embarked on a campaign to improve the living conditions of the working class by raising the taxes on businesses and the wealthy. He sponsored a new constitution in 1936 that included provisions for worker's compensation, trade union recognition, and legalized strikes. His policies brought about a backlash from the right wing, which gained control of Congress and began to stall his legislation. López offered his resignation on May 25, 1937, but the threat of a general strike resulted in the decision of Congress not to accept the resignation and to cooperate more closely with his government. López was constitutionally barred from seeking reelection in 1938, and Eduardo Santos, a rightist member of the Liberal Party, was nominated and elected. López relinquished the presidency to Santos on August 7, 1938. López made plans to seek the presidency again, but a division between the factions of the Liberal Party forced López and his supporters to form a separate party. López was again elected president in May 1942 and took office on August 7, 1942. As president, López joined Colombia with the Allied cause during World War II. López's popularity was seriously diminished due to major inflation brought on by the wartime economy and several scandals in his administration. He offered his resignation on several occasions, and it was finally accepted in July 1945. López left office on August 7, 1945, and subsequently represented Colombia at the United Nations. In 1947 he was elected president of the United Nations Security Council. He remained a leading member of the Liberal Party and was the victim of right-wing extremism when his house was set on fire in 1952. López went into exile in Mexico during the presidency of Gustavo Rojas Pinilla. López returned to Colombia in 1958 following the ouster of Rojas Pinilla and was appointed ambassador to Great Britain in June 1959. He died of a kidney ailment in London on November 20, 1959.

EDUARDO SANTOS MONTEJO (President; August 7, 1938–August 7, 1942). Eduardo Santos Montejo was born to a wealthy family in 1888. He was educated at the College of the Holy Ghost and in Paris. He returned to Colombia in 1913 and became involved with the Liberal Party. He founded the Bogotá daily newspaper *El Tiempo* and became one of South America's most respected journalists. During the administration of Enrique Olaya Herrera, Santos served in the government as foreign minister and head of the Colombian delegation to the League of Nations. He was also the governor of Sanander Province. Santos was elected to the presidency in succession to Alfonso López Pumarejo and took office on August 7, 1938. He led a moderate administration that halted some of the reforms initiated by his predecessor. He allied Colombia with the United States against the Axis powers after the bombing of Pearl Harbor by Japan in December 1941. He completed his term of office on August 7, 1942. Santos remained a leading force in the Liberal Party. He was named to serve as a deputy general of the United Nations Relief and Rehabilitation Administration in 1944 and retained that position until 1948. He was an opponent of the dictatorship of General Gustavo Rojas Pinilla, and his newspaper was shut down for twenty-two months by the government from 1955 until Rojas Pinilla's ouster in 1957. Santos continued to be involved in political affairs. He was a supporter of the Liberal-Conservative alliance that followed Rojas Pinilla's ouster. He was also a strong supporter of the government of Carlos Lleras Restrepo in the early 1960s. Santos died in Bogotá on March 27, 1974.

ALFONSO LÓPEZ PUMAREJO (President; August 7, 1942–August 7, 1945). *See earlier entry under Heads of State.*

ALBERTO LLERAS CAMARGO (President; August 7, 1945–August 7, 1946). Alberto Lleras Camargo was born in Bogotá on July 3, 1906. He attended the National University of Bogotá but left without receiving a degree. He then went to work as a journalist at various liberal newspapers. Lleras entered politics in the late 1920s and was named secretary general of the Liberal Party by Alfonso López in 1929. The following year Lleras was elected to the chamber of deputies, where he served as speaker in 1931 and 1933. He remained a close associate of López and was appointed general secretary to the president when López won the presidency in 1934. Lleras joined the cabinet as minister of the interior the following year and remained in that position until 1938, when he also served as minister of education. When López left office in 1938, Lleras returned to journalism. He was reelected to the chamber of deputies in 1941, where he again served as speaker. In 1943 he was elected to the senate. When López was reelected president in 1942, Lleras was appointed ambassador to the United States. He returned to Colombia in October 1943 to rejoin the cabinet as minister of the interior, and the following year he was appointed foreign minister. In this capacity he signed the United Nations Charter on behalf of Colombia in 1945. When López resigned the presidency in July 1945, Lleras was selected president-designate by the Colombian congress. He took office on August 7, 1945, and formed a coalition cabinet with the Conservative Party. Lleras was constitutionally barred from succeeding himself and relinquished the presidency to Mariano Ospina Pérez on August 7, 1946. After leaving office, he returned to journalism briefly before being elected director-general of the Pan American Union in Washington, D.C., the following year. Lleras returned to Colombia in 1948 and was selected as the first secretary-general of the Organization of American States. He remained in that position until August 1954, when he accepted the post of president of the University of Los Andes. In 1956 he served briefly as editor of the *El Independiente* newspaper before being sent to Hungary to investigate the revolt there on behalf of the United Nations. Lleras was also elected director of the Liberal Party in 1956, and he reached an agreement with the Conservative Party that forced the ouster of President Gustavo Rojas Pinilla in May 1957. The two major parties formed the National Front, which called for a division of power between the Liberals and Conservatives.

Lleras was chosen as the candidate for the Front in the elections scheduled for 1958. Lleras and other government officials were kidnapped on May 2, 1958, by a group of military officers that opposed the election, but Lleras was freed later the same day by troops loyal to the government. Two days later he was again elected president of Colombia, and he took office on August 7, 1958. Lleras began his term of office by restoring civil liberties that had been denied during the rule of Rojas Pinilla. He also established an agrarian reform program and began a number of public works projects. In 1961 he was instrumental in the creation of the Latin American Free Trade Association to help reduce tariffs in the region. Lleras left office on August 7, 1962, and became editor of the news magazine *Vision*. He died in Bogotá after a long illness on January 4, 1990.

Costa Rica

Costa Rica is a country in Central America occupying the narrow isthmus between Nicaragua and Panama. It was granted independence from Spain on September 15, 1821.

HEADS OF STATE

RAFAEL IGLESIAS Y CASTRO (President; May 8, 1894–May 8, 1902). Rafael Iglesias y Castro was born on April 18, 1861. He received a degree in law from the University of Santo Tomas. He became active in politics in 1889 when he supported the presidential candidacy of his future father-in-law, José Joaquín Rodríguez. He subsequently served as minister of war in Rodríguez's government. Iglesias was named minister of finance and commerce in 1893 and was elected to the presidency to succeed Rodríguez the following year. He took office on May 8, 1894. He won a second

term of office with little opposition in 1898. Iglesias placed Costa Rica on the gold standard during his administration. He also sponsored numerous civic improvements, constructed schools and hospitals, improved railways and roads, and constructed the National Theater. He stepped down on May 8, 1902, when Ascensión Esquivel assumed office. Iglesias was an unsuccessful candidate for president in 1910 and 1914. He died on April 11, 1924.

ASCENSIÓN ESQUIVEL (President; May 8, 1902–May 8, 1906). Ascensión Esquivel was born in 1848. He entered politics and was a leading member of the liberal Costa Rican group known as the *Olimpo* or the "Generation of '89." Esquivel was an unsuccessful candidate for president in 1889. He was again a candidate in 1902 and was supported by a liberal coalition. He was victorious and took office on May 8, 1902. Esquivel completed his term of office on May 8, 1906, relinquishing the presidency to Cleto González Víquez. Esquivel died in 1927.

CLETO GONZÁLEZ VÍQUEZ (President; May 8, 1906–May 8, 1910). Cleto González Víquez was born to a leading family in Barba de Heredia on October 13, 1858. He was educated at the University of Santo Tomas, where he received a degree in law. He had a distinguished career as a lawyer before entering politics. He served in the congress, where he became a leading liberal. González Víquez was elected president in a controversial election in 1906, taking office on May 8, 1906. He held office until May 8, 1910, when he was succeeded by his colleague, Ricardo Jiménez Oreamuno. González Víquez returned to congress and was a leading opponent of the government of Alfredo González Flores. He supported the coup that ousted González Flores in 1917. González Víquez remained a leading figure in the National Republic Party and was again elected president in 1928, taking office on May 8, 1928. During his second term he instituted Costa Rica's first income tax. He also enacted many reform laws and supported improvements in public education. His government was threatened by a revolt in February 1932 when Manuel Castro Quesada, a defeated candidate to succeed González Víquez to the presidency, led an uprising. The army remained loyal to the government and the revolt was put down after several days of fighting. González Víquez completed his term of office and stepped down on May 8, 1932. He died in San

José on September 23, 1937, after a long illness.

RICARDO JIMÉNEZ OREAMUNO (President; May 8, 1910–May 8, 1914). Ricardo Jiménez Oreamuno was born in Cartago on February 6, 1859. He received a degree in law from the University of Santo Tomas in 1884. He soon became active in politics, serving as minister to Nicaragua and Salvador. He gained a reputation as a leading liberal and was named secretary of state for the interior, police, and public works in 1886. He was appointed minister of foreign relations, finance, and the interior in 1889. He became president of the supreme court in 1890. Jiménez resigned two years later in opposition to the dictatorship of José Joaquín Rodríguez. Jimenez was elected to congress in 1906, where he was a critic of the United Fruit Company. He was elected president and succeeded Cleto González Víquez on May 8, 1910. He completed his term on May 8, 1914. He returned to politics in 1921 to again serve in the congress. He again served as president from May 8, 1924, until May 8, 1928. Jiménez was elected to the presidency in 1932. A rebellion tried to prevent his assuming the office, but the revolt was quelled. He served his third term from May 8, 1932, until May 8, 1936. He remained a leading political figure and considered a race for a fourth term in 1939 before withdrawing from the contest. Jiménez died in San José on January 4, 1945.

ALFREDO GONZÁLEZ FLORES (President; May 8, 1914–January 27, 1917). Alfredo González Flores was born in Heredia on June 15, 1877. He was educated as a lawyer. He became president of Costa Rica on May 8, 1914, when the congress chose him after elections failed to produce a victor. His government was beset by economic difficulties when coffee sales to Europe fell during World War I. His austerity measures to alleviate the problem caused widespread discontent.

González Flores was ousted in a military coup led by his minister of defense, General Federico Tinoco Granados, on January 27, 1917. González Flores went into exile in the United States, where he persuaded President Woodrow Wilson to deny recognition to General Tinoco's regime. González Flores subsequently returned to Costa Rica and to his native city of Heredia, where he remained a leading figure until his death on December 28, 1962.

FEDERICO TINOCO GRANADOS (President; January 27, 1917–August 13, 1919). Federico Tinoco Granados as born in 1870. He served in the Costa Rican army and was minister of war and the navy under President Alfredo González Flores. Tinoco and his brother, José Joaquín, led a military coup against González Flores and established a military regime on January 27, 1917. Tinoco's actions initially had the support of powerful interests in the country who had opposed González Flores's financial policies, but his government was refused recognition by President Woodrow Wilson of the United States. Tinoco presided over a repressive regime that established press censorship and brutally crushed opposition to his government. As criticism of his regime increased, José Joaquín Tinoco, Federico's brother and war minister, was assassinated in August 1919. Soon after, Tinoco appeared before congress to announce his resignation on August 13, 1919. He went into exile in Europe and died in Paris in 1931.

JUAN BAUTISTA QUIRÓS (President; August 13, 1919–September 2, 1919). Juan Bautista Quirós was born in 1853. He served in the revolutionary government of Federico Tinoco Granados and was Tinoco's hand-picked successor when he resigned on August 13, 1919. The United States refused to recognize Bautista Quirós' government, and

he was forced to step down on September 2, 1919. He died in 1934.

FRANCISCO AGUILAR BARQUERO (President; September 2, 1919–May 8, 1920). Francisco Aguilar Barquero was born in 1857. He served in the government of Alfredo González Flores from 1917. He was González Flores' constitutional successor and, with pressure from the United States, he became president following the resignation of Juan Bautista Quirós. Aguilar conducted new elections and stepped down on May 8, 1920, to allow the victor, Julio Acosta García, to assume office. Aguilar died in 1924.

JULIO ACOSTA GARCÍA (President; May 8, 1920–May 8, 1924). Julio Acosta García was born on May 23, 1872. He was the nephew of Braulio Carillo, who served as Costa Rica's president from 1834 until 1842. Acosta García became active in politics and was a delegate to the congress from 1902 until 1906. He served as governor of Alajuela in 1907 and was consul to El Salvador from 1912 until 1915. He was the Liberal Party's candidate for president in 1920. His election restored constitutional rule to the country, and he took office on May 8, 1920. He completed his term on May 8, 1924. Acosta García remained a leading political figure in the country. He served as foreign minister during the 1940s and headed the Costa Rican delegation to the United Nations organizational meeting in San Francisco in 1945. Acosta García died in San José on July 6, 1954.

RICARDO JIMÉNEZ OREAMUNO (President; May 8, 1924–May 8, 1928). *See earlier entry under Heads of State.*

CLETO GONZÁLEZ VÍQUEZ (President; May 8, 1928–May 8, 1932). *See earlier entry under Heads of State.*

RICARDO JIMÉNEZ OREA-MUNO (President; May 8, 1932–May 8, 1936). *See earlier entry under Heads of State.*

LEÓN CORTÉS CASTRO (President; May 8, 1936–May 8, 1940). León Cortés Castro was born in Alajuela on December 8, 1882. He was educated at the San José School of Law. He entered politics during the military regime of General Federico Tinoco Granados and served as commander of the Alajuela Garrison. Cortés was president of the national assembly from 1925 until 1926 and minister of education from 1929 until 1930. He served as minister of public works in 1930 and again from 1932 until 1936. He was subsequently chosen as the National Republican Party's presidential candidate. He was elected and took office on May 8, 1936. His government opposed the labor movement and suppressed the Communist Party. He instituted the expansion of the highway system and founded the National Bank of Costa Rica. Cortés completed his term of office on May 8, 1940, and was succeeded by Rafael Calderón Guardia. Cortés broke with Calderón soon after the latter's inauguration and led the opposition to Calderón's government. Cortés again ran for the presidency in 1944, but was defeated by Teodoro Picado Michalski in a controversial election. Cortés continued to lead the opposition until his death in San José of a heart attack on March 2, 1946.

RAFAEL ÁNGEL CALDERÓN GUARDIA (President; May 8, 1940–May 8, 1944). Rafael Ángel Calderón Guardia was born in San José on March 10, 1900. He was educated in Belgium where he received a medical degree. He graduated from the Free University of Brussels as a surgeon in 1927. He returned to Costa Rica, where he began a medical practice. He entered politics in 1930 and was elected to the San José municipal council. He was elected to congress in 1934 and became president of the congress in 1938. He was the National Republican Party's candidate for president in 1939 and was elected with little opposition. He took office on May 8, 1940. He introduced social reforms, such as a labor code and a social security system. He incurred the opposition of his predecessor, León Cortés Castro. Calderón was instrumental in securing the election of his successor, Teodoro Picado Michalski, and relinquished his office on May 8, 1944. He again ran for the presidency in 1948, but was defeated by Otilio Ulate. Calderón demanded that the results of the election be nullified and the congress complied. Costa Rica erupted into a civil war. The opposition to Calderón, led by José Figueres, was triumphant, and Calderón went into exile in Nicaragua in April 1948. He led unsuccessful attempts to invade Costa Rica in 1948 and 1955, both of which were supported by Nicaraguan President Anastasio Somoza. Calderón subsequently went to Mexico until 1958, when he returned to Costa Rica. He was elected to congress, but was again defeated for the presidency in 1962. He served as Costa Rica's ambassador to Mexico from 1966 until 1970. Calderón died after a brief illness in San José on June 9, 1970.

TEODORO PICADO MICHALSKI (President; May 8, 1944–April 20, 1948). Teodoro Picado Michalski was born in San José on January 10, 1900. He was educated as a lawyer and worked for the United Fruit Company until 1932, when he entered government service. He served as secretary of public education and in 1938 was elected to the Costa Rican national assembly. Picado subsequently served as president of the assembly. He was the candidate of the ruling National Republican Party in the presidential elections in 1944. He won by a large margin and was sworn into office on May 8, 1944. Picado allowed Communists to serve in his government and established diplomatic relations with the Soviet Union. In July 1947 his government was threatened by a general strike organized by the political opposition. Since Picado was prevented by the constitution from succeeding himself, he supported former president Rafael Calderón Guardia in the elections in February 1948. When Calderón was defeated by Otilio Ulate Blanco, Picado's government nullified the election. Supporters

of Ulate went into rebellion against the government, and in March 1948 José Figueres Ferrer joined forces with the rebels. Picado was forced from office on April 20, 1948, and went into exile in Guatemala. He subsequently went to Nicaragua, where he served as secretary to President Anastasio Somoza. Picado died in Managua, Nicaragua, on June 1, 1960.

Croatia

Croatia was a part of Hungary from 1102 to the 1800s when it became semi-autonomous. After World War I, Croatia was incorporated into the kingdom of the Serbs, Croats, and Slovenes on December 1, 1918. When Germany and Italy conquered Yugoslavia in April 1941, an independent Croatia was established. The state ceased to exist in May 1945 when the area was reclaimed by Yugoslavia.

HEADS OF STATE

ANTE PAVELIC (Polgavnik; April 1941–May 1945). Ante Pavelic was born in Brading, Herzegovina, on July 17, 1889. He was educated at Zagreb University, where he studied law. He became a member of the nationalist Croatian Party of Rights. He was elected to the Zagreb city council in 1920 and served in the Yugoslav Skupstina (parliament) from 1923 to 1929. He left Yugoslavia for Italy in 1929 after King Alexander formed a dictatorship. Pavelic organized the Ustasa, a radical Croatian nationalist movement that was responsible for King Alexander's assassination in October 1934. He was tried and sentenced to death in absentia by the Royalist Yugoslav government. Italy refused to extradite Pavelic, but he was arrested and imprisoned for over a year. During this time he was also sentenced to death in absentia by France for his role in the as-

sassination of King Alexander and French Foreign Minister Louis Barthou. Yugoslavia was defeated by Germany and Italy in April 1941, and Croatia was declared an independent state with Pavelic as *polgavnik*, or leader. His dictatorial regime was marked by brutal repression. After the Allied victory in World War II, Croatia was reabsorbed into Yugoslavia in May 1945. Pavelic evaded the Yugoslavi authorities and lived in hiding in Italy and Austria. He was tried and sentenced to death for a third time by the Yugoslavi Communist government in 1945. Pavelic fled to Argentina in 1948. Juan Perón's government denied requests by Yugoslavia for his extradition. Pavelic was injured in an assassination attempt in Buenos Aires on April 10, 1957. He subsequently went to Spain and died in Madrid on December 28, 1959.

HEADS OF GOVERNMENT

COUNT KÁROLY KHUEN-HÉDERVÁRY (Ban; 1883–July 1903).
See entry under Hungary: Heads of Government.

COUNT TEODOR PEJAČEVIC
(Ban; July 1, 1903–June 26, 1907). Count Teodor Pejačevic was born in Nasice on September 24, 1855. He succeeded Károly Khuen-Héderváry as ban (governor) on July 1, 1903. Pejačevic called for new elections to the Sabor (parliament) in April 1906. The ruling National Party won a very narrow victory. Pejačevic continued to head the government until a dispute with Hungary over the use of Magyar as the official language on Croatian railways forced his resignation on June 26, 1907. He died in Vienna on July 25, 1928.

ALEKSANDAR RAKODCZAY
(Ban; July 1907–January 8, 1908). Aleksandar Rakodczay was born in Bratislava on September 25, 1848. He was president of the Zagreb Supreme Court when he was nominated to replace Count Teodor Pejačevic as ban in July 1907. He was replaced by Baron Pavao Rauch on January 8, 1908.

BARON PAVAO RAUCH (Ban;
January 8, 1908–January 11, 1910). Baron Pavao Rauch was born in Zagreb on February 20, 1865. He was the son of Levin Rauch, a former Croatian ban. The younger Rauch was an ally of Austria and an opponent of Count Károly Khuen-Héderváry. He called for new elections to the Sabor soon after taking office. He remained in power despite an electoral defeat for his newly formed Constitutional Party. His government instigated the persecution of the Serb minority in Croatia. He resigned as ban on January 11, 1910, when Khuen-Héderváry became prime minister of Hungary.

Rauch died in Martijanec on November 29, 1933.

NIKOLA TOMAŠIC (Ban; February 5, 1910–January 19, 1912). Nikola Tomašić was born in Zagreb on January 13, 1864. He was a descendant of the noble Mogorovici family. He was a leader of the Magyarons in Croatia. He was a leading historian and professor of constitutional law at the University of Zagreb. He replaced Baron Pavao Rauch as ban on February 5, 1910. He resigned on January 19, 1912, following new elections to the Sabor. Tomašić died in Treščerovac on May 29, 1918.

SLAVKO CUVAJ (Royal Commissary; January 20, 1912–July 1913). Slavko Cuvaj was born in Bjelovar on February 26, 1851. He served as head of the department of the interior in the government of Nikola Tomašić. He succeeded Tomašić as ban on January 20, 1912. Cuvaj dissolved the Sabor and ruled as Royal Commissary from April 5, 1912, until July 1913. He was badly injured in an assassination attempt by a bomb-throwing young Croat student on June 8, 1912. He subsequently left the country and was replaced as Commissary in July 1913. He died in Vienna on January 31, 1931.

BARON IVAN SKRLEC (Royal Commissary; July 1913–November 29, 1913; Ban; November 29, 1913–June 29, 1917). Baron Ivan Skrlec was a high ranking member of the Hungarian government. He was chosen to replace Slavko Cuvaj as Royal Commissary in July 1913. Constitutional government was reinstated and Skrlec became ban on November 29, 1913. New elections to the Sabor were held the following December. Archduke Francis Ferdinand was assassinated in June 1914, which led

to Austria-Hungary declaring war on Serbia. That conflict led to World War I, with Croatia as a participant. Constitutional rule was suspended during the war. Karl I succeeded to the throne of Austria-Hungary upon the death of his grand-uncle Franz Josef on November 21, 1916. Skrlec was replaced as ban by Anton Mihalovic on June 29, 1917.

ANTON MIHALOVIĆ (Ban; June 29, 1917–October 29, 1918). Anton Mihalovic was born in Feričanci in 1868. He was a former Magyaron and a leader of the coalition supported by Hungary. He was named ban on June 29, 1917. Croatia severed its ties with Austria-Hungary on October 29, 1918, joining the newly formed independent state of the Slovenes, Croats, and Serbs.

Cuba

Cuba is the largest island in the Caribbean Sea. It was under Spanish rule from the time of Christopher Columbus until the Spanish-American War of 1898. The United States occupied the island from 1898 to 1902, when the Republic of Cuba was formed.

HEADS OF STATE

TOMÁS ESTRADA PALMA (President; May 20, 1902–September 28, 1906). Tomás Estrada Palma was born in Bayamo on July 9, 1835. He was educated in Havana and studied law at the University of Seville in Spain. He returned to Cuba and participated in the Ten Years' War against Spain (1868–78), and attained the rank of general. He was proclaimed president of the revolutionary Republic in Arms in 1876, but was captured by the Spanish the following year. He was imprisoned in Spain until 1878. He remained in exile in Paris for the next decade before going to Central America in the late 1880s. He subsequently moved to New York City where he joined with Cuban revolutionary leader José Martí to form the Cuban Revolutionary Party in 1892. Martí was killed in action by the Spanish in Cuba in May 1895, and Estrada Palma succeeded him as leader of the revolutionary government-in-exile. After the defeat of Spain in the Spanish-American War in 1899, Cuba was governed by a United States occupation force under General Leonard Wood. Cuba was granted independence in 1902, and Estrada Palma was elected president without opposition in Cuba's first independent election. He took office on May 20, 1902. He was known for his honesty and integrity, and his government instituted reforms, such as construction of new roads, expansion of educational programs, and improvement of sanitation. He was a candidate for reelection on the Conservative Party ticket in 1905. The Liberal Party boycotted the election and went into revolt. Estrada Palma asked the United States to intervene under the Platt Amendment. When the United States was hesitant to step in, Estrada Palma resigned on September 28, 1906, forcing United States Secretary of War William Howard Taft to send marines to Cuba to restore order. Taft led a provisional occupation government until October 13, 1906, when he installed Charles Edward Magoon to head the occupation government. Estrada Palma retired from politics and returned to his home in Bayamo, where he died on November 4, 1908.

U.S. OCCUPATION (September 28, 1906–January 28, 1909).

JOSÉ MIGUEL GÓMEZ (President; January 28, 1909–May 20, 1913). José Miguel Gómez was born in Santa Clara, Las Villas, on July 6, 1858. He served in the Cuban revolutionary army during the wars of independence and attained the rank of major general. He was named governor of Las Villas during the first occupation by the United States from 1899 until 1902, and he retained that position after the formation of the Cuban Republic. Gómez joined the Liberal Party in 1906 and participated in the insurrection against President Tomás Estrada Palma. He was arrested and imprisoned in Havana but was released after the occupation later in the year. Gómez was the Liberal Party nominee for the presidency following the restoration of constitutional rule in 1908. He was elected president, taking office on January 28, 1909. Gómez's administration was accused of corruption with Gómez becoming known as *El Tiburón*, or the Shark, for his personal involvement in graft and patronage. He was denied the Liberal Party's nomination for reelection in 1913 and supported the Conservative Party's nominee Mario García Menocal. Gómez relinquished his office to Menocal on May 20, 1913, but went into rebellion against Menocal when he ran for reelection in 1917. Gómez and his supporters were captured and imprisoned in Havana for nearly a year. He again plotted a rebellion against the government of Alfredo Zayas y Alfonso in 1920. He subsequently went to the United States in an attempt to arrange another intervention in Cuba. He met with little success and died of pneumonia in New York City hospital on June 13, 1921.

MARIO GARCÍA MENOCAL (President; May 20, 1913–May 20, 1921). Mario García Menocal was born in Matanzar Province on December 17, 1868. He accompanied his family to the United States after the Ten Years War broke out in 1868. Menocal received a degree in engineering from Cornell University in 1888. He subsequently worked as an engineer in Nicaragua before returning to Cuba in 1891. He joined José Martí's rebellion against Spain in 1895 and was promoted to the rank of general during the conflict. Menocal served as Havana's chief of police from 1898 to 1900. He subsequently became a successful businessman and was a cofounder of the Cuban-American Sugar Company. Menocal was an unsuccessful candidate for president against José Miguel Gómez in 1908. He gained the Conservative Party nomination in 1912 and defeated Liberal Alfred Zayas y Alfonso. Menocal took office on May 20, 1913. Cuba's economy suffered during World War I as the European sugar market declined. Menocal joined with the United States in declaring war on Germany in April 1917. He was reelected in 1917 and put down a rebellion by former President Gómez. Menocal profited greatly during his terms as president due to widespread graft and corruption. He relinquished office to Alfredo Zayas on May 20, 1921. Menocal was defeated in a reelection bid in 1924. He made an unsuccessful attempt to oust President Gerardo Machado in 1931. He was arrested and imprisoned for over six months before going into exile in the United States where he remained until 1933. Menocal was again defeated for the presidency in 1936. He was named to the commission that drafted Cuba's new constitution in 1940. He died at his home in Havana on September 7, 1941.

ALFREDO ZAYAS Y ALFONSO (President; May 20, 1921–May 20, 1925). Alfredo Zayas y Alfonso was born in Havana on September 21, 1861. He received a degree in law from the University of Havana. As a result of his involvement in the Cuban independence movement, he was imprisoned in 1896.

Zayas was sent into exile the following year but returned to Cuba in 1898 after the ouster of the Spanish. Zayas subsequently entered politics and served as acting mayor of Havana in 1901. He was elected president of the senate in 1905. He was a leader in the revolt against Tomás Estrada Palma in 1906 and served as an advisor to the American occupation government from 1907 to 1909. He was vice president under President José Miguel Gómez from 1909 until 1913. He was defeated for the presidency in 1913, when Gómez backed Conservative Party nominee Mario García Menocal. Zayas was elected president in 1921 and took office on May 20, 1921. Zayas' administration was advised by U.S. presidential envoy, General Enoch Crowder to accept his choices for the "Honest Cabinet" in 1922. Zayas dismissed Crowder's cabinet in 1923. His government, despite widespread graft and corruption, succeeded in improving Cuba's financial situation through a reduction of the budget and fiscal reforms. Zayas survived a revolt led by Colonel Federico Laredo Brú in 1924. Zayas was denied the Conservative Party's nomination for reelection and relinquished office to Gerardo Machado on May 20, 1925. He retired to private life. Zayas died at his home in Havana on April 11, 1934, after a long illness.

GERARDO MACHADO DE MORALES (President; May 20, 1925–August 12, 1933). Gerardo Machado de Morales was born in Santa Clara, Las Villas, on September 28, 1871. He joined in the revolutionary movement against the Spanish in 1895, rising to the rank of brigadier general. He served as mayor of Santa Clara during José Miguel Gómez's presidency from 1909 to 1913 and then joined Gómez's cabinet as secretary of the interior. Machado was nominated for president by the Liberal Party in 1924 and was easily elected. He took office on May 20, 1925. The early years of his administration were marked by economic

prosperity and the elimination of much of the corruption of his predecessors. He sponsored numerous public works projects and passed regulations to control sugar production. He persuaded congress to amend the constitution to allow him to run for reelection in 1928. He won handily and began his second term in a more autocratic manner. Student protests at the University of Havana broke out in September 1930, and Machado closed the campus. He also banned public meetings of political groups. Further protests erupted and Machado began the wholesale arrest of leftist critics of his regime. Moderate leaders Carlos Mendieta and Mario García Menocal led a failed rebellion against the government in August 1931. A general strike paralyzed the nation in 1933 and, on August 12, 1933, the military, fearing American intervention, ousted Machado from power. Machado was flown to the Bahamas and settled into exile in the United States. He died of cancer in a Miami Beach hospital on March 29, 1939.

CARLOS MANUEL DE CÉSPEDES Y QUESADA (President; August 12, 1933–September 5, 1933). Carlos Manuel de Céspedes y Quesada was born in New York City on August 12, 1871. He was the son of Cuban revolutionary leader Carlos Manuel de Céspedes y Castillo, who was killed in battle against the Spanish during the revolutionary war. The younger Céspedes was educated in the United States, France, and Germany. He returned to Cuba in the mid–1890s to serve as a colonel in the Cuban army. He also served as governor of Santiago Province from 1895 until 1898. Céspedes received a degree in law from the University of Havana in 1901. He was elected vice president of the House of Representatives in 1902 and served until 1908. The following year he entered the Cuban diplomatic corps. He represented Cuba in Italy from 1909 to 1912 and in Argentina from 1912 to 1913.

Céspedes was named minister to the United States in 1913. He remained in the United States until 1922, when he returned to Havana to serve as secretary of state. He resigned from the cabinet in 1926 over a disagreement with President Gerardo Machado. He was ambassador to France from 1930 to 1933. Machado was ousted as president in a military coup on August 12, 1933, and Céspedes was installed as interim president. He called for the return of the Cuban Constitution of 1901 and began plans for a general election the following year. The ruling revolutionary junta forced Céspedes' resignation on September 5, 1933, and Ramón Grau San Martín was installed in his stead. Céspedes subsequently served as ambassador to Spain until August 1935. He was the Centrist Party's nominee for president in 1935, but the party halted political activities, and Céspedes did not run in the election. He died of a heart attack at his home in Vedado on March 28, 1939.

RAMÓN GRAU SAN MARTÍN (President; September 10, 1933–January 15, 1934). Ramón Grau San Martín was born in Pinar del Rio on September 13, 1882. He studied medicine at the University of Havana and received his degree in 1908. He continued his studies throughout Europe before returning to the University of Havana to serve on the faculty. He became involved in politics during a campus demonstration against General Gerardo Machado, the dictator of Cuba. He resigned his position in solidarity with the students. He was arrested by the Machado government in 1929. He was released shortly thereafter, and went to the United States. Grau was offered the presidency by the ruling military junta following the overthrow of Carlos Manuel de Céspedes and took office on September 10, 1933. During his brief term of office he instituted a progressive labor policy, granted voting rights to women, and attacked the Platt Amendment that granted the United

States the right to intervene in Cuban affairs. He also demanded that the workforce of businesses operating in Cuba must be 50 percent Cuban. The United States refused to recognize Grau's government, and he was ousted by his chief of staff, Fulgencio Batista y Zaldívar, on January 15, 1934. Grau was a critic of Batista and the succession of puppet presidents he installed. Grau challenged Batista in the presidential election of 1940 and was defeated, though allegations of election fraud were made. Batista chose not to run for reelection in 1944, and Grau was again the candidate of the opposition. He defeated Batista's designated successor, Carlos Saladrigas Zayas, and took office on October 10, 1944. Grau implemented an economic policy that increased workers' wages and nationalized some businesses. His term of office was also marked by graft and corruption. Grau was ineligible to succeed himself under the Cuban Constitution and he relinquished office to Carlos Prío Socarrás on October 10, 1948. When Prió Socarrás was ousted by Batista four years later, Grau was again a leading critic of the regime. Batista was ousted by Fidel Castro in January 1959, and Grau was virtually ignored by the new revolutionary regime. He lived in seclusion in Havana until his death of cancer on July 28, 1969.

CARLOS HEVIA (President; January 15, 1934–January 18, 1934). Carlos Hevia was born in 1900, the son of Colonel Aurelio Hevia, a former Cuban secretary of the interior. The younger Hevia graduated from the United States Naval Academy at Annapolis in 1919 and returned to Cuba to work as an engineer. He became active in politics and opposed the dictatorship of President Gerardo Machado. He was arrested and sent into exile following a revolt against Machado in 1931. Hevia returned to Cuba after Machado's ouster and served as minister of agriculture under President Ramón Grau San Martin in 1933.

Hevia assumed the presidency when Grau was removed from office on January 15, 1934. Fulgencio Batista, the leader of the revolutionary junta, forced Hevia's resignation three days later. Hevia was a founder of the Authentic Cuban Revolutionary Party in February 1934. He entered President Carlos Prió Socarrás cabinet as minister of state in 1948. He also served as foreign minister from 1949 to 1950, and he was minister of agriculture from 1950 to 1951. The Authenticos nominated Hevia for president in 1952, but Batista seized direct control of the country in March 1952 and canceled the elections. Hevia engaged in several plots against Batista's dictatorship in the 1950s and was briefly imprisoned. When Fidel Castro seized power in 1959 Hevia went into exile in the United States. He was active in the Revolutionary Council that plotted the Bay of Pigs invasion to overthrow Castro in 1961. Hevia died at his home in Lantana, near West Palm Beach, Florida, on April 2, 1964.

MANUEL MÁRQUES STER-LING (President; January 18, 1934). Manuel Márques Sterling was born in Lima, Peru, in 1872, while his parents were in exile from the Spanish rule in Cuba. Márques Sterling returned to Cuba as a young man and was educated at the University of Havana. He participated in the negotiations with the United States that established the Cuban Republic in 1902. He subsequently became a journalist and served as editor of *El Mundo* in Havana. He was also the founder and editor of *Heraldo de Cuba* and *La Nacion*. Márques Sterling was sent to Argentina as chargé d'affaires in 1907. He served as minister to Brazil from 1909 to 1911 and to Peru from 1911 to 1912. He was sent to Mexico in 1912 and retired from the diplomatic corps the following year. He resumed his career in journalism until the early 1930s, when he was again sent to Mexico as Cuba's ambassador. He was appointed foreign

minister by President Ramón Grau San Martín in 1933. Following the ouster of Grau and the short-lived provisional presidency of Carlos Hevia, Márques Sterling was called on to head the government on January 18, 1934. Military strongman Fulgencio Batista refused to accept Márques Sterling's appointment as provisional president and forced his resignation after less than a day in office. Márques Sterling was subsequently appointed ambassador to the United States. He died of complications from an asthmatic condition at the Cuban embassy in Washington later on December 9, 1934.

CARLOS MENDIETA Y MON-TEFUR (President; January 18, 1934–December 11, 1935). Carlos Mendieta y Montefur was born in La Matilde, Santa Clara, on November 4, 1873. He entered the University of Havana to study medicine in 1895. He abandoned his studies the following year to enter the revolutionary movement. He rose to the rank of colonel before retiring from the military during the United States occupation and completing his medical degree in 1901. He was elected to the congress the following year and served as inspector of health in the provisional government. He was the Liberal Party's unsuccessful nominee for vice president in 1916. He became editor of the newspaper *Heraldo de Cuba* in 1919. He was initially a supporter of President Gerardo Machado, but became a critic of his regime in the early 1930s. He and former president Mario García Menocal led an unsuccessful revolt against Machado in 1931. He was captured and imprisoned for several months and then expelled from the country. He lived in New York City until Machado's ouster in 1933. Mendieta was chosen by military strongman Fulgencio Batista to serve as provisional president on January 18, 1934. During his administration a treaty was signed with the United States in May 1934 abrogating the Platt Amendment, which had granted the United States the right to intervene in Cuba. Mendieta's government was largely controlled by Batista and he resigned on December 11, 1935. He retired from political life, and died in Havana on September 29, 1960.

JOSÉ A. BARNET Y VINAGERAS (President; December 11, 1935–May 20, 1936). José Agripino Barnet y Vinageras was born in Spain in 1864. He entered the diplomatic corps soon after the establishment of the Cuban Republic in 1902 and held numerous positions, including minister to Brazil. Barnet was named to Carlos Mendieta's cabinet as secretary of state in 1934. Mendieta resigned from the presidency on December 11, 1935, and Barnet was installed as provisional president. His government was largely controlled by military strongman Fulgencio Batista. Barnet oversaw elections in January 1936 and relinquished office to the elected president, Miguel Mariano Gómez, on May 20, 1936. Barnet died on September 19, 1945, at his home in Vedado, outside of Havana, after a long illness.

MIGUEL MARIANO GÓMEZ Y ARIAS (President; May 20, 1936–December 24, 1936). Miguel Mariano Gómez y Arias was born in Sancti Spiritus, Santa Clara Province, on October 6, 1889. He was the son of José Miguel Gómez, Cuba's president from 1909 to 1913. The younger Gómez entered politics at an early age and served several terms in the House of Representatives in the early 1920s. Gómez was elected mayor of Havana in 1926. He was involved in an unsuccessful revolt against President Gerardo Machado in 1931 and subsequently went into exile in New York City. Gomez returned to Cuba shortly before Machado's ouster in 1933. He again briefly served as mayor of Havana in 1934. Gómez was supported by Fulgencio Batista in the presidential election in January 1936. He assumed office on May 20, 1936. Gómez soon

broke with Batista and vetoed a bill favored by Batista that would have created military schools in rural areas. Batista arranged Gómez's impeachment, and he was forced from office on December 24, 1936. He was subsequently inactive in politics. Gómez died from a brain tumor on October 26, 1950, in Vedado, outside of Havana.

FEDERICO LAREDO BRÚ (President; December 24, 1936–October 10, 1940). Federico Laredo Brú was born in Santa Clara Province on April 23, 1875. He fought in Cuba's war for independence against Spain in 1895, rising to the rank of colonel. He held several judicial positions after the establishment of the Cuban Republic in 1902. Laredo Brú was named to President José Miguel Gómez's cabinet as secretary of the interior in 1911. He retired from politics to practice law in 1913. Laredo Brú led a rebellion against President Alfredo Zayas in 1923. He was named president of the council of state by President Carlos Mendieta in 1934 and was elected Cuba's vice president under Miguel Mariano Gómez in January 1936. He succeeded to the presidency following Gómez's impeachment on December 24, 1936. His government was largely controlled by military strongman Fulgencio Batista, and Laredo Brú stepped down on October 10, 1940, following Batista's election as president. Laredo Brú served as Batista's minister of justice from 1940 to 1944. He died suddenly in Havana on July 7, 1946.

FULGENCIO BATISTA Y ZALDÍVAR (President; October 10, 1940–October 10, 1944). Fulgencio Batista y Zaldívar was born in Banes, Oriente Province, on January 16, 1901. He attended a missionary school and worked in a variety of jobs before entering the Cuban national army in 1921. He attended night school and was promoted to sergeant first class. He was assigned as a stenographer at army headquarters in 1928. He served as chief clerk at the military trials of political opponents of Cuban dictator Gerardo Machado. He soon became involved in a conspiracy of military men plotting Machado's ouster. Machado fled Cuba after a general strike spurred a coup against him in 1933. Manuel de Céspedes became provisional president, but he was unable to settle the rampant disorder in the country. Batista led a group of army sergeants in a coup to oust the provisional government on September 4, 1933. The military junta installed Ramón Grau San Martín as president, and Batista was made chief of staff of the army with the rank of colonel. When the Grau regime was refused recognition by the United States, Batista removed Grau from office. Carlos Hevia and Manuel Márques Sterling each served as president for a period of several days before Batista installed Carlos Mendieta as president on January 18, 1934. Batista remained in control of the government, however. Mendieta was replaced by José Barnet in December 1935, who was followed by Miguel Mariano Gómez in May 1936. Gómez gave way to Federico Laredo Brú in December 1936. Batista sponsored a new constitution in 1940 that liberalized Cuba's political process. He allowed the formation of opposition parties and declared himself a candidate in the presidential election to be held that year. Batista defeated Ramón Grau San Martín and took office as president on October 10, 1940. He supported the Allies during World War II and initi-

ated some social reforms. He was barred by the constitution from seeking a second term and supported the candidacy of Carlos Saladrigas Zayas in the election of 1944. Saladrigas was defeated by Grau, and Batista stepped down from office on October 10, 1944. He left Cuba and eventually settled in Florida. He returned to Cuba in 1948 to win election to the senate. He announced his candidacy for president in the 1952 election, accusing the government of President Carlos Prío Socarrás of corruption. He staged a military coup on March 10, 1952, and ousted Prío from office. Batista was again sworn into office as president. He clamped down on political dissidents, canceled elections, and banned strikes. Cuba became a tourist resort and gambling center, but his government was charged with corruption and abuse of power. Batista was faced with growing discontent among the populace throughout the 1950s. Fidel Castro launched a guerrilla revolt against the government in December 1956. The rebellion eventually reached Havana, and Batista fled the country on January 1, 1959. He went into exile and settled in Estoril, Portugal. He died of a heart attack in Guadalmina, Spain, on August 6, 1973.

RAMÓN GRAU SAN MARTÍN (President; October 10, 1944–October 10, 1948). *See earlier entry under Heads of State.*

Czechoslovakia

Czechoslovakia is a country in central Europe. It received independence from the Austro-Hungarian Empire on October 28, 1918.

HEADS OF STATE

TOMÁŠ MASARYK (President; October 28, 1918–December 18, 1935).

Tomáš Garrigue Masaryk was born in Hodonin on March 7, 1850. He was educated at the University of Vienna, where he received a doctorate in philosophy in 1876. He became a teacher there three years later and joined the faculty of the University of Prague in 1882. Masaryk began his political career as a journalist on the weekly magazine *Cas*. He was elected to the Austrian Reichsrat (parliament), as a Liberal in 1891 but resigned two years later. He founded the Progressive, or Realist, Party in 1900. He was again elected to the Reichsrat in 1907 and opposed the annexation of Bosnia-Herzegovina by the Austro-Hungarian Empire the following year. During World War I Masaryk became an advocate of Czechoslovakia's independence. He traveled throughout Europe and the United States to gain support for his position. He formed the Czechoslovak National Council in Paris in 1915, and it achieved recognition as the provisional government of independent Czechoslovakia during the last year of the war. Masaryk was elected Czechoslovakia's first president after the establishment of the republic on October 28, 1918, and he returned to Prague the following month. He was hailed as the liberator of Czechoslovakia and was reelected in 1920, 1927, and 1934. Masaryk stepped down from office due to poor health on December 18, 1935, and allowed his ally, Eduard Beneš, to succeed him. He died at Lány Castle on September 14, 1937.

EDUARD BENEŠ (President; December 18, 1935–October 5, 1938). Eduard Beneš was born in Kozlany, Bohemia, on May 28, 1884. He attended the Royal Czech College at Vinohrady and received a degree in philosophy from Charles University. He continued his education in Paris, where he received a doctorate in sociology at the Sorbonne. In 1909 he returned to Czechoslovakia and joined the Progressive Party led by Tomáš Masaryk. He joined with Masaryk in 1914, after the start of World War I, to campaign for the liberation of

Czechoslovakia from Austrian rule. Beneš became secretary-general of the Czechoslovak national council in January 1916. This council served as the forerunner of the Czech provisional government established on October 14, 1918. Beneš served as foreign minister and led the Czech delegation to the Paris Peace Conference the following year. He remained foreign minister in the Czech republic government. He also served as premier from September 27, 1921, until October 7, 1922. Beneš led the Czech delegation to the League of Nations, and in 1929 he entered his government into an alliance with Romania and Yugoslavia known as the Little Entente. He became president of Czechoslovakia on December 18, 1935, and succeeded the retiring Masaryk. Beneš was faced with the threat of German aggression in 1938, when Adolf Hitler demanded that the German-speaking districts of Czechoslovakia be ceded to Germany. The Munich Agreement between Hitler and Great Britain's prime minister Neville Chamberlain offered little recourse for Beneš but to grant Hitler's demands. He resigned as president on October 5, 1938, and went into exile in France. Following the fall of France, Beneš established a Czech government-in-exile in Great Britain and became its president on July 23, 1940. He signed a treaty with the Soviet Union in 1943 and attempted to serve as an arbitrator on issues of dispute between Moscow and the West. Beneš became president of the Czech provisional government established in Kosice on March 17, 1945. His health failed when he suffered several strokes in 1947. In February 1948 the Communists in the Czech government, led by Premier Klement Gottwald, demanded that a Communist-dominated government be established. Beneš refused to sign the new Czech constitution and resigned office on June 7, 1948. Three months later, on September 3, 1948, he died of a stroke at his home in Sezimovo Usti.

JAN SZROVÝ (President; October 5, 1938–December 1, 1938). Jan Szrový was born in Třebic on January 24, 1888. He served in the Czech army, rising to the rank of general. He was appointed prime minister by President Eduard Beneš on September 21, 1938. He became acting president of Czechoslovakia after the resignation of Beneš on October 5, 1938, during the early period of the German occupation until December 1, 1938. During his term of office he granted autonomy to Slovakia in October 1938. He subsequently served as minister of defense in Emil Hacha's government. Szrový was arrested after the war and charged as a war criminal. He was sentenced to 20 years imprisonment for his collaboration with the Germans. He died in June 1971.

EMIL HACHA (President; December 1, 1938–March 14, 1939). Emil Hacha was born in Trhové Sviny on July 12, 1872. He received a degree in law from Prague University. He worked in the Austrian bureaucracy beginning in 1898 and served as a judge on the Austrian High Court of Administration from 1916 until 1918. Following the establishment of the Czechoslovakian Republic in 1918, Hacha served on the High Court of Administration. He was president of the court from 1925 until 1938. He also served as a member of the International Court of Justice in Hague. Following the Munich Agreement of 1938 that dismembered Czechoslovakia, Hacha was elected president under pressure from Nazi Germany. He took office on December 1, 1938. Hacha signed the document with Germany that liquidated Czechoslovakia's independence on March 15, 1939. The country became a German protectorate, and Hacha was appointed state president of the puppet government of the Protectorate of Bohemia and Moravia. He retained the position until near the end of World War II. In May 1945 he was arrested after Soviet troops liberated the country. He headed the list of Czech war criminals accused of collaboration and treason. He died in a Prague prison on June 27, 1945, while awaiting trial.

EDUARD BENEŠ (President; July 21, 1940–June 7, 1948). *See earlier entry under Heads of State.*

HEADS OF GOVERNMENT

KAREL KRAMÁŘ (Prime Minister; November 14, 1918–July 8, 1919). Karel Kramář was born in Vysoké nad Jizerou on December 27, 1860. He was educated as a lawyer and was a leader of the Young Czech Party in 1890. He was a deputy to the Austrian Reichsrat from 1891 until 1914, and he was a supporter of an alliance between Austria-Hungary and Czarist Russia. He was arrested on charges of treason in 1915 but was released two years later. Kramář was a founder of the rightist National Democratic Party following the establishment of the Czechoslovakian Republic in 1918. Kramář became prime minister of the first Czechoslovakian government on November 14, 1918. He headed the Czech delegation to the Paris Peace Conference in June of the following year. He stepped down on July 8, 1919. Kramář remained active in politics and served in the Czechoslovak national assembly. He was an unsuccessful candidate to succeed Tomáš Masaryk for the presidency in 1935. He was supported by the extreme right and Fascist parties, but was defeated by Eduard Beneš. Kramář died in Prague on May 26, 1937.

VLASTIMIL TUSAR (Prime Minister; July 8, 1919–September 15, 1920).

Vlastimil Tusar was born in Prague on October 23, 1880. He was a leader of the Czech nationalist movement. He led the Social Democratic Party after the establishment of the Czechoslovakian Republic in 1918. He became prime minister on July 8, 1919. His government was responsible for Czechoslovakia's first budget and the establishment of the constitution. The first general election was held during his term of office. He served until September 15, 1920, when he resigned over his failure to gain the support of the German Social Democrats. He subsequently served as Czechoslovakia's minister to Germany. He died in Berlin on March 22, 1924.

JAN ČERNY (Prime Minister; September 15, 1920–September 26, 1921). Jan Černy was born in Uherský Ostroh on March 4, 1874. He was provincial president of Moravia before being called upon to head a non-party government on September 15, 1920. He relinquished office to Eduard Beneš on September 2, 1921. Cerny again headed a non-party interim government from March 18, 1926, until October 12, 1926. He died in Uherský Ostroh on April 10, 1957.

EDUARD BENEŠ (Prime Minister; September 2, 1921–October 7, 1921). *See earlier entry under Heads of State.*

ANTONIN ŠVEHLA (Prime Minister; October 8, 1922–March 17, 1926). Antonin Švehla was born in Hostivař on April 15, 1873. He was a founder of the Czech independence movement and a leader of the coup that established the Czechoslovak Republic in October 1918. He served as vice president of the first Czechoslovak national council. He was a leader of the Agrarian Party and served as prime minister from October 8, 1922, until March 17, 1926. On October 23, 1926, Švehla again became prime minister, but he suffered a heart attack a year later. A second attack in March 1928 left him unable to perform many of his du-

ties. His government resigned on February 1, 1929. Švehla had been considered by many a likely successor to Tomáš Masaryk for the presidency, but he died in Hostivař of influenza on December 12, 1933.

JAN ČERNY (Prime Minister; March 18, 1926–October 12, 1926). *See earlier entry under Heads of Government.*

ANTONIN ŠVEHLA (Prime Minister; October 23, 1926–February 1, 1929). *See earlier entry under Heads of Government.*

FRANTIŠEK UDRŽAL (Prime Minister; February 1, 1929–October 2, 1932). František Udržal was born in Dolni Roveň on January 3, 1866. He was a prosperous farmer and a leader of the Agrarian Party. He was appointed minister of defense under Eduard Beneš in September 1921 and retained that position in several successive cabinets. He was named to head the government on February 1, 1929, but was forced to resign when his government proved unable to cope with the economic problems arising from the Great Depression. Udržal died in Prague on September 25, 1938.

JAN MALYPETR (Prime Minister; October 30, 1932–November 5, 1935). Jan Malypetr was born in Klobúky on December 20, 1873. He was a member of the Bohemian wing of the Agrarian Party. He served in Antonin Švehla's government as minister of the interior from 1922 until 1926. He was chairman of the chamber of deputies before becoming a compromise choice to head the government on October 30, 1932. He stepped down on November 5, 1935, to resume the chairmanship of the chamber of deputies. He died at his home, near Slany, Bohemia, on September 28, 1947.

MILAN HODŽA (Prime Minister; November 5, 1935–September 21, 1938).

Milan Hodza was born in Sučany on February 1, 1878. He represented the Slovaks in the Hungarian parliament from 1905. He was a leader of the Slovakian nationalist movement and was arrested for criticism of the government in 1914. He remained interned during World War I. Following the establishment of the Czechoslovakian Republic in 1918, he served as minister to Budapest. He was elected to the parliament the following year and served in Vlastimil Tusar's government as minister of coordination from 1919 until 1920. He was minister of agriculture from 1922 to 1926 and minister of education from 1926 to 1929. He again headed the agriculture ministry from 1932 until 1935. He became prime minister on November 5, 1935. He resigned on September 21, 1938, shortly before the Munich agreement that led to Czechoslovakia's dismemberment. Hodža left the country and while in exile in London, he served as vice president of the Czech state council. Conflict with exile leader Eduard Beneš forced Hodža's resignation from the council. He went into exile in the United States in 1942 and died in Clearwater, Florida, on January 27, 1944.

JAN SZROVÝ (Prime Minister; September 21, 1938–December 1, 1938). *See earlier entry under Heads of State.*

RUDOLF BERAN (Prime Minister; December 1, 1938–March 14, 1939). Rudolf Beran was born on December 28, 1887. He was a member of the Agrarian Party and succeeded Antonin Švehla as head of the party in 1933. On December 1, 1938, he was appointed by President Emil Hacha to head a pro–German government during the occupation. He remained prime minister until Czechoslovakia was declared a protectorate of Germany on March 14, 1939. After the war Beran was arrested and charged as a war criminal. He was sentenced to twenty years imprisonment for his col-

laboration with Germany. Beran died in Leopoldstadt Prison on April 23, 1954.

JAN ŠRAMEK (Prime Minister; July 18, 1940–April 4, 1945). Jan Šrámek was born in Grygova on August 11, 1870. He was a Catholic priest in Moravia. He led the Moravian wing of the Czechoslovak Populist Party and became party chairman in 1922. He served in Antonin Švehla's cabinet as minister of public health from 1922 until November 1925. He again joined Švehla's government in October 1926. He became acting premier in March 1928 after Švehla suffered a heart attack. The government resigned in February 1929. He fled into exile following the German occupation of Czechoslovakia in the fall of 1938. Šrámek became head of the Czechoslovakian government-in-exile in London on July 18, 1940. He stepped down on April 4, 1945, when a postwar government was formed under Zdeněk Fierlinger. He became deputy premier in Klement Gottwald's government in July 1946. He was arrested by the Communist regime in March 1948 while trying to escape from Czechoslovakia. Šrámek remained interned until his death on August 21, 1955.

ZDENĚK FIERLINGER (Prime Minister; April 4, 1945–July 3, 1946). Zdeněk Fierlinger was born in Olomouc, Moravia, on July 1, 1891. He joined Tomáš Masaryk to fight for Czechoslovak independence during World War I. Following his country's independence, he served in the Czech foreign service. Fierlinger held diplomatic positions in various countries, including the Netherlands, Switzerland, Austria and the United States. He represented the Czech government in Moscow before World War II and retained that position under the Czech government-in-exile during the war. Fierlinger was leader of the Social Democratic Party and became premier in the first postwar government under President Eduard Beneš on April 4,

1945. Fierlinger stepped down on July 3, 1946, when Communist leader Klement Gottwald was elected to the office. He remained in the national assembly and merged his Social Democratic Party with the Communists when Czechoslovakia became a one-party state in 1948. Fierlinger served as president of the national assembly from 1953 until 1964. He also served as chairman of the Committee for Czechoslovak-Soviet Friendship. He resigned his chairmanship in 1968 following the Soviet-led invasion of his country. Fierlinger died in Prague on May 2, 1976.

Denmark

Denmark is a country in northern Europe.

HEADS OF STATE

CHRISTIAN IX (King; November 15, 1863–January 29, 1906). Christian was born at Gottorp on April 8, 1818. He belonged to the house of Glucksbourg and was a younger son of Prince Vilhelm of Schleswig-Holstein-Sonderburg-Beck. Christian married Louise of Hesse-Kassel in 1842. The reigning monarch of Denmark, Frederik VII, was childless and the Oldenburg line was in danger of becoming extinct. Christian's wife was a cousin of King Frederik, and it was agreed that Christian would become heir to the throne, uniting Denmark with Schleswig-Holstein. Frederik died on November 15, 1863, and Christian assumed the throne. Denmark soon found itself at war with the German powers over the rights to Schleswig-Holstein. Denmark was defeated in the war, and the duchies were relinquished in 1864. Christian supported conservative governments during his reign and often found himself at odds with the parties of the left in the Folketing (lower house of parliament). The constitutional crisis was addressed in 1901 when Christian allowed the formation of Denmark's first parliamentary government. Christian died in Copenhagen on January 29, 1906.

FREDERIK VIII (King; January 29, 1906–May 14, 1912). Frederik was born in Copenhagen on June 3, 1843. He was the eldest son of the future King Christian IX of Denmark and Louisa of Hesse-Kassel. He saw action in Denmark's war against Prussia and Austria in 1864. He served as a leading advisor to his father during his rule and succeeded to the throne as Frederik VIII upon his father's death on January 29, 1906. He was a popular monarch with the Danish people. Frederik was in Hamburg, Germany, on May 14, 1912, while returning from a trip to Nice, France. He was stricken with an illness while taking an evening walk alone. He died en route to the hospital. The king was not recognized by the authorities until his body was found in the hospital mortuary by his aides.

CHRISTIAN X (King; May 14, 1912–April 20, 1947). Carl Frederik Albert Alexander William was born in Charlottenlund Castle near Copenhagen on September 26, 1870. He was the eldest son of Crown Prince Frederik and Princess Louise of Sweden. He entered the Royal Guards in 1889 and became chief of the guard in 1898. His father ascended the throne as King Frederik VIII following the death of King Christian IX in 1906. Christian became Crown

Prince and was promoted to major general in the guard. He served as Denmark's ruler while his father was out of the country. He ascended to the throne as King Christian X upon the death of his father on May 14, 1912. Christian maintained Danish neutrality during World War I. He granted home rule to Iceland, which became a sovereign state in November 1918. The king of Denmark also ruled as king of Iceland. Christian remained on the throne during the German occupation of Denmark in 1940. He refused to be intimidated by the Ger-

mans or to form a government favoring them, gaining much respect from the Danish people. The king became seriously ill following a fall from his horse in 1942. He was placed under palace arrest by the Nazis in August 1943 following a rebellion against the occupation forces. He remained imprisoned until the defeat of the Germans. Iceland severed its ties with Denmark in May 1944. Christian suffered a heart attack and died shortly thereafter at Amalienborg Palace on April 20, 1947.

HEADS OF GOVERNMENT

HUGO EGEMONT HORRING (Prime Minister; May 23, 1897–April 27, 1900). Hugo Egemont Horring was born in Copenhagen on August 17, 1842. He was a leading member of the Danish government and served in the cabinet as minister of the interior. He was called upon to head a Right government on May 23, 1897, following the resignation of Tage Reetz-Thott. The rightist parties were badly defeated in elections to the Rigsdag in the 1898 elections. Horring continued to head the government until April 27, 1900, when his cabinet resigned over the issue of taxation. Horring remained a state councilor until his death in Copenhagen on February 13, 1909.

HANNIBAL SEHESTED (Prime Minister; April 27, 1900–July 24, 1901). Hannibal Sehested was born in Broholm on November 16, 1842. He was a Rightist member of the Rigsdag. He was chosen to head the government on April 27, 1900. Elections were held in April 1901 after the introduction of the secret ballot. The Left Reform Party was victorious in the elections, and Sehested stepped down on July 24, 1901. He died in Broholm on September 19, 1924.

JOHAN HENRIK DEUNTZER (Prime Minister; July 24, 1901–January 14, 1905). Johan Henrik Deuntzer was born in Copenhagen on May 21, 1845. He was a law professor with little background in politics when he was chosen to head a Left government on July 24, 1901, after the introduction of parliamentary democracy in Denmark. Deuntzer's government was forced to resign on January 14, 1905, after the Radicals defected from the cabinet. Deuntzer remained active in politics, serving in the Landsting from 1913. He died in Charlottenlund on November 16, 1918.

JENS C. CHRISTENSEN (Prime Minister; January 14, 1905–October 12, 1908). Jens Christian Christensen was born in Paabol on November 21, 1856. He was a schoolteacher before entering politics in the 1890s. He became leader of the Reform Party in the Rigsdag. He was named to Johan Deuntzer's Liberal cabinet as minister of education in July 1901. The Liberal Party split in 1905, and Christensen formed a Left government on January 14, 1905. He was forced to resign on October 12, 1908, over a financial scandal involving his justice minister, Peter Adler Alberti. Christensen was acquitted of any personal wrongdoing and returned to the government as defense minister in Count Holstein-Ledreborg's government in 1909. He served as minister of control in Carl Zahle's government in 1910. Christensen again served as minister of education in Niels Neergaard's government from 1920 until his resignation for reasons of health in 1922. He retired from politics two years later and died in Hee on December 19, 1930.

NIELS T. NEERGAARD (Prime Minister; October 12, 1908–August 16, 1909). Niels Thomasins Neergaard was born in Ugilt on April 27, 1854. He was a leader of the Moderate Left and a leading Danish historian. He was called upon to form a Left government on October 12, 1908, following the resignation of Jens Christensen. He stepped down on August 16, 1909, when the government could not reach an agreement on a defense issue. Neergaard formed another Liberal government on May 5, 1920. He sponsored numerous social reforms, including disability insurance and fixed old-age pensions. Economic problems caused by the devaluation of the krone forced Neergaard to hold new elections. The Social Democrats were victorious and Neergaard stepped down on April 23, 1924. He remained a leading figure in Danish politics until his death in Copenhagen on September 2, 1936.

JOHAN LUDWIG, COUNT HOLSTEIN-LEDREBORG (Prime Minister; August 16, 1909–October 28, 1909). Johan Ludwig, Count Holstein-Ledreborg, was born Carl Christian Tido in Hochberg on June 10, 1839. He formed a minority Left cabinet on August 16, 1909. He stepped down on October 28, 1909, when his government received a vote of no confidence from the Rigsdag. He died in Ledreborg on March 11, 1912.

CARL THEODOR ZAHLE (Prime Minister; October 28, 1909–July 5, 1910).

Carl Theodor Zahle was born in Roskilde on January 19, 1866. He formed the first Radical government on October 28, 1909. He led a minority government with the support of the Social Democrats. He attempted a constitutional effort for electoral reform, including granting the parliamentary vote to women. He resigned on July 5, 1910, when his policies were defeated. The Radicals and Social Democrats gained a majority in the Folketing in elections in 1913, and Zahle again formed a government on June 21, 1913. He led the government throughout World War I, maintaining Denmark's neutrality during the conflict. Zahle's government received a new mandate in the 1918 elections. He was dismissed by King Christian on March 29, 1920, over a dispute concerning proportional representation in rural districts but remained a leader of the Radical Party. He died in Lyngby on February 5, 1946.

KLAUS BERNTSEN (Prime Minister; July 5, 1910–June 21, 1913). Klaus Berntsen was born in Eskildstrup on June 12, 1844. He became prime minister of a Left government on July 5, 1910. The Left suffered setbacks in elections in 1913, and Berntsen stepped down on June 21, 1913. He served as minister of defense in Niels Neergaard's cabinet from 1920 until 1924. He retired from the Rigsdag in December 1926 and died the following year in Copenhagen on March 27, 1927.

CARL THEODOR ZAHLE (Prime Minister; June 21, 1913–March 29, 1920). *See earlier entry under Heads of Government.*

OTTO LIEBE (Prime Minister; March 30, 1920–April 5, 1920). Karl Julius Otto Liebe was born in Copenhagen on May 24, 1860. He was a leading Danish lawyer who was chosen by King Christian to head a caretaker government on March 30, 1920, and mandated to hold new elections. His government was forced to resign on April 5, 1920, following widespread demonstrations by labor and the Socialists and the threat of a general strike. Liebe died in Copenhagen on March 21, 1929.

AAGE FRIIS (Prime Minister; April 5, 1920–May 5, 1920). Aage Friis was born in Halskov on August 16, 1870. He was named to head a caretaker cabinet supported by the major political parties on April 5, 1920. He oversaw new elections and stepped down when a Left cabinet was formed by Niels Neergaard on May 5, 1920. Friis died on October 5, 1949.

NIELS T. NEERGAARD (Prime Minister; May 5, 1920–April 23, 1924). *See earlier entry under Heads of Government.*

THORVALD STAUNING (Prime Minister; April 23, 1924–December 14, 1926). Thorvald August Marinus Stauning was born in Copenhagen on October 26, 1873. He worked as a cigar sorter and was active in the trade union movement. He became involved in the Danish Social Democratic Party in the 1890s. He was elected to the Folketing, the lower house of the Danish parliament, in 1906. He led the Socialist Party in parliament in 1910 and served in Carl Zahle's Radical cabinet as minister without portfolio from 1916 to 1920. He was also chairman of the Copenhagen city council from 1919 to 1924. After a victory by the Socialists in the elections of 1924, Stauning formed a Social Democratic-Radical coalition cabinet on April 23, 1924. His government fell over a tax issue on December 14, 1926. The Socialists returned to power three years later, and Stauning again became prime minister on April 30, 1929. He was instrumental in keeping Denmark's military weak during the 1930s. Stauning's government accepted Germany's ultimatum to surrender on April 9, 1940, and Germany occupied Denmark during World War II.

Stauning led a coalition government during the war, and attempted to maintain the political integrity of Denmark during the occupation. He retained office until his death in Copenhagen on May 3, 1942.

THOMAS MADSEN-MYGDAL (Prime Minister; December 14, 1926–April 30, 1929). Thomas Madsen-Mygdal was born in Mygdal on December 24, 1876. He was the chairman of the Danish National Farmers' Union. He served in Niels Neergard's Left government from 1920 until 1924, and formed a Left cabinet on December 14, 1926, with the support of the Conservatives. The Conservatives broke with the government on a budgetary issue, and Madsen-Mygdal stepped down on April 30, 1929. He remained active in political affairs. Madsen-Mygdal died in Hellerup during the German occupation of Denmark in 1943.

THORVALD STAUNING (Prime Minister; April 30, 1929–May 3, 1942). *See earlier entry under Heads of Government.*

VILHELM BUHL (Prime Minister; May 3, 1942–November 9, 1942). Vilhelm Buhl was born in Fredericia on October 16, 1881. He attended Copenhagen University and received a degree in law. He joined the finance department in Copenhagen in 1908, rising to the position of director of taxes in 1924. He was elected to the Folketing as a member of the Social Democratic Party in 1932. He was named minister of finance in the cabinet of Prime Minister Thorvald Stauning in 1937 and initiated a series of tax reforms. Buhl was selected as prime minister on May 3, 1942, during the German occupation of Denmark. He stepped down from office on November 9, 1942. He again became prime minister on May 5, 1945, and guided Denmark's return to democracy in the postwar period. He presided over parliamentary elections and relinquished office on November 7, 1945. He subsequently served as chairman of the Social Democratic Party's parliamentary group. He was appointed minister of economic coordination in November 1947 and retained that position until March 1950, when he was appointed minister of justice. He left the cabinet in September 1950 and died in Copenhagen on December 18, 1954.

ERIK SCAVENIUS (Prime Minister; November 9, 1942–August 30, 1943). Harold R. Erik Scavenius was born to a wealthy family on June 13, 1877. He graduated from the University of Copenhagen with a degree in political economics. He subsequently entered the Danish diplomatic corps and served in the Danish legation in Berlin in 1906. Scavenius was foreign minister from 1909 to 1910 and from 1913 to 1920. He was instrumental in maintaining Denmark's neutrality during World War I. He was appointed minister to Sweden in 1924, where he remained until his retirement in 1932. He returned to the government as foreign minister after the German occupation of Denmark in April 1940. He was chosen to head the government as prime minister on November 9, 1942. He retained office until August 30, 1943, when the German occupation administration removed the government and installed a German governor. Scavenius was criticized after the war for his cooperation with the occupation authorities. He dropped out of pol-

itics and died in Copenhagen on November 29, 1962.

VILHELM BUHL (Prime Minister; May 5, 1945–November 7, 1945). *See earlier entry under Heads of Government.*

KNUD KRISTENSEN (Prime Minister; November 5, 1945–November 13, 1947). Knud Kristensen was born on July 13, 1880. He entered politics and became active in the Agrarian Party. In 1920 he was elected to the Danish parliament. He served on the finance committee from 1927 until he left parliament in 1929. Kristensen returned to the parliament in 1932 and was appointed to the cabinet as minister of the interior in 1940. He resigned from the government two years later in protest of the German occupation forces' demand that Erik Scavenius be named prime minister. Kristensen returned to the cabinet following Denmark's liberation and became head of a Liberal-Agrarian coalition government on November 5, 1945. He promoted the incorporation of the German province of South Schleswig into Denmark. His support for a plebiscite on the issue brought down his government on November 13, 1947. Kristensen left the Agrarian Party in 1953 in opposition to plans to revise the Danish constitution to eliminate the upper house of parliament. Kristensen formed the Independent Party, but failed to win any seats in the parliament. He subsequently retired from politics. Kristensen died in Copenhagen on September 29, 1962.

Dominican Republic

The Dominican Republic is a country on the eastern portion of the island of Hispaniola in the Caribbean Sea. It was granted independence from Haiti on February 27, 1844.

HEADS OF STATE

JUAN ISIDRO JIMÉNEZ (President; November 15, 1899–May 1, 1902). Juan Isidro Jiménez was born in 1846. He became a leading political figure in the Dominican Republic, with followers known as Jiménistas. He served as president of the Dominican Republic from November 15, 1899, until May 1, 1902. Jiménez was the victor in elections in 1914 imposed by a plan of the United States to stabilize the nation. Jiménez took office on December 5, 1914. The United States continued to involve itself in the government by imposing conditions for further economic assistance. The Dominican government was instructed to include American citizens as director of public works and financial advisor to the government. Jiménez accepted the conditions, but the congress refused to concur. The government was besieged with threats of rebellion, and the United States sent a naval force to preserve Jiménez's presidency and impose the terms of the agreement. The United States increased its demands on the Dominican Republic and criticism of Jiménez's presidency increased to the point of rebellion. Despite Jiménez's opposition, United States marines landed in Santo Domingo in May 1916. Jiménez resigned from office on May 7, 1916, and the United States occupied the country. Jiménez died in 1919.

HORACIO VÁSQUEZ (President; May 1, 1902–April 18, 1903). Horacio Vásquez was born in Ciudad Moca on October 22, 1860. He was an opponent of President Ulíses Heureaux and was involved in several plots against the government. Vásquez briefly served as provisional president from August 30, 1899, until November 15, 1899, following the assassination of Heureaux. He again served as president from May 1, 1902, until April 18, 1903. His supporters, known as "Horacistas" became a leading political force in the country. The Dominican Republic was occupied by the United States in 1916, and Vásquez served on the committee that negotiated the withdrawal of United States marines in 1924. He was the winner in elections held preceding the marines' withdrawal and took office on March 15, 1924. He was widely viewed as a puppet of the United States. He announced a two-year extension of his term of office in 1928. This, along with economic difficulties brought on by the worldwide economic depression, resulted in his ouster in a military coup led by Rafael Trujillo on March 2, 1930. Vásquez went into exile in the United States. He was allowed to return to the Dominican Republic soon after, but refrained from political activity. He died in Ciudad Trujillo on March 25, 1936.

ALEJANDRO WOSS Y GIL (President; April 18, 1903–November 4, 1903). Alejandro Woss y Gil served as president of the Dominican Republic under the dictatorship of Ulíses Heureaux from May 16, 1885, until January 6, 1887. Woss y Gil again became president on April 18, 1903, but relinquished office to Carlos Morales on November 4, 1903.

CARLOS F. MORALES (President; November 4, 1903–January 13, 1906). Carlos F. Morales was born in 1867. He was selected as president of the Dominican Republic on November 4, 1903. He resigned from office on January 13, 1906, and was succeeded by his vice president, Ramón Cáceres. Morales died in 1914.

RAMÓN CÁCERES (President; January 13, 1906–November 19, 1911). Ramón Cáceres was born to a prosperous family in Moca on December 15, 1866. He was a leading opponent of the regime of President Ulíses Heureaux in the 1890s. Cáceres assassinated Heureaux at a rally in Moca on July 26, 1899. The nation's political situation remained unstable over the next several years, and Cáceres briefly went into exile in 1903. He returned to the Dominican Republic to serve as Carlos Morales' vice president in 1904. Cáceres succeeded to the presidency following Morales' resignation on January 13, 1906. He presided over a period of peace and prosperity in the Dominican Republic. He initiated numerous public works programs and reformed the constitution. He withstood several plots against his administration until November 19, 1911, when he was assassinated by political opponents.

ELADIO VICTORIA (President; November 19, 1911–November 26, 1912). Eladio Victoria was the uncle of Colonel Alfredo Victoria, the military commander of Santo Domingo. He was installed as president on November 19, 1911, following the assassination of Ramón Cáceres. Pressure on his government from the United States to settle a longstanding border dispute with Haiti led to the forced resignation of Victoria on November 26, 1912.

ADOLFO NOUEL Y BOBADILLA (President; December 2, 1912–March 31, 1913). Adolfo Alejandro Nouel y Bobadilla was born in 1862. He was a leading Roman Catholic prelate in the Dominican Republic. He became archbishop of Santo Domingo in 1904. He was chosen as a compromise candidate for interim president of the Dominican Republic on December 2, 1912. Civil disorders continued, and Nouel was unable to control the country's military leaders. He resigned on March 31, 1913, and went to Europe. He served as apostolic delegate to Cuba and Puerto Rico from 1913 until 1915. Nouel was named by the United States Department of State to serve on a consulting commission during the occupation of the Dominican Republic in November 1919. He subsequently became a critic of the occupation forces, which left the country in 1924. Nouel died in Santo Domingo on June 26, 1937.

JOSÉ BORDAS VALDEZ (President; April 14, 1913–August 27, 1914). José Bordas Valdez was a general in the Dominican army when he became provisional president of the Dominican Republic on April 14, 1913. He attempted forceful measures to quell revolutionary activity in the country. His regime was unpopular with the American authorities, which cut off aid to the country to force political reforms. Bordas resigned from office on August 27, 1914.

RAMÓN BÁES (President; August 27, 1914–December 5, 1914). Ramón Báes was chosen as provisional president under the terms of an American plan to stabilize the country. His government was charged with holding democratic elections. Báes' government complied with the agreement, and Juan Isidro Jiménez was victorious in the election. Báes relinquished office to Jiménez on December 5, 1914.

JUAN ISIDRO JIMÉNEZ (President; December 5, 1914–May 7, 1916). *See earlier entry under Heads of State.*

FRANCISCO HENRÍQUEZ Y CARVAJAL (President; July 26, 1916– December 9, 1916). Francisco Henríquez y Carvajal was born on January 14, 1859. He was chosen by the Dominican congress to serve as provisional president on July 26, 1916, after the invasion of the Dominican Republic by United States marines. The United States allowed Henríquez to assume office under conditions set forth by the occupation forces. Henríquez was unwilling to accept such restrictions and resigned from office on December 9, 1916, and left the country. He died in 1935.

U.S. OCCUPATION (May 1916–March 1924).

JUAN BAUTISTA VICINI BURGOS (President; October 21, 1922–March 15, 1924). Juan Bautista Vicini Burgos was a wealthy sugar plantation owner. Though not active in politics, he was chosen as provisional president of the Dominican Republic on October 21, 1922, following an agreement by the United States to withdraw its occupation forces. Burgos worked with the new United States military governor, General Harry Lee, to oversee democratic elections prior to the withdrawal of the United States. Horacio Vásquez was chosen as president and Vicini Burgos relinquished office on March 15, 1924. Vicini Burgos led the opposition to Vásquez through the late 1920s.

HORACIO VÁSQUEZ (President; March 15, 1924–March 2, 1930). *See earlier entry under Heads of State.*

RAFAEL ESTRELLA URENA (President; March 3, 1930–April 22, 1930). Rafael Estrella Urena was chosen as provisional president on March 2, 1930, following the military coup that ousted Horacio Vásquez. The leader of the coup, Rafael Trujillo, remained the most powerful figure in the government. Estrella stepped down on April 22, 1930, but resumed office on May 21, 1930. He again stepped down on August 16, 1930, when Trujillo assumed the presidency.

Estrella was sent into exile by Trujillo, but he was allowed to return to the Dominican Republic in 1935.

JACINTO B. PEYNADO (President; April 22, 1930–May 21, 1930). Jacinto B. Peynado was born on February 15, 1878. He was educated in Santo Domingo as a lawyer and worked as a law professor at Santo Domingo University. He was appointed minister of justice by President Ramón Báes in 1914 and retained that position in Juan Isidro Jiminéz's government and also served as secretary of the interior and the police. He assumed office as provisional president on April 22, 1930, during the dictatorship of Rafael Trujillo. He stepped down on May 21, 1930. He was appointed secretary of the interior, police, and war in General Trujillo's government. He was appointed secretary to the president in 1932 and was elected Trujillo's vice president in 1934. Peynado was Trujillo's hand-picked candidate in elections held in 1938. He again assumed the presidency on August 16, 1938, though Trujillo continued to control the country. Peynado retained office until his death in Ciudad Trujillo on February 24, 1940.

RAFAEL ESTRELLA URENA (President; May 21, 1930–August 16, 1930). *See earlier entry under Heads of State.*

RAFAEL L. TRUJILLO (President; August 16, 1930–August 16, 1938). Rafael Leónidas Trujillo y Molina was born in San Cristobal on October 24, 1891. He joined the Dominican National Guard in 1918, following the American occupation. He rose to the rank of major in 1924 and became chief of staff in 1928. President Horacio Vásquez was ousted in a revolt in February 1930, and Trujillo seized power in the country. He was a candidate of the Confederation of Parties in the subsequent elections. The opposition candidate withdrew from the election under duress, and Trujillo was elected president. He took office on August 16, 1930, and ruled the country in a ruthless fashion, eliminating civil and political rights. Numerous political opponents were arrested or murdered during his regime. Trujillo ordered the slaughter of over 15,000 Haitian immigrant workers in 1937. He stepped down as president on August 16, 1938, and allowed his hand-picked candidate, Jacinto Peynado, to take office. Trujillo remained firmly in control of the country as commander of the army during the presidency of Peynado and Manuel de Jesus Troncoso. Trujillo again became president on May 18, 1942. He was a competent administrator who brought prosperity to the Dominican Republic despite the corruption and brutality of his government. His administration built hospitals, schools, and roads throughout the country. He again stepped down as president on May 16, 1952, and allowed his younger brother, Hector Trujillo, to take office. Rafael Trujillo retained power in the country despite growing opposition to his regime. The Organization of American States imposed economic sanctions and severed diplomatic relations with the Dominican Republic in August 1960 after Trujillo was implicated in an assassination attempt against Venezuelan president Romulo Betancourt. Trujillo retained absolute control of the country until he was assassinated by machine-gun fire while driving outside the capital on May 30, 1961.

JACINTO B. PEYNADO (President; August 16, 1938–February 24, 1940). *See earlier entry under the Heads of State.*

MANUEL DE JESÚS TRONCOSO DE LA CONCHA (President; February 24, 1940–May 18, 1942). Manuel de Jesús Troncoso de la Concha was born in Santo Domingo on April 3, 1878. In 1899 he received a degree in law from the University of Santo Domingo and later worked there as a law professor. He entered politics in 1911 and held various government positions, including minister of justice and the interior. He also served as minister of war and naval affairs. He became vice president under Jacinto B. Peynado during the dictatorship of Rafael Trujillo. He succeeded to the presidency on February 24, 1940, following Peynado's death. He served as nominal head of state, though Trujillo remained the real leader of the country. Troncoso relinquished the presidency to Trujillo on May 18, 1942. He subsequently served as president of the Dominican senate. He died in Ciudad Trujillo on May 30, 1955.

RAFAEL L. TRUJILLO (President; May 18, 1942–March 1, 1951). *See earlier entry under Heads of State.*

Ecuador

Ecuador is a country in northwestern South America. Formerly a Spanish colony, Ecuador became an independent republic in 1830.

HEADS OF STATE

ELOY ALFARO (President; June 18, 1895–August 31, 1901). José Eloy Alfaro Delgado was born in Monteristi, Manabí, Ecuador, on June 25, 1842. He was a supporter of General José Maria Urvina and was instrumental in the revolts against the regime of President Gabriel García Moreno in 1865 and 1871. The failure of the revolts led to Alfaro's exile in Panama, where he continued to promote liberal causes in Ecuador and throughout Latin America. He returned to Ecuador in 1893 to lead a revolt against President Luis Cordero. Cordero was ousted in April 1895, and Alfaro became Ecuador's leader on June 18, 1895. He convened a constituent assembly, which authored a new constitution, and Alfaro was elected president of Ecuador in 1897. He completed his term of office on September 1, 1901, and was succeeded by Leónidas Plaza Gutiérrez. Alfaro led the revolt against the subsequent presidency of Lizardo García and became president after his defeat of the government troops on January 16, 1906. He again convened a constitutional convention, which chose him as president on January 2, 1907. His second term of office was marked by an attempt to reduce the power of the Roman Catholic church in Ecuador. He instituted laws to separate church and state, and church property not used for religious purposes was seized in 1908. He instituted reforms in education and public health and oversaw the opening of the Quito and Guayaquil Railroad. Alfaro stepped down from office on August 11, 1911, and Emilio Estrada was elected as his successor. Alfaro went into exile in Europe but when Estrada died several months later, a civil war ensued, and Alfaro returned to Ecuador in an attempt to return to power in January 1912. He was arrested and imprisoned in Guayaquil with other rebel leaders shortly after his return. They were dragged from their jail cells by an angry mob and lynched on January 28, 1912.

LEÓNIDAS PLAZA GUTIÉRREZ (President; September 1, 1901–August 31, 1905). Leónidas Plaza Gutiérrez was born in Charapotó, Manabí Province, on April 18, 1865. He began a career in the military in 1883 and fought with rebel troops in the liberal rebellion that year. He fled to Central America after

the failure of the revolt and worked in the governments of Costa Rica, Nicaragua, and El Salvador. He returned to Ecuador in 1895 to join Eloy Alfaro's successful liberal revolt. He served in the constituent assembly the following year. He became governor of Azuay Province in 1896 and served as president of the chamber of deputies in 1900. Plaza was chosen by President Alfaro to succeed him, but Alfaro subsequently withdrew his support. Plaza was elected despite Alfaro's opposition and took office on September 1, 1901. He led a moderate regime that respected civil liberties and constitutional government. He completed his term and stepped down in favor of Lizardo García on August 31, 1905. He subsequently left the country and stayed away following Eloy Alfaro's ouster of García's government. He returned to Ecuador to serve as minister of finance in Emilio Estrada's cabinet in 1911. Estrada died later in the year, and Plaza participated in the resulting civil war. The defeat and murder of his rival, Eloy Alfaro, allowed for Plaza's election to a second term as president. He took office on September 1, 1912, and continued to govern in a constitutional fashion. He completed his term on August 31, 1916, after the election of Alfredo Baquerizo Moreno. Plaza remained a leading force in Ecuadorean politics until his retirement in 1925. He died in Huigra, Tungurahua Province, on September 18, 1932.

LIZARDO GARCÍA (President; September 1, 1905–January 15, 1906). Lizardo García was born in Guayaquil on April 26, 1842. He was educated in Ecuador and worked as a merchant and banker. He was a founding member of the Guayaquil Chamber of Commerce in 1889 and became minister of the treasury in 1895. He was elected senator from Guayas Province in 1898 and remained in the senate until 1904. He was elected to succeed Leónidas Plaza Gutiérrez as president and took office on

September 1, 1905. His term of office was cut short by a revolt led by Eloy Alfaro and García was forced to step down on January 15, 1906. He died in Guayaquil on May 28, 1927.

ELOY ALFARO (President; January 16, 1906–August 11, 1911). *See earlier entry under Heads of State.*

CARLOS FREILE ZALDUMBIDE (President; August 11, 1911–August 31, 1911). Carlos Freile Zaldumbide was born to an affluent family in Quito in 1851. He entered politics and was named minister of public instruction in 1896. He was elected to the constituent assembly in 1906 and served as president of the senate in 1911. He replaced Eloy Alfaro as president August 11, 1911, following the election of Emilio Estrada. He stepped down on August 31, 1911, to allow Estrada to take office. He was again called upon to serve as president following Estrada's death on December 21, 1911. Freile was unable to restore order to the country and was forced to resign on March 6, 1912. Freile subsequently went to Europe and died in Paris on August 21, 1926.

EMILIO ESTRADA (President; August 31, 1911–December 21, 1911). Emilio Estrada was born in Quito on May 28, 1855. He was educated in Guayaquil and became a leading business figure in Ecuador. He entered politics in 1895 and served as governor of Guayas Province several times. He was elected to the chamber of deputies in 1899 and served as vice president of the chamber. He was elected president of Ecuador, despite the opposition of President Eloy Alfaro, and took office on August 31, 1911. Estrada died in office on December 21, 1911.

CARLOS FREILE ZALDUMBIDE (President; December 21, 1911–March 6, 1912). *See earlier entry under Heads of State.*

FRANCISCO ANDRADE MARÍN (President; March 6, 1912–August 31, 1912). Francisco Andrade Marín was born in Ibarra on February 15, 1841, He was educated in Quito, where he studied law. He was elected to the constituent convention in 1883 and served in Eloy Alfaro's cabinet as minister of public works in 1892. He subsequently served as minister of the treasury and was elected president of the chamber of deputies in 1911. Andrade Marín succeeded Carlos Freile Zaldumbide as Ecuador's president when Freile resigned on March 6, 1912. Andrade Marín called for new elections, and stepped down on August 31, 1912, following Leónidas Plaza Gutiérrez's selection as president. Andrade Marín died in Quito on September 26, 1935.

LEÓNIDAS PLAZA GUTIÉRREZ (President; September 1, 1912–August 31, 1916). *See earlier entry under Heads of State.*

ALFREDO BAQUERIZO MORENO (President; September 1, 1916–August 31, 1920). Alfredo Baquerizo Moreno was born in Guayaquil on September 28, 1859. He received a degree in law in 1884. He became a leading Ecuadorean writer and poet, best known for his novels *El señor Penco* and *Tierra adentro*. He entered politics and was elected mayor of Guayaquil in 1890 and remained in office until 1896. He also served as secretary to the minister of the Guayaquil superior court from 1894 until 1901. He was named foreign minister in 1902 and retained that position until 1912. He was also Ecuador's ambassador to Peru from 1903 until 1907 and vice president of Ecuador from 1903 until 1906. He was elected to the senate from Guayas in 1912, and served as president of the senate until his election as Ecuador's president. He took office on September 1, 1916. His administration passed a law against forced labor in 1918. He completed his term and stepped down from office on August 31, 1920. Baquerizo was again called upon to serve as president following the ouster of Luis Larrea Alba on October 15, 1931. He retained office until August 27, 1932. Baquerizo died in New York City on March 20, 1951.

JOSÉ LUIS TAMAYO (President; September 1, 1920–August 31, 1924). José Luis Tamayo was born in Chanduy, Guayas Province, on July 29, 1858. He received a degree in law in 1886. Tamayo served as governor of Manabí Province in 1895. He was subsequently appointed minister of the interior and was elected president of the chamber of deputies in 1898. He was elected to the senate from Esmeraldas Province and served from 1902 to 1905. He was elected president of Ecuador and succeeded Alfredo Baquerizo Moreno on September 1, 1920. He completed his term and stepped down on August 31, 1924. Tamayo died in Guayaquil on July 7, 1947.

GONZALO S. CÓRDOVA RIVERA (President; September 1, 1924–July 9, 1925). Gonzalo S. Córdova Rivera was born in Cuenca on July 15, 1863. He attended the University of Cuenca, where he received a degree in law. He was elected to the chamber of deputies from Canar Province in 1892, serving until 1897. He was governor of Canar from 1898 to 1902. He served as minister of the interior from 1903 until 1906. He was elected to the senate from Carchi Province in 1912 and served as vice president of the senate. He also served as Ecuador's minister to the United States, Chile, and Argentina from 1911 until 1913. He was named Ecuador's minister to Venezuela in 1922. Córdova was elected president of Ecuador and took office on September 1, 1924. He was ousted in a military coup on July 9, 1925. He subsequently went into exile and died in Valparaiso, Chile, on April 23, 1938.

ISIDRO AYORA (President; April 1, 1926–August 24, 1931). Isidro Ayora Cueva was born in Loja on August 31, 1879. He studied medicine at the University of Quito and completed his studies in Berlin and Dresden before returning to Ecuador in 1909. In 1912 he began practicing medicine and teaching obstetrics at the Central University. He was appointed rector of the university in 1925. Ayora was chosen as a member of the ruling provisional junta following the coup that ousted Gonzalo Cordova Rivera on July 9, 1925. He also served as minister of social welfare, labor and agriculture. He was chosen as provisional president of Ecuador on April 1, 1926. Ayora initiated many economic reforms to ease Ecuador's financial problems. He worked to eliminate budget deficits and revamped the country's customs system. Ayora convened a constituent convention in 1929 and was reelected to the presidency. Ecuador's economy continued to suffer during the world financial crisis of 1929, and Ayora endured public criticism of his policies. He resigned from office on August 24, 1931, after mass demonstrations against his government. He subsequently returned to his medical practice. Ayora retired to Los Angeles in the early 1970s and died there on March 22, 1978.

LUIS LARREA ALBA (President; August 24, 1931–October 15, 1931). Luis Larrea Alba was born in Guayaquil on October 25, 1895. He received a military education in Quito and Santiago, Chile. He served in Ecuador's army and was a military attaché in Italy and Peru. Larrea headed the police in Guayas Province from 1925 until 1929. He was selected as a deputy from El Oro Province for the constituent assembly in 1928. Larrea became president of Ecuador on August 24, 1931, following the resignation of Isidro Ayora. He was unsuccessful in his attempt to establish a dictatorship in Ecuador and was forced from power on October 15, 1931.

ALFREDO BAQUERIZO MORENO (President; October 15, 1931–August 27, 1932). *See earlier entry under Heads of State.*

CARLO FREILE LARREA (President; August 27, 1932–September 2, 1932). Carlo Freile Larrea was born in Quito on July 15, 1892. He was educated in Quito and London, and received a degree in civil engineering. He was president of the Guayaquil and Quito Railway Company before entering government as minister of public works in 1939. He was chosen to replace Alfredo Baquerizo Moreno as president of Ecuador on August 27, 1932, but was forced from office five days later on September 2, 1932.

ALBERTO GUERRERO MARTINEZ (President; September 2, 1932–December 4, 1932). Alberto Guerrero Martinez was born in Guayaquil in 1878. He attended the University of Guayaquil, where he received a degree in law. Guerrero was elected to the chamber of deputies from Los Rios Province in 1914. He was subsequently elected to the senate and served as president of the chamber from 1923 until 1924. Guerrero was chosen as Ecuador's president on September 2, 1932, following a civil uprising. He headed a caretaker administration that called for new elections and stepped down on December 4, 1932, following the election of Juan Martinez Mera. Guerrero died in Guayaquil on May 21, 1941.

JUAN DE DIOS MARTINEZ MERA (President; December 5, 1932–October 20, 1933). Juan de Dios Martinez Mera was born in Guayaquil on March 9, 1875. He received a degree in law from the University of Guayaquil. He became active in politics when he was appointed secretary of the Guayaquil council and president of the chamber of deputies. He also served in the cabinet as minister of the treasury. Martinez was elected president of Ecuador and took office on December 5, 1932. He was impeached by congress the following year and forced to step down on October 20, 1933. Martinez died in Guayaquil on October 27, 1955.

ABELARDO MONTALVO (President; October 20, 1933–August 31, 1934). Abelardo Montalvo was born in Quito on June 1, 1876. He attended the University of Quito and received a degree in law. He entered politics and was elected to the senate from Pichincha Province. Montalvo was a deputy to the constituent convention in 1906. He was subsequently on the faculty of the Central University as a professor of law. He was also the rector of the Colegio Nacional Mejia. He was chosen to be president of Ecuador on October 20, 1933, following the impeachment of Juan Martinez Mera. He headed a caretaker administration that called for new elections. Montalvo stepped down on August 31, 1934, following the election of José María Velasco Ibarra. He died in Quito on December 26, 1950.

JOSÉ MARÍA VELASCO IBARRA (President; September 1, 1934–August 30, 1935). José María Velasco Ibarra was born in Quito on March 19, 1893. He was educated at the University of Quito and the University of Paris, where he received a degree in law. He returned to Ecuador to serve in the Public Welfare Society. He subsequently became attorney general of Quito. He was also elected to the chamber of deputies and became president of that body. Velasco was a leader of the opposition to President Juan de Dios Martinez Mera. Impeachment charges were brought against Martinez, and he was removed from office in December 1933. Velasco was a candidate in the subsequent elections and received the support of the Conservative Party. He was victorious and took office on September 1, 1934. He was unable to win the support of congress for his economic legislation and offered his resignation later in the year but Congress refused to accept it, and he remained in office. Velasco became increasingly dictatorial in his rule. He imposed censorship restrictions on the newspapers and had opposition leaders arrested. He was ousted by a military coup on August 20, 1935. He was briefly imprisoned before going into exile in Colombia. Velasco was again arrested in 1938 when he tried to reenter Ecuador. He led an unsuccessful revolt against the government of Carlos Arroyo del Río in January 1940 before returning to exile in Colombia. He was refused permission to reenter Ecuador to contest the presidential elections planned for June 1944. He carried out a presidential campaign from exile. Velasco's supporters initiated a revolt in May 1944 and President Arroyo del Río's government resigned. Velasco returned to Quito on May 31, 1944, to take control of the government. His inability to cope with Ecuador's declining economy cost him popularity among many of his former supporters. He resigned the presidency when threatened by a military coup on August 23, 1947 and he went into exile in Argentina. He returned in 1952 and entered the presidential campaign. He was again elected president and took office on September 1, 1952. Velasco completed his term of office on August 21, 1956, and returned to Argentina. He came back to Ecuador to again run for president in 1960, won the election, and took office on September 1, 1960. Velasco was faced with general strikes and violent demonstrations against the government. He was ousted by the military on November 9, 1961. He sought asylum in the Mexican embassy before going into exile in Argentina. He returned to Ecuador after the military junta was ousted in March 1966. Despite attempts by the opposition to prevent Velasco from again becoming president, he was victorious in the 1968 election and took office on September 1, 1968. He faced growing opposition and claimed dicta-

torial powers in mid-1970. Velasco was again ousted by a military coup on February 15, 1972, shortly before his term was scheduled to come to an end. The army's fear of the election of Asaad Bucaram as Velasco's successor prompted the ouster of the government. Velasco again went to Argentina, where he remained until February 1979 when he returned to Quito to bury his wife after she had been killed in an automobile accident. Velasco's health deteriorated, and he was hospitalized with a heart ailment. He died of a heart attack in Quito on March 30, 1979.

ANTONIO PONS (President; August 21, 1935–September 26, 1935). Antonio Pons was born on November 10, 1897. He earned a degree in medicine before entering the government of José María Velasco Ibarra as minister of the interior in 1935. He became Ecuador's president on August 21, 1935, following the ouster of Velasco. Pons relinquished power to the military on September 26, 1935.

FEDERICO PÁEZ (President; September 26, 1935–October 22, 1937). Federico Páez was born in Quito on June 6, 1876. He was educated in Quito, Paris, and Brussels, and received a degree in civil engineering. He began working as a civil engineer in Quito in 1913 and was elected to the chamber of deputies from Pichincha Province in 1916. He was elected to the senate in 1932 and became minister of public works in 1935. He was chosen by the military to serve as Ecuador's interim president on September 26, 1935. Páez established Ecuador's social security system and instituted the public works inspection. He ruled as a dictator and suppressed opposition to the government. Páez resigned from power on October 22, 1937, following dissent within the army. Páez subsequently went to Costa Rica, where he worked as a professor of geophysics in the early 1940s. He died in 1974.

ALBERTO ENRÍQUEZ GALLO

(President; October 23, 1937–August 10, 1938). Alberto Enríquez Gallo was born in Tanicuchi, León Province, on July 24, 1895. He received a military education in Quito and served in the Ecuadorean army starting in 1912. He became general in 1937. Enríquez served as minister of defense in the military government in 1935. He was chosen to replace Federico Páez as interim president of Ecuador on October 23, 1937. He stepped down from office on August 10, 1938, after convening a constituent convention. He remained active in the army and politics and was an unsuccessful candidate for the presidency in 1948. He died in Quito on July 13, 1962.

MANUEL MARIA BORRERO

(President; August 10, 1938–December 2, 1938). Manuel Maria Borrero was born in Cuenca in 1883. He studied law and served as a minister in the Quito superior court. He entered politics and was elected to the chamber of deputies from Azuay Province. He subsequently served as governor of Azuay and as minister on the supreme court. He succeeded Alberto Enríquez Gallo as interim president of Ecuador on August 10, 1938 and stepped down on December 2, 1938, when Aurelio Mosquera Narvaez was chosen as president by the constituent convention.

AURELIO MOSQUERA NARVÁEZ

(President; December 2, 1938–November 15, 1939). Aurelio Mosquera Narváez was born in Quito on August 2, 1883. He was educated in Quito and received a degree in medicine from the Central University. He opened a medical practice before entering politics. He was elected to the chamber of deputies from Pichincha Province in 1914. He again was elected to the chamber in 1928 and was vice president of that body in 1930. He was elected vice president of the senate in 1935. He was elected president of Ecuador by a constituent convention and took office on December 2, 1938. He died in office on November 15, 1939.

CARLOS ARROYO DEL RÍO

(President; November 17, 1939–December 10, 1939). Carlos Alberto Arroyo del Río was born in Guayaquil on November 27, 1893. He received a degree in law and began a private practice in Guayaquil. He was elected to the municipal council in 1917 as a member of the Liberal Radical Party. He was elected to the chamber of deputies in 1922 from Guayas Province and became president of the chamber the following year. He was elected to the senate in 1924 and opposed the military junta that took power in July 1925. He was a leading opponent of President José María Velasco Ibarra in 1934. He served as president of the senate after Velasco Ibarra's ouster and succeeded to the presidency of Ecuador on November 17, 1939, following the death of President Aurelio Mosquera Narváez. He was instrumental in the abrogation of the new constitution and reinstated the constitution of 1906. He stepped down from office on December 10, 1939, to run for the presidency. He was elected president and again took office on September 1, 1940. His political opponents, including Velasco Ibarra, claimed electoral fraud and attempted to stage a coup. They were unsuccessful, and Velasco Ibarra and his leading supporters were forced into exile. Shortly after Arroyo del Río's inauguration, Ecuador was invaded by Peru. Peru seized a large portion of Oriente Province, and the government was blamed for the loss of territory. Arroyo del Río was a staunch supporter of the United States during World War II. He used wartime powers to suppress his opponents. Civil unrest ensued, and he was forced from office on May 28, 1944, and took asylum in the United States embassy. He went into exile in Colombia and, later, New York City. He returned to Ecuador in 1948 to practice law in Guayaquil. He died there on October 31, 1969.

ANDRÉS F. CÓRDOVA NIETO (President; December 11, 1939–August 10, 1940). Andrés F. Córdova Nieto was born in Canar on May 8, 1892. He was educated at the University of Azuay, where he received a degree in law in 1919. He entered politics and was elected to the chamber of deputies from Azuay Province in 1922. He served until 1925, and was elected to the senate in 1930. He was again a member of the chamber of deputies from 1934 until 1935. He succeeded to the presidency on December 11, 1939, following the resignation of Carlos Arroyo del Río. He stepped down on August 10, 1940.

JULIO E. MORENO (President; August 10, 1940–August 31, 1940). Julio E. Moreno Peñaherera was born in Quito on October 20, 1880. He studied law at the Central University in Quito. He served in the government as minister of the interior from 1926 until 1930 and was chosen as president of the senate in 1939. Moreno briefly took office as interim president of Ecuador on August 10, 1940. He stepped down on August 31, 1940, following the reelection of Carlos Arroyo del Río.

CARLOS A. ARROYO DEL RÍO (President; September 1, 1940–May 28, 1944). *See earlier entry under Heads of State.*

JOSÉ MARÍA VELASCO IBARRA (President; June 1, 1944–August 23, 1947). *See earlier entry under Heads of State.*

Egypt

Egypt is located in northeastern Africa. It was granted independence from Great Britain on March 16, 1922.

HEADS OF STATE

ABBAS II (Khedive; January 1, 1892–December 19, 1914). Abbas Hilmi Pasha was born on July 14, 1874, in Cairo. He was the eldest son of Mohammed Tewfik Pasha. He became khedive (viceroy) of Egypt on January 1, 1892. Two years after taking power as Abbas II, he was openly critical of the British in Egypt, which resulted in a strained relationship between the Egyptian and British governments. He quietly supported nationalist interests in opposing British occupation. His relationship with the nationalists had deteriorated by 1904, when they began advocating a more liberal government in Egypt. Abbas was shot and wounded in an assassination attempt by an Egyptian student while visiting Constantinople in July 1914. The British deposed him on December 19, 1914, following the Ottoman Empire's entry into World War I. His uncle, Hussein Kemal was installed as sultan. Abbas spent the remainder of his life in exile. He died in Geneva, Switzerland, on December 21, 1944.

HUSSEIN KEMAL (Sultan; December 29, 1914–October 7, 1917). Hussein Kemal was born in Cairo on December 20, 1853, a son of Khedive Ismail. He was educated in Egypt and, from 1867, Paris. He returned to Egypt to serve in various ministerial positions from 1872 through 1878. He accompanied his father into exile in Naples following Ismail's deposition in June 1879. He was soon allowed to return to Egypt where he reinvolved himself in matters of state. Hussein Kemal was named president of the legislative council and the general assembly in January 1909. He resigned from the post in March of the following year. Abbas II, the nephew of Hussein Kemal, was deposed as khedive by the British when the Protectorate was established in December 1914 after the Ottoman Empire's entry into World War I. Hussein Kemal was installed as Egypt's first sultan on December 29, 1914. He survived two assassination attempts by nationalists in 1915. His reign was largely dominated by the British, though he gave support to reforms in education and the promotion of agriculture. Hussein Kemal suffered from poor health during the latter part of his reign and died on October 17, 1917.

FUAD I (Sultan; October 17, 1917–March 16, 1922; King, March 16, 1922–April 28, 1936). Fuad was born in Giza Palace in Cairo on March 26, 1868, the youngest son of Khedive Ismail. He spent much of his youth in Italy after his father was deposed in 1879. Ismail died in 1895, and Fuad returned to Egypt several years later to serve in the court of Khedive Abbas II as aide-de-camp. Abbas was deposed by the British in 1914, and Fuad's older brother, Hussein Kemal, was installed as Egypt's first sultan. Fuad succeeded to the throne upon the sultan's death on October 17, 1917, after Hussein Kemal's son, Prince Kemal al-Din, rejected the rights of succession. Fuad married the Princess Nazli in May 1919, and his son and heir, Farouk, was born the following February. Fuad became Egypt's first king following Britain's acknowledgement of Egyptian independence on March 16, 1922. During his reign he often came into conflict with the aims of the Wafds, the dominant political party in Egypt. The King's opposition to a constitutional government also brought him into conflict with the British. He abrogated the constitution of 1923 in October 1930, ruling for the next four years with a parliament that had diminished powers. Fuad's failing health led to the restoration of the earlier constitution in November 1934. During most of his reign Fuad maintained an active interest in charitable pursuits, and he was a leading force in the advancement of Egypt's educational facilities. Fuad died in Cairo of a heart attack on April 28, 1936.

FAROUK (King; April 28, 1936–July 26, 1952). Farouk was born in Cairo on February 11, 1920. He was the son of Fuad I and Queen Nazli. His father was sultan of Egypt at the time of Farouk's birth. Fuad became king following Egypt's independence from Great Britain on March 16, 1922. Farouk was raised by an English governess. He was educated by tutors before attending Kenry House and the Royal Military Academy in England. Farouk returned to Egypt following the death of his father on April 28, 1936. He ruled under a regency until he reached his majority on July 29, 1937. Soon after his coronation, he engaged in a bitter dispute with the Wafd Party under Mustafa el-Nahas. He encouraged the formation of anti-Wafd parties. Egypt attempted to remain neutral during World War II, though Great Britain was allowed to maintain military bases in the country. Farouk appointed Hussein Sirry as prime minister in November 1940, and the British viewed the government with suspicion. British troops invaded Farouk's palace in February 1942 and demanded that he appoint a Wafdist government more favorable to the British war effort. Farouk dismissed the Wafd government in October 1944 when the British no longer intervened in Egyptian politics. He was instrumental in the decision to involve the Egyptian army in the war in Palestine in May 1948. Egypt's defeat in that action contributed to Farouk's unpopularity with the army. His regime was also viewed as corrupt, and the King's self-indulgent playboy lifestyle did little to endear him to the Egyptian people. Farouk was forced to abdicate in favor of his infant son, Ahmed Fuad, on July 22, 1952, following a military coup led by General Mohammed Naguib and Colonel Gamal Ab-del Nasser. Farouk went into exile in Italy, where the corpulent ex-King became well known for his frequent visits to night clubs and gambling houses. Farouk suffered a massive heart attack while dining at a restaurant near Rome. He died in a Rome hospital at the age of 45 on March 18, 1965.

HEADS OF GOVERNMENT

MUSTAFA FAHMI (Prime Minister; November 1895–1908). Mustafa Fahmi Pasha first came to prominence in Egyptian politics as foreign minister in the early 1880s. He served as a negotiator between the ruling Turco-Circassians and the nationalist interests during the Arabi Revolt of 1882. He succeeded Riyad Pasha as prime minister in 1891, but was distrusted by the new khedive, Abbas II, who came to power the following year. Fahmi had the support of the British high commissioner, Lord Cromer, who preempted Abbas' attempts to replace Fahmi with Tigane Pasha and Husayn Fakhri in 1893 during the prime minister's period of illness. Fahmi stepped aside when his predecessor, Riyad, was named to head the government. Riyad was in turn succeeded by Nubar, both of whom came into conflict with Abbas and Lord Cromer. The high commission forced Fahmi's reappointment in November 1895. He retained the position for the next thirteen years to the displeasure of Abbas, who viewed Fahmi as a tool of the British. Lord Cromer was replaced as High Commissioner by Sir Eldon Gorst in 1907, and Abbas succeeded in replacing Fahmi with Butrus Ghali Pasha as prime minister the following year. Fahmi exercised little political power over the next several years, though he was still viewed with favor by the British. He was again asked to head a government in 1914, but died before he could resume power.

BUTRUS GHALI (Prime Minister; 1908–February 10, 1910). Butrus Ghali Pasha was born in 1846. He was an influential leader in the Coptic Church and was instrumental in attempts to modernize the church in the late 1800s. He began his career in government service during the reign of Khedive Tewfik, serving as minister of justice, finance, and foreign affairs in various governments. Butrus served as foreign minister in the government of Mustafa Fahmi, and was involved in negotiations with the British over the Sudan. He succeeded Fahmi as prime minister in 1908 with the support of the British. He earned the enmity of the nationalists because of his conciliatory attitude toward the British, typified by his willingness to begin negotiations to extend the lease for the Suez Canal. Butrus was assassinated by Ibrahim Warddani, a young Moslem nationalist, on the steps of the ministry of justice on February 10, 1910. His death caused a long-standing rift between the Muslims and Copts in the nationalist movement.

MUHAMMAD SA'ID (Prime Minister; February 1910–May 1914). Muhammad Sa'id Pasha was appointed minister of the interior in the cabinet of Butrus Ghali in 1908. He succeeded to the office of prime minister when Butrus was assassinated in 1910. Like his predecessor, Sa'id was distrusted by the nationalists, whose continual attacks forced his resignation in May 1914. Sa'id remained active in Egyptian politics as an opponent of nationalist leader Said Zaghlul. Sa'id also served as the Wafd party's liaison with the khedive. He was again called upon to form a government in May 1919, succeeding Husayn Rushdi. He survived an assassination attempt the following September. Sa'id resigned from office two months later. He remained active in Egyptian politics, serving in Zaghlul's cabinet in 1924 before breaking with the Wafd party the following year. Sa'id died on July 20, 1928.

HUSAYN RUSHDI (Prime Minister; May 1914–May 21, 1919). Husayn Rushdi was born in 1864. He entered Butrus Ghali's cabinet as minister of justice in 1908 and remained in Muhammad Sa'id's government as foreign minister from 1910 until 1912. Rushdi briefly served as regent after the deposition of Khedive Abbas II, and was called upon to form a government as prime minister in May 1914, after Sa'id was forced to resign. Rushdi's government was under the near total control of the British during World War I. The unpopular policies of the wartime government, which included conscription of animals and men and the imposition of martial law, led to an assassination attempt against Rushdi in 1915. Rushdi supported Zaghlul and the nationalist's demands to end the British protectorate after the war in 1918. The initial delegation, which was to be headed by Rushdi, was rejected by the British. Rushdi's government resigned in January 1919, but the palace refused to accept the resignation until the following March, when nationalist elements carried out massive demonstrations in support of the recently deported Zaghlul. Allenby, the British high commissioner, asked Rushdi to form a new government in April 1919 during the rebellion. He was unable to restore order and again stepped down two weeks later. He remained active in Egyptian politics, serving in Adli Yegen's cabinet in 1921 and as chairman of the Constitutional Committee in 1922. He was named to the new Egyptian parliament by King Fuad in 1924, a position he held until his death on March 13, 1928.

MUHAMMAD SA'ID (Prime Minister; May 21, 1919–November 17, 1919). *See earlier entry under Heads of Government.*

YUSOF WAHBA PASHA (Prime Minister; November 23, 1919–May 19, 1920). Yusof Wahba Pasha served in Muhammad Sa'id's government as minister of foreign affairs from 1912 until 1914. He was again named to the cabinet as minister of finance in May 1919 during Sa'id's second government. He replaced Sa'id as prime minister on November 23, 1919. The Milner Mission arrived in Egypt shortly after Wahba took office. The mission was to conduct an inquiry into Egypt's recent civil unrest and was boycotted by members of the Wafd Party and other nationalists. Shortly after taking office, Wahba narrowly escaped an assassination attempt by nationalists, who were opposed to the mission. Wahba stepped down on May 19, 1920, for reasons of health. He died several years later in 1924.

MOHAMMED TAWFIQ NESSIM (Prime Minister; May 21, 1920– March 15, 1921). Mohammed Tawfiq Nessim was born in 1875. He served as public prosecutor in the late 1910s before being called upon to form a government as prime minister in May 1920. Nessim survived an assassination attempt the following month by militant nationalists who opposed his close relationship with the palace and the moderates. He resigned his office in March 1921, relinquishing the government to Adli Yegen. He was named chief of the royal cabinet by King Fuad in April 1922. Nessim again formed a government on November 20, 1922, but resigned on February 9, 1923, in protest against Britain's refusal to acknowledge King Fuad's claim on the Sudan. Nessim was minister of finance in Said Zaghlul's cabinet in 1924 and returned to the royal cabinet after the collapse of Zaghlul's government at the end of the year. He was subsequently instrumental in the formation of the pro–Fuad Ittihad Party. He returned to office of prime minister of November 15, 1934, following the abrogation of the 1923 constitution. The Wafd Party began a vigorous campaign for the restoration of the constitution that forced the government to negotiate with the Wafd and other opposition parties. Anti-British riots in Cairo precipitated a restoration of the 1923 constitution by Nessim in December 1935. He resigned on January 22, 1936 to allow the formation of a caretaker government under Ali Maher in preparation for new elections. Nessim died two years later on March 6, 1938.

ADLI YEGEN (Prime Minister; March 15, 1921–December 10, 1921). Adli Yegen was born in 1865. He was active in Egyptian politics in the early 1900s. He was named vice president of the 1914 legislative assembly, where he came into conflict with Said Zaghlul, the second vice president. Adli became a leader of moderate nationalist interests in Egypt that opposed Zaghlul's more militant views. Adli served as minister of education in Rushdi's cabinet in 1918. He was called upon to form a government as prime minister in March 1921, and he again came into conflict with Zaghlul, who had recently returned from exile. Adli was supported by the newly formed moderate organization, the Society of Independent Egypt. Adli headed negotiations with the British to gain Egypt's independence. The talks broke down in the summer of 1921. Zaghlul's nationalists continued to attack the government, forcing Adli's resignation on December 10, 1921. He formed the Liberal Constitutional Party the following year in support of Abdul Khaliq Sarwat's government. Adli was named to the Egyptian Parliament as a senator in 1923, and was again called upon to form a government on June 7, 1926, despite a massive victory by Zaghlul and the Wafd Party. Adli's conflict with the Wafd-dominated legislature forced his resigna-

tion on April 18, 1927, despite continued support by the British. He backed the subsequent government of Sarwat and was again called upon to head a caretaker government in October 1929, following the resignation of Mohammed Mahmud. He retained office until December 30, 1929, when Mustafa el-Nahas took office following a victory in elections by the Wafd Party. Adli remained active in politics and opposed the government of Ismail Sidky in the early 1930s. He was attempting to form a coalition government when he died in Paris on October 22, 1933.

ABDUL   KHALIQ   SARWAT (Prime Minister; December 11, 1921–November 29, 1922). Abdul Khaliq Sarwat was born in 1873. He served in Butrus Ghali's government as procurator-general from 1908 until Butrus' assassination in 1910, when he served as prosecutor of the assassins. Sarwat was called upon to form a government following the collapse of Adli's government in December 1921. He was unable to do this until after the termination of Egypt's protectorate status under Britain in March 1922. Sarwat's support for provisions of the constitution that would make the king a constitutional monarch brought him into disfavor with King Fuad, who forced his resignation on November 29, 1922. Sarwat again headed a government on April 23, 1927, following the resignation of Adli Yegen's government. The Wafd Party's opposition to a treaty Sarwat negotiated with the British Foreign Office, coupled with King Fuad's objection to the Egyptian army remaining under British rule forced the rejection of the treaty and Sarwat's resignation on March 4, 1928. He died on September 22, 1928.

MOHAMMED TAWFIQ NESSIM (Prime Minister; November 20, 1922–February 9, 1923). *See earlier entry under Heads of Government.*

YEHIA IBRAHIM PASHA (Prime Minister; March 15, 1923–January 17, 1924). Yehia Ibrahim studied law in Egypt and served on the Cairo court of appeals, becoming its president in 1907. He served in Wahab Pasha's government as minister of justice in 1919. He was named to replace Mohammed Nessim as prime minister on March 15, 1923. Under his government martial law ended, and a new Egyptian constitution was enacted. He stepped down from office on January 17, 1924, to allow Said Zaghlul, who had recently returned from exile, to form a government. Yehia Ibrahim subsequently became president of the Ittihad Party. He later became involved in the movement to restore constitutional government during the mid-1930s. Yehia Ibrahim died in March 1936.

SAID ZAGHLUL (Prime Minister; January 28, 1924–November 24, 1924). Said Zaghlul was born in 1852 to a peasant family in the Al Gharbiyah province of Egypt. He attended the Muslim University of Al Azhar in Cairo, where he studied law. He entered government service in the interior ministry. Zaghlul was detained in 1882 after the British occupation of Egypt. He subsequently began a legal practice and joined the native court of appeals as a judge in 1893. He also became associated with the nationalist movement during the 1890s. Zaghlul entered Mustafa Fahmi's government as minister of education in 1906. He remained in that position in the subsequent government of Butrus Ghali. He was appointed minister of justice after the assassination of Butrus in 1910. He resigned three years later to become vice president of the legislative assembly. He was a leader in the movement for Egyptian independence after World War I. The British government refused to allow Zaghlul to serve on the Egyptian delegation to the Versaille Peace Conference. Britain's refusal to end the Protectorate led to the formation of the Wafd Party,

with Zaghlul as its leading spokesman. The British deported Zaghlul in March 1919. He returned from exile in Malta the following month. He spent the next two years in Paris, but he retained the leadership of the Wafd Party while abroad. He returned to Egypt in April 1921 and opposed the moderate nationalist government of Adli Yegen. His support for civil disorder against the government resulted in Zaghlul again being deported. He was sent to Aden in December 1921. He was subsequently transferred to the Seychelles and Gibraltar before being released in April 1923. He returned to Egypt later that year to participate in the first elections under the new constitution. The Wafd Party was the overwhelming victor in the elections. Zaghlul formed a government as prime minister on January 28, 1924. He again came into conflict with the British over the disposition of the Sudan. He went to London in September 1924 to negotiate the issue, but had no success. The assassination of Sir Lee Stack, the British governor-general of the Sudan, in November 1924 led to further British demands on the Egyptian government. Zaghlul refused to accept the British position and resigned on November 24, 1924. The Wafd Party dominated elections held in March 1925 and May 1926. Zaghlul remained the party's leader and president of the legislature, though the British refused to allow him to form a government. He led the opposition to the governments of Adli and Sarwat until his death in Cairo on August 23, 1927.

AHMED ZIWAR (Prime Minister; November 24, 1924–June 6, 1926). Ahmed Ziwar was born in 1864. He entered government as minister of education in Rushdi's cabinet in 1919. He served as minister of communications in the subsequent governments of Wahba and Nessim. He remained minister of communications under Adli from 1921 until January 1924. He subsequently served as president of the senate. He was called upon to succeed Said Zaghlul as prime minister on November 24, 1924, following the assassination of Sir Lee Stack. His government was primarily concerned with appeasing the British, who had made numerous demands following Stack's murder. Ismail Sidky, Ziwar's powerful interior minister, largely controlled the government. The Wafd Party was successful in elections in May 1926 and Ziwar stepped down to allow the more moderate Adli to form a government on June 7, 1926. Ziwar later served as chief of the royal cabinet from 1934 until his resignation from the government in November of that year. He died on August 21, 1945.

ADLI YEGEN (Prime Minister; June 7, 1926–April 18, 1927). *See earlier entry under Heads of Government.*

ABDUL KHALIQ SARWAT (Prime Minister; April 23, 1927–March 4, 1928). *See earlier entry under Heads of Government.*

MUSTAFA EL-NAHAS (Prime Minister; March 16, 1928–June 25, 1928). Mustafa el-Nahas was born in Cairo on June 15, 1876. He attended the Cairo School of Law and graduated in 1900. He became a judge in 1914 but was dismissed from government service in 1919 for his political activities. He was deported to Malta in 1921, and released from exile in 1923, following Egyptian independence. He was elected to the national assembly in 1924 and served as minister of communications in the subsequent cabinet of Said Zaghlul. He was elected vice president of the chamber of deputies in 1927 and succeeded Zaghlul as leader of the Wafd Party later in the year. He led opposition to the Anglo-Egyptian treaty of 1928 and demanded that British troops leave Egypt. He was named prime minister on March 16, 1928, but was forced by the palace to resign on June 25, 1928. New elections

were held in 1929 and the Wafdists were victorious. Nahas returned as prime minister on January 1, 1930. He stepped down on June 20, 1930, when negotiations with the British concerning the status of the Sudan collapsed. He was again named prime minister on May 10, 1936, and negotiated the Anglo-Egyptian Treaty of Alliance in 1936. He also presided over Egypt's entry into the League of Nations. Friction developed between the prime minister and King Farouk, and Nahas was dismissed on December 30, 1937. The Wafd Party was badly defeated in the elections of 1938. Nahas claimed electoral fraud and refused to serve in subsequent governments. Nahas was again named prime minister on February 8, 1942, when the British pressured King Farouk for his appointment. Nahas cooperated with the British during World War II and laid the foundation for the formation of the Arab League in October 1944. Nahas was again dismissed by King Farouk on October 8, 1944. The Wafd Party boycotted the elections in January 1945 and went into opposition. Nahas demanded the withdrawal of all British troops from Egypt. He was the target of an unsuccessful assassination attempt in April 1946. Nahas and the Wafds refused to participate in negotiations with Great Britain the following month. The Wafds returned to power in the 1950 elections, and Nahas again became prime minister on January 12, 1950. He proposed social reforms, including the establishment of a social security system. He also abrogated the Anglo-Egyptian treaty of 1936, which caused tense relations with Great Britain in 1951. Rioting broke out in Cairo in 1952, and King Farouk dismissed Nahas on January 27, 1952 for his failure to maintain security. Nahas was placed under house arrest following the coup that deposed Farouk in July 1952. He was deprived of his political rights in 1954. His rights were restored in 1960, but he continued to live in obscurity in Alexandria. Nahas died in Cairo after a long illness at the age of eighty-six on August 23, 1965.

MOHAMMED MAHMUD (Prime Minister; June 27, 1928–October 2, 1929). Mohammed Mahmud was born in 1884. He was an early supporter of Said Zaghlul and was deported with him to Malta in 1919. Mahmud broke with Zaghlul the following year and became vice president of the moderate nationalist Liberal Constitutional Party. He was named to Adli's government as minister of communications in June 1926. He was appointed minister of finance in Sarwat's subsequent government in April 1927. He was again named finance minister in Nahas's Wafd government in March 1928. Mahmud was called upon to form a government as prime minister on June 27, 1928, when Nahas was dismissed. He entered into negotiations with the British to reach a settlement on disputes between the two countries. The British government felt that the Wafd Party was the only group that held enough popular support to ratify an agreement, and Mahmud stepped down on October 2, 1929, to make way for a Wafd-dominated government following new elections. Mahmud remained active in Egyptian politics as president of the Liberal Constitutionalist Party, allying himself with the Wafds to oppose Ismail Sidky's government from 1930 until 1933. Mahmud was again called upon to form a government on December 30, 1937, after the dismissal of Nahas's Wafd government. Mahmud was criticized for agreeing to head a government without calling an election, and he governed against opposition from the Wafdists and even members of his own party. Mahmud was forced to resign on August 18, 1939, when Ali Maher formed a government. Mahmud died on February 2, 1941.

ADLI YEGEN PASHA (Prime Minister; October 3, 1929–December 30, 1929). *See earlier entry under Heads of Government.*

MUSTAFA EL-NAHAS (Prime Minister; January 1, 1930–June 20, 1930). *See earlier entry under Heads of Government.*

ISMAIL SIDKY (Prime Minister; June 20, 1930–March 21, 1933). Ismail Sidky was born in 1875. He was educated in Cairo and attended the Cairo Law School. He served on the Municipal Council of Alexandria in 1899. He later worked in the ministry of the interior before being named minister of Muslim religious institutions. He was a leader in the Egyptian nationalist movement and was a founder of the Wafd Party. He was deported to Malta by the British in 1917 after anti-British riots. He returned to Egypt to establish the Liberal Constitution Party in 1922. He served as deputy minister of the interior from 1924 until 1926. Sidky became prime minister on June 20, 1930. He survived several assassination attempts over the next year. He implemented a conservative constitution to provide for greater power for the monarchy and instituted harsh measures against dissidents to the government. He resigned as prime minister on March 21, 1933. He subsequently served as the Egyptian delegate to meetings that resulted in the Anglo-Egyptian Alliance. He served as minister of finance from 1937 until 1939, when he retired from politics. He was recalled to again serve as prime minister on February 15, 1946, following the resignation of Mahmoud Fahmy el-Nokrashy after student riots in Cairo. Sidky settled the disturbances by demanding the removal of the British military from Egypt and using dictatorial methods to crush demonstrations. Sidky went to London to negotiate an agreement with the British over the Sudan. Conflicting interpretations of what the agreement stated forced Sidky to resign as prime minister on December 8, 1946. Sidky remained in the senate, where he opposed Egypt's invasion of Palestine in 1948. He died of a stroke in a Paris hospital on July 9, 1950.

ABDUL-FATTAH YEHYA PASHA
(Prime Minister; March 24, 1933–November 6, 1934). Abdul-Fattah Yehya Pasha was born in 1876, the son of Abdul Yehya Pasha. Yehya received legal training and served as minister of justice in Adli Yegen's government in 1929. He served as minister of foreign affairs in Ismail Sidky's government from 1930 until 1933. He was vice president of the Sha'b Party and was called upon to form a government as prime minister on March 24, 1933, following Sidky's resignation. His government was dominated by King Fuad and the royal palace until the king fell ill in late 1934. Yehya was forced to step down on November 6, 1934. He returned to the government in 1938 to serve for two years as minister of foreign affairs in Mohammed Mahmud's government. He subsequently retired from politics to serve in the upper chamber. Yehya died in Alexandria on September 27, 1951.

MOHAMMED TAWFIQ NESSIM
(Prime Minister; November 15, 1934–January 22, 1936). *See earlier entry under Heads of Government.*

ALI MAHER
(Prime Minister; January 30, 1936–May 10, 1936). Ali Maher was born in Cairo in 1883. He received a degree in law from the Khedive School of Law and became a judge in 1907. He served on the Egyptian delegation to London that negotiated the independence of Egypt in 1922. He was elected to the Egyptian parliament in 1924 and served as undersecretary of state for education. He was named minister of education in 1925 and served in this post until the following year. He returned to the cabinet as minister of finance in 1928. Maher was elected to the senate in 1930 and was named minister of justice, a position he retained until 1932. Maher was appointed chief of the royal cabinet in 1935 during the illness of King Fuad. He was also named prime minister, minister of the interior, and minister of for-

eign affairs on January 30, 1936. He stepped down on May 10, 1936, after elections were held. He was again named chief of the royal cabinet after King Farouk, who had succeeded his father to the throne in April 1936, came of age in July 1937. Maher represented Egypt in London at the Palestine Conference in 1939. He also returned to the senate in 1939 and formed a cabinet as prime minister after the resignation of Mohammed Tawfiq Nessim on August 18, 1939. He served as military governor of Egypt after the start of World War II. He tried to maintain his country's neutrality during the war, despite Italy's declaration of war against Egypt. He sought a diplomatic solution to the conflict with Italy but was forced to resign on June 22, 1940. Maher was placed under house arrest during the administration of Mustafa el-Nahas because the British believed that Maher had turned over Egyptian defense plans to the Italians. He was released when his brother, Ahmed Maher, became prime minister in October 1944. His brother was assassinated in February of the following year. Ali Maher opposed the Anglo-Egyptian treaty drafted in 1946. He remained out of the government until January 27, 1952, when he was again called upon to form a cabinet following anti-British riots in Cairo. Maher also became military governor, foreign minister, and minister of the army and navy. He ruled under martial law and demanded that British military forces withdraw from the Suez Canal. He also supported Egypt's claim for a union with the Sudan. He was replaced on March 1, 1952, but Maher was again appointed prime minister on July 24, 1952, following the coup that ousted King Farouk. Maher's opposition to the ruling junta's agrarian reform program and revolutionary policies led to his resignation on September 7, 1952. Maher died of a heart attack at the age of 77 August 23, 1960, while vacationing in Geneva.

MUSTAFA EL-NAHAS (Prime Minister; May 10, 1936–December 30, 1937). *See earlier entry under Heads of Government.*

MOHAMMED MAHMUD (Prime Minister; December 30, 1937–August 18, 1939). *See earlier entry under Heads of Government.*

ALI MAHER (Prime Minister; August 18, 1939–June 22, 1940). *See earlier entry under Heads of Government.*

HASSAN SABRY (Prime Minister; June 28, 1940–November 14, 1940). Hassan Sabry was born in 1879. He was active in Egyptian politics, joining Abdul-Fattah Yehya's government as minister of finance in 1933. He also served in Mohammed Mahmud's government as minister of war from January 1938 until his resignation the following year. Sabry formed a government on June 28, 1940, following the resignation of Ali Maher. He served as prime minister and foreign minister for several months until his death on November 14, 1940.

HUSSEIN SIRRY (Prime Minister; November 14, 1940–February 8, 1942). Hussein Sirry was born in Cairo in 1892. He was educated in Egypt and France, and received a degree in engineering. He was considered a leading authority on irrigation and an expert on the flow of the Nile River because he had traveled to its source in the 1920s. He was also responsible for planning the transformation of the Qattara depression near Cairo into a lake. Sirry entered the Egyptian cabinet as minister of public works in 1938. He was elected to the senate in 1939 and served as minister of war. He was named minister of finance and communications later in the year and served until 1940. He was appointed prime minister on November 14, 1940, and attempted to maintain Egypt's neutrality during World War II. He was dismissed on February 8, 1942, when the British military

forced King Farouk to name a prime minister from the Wafd Party. Sirry was named to head a caretaker coalition cabinet on July 26, 1949. He stepped down on January 12, 1950. He also served as foreign minister in 1950. He was again named prime minister on July 2, 1952. He resigned on July 20, 1952, several days before a military coup ousted King Farouk. Sirry subsequently retired from politics. He died in Cairo on January 6, 1961.

MUSTAFA EL-NAHAS (Prime Minister; February 8, 1942–October 8, 1944). *See earlier entry under Heads of Government.*

AHMED MAHER (Prime Minister; October 9, 1944–February 24, 1945). Ahmed Maher was born in 1886. He was a leading Egyptian scholar, holding doctorates in law and economics. He was an early leader of the Nationalist Party, a supporter of Said Zaghlul, and was involved in the formation of the Wafd Party after World War I. Maher served as minister of education in Zaghlul's first Wafd government in 1924. He was accused of complicity in the assassination of Sir Lee Stack, the British governor-general of the Sudan, and was removed from the government. Though acquitted, the British still viewed Maher with suspicion and vetoed his role in national politics. He resumed an active role in the Wafd leadership in 1927 and served as the secretary of the party's parliamentary group. He became a close ally of Mahmoud Fahmy el-Nokrashy and left the Wafd Party with him in January 1938 following a conflict with Wafd leader Mustafa el-Nahas. He and Nokrashy formed the Sa'adist Party and joined the government of Maher's brother, Ali Maher, in 1939. Ahmed Maher was a supporter of Egypt joining the Allies in World War II and resigned from the government with other members of his party in September 1940. Maher formed a government to replace Nahas in October 1944, and retained office following elections in January 1945 that were boycotted by the Wafds. Maher announced his government's intentions to enter World War II against Germany in February 1945. He was assassinated in the Egyptian Parliament in Cairo the following day on February 24, 1945, by Mahmoud Essawy, a Fascist sympathizer.

MAHMOUD FAHMY EL-NOKRASHY (Prime Minister; March 7, 1945–February 16, 1946). Mahmoud Fahmy el-Nokrashy was born in Alexandria in 1882. A former teacher, he joined the Egyptian government in 1920 and served in various posts during the 1920s and 1930s. He was Egyptian minister of the interior, education, and finance from 1938 to 1940. He served as foreign minister from 1944 until 1945, when he was elected president of the Sa'adist Party and became prime minister of Egypt on February 25, 1945, following the assassination of Ahmed Maher. He resigned on February 15, 1946, following riots in Cairo and Alexandria, but was again appointed prime minister on December 9, 1946. Nokrashy was named Egypt's military governor following Egypt's invasion of Palestine on May 14, 1948. He was a supporter of Egypt's policy advocating the elimination of the state of Israel and was a proponent of the withdrawal of English forces from the Anglo-Egyptian Sudan. Nokrashy outlawed the Muslim Brotherhood in 1948 after that organization had been involved in violent confrontations with the government. Nokrashy was shot to death in the ministry of the interior in Cairo by a member of the Muslim Brotherhood on December 28, 1948.

El Salvador

El Salvador is a country on the Pacific coast of Central America. It was granted independence from Spain on September 15, 1821.

HEADS OF STATE

TOMÁS REGOLADO (President; November 13, 1898–February 28, 1903). Tomás Regolado was born in 1864. He served in the Salvadoran army and participated in the revolt that ousted President Carlos Ezeta in June 1895. He led a military coup against the subsequent government of Rafael Antonio Gutiérrez on November 13, 1898, and assumed the presidency. Regolado granted an amnesty for all political prisoners during his term of office. He also succeeded in paying off all of El Salvador's foreign debts. Regolado relinquished office to Pedro José Escalón on February 28, 1903. He continued to serve in the military and led Salvadoran troops into battle with Guate-

mala in 1906. He was killed during the fighting at El Jícaro on July 11, 1906.

PEDRO JOSÉ ESCALÓN (President; February 28, 1903–February 28, 1907). Pedro José Escalón was born in 1847. He succeeded to the presidency on February 28, 1903. El Salvador supported Guatemalan rebels in their attempt to oust the government of Manuel Estrada Cabrera in June 1906. This led to a brief but bloody war with Guatemala. The conflict ended when the United States convinced the two nations to sign an armistice on July 20, 1906. Escalón left office on February 28, 1907. He died on September 6, 1923.

FERNANDO FIGUEROA (President; February 28, 1907–February 28, 1911). Fernando Figueroa was born in 1849. He served in the Salvadoran army and eventually became a general. He briefly served as acting president of El Salvador from May 15, 1885, until June 18, 1885. Figueroa served as commander-in-chief of the Salvadoran army. He again became head of the Salvadoran government on February 28, 1907. A revolt led by Prudencio Alfaro resulted in a state of siege that lasted throughout Figueroa's term of office. He stepped down on February 28, 1911. Figueroa died on June 18, 1919.

MANUEL ENRIQUE ARAUJO (President; February 28, 1911–February 8, 1913). Manuel Enrique Araujo was trained as a physician. He entered politics and served in the national assembly. He also served as mayor of San Salvador. He became president of El Salvador on February 28, 1911. During his term of office he established the national guard and reorganized the army. He also encouraged industrial development in the country. Araujo was stabbed by an assassin on February 4, 1913, and died four days later on February 8, 1913.

CARLOS MELÉNDEZ (President; February 8, 1913–August 28, 1914). Carlos Meléndez was born in San Salvador on February 1, 1861. He was installed as president of El Salvador on February 8, 1913, following the assassination of Manuel Enrique Araujo and the resignation of his vice president, Onofre Duran. He challenged Nicaragua's right to grant a naval base to the United States in the Gulf of Fonseca. The Central American Court of Justice ruled in favor of El Salvador, but the United States and Nicaragua ignored the decision. He stepped down in favor of his brother-in-law, Alfonso Quiñónez y Molina, on August 28, 1914, to become a candidate in the presidential election. He was victorious and resumed office on February 28,

1915. Meléndez maintained El Salvador's neutrality during World War I. He remained in office until December 21, 1918, when he stepped down for reasons of health after arranging the succession of his younger brother Jorge Meléndez. Carlos Meléndez died of cancer in a New York City clinic on October 9, 1919.

ALFONSO QUIÑÓNEZ Y MOLINA (President; August 18, 1914–February 28, 1915). Alfonso Quiñónez y Molina was born in 1873. He received a medical degree from the University of San Salvador in 1897, and later served as a faculty member there. He entered politics and served as mayor of San Salvador. He served in Manuel Enrique Araujo's cabinet as minister of war from 1911 until 1913. Quiñónez became acting president on August 18, 1914, when his brother-in-law, Carlos Meléndez, stepped down to run for reelection. He relinquished the presidency back to Meléndez on February 28, 1915, and became Meléndez's vice president. Quiñónez again became acting president when Meléndez stepped down on December 21, 1918. Quiñónez was succeeded by the younger Meléndez brother, Jorge, on February 28, 1919. Quiñónez was elected president in his own right and succeeded Jorge Meléndez on February 28, 1923. With the help of foreign loans, he initiated several public works programs, including the paving of San Salvador's streets. He completed his term of office on February 28, 1927. Quiñónez was subsequently sent into exile in Paris. He was allowed to return to El Salvador in 1935. Quiñónez died in San Salvador on May 22, 1950, after a long illness.

CARLOS MELÉNDEZ (President; February 28, 1915–December 21, 1918). *See earlier entry under Heads of State.*

ALFONSO QUIÑÓNEZ Y MOLINA (President; December 21, 1918–February 28, 1919). *See earlier entry under Heads of State.*

JORGE MELÉNDEZ (President; February 28, 1919–February 28, 1923). Jorge Meléndez was born on April 15, 1871. He was the brother of the former president, Carlos Meléndez. He was a noted agonomist and agriculturist. He was sworn in as president on February 28, 1919. On January 19, 1921, he signed the Pact of San José with Guatemala that established the Central American Federation. Guatemala withdrew from the union on January 14, 1922, and the federation dissolved on February 4, 1922. Meléndez retained office until February 28, 1923. After a long illness, he died on November 22, 1953.

ALFONSO QUIÑÓNEZ Y MOLINA (President; February 28, 1923–February 28, 1927). *See earlier entry under Heads of State.*

PIO ROMERO BOSQUE (President; February 28, 1927–February 28, 1931). Pio Romero Bosque served as chief justice of the El Salvadoran Supreme Court. He was minister of war in Alfonso Quiñónez y Molina's cabinet from 1923 until 1927. He was elected to succeed Quiñónez to the presidency and took office on February 28, 1927. He completed his term of office and stepped down on February 28, 1931. Romero Bosque died in Managua, Nicaragua, on December 10, 1934.

ARTURO ARAUJO (President; February 28, 1931–December 2, 1931). Arturo Araujo was born in 1878. He was educated in England as an engineer. Upon his return to El Salvador he became involved in the labor movement. He was defeated for the presidency in 1919 and made an unsuccessful attempt to invade El Salvador from Honduras in 1922. Araujo was the Labor Party's nominee for the presidency in 1930 and was elected on a platform of agrarian reform and government assistance to the needy. He took office on February 28, 1931. The economic depression continued to plague El Salvador, and he was ousted in a military coup and replaced by his vice president, General Maximiliano Hernández Martínez, on December 2, 1931. Araujo died on December 1, 1967.

MAXIMILIANO HERNÁNDEZ MARTÍNEZ (President; December 4, 1931–August 29, 1934). Maximiliano Hernández Martínez was born San Salvador in 1882. He was educated at the Guatemalan military academy and entered the Salvadoran army in 1899. He rose through the ranks and became a brigadier general in 1919. Hernández Martínez entered politics and was elected vice president under Arturo Araujo in January 1931. He also served as minister of war in Araujo's government. A military coup ousted Araujo, and Hernández Martínez became provisional president on December 4, 1931. His government was challenged by a leftist peasant rebellion in January 1932 and Hernández Martínez used brutal methods to suppress the revolt. The United Nations initially refused to grant recognition to his regime but finally did so in January 1934. Hernández Martínez stepped down on August 29, 1934, to run in the presidential election. He was victorious and resumed office on February 28, 1935. He ruled El Salvador as a virtual dictator for nearly a decade. He initiated public works programs and eliminated much of the corruption in the government. He extended his term of office by a constitutional amendment in 1939. Another attempt to extend his term in 1944 was met with by a general strike, which forced Hernández Martínez's resignation on May 9, 1944. He went into exile in Honduras, where he remained for the rest of his life. Hernández Martínez was stabbed to death by his chauffeur in an apparent robbery on May 17, 1966, at his farm in eastern Honduras.

ANDRES IGNACIO MENÉNDEZ (President; August 29, 1934–February 28, 1935). Andres Ignacio Menéndez was born in 1879. He became acting president on August 29, 1934, when Maximiliano Hernández Martínez stepped down to be a candidate in the presidential election. Menéndez relinquished office to Hernández on February 28, 1935, following his election. He served in Hernández Martínez's government as minister of war. He again became acting president on May 9, 1944, following Hernández Martínez's resignation. Menéndez was ousted in a coup led by Osmin Aguirre y Salinas on October 21, 1944.

MAXIMILIANO HERNÁNDEZ MARTÍNEZ (President; February 28, 1935–May 9, 1944). *See earlier entry under Heads of State.*

ANDRES IGNACIO MENÉNDEZ (President; May 9, 1944–October 21, 1944). *See earlier entry under Heads of State.*

OSMÍN AGUIRRE Y SALINAS (President; October 21, 1944–February 28, 1945). Osmín Aguirre y Salinas was born in 1889. He became a colonel in the Salvadoran military. Aguirre was a leader of the coup that forced the resignation of Salvadoran leader Maximiliano Hernández Martínez in May 1944. Aguirre led another coup against Hernández's vice president and successor, Andres Ignacio

Menéndez, on October 21, 1944. Aguirre served as president of the subsequent military regime. He presided over new elections and relinquished office to the victor, Salvador Castañeda Castro, on February 28, 1945. After an unsuccessful coup against his successor the following year, Aguirre retired from politics. He was shot to death near his home in San Salvador at the age of 88 on July 12, 1977. His assassins were presumed to be members of a leftist terrorist organization.

SALVADOR CASTAÑEDA CASTRO (President; February 28, 1945–December 14, 1948). Salvador Castañeda Castro was born in Cojutedeque on August 6, 1888. He served in the El Salvadoran military and was minister of the interior in the cabinet of Maximiliano Hernández Martínez from 1935 until 1944. He was elected president and took office on February 28, 1945. His government suspended constitutional freedoms in September 1946. Castañeda Castro survived several plots to overthrow his government in 1947. He scheduled elections for the constituent assembly to gain an extension on his term of office that was scheduled to end in 1949, but he was deposed in a military coup on December 14, 1948, and was imprisoned until September 16, 1949. He died in San Salvador on March 5, 1965.

Estonia

Estonia is a country in northern Europe on the Baltic Sea. It proclaimed its independence from Russia on February 24, 1918. Estonia was incorporated into the Union of Soviet Socialist Republics on August 6, 1940.

HEADS OF STATE

KONSTANTIN PÄTS (Riigivanem [head of state]; February 24, 1918–May 8, 1919). Konstantin Päts was born on

February 23, 1874. Päts was a leader of the Farmers' and United Agrarian parties. He was selected as Estonia's first head of state following independence on February 24, 1918, and was succeeded by Otto Strandmann on May 8, 1919. Päts remained a leading political figure in Estonia, serving as Riigivanem (head of state) on five more occasions. He led the country from January 25, 1921, to October 23, 1922, and from August 2, 1923, to March 10, 1924, when he was forced to resign under criticism of the State Bank's liberal credit policies. He was again chosen to head the nation on February 12, 1931, until January 29, 1932. He regained office on November 7, 1932, and headed a coalition cabinet until April 26, 1933. Päts returned to power on October 21, 1933. He suspended the constitution and postponed elections in March 1934, effecting a coup d'état with the assistance of General Johan Laidoner, whom he named commander-in-chief of the armed forces. The country remained under martial law during Päts' rule, and he eliminated his opponents in the League of Veterans movement. The government forbade participation of opposition parties in elections held in December 1936, and Päts pushed a new constitution through the assembly the following July. He continued to rule as a dictator despite the return to constitutional rule. Päts was forced by the Soviet Union to appoint a government friendly to Moscow in June 1940 and was forced from office on July 21, 1940, by the Soviet Union. His duties were taken over by Prime Minister Johannes Vares. Päts was deported to the Soviet Union on July 30, 1940. He died on January 18, 1956. His body was returned to Estonia for a ceremonial burial in October 1990.

OTTO STRANDMANN (Riigivanem [head of state]; May 8, 1919–November 11, 1919). Otto Strandmann was born on November 30, 1875. He served as head of state of Estonia from May 8, 1919, until November 11, 1919. A leader of the Labor Party, Strandman served as minister of finance in Friedrich Akel's cabinet in 1924. He was again chosen as

Estonia's head of state on July 9, 1929, and served until he was forced to resign on February 3, 1931. He died in 1941.

JAAN TÕNISSON (Riigivanem [head of state]; November 11, 1919–October 8, 1920). Jaan Tõnisson was born on December 22, 1868. He represented Estonia in the first Russian Duma in 1906. He was a leader in the Estonian independence movement and a member of Estonia's foreign delegation to Scandinavia in 1917. He headed the government from November 11, 1919, until October 8, 1920. He returned to his position on December 9, 1927, serving until November 12, 1928, and again from May 18, 1933, to October 17, 1933. He was a critic of the government of Konstantin Päts, who forced his removal as editor of the *Postimees* newspaper in 1935. He unsuccessfully challenged Päts for the presidency in 1938.

ANTS PIIP (Riigivanem [head of state]; October 26, 1920–January 4, 1921). Ants Piip was born in Tuhalaane on February 28, 1884. He was sent by the Committee of Elders as a representative of the foreign delegation to Great Britain in January 1918. He obtained Britain's support for Estonia's self determination. Piip was chosen as Estonia's head of state on October 26, 1920. He was succeeded by Konstantin Päts on January 4, 1921, but remained a leading figure in Estonian politics. He served as a member of the delegation that negotiated the treaty of mutual assistance between Estonia and the Soviets in 1939 and was subsequently named foreign minister in October 1939. He resigned following the annexation of Estonia by the Soviet Union in July 1940. He died on October 1, 1942.

KONSTANTIN PÄTS (Riigivanem [head of state]; January 25, 1921–October 23, 1922). *See earlier entry under Heads of State.*

JAAN KUKK (Riigivanem [head of

state]; October 23, 1922–August 2, 1923). Jaan Kukk was born on April 13, 1885. Kukk headed the government from October 23, 1922, until he was replaced by Konstantin Päts on August 2, 1923. He died in December 1945.

KONSTANTIN PÄTS (Riigivanem [head of state]; August 2, 1923–March 10, 1924). *See earlier entry under Heads of State.*

FRIEDRICH KARL AKEL (Riigivanem [head of state]; March 26, 1924–December 16, 1924). Friedrich Karl Akel was born in Parnumaa on September 5, 1871. He served as foreign minister in the government of Kontantin Päts in early 1924. He was chosen to head a coalition government of the Democratic Union and Labor Parties after Päts's resignation on March 26, 1924. Akel's government resigned on December 16, 1924, following an abortive Communist rising in Reval. Akel remained a leading figure in Estonian politics, serving as foreign minister several times before the country was annexed by the Soviet Union in 1940.

JÜRI JAAKSON (Riigivanem [head of state]; December 16, 1924–November 25, 1925). Jüri Jaakson was born in Fellin on January 16, 1870. Jaakson was chosen to head a coalition cabinet on December 16, 1924, following the resignation of Friedrich Karl Akel. His government stepped down on December 15, 1925. He died during the German occupation of Estonia in late 1943.

JAAN TEEMANT (Riigivanem [head of state]; December 15, 1925–February 22, 1927). Jaan Teemant was born in Vigala on September 24, 1872. He was elected leader of the All-Estonian Congress in 1905. He was forced into exile when Russian authorities declared martial law. He was active in the nationalist movement and became a leader of the rightist parties after independence in

1918. Teemant served as Estonia's head of state from December 15, 1925, until his resignation on February 22, 1927. He also served in the government as minister of foreign affairs. He again served as head of state succeeding Konstantin Päts on February 19, 1932. He oversaw elections to the Diet that resulted in Karl Einbund's selection as head of the government on June 20, 1932. He was a critic of Konstantin Päts's dictatorial rule during the 1930s.

JÜRI ULUOTS (Riigivanem [head of state]; February 22, 1927–November 22, 1927). Jüri Uluots was born in 1890. He served as Estonia's head of state from February 22, 1927, until November 22, 1927. He was a member of the delegation that negotiated a mutual assistance treaty with the Soviet Union in 1939. Uluots was chosen as prime minister on October 12, 1939, but was forced to resign following the formation of a pro–Soviet puppet government on June 21, 1940. He attempted to persuade German occupation forces during World War II to allow self-government for Estonia. When his attempts failed, Uluots went into exile in 1944 and died in Sweden in 1945.

JAAN TÕNISSON ([Riigivanem [head of state]; December 9, 1927–November 13, 1928). *See earlier entry under Heads of State.*

AUGUST REI (Riigivanem [head of state]; July 9, 1929–February 3, 1931). August Rei was born in Pilistvere on March 22, 1886. He was a lawyer and a leader of the Estonian nationalist movement from the early part of the century. He was a major figure in Estonia's independence movement and was chosen as speaker of the national assembly in 1919 following the nation's independence from Russia. He was chosen as Estonia's head of state on July 9, 1929, serving as head of a coalition government until February 3, 1931. Rei was foreign minister in 1932 and Estonia's ambassador to the Soviet Union from 1938 to 1940. Rei went into exile following Estonia's incorporation into the Soviet Union in 1940. He was chosen as foreign minister of the Estonian government-in-exile following the German occupation in 1944. He became head of the government-in-exile the following year. He remained in that position until his death in Stockholm, Sweden, on March 29, 1963.

OTTO STRANDMANN (Riigivanem [head of state]; July 9, 1929–February 3, 1931). *See earlier entry under Heads of State.*

KONSTANTIN PÄTS ([Riigivanem [head of state]; February 12, 1931–January 29, 1932). *See earlier entry under Heads of State.*

JAAN TEEMANT (Riigivanem [head of state]; February 19, 1932–June 20, 1932). *See earlier entry under Heads of State.*

KARL EINBUND (Riigivanem [head of state]; July 19, 1932–October 3, 1932). Karl Einbund (Kaarel Eenapalu after 1935) was born in 1888. He was appointed to the government as interior minister in December 1924. He served as head of state from July 19, 1932, until his resignation on October 3, 1932. Einbund was the leading spokesman of the dicatorial regime of Konstantin Päts during the 1930s and was chosen as prime minister on April 24, 1938. He resigned on October 12, 1939, and was succeeded by Juri Uluots. He died in 1942.

KONSTANTIN PÄTS (Riigivanem [head of state]; November 7, 1932–April 26, 1933). *See earlier entry under Heads of State.*

JAAN TÕNISSON (Riigivanem [head of state]; May 18, 1933–October 17, 1933). *See earlier entry under Heads of State.*

KONSTANTIN PÄTS (Riigivanem [head of state]; October 21, 1933–July 21, 1940). *See earlier entry under Heads of State.*

HEADS OF GOVERNMENT

KARL EINBUND (Prime Minister; April 24, 1938–October 12, 1939). *See entry under Heads of State.*

JÜRI ULUOTS (Prime Minister; October 12, 1939–June 21, 1940). *See entry under Heads of State.*

JOHANNES VARES (Prime Minister; June 21, 1940–August 6, 1940). Johannes Y. Vares was born in Kheimtali Volost, Vil'iandi District, on January 12, 1890. He studied medicine at the University of Kiev and was a doctor in Pi-arnu from 1920 until 1939. He was also a leading poet who became active in politics as a Socialist in the 1930s. He was chosen to head a puppet government under the control of the Soviet Union on June 21, 1940. He presided over elections that resulted in the incorporation of Estonia into the Union of Soviet Socialist Republics on August 6, 1940. He subsequently served as president of the Presidium of the Supreme Soviet of the Estonian SSR until his death in Tallin on November 29, 1946.

Ethiopia

Ethiopia is a country in northeastern Africa.

HEADS OF STATE

MENELEK II (King; November 6, 1889–December 12, 1913). Menelek was born in August 1844. His father, Haile Malakot, became King of Shoa in 1847 and died in 1855. Menelek was taken hostage by Theodore II, who kept him a virtual prisoner in Magdala. Menelek escaped in 1865, three years before Theodore's suicide. He proclaimed himself King of Shoa and was one of three claimants to the imperial throne after Theodore's death. Menelek dropped his claims in support of John IV, but Menelek was allowed to rule in the south while John reigned in the north. John was killed in battle at Metamma by the dervishes in 1889, and Menelek claimed the throne as Ethiopia's most powerful leader. Shortly after taking power, he negotiated a treaty with the Italians that allowed their presence in Eritrea. Disagreements about the treaty soon developed, resulting in a war that ended with the Italians' defeat at Aduwa in 1896. A subsequent treaty resulted in recognition of Ethiopian independence. Menelek increased his territory by conquest during his reign, incorporating Sidama, Janjero, the Awash Valley, and the Kingdom of Kafa. He sought recognition of his empire's borders from the neighboring colonial powers, Britain, France, and Italy. Menelek suffered a cerebral hemorrhage in 1906. He recovered with diminished strength, but was again incapacitated by a paralyzing stroke in October 1909. He named his grandson, Lij Yasu, as his heir. Menelek's wife, Taytu, assumed the powers of a regent during his illness until a palace coup removed her from power. Menelek died in the new capital of Addis Ababa on December 12, 1913.

LIJ YASU (King; December 12, 1913–September 27, 1916). Lij Yasu was born in 1894, the son of King Menelek II's daughter, Shewa Regga, and Ras Mikael of Wello. He was named his grandfather's apparent on May 18, 1909. He took on some imperial duties during the incapacitation of Menelek, though his official coronation was blocked even after Menelek's death on December 12, 1913. Lij Yasu was an unpopular leader with the Shoan elite, who distrusted his presumed support of the Muslim religion and the Axis Powers during World War I. Lij Yasu was forced from power on September 27, 1916, and was eventually captured by Ras Gugsa Araya in 1921. He remained imprisoned until his death on November 7, 1935.

WAIZERU ZAUDITU (Empress; September 27, 1916–April 2, 1930). Waizeru Zauditu was born in 1876, the daughter of King Menelek II. She was chosen to become empress after her nephew, Lij Yasu, was deposed. She was crowned as empress on September 27, 1916, becoming the only woman to rule the modern empire. Zauditu's second cousin, Haile Selassie, was named regent and heir, and exercised much power during her reign. The early years of her reign were marked by domestic stability. Ethiopia entered the League of Nations in 1923. Relations with Italy became strained in the mid–1920s, but the conflicts were resolved by a treaty of friendship in 1928. On October 6, 1928, Zauditu was forced to grant Haile Selassie the title of nagus, or king, giving him full authority to rule. An uprising by feudal chiefs, including Zauditu's ex-husband Gugsa Wele, dominated the last few years of her reign. She died of pneumonia and complications from diabetes on April 2, 1930, several days before Gugsa Wele was killed in battle.

HAILE SELASSIE (Emperor; April 3, 1930–September 12, 1974). Haile Selassie was born Lij Tafari Makonnen on July 23, 1892, at Ejarsa Gora in Harar. He was the son of Ras Makonnen, the cousin and leading adviser of King Menelek II. Tafari was educated by clerical tutors and Roman Catholic missionaries in Harar. His father died in 1906 and, two years later, Tafari was summoned to the capital of Addis Ababa by the king. He was appointed governor of the Sidamo province in southern Ethiopia. His effectiveness in this position resulted in his appointment as governor of Harar, a position formerly held by his father. King Menelek died in 1913 and was succeeded by his grandson Lij Yasu. Yasu proved an unpopular leader, and he was deposed in 1916. Menelek's daughter, Princess Zauditu, assumed the throne as Empress and Tafari was named regent and heir apparent. Tafari was a powerful influence during the reign of Zauditu. He actively sought international recognition for Ethiopia and led the country into the League of Nations in 1923. He also sought to expand educational opportunites in the country and to end slavery. Despite efforts to remove Tafari, he assumed the throne as Emperor Haile Selassie on April 3, 1930, soon after the death of Zauditu. His efforts for further reform in the country were interrupted by the Italian invasion in October 1934. Haile Selassie led the army against the Italians, but was forced to flee the country when the invaders seized the capital in May 1936. He went to Geneva where he addressed the League of Nations in an unsuccessful attempt to obtain sanctions against Italy. He then settled in Bath, England, where he worked for foreign intervention to reclaim his country. Following the libera-

tion of Ethiopia by British troops in May 1941, Haile Selassie returned to Addis Ababa. His immediate problem was to maintain Ethiopian independence from Britain, which continued to administer several provinces well into the 1950s. He was also faced with several internal insurrections that were successfully put down. Haile Selassie continued his efforts to modernize the political structure of Ethiopia and presented a new constitution in 1955. Two years later elections were held for the first time, though most of the real power in the country was retained by the emperor. Haile Selassie also became a leading figure in African affairs, hosting the Economic Commission for Africa in 1958. In December 1960, while the emperor was out of the country, members of the Imperial Guard staged a coup d'état and attempted to install Haile Selassie's son, Asfa Wossen, as emperor. Troops loyal to Haile Selassie defeated the revolutionaries and, after four days, the emperor returned to Addis Ababa. He attempted to institute further liberalization in the country to quell liberal sentiments. In November 1962 he succeeded in reunifying Eritrea with Ethopia. In May 1963 he hosted the first meeting of the Organization for African Unity, which established its headquarters in Addis Ababa. He had little success in resolving the conflict with Somalia over the Ogaden region and was faced with continued unrest in Eritrea by factions wanting independence for the region. He continued with political reforms and, in 1966, allowed the prime minister to choose his own cabinet for the first time. Discontent worsened in the country in 1973, following a severe drought and the resultant exhibition of corruption and ineffeciency in the government's handling of relief efforts. The military in Eritrea revolted in February 1973, and Haile Selassie was forced to proceed with even more reforms in the government. He appointed Endalkachew Makonnen, a young progressive, as prime minister and oversaw the drafting of a new, more democratic, constitution. The reforms were unable to stymie the unrest in the country and, on September 13, 1974, he was deposed by a coup led by junior military officers. Two months later over 60 of his closest

aides and advisors were executed. Haile Selassie was placed under house arrest, and the harsh conditions of his imprisonment led to his death on August 27, 1975, at the age of 80.

Finland

Finland is a country in northern Europe. It received independence from Russia on December 6, 1917.

HEADS OF STATE

PEHR E. SVINHUFUD (Regent; May 18, 1918–December 12, 1918). Pehr Evind Svinhufud was born in Sääksmäki on December 15, 1861. He attended the University of Helsinki where he received a degree in law in 1886. He took his seat in the Finnish Diet in 1894. He entered the judiciary and took the position of assessor in the lower court of appeal in 1901. He was dismissed two years later over his refusal to accept directives he felt were in violation of the Finnish legal system. He became involved in Finnish nationalist activities and was active in the general strike in 1905. He was selected as president of the Diet when it was re-formed in 1907, serving until 1912. He was exiled to Siberia in 1914 after his dismissal from another judicial appointment. He returned to Finland after the Russian Revolution in 1917. He worked toward Finnish independence and was elected prime minister of the provisional government on November 27, 1917. A civil war began in 1918, when Red Guard forces took power in southern Finland. Svinhufud escaped to Ostrobothnia where he continued to lead the government during the civil war. The government returned in May 1918, and Svinhufud was elected regent on May 18, 1918, when a new constitution proclaimed Finland a constitutional monar-

chy. Svinhufud was considered pro-German, and the collapse of Germany at the end of World War I forced Svinhufud's resignation on December 12, 1918. He retired from politics until July 6, 1930, when President Lauri Relander called upon him to form a government as prime minister. Svinhufud defeated Kaarlo Stahlberg for the presidency the following year, taking office on March 2, 1931. During his term of office he banned the Communist Party. He also successfully halted the Fascist Lapua movement from destroying democratic institutions in the country. Svinhufud was defeated for reelection in 1937, and Kyösti Kallio replaced him as president on March 1, 1937. Svinhufud retired to his country estate in Luumäki where he died of cancer on February 29, 1944.

CARL GUSTAV MANNERHEIM (Regent; December 12, 1918–July 25, 1919). Carl Gustav Emil Mannerheim was born in Villnas on June 4, 1867. He was educated at the Nikolaev Cavalry School and joined the Russian cavalry as a second lieutenant in 1889. He served with distinction in the Russo-Japanese War and World War I and returned to Finland after the Russian Revolution with the rank of lieutenant general in December 1917. Mannerheim assumed command of the Finnish Civil Guard and defeated an attempt by Bolshevik forces to take control of Finland. He became Finland's regent on December 12, 1918. He was defeated by Kaarlo J. Stahlberg in the election for Finland's first president. He retired from his position following the establishment of the Finnish Republic on July 25, 1919. Mannerheim authored several books on military strategy during his retirement. He returned to active duty as president of the council of defense in 1931. He was promoted to the rank of marshal two years later. He led the Finnish forces against an attack by the Soviet Union in November 1939. A peace settlement was reached the following March, but Finland again clashed with the Soviets following a new attack in June 1941. Finland also participated in Germany's attack on Leningrad during World War II. Mannerheim became president of Finland August 4, 1944, following the resignation of pro-German President Risto Ryti. He negotiated a peace settlement with the Soviet Union and later declared war on Germany. Mannerheim remained president following Soviet-controlled elections in March 1945. He became ill in September 1945 and went to Lisbon, Portugal, for medical treatment. He returned to Finland in January 1946 and resigned from office for health reasons on March 4, 1946. He retired to Sweden and Switzerland to write his memoirs. Mannerheim died following abdominal surgery in Lausanne, Switzerland, on January 27, 1951.

KAARLO J. STAHLBERG (President; July 25, 1919–March 1, 1925). Kaarlo Juho Stahlberg was born in Suomussalmi on January 28, 1865. He was educated as a lawyer and joined the Finnish civil service. He was dismissed from his civil service position in 1903 for his opposition to Russification measures. He entered politics as a member of the Constitutional Party. He was elected to the Diet in 1904. He was law professor

at the University of Helsinki from 1908 to 1918. He was instrumental in drafting the republican constitution that was enacted in 1919. He was elected the first president of the Finnish Republic, and took office on July 25, 1919. He retired from office at the end of his term on March 1, 1925. He subsequently served on the legislative board. Stahlberg and his wife were victims of an abduction from Helsinki in October 1930 in what was believed to be part of a right-wing plot; the couple were released safely the following day. He was narrowly defeated for another term as president in 1931 and again in 1937. Stahlberg remained a member of the legislative board until 1945. He died in Helsinki on September 22, 1952.

LAURI RELANDER (President; March 1, 1925–March 2, 1931). Lauri Kristian Relander was born in Karelia on May 31, 1883. He was educated at the University of Helsinki and continued to study agriculture in Sweden, Norway, Denmark, Germany, and Russia from 1907. He was elected to the Finnish Diet in 1910, serving until 1913. He was returned to the Diet in 1917. He was minister of agriculture from 1918 to 1920. He was governor of Viipuri Province from 1920 to 1925, and the nominee of the Agrarian Party in the 1925 presidential election. He was elected and took office on March 1, 1925. He completed his term of office and stepped down on March 2, 1931. Relander retired from politics and died on February 9, 1942, in Helsinki after a long illness.

PEHR E. SVINHUFUD (President; March 2, 1931–March 1, 1937). *See earlier entry under Heads of State.*

KYÖSTI KALLIO (President; March 1, 1937–December 19, 1940). Kyösti Kallio was born in Ylivieskä on April 10, 1873. He was a successful farmer in Nivala when he entered politics in 1904, while Finland was an autonomous grand duchy of Russia. He was elected to the Diet in 1907 and was a leader in the independence movement in 1917. Kallio headed the government as prime minister from November 14, 1922, until January 18, 1924, from January 1, 1926, until November 23, 1926, and again from August 16, 1929, to July 1, 1930. He formed another government on October 6, 1936, and continued in that position until March 1, 1937, when he took office as president after defeating the incumbent, Pehr Svinhufud. The Soviet Union invaded Finland in November 1939 and, after several months, the government was forced to sign a peace treaty that ceded the Karelian Isthmus and eastern territory to the Soviet Union. Kallio's health failed, and he announced his resignation on November 28, 1940. Risto Ryti was selected by the electoral college to succeed Kallio to the presidency on December 19, 1940. Kallio was preparing to depart Helsinki by train to his country home in Nivala when he was stricken with a heart attack. He collapsed and died in the arms of Marshal Carl Gustav Mannerheim at the Helsinki railroad station on the evening of December 19, 1940.

RISTO HEIKKI RYTI (President; December 21, 1940–August 1, 1944). Risto Heikki Ryti was born in Huittinen on February 3, 1889. He studied law at the University of Finland. He entered politics and was elected to the Diet as a member of the Progressive Party in 1919.

He served as minister of finance from 1921 to 1924 and also became the president of the Bank of Finland in 1923. Ryti was defeated by Lauri Relander for the presidency of Finland in 1925. President Kyösti Kallio appointed Ryti prime minister on December 1, 1939, at the outbreak of the Soviet Union's invasion of Finland. As Kallio's health declined, Ryti often served as acting president. He was elected to succeed to the presidency, taking office upon Kallio's death on December 19, 1940. The government entered into negotiations with Nazi Germany and entered World War II as a cobelligerent against the Soviet Union in June 1941. Ryti claimed the attack of the Soviet Union was a defensive war for Finland. Ryti stepped down from office on August 1, 1944, to allow Marshal Carl Gustav Mannerheim to assume office and negotiate a peace treaty with the Soviet Union. Ryti was arrested and charged with war crimes by a special people's court in 1945. He was convicted on charges of leading Finland into the war on Germany's side and was sentenced to ten years in prison. Ryti was released after five years for reasons of health. He retired from public life and died of cancer at his home in Helsinki on October 25, 1956.

CARL GUSTAV MANNERHEIM (President; August 4, 1944–March 9, 1946). *See earlier entry under Heads of State.*

HEADS OF GOVERNMENT

PEHR E. SVINHUFUD (Prime Minister; November 27, 1917–May 27, 1918). *See earlier entry under Heads of State.*

JUHO K. PAASIKIVI (Prime Minister; May 27, 1918–November 27, 1918). Juho Kusti Paasikivi was born in Tam-

pere on November 27, 1870. He was educated in Finland, Sweden, Germany, and Russia. He received a doctorate in law in 1901 and worked in the banking industry. He entered politics and was elected to the Finnish parliament in 1907. He served in the cabinet as minister of finance from 1908 until 1909. Finland declared its independence in July 1917, following the Russian Revolution. Paasikivi served as the first prime minister of the independent government from May 27, 1918, until November 27, 1918. Finland engaged in a war with Bolshevik forces intent on establishing a Socialist government. Finland was declared a republic in June 1919, and Paasikivi headed the Finnish delegation that negotiated a peace treaty with the Soviet Union in October 1920. He subsequently retired from political activities, serving in the Finnish Chamber of Commerce. He was appointed Finland's minister to Sweden in 1936. He headed a Finnish delegation to the Soviet Union in 1939 in the hopes of preempting a conflict between the two countries. The negotiations were unsuccessful, and the Soviet Union attacked Finland in November 1939. He was named minister to Moscow in March 1940 and negotiated a peace settlement. He remained in Moscow until his resignation in May 1941. He opposed Finland's alliance with Germany during World War II and negotiated an armistice with the Soviets and his country's exit from the conflict in 1944. He again became prime minister on November 17, 1944, and pledged peaceful cooperation with the Soviets. He formed a new government in April 1945 that included Communists in the cabinet. He remained prime minister until March 9, 1946, when he succeeded retiring President Carl Gustav Mannerheim. He supported a mutual defense pact with the Soviet Union in 1948. He defeated the Communist opposition by a wide margin and was reelected president in 1950. Paasikivi renegotiated the defense pact with the Soviets in 1955 and gained Finland's admittance to the United Nations later in the year. He retired from office after completing his term on March 1, 1956. He died in Helsinki on December 14, 1956, after a long illness.

LAURI J. INGMAN (Prime Minister; November 27, 1918–April 17, 1919).

Lauri Johannes Ingman was born in Teuva on June 30, 1868. He was a leading educator and clergyman. Ingman was a member of the Swedish Party and served as vice speaker of the Diet in 1914. He was named prime minister on November 27, 1918. He stepped down on April 17, 1919. Ingman served in several cabinets before returning to office as prime minister from November 22, 1924, to March 18, 1925. Ingman was named Roman Catholic Archbishop of Finland in 1930. He died in Turku on October 25, 1934.

KAARLO CASTRÉN (Prime Minister; April 17, 1919–July 25, 1919). Kaarlo Castrén was born in Turtola on August 28, 1860. He was called on to head a government on April 17, 1919. His government supported the election of the Finnish president by parliament, but the parliament rejected the proposal in favor of the indirect method of using electors. Castrén stepped down when President Kaarlo Stahlberg assumed the presidency on July 25, 1919. Castrén died in Helsinki on November 19, 1938.

JUHO HEIKKI VENNOLA (Prime Minister; July 25, 1919–March 15, 1920). Juho Heikki Vennola was born in Oulu on June 19, 1872. He was a founder of the Finnish Progressive Party and headed the government as prime minister from July 25, 1919, to March 15, 1920, and from April 9, 1921, to June 2, 1922. He subsequently served in the government as foreign minister and minister of finance. Vennola died in Helsinki on December 3, 1938.

RAFAEL WALDEMAR ERICH (Prime Minister; March 15, 1920–April 9, 1921). Rafael Waldemar Erich was born in Turku on June 10, 1879. He was a professor of law at Helsinki University. He headed the Finnish government as prime minister from March 15, 1920, until April 9, 1921. Erich also served as Finland's minister to Sweden and Italy and represented his country at the International Court of Justice at the Hague. He died in Helsinki on February 19, 1946.

JUHO HEIKKI VENNOLA (Prime Minister; April 9, 1921–June 2, 1922). *See earlier entry under Heads of Government.*

AIMO KAARLO CAJANDER (Prime Minister; June 2, 1922–November 14, 1922). Aimo Kaarlo Cajander was born in Uusikaupunki on March 4, 1879. He was educated at Helsinki University and taught botany there from 1904 until 1911. He later served as professor of forestry at the university. Cajander headed the government as prime minister from June 2, 1922, until November 14, 1922, and from January 19, 1924, until November 22, 1924. He was minister of defense from 1928 until 1929 and deputy prime minister from 1929 until 1933. He was again named to head the government on March 13, 1937. The Soviet Union invaded Finland in November 1939, and Cajander stepped down to allow Risto Ryti to form a government on December 1, 1939. Cajander was named by the new government to head a committee to administer United States relief funds during the conflict. Cajander subsequently headed Finland's forest administration. He died of a heart attack in Helsinki on January 21, 1943.

KYÖSTI KALLIO (Prime Minister; November 14, 1922–January 18, 1924). *See earlier entry under Heads of State.*

AIMO KAARLO CAJANDER (Prime Minister; January 19, 1924–November 22, 1924). *See earlier entry under Heads of Government.*

LAURI J. INGMAN (Prime Minister; November 22, 1924–March 18, 1925). *See earlier entry under Heads of Government.*

ANTTI A. TULLENHEIMO (Prime Minister; March 31, 1925–December 10, 1925). Antti Agaton Tullenheimo was born in Kangasala on December 4, 1879. He was elected to the Finnish parliament in 1914. Tullenheimo headed the government as prime minister from March 31, 1925, until December 10, 1925. He remained in the parliament until 1932. Tullenheimo also served as chancellor of Helsinki University. He died in Helsinki on September 3, 1952.

KYÖSTI KALLIO (Prime Minister; January 1, 1926–November 23, 1926). *See earlier entry under Heads of State.*

VÄINÖ A. TANNER (Prime Minister; December 11, 1926–December 9, 1927). Väinö Alfred Thomasson was born in Helsinki on March 12, 1881. His family changed its name to Tanner in 1895. Tanner attended the University of Helsinki, where he received a degree in law in 1911. He became active in the Finnish cooperative movement and was elected to the parliament as a Social Democrat in 1907. He became speaker of the parliament in 1919 and served until 1926. Tanner was defeated for the presidency in 1925. He headed the government as prime minister from December 11, 1926, until December 9, 1927. He returned to the position of speaker of the parliament in 1930. He was again defeated for the presidency in 1931. He served as chairman of the Bank of Finland from 1933 until 1935 and was named to the cabinet as minister of finance in 1938. He was appointed foreign minister in November 1939 following the Soviet invasion of Finland. He negotiated a peace settlement under the Treaty of Moscow in March 1940. He resigned from office at the end of the year. He reentered the government as minister of commerce and industry during World War II in 1941. He was again named finance minister in 1942. After Finland's defeat by the Soviet Union in

1944, the Soviets insisted that Tanner and other wartime leaders be tried for war crimes. Tanner was sentenced to five years imprisonment but was pardoned and released in 1949. He returned to parliament in 1951 and became head of the Social Democratic Party in April 1957. His party was excluded from subsequent Finnish governments by threats from the Soviet Union. He retired from politics in 1963. Tanner died in a Helsinki hospital on April 19, 1966.

JUHO EMIL SUNILA (Prime Minister; December 17, 1927–December 13, 1928). Juho Emil Sunila was born in Liminka on August 16, 1875. He was a leader of the Agrarian Party and was called upon to head an Agrarian government on December 17, 1927. His government resigned on December 13, 1928, over a budgetary matter. Sunila was called upon to form a coalition government on March 24, 1931, while the country was in an economic crisis. Sunila resigned on December 7, 1932, when President Pehr Evind Svinhufud refused to support the cabinet's proposal of regulating interest rates. Sunila died in Helsinki on October 2, 1936.

OSKARI MANTERE (Prime Minister; December 22, 1928–July 3, 1929). Oskari Mantere was born in Hansjärvi on September 18, 1874. He was called upon to head a Progressive coalition ministry on December 22, 1928. His government acted to prevent a Communist street demonstration in the summer of 1929. Mantere's party was defeated in the most elections, and he stepped down from office on July 3, 1929. He died in Helsinki on December 9, 1942.

KYÖSTI KALLIO (Prime Minister; August 16, 1929–July 1, 1930). *See earlier entry under Heads of State.*

PEHR E. SVINHUFUD (Prime Minister; July 6, 1930–March 2, 1931). *See earlier entry under Heads of State.*

JUHO EMIL SUNILA (Prime Minister; March 24, 1931–December 7, 1932). *See earlier entry under Heads of Government.*

TOIVO KIVIMAKI (Prime Minister; December 14, 1932–September 25, 1936). Toivo M. Kivimaki was born on June 5, 1886. He was a leader of the Progressive Party and formed a coalition government with the Social Democrats on December 14, 1932. Kivimaki declared the government's policy of neutrality in 1935. He stepped down on September 25, 1936, after the defeat of his government's bill amending the criminal codes. Kivimaki subsequently served as Finland's minister to Berlin. He was arrested after World War II and charged with war crimes. He was convicted and briefly imprisoned and died in Helsinki on May 7, 1968.

KYÖSTI KALLIO (Prime Minister; October 6, 1936–March 1, 1937). *See earlier entry under Heads of State.*

AIMO KAARLO CAJANDER (Prime Minister; March 13, 1937–December 1, 1939). *See earlier entry under Heads of Government.*

RISTO HEIKKI RYTI (Prime Minister; December 1, 1939–January 3, 1941). *See earlier entry under Heads of State.*

JOHAN WILHELM RANGELL (Prime Minister; January 3, 1941–March 1, 1943). Johan Wilhelm Rangell was born on October 25, 1894. Rangell served as director of the Bank of Finland and was called upon to head the government as prime minister on January 3, 1941, during World War II. Rangell stepped down on March 4, 1943, to allow Edwin Linkomies to form a government. Rangell was arrested after Finland's defeat in the war and was tried for war crimes. He was convicted and spent several years in prison at the insistence of the Soviet Union.

EDWIN LINKOMIES (Prime Minister; March 4, 1943–August 4, 1944). Edwin Johan Hildegard Linkomies was born in Viborg on December 22, 1894. He was appointed professor of philology at Helsinki University in 1923. He served as dean of the university from 1930 until 1931 and was named rector in 1932. He entered politics and served in the parliament as vice president from 1939 until 1943. He also became president of the Coalition Party in 1942. He headed Finland's wartime government as prime minister from March 4, 1943, until August 4, 1944. After the war Linkomies was tried for war crimes at the insistence of the Soviet Union. He was sentenced to five years of imprisonment in February 1946 but was pardoned the following year. He was appointed deputy chancellor of Helsinki University after his release. He became chancellor in 1962. Linkomies died of a heart attack in Helsinki on September 8, 1963.

ANDERS HACKZELL (Prime Minister; August 8, 1944–September 22, 1944). Anders Werner Antil Hackzell was born in Mikkeli on September 20, 1881. He was educated in law and served as governor of Wiborg Province from 1918 until 1920. Hackzell served as Finnish minister to Moscow from 1922 until 1927. He was foreign minister from 1932 to 1936. Hackzell was called upon to form a government on August 8, 1944, and to seek an armistice with the Soviet Union during World War II. He was forced to resign on September 22, 1944, when he suffered a stroke while in Moscow negotiating a peace settlement. He also developed pneumonia, but recovered sufficiently to return to Helsinki, though he remained partially paralyzed. Hackzell died soon after in Helsinki on January 14, 1946.

URHO CASTRÉN (Prime Minister; September 21, 1944–November 11, 1944). Urho Jonas Castrén was born on December 30, 1886. He became head of the government on September 21, 1944, when Anders Hackzell was forced to resign due to ill health. Castrén's government continued to negotiate a peace settlement with the Soviet Union. He was forced to step down on November 11, 1944, when members of his cabinet resigned because they felt the government was not making sufficient effort to establish satisfactory relations with the Soviet Union. Castrén died in Helsinki on March 8, 1965.

JUHO K. PAASIKIVI (Prime Minister; November 17, 1944–March 9, 1946). *See earlier entry under Heads of Government.*

France

France is a country in western Europe.

HEADS OF STATE

EMILE LOUBET (President; February 18, 1899–February 18, 1906). Emile Loubet was born in Marsanne, in the department of Drome, on December 31, 1838. His father was a prosperous farmer and the mayor of Marsanne. Loubet was educated in Paris, where he studied law. He entered politics in 1870 and was elected mayor of Montelimar. He was elected to the chamber of deputies in 1876, where he supported the republican cause. He was elected to the senate in 1885 and was named to Pierre-Emmanuel Tirard's cabinet as minister of public works two years later. President Marie Sadi-Carnot asked Loubet to form a government as prime minister on February 28, 1892. Loubet also served as minister of the interior. His government's attempt to cover up the Panama scandal forced Loubet's resignation as premier on December 14, 1892, though he remained minister at the interior for some brief time under the subsequent government of Alexandre Ribot. Loubet was elected president of the senate in 1896. He became a candidate for president of France following the death of President Felix Faure, and took office on February 18, 1899. Early in his presidency Loubet pardoned Alfred Dreyfus, whose court-martial conviction at Rennes had been a cause célèbre in France. Tension between France and the Vatican heightened in 1904 when Pope Pius X protested Loubet's state visit to the king of Italy. A controversial decision to enact laws separating church and state was executed the following year. The entente cordiale eased tensions between France and Great Britain, and France entered into an alliance with Russia during Loubet's term of office. He stepped down after completing his term on February 18, 1906, and retired to Montelimar. He died at his country home there of uremic poisoning on December 20, 1929.

ARMAND FALLIERES (President; February 18, 1906–February 18, 1913). Clement Armand Fallieres was born in Mezin, Lot-et-Garonne, on November 6, 1841. He received a degree in law and began a practice in Nerac. He was elected a town councilor there in 1871 and entered the chamber of deputies in 1876. He served in Jules Ferry's cabinet in 1880 and was named minister of the interior in Charles Duclerc's government

in 1882. Fallieres was chosen to head the government as prime minister on January 29, 1883. He resigned on April 6, 1885, in protest against the senate's rejection of his compromise proposal to deal with the expulsion of the pretender to the throne of France. He remained in the government as minister of education and justice in successive governments. He was elected to the senate in June 1890, becoming president of the senate in 1899. He ran for the French presidency, defeating Paul Doumer, on February 18, 1906. France experienced growth and prosperity during his term of office. His expertise in foreign affairs was instrumental in strengthening France's ties with Russia and England. He completed his term of office on February 18, 1913, and was succeeded by Raymond Poincaré. Fallieres retired to his home, Loupillon, near Agren, in southwest France, where he died of a heart attack on June 22, 1931.

RAYMOND POINCARÉ (President; February 18, 1913–February 18, 1920). Raymond Poincaré was born in Bar-le-Due, Lorraine, on August 20, 1860. The son of an engineer, he studied law in Paris and began a law practice in 1882. He soon entered politics and was elected to the chamber of deputies in 1887. He sat with the center left and was appointed to the cabinet as minister of education in 1893. He was minister of finance in Charles Dupuy's government the following year. Poincaré returned to the position of minister of education in Alexandre Ribot's government in January 1895. He left the government the following October to become vice president of the chamber of deputies. He also concentrated on his prospering law practice. He was elected to the senate in 1903 and returned to the government as minister of finance in Ferdinand Sarrien's cabinet in March 1906. He resigned his position the following October when Georges Clemenceau became prime minister. Poincaré remained a leading member of the parliament, though he declined further cabinet appointments. He was called upon by President Armand Fallieres to form a government as prime minister on January 14, 1912, succeeding Joseph Caillaux. He also headed the foreign ministry and sought to strengthen France's ties with Great Britain and Russia during the Balkan Wars of 1912 and 1913. Poincaré was elected president of France, succeeding Failliers on February 18, 1913. As tensions increased throughout Europe prior to World War I, Poincaré supported legislation to increase compulsory military service from two to three years in France. As war became inevitable, Poincaré consulted with King George V of England to ensure the Anglo-French entente would stand together against German aggression. Germany declared war on France on August 3, 1914. Poincaré performed his duties with distinction throughout the war and insisted on an honorable peace. He granted the premiership to his political foe, Georges Clemenceau, in November 1917. His relationship with Clemenceau further deteriorated during the subsequent peace negotiations when the prime minister refused to accept Poincaré's advice. Poincaré completed his term of office on February 18, 1920. He returned to the senate, where he chaired the commission on war reparations. Poincaré again accepted the position of premier on January 16, 1922, when he succeeded Aristide Briand. He rejected British attempts to compromise on the issue of Germany's reparation payments and, with the support of Belgium and Italy, France occupied the Ruhr. He later agreed to accept the proposal from the United States and Great Britain to implement the Dawes Plan, allowing a commission of experts to deal with the reparation question. Poincaré supported the enactment of a tax increase to aid France's financial difficulties in 1924. This met with opposition by the parties of the left, who achieved a majority in the general election in May 1924. Poin-

caré stepped down from office on June 8, 1924. He returned to head the government on July 24, 1926, as leader of a coalition cabinet to deal with the monetary crisis. His government restored confidence in the franc, and in 1928 he sponsored a bill reestablishing the gold standard for the franc. He continued as premier after the general election of 1928 when the Radical ministers resigned from the cabinet. He was in the midst of negotiating an Inter-Allied debt agreement with the United States and Great Britain when failing health forced his resignation on July 28, 1929. He returned to head the government for several weeks from October 11, 1929, until November 2, 1929. He subsequently retired from political activity to write his memoirs. He refused several further invitations to head the government as his health improved. Poincaré died at his home in Paris on October 15, 1934.

PAUL DESCHANEL (President; February 18, 1920–September 21, 1920). Paul Eugene Louis Deschanel was born on February 13, 1856, in Brussels, Belgium, where his father, the distinguished professor Emile Deschanel, was living in political exile because of his opposition to Napoleon III. Paul Deschanel studied law and entered politics as an aide to Prime Minister Jules Simon. He was elected to the chamber of deputies in October 1885 as a member of the Progressive Republican Party. He was elected vice president of the chamber in 1896 and president two years later. He retained that position until 1902 and subsequently headed the chambers' foreign affairs committee. He again became president of the chamber in 1912, retaining office throughout World War I. Deschanel was elected president of France over Georges Clemenceau by a wide margin and took office on February 18, 1920. Several months after his election, Deschanel fell from a moving train on route from Paris to Montbrison. Though his injuries were regarded as slight,

Deschanel suffered a breakdown and resigned from office on September 21, 1920. He was subsequently elected to the senate where he remained until he died of pneumonia in Paris on April 28, 1922.

ALEXANDRE MILLERAND

(President; September 23, 1920–June 25, 1924). Alexandre Millerand was born in Paris on February 10, 1859, the son of a wine merchant. He studied law and achieved prominence for his defense of the Decazeville strike leaders in 1883. He was elected to the chamber of deputies as a Socialist two years later. He served as leader of the socialist Left in the chamber and was editor of the party newspaper. He joined the cabinet as minister of commerce under Pierre Waldeck-Rousseau in 1899, drawing criticism from other party members for serving in a non-Socialist government. He was an outspoken opponent of the subsequent government of Emile Combes. Millerand returned to the cabinet under Aristide Briand as minister of public works in 1909, where he reorganized the state railways. He was minister of war under Raymond Poincaré in 1912 and retained that position in René Vivani's cabinet in 1914. He played an important role in the introduction of light-heavy artillery to the war effort. He resigned, along with other members of Vivani's cabinet, in October 1915. Millerand was named to the position of commissioner general for Alsace-Lorraine in March 1919. He was called upon to form a government on January 19, 1920, following the resignation of Georges Clemenceau. He was elected president of France on September 23, 1920, after poor health forced the resignation of Paul Deschanel. Millerand's attempts to change the constitution to strengthen the power of the president brought him into conflict with the Radicals and Socialists, who repeatedly called for his resignation. Millerand was forced to step down on June 25, 1924, when the opposition refused to approve the formation of a new government. He was defeated for a senate seat in January 1927. He was elected to the senate in a by-election several months later. He remained an outspoken and often controversial statesman until his death in Versailles on April 7, 1943.

GASTON DOUMERGUE

(President; June 25, 1924–June 25, 1931). Gaston Doumergue was born in Aigues-Vives, Gard, on April 1, 1863. He studied law in Paris and practiced in Nimes from 1885 until 1890. He spent the next several years as a jurist in France's colonial territories in Indochina and Algeria. He was elected to the chamber of deputies in 1893 as a Radical. He served in Emile Combes's government as minister of colonies from 1902 until 1905. He was named minister of commerce in Ferdinand Sarrien's cabinet in 1906 and retained the position under Georges Clemenceau from 1908 until his election to the senate in 1910. Doumergue was called upon to form a government to succeed Louis Barthou on December 10, 1913, but results of a general election the following spring forced his resignation on June 9, 1914. Doumergue again served as minister of the colonies during much of World War I. He was sent to Russia in early 1917 to try and prevent the Kerensky government from making a separate peace with the Germans. Doumergue was elected president of the senate in February 1923. The following year he defeated Paul Painlevé for the presidency of France, and took office on June 25, 1924. Doumergue was respected for his ability to mediate between differing political points of view. He completed his term of office on June 25, 1931, and retired to his country home in Nimes. After rioting in Paris forced the resignation of Edouard Daladier's government Doumergue emerged from retirement to head a coalition government on February 9, 1934. He was unable to accomplish his planned constitutional reforms that would increase the power of the premier, and again retired to Tournefeuille on November 10, 1934. Doumergue died suddenly of a heart attack on June 18, 1937, while visiting his hometown of Aigues-Vives.

PAUL DOUMER (President; June 25, 1931–May 6, 1932). Paul Doumer was born in Aurillac, Cantal, on March 22, 1857. He was taken by his mother to Paris at the age of eleven after the death of his father. After receiving his education, he worked as a teacher and journalist. He became involved in politics and was elected to the chamber of deputies as a Radical in 1888. He served as minister of finance in Léon Bourgeois' government in 1895 and 1896. He was appointed governor of Indochina in January 1897, where he remained for five years. He returned to France in 1902 where he formed a Radical Party dissident group in opposition to the government of Émile Combes. He was elected president of the chamber of deputies in January 1905. He was defeated for the presidency of France by Armand Fallieres in 1906. He served on the senate committee for military affairs during World War I, during which four of his sons were killed. Doumer served in several cabinets as minister of finance in 1921 through 1922 and 1925 through 1926. He was elected president of the senate in 1927. Doumer succeeded Gaston Doumergue as president of France on June 13, 1931. His administration was cut short by his assassination by fanatic Russian emigré Pavel Gorgulov on May 6, 1932. Doumer was shot in the head and arm by Gorgulov while attending a charity book auction in Paris. He died of his wounds fourteen hours later.

ALBERT LEBRUN (President; May 10, 1932–June 11, 1940). Albert Lebrun was born in Mercy-le-Haut, Lorraine, on August 29, 1871. He received an engineering degree and worked as a mining engineer before entering politics. He was elected to the chamber of deputies in 1900. He served in the cabinet as minister of colonies from 1911 until 1912 and in Raymond Poincaré's government as minister of war from January 1912 until January 1913. He subsequently served again as minister of colonies until 1914. He was minister of liberated regions in Georges Clemenceau's government from 1917 until Clemenceau forced his resignation in 1919. Lebrun was elected president of the senate in 1931. He was elected to succeed Paul Doumer, the assassinated president of France, on May 10, 1932. He was reelected to a second term in April 1939. Lebrun exercised little power over the various governments that served during his administration, accepting the cabinet's decision for an armistice with the Axis Powers in June 1940. He retired to Vizille on June 11, 1940, after the Vichy government of Henri-Philippe Pétain was installed. Lebrun was interned by the Germans during the occupation of France in 1943 and 1944. He supported General Charles de Gaulle as provisional president after the war. Lebrun remained in retirement and died after a long illness in Paris on March 6, 1950.

HENRI-PHILIPPE PÉTAIN (President; June 11, 1940–August 20, 1944). Henri-Philippe Pétain was born in Cauchy-à-la-Tour, Pas-de-Calais, on April 24, 1856. He was educated at Saint-Cyr and Ecole de Guerre, where he received military training. He served in various staff positions until the outbreak of World War I in 1914. He was placed in command of the 33rd Army Corps in Artois in October 1914 and rose to the rank of general commanding the Second Army in June 1915. He became the "savior of Verdun" in 1916 when, despite suffering massive casualties, the French army halted the German advance at Verdun. He was appointed chief of general staff and commander-in-chief, and prepared the French army to engage the Germans during the final offensive in 1918. He led the French as they pushed the Germans back to the Ardennes in September 1918. He was regarded as France's leading military authority after the war and was granted the rank of marshal. He served on the Supreme War Council and was inspector general of the army during the 1920s. He resigned from office in January 1931. He briefly served as minister of war in Gaston Doumergue's government from February until November 1934. Pétain viewed parliamentary governments with disdain, particularly in regard to the military, preferring authoritarian rule. He was named minister to Spain in March 1939, but was recalled in May 1940 after the French forces suffered heavy losses against the Germans in the early part of World War II. Pétain formed a government to negotiate an armistice with the Axis Powers in June 1940. He summoned the French national assembly to Vichy where he was granted emergency powers as chief of state on June 11, 1940, bringing an end to the French Third Republic. The terms of the armistice with Germany left northern France and the Atlantic coast under German occupation, with the Vichy government in control of southern France and the Mediterranean coastline. Pétain's premier, Pierre Laval, held most of the power during the Vichy government, with Pétain serving as a popular figurehead. Petain suffered from poor health and periods of senility while in office. He was arrested by the Germans on August 20, 1944, and taken to Germany. He returned to France in April 1945, and was arrested by the provisional government of Charles de Gaulle. Pétain was tried and convicted of treason during the war because of his collaboration with the Nazis and was sentenced to death on August 15, 1945. His sentence was commuted to life imprisonment. He was held at Portalet and, later, in a fortress on Ile d'Yea. He was subsequently moved to a villa on Ile d'Yea due to his poor health. He died there after a long illness on July 23, 1951.

CHARLES DE GAULLE (President; September 10, 1944–June 19, 1946). Charles André Joseph Marie de Gaulle was born in Lille on November 22, 1890. He graduated from Saint-Cyr, the French military school, in 1911 and was commissioned as a second lieutenant. He served under Colonel Henri-Philippe Pétain during World War I. He was wounded in 1916 and was taken prisoner by the Germans. Following his repatriation he served as a commandant with the French army in Poland. He subsequently attended the War College in Paris and, in 1927, he was named to the general staff of the Army of the Rhine. He headed the French military missions to Egypt, Syria, Iraq, and Persia from 1929 until 1932. Upon his return to France he was promoted to lieutenant colonel and became secretary general of the High Council of National Defense. De Gaulle advocated a mobile mechanized force for the French armed forces and questioned the French strategy of warfare based on the impregnability of the Maginot Line. He authored a book, *The Army of the Future*, in 1934 to voice his opinions. De Gaulle's theories were proved correct when the German army overran the French forces in May 1940. De Gaulle was promoted to brigadier general and named undersecretary of national defense and war in June 1940. He refused to accept the truce negotiated by Premier Henri-Philippe Pétain with the Germans. Following the German occupation, de Gaulle went to London where he became president of the French government-in-exile and commander of the Free French Army. Following the Allied victory in North Africa in 1943, de Gaulle served as copresident of the French Committee of National Liberation with Henri Giraud. Giraud resigned following a power struggle with de Gaulle and, following the liberation of France in 1944, de Gaulle became president and premier of the provisional government on September 10, 1944. He relinquished his position as premier on

January 27, 1946. When de Gaulle's proposal for a strong executive presidency was rejected, he resigned from office on June 19, 1946. The following year he founded the Rally of the French People's Party. When he suffered electoral defeat in 1953, he retired from politics. De Gaulle resumed power as premier on June 1, 1958, following a revolt by the French army in Algeria. The French national assembly granted de Gaulle broad powers to deal with the threat of civil war. He was inaugurated as president of the French Fifth Republic on January 8, 1959. He disappointed right-wing elements in the army by granting independence to Algeria in 1962. He was later the target of several assassination attempts by the Secret Army Organization in the early 1960s. De Gaulle governed in an authoritarian manner and sought to secure France's position as the leading power in European affairs. He vetoed the admission of Great Britain to the European Community on several occasions. Though forced into a runoff, he was reelected to the presidency in 1965. In 1966 de Gaulle removed French military forces from the North Atlantic Treaty Organization and ordered that NATO's headquarters leave France. He was also a frequent critic of the United States policy in Southeast Asia. He also created a furor in July 1967 when he shouted "Long live free Quebec" while on a visit to Canada. The incident outraged the Canadian government, and de Gaulle was forced to cut his trip short. De Gaulle's government was faced with a crisis in May and June 1968 when a students and workers strike resulted in violent street rioting. De Gaulle dissolved parliament and called for new elections, which resulted in an overwhelming victory for him. He promised reforms in France's educational policies and labor relations to help settle the crisis. In April 1969 de Gaulle supported a referendum to centralize the government and reorganize the French senate. He said that he would resign from office if the referendum failed and, following the defeat of the referendum, he stepped down as president on April 27, 1969. He returned to his home in Colomby-les-deux Eglises, to write his memoirs. He died of a heart attack at his home on November 9, 1970.

HEADS OF GOVERNMENT

PIERRE WALDECK-ROUSSEAU
(Premier; June 22, 1899–June 7, 1902). Pierre-Marie Rene Waldeck-Rousseau was born in Nantes on December 2, 1846. He studied law in Paris and began his practice in 1870. He was elected mayor of Nantes the same year. He was elected to the chamber of deputies from Renness in 1879. He was an ally of Leon Gambetta and served in his cabinet as minister of the interior from November 1881 until January 1882. He again held that position in Jules Ferry's cabinet from February 1883 to March 1885. He was best known during this period for the legalization of trade unions in 1884. He remained in the chamber of deputies until 1889, when he returned to practice law in Paris. He was elected to the senate from Loire in 1894 and was an unsuccessful candidate for president of France the following year. Waldeck-Rousseau was called upon to form a government as prime minister on June 22, 1899. He formed a Republican-dominated cabinet and was largely responsible for the granting of amnesty against further prosecutions in the Dreyfus affair in December 1900. His government was also responsible for laws allowing freedom of association, except for religious purposes, in July 1901. His government was successful in the May 1902 elections, but Waldeck-Rousseau stepped down

from office for reasons of health on June 7, 1902. He retired to his country home in Corbeil, near Paris, where he died after liver surgery on August 10, 1904.

EMILE COMBES (Premier; June 7, 1902–January 24, 1905). Justin Louis Emile Combes was born in Roquecourbe, Tarn, on September 6, 1835. He was educated at the Castres seminary and the Ecole des Carmes in Paris, where he received a doctorate in divinity. He taught philosophy, but was refused ordination to the priesthood. He subsequently studied medicine and became a doctor in 1867. He was elected mayor of Pons in 1875 and sat with the Radical Party. He was elected to the senate in 1885 and served in Léon Bourgeois' cabinet as minister of education and public worship in 1895 and 1896. He was selected to succeed Pierre Waldeck-Rousseau as prime minister on June 7, 1902. He also served as minister of the interior and public worship and began a vigorous anticlerical campaign to limit the rights of religious orders to teach. He advocated the separation of church and state, and diplomatic relations with the Vatican were severed by France. Combes resigned from office on January 24, 1905. He remained a leading political figure in France and served in Aristide Briand's cabinet as minister without portfolio in 1915 and 1916. Combes died in Pons on May 25, 1921.

MAURICE ROUVIER (Premier; January 24, 1905–March 14, 1906). Maurice Rouvier was born in Aix-en-Provence on April 17, 1842. He worked at a leading Greek commercial house before entering politics. He was elected to the national assembly from Marseilles in 1871. He was recognized as an expert in financial matters and served on numerous budget committees. He was named to Leon Gambetta's cabinet as minister for commerce and the colonies in 1881. He again served as commerce minister in Jules Ferry's government in 1884 and

1885. Rouvier formed a government as prime minister on April 18, 1887. He dismissed General Boulanger from his position as minister of war. Rouvier resigned on November 19, 1887, to force the resignation of French president Jules Grevy, who was implicated in the selling of honors. Rouvier served in several cabinets as minister of finance from 1889 until 1892. He was forced to resign from the government in December 1892 when he was implicated in the Panama scandal, though he was not convicted of misdeeds. He was elected to the senate from Alpes-Maritimes in 1902 and subsequently served in Emile Combes' government as minister of finance. Rouvier again became prime minister on January 24, 1905, also serving as minister of finance and later that year took on the responsibilities of minister of foreign affairs. Conflicts over the government's actions in regard to the separation of church and state forced his resignation on March 14, 1906. He died of pulmonary congestion at his home in Neuilly on June 7, 1911.

FERDINAND SARRIEN (Premier; March 14, 1906–October 23, 1906). Jean Marie Ferdinand Sarrien was born in Bourbon-Lancy on October 15, 1840. He saw action in the war of 1870 as a captain of the militia. He was elected to the chamber of deputies in 1876 and was named to Henri Brisson's cabinet as minister of post and telegraph in 1885. He served as minister of the interior in 1887. Sarrien was elected vice president of the chamber of deputies in 1896. He returned to the cabinet as minister of the interior in 1898 and was named minister of justice later in the year. Sarrien was an unsuccessful candidate for the French presidency in 1906. He succeeded Maurice Rouvier as prime minister on March 14, 1906. He stepped down on October 23, 1906, when Georges Clemenceau formed a government. He then played no major role in French politics and died of a brain hemorrhage on November 28, 1915.

GEORGES CLEMENCEAU (Premier; October 23, 1906–July 25, 1909). Georges Clemenceau was born in Mouilleron-en-Pareds, Vendee, on September 28, 1841. He studied medicine in Nantes and Paris. Clemenceau went to the United States in 1865, where he studied United States political thought and taught French at a private school in Connecticut. He returned to Paris in 1869. Two years later he was elected to the national assembly in Bordeaux, sitting with the Radicals. He stepped down from his seat in the assembly in March 1871 when he was unable to negotiate an agreement between the national assembly and the central committee of the National Guard, which ruled Paris. Clemenceau was elected to the Paris municipal council in July 1871, becoming president of the council in 1875. He was elected to the chamber of deputies the following year and became a leader of the Radicals. He founded the leftist newspaper *La Justice* in 1880 in Paris. During the 1880s Clemenceau was responsible for bringing down several governments and was an outspoken opponent of General Georges Boulanger and the Boulangist movement. Clemenceau did not stand for reelection in 1893 due to a duel he fought with Boulangist Paul Deroulede. Clemenceau subsequently worked primarily as a journalist and became involved with the Dreyfus case. He supported Emile Zola's position against the nationalist and anti-Semitic sentiments that persecuted Dreyfus. Clemenceau returned to active politics in 1902, when he was elected to the senate. He was a proponent of the separation of church and state and was named minister of the interior in Ferdinand Sarrien's government in March 1906. His decision to use the military to settle a labor disorder in Pas-de-alais in May 1906 cost him the support of the Socialists. Clemenceau became prime minister on October 23, 1906, when Sarrien's cabinet resigned. For the next two years Clemenceau helped to strengthen ties between France and Great Britain and led his country to a greater role in Europe. His government resigned on July 25, 1909, when he lost a vote in the chamber of deputies in regard to the state of the French navy. He returned to the senate in 1911, where he campaigned to strengthen the French military in the face of a growing German threat. When World War I commenced in August 1914, Clemenceau was an outspoken critic of the government's in efficiency in waging the war, demanding that more armaments, ammunition, and soldiers be deployed. The morale of the French army and people was at a low ebb by November 16, 1917, when Clemenceau was asked by President Raymond Poincaré to form a government. He did much to restore the nation's confidence, serving as both head of the government and minister of war until the German armistice in November 1918. After the war Clemenceau concentrated on the negotiations of a peace settlement. He served as president of the peace conference at Versailles and tried to reconcile France's position with those of its allies, Great Britain and the United States. A peace treaty was signed in June 1919, and Clemenceau remained in power following elections in November of that year. He was challenged by both the extreme Right and Left in the chamber and was forced to step down on January 19, 1920. Two years later, Clemenceau undertook a tour of the United States as a private citizen to strengthen ties between the French and American people. He subsequently returned to Paris where he spent his remaining years writing several books. Clemenceau died of uremia in Paris on November 24, 1929.

ARISTIDE BRIAND (Premier; July 25, 1909–March 5, 1911). Aristide Briand was born in Nantes on March 28, 1862. He began his political career as a journalist while in law school. Briand moved to Paris in 1893 and became involved in the Socialist Party. He was defeated several times for a seat in the chamber of deputies before his election in 1902. He was instrumental in drafting the law separating church and state. He resigned from the Socialist Party to accept the education and religion ministries in Ferdinand Sarrien's cabinet in March 1906. He remained in Georges Clemenceau's subsequent government, and was named minister of justice in January 1908. Briand was called upon to form a government when Clemenceau stepped down on July 25, 1909. He simultaneously served as minister of home policy and religion. Briand stopped a possible railroad strike by mobilizing railway workers into the army. He formed a new cabinet in November 1910, but was forced to resign on March 5, 1911. He was named to Raymond Poincaré's cabinet as minister of justice in January 1912 and he succeeded as premier on January 21, 1913, when Poincaré was elected president. He was responsible for the adoption of the three-year military service law. His government resigned on March 21, 1913, over Briand's attempts to alter voting procedures. He returned to the government in René Vivani's cabinet as minister of justice in August 1914. Briand replaced Vivani as head of a national coalition government on October 31, 1915. He also served as foreign minister and advocated closer allied relations with Greece during World War I. Briand re-formed his cabinet in the autumn of 1916, appointing General Hubert Lyautey as minister of war. Lyautey resigned in March 1917 and Briand stepped down on March 19, 1917. He was inactive politically for the next three years but was called upon to again head a government on January 16, 1921. Also serving as foreign minister, Briand worked to insure the Versaille Treaty was upheld by Germany. He was criticized by the Conservatives in the chamber of deputies for the Anglo-French mutual defense treaty he negotiated with Britain's David Lloyd George. He resigned from office on January 16, 1922.

He returned to the cabinet as Paul Painlevé's foreign minister in April 1925. He was instrumental in negotiating the Locarno Treaty in October 1925 that confirmed Germany's borders and was the start of Franco-German reconciliation. Briand shared the 1926 Nobel Peace Prize with German Gustav Stresemann for his efforts. Briand again led the government from November 29, 1925, until July 20, 1926, when the chamber of deputies refused to grant the government special powers to deal with economic problems. Raymond Poincaré named Briand foreign minister in his subsequent coalition government. He remained France's leading spokesman on foreign affairs for the next five and a half years. He negotiated the Kellogg-Briand Pact in 1928, which ensured Franco-American nonagression, and he also supported a European union and Franco-German economic cooperation. He also briefly headed the government from July 28, 1929, until October 11, 1929. Briand stepped down as foreign minister due to poor health in January 1932. He died of a heart attack in Paris on March 7, 1932.

ERNEST MONIS (Premier; March 5, 1911–June 29, 1911). Antoine Emmanuel Ernest Monis was born in Chăteauneuf-sur-Charente on May 29, 1846. He became a leading attorney in Paris. Monis was elected to the chamber of deputies from Gironde in 1885 and served until 1889. He was elected to the senate in 1891. Monis was named minister of justice in Rene Waldeck-Rousseau's cabinet in June 1899. He remained in the government until June 1902. He was elected vice president of the senate in 1906 and was appointed premier by President Armand Fallieres on March 5, 1911. Monis's government sent French troops to Morocco to assist the sultan against rebellious tribesmen in April 1911. Monis and other officials were attending an airplane race at Issy-les-Moulineaux on May 21, 1911, when a plane crashed into the spectators. War

Minister Maurice Berteaux was killed and Monis's thigh was broken. He attempted to govern from his sickbed but was forced to step down on June 29, 1911. Monis was appointed minister of marine in December 1913. He was forced to resign in March 1914 when he and Joseph Caillaux were censured by the chamber of deputies for interfering in the trial of a stock swindler several years earlier. His political career floundered, and he was defeated for reelection to the senate in 1920. His final years were spent in relative poverty; he worked as a lawyer before small local courts. When his situation became known, he was voted a state pension. Monis died at his home in Chateauneuf-sur-Charente on May 26, 1929.

JOSEPH CAILLAUX (Premier; June 29, 1911–January 14, 1912). Joseph Marie Auguste Caillaux was born in Le Mans on March 30, 1863. He was the son of French statesman Eugene Caillaux. The younger Caillaux entered civil service as inspector of finance in 1882. He was elected to the chamber of deputies in 1898, sitting with the Radical Socialists. He was named to Rene Waldeck-Rousseau's cabinet as minister of finance in 1899 and served until 1902. He again held the ministry in Georges Clemenceau's government from 1906 to 1909, during which time he introduced the income tax. Caillaux was named premier on June 29, 1911. He negotiated a settlement with Germany over the question of Morocco early in his term. He also introduced several social reform programs and supported state control of the railways. This position garnered major opposition in the chamber of deputies and forced his resignation on January 14, 1912. He was appointed minister of finance in December 1913 and became the object of a vicious slander attack in the newspaper *Le Figaro*. Caillaux's wife shot and killed editor Gaston Calmette when love letters between her and Caillaux, written while she was still married to her first husband, were pub-

lished in *Le Figaro*. She was acquitted of the crime, but Caillaux was forced to resign from the government. He continued to serve in the chamber of deputies during World War I, though he was not invited to serve in any wartime governments. Caillaux supported an early end of the war and met with German agents to seek a negotiated peace. He was accused of treason by Clemenceau and was stripped of parliamentary immunity in December 1917. He was arrested on January 4, 1918, and was tried by the senate two years later. He was acquitted of the more serious crimes but was found guilty of communicating with the enemy during the war. He was sentenced to three years in prison, which he had already served. He was released and retired to Mamers. Caillaux's political rights were restored in the amnesty of 1924. He returned to the government as minister of finance in Paul Painlevé's government in April 1925, but was dismissed the following October. He was elected to the senate in 1925 and returned to the finance ministry under Aristide Briand in June 1926. He resigned several weeks later when the chamber refused to grant him extraordinary powers to deal with the economic crisis. He served as finance minister for several days in Fernand Bouisson's short-lived government in June 1935. He continued to head the Senate's finance committee. He was politically inactive during World War II and the establishment of the Vichy regime. He died at his home in Mamers on November 21, 1944.

RAYMOND POINCARÉ (Premier; January 14, 1912–January 21, 1913). *See earlier entry under Heads of State.*

ARISTIDE BRIAND (Premier; January 21, 1913–March 21, 1913). *See earlier entry under Heads of Government.*

LOUIS BARTHOU (Premier; March 21, 1913–December 10, 1913). Jean-Louis Barthou was born in Oloron-

Sainte-Marie on August 25, 1862. He was educated as a lawyer and elected to the chamber of deputies in 1889. He entered Charles Dupuy's cabinet as minister of public works in 1894. He served as minister of the interior under Jules Meline in 1896. He returned to head the public works ministry in 1906 under Ferdinand Sarrien, retaining that position under Georges Clemenceau through 1909. He was named to head the government as premier on March 21, 1913. He enacted legislation that mandated three-year military service. Barthou's government resigned on December 10, 1913. He served as minister of state in 1917 and became minister of war under Aristide Briand in 1921. He served as minister of justice in 1922 and represented France at the Genoa Conference later in the year. He was subsequently elected to the senate. He returned to the ministry of justice in 1926. Barthou was named foreign minister in Gaston Doumergue's coalition government in 1934. He attempted to negotiate a pact between France and Yugoslavia. Barthou arranged a state visit to France by Yugoslavia's King Alexander I. During the visit Barthou was killed while unsuccessfully attempting to thwart the assassination of the king by a Croation terrorist in Marseille on October 9, 1934.

GASTON DOUMERGUE (Premier; December 10, 1913–June 9, 1914). *See earlier entry under Heads of State.*

ALEXANDRE RIBOT (Premier; June 9, 1914–June 14, 1914). Alexandre-Felix-Joseph Ribot was born in Saint-Omer on February 7, 1842. He was educated in the law and served as a state councilor with the ministry of justice. Ribot was elected to the chamber of deputies in 1878 from Pas-de-Calais. He was defeated for reelection in 1885, but returned to the chamber two years later. He served in the cabinet as minister of foreign affairs from March 1890 to February 1892. Ribot headed the govern-

ment as premier from December 14, 1892, until the Panama Canal scandal brought down his government on March 30, 1893. He again served as premier from January 26, 1895, while also holding the finance portfolio, until his government fell because of a financial scandal on October 30, 1895. He remained a member of the moderate republican opposition for the next eighteen years. Ribot was elected to the senate in 1909. He again briefly served as premier from June 9, 1914, until June 14, 1914. He served in René Vivani's subsequent government as minister of justice. He was again named minister of finance after the outbreak of World War I in August 1914. Ribot held that position until 1916. He was again called upon to head the government as premier and foreign minister on March 19, 1917, and served until September 18, 1917. He remained in Paul Painlevé's subsequent government as foreign minister for several months. He held no further political position. Ribot died in Paris on January 13, 1923.

RENÉ VIVANI (Premier; June 14, 1914–October 31, 1915). René Vivani was born in Sidi Bel Abbes, Algeria, on November 8, 1863. He was educated as a lawyer and practiced in Algeria and Paris. He became involved with the Socialist Party and was elected to the chamber of deputies in 1893. He was defeated for reelection in 1902, but was returned to the chamber in 1906. He was named France's first minister of labor in the government of Georges Clemenceau in October 1906 and retained that position in Aristide Briand's government from 1909 to 1910. He served as minister of education under Gaston Doumergue from 1913 until he was called upon to head the government as premier on June 14, 1914. He also served in the government as foreign minister until the start of World War I in August 1914. Criticism over munition shortages in the early stages of the war compelled Vivani's resignation as premier on October 31, 1915.

He remained in Briand's government as justice minister until March 1917. He headed France's delegation to the League of Nations in 1920 and 1921. He was elected to the senate the following year but held no further government positions. Vivani died in Le Plessis-Robinson, Seine, on September 7, 1925.

ARISTIDE BRIAND (Premier; October 31, 1915–March 19, 1917). *See earlier entry under Heads of Government.*

ALEXANDRE RIBOT (Premier; March 19, 1917–September 18, 1917). *See earlier entry under Heads of Government.*

PAUL PAINLEVÉ (Premier; September 18, 1917–November 16, 1917). Paul Painlevé was born in the Latin Quarter of Paris on December 5, 1863. He received a doctorate in mathematics from the University of Paris in 1887. He later taught at the universities of Paris and Lille and at the École Polytechnique. He was a pioneer in the science of aviation and became the first Frenchman to fly with Wilbur Wright in 1908. He began teaching a course in aviation at the École Aeronautique the following year. Painlevé also became involved in politics. He was elected to the chamber of deputies in 1906 and was a leader of the Republican socialist group. He was named to Aristide Briand's wartime government as minister of education and inventions in October 1915. He served as minister of war from March to September 1917. He was called upon to head the government as premier on September 18, 1917. He stepped down on November 16, 1917, and was replaced by Georges Clemenceau. Painlevé served as president of the chamber of deputies in 1924 and was narrowly defeated for the presidency of the republic by Gaston Doumergue in 1924. Painlevé again headed a Socialist coalition government from April 17, 1925, until his government was forced to resign on November 2, 1925, over its inability to settle a financial cri-

sis brought on by the devaluation of the franc. He subsequently served as minister of war under Aristide Briand and Raymond Poincaré in 1929. He also served as air minister from 1930 until 1932. Painlevé died of a heart attack in Paris on October 29, 1933.

GEORGES CLEMENCEAU (Premier; November 16, 1917–January 19, 1920). *See earlier entry under Heads of Government.*

ALEXANDRE MILLERAND (Premier; January 19, 1920–September 3, 1920). *See earlier entry under Heads of State.*

GEORGES LEYGUES (Premier; September 3, 1920–January 16, 1921). Georges Leygues was born in Villeneuve-sur-Lot on November 28, 1858. He studied law at the University of Bordeaux. He entered politics in 1885 and was elected to the chamber of deputies. He was named minister of public instruction and fine arts in Charles Dupuy's government in May 1894. He remained in the subsequent government of Alexandre Ribot as minister of the interior from January to October 1895, when he resumed the post of minister of public instruction and fine arts. He remained in the cabinet until June 1902. He became colonial minister in March 1906 and served until October 1906. He was politically inactive for the next decade, but returned to the government as minister of marine in 1917. He succeeded Alexandre Millerand as premier on September 3, 1920. His government fell on January 16, 1921. Leygues again served as minister of marine from 1925 to 1926 and from 1929 to 1930 and again from 1932 until his death at his home in Saint Cloud on September 2, 1933.

ARISTIDE BRIAND (Premier; January 16, 1921–January 16, 1922). *See earlier entry under Heads of Government.*

RAYMOND POINCARÉ (Premier; January 16, 1922–June 8, 1924). *See earlier entry under Heads of State.*

FRÉDÉRIC FRANÇOIS-MARSAL (Premier; June 8, 1924–June 14, 1924). Frédéric François-Marsal was born in Paris on March 15, 1874. He was educated at the Lycée Louis-le-Grand and St. Cyr and entered the army. He served on the staff of the governor-general of Indochina before leaving the army and becoming a leading banker. He was named to the cabinet as minister of finance in January 1920 and retained that position until January 1921. He was again named finance minister in Raymond Poincaré's cabinet in March 1924. President Alexandre Millerand appointed François-Marsal premier on June 8, 1924. His cabinet fell six days later on June 14, 1924, precipitating Millerand's resignation as president. François-Marsal returned to his career in banking. He was found guilty of having misused funds of a charitable organization he was director of in 1935. He was fined and sentenced to eighteen months in prison. François-Marsal died at his home in Gisors on May 28, 1958.

EDOUARD HERRIOT (Premier; June 14, 1924–April 17, 1925). Edouard Herriot was born in Troyes on July 5, 1872. He graduated from the École Normal Superieure in 1894. He worked as a teacher and gained a reputation as a leading scholar and educator. Herriot entered politics in 1904 and was elected to the Lyons municipal council. He became mayor of Lyons the following year and retained that position for the remainder of his life. He was elected to the senate as a member of the Radical Party in 1912. He served in Aristide Briand's cabinet as minister of public works, transport, and supplies from December 1916 until March 1917. Herriot stepped down from the senate in 1919 to serve in the chamber of deputies, where he became the leader of the Radicals. He led the oppo-

sition until June 14, 1924, when his left-wing coalition won control of the government. His administration agreed to evacuate French troops from the Ruhr and accepted the Dawes Plan on wartime reparations. His cabinet fell on April 17, 1925. He briefly headed the government for several days from July 20 until July 24, 1926. He was subsequently named minister of education in Raymond Poincaré's cabinet. He retained that position until 1928. He returned to head the government as premier on June 4, 1932, also serving as foreign minister. His cabinet fell on December 20, 1932, when the chamber of deputies refused to pay an installment of France's war debt to the United States. Herriot remained in the government as vice premier under Gaston Doumergue and Pierre Flandin until 1935. He was elected president of the chamber of deputies in June 1936, retaining that office until the German occupation in June 1940. Herriot remained in France after the occupation. His criticism of the Vichy government of Henri-Philippe Pétain resulted in his arrest and deportation to Germany. He remained imprisoned in Germany until his rescue by Soviet troops in April 1945. He resumed his political career and was elected president of the new national assembly in 1947. He retained that position until his retirement in 1954. Herriot died in Lyons of heart failure on March 26, 1957.

PAUL PAINLEVÉ (Premier; April 17, 1925–November 2, 1925). *See earlier entry under Heads of Government.*

ARISTIDE BRIAND (Premier; November 29, 1925–July 20, 1926). *See earlier entry under Heads of Government.*

EDOUARD HERRIOT (Premier; July 20, 1926–July 24, 1926). *See earlier entry under Heads of Government.*

RAYMOND POINCARÉ (Premier; July 24, 1926–July 28, 1929). *See earlier entry under Heads of State.*

ARISTIDE BRIAND (Premier; July 28, 1929–October 11, 1929). *See earlier entry under Heads of Government.*

RAYMOND POINCARÉ (Premier; October 11, 1929–November 2, 1929). *See earlier entry under Heads of State.*

ANDRÉ TARDIEU (Premier; November 2, 1929–February 21, 1930). André-Pierre-Gabriel-Amédée Tardieu was born in Paris on September 22, 1876. He was educated at the Ecole Normale Superieur. He began his career in the diplomatic service as an attaché at the French embassy in Berlin in 1897. He returned to Paris the following year to work in the foreign ministry. Tardieu achieved prominence writing for *Figaro* in 1901 and for *Le Temps* beginning in 1903, often under the pseudonym of George Villiers. He became foreign editor of *Le Temps*, where he remained until his election to the chamber of deputies in 1914. He became a close ally of Georges Clemenceau and was a member of the French delegation to the Paris Peace Conference in 1919. He was defeated for reelection to the chamber in 1924, but regained his seat two years later. He was subsequently named to Raymond Poincaré's cabinet as minister of public works. He became minister of the interior in 1928. Tardieu was the leader of the center-right in the chamber of deputies and formed a government as prime minister on November 2, 1929. He stepped down on February 21, 1930, over a budgetary question in the chamber. He was again called upon to head the government on March 2, 1930, serving until December 13, 1930. He remained in the government, serving as minister of agriculture from 1931 until 1932 and minister of war in 1932 under Pierre Laval. Tardieu formed his third government on February 23, 1932, serving as prime minister and minister of foreign affairs. His coalition was defeated in subsequent elections and he relinquished office on June 4, 1932. He re-

turned to the government as minister of state without portfolio in Gaston Doumergue's government of national union in 1934. He retired from active politics the following year. Tardieu's health declined, and he suffered a nervous breakdown and a stroke in 1939. His illnesses left him largely paralyzed. He died in a hospital in Mento on September 15, 1945.

CAMILLE CHAUTEMPS (Premier; February 21, 1930–March 2, 1930). Camille Chautemps was born in Paris on February 1, 1885. He was the son of Emile Chautemps, a former vice president of the French senate. Chautemps was educated in Paris, where he received a degree in law. He entered politics as a member of the Radical Party and was elected mayor of Tours. He was elected to the chamber of deputies in 1919 and was named to Edouard Herriot's cabinet as minister of the interior in 1925. Chautemps became premier on February 21, 1930, but his government lost a vote of confidence in the chamber of deputies two days later and he was replaced on March 2, 1930. He again headed the government from November 22, 1933, to January 30, 1934. He served in Léon Blum's government and opposed giving aid to the Spanish Republic during the civil war in 1937. He replaced Blum as premier on June 23, 1937. He resigned on March 12, 1938, and was succeeded by Blum's second government. Chautemps supported a negotiated peace with Adolf Hitler's Germany at the start of World War II. He served as vice premier in Henri-Philippe Pétain's Vichy government in June 1940 and was sent on a mission to the United States. He broke with the Vichy regime while in the United States and offered his support to Charles de Gaulle's Free French provisional government. Chautemps remained in the United States after the war. He was tried and convicted in absentia for collaborating with the enemy. He received a five-year prison term that was eventually set aside. He was allowed to visit France in later years, but continued to reside in the United States. He died at his home in Washington, D.C., on July 1, 1963, after a long illness.

ANDRÉ TARDIEU (Premier; March 2, 1930–December 13, 1930). *See earlier entry under Heads of Government.*

THEODORE STEEG (Premier; December 13, 1930–January 27, 1931). Theodore Steeg was born in Libourne on December 9, 1868. He entered politics and was elected to the chamber of deputies as a Radical in 1904. He was elected to the senate in 1914. Steeg served in several cabinets as minister of education and minister of the interior. He was governor-general of Algeria in the early 1920s, before replacing General Hubert Lyautey as resident-general of Morocco in September 1925. He headed the French government there when Abdelkrim surrendered, ending the Rift rebellion. Steeg returned to Paris to form a government on December 13, 1930. He served as premier for slightly over a month, stepping down on January 27, 1931. He was minister of colonies under Camille Chautemps in 1933 and minister of state in Léon Blum's government later in the year. He refused to give his support to the Vichy government during World War II. Steeg was the leader of the Radical Party after the war and served in the first constituent assembly. He died in Paris on December 10, 1950.

PIERRE LAVAL (Premier; January 27, 1931–February 23, 1932). Pierre Laval was born in Chateldon, Pyu-de-Dome, on June 28, 1883. He was elected to the chamber of deputies from Aubervilliers in 1914. He began his political career on the extreme left, but moved to the right after becoming a senator in 1926. He served in several governments before becoming premier on January 27, 1931. He stepped down on February 23, 1932. He subsequently served as minis-

ter of labor in Andre Tardieu's government from February to June 1932. Laval was minister of colonies from February to October 1934 and foreign minister from October 1934 to May 1935. He again headed the government as premier from June 7, 1935, until January 25, 1936, while also retaining the position of foreign minister. During this term of office he supported an agreement that recognized Italy's claims on Abyssinia. He remained out of the government until after Germany's defeat of France in June 1940. He entered Henri-Philippe Pétain's Vichy government as premier on July 11, 1940. Pétain distrusted Laval's ambition and dismissed him in December 1940. He was subsequently arrested and imprisoned until the Germans arranged his release. He subsequently went to German-occupied Paris. He returned to power to lead the Vichy government on April 9, 1942. Laval was granted dictatorial powers by Pétain shortly after resuming office. The Allies began achieving victory over the German forces, and Laval was forced to retreat with the Germans on August 17, 1944. He escaped to Switzerland the following year. He then went to Spain before returning to France to stand trial for treason in July 1945. He was sentenced to death, and after a failed suicide attempt by poison in the prison of Fresnes, he was shot to death on October 15, 1945.

ANDRÉ TARDIEU (Premier; February 23, 1932–June 4, 1932). *See earlier entry under Heads of Government.*

EDOUARD HERRIOT (Premier; June 4, 1932–December 20, 1932). *See earlier entry under Heads of Government.*

JOSEPH PAUL-BONCOUR (Premier; December 20, 1932–January 31, 1933). Joseph Paul-Boncour was born in Saint-Aignan, on August 4, 1873. He attended the University of Paris, where he received a degree in law. He served as private secretary to Premier Pierre

Waldeck-Rousseau from 1898 until 1902. Paul-Boncour was elected to the chamber of deputies in 1906 and was named to the cabinet as minister of labor in 1911. He was defeated for reelection to the chamber in 1914, but was returned to office after World War I as a Socialist. He was elected to the senate in 1931 and was named France's permanent representative to the League of Nations in 1932. He also served as minister of war in Edouard Herriot's cabinet in 1932 and briefly served as premier from December 20, 1932, until January 31, 1933. He also served in the government as foreign minister, and retained that position in the subsequent government until January 1934. He again served as foreign minister from January until June 1936 and in March 1938. He refused to support Marshal Henri-Philippe Pétain's Vichy government, favoring the continuation of France's war against Germany in July 1940. Paul-Boncour supported the Resistance during the occupation. He was elected to the consultative assembly after the war in 1944 and headed the French delegation to the United Nations Charter Conference in San Francisco. He again served in the senate from 1946 until his retirement in 1948. He died in Paris at the age of 98 on March 28, 1972.

EDOUARD DALADIER (Premier; January 31, 1933–October 24, 1933). Edouard Daladier was born in Carpentras, near Vaucluse, on June 18, 1884. He was educated at the Lycée Duparc in Lyons and became a history professor at several universities. He entered politics in 1912 and was elected mayor of Carpentras. He served with distinction in the French army during World War I. He was elected to the chamber of deputies in 1919 as a Radical. He was named to Edouard Herriot's cabinet as minister of colonies in 1924 and he participated in subsequent Radical governments in various positions, including minister of war, education, and foreign affairs. He led the

government as premier from January 31, 1933, until October 24, 1933. He remained in the cabinet as minister of war until January 30, 1934, when he again became premier. He was forced to step down after ten days on February 9, 1934, following violent riots that took place in Paris over a financial scandal. Daladier served in several successive governments as minister of national defense from June 1936 until April 1938. He then resumed the position of premier on April 10, 1938. Daladier led the government to the right, using force to break strikes and refusing to support the Spanish Republic during the civil war. He joined with British Prime Minister Neville Chamberlain to sign the Munich agreement in September 1938 that gave Czechoslovakia to the Axis powers. Daladier continued to head the government when France declared war on Germany on September 3, 1939. He stepped down on March 21, 1940, when his government was criticized for not assisting Finland during the Soviet invasion. He remained in the cabinet as minister of war under Paul Reynaud until May 1940 and briefly served as foreign minister until June 1940. Daladier was interned by the Vichy government in September 1940. He was deported to Germany in 1943, where he remained imprisoned until he was liberated by American troops in 1945. Daladier was reelected to the chamber of deputies in 1946, where he remained until his retirement in 1958. He died at his home in Paris on October 10, 1970.

ALBERT SARRAUT (Premier; October 24, 1933–November 22, 1933). Albert Pierre Sarraut was born in Bordeaux on July 28, 1872. He studied law in Carcassone and Toulouse. He entered politics and was elected to the chamber of deputies in 1902. He served as undersecretary of state from 1906 until 1910. Sarraut was governor-general of Indochina from November 1911 until January 1914. He returned to France to serve as minister of education in René Vivani's cabinet until 1915. He returned to In-dochina as governor-general from January 1917 until May 1919. He was minister of colonies from 1920 to 1924 and was France's ambassador to Turkey from 1925 to 1926. He was elected to the senate in 1926 and served as minister of the interior from 1926 to 1928. He was minister of the navy from 1930 to 1931 and was again minister of colonies from 1932 to 1933. He headed the government as premier from October 24, 1933, until November 22, 1933, when he resigned over a financial issue. He served as minister of the interior in 1934 and again became premier on January 25, 1936. He gained approval in the chamber of deputies for the Franco-Soviet mutual assistance treaty. He continued to head the government when Germany violated the Treaty of Versailles by sending troops into the Rhineland. Sarraut stepped down on June 3, 1936. He served in several governments as minister of the interior between June 1937 and June 1940. Sarraut was largely inactive during the early years of the occupation. He became editor of the *Depeche de Toulouse* in 1943 after his brother, Maurice, was murdered by Nazis. He was arrested by the Gestapo in 1944 and deported to Germany. He was liberated by the Allies the following year. Sarraut failed to secure a seat in the parliament after the war. He became president of the French Union in 1949 and served until his retirement in 1958. He died at his home in Paris on November 26, 1962.

CAMILLE CHAUTEMPS (Premier; November 22, 1933–January 30, 1934). *See earlier entry under Heads of Government.*

EDOUARD DALADIER (Premier; January 30, 1934–February 9, 1934). *See earlier entry under Heads of Government.*

GASTON DOUMERGUE (Premier; February 9, 1934–November 10, 1934). *See earlier entry under Heads of State.*

PIERRE-ÉTIENNE FLANDIN (Premier; November 10, 1934–May 30, 1935). Pierre-Étienne Flandin was born to a wealthy family in Paris on April 12, 1889. He entered politics and was elected to the chamber of deputies in 1914. He was named to the cabinet as minister of commerce in 1924. He again headed the commerce ministry from 1929 until 1930 and became minister of finance in 1931. He remained in the cabinet until November 10, 1934, when he became premier and foreign minister. His government collapsed over a financial issue on May 30, 1935. He served as minister without portfolio under Pierre Laval from 1935 until 1936. He was foreign minister in Albert Sarraut's government from January to June 1936. He was unable to persuade the government to react against Germany when the Rhineland was invaded in March 1936, and he subsequently resigned himself to a view that Germany would be the dominant power in Europe. He served in Pierre Laval's Vichy government as foreign minister from December 1940 until February 1941. After the war he was tried for treason. He was acquitted of treason but sentenced to five years of national indignity for collaborating with the Vichy regime. The sentence was subsequently suspended. Flandin was elected to the council of the Yonne Department in 1955. He died at Saint Jean-Cap-Ferrat on the Riviera on June 13, 1958.

FERNAND BOUISSON (Premier; June 1, 1935–June 4, 1935). Fernand Emile Honore Bouisson was born in Constantine on June 16, 1874. He served in the chamber of deputies as a member of the Socialist Party and became president of the chamber in 1927. He resigned from the Socialist Party after the riots in February 1934. Bouisson headed the government as premier for four days from June 1, 1935, until June 4, 1935. He remained president of the chamber of deputies until 1936. He was a supporter of the Vichy regime during World War II and was arrested in 1944 as a collaborationist. He was imprisoned for a time after the war. Bouisson died of a heart attack at his Riviera villa in Antibes on December 28, 1959.

PIERRE LAVAL (Premier; June 7, 1935–January 25, 1936). *See earlier entry under Heads of Government.*

ALBERT SARRAUT (Premier; January 25, 1936–June 3, 1936). *See earlier entry under Heads of Government.*

LEÓN BLUM (Premier; June 3, 1936–June 23, 1937). León Blum was born in Paris to an Alsatian Jewish family on April 9, 1872. He received a degree in law from the Sorbonne in 1894. He subsequently worked as a drama critic. Blum joined the Socialist Party in 1899 and was a supporter of the Republicans during the Dreyfus affair. He was elected to the chamber of deputies in 1919 and served as chairman of the Socialist Party's executive board. He broke with the Socialists in 1921 when the Communists took control of the party. Blum founded the Moderate Socialist Party and created the journal *Le Populaire*. Blum was defeated for reelection to the chamber of deputies in 1928, but was returned the following year. He formed the Popular Front, a coalition of leftist parties opposed to fascism, in 1936 and led the coalition to victory. He became premier on June 3, 1936. His government carried out a number of social reforms, including nationalizing the leading French armament industries and the Bank of France and instituting a 40-hour work week. His reforms were bitterly opposed by the business community and the right wing. He tried to maintain France's neutrality during the Spanish Civil War, alienating many of his leftist supporters. Blum resigned on June 23, 1937, when the French senate refused to grant him special powers to deal with the economic crisis. He served as vice premier in the subsequent government of Camille Chautemps and returned as premier on March 12, 1938. He was again forced to resign on April 10, 1938, and refused to participate in the government of Radical leader Edouard Daladier. Following the defeat of France by the Germans in October 1940, Blum was charged with betrayal of his office by the Vichy authorities. He was brought to trial in February 1942. The trial was suspended after several months because of the spirited defense offered by Blum and his codefendants. He was returned to prison in a German concentration camp, where he remained until he was freed by American troops in May 1945. He returned to France and again became premier of an interim Socialist government on December 16, 1946. He stepped down on January 22, 1947, following the election of a president for the new French Fourth Republic. He was narrowly defeated for another term as premier in November 1947, and joined the government of André Marie as vice premier in August 1948. Despite ill health, Blum remained a leading political figure in France. He died of a heart attack at his country cottage in Jouy-en-Josas on March 30, 1950.

CAMILLE CHAUTEMPS (Premier; June 23, 1937–March 12, 1938). *See earlier entry under Heads of Government.*

LÉON BLUM (Premier; March 12, 1938–April 10, 1938). *See earlier entry under Heads of Government.*

EDOUARD DALADIER (Premier; April 10, 1938–March 21, 1940). *See earlier entry under Heads of Government.*

PAUL REYNAUD (Premier; March 21, 1940–June 11, 1940). Paul Reynaud was born in Barcelonnette, Basses-Alpes, on October 15, 1878. He was educated in Paris, where he became a lawyer. Reynaud saw action on the western front during World War I. He was elected to the chamber of deputies in 1919. He was out of the chamber from 1924 until 1928. He was named to the cabinet in 1930 as minister of finance. He also served as minister of the colonies and minister of justice over the next two years. He became minister of justice under Edouard Daladier in April 1938, and he opposed the Munich agreement that gave Czechoslovakia to Germany. He was named minister of finance in 1938 and devalued the franc in an attempt to prepare France's economy for a possible war. He became premier of France on March 21, 1940. He supported the continuation of the war as France's forces were collapsing. When an armistice seemed inevitable, he resigned on June 11, 1940, rather than be a party to it. He was arrested by the Vichy government in September 1940 and remained in captivity throughout the war until the liberation. He returned to politics after the war as a member of the chamber of deputies. He was minister of finance and economic affairs in André Marie's short-lived coalition government in July 1948. He was unsuccessful in forming a government in 1953, but served as vice premier in Joseph Laniel's cabinet. He supported Charles de Gaulle's government in 1958 and was instrumental in drafting the Fifth Republic's constitution. He broke with de Gaulle over his increased powers as president in 1962 and retired from office. Reynaud died of a heart attack at the American Hospital in Neuilly, outside of Paris, on September 21, 1966.

HENRI-PHILIPPE PÉTAIN (Premier; June 17, 1940–July 11, 1940). *See earlier entry under Heads of State.*

PIERRE LAVAL (Premier; July 11, 1940–December 1940). *See earlier entry under Heads of Government.*

JEAN DARLAN (Premier; February 11, 1941–April 9, 1942). Jean Louis Xavier François Darlan was born in Nerac, Lot-et-Garonne, on August 7, 1881. He entered the French naval school in 1899 and served in the French navy. He served as a commander during World War I and rose through the ranks to rear admiral in 1929. He was named chief of staff of the navy in December 1936 and, following his promotion to admiral of the fleet, he became commander in chief of the French navy in August 1939. Following the fall of France in 1940, Darlan served Henri-Philippe Pétain's Vichy regime as vice premier. He headed the government from February 11, 1941, until April 9, 1942. He subsequently became commander-in-chief of all Vichy French military forces. He was sent to North Africa to serve as high commissioner in November 1942. The Allied invasion of Morocco and Algeria began soon after, and Darlan ordered the local Vichy French forces not to resist the invasion. He negotiated an armistice with the Allies and brought his forces under the command of the Free French. Darlan was granted authority as chief of state for French Africa and was to be placed in charge of all French Resistance forces. But Darlan was shot and killed in Algiers on December 24, 1942, by Bonnier de la Chappille, a French antifascist, who viewed Darlan as a traitor to France for his earlier collaboration with the Germans.

PIERRE LAVAL (Premier; April 9, 1942–August 17, 1944). *See earlier entry under Heads of Government.*

CHARLES DE GAULLE (Premier; September 10, 1944–January 27, 1946). *See earlier entry under Heads of State.*

Germany

Germany is located in north central Europe.

HEADS OF STATE

WILHELM II (Kaiser; June 15, 1888–November 28, 1918). Friedrich Wilhelm Viktor Albert was born in Potsdam on January 27, 1859, the eldest son of Crown Prince Frederick of Prussia and British Princess Victoria, eldest daughter of Queen Victoria. He was born with a crippled left arm and was estranged from his mother at an early age. He had a military education and began serving in the army in 1879. His father succeeded to the throne as emperor of Germany and king of Prussia on March 9, 1888, but died shortly thereafter on June 15, 1888. His son succeeded to the throne as Kaiser Wilhelm II. Wilhelm came into conflict with Otto von Bismarck, the architect of the German empire and the leading political figure in Germany. He dismissed Bismarck as chancellor in March 1890. Wilhelm exercised great influence on subsequent governments and sought to eliminate the growing strength of the Social Democrats. Wilhelm's foreign policy was geared toward expansion of the German empire. He drew the ire of the British for his telegram of support for Paul Kruger, president of the South African Republic, in 1896. The British were also concerned about Germany's naval policy under Admiral Alfred von Tirpitz. The Kaiser sought to drive a wedge between the British and French by supporting the independence of Morocco in 1905, but he was forced to accept France's control there in a conference the following year. He further antagonized the British with an interview in the *Daily Telegraph*, in which he claimed much of Germany was anti-British. His actions embarrassed the government of Chancellor Prince Bernhard von Bülow, and the Kaiser promised to be more circumspect in future statements. A war between Germany and France over the Moroccan question was narrowly averted in 1911 following the Agadir crisis. Germany's support for Austria-Hungary against Serbia drew it into World War I in 1914. The Kaiser largely deferred to his general staff in the conduct of the war and refused to accept the possibility of a negotiated peace until late in the war. There was much sentiment within Germany for Wilhelm's abdication as the war ended. Though he initially resisted, he was persuaded to seek asylum in the Netherlands on November 9, 1918. Wilhelm signed his abdication on November 28, 1918, and spent the remainder of his life in exile. He died at his estate in Doorn, the Netherlands, of an intestinal ailment on June 4, 1941.

FRIEDRICH EBERT (President; February 6, 1919–February 28, 1925). Friedrich Ebert was born in Heidelberg on February 4, 1871. He was apprenticed to a saddler at the age of 14 and worked his trade throughout Germany as a young man. He became involved in the trade union movement and the Social Democratic Party, and edited the Socialist newspaper in Bremen, the *Bürgerzeitung*. He became secretary general of the Social Democratic Party in 1905 and succeeded August Bebel as chairman of the party in 1913. Ebert had been elected to the Reichstag the previous year. The party grew in strength under Ebert and supported the government's war policy in 1914. Leftist members of the party broke with the Social Democrats in 1917. As Germany's hopes of a military victory in World War I diminished, revolutionary movements took hold throughout the country. The Kaiser was forced from the throne in November 1918. Ebert replaced Prince Max of Baden as head of the government, which he named "Council of People's Representatives," on November 9, 1918. Ebert was elected the first president of the new German Republic and took office on February 6, 1919. The new republic was besieged by civil strife and revolutionary activity from the Left. The Communist uprisings were suppressed with the use of volunteer military units, known as the Freikorps. The harsh settlements imposed on Germany as a result of the Treaty of Versailles led to further problems for the new republic. Wolfgang Kapp led an unsuccessful coup attempt known as the Kapp Putsch against the government in March 1920 with the goal of restoring the monarchy. Germany appealed to the Allies for a moratorium on war reparations due to a severe economic crisis. France seized the German industrial center, the Ruhr region, and Ebert supported a general strike in that area. The strike further damaged the country's economy, and Ebert's political reputation suffered as well. His own party deserted him over his appointment of Gustav Stresemann as chancellor in August 1923. The republic survived the crisis and the economy improved through monetary reform and the negotiation of a reduction of reparations. Ebert continued to serve as president until his death in a Berlin hospital of peritonitis after surgery for appendicitis on February 28, 1925.

WALTER SIMONS (President; February 28, 1925–May 12, 1925). Walter Simons was born in Elberfeld in 1861. He studied history, philosophy and law and became a judge in 1893. He began working at the ministry of justice in 1905 and at the foreign ministry in 1910. Simons was the director of the Reich chan-

cellery at the start of World War I. He was a member of the German delegation to the Versailles Peace Conference in 1919. He rejected the terms of the settlement and the admission of Germany's guilt in starting the war. Simons resigned from the foreign office in June 1919 and continued to denounce the terms of the Treaty of Versailles. Simons was foreign minister in Konstantine Fehrenbach's cabinet in June 1920 and headed the German delegation to the London war reparations conference in the spring of 1921. He refused to accept the reparations plan, citing Germany's inability to pay. He won praise from the German people for his stance, but the cabinet was forced to resign in May 1921 when France pressured the government into submission with troop movements in the Ruhr region. Simons was named to the federal court in Leipzig in 1922. As president of the German Supreme Court, he served as interim president of the republic upon the death of Friedrich Ebert on February 28, 1925, until the election of Paul von Hindenburg on May 12, 1925. Simons remained chief justice of the Supreme Court until his resignation in December 1929. He subsequently served as president of the German Society for International Law until 1934. Simon died at his home in Nowaweson on July 14, 1941.

PAUL VON HINDENBURG (President; May 12, 1925–August 2, 1934). Paul Ludwig Hans Anton von Beneckendorff und von Hindenburg was born in Posen, Prussia, on October 2, 1847. He entered the Prussian military at the age of 11, serving in the Austro-Prussian War in 1866. He also saw action during the Franco-German War of 1870 and 1871. Hindenburg attained the rank of major general in 1896. He was placed in command of the Fourth Army Corps at Magdeburg in 1903, where he remained until his retirement in 1911. He settled in Hanover until he was called back into service in August 1914. He was credited with the success of the German army in opposing the invading Russian forces in East Prussia. He was promoted to the rank of field marshal general and became chief of the general staff in August 1916. After the defeat of the German army, Hindenburg led the troops home. He again retired in 1919. He was approached by the Rightist parties to run for the presidency of the Republic following the death of Friedrich Ebert in February 1925. He was successful in the election on April 26, 1925, and took office on May 12, 1925. He initially governed in accordance with the constitution until the economic crisis of 1929. He began a period of government by decree in June 1930, when the Reichstag proved uncooperative with the government of chancellor Heinrich Brüning. The Nazi Party under Adolf Hitler made major gains in the 1930 elections and orchestrated a campaign of civil unrest throughout Germany. Hindenburg was persuaded to seek a second term of office in April 1932. He defeated Hitler for the presidency but had difficulty in forming a government. Hitler refused to allow the Nazis to participate in any government of which he was not the chancellor. Hindenburg distrusted Hitler and refused to name him to head the government. When the government of General Kurt von Schleicher fell in late January 1933, Franz von Papen convinced Hindenburg to appoint Hitler as chancellor of a coalition cabinet. Hitler quickly seized power in the new government. Hindenburg, whose power was eclipsed by that of his chancellor, adjusted to the new situation and became a supporter of Hitler. He continued to serve as president until his death in Neudeck on August 2, 1934.

ADOLF HITLER (President; August 2, 1934–April 30, 1945). Adolf Hitler was born in Braunau-am-Inn, Austria, near the Bavarian border, on April 20, 1889. He received his secondary education in Linz. For several years he worked as an artist, but without much success. He went to Munich in 1913, but was recalled to Austria the following year for military service. He was rejected as unfit, but joined the German army when World War I broke out. He served as a corporal on the front lines and was given the Iron Cross for bravery in action. He was wounded in 1916 and was hospitalized for exposure to gas. Hitler entered politics after the war, joining the German Workers' Party in 1919. The party was renamed the Nationalsozialistische Deutsche Arbeiterpartei, or Nazi Party, in August 1920. Hitler directed the party's propaganda department in Munich. He became associated with Ernst Roehm, who organized the *Sturmabteilungen* (SA), which served as the party's paramilitary unit. Hitler greatly strengthened the small party through his use of propaganda and by blaming many of Germany's problems on the Jews and Communists. Despite friction with other party leaders, he became the chairman of the party in July 1921. The growth of the party under Hitler led him to join with General Erich Ludendorff in a coup attempt against the Weimar Republic in Munich in November 1923. The Munich Putsch was unsuccessful, and Hitler was arrested and sentenced to a five-year prison term. He only served nine months at Landsberg, where he wrote the first volume of his political treatise *Mein Kampf*. The party's fortunes diminished while Hitler was imprisoned. He dedicated himself to rebuilding the party despite rulings that he was not to give speeches in Bavaria and other German states. He formed an alliance with Alfred Hugenberg's Nationalists in 1929 during the worldwide economic depression that engulfed Germany. Hitler's brand of right-wing authoritarianism appealed to the business and industrial leaders of Germany, who helped to fund his political endeavors. The party's strength grew rapidly in the face of the government's inability to control the many problems besetting Germany. Hitler drew over 36 percent of the vote in the

1930 presidential election against Paul von Hindenburg. His strong following led to a growing personal mystique that garnered him the chancellorship on January 30, 1933. Hitler persuaded von Hindenburg to call for new elections once he had taken power. The Reichstag fire, allegedly set by Communists on February 27, 1933, gave Hitler an excuse to seize greater power and suspend civil liberties. Hitler needed to solidify the support of the army for his regime. Ernst Roehm and his supporters, who continued to press for more revolutionary action, caused problems between the government and the army. Unable to convince Roehm to moderate his position, Hitler moved against Roehm and the SA, as well as other political rivals, on June 29, 1934. During what became known as "the night of the long knives," Roehm, his top lieutenants, Nazi rival leader Gregor Strasser, former prime minister General Kurt von Schleicher, and numerous others were arrested and summarily executed by order of Hitler with the support of his lieutenants, Hermann Goering, and Heinrich Himmler. This action brought the army firmly into Hitler's camp and, when von Hindenburg died on August 2, 1934, they supported the merger of the chancellorship with the presidency, giving Hitler supreme command of the armed forces. As Germany's economy rebounded, Hitler turned his attention to foreign affairs. On the international stage Hitler attempted to allay the fears of the Western powers and establish himself as a bastion against communism. He began to expand Germany's military strength despite the opposition of Britain, France, and Italy. He negotiated a naval treaty with England in June 1935 and remilitarized the Rhineland in March 1936. He considered Benito Mussolini's Fascist regime in Italy as a natural ally for Germany, and the Rome-Berlin Axis was established in October 1936. He also approved a treaty of alliance with Japan later in the year. Hitler sent troops to

Austria in February 1938, effecting the annexation of that country by the German state. He was able to acquire the Sudentenland from Czechoslovakia as a result of the Munich agreement with Britain and France in September 1938. Not satisfied, Hitler's forces invaded and occupied the rest of Czechoslovakia in March 1939. His next move, against Poland, met with opposition from Britain and France. Hitler signed a nonaggression pact with the Soviet Union in August 1939 and began the invasion of Poland on September 1, 1939. Britain and France declared war on Germany two days later. The German forces quickly triumphed in Poland and occupied Denmark and Norway in April 1940. Italy entered the conflict on Germany's side on June 10, 1940, and France capitulated later in the month. Hitler's hope for a quick victory over Britain did not materialize, despite Germany's devastating aerial attacks on the island. Hitler was forced to come to Italy's aid in the invasion of Greece and the Balkans and invaded Yugoslavia in March 1941. Germany began its war on the eastern front against the Soviet Union on June 22, 1941. Hitler's hope for a quick victory there also did not come to pass. The Japanese attack on Pearl Harbor in December 1941 brought the United States into the conflict against the Axis Powers. During this period the Nazi state expanded concentration camps for the internment of Jews from Germany and other occupied territories. Extermination camps at such places as Auschwitz and Mauthausen began the liquidation of the Jews in what was viewed by Hitler as a "final solution" to the Jewish question. It is estimated that nearly six million Jews and over a million other ethnic minorities were cruelly slaughtered in these camps. Germany suffered military defeats at El Alamein in North Africa and Stalingrad in the Soviet Union near the end of 1942. Mussolini was ousted in July 1943, and Germany was forced to occupy northern Italy and rescue the captured dictator. As Germany's military position weakened, some people in the military and civilian population plotted for Hitler's removal in order to negotiate a peace. Hitler survived an assassination attempt at his headquarters in East Prussia when Colonel Graf Claus von Stauffenberg detonated a bomb during a conference there. Hitler was only slightly injured and immediately instituted a purge of his opponents, executing most of the plotters and many other critics of his regime as well. The German army continued to be driven back, though Hitler refused to consider a negotiated surrender. An offensive by the German forces in the Ardennes in December 1944 met with failure, and Hitler spent the remainder of the war sequestered in the chancellery and the bunker beneath it. His mental and physical health had declined during the war and, as the Russian army advanced on Berlin, Hitler began to accept the likelihood of defeat. On April 30, 1945, Hitler married his longtime mistress, Eva Braun, in the bunker. He appointed Admiral Karl Doenitz as his successor and shot himself, while his new wife took poison. According to his instructions, their bodies were burned to prevent desecration by the Russian troops.

KARL DOENITZ (President; April 30, 1945–May 23, 1945). Karl Doenitz was born in Berlin on September 16, 1891. He joined the German navy in 1909 and served as a submarine officer during World War I. He was captured by the British during the war and was confined to a mental institution in Manchester, England, though it was generally believed he had only feigned insanity. He was eventually repatriated to Germany.

Between the wars Doenitz secretly worked on submarine designs and training plans in anticipation of the time when Germany could rearm itself. Doenitz was promoted to rear admiral in 1935 and supervised the construction of a new U-boat fleet. As commander of this fleet during World War II, Doenitz was responsible for sinking nearly 3,000 Allied ships before the convoy system rendered the submarines largely ineffective. Doenitz was named to succeed Admiral Erich Raeder as commander-in-chief of the navy on January 30, 1943. Adolf Hitler appointed Doenitz as head of the northern military and civil command on April 20, 1945. He was named by Hitler as his successor as head of state before his suicide on April 30, 1945. Doenitz initially resisted the Allied call for an unconditional surrender in the hopes of arranging for the majority of the German armed forces to surrender to the British and Americans rather than to the Soviets. His attempts proved futile, and Doenitz surrendered unconditionally on May 23, 1945. He was held by the Allies and tried for war crimes at the International Military Tribunal at Nuremberg with other major figures in the Nazi regime. Doenitz was not implicated in the Nazi policy of genocide and crimes against humanity, but was convicted of his role in the war and sentenced to ten years in prison on September 30, 1946. He was released from Spandau Prison in West Berlin in 1956. He retired on a government pension and completed his memoirs two years later. Doenitz settled in an old villa in Auhmuehle, where he lived in relative obscurity. He died of progressive heart disease in Grunau bei Berlin on December 24, 1980.

HEADS OF GOVERNMENT

PRINCE VON HOHENLOHE-SCHILLINGFÜRST (Chancellor; October 29, 1894–October 17, 1900). Chlodwig Carl Victor, Prince von Hohenlohe-

Schillingfürst and Prince of Ratibor and Corvey was born in Rothenburg, Bavaria, on March 31, 1819. He succeeded his eldest brother to his princely title in 1846. Prince von Hohenlohe took his place in the Bavarian House of Peers, where he distinguished himself. He held various government positions and ambassadorial posts before his appointment as minister president of Bavaria in December 1866. Hohenlohe's opposition to the acceptance of the Vatican's dogma of papal infallibility led to his resignation in February 1870. The following year he became a leading advocate of Bavaria's incorporation into the German Empire and was elected to the Reichstag (German Parliament). He served as vice president of that body, sitting with the Free Conservative Party. He was sent to France as Germany's ambassador in 1874. He was appointed governor of Alsace-Lorraine in 1885, serving until 1894. Hohenlohe was named by Kaiser Wilhelm II to succeed Prince George von Caprivi as chancellor on October 29, 1894. The aging Hohenlohe largely deferred to the wishes of the imperial court in regard to Germany's domestic and foreign policies. He also served as a moderating influence on the rivalries of the more powerful figures in the government. He continued to head the government until October 17, 1900, when he stepped down for reasons of health. He died suddenly the following year in Ragatz, Switzerland, on July 6, 1901.

PRINCE BERNHARD VON BÜLOW (Chancellor; October 17, 1900–July 14, 1909). Prince Bernhard von Bulow was born in Klein-Flottbeck, near Altona, on May 3, 1849, the son of Bernhardt Ernst von Bülow, a close associate of Otto von Bismarck. The younger von Bülow served in the army during the Franco-German War in 1870 and entered the civil service two years later. He served as the assistant to the administrator of Metz. He entered diplomatic service in 1874, serving as chargé d'affaires in Athens. He subsequently served at the Germany embassy in Paris as secretary and at St. Petersburg, Russia, as councilor. He was named minister to Bucharest in 1888 and ambassador to Rome in 1894. He returned to Berlin to serve in the imperial cabinet as foreign minister in 1897. He supervised the emperor's policy of German colonial expansion. He succeeded Prince von Hohenlohe-Schillingfürst as chancellor on October 17, 1900. His chancellery was widely known throughout Europe as a gathering place for the cultural and social elite, presided over by the Prince and his Italian-born wife Countess Dönhoff, Princess Camporeale. Von Bülow's efforts to maintain friendship with the British were compromised by a statement made by the Kaiser in the London *Daily Telegraph* in October 1908 saying the German people were hostile to Great Britain. Von Bülow threatened to resign over the incident, but the Kaiser persuaded him to remain in office by promising to "henceforth observe strict reserve" in his statements. Von Bülow retired from office on July 14, 1909. He was recalled by the Kaiser to serve on a diplomatic mission to Italy in 1914 to ensure that country's neutrality during World War I. His mission ultimately failed, as Italy declared war on Austria in May 1915. Von Bülow returned to Berlin, where he was sometimes called upon to advise the government on diplomatic affairs during the war. There was some sentiment to again name von Bülow chancellor near the end of the war, but the Socialists opposed his reinstatement. The Kaiser was forced to leave the country in November 1918, and after the revolution that instituted the German republic, von Bülow went into exile in Rome. He died at his wife's villa there on October 28, 1929, after a brief illness.

THEOBALD VON BETHMANN-HOLLWEG (Chancellor; July 14, 1909–July 14, 1917). Theobald Theodore Frederic Alfred von Bethmann-Hollweg was born in Hohenfinow, Brandenburg, on November 29, 1856. He was educated at the universities of Strassbourg, Leipzig, and Berlin, where he studied law. He entered the civil service in 1890 and was soon made a deputy in the Reichstag. He was named governor of Brandenburg Province in 1896 and was appointed Prussia's minister of the interior in March 1905. He succeeded Prince Bernhard von Bülow as imperial chancellor on July 14, 1909. Von Bethmann-Hollweg sought without success to improve Germany's relationship with Great Britain during the early years of his government. He tried to avoid a European war but after the outbreak of World War I, he largely deferred to the military in matters of policy. He opposed the use of unlimited U-boat warfare, realizing that the entry of the United States into the conflict would be damaging to Germany. Von Bethmann-Hollweg remained in office despite the rejection of his position. He was forced to step down on July 14, 1917, during debate over peace negotiations. He subsequently retired from politics and died of pneumonia in Hohenfinow on January 2, 1921.

GEORG MICHAELIS (Chancellor; July 14, 1917–October 31, 1917). Georg Michaelis was born in Hanau, near Frankfurt, on September 8, 1857. He studied law and entered the Prussian administration in 1879. He went to Tokyo, Japan, in 1885 and taught law there for four years. He returned to Prussia in 1889 and worked as a public prosecutor. He rose to the position of undersecretary of state in the Prussian ministry of finance in 1909. Michaelis served in several administrative positions during the early years of World War I, becoming commissioner for the national food supply in early 1917. He was supported by the military to succeed Theobald von Bethmann-Hollweg as chancellor and, on July 14, 1917, he became the first commoner to hold that position. His government failed to gain a negotiated peace settlement for Germany, despite the assistance of the Vatican. His lack of success led to his resignation on October 31, 1917. Michaelis subsequently served as governor of Pomerania from March 1918 to April 1919. He then retired from politics and spent the remainder of his life involved in Protestant church activities. He died of a heart attack in Bad Saarow, near Berlin, on July 24, 1936.

GEORG VON HERTLING (Chancellor; November 3, 1917–October 3, 1918). Georg F. von Hertling was born in Darmstadt on August 31, 1843. He was educated in Münster, Munich, and Berlin, where he studied philosophy and theology. He accepted a professorship in the philosophy department of the University of Berlin in 1867. Von Hertling was also a respected author of numerous books on Catholic theology. He became a member of the Reichstag in 1875 and the leader of the Centre Party following the death of Count Hompesch in 1909. Von Hertling was named minister president of Bavaria in 1912 and was created a count by King Ludwig III two years later. He was appointed chancellor of Germany and premier of Prussia on November 3, 1917. Von Hertling attempted to gain a peace settlement with the Entente Powers, and a treaty was arranged with Russia and Rumania in July 1918. His government was criticized by the left for its lack of support for workers' rights. He was also assailed for his inability to cope with the growing crisis of food shortages in the country. Von Hertling resigned on September 30, 1918. He died after a brief illness at his home in Ruhpolding, Upper Bavaria, on January 4, 1919.

PRINCE MAX VON BADEN (Chancellor; October 3, 1918–November 9, 1918). Prince Maximilian Alexander Friedrich Wilhelm von Baden was born on July 10, 1867, the son of Prince William and heir to the Grand Duchy of

Baden. Prince Max entered politics after completing his education and serving in the military. He served as president of the upper chamber of the Baden diet in 1910. During World War I Prince Max worked with the Baden Red Cross in the caring of prisoners of war. He was also the organizer of the German-Russian Prisoner of War Conference in 1915. Considered a moderate, Prince Max was called upon by the Kaiser to serve as chancellor on October 3, 1918. The final German offensive during the war had failed, and his government was given the task of arranging an armistice. There was great sentiment in the country for the abolition of the monarchy, and Prince Max relinquished the reins of government to Friedrich Ebert on November 9, 1918. His actions were severely criticized by the right-wing militarists, who felt Prince Max acted in haste in regard to both the armistice and the Kaiser's abdication. Prince Max renounced his claims to the throne of Baden following the abdication of his uncle, Grand Duke Frederick I, on November 22, 1918. He was named regent on November 28, 1918, following Kaiser Wilhelm's abdication, but refused to accept the appointment as the German Republic had already been proclaimed. He retired to Switzerland, where he was a vocal critic of the harsh settlement imposed on Germany by the Treaty of Versailles. He returned to Germany and authored his memoirs *Reminescences and Documents* in 1927. Prince Max's health rapidly declined due to an arterial disease during the summer of 1929. He suffered a fall in October of that year and died the following month at his home in Schloss Salem, on Lake Constance, on November 6, 1929.

FRIEDRICH EBERT (Chancellor; November 9, 1918–February 6, 1919). *See earlier entry under Heads of State.*

PHILIPP   SCHEIDEMANN (Chancellor; February 13, 1919–June 19,

1919). Philipp Scheidemann was born in Kassel on July 26, 1865. He joined the Socialist Party as a young man and served as an editor for various party newspapers and journals in the late 1800s. He was elected to the Reichstag from Solingen in 1903. The Socialists made impressive gains in the elections of 1912, and Scheidemann became vice president of the Reichstag, though he only held the position for several weeks. He was an outspoken critic of the imperial government's foreign policy leading up to World War I. He was again elected vice president of the Reichstag in June 1918. Scheidemann was called upon to serve as secretary of state without portfolio at the foreign office in the cabinet of Prince Max von Baden in October 1918, when the government invited the Socialists to participate in anticipation of the end of the war. A general strike supporting the abdication of the Kaiser began on November 9, 1918, and Scheidemann resigned from the government. To preempt a call by German Communist leader Karl Liebknecht to proclaim Germany as a Soviet Republic, Scheidemann announced the formation of the German Republic at the parliament building. The government relinquished power to the Council of People's Representatives, with Friedrich Ebert as leader. Scheidemann was elected chancellor on February 13, 1919, after the national constituent assembly was convened. He resigned from office on June 19, 1919, due to conflicts with President Ebert over his refusal to sign the Treaty of Versailles. He subsequently retired to Kassel, where he served as mayor until 1925. When Adolf Hitler came to power in the early 1930s, Scheidemann was forced to flee into exile. He went to Czechoslovakia, where he formed the German Social Democrat Party in Prague. He settled in Copenhagen, Denmark, in 1934. His criticism of the Nazi regime led to the loss of his citizenship and confiscation of his property. Many of his relatives were arrested and placed in concentration camps during the 1930s. Scheidemann died at his daughter's home in Copenhagen on November 29, 1939.

GUSTAV BAUER (Chancellor; June 19, 1919–March 26, 1920). Gustav Adolf Bauer was born on January 6, 1870. He joined the trade union movement in 1903 and became active in politics, working with the Socialists. He served as secretary of state in Max von Baden's cabinet in 1918 and served in Philipp Scheidemann's cabinet as minister of labor. He succeeded Scheidemann as chancellor on June 19, 1919. Wolfgang Kapp led a coup attempt against the government in March 1920. The Kapp putsch was put down after several days, but these events led to Bauer's resignation on March 26, 1920. He remained in the government, serving as minister of transport in Hermann Müller's cabinet until June 1920. Bauer served as vice chancellor and minister of the treasury in Josef Wirth's government from May 1921 to November 1922. Bauer remained in the Reichstag until February 1925, when he was accused of profiting financially in a credit controversy involving the Barmat Brothers of Holland and the Prussian State Bank. He was expelled from the Socialist Party soon after and retired from politics. He died on September 6, 1944.

HERMANN MÜLLER (Chancellor; March 27, 1920–June 8, 1920). Hermann Müller was born in Mannheim on May 18, 1876. He joined the Socialist Party at an early age. He became the editor of the Socialist newspaper *Goerlitzer Volkszeitung* in Silesia in 1899. He became a member of the Goerlitz municipal government in 1903 and of the Social Democratic Party's central executive committee in 1906. He rose to be a leading figure in the party and was elected to the Reichstag in 1916. He was named to Gustav Bauer's cabinet as foreign minister in June 1919. He and Dr. Johannes Bell were designated by the national assembly to represent Germany as signatories for the Treaty of Versailles on June 28, 1919. He was chosen to succeed Bauer as head of a coalition government on March 27, 1920, after the abortive rightwing Kapp putsch. During his brief term of office he undertook the introduction of various social reforms. His government resigned on June 8, 1920, after new elections to the national assembly were held. Müller remained a prominent figure in the Social Democratic Party and briefly served as minister of agriculture in the government of Wilhelm Cuno in November 1922. He remained in the opposition until he was again called upon to head the government following the collapse of Wilhelm Marx's rightist cabinet on June 28, 1928. However, he had difficulty in forming a coalition cabinet at that time, and Germany was faced with numerous internal difficulties over the next two years. Müller was forced to resign on March 29, 1930, when the coalition dissolved. He returned to the Reichstag as leader of the Socialists until his death in Berlin of a heart attack following gall bladder surgery on March 20, 1931.

KONSTANTIN FEHRENBACH (Chancellor; June 20, 1920–May 4, 1921). Konstantin Fehrenbach was born in Wellendingen, in the Black Forest, on January 11, 1852. He was educated at Freiburg where he initially intended to study for the priesthood but then went into law instead. He began a practice in Freiburg in 1882 and soon became active in politics. He was elected to the Baden Provincial Assembly in 1885 and entered the Reichstag in 1903. He sat with the Centre Party and was elected president of the Reichstag in 1918. He was elected to the national assembly after the establishment of the German Republic and soon became president of that body. President Friedrich Ebert invited Fehrenbach to form a coalition cabinet on June 20, 1920. His government attended the Spa Conference in July 1920, and the subsequent financial conferences in Brussels and London, where the German government attempted with little success to alleviate some of the harsher aspects of the Treaty of Versailles. Fehrenbach also presided over the internal disarmament of Germany, which led to a rise of paramilitary groups in Bavaria. The country was also beset by rioting in central Germany during his administration. He stepped down from office on May 4, 1921. Fehrenbach became the leader of the Centre Party in November 1923 when Wilhelm Marx was named chancellor. He died at his home in Freiburg three years later on March 26, 1926.

JOSEPH WIRTH (Chancellor; May 9, 1921–November 14, 1922). Karl Joseph Wirth was born in Freiburg, Baden, on September 6, 1879. He was educated at Freiburg University and became a mathematics professor. He became involved in politics and was elected to the Reichstag as a member of the Centre Party in 1914. He was elected to the national assembly in 1919, following the formation of the German Republic. He succeeded Matthias Erzberger as minister of finance in Hermann Müller's coalition government in March 1920. Wirth succeeded Konstantin Fehrenbach as chancellor on May 9, 1921. His government was formed with the mission of fulfilling the terms of the Treaty of Versailles. This was a difficult task, with the partition of Silesia between Germany and Poland sparking much opposition. Wirth resigned on October 22, 1921, but formed a new government several days later. His plans to form a coalition government failed to materialize because of the Socialists' and Conservatives' opposition to the appointment of Walther Rathenau as foreign minister. Wirth headed the German delegation to the Genoa Economic Conference, and his government signed the German-Soviet treaty of friendship at Rapallo in April 1922. Wirth resigned on November 14, 1922, when his government's economic

policies failed to prevent the depreciation of the mark. Wirth returned to the government as minister of occupied provinces in 1929. He served as minister of the interior from 1930 until his retirement to Freiburg in October 1931. He went into exile in Paris and, later, Switzerland, after Adolf Hitler's Nazi Party came to power in 1933. Wirth returned to Germany in 1948. He became a leading advocate of West Germany's neutrality. He opposed West Germany's entry into the North Atlantic Treaty Organization and was defeated for a seat in the Parliament in 1952. He was a founder of the League of Germans in Unity, Peace, and Freedom. He made several visits to the Soviet Union in the early 1950s and was awarded the Stalin Peace Prize in 1955. Wirth died at his home in Freiburg on January 3, 1956.

WILHELM CUNO (Chancellor; November 22, 1922–August 12, 1923). Carl Joseph Wilhelm Cuno was born in Suhl, Thuringia, on July 2, 1876. He entered the civil service in 1900 and served as counselor for the Prussian finance ministry from 1907 to 1916. He also served as food controller from 1916, reorganizing food supplies during World War I. He became director of the Hamburg-America Steamship Line in 1917, and became chairman and general manager of the line the following year. He was a member of the German peace delegation after the war, serving as an advisor on economic matters. Cuno was a member of the German People's Party and was called upon to head the government as chancellor on November 22, 1922. Germany was in the midst of a major economic crisis, and therefore Cuno's government requested a moratorium on repayment of war reparations. France reacted by invading the Ruhr region, Germany's industrial center, in January 1923. The Cuno government began a campaign of passive resistance against the invaders, which gained him the unified support of the country. Germany's continuing economic difficulties forced his government's resignation on August 12, 1923. Cuno remained a prominent figure in business and civic affairs. He was a founder of the Anglo-German Association in 1929 and was chairman of the World Shipping Conference in 1932. He died suddenly of a heart attack in Hamburg on January 5, 1933.

GUSTAV STRESEMANN (Chancellor; August 13, 1923–November 28, 1923). Gustav Stresemann was born in Berlin on May 10, 1878. He studied literature and history at the University of Berlin and received a doctorate in philosophy in 1902. Stresemann involved himself in German commercial enterprise, founding the Saxon Industrialists' Union in 1902. He became involved in politics and joined the National Liberal Party in 1903. He served as a member of the Dresden city council from 1906 until 1912, and was elected to the Reichstag from Annaberg in 1907. His interest in social reforms antagonized the right-wing elements in his party, and he was defeated for reelection in 1912. He returned to the Reichstag from Aurich two years later and served until 1918. He was a leading proponent of Kaiser Wilhelm II's expansionist policy for Germany and strongly supported engaging in World War I to annex territory in France, Belgium, Poland, and Russia. He succeeded Ernst Bassermann as leader of the National Liberals in the Reichstag in July 1917, and became leader of the party the following November. He was an advocate of the use of unrestricted submarine warfare in Germany's conduct of the war and was instrumental in bringing down the government of moderate chancellor Theobald von Bethmann Hollweg in July 1917. He remained active in politics after Germany's defeat in the war and the subsequent abdication of the Kaiser. He formed the German National People's Party and was elected to the national assembly of the German Repub-

lic. Stresemann was chosen to head a coalition government composed of most of the major parties on August 13, 1923. He inherited rampant inflation from his predecessor, Wilhelm Cuno, due to the general strike in the occupied industrial area, the Ruhr region. Stresemann put an end to the conflict there, earning the enmity of right-wing extremists. His government sent troops to Saxony and Thuringia to put down a Communist insurrection in October 1923, and withstood Adolf Hitler's rightist putsch in November 1923. Stresemann and his minister of finance, Hans Luther, were successful in stabilizing the currency and improving the economy. Despite all this, his government was forced to step down on November 28, 1923, when the Social Democrats withdrew from the cabinet. Stresemann was named foreign minister in the cabinet of his successor, Wilhelm Marx, and served in the next several governments in that position. As foreign minister, Stresemann was successful in restoring Germany's international standing and effecting a reconciliation with its neighbors. He negotiated the Pact of Locarno in 1925, which established Germany's western borders. Germany was admitted to the League of Nations in 1926, and Stresemann was the corecipient of the 1926 Nobel Peace Prize with French statesman Aristide Briand for their work in effecting a reconciliation between France and Germany. Stresemann succeeded in gaining a decrease in Germany's war reparation, and he worked toward the evacuation of foreign troops in the Rhineland. Stresemann remained foreign minister until his sudden death of a heart attack in Berlin on October 3, 1929.

WILHELM MARX (Chancellor; November 30, 1923–December 15, 1924). Wilhelm Marx was born in Cologne on January 15, 1863. He studied law and began his career as a jurist in the Elberfeld county court in 1894. He was a member of the Centre Party and was elected to the Prussian Landtag (assembly) in 1899 and to the Reichstag in 1910. He became chairman of the Centre Party in 1921 and was president of the Court of Appeals in Berlin in 1922. He succeeded Gustav Stresemann as chancellor on November 30, 1923, heading a minority government. He was successful in gaining the acceptance of the Dawes Plan in August 1924. Marx stepped down from office on December 15, 1924. He subsequently served as prime minister of Prussia from February until April 1925. He was an unsuccessful candidate for president of the German Republic in 1925, being defeated by Paul von Hindenburg. Marx served in Hans Luther's cabinet as minister of justice and the occupied territories from January 1926 until he replaced Luther as chancellor on May 18, 1926. Marx invited the rightist German nationalists into the government in January 1927. The success of the Social Democrats in the elections of May 1928 led to Marx's resignation on June 28, 1928. He subsequently retired from politics. Marx spent the war years living in a cottage in Neustadt an der Wied. He died in Bonn on August 5, 1946.

HANS LUTHER (Chancellor; January 16, 1925–May 18, 1926). Hans Luther was born in Berlin on March 10, 1879. He studied law and entered the civil service in Berlin. Luther became lord mayor of Essen near the end of World War I. He held that position until 1922. Luther served in the cabinet of Gustav Stresemann and Wilhelm Marx as minister of finance. He was instrumental in halting the rampant inflation in Germany by introducing a new currency. He was selected to succeed Marx as chancellor on January 16, 1925. His government was forced to resign on May 18, 1926, and Luther withdrew from politics. He entered the banking industry and served as president of the Reichsbank from 1930 until 1933. When Adolf Hitler's Nazi Party gained power in

1933, Luther was named Germany's Ambassador to the United States. He retained that position until 1937, when he returned to his farm in Bavaria. He was not active in politics during World War II. After the war he served as an advisor to the West German government on legal and economic affairs. He also accepted a teaching position at the Munich Academy of Political Sciences. Luther authored his memoirs, *Politician Without a Party*, in 1960. He died at a Düsseldorf hospital on May 11, 1962.

WILHELM MARX (Chancellor; May 18, 1926–June 28, 1928). *See earlier entry under Heads of Government.*

HERMANN MÜLLER (Chancellor; June 28, 1928–March 29, 1930). *See earlier entry under Heads of Government.*

HEINRICH BRÜNING (Chancellor; March 29, 1930–May 30, 1932). Heinrich Brüning was born in Münster, Westphalia, on November 26, 1885. He studied history, philosophy, and politics at the universities of Munich, Strassbourg, and Bonn. He also attended the London School of Economics. After serving in the army during World War I he entered politics. He joined the Centre Party and was elected to the Reichstag from Breslau in 1924. His expertise in financial matters brought him to prominence in the party and he became leader of the Centrists in the Parliament in 1929. He formed a government as chancellor on March 29, 1930, during the world economic crisis. He attempted to alleviate Germany's financial problems with a policy of tax increases and budget cuts. His fiscal policies were rejected by the Reichstag but were implemented under presidential decree by President Paul Von Hindenburg. Brüning's inability to check the effects of the economic depression and his failure to gain Allied approval for Germany's rearmament led to his resignation on May 30, 1932. Brüning remained leader of the Centre

Party until June 1934, when he fled the country during Adolf Hitler's bloody purge of political rivals. Brüning spent some time in England before emigrating to the United States. He joined the faculty of the Harvard Graduate School of Business Administration in 1939 as professor of political science. Brüning returned to Germany in November 1952 and accepted the position of professor of political science at the University of Cologne. Brüning retired in the 1960s and returned to the United States. He died in Norwich, Vermont, on March 30, 1970.

FRANZ VON PAPEN (Chancellor; May 31, 1932–November 17, 1932). Franz von Papen was born to a wealthy family in Werl, Westphalia, on October 29, 1879. He chose a career in the German military on the general staff. He was named a military attaché at the Germany embassy in Washington in 1913, where he served during the early days of World War I. Von Papen was implicated in attempts to sabotage American shipments to Germany's opponents in the war. He was declared a persona non grata and expelled from the United States in 1915. He attained the rank of lieutenant colonel and served as chief of staff of the 4th Turkish Army in Palestine in 1918. He resigned from the army after the war and the establishment of the German Republic. He subsequently entered politics and was elected to the Prussian Landtag. He was a member of the far right wing of the Centre Party. He also served as chairman of the board of *Germania*, the Catholic daily newspaper. Von Papen, who was not taken very seriously in German political circles, was President Paul von Hindenburg's surprise choice to head the government following the resignation of Heinrich Brüning on May 31, 1932. His government moved against the Social Democrats and other leftists, proclaiming martial law and deposing the Prussian administration in July 1932. Von Papen was unable to convince Adolf Hitler to bring his Nazi Party into the government, as Hitler wanted to have the chancellorship for himself. Von Papar's government collapsed on November 17, 1932, when General Kurt von Schleicher resigned from the cabinet as defense minister. Von Schleicher subsequently replaced von Papen as chancellor. In January 1933 von Papen reached an accord with Hitler. They arranged for von Schleicher's dismissal as head of the government. Under an arrangement agreed to by President von Hindenburg, Hitler would head the new coalition government and von Papen would serve as his vice-chancellor. Von Papen and his allies felt they could control Hitler, but they were outmaneuvered by the Nazi leader's consolidation of power. When Hitler led a bloody purge of his rivals and opponents on June 30, 1934, von Papen was detained at his office for several days, and many of his closest associates were among the slain. He resigned his position on July 3, 1934. Von Papen was sent by Hitler to serve as Germany's ambassador to Austria the following month, where he worked to arrange the peaceful union, or *Anschluss*, between Germany and Austria. He was successful in undermining the regime of Austrian Chancellor Kurt von Schuschnigg. He returned to Germany in March 1938, immediately before Germany incorporated Austria by force. Von Papen was sent to Turkey as Germany's ambassador in 1939. He worked to ensure Turkey's neutrality during World War II. Constantinople was a hotbed of intrigue during the war, and von Papen, who was code-named "the Fox," used the valet of the British ambassador to ferret out Allied secrets. He returned to Germany when Turkey entered the war on the side of the Allies in 1944. He retired to his estates, where he was captured by the American Ninth Army in April 1945. He was tried by the International Military Tribunal at Nuremberg and, on October 1, 1946, was acquitted of charges of preparing an aggressive war. In February 1947 he was again tried by the German denazification court and convicted of being a major Nazi. He was sentenced to eight years in prison, but was reclassified as a secondary figure in January 1949 and released. He retired on a civil servant's pension to his estate in Saarland. He remained politically inactive, authoring his memoirs in 1952 and an autobiography in 1968. He died after a brief illness at his villa in Obersasbach, Baden-Württemberg, on May 2, 1969.

KURT VON SCHLEICHER (Chancellor; December 2, 1932–January 28, 1933). Kurt von Schleicher was born in Brandenburg on April 7, 1882. He entered the army in 1900 and was named to the general staff in 1913. Von Schleicher rose through the ranks, making many powerful military and political contacts along the way. He was made aide-de-camp to General Hans von Seeckt in 1923 and was promoted to colonel in 1926. He became a leading force in the Reichswehr ministry. His power increased following the appointment of Wilhelm Groener, his former commanding officer, as defense minister in 1928. Von Schleicher was named to the newly created position of chief of the ministerial staff at the Reichswehr, with the rank of major general, in 1929. Von Schleicher was instrumental in bringing about the collapse of Heinrich Brüning's government in June 1932. He served as minister of defense in Franz von Papen's subsequent government. His resignation from the cabinet brought about von Papen's resignation, and von Schleicher was called upon to head the government on December 2, 1932. He was a powerful opponent of Adolf Hitler and the Nazis and worked to ensure that the Reichswehr was in a position to curtail excesses by the Nazis. Von Schleicher was forced to resign on January 28, 1933, following an agreement between Hitler and von Papen that resulted in President Paul von Hindenburg offering the reins of government to the Nazi leader. Von Schleicher retired to private life but was still viewed as a powerful opponent of the Nazis. When Hitler dispatched the *Schutzstaffel* (SS) to eliminate his rivals and opponents on June 29, 1934, in an event known as the "night of the long knives," von Schleicher was high on the list. Accused of conspiring against the government, the SS shot von Schleicher and his wife to death at their Berlin flat, allegedly because they were resisting arrest.

ADOLF HITLER (Chancellor; January 30, 1933–April 30, 1945). *See earlier entry under Heads of State.*

Greece

Greece is a country in southeastern Europe. It received independence from the Ottoman Empire on March 25, 1827.

HEADS OF STATE

GEORGE I (King; October 31, 1863–March 18, 1913). George I was born Prince William of Schleswig-Holstein in Copenhagen, Denmark, on December 24, 1845. He was the second son of King Christian IX of Denmark. When King Otho I of Greece was forced to abdicate in October 1862 and Prince Alfred, Duke of Edinburgh, refused the Greek throne, Prince William was nominated by Great Britain, France, and Russia to ascend to the throne. The

Greek national assembly accepted the nomination on March 30, 1863, and he claimed the throne as king of the Hellenes on October 31, 1863. A new constitution was promulgated the following year and George reigned as a constitutional monarch. He married Olga, daughter of Grand Duke Konstantin Nikolaevich of Russia, in October 1867. During his reign Greece expanded its borders to include the Ionian Islands in 1864; Thessaly and Arta in 1881; and Epirus, Macedonia, and Crete in 1913. George was a popular monarch during most of his 50-year reign. He was assassinated on March 18, 1913, by a Greek named Alexandros Schinas, who shot George to death while the monarch was walking in the streets of Salonika.

CONSTANTINE I (King; March 18, 1913–June 12, 1917). Constantine was born in Athens on August 2, 1868, the eldest son of King George I of Greece. He was educated in Germany at Leipzig University and the Prussian Military Academy. Constantine married Sophia, the sister of Kaiser Wilhelm II, in 1889. Constantine commanded the Greek forces in Thessaly, which were defeated by the Turks in 1897. He was appointed commander-in-chief of the Greek army in 1900. He was pressured to retire from the army after Greece's failure to reclaim Crete in 1909. Constantine returned to the army two years later as inspector general. He succeeded to the throne when his father was assassinated on March 18, 1913. Constantine favored Germany and the Central Powers during World War I and attempted to maintain Greece's neutrality during the war. He came into conflict with Prime Minister Eleutherios Venizelos, who favored the Allied cause. The king's position was jeopardized when the Allies occupied Salonika and began a naval blockade of Greece. The Allies demanded Constantine's abdication, and he stepped down from the throne in favor of his second son, Alexander, on June 12, 1917. Con-

stantine retired to Switzerland until 1920, when Alexander died suddenly. Royalists pressed for a plebiscite on December 5, 1920, which restored Constantine to the throne. He returned to Athens on December 20, 1920. Greece continued its conflict with Turkey in the Greco-Turkish War from 1921 until 1922, when the Greek forces were defeated at Anatolia. A military uprising again forced Constantine's abdication in favor of his eldest son, George, on September 30, 1922. Constantine went into exile in Palermo, Sicily, where he died of heart disease the following year on January 11, 1923.

ALEXANDER (King; June 12, 1917–October 25, 1920). Alexander was born in Athens on August 1, 1893. He was the second son of King Constantine and Queen Sophia. Alexander was educated at Oxford University in England and served as a captain of artillery in the Greek army. When his father was deposed during World War I, Alexander was chosen to succeed to the throne. He was crowned on June 12, 1917, though Prime Minister Eleutherios Venizelos largely was in control of the country. Alexander married commoner Aspasia Manos of Athens in November 1919. The marriage was controversial and the Metropolitan of Athens refused to make the union legally binding. Alexander was bitten and mauled by his pet monkey on October 2, 1920, when he tried to stop a fight between his dog and the monkey. He became seriously ill and died several weeks later from blood poisoning at Tatoi Palace on October 25, 1920.

CONSTANTINE I (King; December 20, 1920–September 30, 1922). *See earlier entry under Heads of State.*

GEORGE II (King; January 11, 1923–April 13, 1924). George was born at Tatoi, near Athens, on July 20, 1890. He was the eldest son of King Constantine of Greece and Queen Sophia. He was bypassed in favor of his younger brother, Alexander, for the succession when his father was deposed in June 1917. He accompanied the royal family into exile. He returned to Greece after the death of Alexander and the restoration of Constantine in December 1920. He succeeded his father to the throne as King George II on January 11, 1923, after King Constantine was again forced to abdicate on September 30, 1922. His rule was marred by uprisings and republican sentiments. George left Greece on December 19, 1923, and traveled to Bucharest. He was officially deposed, and Greece was declared a republic on March 25, 1924. He spent the next decade in exile in various European capitals. In Greece Georgios Kondylis staged a military coup in October 1935. Kondylis abolished the republican constitution and revived the monarchy. George was recalled to Greece and restored to the throne in November 1935. He assumed command of the Greek army following the Italian invasion of Greece in 1940. He fled with his government to Crete in April 1941, shortly before the German army reached Athens. He eventually landed in London, where he established a government-in-exile. Following the expulsion of the Germans from Greece, some elements in the country were unwilling to accept the return of George to the throne. He accepted Archbishop Damaskinos as regent in his stead in December 1944. Following a plebiscite in September 1946, George II was invited to return to the throne. He arrived in Greece later that month. After less than a year on the throne, he died suddenly of a heart attack in Athens on April 1, 1947.

PAUL KONDURIOTIS (President; April 13, 1924–March 19, 1926). Paul Konduriotis was born to a leading Greek family on the island of Hydra on April 4, 1855. He was the grandson of George Konduriotis, who was a leading figure in Greece's war for independence in the 1820s. The younger Konduriotis joined the Greek navy at an early age. He rose through the ranks to admiral and was acclaimed for leading the Greek fleet to victory against the Turks at the battle of Lemnos during the Greco-Turkish War of 1896–1897. He again commanded the Greek fleet against the Turks during the Balkan War of 1912 and 1913, forcing the Turkish fleet to retreat behind the Dardenelles. He was named to the cabinet as minister of marine in 1915. He was a strong supporter of the Allies during World War I, and opposed King Constantine's policy of neutrality. Konduriotis again served as minister of marine in Eleutherios Venizelos's cabinet from 1917 until 1919. He was named regent by the chamber of deputies following the death of King Alexander on October 25, 1920. He resigned the regency on November 18, 1920, in favor of the Queen Mother, Olga, when it appeared likely that deposed King Constantine would reclaim the throne. He subsequently traveled abroad before accepting the chairmanship of the Committee of the National Relief Fund. He survived an assassination attempt when he was shot by three former soldiers at his office on December 21, 1921. King Constantine was deposed in September 1922, and his son and successor, George II, was expelled in December 1923. Konduriotis was again named regent. He became the first president of the newly proclaimed Greek Republic on April 13, 1924. The political situation in Greece remained volatile during Konduriotis' presidency, but he interfered little with the policies of the government. A revolt let by General Theodoros Pangalos led to Konduriotis's resignation on March 19, 1926. Pangalos was himself ousted by General Georgios Kondylis, and Konduriotis resumed the presidency on August 23, 1926. Konduriotis survived another assassination attempt in October 1927. He was elected to a second term by the chamber of deputies in June 1929 despite his wishes to resign. He did step down for reasons of health six months later on December 9, 1929.

Though Konduriotis retired from politics, his son, Theodore, was implicated in a revolt against the government in March 1935. The elder Konduriotis died in Athens on August 22, 1935.

THEODOROS PANGALOS (President; April 19, 1926–August 22, 1926). Theodoros Pangalos was born in Salamis in 1878. He was educated at the Athens Military Academy and entered the Greek army. He commanded a regiment in Macedonia in 1914 and attained the rank of general in 1918. The following year he was named chief of staff of the Greek army. Pangalos headed the commission of inquiry to investigate the Greek army's defeat by the Turks in 1922. He was named minister of law and order in 1924, and became minister of war in Andreas Michalakopoulos' government the following year. He succeeded Michalakopoulos as prime minister on June 26, 1925, when he and Admiral John Hadjikyriakos issued an ultimatum to the government. Pangalos dissolved the chamber of deputies and led a repressive government. President Paul Konduriotis resigned on March 20, 1926, and Pangalos staged a plebiscite to confirm himself as president on April 19, 1926. He abolished the constitution, suppressed the press, and nearly embroiled Greece in a war against Bulgaria over a border incident. Pangalos was ousted in a coup led by General Georgios Kondylis on August 22, 1926. He was captured near Cape Matapan while trying to flee the country and was imprisoned at Fort Izzeddin on Crete. He was held for a lengthy period before receiving a three-year sentence. After his release, he remained under surveillance during the dictatorship of Ioannis Metaxas in the late 1930s. He remained in retirement until his death in Athens on February 22, 1952.

PAUL KONDURIOTIS (President; August 23, 1926–December 9, 1929). *See earlier entry under Heads of State.*

ALEXANDROS ZAIMÏS (President; December 14, 1929–November 3, 1935). Alexandros Zaimïs was born in Athens on October 28, 1855. He was the son of Thrasybulos Zaimïs, who served as prime minister of Greece from 1871 until 1872. The younger Zaimïs studied law and political science in Athens and Paris. He entered politics and was elected to the chamber of deputies in 1885. He was named to the cabinet as minister of justice in 1890. Zaimïs was president of the chamber of deputies before becoming prime minister of Greece on October 3, 1897. He held the position for two years until his resignation on April 14, 1899. He again led the government following the resignation of Georgios Theotakis on November 25, 1901. He stepped down on December 6, 1902, following elections that saw a decline in his support and the selection of his estranged uncle, Theodoros Deliyannis, as prime minister. He subsequently abandoned active politics to accept the position of Greek high commissioner to Crete in 1906. He helped bring stability to the island before stepping down in 1911. He became governor of the Greek National Bank in 1913 and again accepted the premiership on October 7, 1915, after the resignation of Eleutherios Venizelos. Zaimïs' government received a vote of no confidence from the Parliament and he relinquished the government to Stafanos Skouloudis on November 7, 1915. He again briefly headed the government from June 22, 1916, until September 16, 1916. Zaimïs returned to power on May 3, 1917, and was instrumental in securing the abdication of King Constantine in June 1917. He relinquished the premiership to Venizelos shortly after on June 27, 1917. He subsequently returned to the National Bank, where he remained until 1920. He was largely inactive after King Constantine was restored to the throne in 1920. Zaimïs refused another term as prime minister after King Constantine's second abdication in October 1922. He returned to head the government on December 4, 1926, as head of a coalition cabinet. He remained prime minister until June 29, 1928, when he was again replaced by Venizelos. Zaimïs subsequently became president of the senate and was selected to succeed Paul Konduriotis as president on December 14, 1929. He was reelected by the chamber of deputies for a second term in October 1934. Zaimïs resigned on November 3, 1935, when a royalist coup led by General Georgios Kondylis restored King George II to the monarchy. Zaimïs went into exile in Vienna, Austria. His health was failing, and he died in a hospital there on September 15, 1936.

GEORGE II (King; November 3, 1935–April 1, 1947). *See earlier entry under Heads of State.*

HEADS OF GOVERNMENT

GEORGIOS THEOTOKIS (Prime Minister; April 14, 1899–November 25, 1901). Georgios Theotokis was born in Corfu in 1843. He entered politics and was elected to the chamber of deputies in the late 1870s. He was named to the cabinet as minister of marine in 1886, holding that position until 1890. He served as minister of the interior in several governments in the 1890s before being chosen to replace Alexandros Zaimïs as prime minister on April 14, 1899. He led the government for over two years before relinquishing the position to Zaimïs on November 25, 1901. Theotokis again briefly headed the government from June 26, 1903, to July 10, 1903, following the assassination of Theodoros Deliyannis. He was returned to office on December 18, 1903, and served until December 28, 1904. He again became prime minister on December 20, 1905, serving for nearly four years until a constitutional crisis forced his resignation on July 20, 1909. Theotokis remained a leading political figure in Greece, serving as minister of national economy and public instruction. He remained in the cabinet until his death in Athens on January 24, 1916.

ALEXANDROS ZAIMÏS (Prime Minister; November 25, 1901–December 6, 1902). *See earlier entry under Heads of State.*

THEODOROS DELIYANNIS (Prime Minister; December 6, 1902–June 26, 1903). Theodoros Deliyannis was born in Kalavryta in 1826. He was educated in Athens, where he studied law. He entered the government in 1843 and became a leading political figure in Greece. He served in numerous cabinets between 1863 and 1878, often serving as foreign minister and minister of finance. He represented Greece at the Berlin Congress in 1878, which resulted in an increase of Greek territory. Deliyannis became prime minister on April 30, 1885, but his government antagonized other European powers, resulting in a blockade of the Greek coast. He was forced to step down on May 12, 1886. He returned to lead the government on November 5, 1890. His government's inability to cope with Greece's financial problems led to his resignation on March 2, 1892. Deliyannis was again named prime minister on January 25, 1895. Greece's military defeat in a war with Turkey forced his government's resignation on April 30, 1897. He was again called upon to form a government on December 6, 1902. His final term of office was cut short when he was stabbed to death on June 22, 1905, at the main entrance of the chamber of deputies in Athens by a professional gambler named Gherakaris, who opposed the government's policy of closing down the country's gambling houses.

GEORGIOS THEOTOKIS (Prime Minister; June 26, 1903–July 10, 1903). *See earlier entry under Heads of Government.*

DIMITRIOS RALLIS (Prime Minister; July 10, 1903–December 18, 1903). Dimitrios Rallis was born in Athens in 1844. He became active in politics and achieved prominence as the leader of the newly formed Young Greek Party in 1890. Rallis was chosen to head the government on April 30, 1897. His government concluded an unsuccessful war against Turkey and he resigned on October 3, 1897. He was again selected to head the government on July 10, 1903, but was forced to resign on December 18, 1903. Rallis again briefly served as prime minister from June 22, 1905, until December 20, 1905, and from July 20, 1909, until August 28, 1909. He remained out of the government until 1915, when he joined the cabinet as minister of justice. He was named minister of finance the following year. He retired from politics in 1917 after the abdication of King Constantine. Rallis emerged from retirement to head the government on November 17, 1920, shortly before King Constantine was restored to the throne. Failing health forced his resignation on February 6, 1921. Rallis died in Athens on August 19, 1921.

GEORGIOS THEOTOKIS (Prime Minister; December 18, 1903–December 28, 1904). *See earlier entry under Heads of Government.*

THEODOROS DELIYANNIS (Prime Minister; December 28, 1904–June 22, 1905). *See earlier entry under Heads of Government.*

DIMITRIOS RALLIS (Prime Minister; June 22, 1905–December 20, 1905). *See earlier entry under Heads of Government.*

GEORGIOS THEOTOKIS (Prime Minister; December 20, 1905–July 20, 1909). *See earlier entry under Heads of Government.*

DIMITRIOS RALLIS (Prime Minister; July 20, 1909–August 28, 1909). *See earlier entry under Heads of Government.*

KIRIAKOULIS MAVROMICHALIS (Prime Minister; August 28, 1909–January 31, 1910). Kiriakoulis Mavromichalis was born in 1849. A moderate, he served as a minister in the government of Theodoros Deliyannis. He headed the government as prime minister from August 28, 1909, following Dimitrios Rallis's resignation in the face of a military uprising, to January 31, 1910. Mavromichalis's government granted most of the army's demands, ending the immediate threat of a military coup. The newly formed Military League continued to hold great influence over the government, which invariably complied with its demands. In January 1910 the League insisted on the convocation of a national assembly. The proposal was accepted, and Mavromichalis' cabinet stepped down on January 31, 1910. Mavromichalis was in opposition to the government of Eleutherios Venizelos that took power later in the year. He died in Athens in early February 1916.

STEFANOS DRAGOUMIS (Prime Minister; January 31, 1910–October 19, 1910). Stefanos Dragoumis was born in 1842. He became active in politics in the 1880s, serving in the chamber of deputies. He was chosen to serve as prime minister on January 31, 1910, also serving in the government as minister of finance. His government resigned on October 19, 1910, to make way for Eleutherios Venizelos. Dragoumis subsequently served as governor-general of Crete. He was arrested and charged with treason in 1919 for conspiring to restore King Constantine to the throne. He was subsequently released and Constantine resumed the monarchy in December 1920. Dragoumis died in Athens on September 18, 1922.

ELEUTHERIOS VENIZELOS

(Prime Minister; October 19, 1910–March 10, 1915). Eleutherios Gormer Venizelos was born near Canea, on the island of Crete, on August 23, 1864. He was educated in Syra and at the University of Athens, where he received a degree in law in 1887. He returned to Crete to establish a legal practice and entered politics as a member of the assembly. He briefly fled Crete during the revolt in 1889, but returned soon after. He became leader of the local Liberal Party and was a prominent figure in the Cretan rising against the Turks in 1897. Prince George of Greece was appointed High Commissioner to Crete the following year and Venizelos was named his councilor of justice. Venizelos was displeased by the prince's policies and was dismissed after several disagreements. He subsequently became leader of the opposition on the island and led an armed uprising from the mountains of Therisso in 1905. Prince George left the island in September of the following year and was replaced as high commissioner by Alexandros Zaimïs. Venizelos and Zaimïs reached an accord and the rebellion was quelled. Venizelos remained a leading figure in Cretan politics and was instrumental in unifying Crete with Greece after the first Balkan war. Venizelos was called to Athens in 1910 and was elected to the chamber of deputies. Soon after, he was called upon by King George I to form a government as prime minister on October 19, 1910. He also served in the government as minister of war and marine and was instrumental in revising the Greek constitution in 1911. He reorganized the army and the navy and was also the main force behind the creation of the Balkan League. King George I was assassinated in March 1913 and his son, King Constantine, was hostile toward Venizelos. Their conflict came to a head

when Constantine refused to accept Venizelos' proposal for Greece to enter World War I on the side of the Allies. Constantine, who favored the Central Powers, forced Venizelos's resignation on March 10, 1915. Venizelos briefly returned to head the government on August 12, 1915, but continued conflict with Constantine again brought about his resignation on October 7, 1915. Venizelos and a number of his supporters went to Crete in September 1916 and called upon the Greek citizens to support the Allies during the war. The following month he went to Salonika, where he organized a provisional government that received the recognition of the Allies. King Constantine was forced to abdicate in June 1917, and Venizelos returned to Athens to head the government on June 27, 1917. He led Greece into World War I on the side of the Allies. He was successful in acquiring a large portion of the Turkish Empire in the peace settlement that followed the war. Venizelos was slightly wounded in an assassination attempt by two Royalists on August 12, 1919. Venizelos' support at home waned during his period away from Greece attending peace conferences, and the Turkish war proved unsuccessful and unpopular. King Alexander, the son and successor of King Constantine, died suddenly in October 1920, and sentiment rose for the return of the deposed Constantine. Venizelos stepped down from office on November 17, 1920. He was not politically active for the next two years until Constantine was again deposed in a revolt in September 1922. Venizelos served as Greece's representative to the peace conference in Lausanne, France, which ended the conflict with Turkey. He returned to Athens to again head the government on January 12, 1924. He stepped down on February 6, 1924, due to poor health. He remained inactive for the next four years, recuperating and resting in Cannes, France. He returned to Greece to again head the government on July 4, 1928. His government signed a pact of friendship with

Benito Mussolini's Italy and trade treaties with Yugoslavia and Turkey. Royalists staged an unsuccessful coup against the government in October 1930. Venizelos was forced to relinquish office to Royalist leader Panayiotis Tsaldaris on November 4, 1932, but returned to power two months later on January 15, 1933. Elections held soon afterward went badly for Venizelos and he stepped down on March 6, 1933. The following day General Nicholas Plastiris, a friend and supporter of Venizelos, led a coup against the government in an attempt to establish a military dictatorship. The coup attempt was crushed in less than a day, and the government considered bringing charges against Venizelos for complicity in the revolt. An assassination attempt against him that injured his wife, the former Helena Schilizzi, made further action against him unpopular with the public, and he was never charged. Following an unsuccessful candidacy for the presidency against Alexandros Zaimïs in October 1934, Venizelos retired to Crete. In March 1935 his supporters staged a revolt in Athens and Crete. Venizelos briefly controlled Crete as head of a provisional government before the rising was crushed two weeks later by Royalist forces under General Georgios Kondylis. Venizelos left Crete for the island of Rhodes before settling in exile in France. He was sentenced to death in absentia with other leaders of the revolt but received an amnesty from King George II in November 1935 after the restoration of the monarchy. He died in Paris of pneumonia on March 18, 1936.

DIMITRIOS GOUNARIS (Prime Minister; March 10, 1915–August 23, 1915). Dimitrios Gounaris was born in 1866. He became active in politics and served in Dimitrios Rallis's cabinet as minister of finance from 1908 until 1909. He became a leader of the Royalist Party and briefly headed the government as prime minister. He served from March 10, 1915, until August 23, 1915, following

Eleutherios Venizelos's resignation because of a conflict with King Constantine over Greece's participation in World War I. Gounaris was deported after the abdication of King Constantine in June 1917. He returned to Athens after Constantine reclaimed the throne in December 1920. He returned to the government as minister of war before replacing Nikolaos Kalogeropoulos as prime minister on April 2, 1921. The Allies were unable to achieve a peace settlement between Greece and Turkey, and conflicts continued in Asia Minor. Gounaris resigned the premiership in March 1922, but quickly resumed his position. He again resigned on May 16, 1922. He was arrested in September 1922 when a military revolt forced the abdication of King Constantine. On November 27, 1922, a trial by the Revolutionary Court Martial was concluded and Gounaris and several other leading Royalist politicians were condemned to death for high treason in connection with the Greek military disaster in Asia Minor. Gounaris and the others were executed in Athens on November 28, 1922.

ELEUTHERIOS VENIZELOS (Prime Minister; August 23, 1915–October 7, 1915). *See earlier entry under Heads of Government.*

ALEXANDROS ZAIMÏS (Prime Minister; October 7, 1915–November 7, 1915). *See earlier entry under Heads of State.*

STEFANOS SKOULOUDIS (Prime Minister; November 7, 1915–June 22, 1916). Stefanos Skouloudis was born in 1836 in the Ottoman Empire. He became a successful businessman and a founder of the Bank of Constantinople before settling in Athens. He entered politics and was elected to the chamber of deputies. Skouloudis served as Greece's minister to the court of Spain in 1883. He was named to Charilaos Trikoupis' cabinet as minister of marine in

1892. He served as foreign minister in Dimitrios Rallis' cabinet in 1897. He remained a leading political figure and was chosen to head the Greek delegation to the Balkan League at the London peace conference to negotiate a settlement with the Turks in 1912. He was appointed to head the government as prime minister on November 7, 1915. His government supported Greece's neutrality during World War I. Skouloudis was unable to control Greece's political or economic problems and stepped down on June 22, 1916, after the occupation of Salonika by the Allies. Skouloudis' political career largely ended with the abdication of King Constantine in 1917. He was briefly detained in early 1919 for his participation in a Royalist coup in support of Constantine. Skouloudis died in Athens on August 20, 1928.

ALEXANDROS ZAIMÏS (Prime Minister; June 22, 1916–September 16, 1916). *See earlier entry under Heads of State.*

NIKOLAOS KALOGEROPOU-LOS (Prime Minister; September 16, 1916–October 10, 1916). Nikolaos Kalogeropoulos was born in 1853. He received a degree in law from the University of Paris and entered politics. He briefly served as minister of finance in 1904 and 1905. He was minister of the interior in Georgios Theotakis' cabinet from 1908 to 1909. Kalogeropoulos was called upon to head the government as prime minister on September 16, 1916, and to serve simultaneously as minister of war and finance. He attempted to maintain Greece's neutrality during World War I, but pressure by the Allies to join the conflict forced his government's resignation on October 10, 1916. Kalogeropoulos was politically inactive after the abdication of King Constantine in June 1917. Constantine was restored to the throne in December 1920, and Kalogeropoulos was again called upon to head the government on February 6,

1921. He headed the Greek delegation to the Near East Conference in London in 1921, where he pressed Greece's claim for Asia Minor. Military setbacks against the Turks in the region forced his government's resignation on April 8, 1921. He was again called upon to form a government after Greece's defeat in the war against Turkey in September 1922, but was unable to gain a mandate. He was arrested and charged with treason following the coup that ousted King Constantine in September 1922, though the charges were never pressed. Kalogeropoulos retired from politics and died in Athens on January 11, 1927.

SPYRIDON LAMBROS (Prime Minister; October 10, 1916–May 3, 1917). Spyridon Lambros was born in 1851. He was a leading Greek academic who was called upon by King Constantine to form a government when Nikolaos Kalogeropoulos's ministry collapsed. Greece's position of neutrality during World War I created numerous problems for the country, with the Bulgarian army crossing the border and the Allies recognizing the provisional government of Eleutherios Venizelos in Salonika. The French imposed a naval blockade of Greece in December 1916. Lambros' government was forced to accept concessions from the Allies. He stepped down on May 3, 1917, and was succeeded by Alexandros Zaimïs. He died on July 23, 1919.

ALEXANDROS ZAIMÏS (Prime Minister; May 3, 1917–June 27, 1917). *See earlier entry under Heads of State.*

ELEUTHERIOS VENIZELOS (Prime Minister; June 27, 1917–November 17, 1920). *See earlier entry under Heads of Government.*

DIMITRIOS RALLIS (Prime Minister; November 17, 1920–February 6, 1921). *See earlier entry under Heads of Government.*

NIKOLAOS KALOGEROPOU-LOS (Prime Minister; February 6, 1921–April 8, 1921). *See earlier entry under Heads of Government.*

DIMITRIOS GOUNARIS (Prime Minister; April 8, 1921–May 16, 1922). *See earlier entry under Heads of Government.*

NIKOLAOS STRATOS (Prime Minister; May 16, 1922–May 22, 1922). Nikolaos Stratos was born in 1872. He entered politics in 1909. He was named to Eleutherios Venizelos's cabinet as minister of marine the following year. He subsequently left the Venezelist party to become an Independent Royalist. Stratos headed a brief interim government from May 16, 1922, until May 22, 1922, following the resignation of Dimitrios Gounaris. He was arrested and tried with Gounaris and other government figures for high treason in connection with the Greek military defeat by the Turks in Asia Minor. He was executed in Athens on November 28, 1922.

PETROS PROTOPAPADAKIS (Prime Minister; May 22, 1922–September 10, 1922). Petros Protopapadakis was born in 1860. He served in Dimitrios Gounaris' cabinet as minister of finance in 1915. He returned with the cabinet in Gounaris' second government in 1921, serving as minister of finance of supplies. Protopapadakis became prime minister on May 22, 1922. He was forced to resign on September 10, 1922, and was arrested. He was tried with Gounaris and other government figures for high treason and was executed in Athens on November 28, 1922.

NIKOLAOS TRIANDAFILLAKOS (Prime Minister; September 10, 1922–September 27, 1922). Nikolaos Triandafillakos was born in 1855. He was a leading diplomat and served as Greece's high commissioner to Turkey. The Greek military defeat by Turkey in Asia Minor caused the collapse of several governments, and Triandafillakos was called upon to serve as prime minister on September 10, 1922. The government was faced with growing civil and military unrest, and martial law was imposed on September 26, 1922. A military revolt took place in Salonika and spread throughout the country, calling for the abdication of the king. Triandafillakos' cabinet resigned on September 27, 1922, and King Constantine abdicated on September 30, 1922. Triandafillakos was inactive in subsequent governments and died on 1939.

SOTIRIOS KROKIDAS (Prime Minister; September 29, 1922–November 27, 1922). Sotirios Krokidas was born in the village of Perigali in 1852. He was a former governor of Crete when he was called upon to form a transition government on September 29, 1922, preceding the abdication of King Constantine and his succession by King George II. Krokidas' government resigned on November 27, 1922, to make way for the revolutionary cabinet of General Stylianos Gonatus. Krokidas died at his home in Perigali on July 28, 1924.

STYLIANOS GONATUS (Prime Minister; November 27, 1922–January 12, 1924). Stylianos Gonatus was born in Patras in southern Greece on August 15, 1875. He graduated from the Army Officers Cadet School in 1897 and served in the Greek army as a second lieutenant in the Greek-Turkish War that year. Gonatus fought in numerous military campaigns and attained the rank of colonel in 1917. Gonatus and Nicholas Plastiras led a military rising which forced the abdication of King Constantine in September 1922. Gonatus became premier of the revolutionary government on November 27, 1922. He was an opponent of the monarchy and was instrumental in the ouster of King George II and the establishment of the Greek Republic in April 1924. Gonatus stepped down as head of the government on January 12, 1924, in favor of Eleutherios Venizelos. He was promoted to lieutenant general later in the year. Gonatus was elected to the senate in April 1929 and served as minister of communications in Venizelos' government. He was named governor-general of Macedonia later in the year and retained that position until 1932. Gonatus subsequently served as president of the senate until November 1935, when the monarchy was reestablished. He was detained for several months by the Nazi occupation forces in Greece during World War II. After the war Gonatus returned to the Parliament and served in several cabinets in 1946 and 1947. He subsequently retired from politics. Gonatus died in Athens on March 29, 1966, after a long illness.

ELEUTHERIOS VENIZELOS (Prime Minister; January 12, 1924–February 6, 1924). *See earlier entry under Heads of Government.*

GEORGE KAPHANDARIS (Prime Minister; February 6, 1924–March 11, 1924). George Kaphandaris was born in 1873. He entered politics and was widely respected as a leading orator and economic expert in the chamber of deputies. He served in several governments, heading the ministries of the interior and finance. He was a leading member of the Progressive Party and was chosen to head the government as prime minister on February 6, 1924, when Eleutherios Venizelos stepped down for reasons of health. He was replaced as prime minister by Alexandros Papanastasiou a month later on March 11, 1924. He remained active in politics and was a critic of the dictatorship of Ioannis Metaxas. He was exiled several times during Metaxas's rule. Kaphandaris was named deputy prime minister in Themistocles Sophoulis' postwar government in August 1945. He and several other ministers resigned in March 1946

in opposition to the holding of elections the following month. He died suddenly in Athens on August 28, 1946.

ALEXANDROS PAPANASTASIOU (Prime Minister; March 11, 1924–July 19, 1924). Alexandros Papanastasiou was born in 1876. He was a leader of the Greek Labor Party. He briefly served as prime minister from March 11, 1924, until July 24, 1924, when he was forced to resign following allegations of Communist sympathies. He was threatened with a court-martial the following year for his opposition to the government, but the trial was canceled. Papanastasiou was arrested in 1926, but was ordered released after two months by President Theodoros Pangalos. He was again arrested later in the year for complicity in a plot against the government and banished to the island of Naxos. He returned to Athens near the end of the year to again serve in the government. He was instrumental in the creation of the Balkan League as chairman of the Balkan states conference. Papanastasiou was detained in 1935 during Eleutherios Venizelos' revolt, and was again briefly exiled. He died of a heart attack at his country estate near Athens on November 17, 1936.

THEMISTOCLES SOPHOULIS (Prime Minister; July 24, 1924–October 1, 1924). Themistocles Sophoulis was born in Vathy, on the island of Samos, on November 25, 1861. He was an archaeologist and writer and served as a leader of the opposition to Turkish rule on Samos. When Samos was granted its liberty from Turkey, Sophoulis became the leader of the island's government and led the island into union with Greece. In 1914 he was appointed governor-general of Macedonia, and the following year he was elected to the Greek Parliament as the representative from Samos. Sophoulis was an ally of Liberal leader Eleutherios Venizelos, and in 1916 he joined with him in the revolutionary pro–Allied government at Salonika. He returned to Athens in 1917 after King Constantine was deposed. He was elected president of the chamber of deputies that same year and retained that office until 1920. Sophoulis was elected prime minister of the new Greek Republic on July 24, 1924, and served until October 1, 1924. He succeeded Venizelos as leader of the Liberal Party upon the latter's death in 1936. During the dictatorship of Ioannis Metaxas from 1936 until 1941, Sophoulis held no public office. He was arrested in 1944 following the German occupation of Greece and remained in the Haidari concentration camp until the liberation. He became prime minister of the postwar government on November 21, 1945, and remained in office until April 1, 1946, following the election victory of the Populist Party. He again formed a government on September 7, 1947, and presided over a coalition cabinet of Liberals and Populists. He retained the office of prime minister until his death in Kifissia, Greece, on June 24, 1949.

ANDREAS MICHALAKOPOU-LOS (Prime Minister; October 7, 1924–June 25, 1925). Andreas Michalakopoulos was born in 1876. He received a degree in law from the University of Athens. He was elected to the chamber of deputies from Patras in 1910. He was named to the cabinet as minister of agriculture in 1918 and was appointed minister of state the following year. Michalakopoulos was named to head the government as prime minister on October 7, 1924. He was forced from office by General Theodoros Pangalos on June 25, 1925. He returned to the government as foreign minister in 1926. He again served as foreign minister in Eleutherios Venizelos' governments in 1932 and 1933. Michalakopoulos was leader of the Conservative Republican Party until 1935, when he dissolved the party and retired from politics. He died in Athens on March 27, 1938.

THEODOROS PANGALOS (Prime Minister; June 26, 1925–August 22, 1926). *See earlier entry under Heads of State.*

GEORGIOS KONDYLIS (Prime Minister; August 22, 1926–December 4, 1926). Georgios Kondylis was born in Proussos, Southern Eurytanis, in 1879. He fought against the Turks in Crete in 1896 and joined the Greek army the following year as a private. Kondylis fought in Macedonia from 1905 through 1908 and in the Balkan wars of 1912 and 1913. He supported Eleutherios Venizelos's provisional government in Salonika in 1916 in opposition to King Constantine's pro–German policies. Kondylis fought in Macedonia during World War I and saw action at Anatolia in Asia Minor during the Greek-Turkish war in 1919. Kondylis resigned from the army when King Constantine was restored to the throne in 1920. He supported the revolutionary government that again ousted Constantine in 1923 and was instrumental in crushing a countercoup in October 1923. He supported the elimination of the monarchy and the establishment of the Greek Republic. He joined Alexandros Papanastasiou's cabinet as minister of war in March 1924, but resigned three months later over the government's inability to deal harshly with labor strikes and Communist insurgents. He returned to the cabinet as minister of the interior under Andreas Michalakopoulos in October 1924. Kondylis was arrested and imprisoned in Santorin in February 1926 for his opposition to the dictatorship of General Theodoros Pangalos. He was amnestied two months later and led the coup that ousted Pangalos on August 22, 1926. He restored Admiral Paul Konduriotis to the presidency and took the office of prime minister. Following general elections, Kondylis stepped down to allow Alexandros Zaimïs to head the government on December 4, 1926. He subsequently retired from politics, but returned in May 1927, re-forming the

National Republican Party. He was arrested in March 1933 when General Nikolas Plastiras led a military coup after the Royalists were successful in the elections. Kondylis was instrumental in crushing the coup the following day, allowing Royalist leader Panayiotis Tsaldaris to take over the reigns of government. He again served in the cabinet as minister of war in 1935, quickly crushing Venizelos' rebellion in Salonika in March 1935. He became deputy prime minister under Tsaldaris and became an advocate of the restoration of the monarchy. He met with Italian leader Benito Mussolini in June 1935 and was impressed with Mussolini's Fascist dictatorship. Kondylis led another coup against the government on October 10, 1935, and became prime minister. He proclaimed himself regent and brought about the restoration of King George II to the throne the following month. Kondylis hoped to rule Greece as a dictator, but King George favored a constitutional monarchy and dismissed him on November 30, 1935. He remained active in political affairs and was a bitter opponent of the Venezelists. He died suddenly of a heart attack at his home in Athens on January 31, 1936.

ALEXANDROS ZAIMÏS (Prime Minister; December 4, 1926–June 29, 1928). *See earlier entry under Heads of State.*

ELEUTHERIOS VENIZELOS (Prime Minister; July 4, 1928–November 4, 1932). *See earlier entry under Heads of Government.*

PANAYIOTIS TSALDARIS (Prime Minister; November 4, 1932–January 11, 1933). Panayiotis Tsaldaris was born in 1868. He entered politics and was elected to the chamber of deputies in 1910. He became affiliated with the Royalist Party and was a close associate of Royalist leader Dimitrios Gounaris. He was named to Gounaris' short-lived cabinet as minister of justice in 1915. He returned to the government as minister of justice and communications after the collapse of Eleutherios Venizelos' government in 1920. The following year he served as a member of The Hague Court of Arbitration. He was arrested and briefly detained by the newly installed revolutionary government upon his return to Greece in 1922. Tsaldaris succeeded Gounaris as leader of the Royalists when the latter was executed by the revolutionary government later in the year. Tsaldaris served as minister of the interior in Alexandros Zaimïs's coalition government in 1926. The Royalists suffered a major electoral setback in 1928 but resurged in 1932, and Tsaldaris formed a coalition government with Ioannis Metaxas and Georgios Kondylis. Tsaldaris headed the government from November 4, 1932, until January 11, 1933. He again led the government as prime minister and minister of foreign affairs from March 10, 1933. His government faced a rebellion by supporters of Venizelos in March 1935. The rebellion was crushed by Royalist troops led by General Kondylis. The government supported a plebiscite to restore the monarchy. Tsaldaris, who was criticized for his leniency toward the rebels, was ousted on October 10, 1935, in a bloodless coup led by General Kondylis to expedite King George II's return to the throne. Tsaldaris was called upon by King George to return as prime minister in March 1936, but was unable to organize a new government. He remained a leading figure in Greek politics until his sudden death of a heart attack at his home in Athens on May 17, 1936.

ELEUTHERIOS VENIZELOS (Prime Minister; January 15, 1933–March 6, 1933). *See earlier entry under Heads of Government.*

ALEXANDER OTHONAOS (Prime Minister; March 6, 1933–March 8, 1933). Alexander Othonaos was born in 1879. He entered the Greek army in the early 1900s. He saw action in the Balkan wars and participated in the 1909 revolution. He rose through the ranks of the army and served as president of the 1922 military tribunal to assess responsibility for Greece's military defeat by Turkey. The tribunal sentenced five leading Royalist politicians to death, including former prime ministers Dimitrious Gounaris, Nikolaos Stratos, and Petros Protopapadakis. Othonaos briefly headed the government as prime minister from March 6, 1933, until March 8, 1933, following General Nikolas Plastiras's short-lived revolt. Othonaos returned to prominence as commander-in-chief of the Greek army following the liberation of Greece from the German occupation forces in 1944. He resigned his position soon after in opposition to Greece's dependence on the British for military assistance. Othonaos died in Athens on September 20, 1970.

PANAYIOTIS TSALDARIS (Prime Minister; March 10, 1933–October 10, 1935). *See earlier entry under Heads of Government.*

GEORGIOS KONDYLIS (Prime Minister; October 10, 1935–November 30, 1935). *See earlier entry under Heads of Government.*

KONSTANTINOS DEMERDIS (Prime Minister; November 30, 1935–April 13, 1936). Konstantinos Demerdis was born in Athens in 1876. He was educated at the University of Athens and studied law in Germany. He entered politics and was elected to the chamber of deputies in 1911. Demerdis was also a leading Greek academician and a professor at the University of Athens. He was called upon by the newly restored King George II to head a neutralist cabinet on November 30, 1935. Demerdis served as prime minister and minister of foreign affairs in a government designed to revise the constitution and hold new

elections. An amnesty for supporters of Eleutherios Venizelos involved in the rebellion of March 1935 was issued, and new elections were called. Demerdis formed a new nonpartisan cabinet on March 15, 1936. He died suddenly of heart disease in Athens on April 12, 1936.

IOANNIS METAXAS (Prime Minister; April 22, 1936–January 29, 1941). Ioannis Metaxas was born in Ithaca on April 12, 1871. He graduated from the Athen's Military Academy in 1890 and served with distinction in the Greco-Turkish War in 1897. He subsequently went to Germany where he received further military training. He returned to Greece in 1903 and continued to advance his military career. He was named to the general staff in 1913. He supported King Constantine's policy of neutrality during World War I, and often came into conflict with Prime Minister Eleutherios Venizelos, who advocated Greece's participation in the conflict on the side of the Allies. Metaxas offered to resign in 1915, but the king dismissed Venizelos and refused to accept Metaxas's resignation. He was promoted to general in 1916 and remained chief of staff until Constantine was deposed in June 1917. Metaxas went into exile and was tried for treason in absentia in 1920. He was pardoned and returned to Greece the following year when Constantine reclaimed the throne. He founded the Free Thinker's Party in 1921. Metaxas again went into exile in Italy after leading an unsuccessful coup attempt when Constantine was again deposed in September 1922. He returned to Greece several years later and accepted the post of minister of communications in the cabinet in 1928. He soon resigned and spent the next seven years in parliament in opposition. He refused to accept another ministerial position until 1935, when the monarchy was restored under King George II. Metaxas was named prime minister on April 22, 1936, following the sudden death of four of Greece's leading political figures. He suspended the constitution and dismissed the Parliament on August 4, 1936. Metaxas governed as a dictator with the support of King George II. He was successful in improving Greece's financial and military positions at the expense of civil liberties. Greece was invaded by Italy in October 1940, but Metaxas succeeded in unifying the country in a successful campaign against the invader. Metaxas died in Athens after a brief illness on January 29, 1941.

ALEXANDROS KORIZIS (Prime Minister; January 29, 1941–April 18, 1941). Alexandros Korizis was born on the island of Poros off the east coast of southern Greece on April 15, 1885. Korizis studied law and finance and was employed by the Bank of Greece in 1903 and rose to the position of general controller of the bank in 1915. He served as an advisor to the Greek government on financial affairs during the 1920s and became vice governor of the bank in 1929. He was named to Ioannis Metaxas's cabinet as minister of health and social welfare in 1936. He was appointed to chair the Athens administration committee of the Greek War Relief Association after the Italian invasion of Greece in the fall of 1940. He stepped down from the cabinet to become governor of the Bank of Greece in 1940. Korizis was a close friend and advisor to Greek dictator Metaxas. He was chosen to head the government on January 29, 1941, following Metaxas's death. He carried on Greece's fight against the Italian invaders for several months before Germany launched an attack on Greece. Korizis commited suicide in Athens on April 18, 1941, presumably over his government's inability to unify the country in the face of the German invasion.

EMMANOUIL TSOUDEROS (Prime Minister; April 21, 1941–May 26, 1944). Emmanouil Tsouderos was born in 1882. He was educated in Athens, Paris, and London. He entered politics and was elected to the chamber of deputies from Crete. He was a leading financial expert and accompanied the Greek delegation to the Paris Peace Conference in 1918. He served on the Vienna Committee of Reparations in 1920 and 1921. Tsouderos was a supporter of Eleutherios Venizelos and served in several cabinets as minister of finance and communications in the 1920s. He also served as Greece's delegate to the League of Nations. Tsouderos was governor of the National Bank of Greece from 1931 until 1938. He was named to head the government as prime minister on April 21, 1941, shortly before the German invasion of Greece. Tsouderos and his cabinet fled to Egypt, where he continued to head the government-in-exile. He stepped down as prime minister on May 26, 1944, and remained in the government as deputy premier after Greece's liberation. He remained active in politics until January 1956, when he went to rest in Paris for reasons of health. Tsouderos died in Genoa, Italy, on February 10, 1956.

GEORGIOS PAPANDREOU (Prime Minister; May 26, 1944–December 31, 1944). Georgios Papandreou was born in Kalentzi on February 13, 1888. He received a degree in law from the University of Athens. He entered politics in 1915 and became prefect of Chios. He served as governor-general of the Aegean Islands from 1917 until 1920. He was elected to the Greek Parliament in 1923 and was named minister of the interior in the government of General Nikolas Plastiras. He served as minister of education from 1929 until 1933. Two years later he founded the Democratic Socialist Party. He was sent into exile during the dictatorship of Ioannis Metaxas. He was an opponent of the Italian-German occupation of Greece during World War II. He was arrested by the Italians, but escaped to Egypt where he joined the government-in-exile. He was named prime minister in King George II's exile government on May 26, 1944. The government moved to Naples on September 7 and returned to Athens on October 18, 1944. He was asked by the king to remain as prime minister, but declined because of his opposition to the monarchy and resigned on December 31, 1944. He remained active in government, serving as minister of the interior in 1947 and deputy prime minister from 1950 until 1951. He spent the remainder of the 1950s in opposition to the government. He formed the Center Union Party in September 1961 and led the party to victory in the elections in November 1963. He became prime minister on November 7, 1963, but resigned on December 24, 1963, in order to call for new elections to increase his majority. His party was given an absolute majority in the subsequent elections and Papandreou again became prime minister on February 19, 1964. He resigned from office on July 15, 1965, following a dispute with King Constantine II over the question of control of the armed forces. Papandreou's party was again expected to win the elections of 1967, but the government was taken over by the military in April of that year. Papandreou was arrested by the junta leaders and imprisoned. He was in poor health at the time and was sent to a military hospital for treatment. He was released and placed under house arrest, until he was amnestied in December 1967. Papandreou died in Athens following surgery for a bleeding ulcer on November 1, 1968. His funeral served as an occasion for his supporters to express their opposition to the leaders of the ruling junta.

NIKOLAS PLASTIRAS (Prime Minister; January 2, 1945–April 9, 1945). Nikolas Plastiras was born in Kardhitsa, Thessaly, in 1883. He served in the Greek army and fought in the Balkan war. He was promoted to colonel in 1920. In the early 1920s he led a Greek expedition against the Turks in Anatolis and

distinguished himself by successfully leading the Greek evacuation after the Turkish victory. Plastiras returned to Greece to lead a coup on September 2, 1922, that forced the abdication of King Constantine. He organized the ruling revolutionary committee and served as acting prime minister. He stepped down in November 1922 in favor of General Stylianos Gonatus, a fellow coup leader. His political mentor, Eleutherios Venizelos, became prime minister in January 1924, and Plastiras went into political retirement. The following year Venizelos was ousted, and Plastiras was arrested and sent into exile by the government of General Theodoros Pangalos. Plastiras made several attempts to overthrow the Pangalos government and was sentenced to death in absentia. He was allowed to return to Greece following the ouster of Pangalos in August 1926. Venizelos returned as prime minister in 1928, and Plastiras helped to reorganize the army. The Royalist opposition was successful in the elections of 1933, and Plastiras, with the approval of Venizelos, staged a coup on March 7, 1933. His government lasted less than a day before he was ousted by General Georgios Kondylis. Plastiras fled to Bulgaria and eventually to Egypt. He led an unsuccessful uprising when the monarchy was reestablished in 1935. He was a leading opponent of the subsequent dictatorship of General Ioannis Metaxas and led several unsuccessful attempts against the government. Plastiras was politically inactive throughout the German occupation during World War II. He returned to Greece following the liberation of the country from occupation forces and the defeat of Communist insurgents. On January 2, 1945, he became prime minister. He stepped down three months later on April 9, 1945, following general elections. Plastiras reentered politics and again became prime minister as head of a coalition government on April 15, 1950. He was forced to resign on August 18, 1950, following the resignation of the liberal members of his government. Plastiras was again named prime minister on November 1, 1951, when Alexandros Papagos, leader of the majority party, refused to form a coalition government. Plastiras was able to establish a coalition government, but his health deteriorated during his term of office and forced his resignation on October 11, 1952. He recovered sufficiently to run in the elections in November 1952, but his party was defeated and he lost his seat in parliament. Plastiras suffered a series of heart attacks in July 1953. He died in Psychico, near Athens, on July 26, 1953.

PETROS VOULGARIS (Prime Minister; April 9, 1945–October 9, 1945). Petros Voulgaris was born on the island of Hydra in 1884. He attended the Naval Cadet School and served as chief of the naval air force during World War I. Voulgaris was stationed in Ankara, Turkey, as a naval attaché when he was dismissed on charges that he supported a coup against the Greek government in 1935. He went into exile in Egypt following the German occupation of Greece during World War II. He served as air minister in the government-in-exile. He successfully led a group of naval officers on a mission to seize all Greek warships in Alexandria harbor from Communist sympathizers who had control of the ships. Following the liberation of Greece, Admiral Voulgaris was asked to become prime minister on April 9, 1945, as leader of an interim government in anticipation of democratic elections. Voulgaris faced the opposition of the various political parties in Greece and resigned on October 9, 1945. He died of a heart ailment at the Athens Naval Hospital on November 26, 1957.

DAMASKINOS (Prime Minister; October 17, 1945–November 1, 1945). Archbishop Damaskinos was born George Papandreou in Dorvitsa on March 3, 1891. He was educated in Karditsa and at the University of Athens. He was ordained to the priesthood in 1917 and was elected bishop of Corinth in 1922. Damaskinos was a leading opponent of the regime of Prime Minister Ioannis Metaxas, and when he was elected archbishop of Athens and primate of Greece in 1938, the prime minister annulled the election. Damaskinos was exiled to a monastery in the Greek mountains until the German-Italian occupation of Greece in 1942. He was then asked to assume his office and became the primary spiritual leader of Greece. Following the liberation of Greece in 1944, the country broke into civil war between Royalist and Communist elements. Archbishop Damaskinos was asked to serve as regent while King George II remained in exile. He also served as prime minister from October 17, 1945, until November 3, 1945. Following a plebiscite on September 1, 1946, the king was invited to return to the throne. King George II returned to Greece on September 27, 1946, and Archbishop Damaskinos retired from political activities. He died in Psychico, near Athens, on May 20, 1949.

PANAYOTIS KANELLOPOU-LOS (Prime Minister; November 1, 1945–November 20, 1945). Panayotis Kanellopoulos (Canellopoulos) was born in Patras on December 13, 1902. He was educated in Greece and Germany, studying law and sociology. In the late 1920s he taught sociology at Athens University. He left the university to enter politics in 1935 and founded the National Unionist Party in opposition to the restoration of the monarchy. Kanellopoulos was an opponent of the dictatorship of Ioannis Metaxas and spent most of the period between 1936 and 1940 in exile. He joined the Greek military service in 1940 following the Italian invasion of Greece. He was a leader of the Resistance following the German occupation of Greece and left the country for the Middle East in 1942. There he joined the Greek government-in-exile as minister of war. He returned to Greece in 1944 to supervise the German withdrawal. Kanellopoulos was named prime minister on November 1, 1945, but his government could not survive the fighting between the various political factions. He stepped down on November 20, 1945. He was elected to parliament the following year and served in various cabinet positions over the next two decades. Kanellopoulos was minister of war from 1949 until 1950. He joined with Alexandros Papagos's Greek Rally Party in 1952 and served as deputy prime minister and minister of national defense until Papagos's death in 1955. He was a leading contender to succeed Papagos but was bypassed in favor of Konstantine Karamanlis. Kanellopoulos served as deputy prime minister under Karamanlis from 1959 until 1963. When Karamanlis withdrew from politics in 1963, Kanellopoulos was elected leader of the National Radical Union Party. He again served as prime minister when his party withdrew its support from Ioannis Paraskevopoulos' caretaker government. Kanellopoulos was selected to succeed him as prime minister on April 3, 1967. His interim government was given the mandate to hold elections the following May, but a military junta toppled the government on April 21, 1967, and Kanellopoulos and many members of his cabinet were arrested. Following his release, he remained an outspoken critic of the military regime. Kanellopoulos was again elected to parliament after the collapse of the junta in 1974. He was the unsuccessful nominee of the Centre Party for the Greek presidency the following year, and he retired from politics. Kanellopoulos died of a heart attack in Athens on September 11, 1986.

THEMISTOCLES SOPHOULIS (Prime Minister; November 21, 1945– April 1, 1946). *See earlier entry under Heads of Government.*

Guatemala

Guatemala is a country in the northern part of Central America. It was granted independence from Spain on September 15, 1821.

HEADS OF STATE

MANUEL ESTRADA CABRERA (President; September 25, 1898–April 15, 1920). Manuel Estrada Cabrera was born in Quetzaltenango on November 21, 1857. He was educated at the Guatemala City Law School and received a degree in law in 1883. He was named to José Mariá Reina Barrios' cabinet as minister of the interior and minister of justice during the 1890s. He also served as Reina Barrios' vice president. Estrada Cabrera succeeded to the presidency on September 25, 1898, following Reina Barrios' assassination. Estrada Cabrera initiated numerous public works projects, building roads, railways, and bridges. He was an opponent of the labor movement and used the armed forces to crush strikes. He amended the constitution to allow unlimited presidential terms and was reelected in sham elections in 1904, 1910, and 1916. Guatemala engaged in a brief war with El Salvador in 1906 when that country supported a revolt against Estrada Cabrera's government. Popular discontent against his rule increased in the late 1910s. This was compounded by a major earthquake that seriously damaged Guatemala City. The Guatemalan national assembly declared Estrada Cabrera insane and unfit to continue to govern. He was relieved from office on April 15, 1920. Estrada Cabrera died in Guatemala City on September 24, 1924.

CARLOS HERRERA Y LUNA (President; April 15, 1920–December 9, 1921). Carlos Herrera y Luna was born in 1856. He was a leading economist and financier. He was chosen by the Guatemalan national assembly to replace deposed president Manuel Estrada Cabrera on April 15, 1920, but he was ousted in a military coup the following year on December 9, 1921. Herrera died on July 6, 1930.

JOSÉ MARÍA ORELLANA (President; December 9, 1921–September 26, 1926). José María Orellana was born in El Jicaro on July 11, 1872. He was educated at Guatemala's military academy, the Polytechnic School, and entered the military. He served in President Manuel Estrada Cabrera's administration in various military and political positions including director of the Military Academy, chief of staff and minister of education. When Estrada Cabrera was removed from office in April 1920, a Unionist government led by Carlos Herrera was installed. Orellana was a leader of the military coup that ousted Herrera on December 9, 1921, and he served as provisional president. Orellana was the Liberal Party's nominee in elections held the following February and won by an overwhelming margin. During his administration he established the Central Bank of Guatemala. He remained president until his death of a heart attack in Guatemala City on September 26, 1926.

LÁZARO CHACÓN (President; September 26, 1926–December 12, 1930). Lazáro Chacón was born in Zacapa on June 27, 1874. He entered the army in 1892 and saw action in several

Central American campaigns. He rose to the rank of general in 1926. Chacón served as vice president under José María Orellana. He succeeded to the presidency when Orellana died in office on September 26, 1926. Chacón was subsequently elected president in his own right. He suspended the constitution in 1928 in response to civil unrest against his government. Chacón resigned on December 12, 1930, after suffering a stroke. He went to the United States for medical treatment and died at his home in New Orleans on April 10, 1931.

BAUDILIO PALMA (President; December 12, 1930–December 17, 1930). Baudilio Palma was born in 1884. He served as vice president under Lázaro Chacón and was chosen by the council of ministers to serve as acting president when Chacón resigned due to poor health on December 12, 1930. Palma was ousted by a military coup led by General Manuel Orellana on December 17, 1930. He died in San Salvador on June 20, 1946.

MANUEL ORELLANA (President; December 17, 1930–January 2, 1931). Manuel Orellana served in the Guatemalan military, rising to the rank of general. He led a military coup against acting president Baudilio Palma on December 17, 1930, and headed the ruling junta until his resignation on January 2, 1931.

JOSÉ MARÍA REINA ANDRADE (President; January 2, 1931–February 14, 1931). José María Reina Andrade was born in 1860. He began his career in politics as a member of the constitutional congress in 1877. He was educated as a lawyer and held numerous government positions, including chief justice of the Supreme Court. He was chosen by the national assembly to serve as provisional president on January 2, 1931. Reina Andrade oversaw new elections and relinquished office to Jorge

Ubico on February 14, 1931. He died in Guatemala City on August 26, 1947.

JORGE UBICO (President; February 14, 1931–July 1, 1944). Jorge Ubico y Castañeda was born in Guatemala City on November 10, 1878. He was educated at the military academy in Guatemala and entered the army in 1897. He was promoted to the rank of colonel and saw action in Guatemala's border war against El Salvador in 1906. He was appointed governor of Alta Verapaz the following year and became governor of Retalhuleu in 1912. He was subsequently elected to the national assembly and directed relief efforts after devastating earthquakes rocked Guatemala City in 1917 and 1918. He was promoted to brigadier general in 1920 and was a participant in the military coup that ousted President Carlos Herrera in December 1921. He served in José María Orellana's cabinet as minister of war in 1922. He was the Progressive Party's presidential nominee in 1926, but was defeated by Lázaro Chacón. Ubico returned to politics in 1931 as the Liberal and Progressive Party's nominee for president. He was victorious and took office on February 14, 1931. Ubico was successful in stabilizing the Guatemalan economy and attracted United States business interests to the country. He suppressed leftists and labor unions and governed Guatemala as a virtual dictator. He extended his term of office in 1937 and again in 1941. Ubico was a strong supporter of the United States during World War II. Opposition to his regime mounted in the early 1940s, and student protests led to Ubico declaring a state of siege in 1944. A subsequent general strike and ongoing civil disturbances forced Ubico's resignation on July 1, 1944. He went into exile in Mexico before settling in the United States in October 1944. He died in a New Orleans hospital on June 14, 1946.

FEDERICO PONCE (President; July 4, 1944–October 20, 1944). Federico Ponce Vaidés was born in 1889. He served in the Guatemalan military and was governor of several departments during the administration of Jorge Ubico. He was chosen to serve as provisional president on July 4, 1944, following Ubico's resignation. Ponce attempted to retain the presidency and was ousted in a military coup led by Jacobo Arbenz Guzmán on October 20, 1944. Ponce died in Guatemala City on January 28, 1956.

JACOBO ARBENZ GUZMÁN (President; October 20, 1944–March 15, 1945). Jacobo Arbenz Guzmán was born in Quetzaltenango on September 14, 1913. He was educated at the military academy in Guatemala City and served in the Guatemalan army. He was involved in the military rising that forced the ouster of President Jorge Ubico in July 1944. He went into exile in El Salvador in opposition to the subsequent government of General Federico Ponce. Arbenz led coup against Ponce's government on October 20, 1944, and served as leader of the junta until March 15, 1945, when Juan José Arévalo was inaugurated as president. Arbenz served as minister of defense in the Arévalo government and succeeded in putting down numerous attempts to oust the government. His leading rival in the military, Colonel Francisco Javier Araña, was assassinated in July 1949. Arbenz resigned from the government in June 1950 to become a candidate for the presidency. He was elected in November 1950 and took office on March 1, 1951. Arbenz continued the land reform measures of his predecessor. He also established relations with Communist nations and expropriated American-owned businesses including the United Fruit Company. His actions drew the criticism of the United States and rightists in the military who accused his government of being controlled by the Communists. He survived a coup attempt in 1953 and instituted repressive measures against his opponents.

He was ousted following an invasion and right-wing military coup supported by the American Central Intelligence Agency on June 27, 1954. Arbenz went into exile in France. He subsequently lived in Switzerland, Czechoslovakia, and Cuba before settling in Mexico City. Arbenz was found dead in the bathroom of his home on January 27, 1971. He supposedly slipped, fell into the tub, and drowned in the scalding water.

JUAN JOSÉ ARÉVALO (President; March 15, 1945–March 15, 1951). Juan José Arévalo Barmejo was born in Taxisco on September 10, 1904. He was educated at the University of La Plata, where he received a doctorate in education in 1934. He returned to Guatemala and worked in the education ministry briefly before returning to Argentina. He served on the faculty of the University of Tucuman. He again returned to Guatemala following the ouster of President Jorge Ubico in 1944. Arévalo was the presidential candidate of the revolutionaries and was the overwhelming victor in the subsequent election. He took office on March 15, 1945. He lifted restrictions on the press and the labor unions and initiated a program of agrarian reform. He also launched a social security program and began reforms in education, health, and sanitation. He survived numerous attempts to oust his government. Arévalo's likely successor, Colonel Francisco Javier Araña, was assassinated in July 1949. Arevalo completed his term of office on March 1, 1951. He served as ambassador-at-large in the government of his successor, Jacobo Arbenz Guzmán. Arbenz was ousted by a right-wing military coup in 1954, and Arevalo went into exile in Argentina. He authored a book critical of United States policy in Latin America entitled *The Shark and the Sardines* in 1961. Arévalo returned to Guatemala to run for the presidency in 1963, but Colonel Enrique Peralta Azurdia staged a coup to prevent the election. Arévalo again returned to Guatemala following the restoration of a civilian government in 1986. He died in Guatemala City on October 6, 1990.

Haiti

Haiti is a country that occupies the western part of the island of Hispaniola in the northern Caribbean Sea. It was granted independence from France on January 1, 1804.

HEADS OF STATE

TIRÉSIAS SIMON SAM (President; March 31, 1896–May 12, 1902). Tirésias Simon Sam succeeded Florvil Hyppolite as president of Haiti on March 31, 1896, following Hyppolite's death in office. He was an unpopular leader and was criticized for his alleged prejudice against Haiti's mulatto population. He was also accused of selling out Haiti's interests to foreigners. He initially refused to step down at the end of his term, hoping to extend his rule for another year. He was persuaded to step down on May 12, 1902, and intended to place his handpicked successor in the presidency. Opponents of Sam halted his plans with an attack on the chamber of deputies, and Sam was forced into exile. Leading citizens of Haiti formed a committee of safety to govern the country in the absence of a president. Sam remained involved in Haitian affairs through his son, Vilbrun Guillaume Sam, whom he supported politically and financially. The younger Sam briefly served as president of Haiti before his murder in 1915.

ADOLPH BOISROND CANAL (President; May 26, 1902–December 21, 1902). Adolph Boisrond Canal served in the Haitian army, rising to the rank of general. He became president on July 17, 1876, following the ouster of President Michel Dominique several months earlier. Canal was a leader of the Liberal Party and had the support of Haiti's mulatto population. A split in the Liberal Party between Canal and supporters of Boyer Bazelais led to a victory by the National Party in the 1879 elections. Canal stepped down on July 17, 1879, and was replaced by Etienne Salomon several months later. He remained a leading figure in Haitian politics and was chosen as the chairman of the committee of safety and became provisional president of Haiti on May 26, 1902, following the ouster of President Tirésias Simon Sam. His government named Pierre Nord Alexis as minister of war and forced back a rebellion led by Antenor Fermin. He stepped down on December 21, 1902, when Alexis claimed the presidency.

PIERRE NORD ALEXIS (President; December 21, 1902–December 2, 1908). Pierre Nord Alexis was born in 1820. He was the son of Baron Nord, who was a leading figure in the administration of President Henri Christophe in the early 1800s. Alexis entered the army in the late 1830s. He served as an aide-de-camp to President Jean Louis Pierrot. He was sent into exile by President Michel Dominique in 1874, but was allowed to return to Haiti several years later by his successor, Boisrond Canal. Alexis was a leading opponent of President Etienne Salomon and was imprisoned several times in the 1880s. He was a leader of the revolt that ousted Sa-

lomon in August 1888. He was appointed to an administrative position in the military in northern Haiti by President Florvil Hippolyte the following year. He remained there until the resignation of President Tirésias Simon Sam in May 1902. He was initially a supporter of Antenor Firmin and led his troops on a march to the capital in support of Firmin. He was named by the provisional governing committee of Haiti as minister of war and the navy. His own presidential ambitions soon led him to turn on Firmin. Fighting between troops loyal to the two men nearly reduced Haiti to a state of civil war before Firmin's supporters were crushed in Port-au-Prince. Alexis courted the support of American interests in Haiti, and Firminist strongholds in Gonaives and St. Marc were placed under naval blockades. Alexis led his troops to the chamber of deputies in December 1902 and forced the legislature to approve him as president. He took office on December 21, 1902. He ruled for the next six years over an administration marked by corruption and revolt. Alexis planned to be named president-for-life by his hand-picked legislature. Firminists began a new revolt in January 1908. The revolt failed and led to further repression against dissidents. Continuing economic difficulties and a famine in the south led to food riots in June 1908. General Antoine Simon led a rebellion from southern Haiti that ousted Alexis on December 2, 1908. Alexis went into exile aboard a French ship and settled in Kingston, Jamaica. He died there on May 1, 1910.

F. ANTOINE SIMON (President; December 17, 1908–August 2, 1911). F. Antoine Simon served in the Haitian army and was promoted to the rank of general. He headed the military department in southern Haiti and became leader of a coalition that wanted to oust President Pierre Nord Alexis. Simon led a military revolt that captured the capital on December 1, 1908, and took over the presidency. He was soon ruling in an authoritarian fashion, and began repressive measures against the press and opponents of the government in the spring of 1909. He faced a military rising in the north in early 1911, which he crushed in a ruthless fashion. His oppressive measures led to criticism by the United States and the European powers. The north rebelled again in the spring of 1911, and Simon was unable to rally his forces for an adequate defense. He was forced to step down from office on August 2, 1911, and go into exile. Simon died in 1923.

MICHEL CINCINNATUS LECONTE (President; August 14, 1911–August 8, 1912). Michel Cincinnatus Leconte was educated in Haiti and in Europe. He was active in the revolt that ousted President Etienne Salomon in August 1888. He held various government positions and served in the government of Pierre Nord Alexis as minister of the interior in 1906. He was a leading figure in northern Haiti, and was active in the military revolt that deposed President Antoine Simon. Leconte became president of Haiti on August 14, 1911. His regime was beset by opposition from the time he took power. He began making limited reforms in the country, advancing education and building barracks for the military. He also undertook an ambitious public works program and made significant strides against government corruption. The Haitian economy improved marginally during his rule. Leconte was killed on August 8, 1912, by an explosion in the presidential palace. The explosion occurred when a large stockpile of arms and ammunition stored in the basement of the palace was ignited. There is some evidence to suggest that Leconte was murdered before the detonation, as his charred body was found dismembered after the explosion.

TANCRÉDE AUGUSTE (President; August 8, 1912–May 2, 1913). Tancréde Auguste was born in 1859. He was a prosperous planter and businessman from Cape Haitian. He served in President Tirésias Simon Sam's government as minister of the interior and police from 1896 until 1902. He was elected president on August 8, 1912, following the death of Michel Cincinnatus Leconte. Auguste suffered from poor health in the latter part of his term. His death on May 2, 1913, was thought to be the result of poisoning.

MICHEL ORESTE (President; May 4, 1913–January 27, 1914). Michel Oreste was born in Jacmel in 1859. Oreste was educated as a lawyer and was a leading figure in Haiti who had served as a senator and jurist. He was chosen to succeed Tancréde Auguste as president by the national assembly on May 4, 1913. He attempted to improve Haiti's educational facilities but was unable to improve economic conditions in the country. His attempts at military reform caused discontent against his regime. Oreste's government came under siege by forces loyal to Charles and Oreste Zamor and General Davilmar Theodore. Oreste was unable to halt the revolt and the city of St. Marc fell in late January 1914. Oreste was forced to resign on January 27, 1914, and fled the country aboard a German ship. He died in 1919.

ORESTE ZAMOR (President; February 8, 1914–October 29, 1914). Oreste Zamor was a leading military figure in the northern region of Haiti. He and his brother, Charles, led a military revolt against the regime of President Michel Oreste that ousted the government on January 27, 1914. He was chosen by the chamber of deputies to replace Oreste as president on February 8, 1914. Haiti's ecomomy continued to deteriorate under Zamor's rule, and his administration came into conflict with European interests in the country. He was faced with widespread revolt, and was forced to resign on October 29, 1914. Zamor was arrested in early 1915 by the government of

Jean Guillaume Sam and was jailed in Port-au-Prince. As Sam's government began to collapse, the jail commandant ordered the execution of all political prisoners being held, and Zamor was brutally executed on July 27, 1915.

JOSEPH DAVILMAR THÉODORE (President; November 7, 1914–February 22, 1915). Joseph Davilmar Théodore was from Ennery and was a leading military figure in northern Haiti. He was a leader of the military revolt against President Oreste Zamor in January 1914. He was chosen as president of Haiti on November 7, 1914, but was forced to resign on February 22, 1915, because of his inability to raise funds to pay his cacao followers. He died in 1917.

JEAN VILBRUN GUILLAUME SAM (President; March 4, 1915–July 28, 1915). Jean Vilbrun Guillaume Sam was the son of Tirésias Simon Sam, who served as Haiti's president from 1896 to 1902. The younger Sam was the leader of the Haitian revolution in January 1915 and became president of Haiti on March 4, 1915. He was faced with a rebellion in the north led by Rosalvo Bobo and took repressive measures against his political opponents. Sam ordered the execution of several hundred of his political opponents on July 27, 1915, including former president Oreste Zamor. Following a revolution against his oppressive rule, he took refuge in the French legation in Port-au-Prince on July 28, 1915. An angry mob stormed the legation, dragging Sam into the streets. He was then impaled on the iron fence surrounding the legation and torn to pieces. The remnants of his corpse were dragged through the streets. His regime and the subsequent civil disorders led to American military intervention in August 1915.

PHILIPPE SUDRÉ DARTINGUENAVE (President; August 12, 1915–May 15, 1922). Philippe Sudré Dartinguenave was a mulatto born in south-ern Haiti. Dartinguenave was president of the Haitian senate and was chosen by the legislature to serve as Haiti's president following the United States occupation. He took office on August 12, 1915, and tried to reach a balance between the desires of the Haitian Assembly and those of the occupation authorities. He was responsible for signing the treaty that legalized the intervention of the United States. Dartinguenave was widely viewed as a puppet of American interests. A major rebellion against the occupation forces developed in the north under Charlemagne Peralte in 1919. He led a provisional government in the north until he was killed in November 1919. The rebellion continued under Benoit Bertraville until he was also killed in battle in March 1920. Dartinguenave left office on May 15, 1922, and died in 1926.

LOUIS BORNÓ (President; May 15, 1922–May 15, 1930). Joseph Louis E. Antoine François Bornó was born in 1865. He was chosen by General John H. Russell, the United States high commissioner to Haiti, to serve as Haiti's president on May 15, 1922. Bornó served for eight years, and during that time he worked closely with Russell. He stepped down from office on May 15, 1930. Bornó died on July 19, 1942.

EUGÉNE ROY (President; May 15, 1930–November 18, 1930). Eugéne Roy was a leading Haitian banker when he was chosen to serve as interim president of Haiti on May 15, 1930. His administration was charged with the duty of conducting new elections to the national assembly. The new assembly chose Sténio Vincent as president, and Roy stepped down on November 18, 1930. He died on October 27, 1939.

STÉNIO JOSEPH VINCENT (President; November 18, 1930–May 15, 1941). Sténio Joseph Vincent was born in 1874. He served as mayor of Port-au-

Prince before being elected president of Haiti. He took office on November 18, 1930. He was an opponent of the occupation of Haiti by the United States. He came into conflict with the Haitian senate in 1935 and expelled many of his opponents from their seats. He was criticized for his failure to act against the Dominican Republic over the massacre of Haitians in 1937. He left office on May 1, 1941. Vincent died in Port-au-Prince on September 3, 1959.

ÉLIE LESCOT (President; May 15, 1941–January 11, 1946). Élie Lescot was born in Saint Louis du Nord on December 9, 1883. He was active in politics and served as secretary of public education and agriculture in the cabinet of President Louis Bornó from 1922 until 1930. He was subsequently named secretary of

justice and the interior under President Sténio Vincent. Lescot served as Haiti's ambassador to the United States from 1937 until 1941. When President Vincent declined to run for a third term, Lescot was elected president of Haiti and took office on May 15, 1941. He was initially a popular leader, but soon lost favor in the country. He was accused of using his position to allow his sons to acquire government property in an unfair manner. The economy also suffered under his administration, and the cost of living tripled. Lescot ruled by martial law and kept a tight rein on the press and the opposition. His unpopular regime was ousted by the military on January 11, 1946, and he withdrew from political affairs. Lescot died in La Boule, Haiti, on October 22, 1974.

Honduras

Honduras is a country in Central America. It was granted independence from Spain on September 15, 1821.

HEADS OF STATE

TERENCIO SIERRA (President; February 1, 1899–May 5, 1903). Terencio Sierra was a general in the Honduran army. He served as minister of war in the government of Policarpo Bonilla from 1895 until he became the Liberal Party's nominee for president in 1898. He was victorious and took office on February 1, 1899. Sierra attempted to block the selection of his successor and award the presidency to Juan Angel Arias when Manuel Bonilla received the most votes in the 1903 elections, but Bonilla led a revolt against the government, and Sierra fled into exile in El Salvador in May 1903. He died in 1907.

MANUEL BONILLA (President;

May 5, 1903–April 11, 1907). Manuel Bonilla Chirinos was born in 1849. He served in the Honduran military and was promoted to the rank of general. He became vice president under Terencio Sierra in 1899, but he resigned several years later after a dispute with Liberal Party leader and former president Policarpo Bonilla. Manuel Bonilla formed the Nationalist Party and entered the 1903 presidential contest. He received the majority of the votes but was denied the office by President Sierra, who attempted to install his candidate, Juan Angel Arias. Bonilla went to Ampala, where he declared himself president. He returned to oust Sierra and was declared president by congress on May 5, 1903.

Bonilla's disputes with the Liberals under Policarpo Bonilla resulted in his closing the congress in early 1904. Manuel Bonilla extended his term of office at a constitutional convention in 1905. In December 1906 President Jose Santos Zelaya of Nicaragua sent troops into Honduras to support insurgents under Policarpo Bonilla. Manuel Bonilla was forced from office on April 11, 1907. He went into exile in Guatemala and British Honduras. Bonilla returned to Honduras four years later with the support of the Cuyamel Fruit Company president, Samuel Zemurray. His rebellion ousted the government of Miguel Davila and an interim regime under Francisco Bertrand was established to hold new elections. Bonilla was reelected president and took office on February 1, 1912. His term of office was cut short by his death on March 21, 1913.

MIGUEL R. DÁVILA (President; April 18, 1907–March 28, 1911). Miguel R. Dávila was promoted to general in the Honduran military. He was a member of the Liberal Party and was chosen to head the ruling revolutionary junta following the ouster of President Manuel Bonilla on April 18, 1907. Dávila was approved by the constituent assembly as constitutional president on March 1, 1908. He was faced with several rebellions led by Bonilla. Rebel forces captured several towns and the country was threatened with civil war. Dávila and Bonilla agreed to arbitration by the United States, and Dávila stepped down from office on March 28, 1911, to allow the formation of a provisional government under Francisco Bertrand.

FRANCISCO BERTRAND (President; March 28, 1911–February 1, 1912). Francisco Bertrand was born in 1866. He was chosen to head a provisional government on March 28, 1911, to end a rebellion by General Manuel Bonilla against the government of Miguel Dávila. Bertrand stepped down on February 1, 1912, after Bonilla's election as president. Bertrand served in the government as minister of justice and vice president and became interim president following Bonilla's death on March 20, 1913. He stepped down on July 28, 1915, to become a candidate in the presidential election. He was victorious and resumed office on February 1, 1916. Bertrand declared an amnesty of all political prisoners. He attempted to form a union of Central American states, but was unable to convince the other countries to agree to such a plan. Bertrand was a popular leader until he attempted to install his own successor in 1919. A revolt forced Bertrand from office on September 9, 1919. He went into exile in the United States and settled in New Orleans. He returned to Honduras in the spring of 1926 and died in La Ceiba on July 16, 1926.

MANUEL BONILLA (President; February 1, 1912–March 20, 1913). *See earlier entry under Heads of State.*

FRANCISCO BERTRAND (President; March 20, 1913–July 28, 1915). *See earlier entry under Heads of State.*

ALBERTO MEMBREÑO (President; July 28, 1915–February 1, 1916). Alberto Membreño was born in 1858. He served as minister to the United States in 1915. He succeeded to the presidency when Francisco Bertrand stepped down on July 28, 1915, to run in the presidential election. Membreño's government oversaw the election, and he relinquished office on February 1, 1916, following Bertrand's victory. Membreño led unsuccessful revolts against the government in October 1919 and in February 1920. He died in Tegucigalpa on February 4, 1921.

FRANCISCO BERTRAND (President; February 1, 1916–September 9, 1919). *See earlier entry under Heads of State.*

RAFAEL LÓPEZ GUTIÉRREZ

(President; February 1, 1920–February 1, 1924). Rafael López Gutiérrez served in the Honduran military and attained the rank of general. He was selected to succeed Francisco Bertrand as president on February 1, 1920. He withstood several attempts to oust his government during his first year in office. In elections held in 1923 none of the major candidates received an absolute majority. López Gutiérrez planned to extend his term of office, but several factions went into revolt and forced him from office. López Gutiérrez fled the capital in February 1924 and went to Ampala. He was suffering from diabetes and attempted to go to the United States for insulin treatment. He died of complications from his condition on March 10, 1924.

VICENTE TOSTA

(President; April 30, 1924–February 1, 1925). Vicente Tosta was born in 1876. He served in the Honduran military, rising to the rank of general. Tosta was a leader of the military rising that forced Francisco Bertrand from power in September of 1919. He initially supported Bertrand's successor, Rafael Lopez Gutierrez, but broke with López near the end of his term in 1924. He led an uprising that drove López from office in February 1924. The government was briefly controlled by the council of ministers. Tosta became provisional president on April 30, 1924, by an agreement of the various rebel leaders involved in the revolt. Tosta led troops against a rising by General Gregoria Ferrera later in the year, successfully putting down the rebellion. Tosta relinquished office on February 1, 1925, following the election of Miguel Pas Baraona. Tosta served as minister of war and marine in Pas Baraona's government. He was a candidate for the presidency in 1928 but withdrew from the race to support Vicente Mejia Colindres. He served as Mejia Colindres' minister of the interior until his death in Tegucigalpa after a brief illness on August 7, 1930.

MIGUEL PAS BARAONA

(President; February 1, 1925–February 1, 1929). Miguel Pas Baraona was Tiburcio Carias Andino's running mate in the election of 1923. When the election results failed to produce a victor, several rival factions went into revolt, driving President Rafael López Gutiérrez from power. A provisional government was subsequently installed, and new elections were held. Carias Andino supported Pas Baraona's candidacy, and he won the election. He took office on February 1, 1925. His government supported the construction of schools and roads and improved Honduras' economic standing. He completed his term on February 1, 1929. Pas Baraona died two years later in 1931.

VICENTE MEJIÁ COLINDRES

(President; February 1, 1929–February 1, 1933). Vicente Mejiá Colindres was born in 1878. He was educated as a physician. He entered politics and was elected to the national assembly. He served in several governments as minister of education, foreign affairs, and the interior. He was the candidate of the United Liberal Party for president in 1928 and was the surprising victor over Tiburcio Carias Andino's National Party. Mejiá Colindres took office on February 1, 1929. His government initiated reforms in education and the emancipation of the Indian population. He completed his term of office on February 1, 1933. Mejiá Colindres was forced into exile by Carias Andino after he assumed office. He remained in Costa Rica until 1950, when he was allowed to return to Honduras. He spent his remaining years writing books and essays. He died in Tegucigalpa on August 24, 1966.

TIBURCIO CARIÁS ANDINO

(President; February 1, 1933–January 1, 1949). Tiburcio Cariás Andino was born in Tegucigalpa on March 15, 1876. He received a law degree from Central University in 1898 and joined the Honduran army, where he served as commandant and governor of Honduras' northern zone from 1903 until 1907. He subsequently entered politics and was elected as a delegate to the federal convention of Central America in 1921. He was the founder of the Nationalist Party and was a candidate for president of Honduras in October 1923. He received a majority of the popular vote, but the Honduran congress refused to confirm his election. He was a leader of the subsequent revolt that forced President Rafael López Gutiérrez from power in February 1924. He supported Miguel Pas Baraona's candidacy the following year. Carias was again the Nationalist Party's candidate for president in 1928, but he was defeated by Vicente Mejía Colindres in a close election. In 1932 Carias defeated Angel Zuñiga Huete for the presidency, taking office on February 1, 1933. Carias was a popular leader and the economy of Honduras improved during his administration. A new constitution was introduced in 1936 that allowed Cariás to remain in office until 1943. Several years later his term of office was extended until 1949. Cariás relinquished the presidency to his protégé, Juan Manuel Gálvez, on January 1, 1949. He again sought election to the presidency in 1954 but received less than a third of the vote. He boycotted the subsequent congress and a military coup took place. Carías went into retirement to his home in Tegucigalpa where he died at the age of 94 on December 23, 1969.

Hungary

Hungary is a country in eastern Europe. It was part of the Austro-Hungarian Empire until November 1918.

HEADS OF STATE

FRANZ JOSEF (Emperor; December 2, 1848–November 21, 1916). *See earlier entry under Austria: Heads of State.*

KARL (Emperor; November 21, 1916–November 11, 1918). *See earlier entry under Austria: Heads of State.*

MIHÁLY KÁROLYI (President; November 16, 1918–March 21, 1919). Count Mihály Károlyi was born in Budapest on March 4, 1875. He entered politics as a Liberal in 1901 and was elected to parliament as an independent in 1906. He was an advocate of democratic reforms and became leader of the Independence Party after the death of Gyula Justh in 1913. He was interned in France at the start of World War I, but was soon allowed to return to Hungary. He opposed Hungary's alliance with Germany during the war. He was called upon to head the government as prime minister on October 31, 1918, shortly before the armistice. He became president of the Hungarian republic on November 16, 1918. He fled into exile on March 21, 1919, when Béla Kun proclaimed the Hungarian Soviet Republic. Károlyi remained in exile during the subsequent regency of Miklós Horthy. He was an outspoken opponent of Horthy and Fascism. He was the leader of the movement for a democratic Hungary in Great Britain in 1943. He returned to Hungary in 1946 and served as ambassador to France from 1947 until 1949. He opposed the Communist government's death sentence of former Foreign Minister Laszlo Rajk in June 1949. He retired after Rajk was executed and returned to exile. He settled in Paris and died in Vince, on the French Riviera, on March 18, 1955. Károlyi's ashes were returned to Budapest in 1962.

BÉLA KUN (President; March 21, 1919–August 1, 1919). Béla Kun was born in Szilágycseh, Transylvania, on February 20, 1886. He was educated in Cluj and joined the Social Democratic Party in 1902. He served in the army during World War I and was taken prisoner in Russia in 1916. He joined the Bolshevik Party the following year. He became chairman of the International Federation of Communist Prisoners of War and took part in the defense of Petrograd. He returned to Budapest in November 1918 and founded the Communist Party of Hungary. Kun was arrested in February 1919 and remained imprisoned until the Hungarian Soviet Republic was proclaimed on March 21, 1919. Kun became people's commissar for foreign affairs and leader of the country. The Soviet Republic was ousted by the Romanians and counterrevolutionary forces under Admiral Miklós Horthy. Kun emigrated to Austria, where he was interned and expelled to the Soviet Union in 1920. He became a member of the executive committee of the Communist International (Comintern) the following year. Kun reappeared in Vienna in 1928, where he was again arrested before being allowed to return to the Soviet Union. He continued to be an active participant in the Communist movement before falling out of favor with Soviet leader Josef Stalin. He was arrested in May 1937 and imprisoned at Butyrka prison in Moscow. He was executed there November 30, 1939.

GYULA PEIDL (President; August 1, 1919–August 7, 1919). Gyula Peidl was born in Ravazd on April 3, 1873. He was a leader of the Social Democratic Party in Hungary at the end of World War I. He declined to served in the Communist

government of Béla Kun and became leader of a government composed of trade union leaders after Kun's ouster on August 1, 1919. Peidl's government was overthrown in a coup several days later, and Peidl was arrested and exiled by the new government. He was eventually allowed to return to Hungary on the condition he refrain from political activities. Peidl died in Budapest on January 22, 1943.

ISTVÁN FRIEDRICH (President; August 7, 1919–November 17, 1919). István Friedrich was born in Malacka on July 1, 1883. He was a businessman and minor politician. He served as deputy minister of defense in Mihály Károlyi's government in 1918. Friedrich formed a counterrevolutionary government in Budapest on August 7, 1919. Another counterrevolutionary government in Arad, under Count Gyula Andrassy, resigned in favor of Friedrich's Budapest government. The armed forces did not acknowledge the government's control, and Admiral Miklós Horthy remained the most powerful member of the counterrevolutionary movement. Friedrich's government fell on November 17, 1919. He did not take part in subsequent political affairs. He died in 1958.

KÁROLY HUSZÁR (President; November 23, 1919–March 1, 1920). Károly Huszár was born in Nussdorf on September 10, 1882. He was a teacher and member of the Christian Socialist Party. Huszár formed a coalition government on November 23, 1919, whose primary task was to hold an election. Admiral Miklós Horthy was elected regent on March 1, 1920, and Horthy appointed Sándor Simonyi-Samadam to head the government on March 14, 1920. Huszár died in Budapest on October 29, 1941.

MIKLÓS HORTHY (Regent; March 1, 1920–October 15, 1944). Miklós Horthy de Nagybanya was born in Kenderes on June 18, 1868. He was educated at the Austro-Hungarian naval academy. He served in the imperial navy and was naval aide-de-camp to Emperor Franz Josef from 1909 until 1914. He commanded a battleship during World War I and was severely wounded in the battle of Otranto in May of 1917. He was promoted to admiral and made naval chief of staff in January 1918. Horthy returned to Kenderes after the Empire's defeat in the war. Béla Kun formed a Communist government in Hungary, and Horthy was called upon by the counterrevolutionary government in Szeged to serve as minister of defense in opposition to Kun. He led his troops into Budapest on November 16, 1919. The Hungarian parliament declared the restoration of the monarchy on March 1, 1920, and Horthy was elected to serve as regent. He prevented the return of King Karl to the throne on two occasions in 1921. He left the conduct of the government to his prime ministers, notably István Bethlen, over the next decade. He took a larger role in Hungary's rule during the 1930s and attempted to maintain social order in the country. He was forced into an alliance with Nazi Germany, despite a personal distaste for Adolf Hitler's regime. Ruthenia was returned to Hungary after the dismemberment of Czechoslovakia in March 1939. Hungary declared war on the Soviet Union during World War II and was badly defeated by the Soviets at Voronezh in January 1943. Horthy attempted to withdraw Hungary from the conflict and appealed for an armistice on October 11, 1944. He was seized by the Gestapo and forced to abdicate on October 15, 1944. He was interned in Tirol,

Germany, where he remained until he was liberated by American forces in May 1945. The United States refused to turn Horthy over to the Yugoslav government to stand trial for war crimes, and he was allowed to go into exile in Estoril, Portugal. He died at his home there on February 9, 1957.

FERENC SZÁLASI (Head of State; October 16, 1944–April 4, 1945). Ferenc Szálasi was born in Kassa on January 6, 1897. He served in the Hungarian army, was promoted to the rank of major, and served on the general staff. He became the leader of the right-wing Hungarian Life Association in 1930. He was a proponent of fascism and formed the Party of the Nation's Will after retiring from the military in 1935. He united his group with other fascist organizations to form the Hungarian National Socialist Party two years later. The party was banned, and Szálasi was arrested for conspiracy against the government in August 1938. He was released in September 1940 and became the leader of the Arrow-Cross Party. The regent, Miklós Horthy, was forced by the German occupiers to appoint Szálasi as prime minister on October 16, 1944, after Horthy tried to withdraw Hungary from World War II. Horthy was forced to abdicate, and Szálasi became head of state of a fascist government. The Arrow-Cross movement conducted terrorist activities against its opponents during the final months of the war. His government fell when Hungary was liberated on April 4, 1945. Szálasi was arrested and sentenced to death by a people's tribunal. He was executed in Budapest on March 12, 1946.

HEADS OF GOVERNMENT

KÁLMÁN SZÉLL (Prime Minister; February 26, 1899–June 27, 1903). Kálmán Széll was born in Gosztony on June 8, 1845. He was a leading landowner who

was elected to parliament in 1867. Széll served as minister of finance from 1875 until 1878, when he stepped down because of Hungary's growing financial difficulties. He worked as a banker for the next two decades. Széll became prime minister and minister of the interior on February 26, 1899. His government was forced to resign over a military issue on June 27, 1903. He remained active in politics and became chairman of the Constitutional Party. Széll died in Rátót on August 16, 1915.

KÁROLY KHUEN-HÉDERVÁRY (Prime Minister; June 27, 1903–November 3, 1903). Count Károly Khuen-Hedérváry was born in Gräfenberg on May 23, 1849. He was educated in Slavonia at his father's estate and attended the universities in Croatia and Budapest. He was elected to the Hungarian parliament in 1875 and became ban, or governor, of Croatia in 1883. He headed the Croatian government until 1903. Khuen-Hedérváry was chosen as prime minister of Hungary on June 27, 1903, after heading the Croatian government for 20 years. He stepped down as prime minister after five months on November 3, 1903. He again became prime minister on January 17, 1910. His government resigned on April 22, 1912, over the issue of the government's control of the army. He remained a leading advisor to Emperor Franz Josef. Khuen-Hedérváry died in Budapest on February 16, 1918. (See also under Croatia.)

ISTVÁN TISZA (Prime Minister; November 3, 1903–June 18, 1905). István Tisza was born in Budapest on April 22, 1861. He was the son of Kálmán Tisza, who served as Austria-Hungary's prime minister from 1875 until 1890. The younger Tisza worked in the interior ministry and was elected to parliament in 1886. He became president of the Hungarian Industrial and Commercial Bank in 1890, where he remained for the next ten years. He was named prime minister on November 3, 1903, but his government fell on June 18, 1905, over his efforts to override parliamentary obstruction to his policies. He formed the

Party of National Work in 1910 and became speaker of the lower house of parliament in May 1912. He again became prime minister on June 10, 1913. He was initially opposed to Austria-Hungary's war with Serbia in 1914, but soon became a supporter of the war effort. He led Hungary during most of World War I before stepping down on June 5, 1917. Tisza was held responsible for Hungary's misfortunes during the war and was shot to death by soldiers at his home in Pest on October 31, 1918, soon after the revolution broke out.

GÉZA FEJÉRVÁRY (Prime Minister; June 18, 1905–April 8, 1906). Géza Fejérváry was born in Josefstadt on March 15, 1833. He entered the army in 1851 and saw action at the Battle of San Marino in 1862. He became undersecretary of the Hungarian defense army after the establishment of the dual monarchy. He subsequently became minister of national defense and retained that position until 1903. Fejérváry was called upon by Emperor Franz Josef to form a government as prime minister on June 18, 1905. He undertook to preserve the emperor's complete authority of the army, which was being encroached upon by the coalition parties in the parliament. He dissolved the chamber in February 1906 and the members agreed to revise their demands. Fejérváry stepped down on April 8, 1906. He subsequently served as captain of the Hungarian Guard. He died in Vienna on April 25, 1914.

SÁNDOR WEKERLE (Prime Minister; April 8, 1906–January 17, 1910). Sándor Wekerle was born in Mór, Stuhlweissenburg, on November 14, 1848. He was educated at the University of Budapest and entered the ministry of finance in 1870. He became undersecretary of state in 1887, and was named to the cabinet as minister of finance in 1889. He introduced the gold standard and balanced the budget in 1892. Wekerle served as prime minister from November 17, 1892, until January 14, 1895. During his term of office he initiated various reforms including the introduction of civil marriages in Austria-Hungary. He was president of the supreme court in 1896. He subsequently retired from politics for several years. He was again called upon to serve as prime minister of the coalition government on April 8, 1906. He headed the cabinet until the coalition fell on January 17, 1910. He remained a leading member of the opposition until August 20, 1917, when he was called upon to head the government during World War I. He continued to support the war effort and Hungary's union with Austria until he was forced to resign on October 23, 1918, following the fall of Fiume. Wekerle was arrested in 1919 and charged with being involved in a conspiracy against the government but was held only briefly and was released without trial. He died in Budapest on August 26, 1921.

KÁROLY KHUEN-HÉDERVÁRY (Prime Minister; January 17, 1910–April 22, 1912). *See earlier entry under Heads of Government.*

LÁSZLÓ LUKÁCS (Prime Minister; April 22, 1912–June 10, 1913). László Lukács was born in Abrud on November 24, 1850. He served in Dezso Banffy's government as minister of finance from 1895 until 1899. He succeeded Károly Khuen-Héderváry as prime minister on January 17, 1910. He was forced to resign on June 10, 1913, over the issue of borrowing a large sum of money from the National Bank for political purposes. He died in Budapest on February 23, 1932.

ISTVÁN TISZA (Prime Minister; June 10, 1913–June 5, 1917). *See earlier entry under Heads of Government.*

MÓRIC ESTERHÁZY (Prime Minister; June 15, 1917–August 18, 1917). Count Móric Esterházy was born in Pusztamajk on April 27, 1881. He was the

son of Count Nicholas Esterházy. The younger Esterházy was educated at Oxford University in England. He was a political liberal and was called upon by Emperor Karl to form a government as prime minister on June 15, 1917, following the resignation of István Tisza over the issue of universal suffrage. He sought to grant non-Magyars representation in the parliament. Political strife and the continuation of the war effort caused Esterházy great personal strain. He asked the emperor to be relieved from office under the threat of suicide on August 18, 1917. He subsequently suffered a breakdown and spent some time in a Swiss sanatorium. Esterházy was briefly imprisoned with other liberal political figures after the war. He retired from politics and lived quietly until his death in Vienna on June 27, 1960.

SÁNDOR WEKERLE (Prime Minister; August 20, 1917–October 23, 1918). *See earlier entry under Heads of State.*

MIHÁLY KÁROLYI (Prime Minister; October 31, 1918–November 11, 1918). *See earlier entry under Heads of State.*

DÉNES BERINKEY (Prime Minister; January 18, 1919–March 21, 1919). Dénes Berinkey was born in Csáz on October 17, 1871. He was an expert in international law and was appointed by Mihály Károlyi to head the government as prime minister on January 18, 1919. He resigned on March 21, 1919. Berinkey died in 1948.

SÁNDOR GARBAI (Prime Minister; March 22, 1919–June 24, 1919). Sándor Garbai was born in 1879. He was a leader of the Socialists in Hungary and joined the coalition with the Communists under Béla Kun. Garbai became president of the revolutionary governing committee on March 22, 1919, when Hungary was proclaimed a Soviet Republic. Kun remained the preeminent member of the government. Garbai stepped down on June 24, 1919, following an abortive counterrevolutionary uprising. He died in 1947.

ANTAL DOVCSÁK (Prime Minister; June 24, 1919–August 1, 1919). Antal Dovcsák was born on March 11, 1879. He was chosen by Béla Kun to lead the revolutionary governing council on June 24, 1919. His government was forced from power by a counterrevolutionary coup on August 1, 1919.

GYULA PEIDL (Prime Minister; August 1, 1919–August 6, 1919. *See earlier entry under Heads of State.*

ISTVÁN FRIEDRICH (Prime Minister; August 7, 1919–November 17, 1919). *See earlier entry under Heads of State.*

KÁROLY HUSZÁR (Prime Minister; November 23, 1919–March 14, 1920). *See earlier entry under Heads of State.*

SÁNDOR SIMONYI-SAMADAM (Prime Minister; March 15, 1920–June 27, 1920). Sándor Simonyi-Samadam was born in Csesznek on March 23, 1864. He was chosen by the Regent, Admiral Miklós Horthy, to form a government on March 15, 1920, following Károly Huszar's resignation. He gained the support of the Clerical and Agrarian parties. He resigned on June 27, 1920. Simonyi-Samadam died on June 4, 1946.

PÁL TELEKI (Prime Minister; July 19, 1920–April 13, 1921). Pál Teleki was born in Budapest on November 1, 1879. He was educated at the University of Budapest, where he received a degree in law in 1903. He was also a leading geographer and served as secretary-general of the Hungarian Geographical Society and director of the Cartographical Institute. He entered politics and was elected to the parliament in 1911. He served as a member of the Trianon peace delegation

and headed the government as prime minister from July 19, 1920, until April 13, 1921. He resumed his geographical pursuits and chaired the Federation of Social Sciences. He returned to politics in May 1938 to serve as minister of education in Béla Imrédy's cabinet. He succeeded Imrédy as prime minister on February 16, 1939. He supported his predecessor's anti–Jewish policies. He attempted to keep Hungary neutral in the early days of World War II while maintaining cordial relations with Germany. Teleki's government signed a treaty of friendship with Yugoslavia in December 1940. Germany demanded Hungarian support in an attack on Yugoslavia early in 1941, while Great Britain warned Hungary of dire repercussions should it enter the conflict on Germany's side. Teleki shot himself to death in Budapest during the night of April 2, 1941.

ISTVÁN BETHLEN (Prime Minister; April 14, 1921–August 18, 1931). István Bethlen was born in Gernyeszég on October 3, 1874. He was a leading Transylvanian landowner. He entered politics and was a leader of the counterrevolution that ousted Béla Kun's Communist government in 1919. Bethlen became prime minister on April 14, 1921, under the Regency of Miklós Horthy. His government signed a treaty of friendship with Italy in 1927. Bethlen stepped down on August 18, 1931, as Hungary was suffering from financial problems brought on by the worldwide economic depression. He remained an influential political figure, served as a member of the upper house of Parliament and was named privy councilor in 1936. He was an opponent of Hungary's dominance by Germany during World War II. He supported negotiations with the Allies to end Hungary's participation in the war. Bethlen went into hiding following the German occupation of Hungary in March 1944. He was arrested by the Communist regime that gained control of the country after the war. Bethlen was sent to a prison camp in the Soviet Union, where he died on October 5, 1946.

GYULA KÁROLYI (Prime Minister; August 24, 1931–September 21, 1932). Count Gyula Károlyi was born in Nyirbakta on May 7, 1871. He was a member of a leading Hungarian family. He led the national government that was formed in Arad in opposition to Béla Kun's Communist regime in 1919. Károlyi served as foreign minister in István Bethlen's government from December 1930 until he succeeded Bethlen as prime minister on August 24, 1931. His government fell on September 21, 1932, when he was unable to solve Hungary's economic crisis. He died in Budapest on April 23, 1947.

GYULA GÖMBÖS (Prime Minister; October 1, 1932–October 6, 1936). Gyula Gömbös de Jakfa was born in Murga on December 26, 1886. He received a military education and entered the Hungarian army. He served on the general staff during World War I and was military attaché to Zagreb in 1918. He was elected to the national assembly in 1920 after the fall of Béla Kun's Communist government. He was instrumental in preventing the second attempt by deposed Emperor Karl to reclaim the throne in 1921. Gömbös broke with István Bethlen's National Unity Party in 1923 to lead the Party for the Protection of Race. He rejoined the National Union Party in 1928 and joined the government as deputy minister of defense. He became minister of defense, with the rank of major general, the following year. Gömbös succeeded Gyula Károlyi as prime minister on October 1, 1932. He attempted to model his government on the fascist states of Germany and Italy and favored Hungary's alignment with Germany in foreign affairs. Gömbös' health deteriorated in 1936, and he went to Germany for treatment of kidney and gall bladder ailments in September 1936.

He died in Nymphenburg, near Munich, on October 6, 1936.

KALMÁS DARÁNYI (Prime Minister; October 12, 1936–May 13, 1938). Kalmás de Puenta-Szentgorgy es Tetetlen Darányi was born in Budapest on March 22, 1886. He was educated at the University of Budapest. He entered the army as a first lieutenant and saw action with the Royal Thirteenth Hussar's during World War I. He was named secretary of state in István Bethlen's cabinet in 1928 and retained that position in the subsequent government of Gyula Károlyi. Darányi was named minister of agriculture in 1935. He served as deputy premier under Gyula Gömbös and became prime minister on October 12, 1936, following Gömbös' death in office. Darányi favored Hungary's alliance with Italy. His government passed the first anti-Jewish legislation in March 1938. The growing Nazi presence in Hungary and the government's inability to cope with the rising violence associated with it, forced Darányi's resignation on May 13, 1938. He died on November 1, 1939, in Budapest after a long illness.

BÉLA IMRÉDY (Prime Minister; May 14, 1938–February 14, 1939). Béla Imrédy was born in Budapest on December 29, 1891. He was a leading economist and was appointed director of the National Bank in 1928. He served in Gyula Gömbös's government as minister of finance from 1932 until 1935, when he assumed the presidency of the National Bank. He succeeded Kalmás Darányi as prime minister on May 14, 1938. He continued Hungary's policy of alliance with Nazi Germany. He was forced to step down on February 14, 1939, but remained a leading figure in the right-wing of the government party. He formed the Hungarian Revival Party in September 1940 and advocated the transformation of Hungary into a fascist state. He served in Döme Sztójay's government as minister of economic affairs following Germany's occupation of Hungary in March 1944. Imrédy was arrested after the war and tried as a war criminal. He was sentenced to death by the people's tribunal and executed by firing squad at the Marko jail courtyard in Budapest on February 28, 1946.

PÁL TELEKI (Prime Minister; February 16, 1939–April 3, 1941). *See earlier entry under Heads of Government.*

LÁSZLÓ BARDOSSY (Prime Minister; April 4, 1941–March 9, 1942). László Bardossy was born in Szombathely on December 10, 1880. He headed the press department of the foreign ministry from 1924 until 1931. He served as counselor at the Hungarian legation in London from 1931 until 1934. Bardossy was appointed ambassador to Romania in 1934. He returned to Budapest to serve as foreign minister in February 1941. He was also named to head the government as prime minister on April 4, 1941, following the suicide of Pál Teleki. Bardossy's government declared war on the Soviet Union in June 1941. His government stepped down on March 9, 1942. He became chairman of the Fascist United Christian National League the following year. Bardossy collaborated with the Arrow-Cross Party during the German occupation in 1944. He was arrested as a war criminal after the war. He was tried by a people's tribunal and sentenced to death in November 1945. Bardossy was hanged in Budapest on January 10, 1946.

MIKLÓS KÁLLAY (Prime Minister; March 9, 1942–March 19, 1944). Miklós Kallay was born in Kallosemjen in 1887. He was a leading Hungarian landowner and rightist politician. He was named secretary of state for commerce in 1929 and served as minister of agriculture in Gyula Gömbös' government from 1932 until 1935. Kállay succeeded László Bardossy as prime minister on March 9, 1942, and also served as

foreign minister. His government continued to collaborate with Germany in the war against the Soviet Union. After the defeat of the Germans at Stalingrad, Kállay tried to negotiate a separate peace with the Allies in early 1944. Germany quashed his government's efforts and occupied Hungary. Kállay's government collapsed on March 19, 1944. Kállay fled to the Turkish legation, where he remained until November 1944. He was subsequently arrested by the Germans and imprisoned in the Mauthausen concentration camp. He was liberated by American troops after the war and went to Rome. He emigrated to the United States in 1951 and served on the Hungarian national council in exile. Kállay died at his home in New York City on January 14, 1967.

DÖME SZTÓJAY (Prime Minister; March 22, 1944–August 24, 1944). Döme Sztójay was born in Budapest on January 5, 1883. He became a lieutenant general in the Hungarian army. Sztójay served as military attaché in Berlin from 1927 until 1933 and was named Hungary's ambassador to Germany in 1935. He was a leading supporter of Hungary's alliance with Germany during World War II. He returned to Budapest with German troops to assume control of the government as prime minister on March 22, 1944. His government functioned as a puppet of the German occupation forces and allowed the deportation of Hungarian Jews to death camps in Germany. Sztójay was forced to resign by moderate elements in the government on August 24, 1944. He was arrested as a war criminal after the war and sentenced to death by a people's tribunal. Sztójay was executed by a firing squad in Budapest on March 22, 1946.

GÉZA LAKATOS (Prime Minister; August 29, 1944–October 15, 1944). Vitez Géza Lakatos was born on April 30, 1890. Lakatos was commander of the Hungarian forces in Russia during World

War II. He was named to head the government as premier by Regent Miklós Horthy on August 29, 1944. Hungary had been occupied by Germany earlier in the year, and Lakatos' government was to assure Germany of Hungary's allegiance to the Axis Powers. He stepped down on October 15, 1944, and was replaced by Ferenc Szálasi. He left Hungary following the Communist takeover after the war. He moved to Adelaide, Australia, in the mid-1960s and died there on May 21, 1967.

FERENC SZÁLASI (Prime Minister; October 16, 1944–April 4, 1945). *See earlier entry under Heads of State.*

ZOLTÁN TILDY (Prime Minister; April 4, 1945–February 1, 1946). Zoltán Tildy was born in 1889. He was educated in Budapest and became a minister in the Hungarian Reformed Evangelical Church. He entered politics and was elected to parliament as a member of the Smallholders Party. He later became leader of that party. During World War II he was active in the underground resistance to the Germans. He was selected as president of the Budapest national committee following the Soviet occupation of Hungary at the conclusion of the war. The Smallholders Party was victorious in the elections in November 1944 and Tildy became prime minister of Hungary on April 4, 1945. He relinquished the office to become president of the new Hungarian Republic on February 1, 1946. Mátyás Rákosi, the leader of the Hungarian Communist Party, forced Tildy to resign on July 30, 1948. He was put under house arrest and remained politically inactive until October 1956, when he joined the government of Imre Nagy as minister of state. When Nagy's rebellion was crushed by the Soviet Union in November 1956, Tildy was arrested and sentenced to six years in prison. He was released in April 1959 due to poor health. He died in Budapest on August 3, 1961.

Iceland

Iceland is an island nation in the North Atlantic Ocean near the Arctic Circle. In 1874 Denmark granted home rule to Iceland, which became, in 1918, a sovereign state in personal union with Denmark, whose King was also the King of Iceland. It gained independence from Denmark on June 17, 1944.

HEADS OF STATE

CHRISTIAN X (King; November 30, 1918–August 1, 1945). *See earlier entry under Denmark: Heads of State.*

SVEINN BJÖRNSSON (President; August 1, 1945–January 25, 1952). Sveinn Björnsson was born in Copenhagen, Denmark, on February 27, 1881. After his graduation from the University of Copenhagen in 1907, he went to Reyk- javik to practice law. He entered politics and was elected to the Reykjavik town council in 1912. He joined the Independence Party and was elected to the Althing, Iceland's parliament, in 1914. Iceland became a sovereign state united with Denmark under the Danish crown on December 1, 1918. Björnsson served as minister to Denmark from 1920 until 1924 and again from 1926 until 1941. Following the German invasion of Denmark, Björnsson returned to Iceland, where he was elected regent by the Althing on June 17, 1941. Björnsson was elected the first president of the new Icelandic republic on June 17, 1944, and took

office on August 1, 1945. He was returned to office in 1949. Björnsson fell seriously ill with a heart ailment in 1950, but remained president until his death in Reykjavik on January 25, 1952.

HEADS OF GOVERNMENT

JÓN MAGNÚSSON (Prime Minister; November 30, 1918–March 7, 1922). Jón Magnússon was born on January 16, 1859. Magnússon served in Iceland's Althing (parliament). He became Iceland's first prime minister on November 30, 1918, when the country gained autonomy under the Danish crown. He remained head of the government until March 7, 1922. He subsequently served as minister of state. Magnússon died on June 23, 1926, while accompanying the king and queen of Denmark on a tour of Iceland.

SIGURDUR EGGERZ (Prime Minister; March 7, 1922–March 22, 1924). Sigurdur Eggerz was born on February 28, 1875. He succeeded Jón Magnússon as prime minister of Iceland on March 7, 1922. He headed the government for two years, until March 22, 1924. Eggerz died on November 16, 1945.

JÓN THORLAKSON (Prime Minister; March 22, 1924–August 28, 1927). Jón Thorlakson was born on March 3, 1877. He served in the Althing as a member of the Conservative Party. He was named to head the government as prime minister on March 22, 1924. Iceland's agriculture was improved with the passage of new agricultural laws in 1923. He retained office until August 28, 1927, following the defeat of the Conservatives in parliamentary elections. Thorlakson died on March 20, 1935.

TRYGVI THORHALLSON (Prime Minister; August 28, 1927–June 2, 1932).

Trygvi Thorhallson was born on February 9, 1889. He was a leader of the Icelandic Progressive Party. He formed a government as prime minister on August 28, 1927, and attempted to stabilize Iceland's currency. He stepped down as prime minister on June 2, 1932. Thorhallson died on July 31, 1935.

ASGEIR ASGEIRSSON (Prime Minister; June 2, 1932–March 29, 1934). Asgeir Asgeirsson was born in Koranesi on May 13, 1894. He was educated in Iceland and served on the faculty of the Teachers College of Iceland. He entered politics and was elected to the Althing in 1923. Asgeirsson served on various parliamentary committees and was elected speaker in 1930. He was named minister of finance in 1931 and formed a government as prime minister on June 2, 1932. He retained office until March 29, 1934, when he was replaced by Hermann Jonasson. Asgeirsson chaired the government's bureau of education from 1934 until 1938 and then became director of the Fisheries Bank of Iceland. He served as Iceland's representative to the Bretton Woods Economic and Monetary Conference in 1944. He was also elected president of the Althing in 1944. Asgeirsson was named governor of the International Monetary Fund in 1946. He also served in the Icelandic delegation to the United Nations in 1947 and 1948. Asgeirsson was elected president of Iceland in June 1952 and took office on August 1, 1952. He was reelected without opposition to the largely ceremonial position in 1956, 1960, and 1964. He retired after completing his fourth term of office on July 30, 1968. Asgeirsson died in Reykjavik on September 15, 1972.

HERMANN JÓNASSON (Prime Minister; March 29, 1934–May 18, 1942). Hermann Jónasson was born in northern Iceland on December 25, 1896. He was educated at the University of Iceland, where he received a degree in law. He served as a judicial assistant in Reykjavik until 1928 and then became police commissioner of the city. Jónasson left the police in 1934 to enter politics. He was elected to the Althing as a member of the Progressive Party and became prime minister on March 29, 1934. He remained prime minister of a coalition government in 1937. Iceland had been granted independence from Denmark in 1918, but recognized the king of Denmark as its monarch. The Althing granted executive powers to the prime minister in April 1940 following the German occupation of Denmark. Jónasson offered his resignation in October 1941 after Iceland experienced increased inflation. His resignation was not accepted until the following month. He remained as head of the government until Olafur Thors took office on May 18, 1942. Jónasson returned to serve as prime minister of a leftist coalition government that included Communist Ludvig Josepsson on July 21, 1956, and remained in office until December 4, 1958. He died on November 2, 1976.

OLAFUR THORS (Prime Minister; May 18, 1942–December 18, 1942). Olafur Tryggvason Thors was born in Bogarnes on January 19, 1892. He was educated at the University of Copenhagen in Denmark, where he received a degree in philosophy in 1913. He subsequently served as director of an industrial business in Reykjavik. Thors became active in politics in 1924 and served on the central committee of the Conservative Party. He was elected to the Icelandic parliament and was a founding member of the Independence Party in 1928. He served as chairman of the party, and in 1939 he was named to the cabinet as minister of industries. Thors was selected to replace Hermann Jónasson as prime minister on May 18, 1942, and served until December 18, 1942. Thors again formed a government as prime minister on October 21, 1944. His government resigned in October 1946, but Thors remained head of an interim government until February 3, 1947. He was again returned to office on December 6, 1949, and served until March 14, 1950. Thors again formed a coalition government on September 13, 1953. His government resigned on July 21, 1956, following the Progressive Party's withdrawal from the coalition. Thors formed another government on November 20, 1959. He retained office until November 12, 1963, when he resigned for reasons of health. He died after suffering a stroke in Reykjavik on December 31, 1964.

BJORN THORDARSON (Prime Minister; December 18, 1942–October 21, 1944). Bjorn Thordarson was born in 1879. He was educated at the University of Copenhagen, where he received a degree in law. He served as secretary to the supreme court from 1921 until 1926 and became a magistrate in Reykjavik in 1929. Thordarson was chosen to head the government as prime minister on December 18, 1942. Denmark was under German occupation during World War II, and Iceland served as a base for British and American troops during the war. Thordarson's government supported a resolution terminating the union with Denmark in February 1944, and a subsequent plebiscite confirmed this action. Iceland became an independent republic on June 17, 1944. Thordarson stepped down as prime minister on October 21, 1944. He died in 1963.

OLAFUR THORS (Prime Minister; October 21, 1944–February 3, 1947). *See earlier entry under Heads of Government.*

Iran

Iran is a country in western Asia. Prior to 1935 the country was known as Persia.

HEADS OF STATE

MUZAFFAR-AD-DIN (Shah; May 1, 1896–January 8, 1907). Muzaffar-ad-Din was born in Teheran on March 25, 1853. He was the son of the Persian Shah Nasir ad-Din. He was named crown prince of the Qajar dynasty and sent to the province of Azerbaijan as governor in 1861. His relationship with his father was often strained and he was seldom consulted on matters of state. He succeeded to the throne upon the assassination of his father on May 1, 1896. Muzaffar-ad-Din was plagued with poor health and often sought treatment in Europe. His spending habits put a strain on Persia's financial status, leading the shah to make concessions to various foreign interests. Russia soon became Persia's leading creditor and exerted much financial and political control over the government. The shah's policies, along with alleged corruption in the court, brought forth demands for constitutional reforms. Widespread demonstrations forced the shah to establish a national consultative assembly, the Majlis. The Majlis began drafting a constitution that Muzaffar ad-Din signed and that took effect on December 30, 1906. The shah died of a heart attack in Teheran several days later on January 8, 1907.

MOHAMMED ALI QAJAR (Shah; January 8, 1907–July 16, 1909). Mohammed Ali Qajar was born on June 21, 1872. He was the eldest son of Muzaffar-ad-Din. He served as commander of Persia's troops in the province of Azerbaijan in 1892 and was proclaimed crown prince upon the ascension of his father to the throne in 1896. Mohammed Ali also became governor of Azerbaijan. He suc-

ceeded to the throne upon his father's death on January 8, 1907. He continued his father's policy of relying heavily on Russian advisors. He also resented the growing power of the Majlis (legislative assembly). His prime minister, Amin as-Soltan, was assassinated shortly after Mohammed Ali ascended to the throne, and the shah survived an attempt on his own life the following year. He began harsh and repressive measures against reformist elements in the country. He imposed martial law on Teheran and banned the political activities of the constitutionalists. He unleashed the Russian-trained Cossack Brigade to bombard the parliament building in June 1908 and suspended the constitution several days later. Discontent against Mohammed Ali's reign increased, leading to an attack by pro-constitutional forces in July 1909. The shah took refuge in the Russian legation, and he was deposed by the victorious reformists in favor of his 12-year-old-son, Ahmad. Mohammed Ali went into exile in Russia in September 1909. He made an attempt to return to Persia in 1911, leading his forces, composed largely of Turkomans, in the capture of Astarabad. His brother, Salar ad Daukh, also began a revolt in western Persia. Their forces were defeated by the constitutionalists in September 1911. He returned to exile in Russia the following year. He remained in exile until his death on April 5, 1925.

SULTAN AHMAD (Shah; July 16, 1909–October 31, 1925). Sultan Ahmad was born on January 21, 1898, the son of Shah Mohammed Ali. He succeeded to the throne on July 16, 1909, after the ouster of his father by pro-constitutional forces. Ahmad was 12 years old at the time of his ascension and ruled under a regency. During his reign an American financial expert, Morgan Shuster, was brought in to enact economic reforms in the country. The Russians forced the Persian government to dismiss Shuster in November 1911, and the Majlis was dissolved the following month in a coup led by the regent Nasr al-Mulk. Ahmad exercised little real power during his reign. Persia, which was officially neutral during World War I, was occupied by various powers including the Russians, British, and Ottomans during the war. After the war, the British moved in to fill the void left by the Russians following the revolution in 1919. Government corruption and the young shah's incompetence caused growing discontent in the country. A military coup against the government was led by Colonel Reza Khan in February 1921. Ahmad went to Europe in 1923, leaving Reza Khan in control of the country. He was officially deposed on October 31, 1925; that date marked the end of the Qajar dynasty. Ahmad remained in exile until his death in Paris on February 27, 1930.

MOHAMMED REZA KHAN (Shah; December 12, 1925–September 16, 1941). Mohammed Reza Khan was born in Alasht, in the province of Mazanderan on March 16, 1878. He went to Teheran at an early age after the death of his father. He entered the Persian army, where he was trained by Russian instructors. He rose to the rank of colonel in the highly regarded Cossack Brigade. He feared for the fate of the country due to the widespread corruption in the government and the inability of the shah to lead effectively. He joined forces with reformist leader Said Ziya ad-Din Tabataba'i and led his forces into Teheran on February 21, 1921. A new government was formed with Tabataba'i as prime minister and Reza Khan as minister of war and commander-in-

chief. He subsequently renounced the Anglo-Persian Treaty with Britain. He forced the resignation of Tabataba'i several months later. Reza Khan took the office of prime minister on October 29, 1923, and was granted executive authority by the Majlis. The Majlis ended the Qajar dynasty on October 31, 1925, deposing Shah Ahmad. The constitution was also changed to allow Reza Khan to ascend to the throne as Reza Shah Pahlavi on December 12, 1925. His coronation took place in April of the following year. The shah began a policy of Westernization in Persia, introducing a judicial system to replace the jurisdiction of religious courts on civil matters. He used the army to put down various tribal rebellions during his reign. He also instituted policies of education reform and industrialization. Iran became the official name of the country in 1935. Reza Khan's government adopted a policy of neutrality at the onset of World War II, though the shah was sympathetic to the German cause. A large number of German technicians were allowed in the country in the early days of the war, causing concern for Great Britain and Russia. During the war Reza Khan also refused to allow Britain and the Allies to send supplies to Russia across Iranian territory. He rejected an ultimatum from the Allies, which resulted in an invasion of the country by British and Russian troops on August 25, 1941. The occupying powers forced the abdication of Reza Khan on September 16, 1941, and installed his son, Mohammed Reza Pahlavi, on the throne. Reza Khan was exiled to Mauritius and, subsequently, South Africa, where he died in Johannesburg on July 26, 1944.

MOHAMMED REZA PAHLAVI (Shah; September 16, 1941–January 16, 1979). Mohammed Reza Pahlavi was born in Teheran on October 26, 1919. He was the son of Reza Shah Pahlavi, who was chosen as shah of Persia by the National Assembly in 1925. The crown prince was educated in Rolle, Switzerland, from 1931 until 1936, when he returned home to attend the Officers Training Academy. He was subsequently made an officer in the Persian army and became more involved in matters of state. Iran was invaded by British and Soviet troops in 1941 following Reza Shah Pahlavi's refusal to force Axis nationals to leave Iran during World War II. Reza Shah was forced to abdicate on September 16, 1941. Mohammed Reza Pahlavi succeeded to the Peacock Throne and soon thereafter granted greater political power to the Majlis. Early the following year he signed a treaty with Great Britain and the Soviet Union, and in 1943 he extracted a promise that Iranian sovereignty would be preserved after the end of the war. Iran declared war on the Axis Powers in September 1943. Following the war, Iran became involved in a dispute with the Soviet Union over control of the province of Azerbaijan in northwestern Iran. The shah was faced with a revolt led by the Soviet-oriented Tudeh party, but the rebellion was crushed in December 1946. The shah also rejected an oil pact with the Soviet Union in 1947, and this caused further deterioration in the relations between the two countries. The shah was shot during an assassination attempt on February 4, 1949, but recovered from his injuries. In 1950 a financial scandal developed when it was learned that the Anglo-Iranian Oil Company was underpaying the Iranian government on oil royalties. The company was nationalized in April of the following year. Nationalism in Iran escalated during this period, and the shah named Mohammed Mossadegh prime minister in April 1951. The Iranian government broke diplomatic relations with Great Britain in October 1952. Mossadegh threatened the shah's rule with a proclamation of martial law, and the shah fled Iran, going to Baghdad on August 16, 1953. A brief period of civil war followed, with the shah's troops, led by General Fazlolah Zahedi and aided by the United States Central Intelligence Agency, defeating the rebel mobs. The shah returned to Teheran on August 22, 1953. He then began the process of reform in Iran, which was called the White Revolution. He announced a policy of land reform, women's rights, profit-sharing for workers, national health reform, and other programs. The shah survived another assassination attempt on April 10, 1965. In December of 1973 Iran, along with other Persian Gulf oil states, raised its oil prices by a large margin. The shah's modernization plans met with opposition from Muslim fundamentalists within the country. In the face of rising conflict, the shah's regime became increasingly oppressive. He banned all political parties in March 1975 in an attempt to end dissent. The vast increase of oil wealth in the country contributed to widespread inflation and corruption in the government. The shah's regime faced ever greater opposition during the late 1970s. Student protests, strikes, and riots resulted in a declaration of martial law, which only served to increase the opposition to the government. The shah was forced to leave Iran on January 16, 1979. His exit also marked the return of the Ayatollah Ruhollah Khomeini to Iran. The Muslim fundamentalist emerged as the leading figure in the country. The shah went first to Egypt, then on to Morocco, and then to the Bahamas. The new government in Iran demanded his extradition and the return of his vast financial holdings. The shah's health deteriorated during his exile. He went to New York for gall bladder surgery in October 1979, a move that prompted Iranian militants to take over the United States embassy in Teheran. He subsequently continued his exile in Panama and then in Egypt, the only country that would allow him entry. He was again hospitalized for the removal of his enlarged spleen. He died of a hemorrhage in a Cairo hospital on July 27, 1980.

HEADS OF GOVERNMENT

AMIN AS-SOLTAN (Prime Minister; 1898–September 1903). Amin as-Soltan, Ali Asghar Khan, was born in 1858, the son of Aqa Ibrahim, a leading advisor to the shah. He was Persia's most powerful political figure in the 1880s. He served as prime minister under Nasir ad-Din Shah and instituted Persia's pro-Russian policies in 1892. He was dismissed as prime minister following the assassination of Nasir ad-Din Shah in 1896, but returned as premier in 1898. Amin as-Soltan, having been given the title of Atabak, was unpopular with the progressives, who believed he was leading Persia to Russian control. He was again dismissed in September 1903 and embarked on a world tour. In January 1907 he was reappointed as premier by Mohammad Ali Shah, who had succeeded to the throne. Shortly after his appointment, on August 31, 1907, Amin as-Soltan was stabbed to death by members of a radical group.

ABD AL-MAJID MIRZA, 'AIN AL-DOWLEH (Prime Minister; September 1903–July 1906). Abd al-Majid Mirza was born in 1845, the son of Sultan Ahmad Mirza Azod al-Dowleh. He entered government service in the 1880s, serving as governor of various provinces. He was granted the title 'Ain al-Dowleh by Shah Nasr al-Din in 1893. Abd al-Majid Mirza was named prime minister by Shah Muzaffar-ad-Din in September 1903, replacing Amin as-Soltan. His conservative government increased restrictions on the press and instituted other repressive measures against reformists. Supporters of the constitutional movement forced his dismissal in July 1906. He remained a leading political figure in Persia, briefly serving as prime minister in 1915 and 1917. He was arrested and fined following Mohammed Reza Khan's coup in 1921. The 'Ain al-Dowleh died in 1926.

NA'IMI MIRZA NASR ALLAH KHAN AL-DOWLEH (Prime Minister; July 1906–January 1907). Na'imi Mirza Nasr Allah Khan al-Dowleh served in the government as foreign minister in 1899. He replaced the 'Ain al-Dowleh as prime minister in July 1906, serving until his death in January 1907.

AMIN AS-SOLTAN (Prime Minister; January, 1907–August 31, 1907). *See earlier entry under Heads of Government.*

ABU'L KASIM KHAN (Prime Minister; September 1907–1908). Abu'l Kasim Khan was born in 1858. He was the grandson of a former Nasr-ul-Mulk of the Karaguzlu tribe of Hamadan. He was educated in Oxford, England, and returned to Persia in 1882. He became Nasr-ul-Mulk upon the death of his grandfather, and served at the court of the shah. He was appointed ambassador to the courts of Europe in 1897 and was subsequently appointed minister of finance. His opposition to the policy regarding Russian loans forced him from the capital, and he accepted the governorship of Persian Kurdistan in 1899. He was named prime minister by the new shah, Mohammed Ali, following the assassination of Amin as-Soltan on August 31, 1907. He came into conflict with the shah the following year and was imprisoned. He was freed by the British legation and went into exile in England. He was again offered the position of prime minister in 1909 upon the deposition of the shah and the restoration of the constitution, but he refused the appointment. He was offered the regency the following year and returned to Teheran in 1911. He spent much of 1912 out of the country, but never resigned the regency. He relinquished the position in 1913 when Ahmad Mirza came of age. Abu'l Kasim Khan died on December 26, 1927.

MIRZA HOSEIN GHOLI KHAN MAFI, NEZAM AL-SALTANEH

(Prime Minister; 1908). Mirza Hosein Gholi Khan Mafi was born in 1832. At the beginning of his career in government in 1852, he worked in the provincial governor's office in Bushehr. He was named governor of Yazd in 1874. He was subsequently granted the title Nezam al-Saltaneh and became governor of Arabestan, Bakhtyari, and Chahar Mahal. He was appointed minister of justice in 1896, but he soon resigned over a disagreement with Prime Minister 'Ain al-Dowleh. Mirza Hosein Gholi was named head of the Bureau of Taxation in the subsequent government of Amin as-Soltan in 1898. He remained an influential government figure and was named prime minister in 1908. He stepped down from the government after several months and died later in the year.

MIRZA JAVAN KHAN SA'D AL-DOWLEH

(Prime Minister; 1908–1909). Mirza Javan Khan Sa'd al-Dowleh was born to a prominent Persian family in the 1840s. He studied telegraphy in Russia and returned to Persia to work in the Tabriz communications center. He was named minister of post and telegraph in the government in 1880. He was appointed Persia's ambassador to Belgium in 1892. He was a supporter of the constitutional revolution, which forced his resignation as minister of commerce. He held several ministerships after the success of the constitutionalists. Sa'd al-Dowleh was appointed prime minister in 1908 after Shah Mohammad Ali regained power. He was forced to flee from office the following year when the constitutionalists forced Shah Mohammad Ali's abdication. He accompanied the shah into Russian exile. He returned to Persia in 1912. He was denied another term of office as prime minister when the British vetoed his appointment in 1915. He died in Teheran later in the year.

MUHAMMAD WALI KHAN, SIPAHADAR-I AZAM

(Prime Minister; July 1909–1910). Muhammad Wali Khan, Sipahadar-i Azam was a leading figure in the movement that deposed Shah Mohammed Ali. He was called upon to head the first government under shah Ahmad, but he stepped down the following year. He returned to serve as prime minister in March 1916. He arranged an agreement with the entente powers to allow them to raise military forces in Persia in return for financial aid. This agreement led Ottoman forces to advance on Persia and forced Wali Khan's resignation. The government of Vozuq al-Dowleh anulled the agreement in 1919.

MIRZA HASAN KHAN MOSTOWFI AL-MAMALEK

(Prime Minister; 1910). Mirza Hasan Khan Mostowfi al-Mamalek was born to a prominent Persian family in 1875. He studied in Europe, and upon his return in 1907 he served as minister of war in the government of Amin as-Soltan. He remained active in the government following the ouster of Shah Mohammed Ali and served in various cabinets. He briefly headed the government in 1910 and in early 1918. He was selected to head Reza Shah Pahlavi's government on January 20, 1922, and served until May 9, 1922. He again served as prime minister from June 18, 1923, until disagreements with members of parliament forced him to step down in October of that year. He subsequently retired from politics. Mostowfi al-Mamalek died in 1932.

SAMSUN-ES-SULTANEH

(Prime Minister; 1911–January 1913). Najaf Qoli Khan Samsun-es-Sultaneh Bakhtiari was born in 1854 to a prominent Bakhtiari family. He was leader of a tribal army that was instrumental in the ouster of Shah Mohammad Ali in 1909. He was called upon to form a government as prime minister in 1911. Russia and Great Britain tried to force his ouster, but Samsun-es-Sultaneh was able to remain head of the government until January 1913 due to widespread popular support for him. Samsun-es-Sultaneh again headed the government briefly in early 1918. He was appointed governor of Khorasan in 1921, but declined the appointment due to his support for Colonel Mohammad Taqi Khan Pesyan's rebellion in Mashhad. Samsun-es-Sultaneh retired to his home region and died in Bakhtiari in 1930.

MIRZA MOHAMMED ALI KHAN, ALA AL-SULTANEH (Prime Minister; January 1913–July 1913). Mirza Mohammed Ali Khan Ala al-Sultaneh was born in Baghdad in 1838. He was the son of Mirza Ibrahim Khan, a prominent Persian consul, and, like his father, Mirza Mohammed Ali Khan entered the foreign service. He was named ambassador to Britain by Shah Nasir ad-Din in the early 1890s. He was also given the title Ala al-Saltaneh. He served in several cabinets in the early 1900s and was named to succeed Samsun-el-Sultaneh as prime minister in January 1913. He retained office until July 1913. The Ala al-Sultaneh died in 1918.

ABD AL-MAJID MIRZA, 'AIN AL-DOWLEH (Prime Minister; 1915). *See earlier entry under Heads of Government.*

ABD AL-HOSEIN MIRZA FARMAN FARMA (Prime Minister; December 1915–March 1916). Abd al-Hosein Mirza Farman Farma was born to a noble family in 1857. He received a military education in Teheran. He was a leading figure in the royal court and was married to the daughter of Muzaffar-ad-Din, who became shah in 1896. Farman Farma was appointed governor of Teheran and minister of war shortly after Muzaffar-ad-Din took the throne. The shah became concerned about Farman Farma's popularity and sent him into

exile in Iraq. He was allowed to return to Persia in 1906 and was named governor of Kerman. He subsequently served as minister of justice and governor of Azerbaijan. He remained a leading figure in the government and became minister of the interior in 1909. He also served as minister of war and governor of Kermanshah. He was a supporter of British interests during World War I. He returned to lead the interior ministry in 1915 and was appointed to head the government in December of that year. He retained office for several months, stepping down in March 1916. He was subsequently named governor of Fars. Farman Farma's active political career ended soon after that. His son, Nosrat al-Dowleh, was a leading advisor to Reza Shah Pahlavi until his execution in 1937. Farman Farma died in 1939.

MUHAMMAD WALI KHAN, SIPAHADAR-I AZAM (Prime Minister; March 1916–August 1916). *See earlier entry under Heads of Government.*

MIRZA HASAN KHAN VOZUQ AL-DOWLEH (Prime Minister; August 1916–1917). Mirza Hasan Khan was born in 1873. He was the nephew of Mirza Ali Khan Amin al-Dowleh, and the brother of Ahmed Qavam es-Sultaneh. He was appointed to replace his father as tax collector in Azerbaijan in 1892 and was given the title Vozuq al-Dowleh in 1896. He was elected to the parliament in Teheran in 1906 and served in several cabinets. He was named to head the government as prime minister in August 1916. He stepped down the following year, but regained the position in 1918, when he served simultaneously as minister of the interior. His government ratified the Anglo-Persian Agreement of 1919, which made Persia a British protectorate. He stepped down on June 24, 1920. The following year Mirza returned to the government as minister of finance. He remained active in political affairs during the reign of

Reza Shah Pahlavi, and again headed the government from February 15, 1923, to June 12, 1923, and from June 13, 1926, to May 28, 1927. Mirza returned as prime minister on September 17, 1933, when he served until December 3, 1935. He retired from active involvement in politics after Reza's abdication in 1941 and became a successful land speculator. He died in 1950.

ABD AL-MAJID MIRZA, 'AIN AL-DOWLEH (Prime Minister; 1917). *See earlier entry under Heads of Government.*

SAMSUN-ES-SULTANEH (Prime Minister; 1918). *See earlier entry under Heads of Government.*

MIRZA HASAN KHAN MOS-TOWFI AL-MAMALEK (Prime Minister; 1918). *See earlier entry under Heads of Government.*

MIRZA HASAN KHAN VOZUQ AL-DOWLEH (Prime Minister; 1918–June 24, 1920). *See earlier entry under Heads of Government.*

MIRZA HASAN KHAN PIRNIA MOSHIR AL-DOWLEH (Prime Minister; July 1920–October 29, 1920). Mirza Hasan Khan Pirnia Moshir al-Dowleh was born in the Na'in province in 1870. He was the son of former Iranian prime minister Mirza Nasrollah Khan Pirnia Moshir al-Dowleh. Mirza studied law in Moscow. He also attended military school, and was appointed military attaché to the Persian embassy in St. Petersburg. He returned to Persia, where he became a leading reformist in the government. He served in various cabinets and was named to head a government as prime minister in July 1920. He stepped down on October 29, 1920. He retired from public life in 1923 to concentrate on writing a history of Persia. Mirza died in Teheran on November 21, 1935.

MANSUR FATHALLAH KHAN AKBAR (Prime Minister; October 29, 1920–February 21, 1921). Mansur Fathallah Khan Akbar was from a leading family in Rasht. He succeeded his uncle, Akbar Khan, as governor of the province in 1889. He joined the reformist movement and served in the constitutionalists' 1909 cabinet as minister of posts and telegraphs. He served as minister of war in Mirza Hasan Khan Vozuq al-Dowleh's government from 1916 until 1920. He headed the government as prime minister from October 29, 1920, until Reza Khan's military coup on February 21, 1921. He initially sought refuge in the British embassy, and later retired from political affairs. Fathallah died in 1936.

SAID ZIYA AD-DIN TABA-TABA'I (Prime Minister; February 21, 1921–May 24, 1921). Said Ziya ad-Din Tabataba'i was born in Yazd, Persia, in 1888. Working as a journalist, he was an early supporter of constitutional government and political reforms. He began publishing the pro-British journal *Ra'd* (Thunder) in Teheran during World War I, which gained him the confidence of British influences in Iran. In 1920 he became active in the reformist political organization Anjoman-e Pulad (steel committee). He was a leading participant in Reza Khan's overthrow of the Qajar dynasty and was named prime minister in the new government on February 21, 1921. Tabataba'i used his position to crush opposition to the new government and to attack longtime political foes. He lost the confidence of Reza Khan and stepped down from office on May 24, 1921. He went into exile in Switzerland until 1930, and he then spent the next thirteen years in Palestine under the protection of the British government. He returned to Persia in September 1943, several years after the ouster of Reza Khan. He was a founder of the National Will Party, which opposed the remnants of Reza Khan's military government and the emerging Communist Tudeh party. Tabataba'i was elected to the Majlis as a deputy in 1944. He was an opponent of the government of Mohammad Mossadegh in the early 1950s and soon retired from active politics, but he became a close advisor to Shah Mohammed Reza Pahlavi. He died in his home village of Sa'adatabad in 1969.

AHMED QAVAM ES-SULTANEH (Prime Minister; June 4, 1921–January 20, 1922). Ahmed Qavam es-Sultaneh was born in Mazandaran, Azerbaijan, in 1882. He was the nephew of Mirza Ali Khan Amin al-Dowleh, and the brother of Mirza Hasan Khan Vozuq al-Dowleh. Qavam entered government service as a scribe at the shah's court in 1898. He received his first cabinet appointment in 1909 when he was named minister of justice. He was subsequently appointed minister of the interior. Qavam was appointed governor-general of the Korasan province in 1913. He was arrested by order of Prime Minister Said Ziya ad-Din Tabataba'i in 1921. He was released several months later, and Tabataba'i fled the country. Qavam was installed as prime minister on June 4, 1921, in Reza Khan's military government. He stepped down on January 20, 1922, but was asked to form another government on June 10, 1922. He was removed from office on January 26, 1923, and charged with plotting against Reza Shah Pahlavi. Qavam subsequently went into exile in Europe, where he remained until he was allowed to return to Persia in 1929. He reentered politics, and, following the abdication of the shah, he again became prime minister on August 3, 1942. His term of office was a turbulent one, and though he managed to restore order during antigovernment riots in 1942, he was forced to resign on February 15, 1943, after being charged with nepotism. Qavam remained in the Iranian parliament as a leading spokesman of the minority parties. He again emerged

as prime minister on January 26, 1946. He appointed a moderate cabinet but retained the positions of foreign minister and minister of the interior for himself. He was able to negotiate the withdrawal of Russian troops from Iran. He also reached a settlement with pro-independence supporters in the Azerbaijan region, which resulted in Azerbaijan being restored as a province of Iran. In 1947 he sponsored a Soviet-Iranian oil treaty that was rejected by the Iranian parliament. After a vote of no confidence, he was forced from office on December 10, 1947. Following a period of illness that saw him hospitalized in France, Qavam returned to Iran, and in May 1948 he was cleared of charges of misconduct in office. Qavam was again appointed prime minister on July 17, 1952, following the resignation of Mohammed Mossadegh. Qavam resigned four days later after a general strike and riots demanded Mossadegh's return. Qavam was arrested, but charges against him were dismissed. He subsequently went into political retirement and died in Teheran after a lengthy illness on July 23, 1955.

MIRZA HASAN KHAN MOSTOWFI AL-MAMALEK (Prime Minister; January 20, 1922–May 9, 1922). *See earlier entry under Heads of Government.*

AHMED QAVAM ES-SALTANEH (Prime Minister; June 10, 1922–January 26, 1923). *See earlier entry under Heads of Government.*

MIRZA HASAN KHAN VOZUQ AL-DOWLEH (Prime Minister; February 15, 1923–June 12, 1923). *See earlier entry under Heads of Government.*

MIRZA HASAN KHAN MOSTOWFI AL-MAMALEK (Prime Minister; June 18, 1923–October 1923). *See earlier entry under Heads of Government.*

MOHAMMED REZA KHAN (Prime Minister; October 29, 1923–October 31, 1925). *See earlier entry under Heads of State.*

MOHAMMED ALI KHAN FARUGHI (Prime Minister; November 1, 1925–June 6, 1926). Mohammed Ali Khan Farughi was born to a leading Persian family in 1877. He inherited the title Zaka al-Molk from his father in 1908. Farughi was subsequently elected to the Majlis and was named minister of finance in 1911. He was soon named to head the Persian supreme court. He returned to the cabinet as minister of justice in 1915. Farughi was named to head the government on November 1, 1925, as Mohammed Reza Khan's first prime minister after he was enthroned as the new shah. Farughi stepped down on June 6, 1926. He remained in the government until 1935. He was recalled to head the government on September 16, 1941. He resigned on December 21, 1942, shortly before his death.

MIRZA HASAN KHAN VOZUQ AL-DOWLEH (Prime Minister; June 13, 1926–May 28, 1927). *See earlier entry under Heads of Government.*

MIRZA MAHDI GHOLI KHAN HEYDAYAT, MOKHBER AL-SALTANEH (Prime Minister; June 2, 1927–September 13, 1933). Mahdi Gholi Khan Heydayat, Mokhber al-Saltaneh was born in 1863. He was educated in Germany and returned to Persia to teach in Teheran in 1880. He began his career in government service as an advisor to Shah Nasir al-Din in 1893. Heydayat served on the council that oversaw the 1911 elections. He was also governor of several provinces including Fars and Azerbaijan. Heydayat was named prime minister on June 2, 1927. He stepped down from office on September 13, 1933. He retired from the government and wrote his memoirs. Heydayat died in 1950.

MIRZA HASAN KHAN VOZUQ AL-DOWLEH (Prime Minister; September 17, 1933–December 4, 1935). *See earlier entry under Heads of Government.*

MOHAMMED KHAN DJAM, MODIR AL-MOLK (Prime Minister; December 4, 1935–October 27, 1939). Mahmud Khan Djam, Modir al-Molk, was born in Tabriz in 1885. He studied medicine and became a physician to the royal court. He worked in Teheran as a translator in the justice ministry beginning in 1909. He was granted the title Modir al-Molk in 1919. He served in several cabinets during the 1920s and 1930s and was appointed prime minister on December 4, 1935. He retained office until October 27, 1939. Djam was appointed ambassador to Egypt after Reza Shah Pahlavi's abdication in 1941. He was elected to the senate in 1956. Djam died in Teheran in 1969.

AHMAD MATIN DAFTARI (Prime Minister; October 27, 1939–June 27, 1940). Ahmad Matin Daftari was born to a prominent Persian family in 1896. He studied law in Europe in the late 1920s and returned to Iran to serve as minister of justice in 1936. He was named prime minister by Reza Shah Pahlavi on October 27, 1939. He stepped down on June 27, 1940, but remained active in politics. He also taught law at the Teheran University. His political activities were curtailed in the early 1960s due to his active opposition to policies of the government of Reza Shah Pahlavi. His son, Hedayatollah Matin Daftari, was also a leading opponent of the shah. Daftari died in Teheran in 1971.

ALI MANSOUR (Prime Minister; June 27, 1940–August 27, 1941). Ali Khan Mansor was born in 1895. He served as minister of roads and railways prior to World War II and was instrumental in the construction of the Trans-Iranian Railway. He was appointed prime minister on June 27, 1940, and was serving in that position when British and Soviet troops invaded Iran in August 1941. Following World War II, Mansour was appointed to a council to establish Iran's policy in Azerbaijan regarding Soviet troops that remained in the province. Following the withdrawal of Soviet troops, Mansour was named governor-general of Azerbaijan in late 1946. In 1948 he headed a royal commission designed to draw up a seven-year plan for the development of Iran. Mansour was again named prime minister on March 23, 1950, and served briefly until June 26, 1950. He was appointed Iran's ambassador to Turkey in 1953. He was the father of Hassan Ali Mansour, who served as Iran's prime minister from 1964 until his assassination in early 1965. Ali Mansour died in Teheran on December 8, 1974.

MOHAMMED ALI KHAN FARUGHI (Prime Minister; September 16, 1941–March, 1942). *See earlier entry under Heads of Government.*

ALI SUHATILI (Prime Minister; March 1942–July 1942). Ali Suhatili was born in 1897. He was named to head the government in March 1942, but was forced to step down in July of that year. He was again named prime minister on February 15, 1943, and served until February 21, 1944. Suhatili was accused of corruption during his second term of office which prevented his reappointment the following year. He died on May 1, 1958.

AHMED QAVAM ES-SULTANEH (Prime Minister; August 3, 1942–February 15, 1943). *See earlier entry under Heads of Government.*

ALI SUHATILI (Prime Minister; February 15, 1943–February 21, 1944). *See earlier entry under Heads of Government.*

MOHAMMED SAID MARAGHEI (Prime Minister; February 21, 1944–November 9, 1944). Mohammed Said Mara-

ghei was born in 1881. He entered the diplomatic service as a clerk at the Persian consulate in Istanbul, Turkey. He later held positions in Batum and Baku. Said was named ambassador to the Soviet Union prior to World War II. He was serving in that position when Soviet and British troops invaded Iran in 1941. He was subsequently named minister of foreign affairs, and on February 21, 1944, he was named prime minister. During his term of office, he rejected a Soviet proposal to exploit Iran's oil deposits. On November 9, 1944, he was forced to step down as prime minister, to some extent because of pressure from Moscow. Said returned as prime minister on November 9, 1948. The following year he also served on the ruling royal council during the shah's visit to the United States. He resigned on March 23, 1950. Said subsequently retired from politics. He died in Teheran after a long illness on November 1, 1973.

MURTEZA QUALI KHAN BAYATT (Prime Minister; November 25, 1944–April 19, 1945). Murteza Quali Khan Bayatt was born in Arak to a wealthy family in 1886. He supported the constitutionalists during the 1906 revolution and soon joined the moderate E'tedali Party. He was elected to the Majlis in 1922 and supported the installation of Reza Khan as shah in 1925. He subsequently served in the government as minister of finance. Bayatt was named prime minister on November 25, 1944. His government was involved in attempts to remove Allied forces from Iran following World War II. He was also forced to deal with Soviet demands for oil concessions in northern Iran. Bayatt resigned on April 19, 1945. He was elected to the Iranian senate in 1950 and became vice president of that body. He was appointed by Prime Minister Mohammad Mossadegh to lead the new Iranian oil company. Bayatt was the head of the oil consortium from 1955 until his death in 1958.

IBRAHIM HAKIMI (Prime Minister; May 11, 1945–June 4, 1945). Ibrahimi Hakim was born in 1870. He studied medicine in Teheran and Paris and returned to Persia as a physician. He served as the head of the council of physicians in the war ministry from 1907 until 1912. Hakimi served in various pre–World War II cabinets and held the portfolios of finance, foreign affairs, and justice. He also served in the senate as speaker. He first held the office of prime minister from May 11 to June 4, 1945, when he resigned over differences with the cabinet. He was again asked to form a government on November 4, 1945. During his second term of office, Hakimi's government was faced with the threat of Soviet military involvement in the province of Azerbaijan. When he was unable to reach a settlement on the issue with the Soviet government, he sent the matter to the United Nations and resigned on January 21, 1946. Hakimi was again appointed prime minister on December 23, 1947. During his third term of office a confrontation with the Soviet Union developed over Iran's military assistance from the United States. Hakimi accused the Soviets of violating the Russo-Iranian Friendship Treaty of 1921. Hakimi received a vote of no confidence from the Iranian parliament and resigned on June 12, 1948. He later served on the royal council formed in 1949 to rule during the shah's absence from Iran while on a visit to the United States. Hakimi subsequently retired from politics and died in Teheran on October 20, 1959.

MOHSEN SADR (Prime Minister; June 12, 1945–October 22, 1945). Mohsen Sadr was born in 1865. He served as a judge during the rule of Reza Shah Pahlavi. He was an arch conservative and had presided over the execution of liberal intellectuals during the constitutional revolution in the early part of the century. He was chosen as prime minister on June 12, 1945, with the backing of the National Union Party, the royalists, and other conservative elements in the parliament. His selection outraged liberal members, who boycotted parliament for three months. Sadr also took the position of minister of the interior in a cabinet composed primarily of pro–British ministers. His government was faced with a secessionist movement in the Azerbaijan region. Sadr postponed elections to the parliament and greatly increased the military budget before stepping down on October 22, 1945.

IBRAHIM HAKIMI (Prime Minister; November 4, 1945–January 21, 1946). *See earlier entry under Heads of Government.*

Iraq

Iraq is a country in western Asia. It was granted independence under a League of Nations mandate administered by Great Britain on October 3, 1932.

HEADS OF STATE

FAISAL I (King; August 23, 1921–September 8, 1933). Faisal ibn Husain was born in At Ta'if in Hejaz on May 20, 1885. He was the son of Husain ibn Ali, the sharif of Mecca. He received a local education in Arabia until 1891, when he accompanied his father into exile in Constantinople, where Faisal studied politics and became acquainted with Western ways. He returned to Mecca in 1909 and participated in several military expeditions against dissidents. He was elected to the Ottoman parliament in 1913. He subsequently became involved in the Arab nationalist movement due to the harshness of the Ottoman rulers of Syria. He joined the "Arab revolt" of his father and became an ally of Colonel T. E. Lawrence. Faisal became the field commander of the Hejaz and commanded troops in the desert campaign against the Turks under the British command of Field Marshal Allenby. After the capture of Damascus in October 1918 Faisal attempted to create an Arab-controlled state in Syria. He was proclaimed king of Syria in March 1920. French forces seized Damascus and put Syria under French rule on July 26, 1920, and Faisal was expelled from the country. The British supported Faisal's subsequent claim to the throne in Iraq, where he took power on August 23, 1921. Faisal worked diligently to modernize and unify the country. He ruled under a British mandate, with England controlling financial and foreign policies. Faisal supported a pan-Arab union with Syria and Palestine. Great Britain granted Iraq independence, and Iraq entered the League of Nations in 1932. Faisal subsequently suffered from poor health and spent the summer of 1933 in Switzerland to recuperate. He died in Bern, Switzerland, of a heart attack on September 8, 1933.

GHAZI (King; September 9, 1933–April 4, 1939). Ghazi ibn Faisal was born in 1912. He was the son of King Faisal of Iraq and succeeded to the throne on September 9, 1933, following the death of his father. He continued Faisal's policy of modernization in the country. His reign was challenged by dissident elements, who staged an unsuccessful rebellion in 1935. Jafar el-Askari, the

King's defense minister and leading advisor, was killed prior to a military coup led by General Bakr Sidqi in October 1936. Sidqi was assassinated the following year and Nuri as-Said became prime minister and leading advisor to the king. Ghazi signed a treaty of alliance with Saudi Arabia in 1937, while also maintaining close relationships with Great Britain, France, and the United States. He retained the throne until his death in an automobile accident on April 4, 1939. There was some speculation that the death may not have been accidental. The future regent Abdul-Ilah and his sister Aliya, Ghazi's estranged wife, were suspected of involvement.

BAKR SIDQI (Military Dictator; October 30, 1936–August 11, 1937). Bakr Sidqi was born in Kir Tuk, Kurdestan, in 1890. He was the son of the Ottoman provincial governor. He entered the Turkish army in 1908, where he gained a reputation for ruthlessness. He fought with the Ottoman army during World War I. He joined King Faisal's army in Iraq as a general after the war. Sidqi's massacre of unarmed Assyrians in Mosul Province forced his dismissal in 1933, but he was soon reinstated. Sidqi led a military coup against the government on October 30, 1936, during which time defense minister Jafar el-Askari was slain and the government of Yasin al-Hashimi was forced to resign. Sidqi established himself as chief of the general staff and military dictator of Iraq. He controlled the army and the government under a warrant from King Ghazi until August 11, 1937, when he and Major Muhammad 'Ali Jawad, commander of the Iraqi air force, were shot to death at the airport in Mosul. The assassin was identified as Muhammad 'Ali Yallafari, an Iraqi soldier and distant relative of slain defense minister el-Askari.

FAISAL II (King; April 4, 1939–July 14, 1958). Faisal was born in Baghdad on May 2, 1935. He was the son of King

Ghazi, who ruled Iraq from 1933 to 1959. Faisal succeeded his father as king when Ghazi was killed in an automobile accident on April 4, 1939. Faisal II ruled through the regency of his uncle, Abdul-Ilah, while he was being educated at Harrow in Great Britain. His classmates included his cousin, Hussein, who was to become king of Jordan. Faisal returned to Iraq on May 2, 1953, after having come of age. He remained close friends with his cousin, King Hussein, and planned to federate their nations in response to the militant nationalist policies of Gamal Nasser's newly formed United Arab Republic. Faisal and Hussein reached an agreement in February 1958 to unify Iraq and Jordan the following July, with Faisal as head of the federation. The proposed federation was aborted when Faisal was ousted in a nationalist coup led by Brigadier Abdul Karim Kassem. The king surrendered to the coup leaders on July 14, 1958, when he was given a promise of safe conduct. Instead he and many other members of the royal family were slaughtered and their butchered bodies dragged through the streets of Baghdad.

ABDUL-ILAH (Regent; April 4, 1939–May 2, 1953). Abdul-Ilah was born in Taif on November 14, 1913. He was the son of Ali ibn Husain, who had ruled as king of the Hejaz from 1924 until his defeat and ouster by King Saud of Saudi Arabia in 1925. Upon the death of King Ghazi in 1939, Abdul-Ilah was named regent of Iraq for Faisal II, his nephew. The regency was briefly deposed by pro-German Rashid Ali Gailani, following Abdul-Ilah's declared support for the Allies in 1941. Abdul-Ilah returned to Baghdad following Gailani's ouster and proceeded to declare war on the Axis Powers. He was made crown prince in 1943 and following the assassination of Jordan's King Abdullah, he was recognized as head of the Hashemite royal family. Abdul-Ilah's moderate pro-Western policies brought him into conflict with some of the more militant Arab nationalists in the region. After Faisal came of age, Abdul-Ilah continued to serve as the king's close advisor. He was murdered on July 14, 1958, together with Faisal and other members of the royal family, following a nationalist coup.

HEADS OF GOVERNMENT

ABDUR RAHMAN AL-HAIDARI AL-GAILANI (Prime Minister; October 27, 1920–November 17, 1922). Abdur Rahman al-Haidari al-Gailani was born to a leading Baghdad family in 1841. He was head of the Sufi religious order, which had been founded by his family seven centuries earlier. Gailani was chosen as president of Iraq's council of ministers on October 27, 1920. He was initially opposed to the selection of Faisal I as Iraq's king, and resigned his position in August 1921, following Faisal's accession to the throne. Gailani was subsequently appointed by Faisal to serve as prime minister of the first Iraqi govern-

ment. He negotiated the Anglo-Iraqi Treaty with Great Britain, though he opposed the British mandate. He stepped down from office the following year on November 17, 1922. Gailani died in June 1927.

ABDUL MUHSIN ES-SA'DUN (Prime Minister; November 18, 1922–November 15, 1923). Abdul Muhsin es-Sa'dun was born in 1879, the son of Fahd Pasha al-Sa'dun of the ruling house of the Muntafiq tribe. Sa'dun attended the Ottoman Military College and became aide-de-camp to the Ottoman sultan in 1905. He returned to Iraq in 1909 and was elected to the Ottoman parliament the following year. He was a leader of the al-Taqaddum Party (progressive party), which called for Iraq's independence from the British mandate. He served in various cabinets and was selected as prime minister on November 18, 1922, an office he held for a year. He again headed the government from June 19, 1925, until November 1, 1926, also serving as Iraq's principal negotiator for the 1926 Anglo-Iraqi Treaty. He was again prime minister from January 14, 1928, until January 20, 1929. He was reappointed on September 19, 1929, and headed the government until his suicide on November 13, 1929.

JAFAR EL-ASKARI (Prime Minister; November 22, 1923–August 3, 1924). Jafar el-Askari was born in Baghdad in 1887. He was the son of a military leader of the Ottoman Empire. He graduated from the Ottoman Military Academy in 1904 and served in the Ottoman army during World War I. He was captured by the British during the war and made a daring escape from his captors in Egypt. He subsequently joined the Arab nationalist movement with his brother-in-law, Nuri as-Sa'id, and joined T. E. Lawrence's Arab revolt against the Turks. Askari became a close associate of Faisal, who became king of Syria in 1920. Faisal was removed from power by the French, but was supported in his claim of the Iraqi throne in 1921. Askan served as minister of defense in the first Iraqi government. He headed the government from November 22, 1923, until August 3, 1924, and again from November 21, 1926, until December 31, 1927. He remained active in government affairs, serving in the cabinet as minister of defense and foreign affairs in 1931 and 1932. He continued to be a major figure in Iraqi politics and was again serving as minister of defense when he was murdered by insurgent troops under the orders of General Bakr Sidqi on October 30, 1936.

YASIN AL-HASHIMI (Prime Minister; August 4, 1924–June 29, 1925). Yasin al-Hashimi was born Yasin Hilmi Salman in Baghdad. He attended the Istanbul Military Academy, where he was promoted to the rank of general. He began his political career as minister of transportation in 1924. He was named to head the government on August 4, 1924, and served until June 29, 1925. He remained active in government affairs and returned to office as prime minister on March 17, 1935. The military activity of General Bakr Sidqi caused Hashimi's government to fall on October 30, 1936. He was deported to Damascus, Syria, where he died on January 2, 1937.

ABDUL MUHSIN ES-SA'DUN (Prime Minister; June 19, 1925–November 1, 1926). *See earlier entry under Heads of Government.*

JAFAR EL-ASKARI (Prime Minister; November 21, 1926–December 31, 1927). *See earlier entry under Heads of Government.*

ABDUL MUHSIN ES-SA'DUN (Prime Minister; January 14, 1928–January 20, 1929). *See earlier entry under Heads of Government.*

TAUFIQ BEG SUWAIDI (Prime Minister; April 28, 1929–August 25, 1929). Taufiq al-Suwaidi was born in Baghdad in 1891, the son of Yusuf Suwaidi, a leading Arab nationalist and jurist. He was educated as a lawyer in Baghdad, Istanbul, and France. He served as a legal advisor to the Iraqi government from 1921 until 1927. He was named to the cabinet as minister of education in 1927 and served for one year. Suwaidi served as prime minister and foreign minister from April 28 until August 25, 1929, and again from November 18, 1929, until March 9, 1930. He was again foreign minister from 1937 to 1938, and also in 1941 following the ouster of the pro-German regime of Rashid Ali

Gailani. Suwaidi was again prime minister from February 23, 1946, to May 31, 1946, and from February 5, 1950, to September 4, 1950. He served as foreign minister again in 1950 and in 1953. Suwaidi was named deputy prime minister in 1958 and was foreign minister of the Iraqi-Jordanian federation from May until July 1958. He was arrested following the overthrow of the Hashemite monarchy in July 1958 and was sentenced to life imprisonment, but he was released in July 1961. He subsequently went into exile in Lebanon, where he remained until his death in 1968.

ABDUL MUHSIN ES-SA'DUN (Prime Minister; September 19, 1929–November 13, 1929). *See earlier entry under Heads of Government.*

TAUFIQ BEG SUWAIDI (Prime Minister; November 18, 1929–March 29, 1930). *See earlier entry under Heads of Government.*

NURI AL-SAID (Prime Minister; March 23, 1930–October 27, 1932). Nuri al-Said was born in Baghdad in 1888. He attended the Istanbul Military Academy in 1903 and joined the Iraqi army as an officer in 1908. He was an early Arab nationalist and joined the Arab revolt during World War I. He was a close advisor to Emir Faisal, and served as his chief of staff during the Arab revolt led by Lawrence of Arabia. Nuri remained with Emir Faisal during his rule in Syria in 1920 and accompanied him the following year when Faisal was named the first king of Iraq. Nuri was named to the cabinet as minister of defense in November 1922 and again served in that position during three cabinets between 1923 and 1928. For the next twenty-five years, he remained a major political figure in Iraq and served as prime minister from March 23, 1930, until October 27, 1932. During that time he signed the Anglo-Iraqi Treaty of 1930. Nuri served as foreign minister in several cabinets during

the early 1930s. He was forced to flee the country following the coup led by General Bakr Sidqi in October 1936. He returned to Iraq following Sidqi's assassination in August 1937. Nuri served in several diplomatic positions abroad before again serving as prime minister from December 26, 1938, until March 31, 1940. He again fled Iraq following the pro-German coup led by Rashid Ali Gailani. He returned to Iraq following Gailani's ouster and was again named prime minister on October 19, 1941. Nuri led the Iraqi government in declaring war on the Axis Powers during World War II. He retained office until June 4, 1944. He was a leading proponent of Arab unity and a founder of the Arab League. Nuri again formed a government on November 21, 1946, serving until March 30, 1947. He was again prime minister from January 6 until November 7, 1949, and founded the Constitutional Union Party. He served as head of government again from September 16, 1950, until July 9, 1952, when he was forced to resign following student riots. Nuri remained in the government as minister of defense. He was again named prime minister on August 4, 1954. During this term of office, Iraq broke off diplomatic relations with the Soviet Union and signed the Baghdad Pact with Turkey, Pakistan, Iran, and Great Britain. His opposition to Egypt's President Gamal Abdel Nasser, along with his moderate pro-Western policies, met with opposition from nationalists. He stepped down on June 16, 1957, for reasons of health. Nuri's last term as prime minister was from March 3 until May 13, 1958, when he resigned in preparation to become prime minister of the newly formed federation between Iraq and Jordan. Following the ouster of Faisal II, Nuri was captured and brutally killed on July 14, 1958, when he tried to escape from Baghdad dressed as a woman. His body was reportedly dismembered by an angry mob.

NAJI SHAWKAT (Prime Minister; November 3, 1932–March 18, 1933). Naji Shawkat was born in Baghdad in 1891. He served with the Ottoman army during World War I. He subsequently returned to Iraq, where he served as minister of the interior in several cabinets during the 1920s and 1930s. He was named prime minister on November 3, 1932, holding that position until Rashid Ali Gailani formed a government on March 18, 1933. He remained active in Iraqi politics until 1941, when his career ended because of his support for Gailani's pro–Axis policies.

RASHID ALI GAILANI (Prime Minister; March 20, 1933–October 29, 1933). Rashid Ali Gailani was born in Baghdad in 1892. Though a member of the wealthy and powerful Gailani family, Rashid's father had been stripped of privileges, and his branch of the family was of modest means. Rashid entered politics and served as minister of justice in Yasin al-Hashimi's cabinet in 1924. He and Hashimi founded the Party of National Brotherhood in 1930 in opposition to a new treaty with Great Britain. Rashid was named prime minister on March 20, 1933, but was forced to resign on October 29, 1933. He spent the next several years in opposition to the governments of Jamil al-Midfai and Ali Jawdat al-Ayubi. Hashimi formed a new government in March 1935, and Rashid was named minister of the interior. The government was forced from office by General Bakr Sidqi's coup in October 1936. Rashid became increasingly involved with militant nationalists and became an ally of the exiled grand mufti of Jerusalem, Amin al-Husayni. Rashid was again called upon to head the government on March 31, 1940. He refused Great Britain's requests to break off relations with Italy during World War II and refused to allow British troops to travel through Iraq. He was briefly forced to step down on January 31, 1941, but returned to office on April 4, 1941. His pro–German policies led British troops to invade Iraq in May 1941, and the Iraqi army was defeated. Rashid left office on May 29, 1941, fleeing the country for exile in Germany. He went to Saudi Arabia in May 1945, where he remained until 1954. Rashid returned from exile following the ouster of the monarch in September 1958. He made a brief effort to lead a rebellion against the subsequent government of Abdul Karim Kassem and was arrested in December 1958. He was tried and sentenced to death, but was pardoned by Kassem. He eventually returned to exile and died in Beirut, Lebanon, on August 28, 1965.

JAMIL BEG AL-MIDFAI (Prime Minister; November 9, 1933–August 25, 1934). Jamil Beg al-Midfai was born in Mosul in 1890. He attended the Istanbul School of Engineering and served with the Ottoman army during World War I. He deserted the Ottomans to join the Arab revolt in 1916. Midfai served as an advisor to Faisal in Damascus, Syria, from 1918 until 1919. He returned to Iraq in 1920, where he was active in the anti–British nationalist movement. He was forced to leave Iraq later in the year because of his activities. Midfai remained in exile in Transjordan until 1923. He returned to Iraq and served as governor of several provinces. He was named to the cabinet as minister of the interior in 1930. Midfai served as prime minister from November 9, 1933, until August 25, 1934, and again from March 1 to March 16, 1935. He again formed a government on August 17, 1937, following the assassination of military strongman Bakr Sidqi and served until December 26, 1938. He was again prime minister from June 2 until October 10, 1941. Midfai again fled to Transjordan in 1941 following the pro–German coup led by Rashid Ali Gailani. He returned to Iraq following Gailani's ouster and the restoration of the Hashemite monarchy. Midfai served as president of the senate from 1944 until 1945 and was named minister of the interior in 1948. He served another term as prime minister from January 29, 1953, until his resignation on September 1, 1953. He was elected president of the senate again in 1955 and retained that position until his death in 1958.

ALI JAWDAT AL-AYUBI (Prime Minister; August 26, 1934–February 24, 1935). Ali Jawdat al-Ayubi was born in Mosul in 1887 to a Sunni Muslim family. He was educated at the Istanbul Military Academy and subsequently served in the Ottoman army. He deserted the Ottomans and joined Sharif Husain's Arab rebellion in 1916. Ayubi served as governor of Aleppo under Faisal's reign in Syria in 1920. The following year Ayubi returned to Iraq and became a leader of the right-wing nationalist Al-Ikha Party. He was named minister of the interior in 1923 and served until 1924. He returned to the cabinet as minister of finance in 1930 and was an opponent of the Anglo-Iraqi Treaty of that year. Ayubi became chief of the royal household in 1933. He was first named prime minister on August 26, 1934, and served until February 24, 1935. He subsequently served as speaker of the parliament before being named Iraq's minister to London later that year. Ayubi was sent to Paris as Iraq's representative in 1937 and then returned to Iraq to serve as foreign minister in 1939. He left Iraq during the pro–German rule of Rashid Ali Gailani in 1941. He returned following the restoration of the pro–British regime under Nuri al-Said. Ayubi was appointed minister to Washington, D.C., in 1944. He returned to Iraq to serve as foreign minister in 1948. He was again named prime minister on December 10, 1949, and retained that position until February 1, 1950. Ayubi was deputy prime minister from 1953 until 1957 and served another brief term as prime minister from June 17 to December 10, 1957. He fled to Lebanon following the military coup that deposed King Faisal II in

1959. Ayubi published his memoirs in 1967. He died of a heart attack in Beirut, Lebanon, on March 3, 1969.

JAMIL BEG AL-MIDFAI (Prime Minister; March 1, 1935–March 16, 1935). *See earlier entry under Heads of Government.*

YASIN AL-HASHIMI (Prime Minister; March 17, 1935–October 30, 1936). *See earlier entry under Heads of Government.*

SULEIMAN HIKMAT (Prime Minister; October 30, 1936–August 12, 1937). Suleiman Hikmat was born in 1889. He was a leading political figure from the early years of Iraqi independence. He was chosen as prime minister following General Bakr Sidqi's military coup d'état on October 29, 1936. Hikmat was forced to step down on August 12, 1937, following Sidqi's assassination.

JAMIL BEG AL-MIDFAI (Prime Minister; August 17, 1937–December 26, 1938). *See earlier entry under Heads of Government.*

NURI AL-SAID (Prime Minister; December 26, 1938–March 31, 1940). *See earlier entry under Heads of Government.*

RASHID ALI GAILANI (Prime Minister; March 31, 1940–January 31, 1941). *See earlier entry under Heads of Government.*

TAHA EL-HASIMI (Prime Minister; February 1, 1941–April 1, 1941). Taha el-Hasimi was born in 1888. He briefly served as prime minister of Iraq when Rashid Ali Gailani was forced to step down on February 1, 1941. He relinquished the office on April 1, 1941, when Gailani resumed power. Hasimi died on June 1, 1961.

RASHID ALI GAILANI (Prime Minister; April 4, 1941–May 29, 1941).

See earlier entry under Heads of Government.

JAMIL BEG AL-MIDFAI (Prime Minister; June 2, 1941–October 10, 1941). *See earlier entry under Heads of Government.*

NURI AL-SAID (Prime Minister; October 19, 1941–June 4, 1944). *See earlier entry under Heads of Government.*

HAMDI AL-PACHACHI (Prime Minister; June 4, 1944–January 31, 1946). Hamdi al-Pachachi was born to a wealthy family in Baghdad in 1891. He served as minister of social welfare from 1941 until 1944. He subsequently became president of the chamber of deputies. Pachachi was asked to form a cabinet as prime minister on June 4, 1944. He was forced to resign on January 31, 1946. He was named foreign minister in January 1948 and retained that position until his death in Baghdad from a heart attack on March 27, 1948.

Ireland

Ireland is an island country in the North Atlantic west of Great Britain. The Irish Free State was established on December 6, 1922, although the six northern counties maintain their allegiance to the British Crown. The sovereign country of Ireland, or Eire, as it is known in the Gaelic language, was established on December 29, 1937.

HEADS OF STATE

DOUGLAS HYDE (President; December 29, 1937–June 25, 1945). Douglas Hyde was born in Frenchpark, County Roscommon, on January 17, 1860. He attended Trinity College in Dublin and joined the Society for the Preservation of the Irish Language in 1878. He later organized the Gaelic Union in order to publish periodicals in the Irish language. Hyde served as founder and president of the Gaelic League from 1893 until 1915. He wrote numerous books, including *Story of Early Gaelic Literature* (1895), *A Literary History of Ireland* (1899), and *Mediaeval Tales from the Irish* (1899). He also wrote poems and plays and recounted old Irish legends, sometimes under the pseudonym An Craoibhin Aoibhinn, meaning "the delightful little branch." Hyde became a professor of modern Irish at University College in Dublin in 1909 and remained in that position until 1932. He was also elected to the Irish senate in 1925, and when the Irish constitution was created in 1937, he was selected to be the first president of Eire. He took office on December 29, 1937, and retained the position until his retirement on June 24, 1945. He died in Dublin on July 12, 1949.

HEADS OF GOVERNMENT

EAMON DE VALERA (Head of Government; April 1, 1919–December 5, 1921). Eamon De Valera was born in New York City on October 14, 1882. His father was a Spanish musician, and his mother was Irish. De Valera was brought to live with his maternal grandmother in County Limerick, Ireland, following his father's death in 1884. He was educated in Ireland and received a degree in mathematics. He embarked on a career as a teacher and soon became interested in Gaelic studies. De Valera joined the Gaelic League, and in 1913 he became associated with the Irish Volunteers, a group dedicated to Ireland's independence from Great Britain. He was arrested during the Easter Rebellion in 1916 and was spared from the death sentence handed to many of the other leaders of the rebellion because of his American birth. He was sentenced to life imprisonment but was released in June 1917 following a general amnesty. De Valera subsequently was elected president of the Sinn Fein nationalist organization and was also elected to the British Parliament, though he never took office because of his refusal to swear allegiance to the British Crown. He was again arrested in 1918 following his opposition to Ireland's involvement in World War I. He escaped from Lincoln Prison in February 1919 and returned to Ireland. He was selected as head of the provisional government on April 1, 1919. De Valera soon went to the United States on a mission to seek aid for Ireland's independence movement. Upon his return to Ireland he entered into peace negotiations with the British government led by Prime Minister David Lloyd George. De Valera did not personally take part in the meetings that resulted in a treaty granting the 26 counties of southern Ireland limited independence. He stepped down from office on December 5, 1921. He and other nationalist leaders repudiated the treaty, and in June 1922 a bloody civil war resulted. De Valera was instrumental in calling an end to the battle in May 1923 because he felt the Irish Republicans could not defeat the British army through warfare. In 1925 De Valera attempted to get the Sinn Fein to accept election to the Irish parliament regard-

less of the oath to the Crown. His position was rejected by the Sinn Fein, and De Valera formed the Fianna Fail, or "Soldiers of Destiny," as his own political party. Two years later De Valera took his seat in parliament. De Valera's party was successful in subsequent elections, and he took office as Ireland's prime minister on March 9, 1932. He also served as foreign minister during his term of office. He was active in the League of Nations, where he served as president of the council in 1932 and president of the assembly of the league in 1938. De Valera's government drafted a new constitution in December 1937 and established the independent state of Eire the following year. Ireland under De Valera remained neutral during World War II, and the Fianna Fail was again successful in the elections of 1944. Four years later De Valera's party lost its absolute majority, and John Costello replaced him as prime minister on February 18, 1948. After a new election was called in May 1951, De Valera was returned as prime minister by a narrow margin and took office on June 13, 1951. He was again defeated by Costello's Fine Gael Party and was replaced on June 2, 1954. Costello's ruling coalition collapsed in January 1957, and De Valera returned as prime minister on March 20, 1957. De Valera, suffering from failing eyesight, retired from parliamentary politics to take office as the president of the Republic of Ireland on June 25, 1959. He won reelection to the largely ceremonial office in 1966. De Valera retired to a Dublin nursing home on June 25, 1973, where he died there of pneumonia on August 29, 1975.

ARTHUR GRIFFITH (Head of Government; January 10, 1922–August 12, 1922). Arthur Griffith was born in Dublin on March 31, 1872. He became involved with the Irish nationalist movement at an early age. He began writing for the weekly paper the *United Irishman* in 1899 and became an editor two years later. He initiated a policy of passive resistance against Great Britain in 1902 to gain Irish autonomy. His movement was known as the Sinn Fein, which also became the name of his newspaper in 1907. While he was not an active participant in the Easter Rebellion of 1916, he was still arrested by the British and imprisoned in Frongoch, Wales. Eamon De Valera was chosen as Sinn Fein's leader upon their release in 1917, and Griffith continued to edit the movement's newspaper. He was again arrested in 1918. Griffith was elected vice president of the provisional government of the Irish republic under De Valera in December 1918, and he acted in De Valera's stead while the latter traveled abroad in 1919 and 1920. The nationalists continued to fight against the British until a truce was arranged in July 1921. Griffith headed the Irish delegation to London that negotiated the Anglo-Irish treaty at the end of the year. The terms of the treaty met with opposition from De Valera and his followers, who resigned from the assembly when the treaty was narrowly approved. Griffith was selected to head the provisional government on January 10, 1922, with Michael Collins serving as chairman of the provisional government and commander of the army. Griffith died suddenly of a cerebral hemorrhage while en route to his office in Dublin on August 12, 1922.

MICHAEL COLLINS (Head of Government; August 12, 1922–August 22, 1922). Michael Collins was born in Clonakilty, County Cork, on October 16, 1890. He served in the British civil service in London, where he began working as a postal clerk in 1906. He became involved with Irish nationalism and joined the Irish Republican brotherhood in 1909. Collins returned to Dublin in 1916 and took part in the Easter Rebellion. He was captured and interned in Frongoch, Wales, until December 1916. He was elected to the Dail Eireann (assembly), in December 1918

as a member of the Sinn Fein. He declared his support for the Irish Republic and served as the Sinn Fein minister of home affairs. He was instrumental in arranging the escape of nationalist leader Eamon De Valera from prison in February 1919. Collins also served as director of organization and intelligence of the Irish Republican Army. After the truce with Great Britain in July 1921, Collins and Arthur Griffith represented the Irish nationalists at the negotiations in London at the end of the year. He signed the treaty with Great Britain on December 6, 1921, and persuaded the Dail to approve it by a narrow margin. Griffith became president of the Irish republic and Collins became chairman of the provisional government. Civil war soon broke out between the government and followers of Eamon De Valera, who opposed the treaty. Collins became head of state following the death of Griffith on August 12, 1922. He continued to lead the army in putting down the rebellion. His party was ambushed at Beal-na-Blath on August 22, 1922, while traveling from Skibereen to Cork. Collins was shot and killed during the ensuing skirmish.

WILLIAM T. COSGRAVE (Head of Government; September 9, 1922–March 9, 1932). William Thomas Cosgrave was born in Dublin on June 6, 1880. He joined the Sinn Fein movement at an early age. He joined the Irish Volunteers in 1913 and took part in the Easter Rebellion in 1916. He was captured and interned by the British at Frongoch, Wales. He returned to Ireland in 1917 and was elected to the Dail Eireann. Cosgrave supported the treaty with Great Britain in 1921 and served as minister of local government in the subsequent provisional government. Cosgrave became leader of the provisional government on September 9, 1922, following the assassination of Michael Collins. He served as president of the executive council of the Irish Free State and was also minister of finance until 1923. He also served briefly as minister of defense in 1924. Cosgrave attempted to bring stability to the country still in the midst of a civil war. He was also forced to enact heavy taxation to stabilize the economy. His vice president, Kevin O'Higgins, was assassinated in July 1927. Eamon de Valera's party reentered the parliament soon after, and Cosgrave's Fine Gael Party failed to achieve an absolute majority in the elections in September 1927.

Cosgrave continued to head the government until the elections of 1932 produced a victory for De Valera. Cosgrave stepped down on March 9, 1932. He remained leader of the Fine Gael until 1944. Cosgrave died in Dublin on November 16, 1965.

EAMON DE VALERA (Prime Minister; March 9, 1932–February 18, 1948). *See earlier entry under Heads of Government.*

Italy

Italy is a country on a peninsula jutting into the Mediterranean Sea from southern Europe.

HEADS OF STATE

UMBERTO I (King; January 9, 1878–July 29, 1900). Umberto Ranieri Carlo Emmanuele Giovanni Mario Ferdinando Eugenio was born in Turin in Piedmont on March 15, 1844, the son of King Victor Emmanuel II and Adelaide, Archduchess of Austria. After a military education, he entered the army in March 1858. He saw action in Solferino in 1859 and against the Austrians at Custozza in 1866. He held the title Prince of Piedmont, and married Princess Margherita Teresa Giovanna of Savoy in April 1868. A son, the future King Victor Emmanuel III, was born in November 1869. Umberto succeeded his father to the throne of Italy on January 9, 1878. Umberto's reign was initially tranquil, despite conflict with republicans on the Left and Catholic clericals on the Right. In foreign affairs Umberto supported the government's alliances with Germany and Austria-Hungary. He also promoted increased spending for the Italian armed forces. During the later years of his reign Umberto often tried to interfere in parliament's selection of prime ministers,

further alienating republican sentiments. Umberto was shot to death at his summer retreat in Monza by anarchist Gaetano Bresci on July 29, 1900.

VICTOR EMMANUEL III (King; July 29, 1900–May 9, 1946). Victor Emmanuel was born at Capodimonte Palace in Naples on November 11, 1869. He was the only son of King Umberto I and Margherita of Savoy-Genoa. Victor Emmanuel became prince of Naples and heir apparent as a child. He received a military education and was given command of the Naples army corps in 1896. Later in the year he married Princess Helena of Montenegro. He succeeded to the throne of Italy as King Victor Emmanuel III following the assassination of his father by an anarchist on July 29, 1900. Victor Emmanuel was a popular monarch who traveled extensively throughout his kingdom. He survived an assassination attempt by an anarchist in March 1912. The king abrogated Italy's alliance with Germany and Austria at the start of World War I and joined the

Allies in declaring war on Austria in May 1915. The Allies were victorious, and an armistice was signed in November 1917. Italy experienced a growing antimonarchist movement in the years following the war. Victor Emmanuel allowed Benito Mussolini's National Fascist Party to march on Rome and seize political power in October 1922. The king's powers were limited under the subsequent Fascist dictatorship. Victor Emmanuel concentrated on his interest in numismatics by writing books on the subject and acquiring one of the world's most valuable collections of coins. The king opposed Italy's alliance with Germany, but was unable to convince Mussolini to remain neutral during World War II. Italy declared war on Great Britain and France in June 1940. Italy suffered military reversals during the war, and Mussolini was dismissed in July 1943. The king named Marshal Pietro Badoglio as premier, and Italy remained allied with Germany. The new government agreed to a surrender to the Allies in September 1943. At that time Rome was then occupied by the German army. The royal family and the government escaped the city. Rome was captured by the Allies on June 5, 1944, and Victor Emmanuel relinquished power to his son, Crown Prince Umberto. Victor Emmanuel retained the title of king until his abdication on May 9, 1946. He went into exile in Alexandria, Egypt, where he died of lung congestion on December 28, 1947.

HEADS OF GOVERNMENT

LUIGI PELLOUX (Prime Minister; June 29, 1898–June 18, 1900). Luigi Pelloux was born in La Roche, Savoy, on March 1, 1839. He entered the Italian army in 1848 as a sublieutenant. He was active in the unification wars in 1859 and 1866 and was commander of the artillery division that forced the fall of Rome in 1870. Pelloux was elected to the chamber of deputies in 1880. He was promoted to the rank of general in 1885. He served in the cabinets of Antonio Di Rudini and Giovanni Giolitti as minister of war from February 1891 to November 1893. He became a senator in 1896 and returned to the cabinet as Di Rudini's minister of war in July of that year. He retained his position until December 1897. Di Rudini's government fell after civil disturbances in the Bari area, and Pelloux formed a cabinet as prime minister on June 29, 1898. He initially sponsored reformist legislation, but in 1899 he attempted to enact laws that would limit civil liberties. This action cost him the support of the Left in the chamber. The parliament succeeded in obstructing much of his legislation, and the courts overruled his restrictive bills of decree in February 1900. Pelloux called for new elections and stepped down on June 18, 1900, after he failed to receive a popular mandate for his policies. His subsequent political influence was minimal. Pelloux died in Bordigher on October 26, 1924.

GIUSEPPE SARACCO (Prime Minister; June 20, 1900–February 6, 1901). Giuseppe Saracco was born in Bistagno on October 9, 1821. He entered politics as a rightist in the Cavourian Party and was elected to the parliament in 1849. He later sat with the center Left and remained in office until his defeat for reelection in 1865. He was subsequently appointed to the senate. He served in Urbano Rattazzi's cabinet as minister for public works from March until December 1862. He also served as minister of finance under Alfonso La Marmora from October 1864 until December 1865. He was vice president of the senate from March 1878 until February 1880, and again from June 1886 to April 1887. He subsequently returned to the cabinet as minister of public works, where he remained until July 1887. He again held that position under Francesco Crispi from August 1887 until March 1889. He was elected president of the senate in November 1898, and remained in that position until he succeeded Luigi Pelloux as prime minister on June 20, 1900. His government was successful in maintaining calm following the assassination of King Umberto I in July 1900. He also was able to restore a working relationship between the government and the chamber. He stepped down from office on February 6, 1901, and returned to the presidency of the senate. He continued to lead the senate until October 1904. Saracco died in Acqui on January 19, 1907.

GIUSEPPE ZANARDELLI (Prime Minister; February 14, 1901–October 23, 1903). Giuseppe Zanardelli was born in Brescia on October 29, 1826. He was active in Brescia's insurrection against Austria in 1848. After the rebellion's defeat the following year, he went to Pisa and studied law at the University of Pavia. He received his degree and returned to Brescia, but his revolutionary activities provoked the Austrian authorities to keep him from practicing law. He again joined the rebellion against Austrian rule in 1859 and, following the unification of Lombardy and Piedmont, was elected to the chamber of deputies. He sat with the liberal Left and gained a reputation as one of Italy's finest orators. He supported Garibaldi and Mazzini's attempts to further Italian reunification. He was named to Agostio Depretis's cabinet as minister of public works in March 1876. He resigned in November 1877, following a disagreement with Depretis over telegraph censorship. He served as minister of the interior in Benedetto Cairoli's cabinet from March until December 1878. He was criticized by the Right for

his vociferous defense of civil liberties. He again served in Depretis's cabinet as justice minister from May 1881 until March 1883. He subsequently broke with Depretis to join with four other leftists as the Pentarchy. Following his reconciliation with Depretis, he returned to the position of minister of justice in April 1887. He remained in Francesco Crispi's cabinet from August 1887 until February 1891. Under his leadership the penal code was reformed in 1890, and the death penalty was abolished. Zanardelli served as president of the chamber of deputies from November 1892 until February 1894. During this period he unsuccessfully tried to form a government following the fall of Giovanni Giolitti's cabinet in November 1893. He again led the chamber from April until December 1897, when he was named to Antonio Di Rudini's cabinet as minister of justice. He resigned from the government in May 1898 in opposition to Di Rudini's ruthless suppression of civil unrest. He returned to lead the chamber of deputies in November 1898. He resigned the following May in opposition to Luigi Pelloux's repressive legislation. He was instrumental in forcing Pelloux's resignation in June 1900. Zanardelli was chosen to head the government as prime minister on February 14, 1901. He instituted measures to increase political and social reform during his term of office, and sought a closer relationship with France. He stepped down for reasons of health on October 23, 1903. He died two months later at his villa in Maderno on December 26, 1903.

GIOVANNI GIOLITTI (Prime Minister; November 3, 1903–March 4, 1905). Giovanni Giolitti was born in Mondovi, Cureo, on October 27, 1842. He received a degree in law from the University of Turin in 1860. Soon after he entered government service where he distinguished himself in fiscal and administrative departments. He was elected to the chamber of deputies in 1882 and was appointed councilor of state by Agostino Depretis the same year. He was named minister of finance in Francesco Crispi's cabinet in 1889, where he served until the following year. Giolitti was named to head the government as prime minister on May 6, 1892. His government fell on November 30, 1893, over a financial scandal involving the Banco Romano. Though he was cleared of any personal wrongdoing, his political career suffered as a result of the scandal. He returned to power as minister of the interior in Giuseppe Zanardelli's government in 1901, and succeeded as prime minister on November 3, 1903, when poor health forced Zanardelli's resignation. Giolitti stepped down on March 4, 1905, but returned to office when Sidney Sonnino resigned on May 23, 1906. He remained head of the government until December 2, 1909, when opposition to his plan to implement a graduated income tax forced his resignation. He formed a new government on March 30, 1911, and attempted to initiate electoral reform that would grant universal suffrage. He stepped down in favor of Antonio Salandra on March 10, 1914. Giolitti opposed Italy's entry into World War I, and popular sentiment against his position led to his retirement in 1917. He reentered politics two years later and again headed the government from June 15, 1920, until June 26, 1921. Giolitti was initially supportive of Benito Mussolini's Fascist government, but soon became a leading member of the opposition. One of his last political acts was to speak out against the Fascist electoral law of 1928. Giolitti died soon afterwards of uremic poisoning at his family home in Cavour on July 17, 1928.

ALESSANDRO FORTIS (Prime Minister; March 28, 1905–February 2, 1906). Alessandro Fortis was born in Flori on September 16, 1841. He was an early supporter of Giuseppe Garibaldi and participated in the unsuccessful attempt to capture Rome in 1867. Fortis was briefly imprisoned with other radical republicans in 1874. He soon abandoned radicalism and entered mainstream politics. He was elected to the chamber of deputies in 1880. Fortis served as undersecretary of state under Francesco Crispi from 1887 until 1890. He served in Luigi Pelloux's government as minister of agriculture from June 1898 until May 1899. He broke with Pelloux over his repressive policies and became a close ally of Giovanni Giolitti. Fortis succeeded Giolitti as prime minister on March 28, 1905. During his term of office his government nationalized the railroads and negotiated a trade treaty with Spain. He stepped down from office on February 2, 1906. Fortis died after a long illness in Rome on December 4, 1909.

SIDNEY SONNINO (Prime Minister; February 2, 1906–May 17, 1906). Sidney Constantino Sonnino was born in Pisa on March 11, 1847. He was the son of a wealthy Jewish banker and a British mother and spent his early years in Alexandria, Egypt. He returned to Italy with his family in 1850. Sonnino received a degree in law from the University of Pisa at the age of 18. He subsequently entered the diplomatic corps and served in Madrid, Vienna, Berlin, and Versailles. He returned to Italy in 1871 and authored numerous notable works on economic and agrarian issues. He became active in politics and was elected mayor of Montespertoli in 1877. He was elected to the chamber of deputies in 1880, where he sat with the Center. He briefly served as undersecretary of the treasury in Francesco Crispi's cabinet in 1889. Sonnino served as minister of finance and the treasury when Crispi formed a new government in 1893. He was successful in balancing the budget with his innovative taxation policies. He retained his position until 1896. Sonnino led the majority in the chamber during Luigi Pelloux's administration from 1898 until 1900. He was called upon to form a government as prime minister on February 2, 1906, but after only 100 days he was forced to resign on May 17, 1906. After several years of political inactivity Sonnino again formed a cabinet on December 10, 1909. His second government was as brief as his first, and he stepped down on March 21, 1910. He remained an influential leader in the chamber, promoting Italian colonialism. He was initially in favor of Italy's support of the Triple Alliance in the early days of World War I, but soon changed his position in favor of the Triple Entente. He was called upon to serve as foreign minister in November 1914, and was instrumental in drafting the Treaty of London, which allied Italy with England, France, and Russia during the war. He retained his position throughout the war and attended the Paris Peace Conference. He was unsuccessful in obtaining territorial concessions for Italy and left office when Vittorio Orlando's government resigned in June 1919. He did not stand for reelection to the chamber, but was appointed to the senate the following year. He was largely politically active for the remainder of his life. Sonnino died suddenly of a stroke in Rome on November 24, 1922.

GIOVANNI GIOLITTI (Prime Minister; May 23, 1906–December 2, 1909). *See earlier entry under Heads of Government.*

SIDNEY SONNINO (Prime Minister; December 10, 1909–March 21, 1910). *See earlier entry under Heads of Government.*

LUIGI LUZZATTI (Prime Minister; April 1, 1910–March 20, 1911). Luigi Luzzatti was born in Venice on March 1, 1841. He was educated at Padua University. Luzzatti subsequently engaged in an academic career, serving as professor of political economy at Milan in 1863 and professor of constitutional law at Padua in 1866. He entered politics in

1870, and was elected to the chamber of deputies. He served as a vice minister in Marco Minghetti's government from 1873 until 1876. He held four terms as minister of the treasury under Antonio Di Rudini, from 1891 until 1892 and from 1896 until 1898. Luzzatti was credited with saving the country from bankruptcy. He again held the post under Giovanni Giolitti from 1903 until 1905, and under Sidney Sonnino in 1906. He also served in Sonnino's short-lived government from December 1909 until March 1910 as minister of agriculture, industry, and commerce. He succeeded Sonnino as head of the government on April 1, 1910. He initiated education and electoral reforms before stepping down on March 20, 1911. He reemerged from private life to serve again as minister of the treasury in Francesco Nitti's cabinet from March until May 1920. Luzzatti was named to the senate the following year. He died in Rome on March 29, 1927.

GIOVANNI GIOLITTI (Prime Minister; March 30, 1911–March 10, 1914). *See earlier entry under Heads of Government.*

ANTONIO SALANDRA (Prime Minister; March 20, 1914–June 12, 1916). Antonio Salandra was born in Troia, near Foggia, on August 13, 1853. He was educated at the University of Naples, where he received a law degree in 1872. Salandra subsequently became a professor of administrative law at the University of Rome. He entered politics in 1886 and was elected to the chamber of deputies. He sat with the Center Right and served as undersecretary of finance from 1892 until 1893. He was named undersecretary of the treasury in 1893 and held that position until 1896. He was named to the cabinet as minister of agriculture by Luigi Pelloux in 1899 and served until 1900. He also served in Sidney Sonnino's cabinets as minister of finance in 1906 and as minister of the treasury from 1909 until 1910. Salandra succeeded Giovanni Giolitti as prime minister on March 20, 1914. He initially favored Italy's neutrality in the early days of World War I, but gradually began to support Italy's involvement in the conflict on the side of the Allies. He signed the Treaty of London in April 1915, which allied Italy with England, France, and Russia. He offered his resignation in May 1915 in the hopes of easing an ongoing political crisis. King Victor Emmanuel III refused to accept his resignation, and Salandra entered Italy into the conflict by declaring war on Austria later that month. Italy suffered military setbacks at Trentino soon after and Salandra stepped down on June 12, 1916. Salandra served as a delegate to the Paris Peace Conference in 1919 and was Italy's representative to the League of Nations in 1923. He was an early supporter of Fascism, but later called for a return to a constitutional government. Salandra went into retirement in 1925. He was named to the senate in 1928. He died from a heart ailment at his home in Rome on December 9, 1931.

PAOLO BOSELLI (Prime Minister; June 17, 1916–October 30, 1917). Paolo Boselli was born in Savona on June 8, 1838. He received a law degree from the University of Turin. He was elected to the chamber of deputies in 1870. The following year he also served on the faculty of the University of Rome as a professor of finance. He was a founder and president of the Council for the Mercantile Marine in 1881. He was also an international representative of Italian history and culture in his capacity as head of the Dante Aligheri Society. Boselli was named to Francesco Crispi's cabinet as minister of education in 1888 and served until 1891. He held several other cabinet positions, serving as minister of agriculture from 1891 until 1894 and as minister of finance from 1894 until 1896. He was also minister of the treasury from 1899 until 1900 and min-

ister of education in 1906. He was a supporter of Italy's entry into World War I in 1915 and succeeded Antonio Salandra as head of a coalition government on June 17, 1916. Conflicts within the government and Italy's continued military failures, culminating in the military disaster of Caporetto, led to Boselli's resignation on October 30, 1917. He was appointed to the senate in 1921 and was granted honorary membership in the Fascist party. Boselli died of influenza in Rome on March 10, 1932.

VITTORIO ORLANDO (Prime Minister; October 30, 1917–June 19, 1919). Vittorio Emanuele Orlando was born in Palermo, Sicily, on May 19, 1860. He was a renowned legal scholar and served on the faculties of the universities in Modena, Messina, and Palermo. He was elected to the chamber of deputies in 1897 as a supporter of the liberal Left. He also accepted a professorship of public and constitutional law at the University of Rome in 1901, a position he retained for the next thirty years. He was appointed to Giovanni Giolitti's cabinet as minister of education in 1903 and served until 1905, and he was minister of justice from 1907 until 1909. He again held the justice ministry under Antonio Salandra from 1914 until 1916, and was named Paolo Boselli's minister of the interior in 1916. He succeeded to the premiership on October 30, 1917, when Boselli was forced to resign following the military disaster of Caporetto. Orlando's government conducted the remainder of Italy's involvement in World War I. He led the Italian delegation to the Paris Peace Conference in April 1919, where he clashed with U.S. President Woodrow Wilson over territorial concessions to Italy. His inability to obtain what he considered Italy's fruits of victory, including Fiume, led to Orlando's resignation on June 19, 1919. Orlando was again called upon to head a government in 1922, but was twice unable to form a cabinet. He initially supported Benito Mussolini's Fascist movement, but reversed his position in 1925. Orlando withdrew from public life in 1931 in opposition to Mussolini's regime. He was an opponent of Italy's involvement in World War II and served as an advisor to King Victor Emmanuel III regarding the ouster of Mussolini in July 1943. The following year Orlando resumed his teaching position and became president of the chamber of deputies. He was elected to the senate in 1948 but was an unsuccessful candidate for the presidency of the republic later in the year. He continued to be a leading political figure in Italy throughout the remainder of his life. He urged Italy's withdrawal from the North Atlantic Treaty Organization (NATO) in 1950. He was also an early supporter of the World Peace Appeal's advocacy of the destruction of all nuclear weapons. Orlando died in Rome after a brief illness on December 1, 1952.

FRANCESCO NITTI (Prime Minister; June 20, 1919–June 9, 1920). Francesco Savero Nitti was born in Melfi, in the Basilicata, on July 19, 1868. He was a leading economist and was a professor at the University of Naples before his election to the chamber of deputies in 1904. He was named to Giovanni Giolitti's cabinet as minister of agriculture in March 1911, a position he retained until Giolitti's government fell in March 1914. He was a member of Italy's economic mission to the United States during World War I in 1917. He returned to the cabinet as minister of the treasury under Vittorio Orlando from October 1917 until he resigned in January 1919 in opposition to the terms of the peace treaty. Nitti was called upon to form a government as prime minister on June 20, 1919, following Orlando's resignation. His government was unable to control the growing civil unrest in postwar Italy and he offered his resignation on May 12, 1920. He was asked to form a new government on May 21, 1920, but it fell two weeks later on June 9, 1920. He

was an outspoken opponent of the growing strength of the Fascist movement, and his house was vandalized by Fascists when they marched on Rome in October 1922. Nitti went into exile in May 1924, first to Zurich, Switzerland, before settling in Paris. He remained a leading critic of Mussolini's regime. Nitti was arrested by the Germans in 1943 after the occupation of France. He spent the next two years confined in a small Bavarian village until he was liberated by the Allies. He returned to Italy after the war to form the National Union for Reconstruction Party. He subsequently joined the National Democratic Union Party and was elected to the senate in 1948. Nitti died of influenza at his home in Rome on February 20, 1953.

GIOVANNI GIOLITTI (Prime Minister; June 15, 1920–June 26, 1921). *See earlier entry under Heads of Government.*

IVANHOE BONOMI (Prime Minister; June 26, 1921–February 25, 1922). Ivanhoe Bonomi was born in Mantua on October 18, 1873. He was employed as a teacher while he studied law and became affiliated with the Socialists at an early age. He was elected to the chamber of deputies in the 1890s and served as editor of the Socialist newspaper *Avanti!* in 1899. He became a leader of the conservative Socialists following a split in the party in 1902. He worked with Leonida Bissolati to form a reformist labor party and was expelled by the Socialists over his support of the government during the Libyan conflict in 1912. He supported Italy's intervention on the side of the Allies during World War I. He was named minister of labor in Paolo Boselli's cabinet in 1916, and remained in the cabinet during the next several governments. He served as minister of war in Giovanni Giolitti's government in 1920. Bonomi was called upon to form a government as prime minister when Giolitti was forced to resign on June 26, 1921, following widespread civil unrest and labor strikes. Bonomi was able to broker a temporary peace settlement between the battling Socialist and Fascist factions, but the Fascists under Benito Mussolini broke the peace and renewed fighting. Bonomi resigned on February 25, 1922. He subsequently retired from public life. He reemerged in 1942 as a member of the conspiracy to oust Mussolini's government. After Mussolini's ouster in July 1943, Bonomi led the Committee of National Liberation, an anti–Fascist coalition. He was called upon to form a cabinet on December 10, 1944, after the Allied occupation of Rome. Bonomi's government cooperated with the Allies to suppress the Fascists and liberate northern Italy. He was also instrumental in diffusing leftist revolutionary sentiment in the country. He stepped down on June 20, 1945. He remained a leading political figure until his death in Rome on April 20, 1951.

LUIGI FACTA (Prime Minister; February 25, 1922–October 31, 1922). Luigi Facta was born in Pinerolo, Turin, on November 16, 1861. He studied law in Pinerolo and opened a practice there before entering politics. He was elected to the chamber of deputies in 1892. He was a close ally of Giovanni Giolitti and served as his undersecretary of the interior from 1906 until 1909 and as his minister of finance from 1911 until the spring of 1914. He initially supported Italy's neutrality during World War I, but subsequently supported the government's decision to enter the conflict on the side of the Allies. He served in Vittorio Orlando's cabinet as minister of justice from 1917 until 1919. He again served in Giolitti's government as finance minister from June 1920 until July 1921. Facta was called upon to form a government on February 25, 1922. The government collapsed on July 19, 1922, but he was able to form a new cabinet on August 1, 1922. Facta's government attempted a policy of conciliation toward the Fascists and

the Socialists, but civil disorders continued. The Fascists' march on Rome occurred in October 1922, and Facta appealed to King Victor Emmanuel III to grant the government martial law powers to deal with the uprising, as well as a Socialist sponsored general strike. The king refused and Facta's government resigned on October 31, 1922, to make way for Fascist leader Benito Mussolini. Facta retired from public life, though he was named to the senate by Mussolini in 1924. He died at his home in Pinerolo of complications from diabetes on November 5, 1930.

BENITO MUSSOLINI (Prime Minister; October 31, 1922–July 25, 1943). Benito Mussolini was born in Predappion on July 29, 1883. As a young man, he was a journalist and schoolteacher and traveled to Switzerland and Austria. He became active in the Socialist Party and was jailed in 1911 for his opposition to Italy's policy during the Libyan conflict. The following year he became editor of the Socialist newspaper *Avanti!*. He initially favored Italy's neutrality during World War I, but soon called for an alliance with Germany. He was expelled from the Socialist Party for his views. Mussolini served in the Italian army during the war until he was wounded in 1917. In March 1919 he and several other war veterans formed the Fasci di Combattimento (fighting leagues) in Milan. The Fascist movement was initially unsuccessful but soon gained support from leading members of the Right. The Fascists formed their own paramilitary organization known as the Blackshirts, who were active against the Socialists, Communists, and other leftist elements. Mussolini became known as "Il Duce", or the leader, and organized the Fascist march on Rome in October 1922. King Victor Emmanuel III entrusted the government to Mussolini on October 31, 1922, to prevent further violence in the capital. Mussolini faced an early crisis following the assassination of

Socialist journalist Giacomo Matteotti in June 1924. The following year Mussolini began the establishment of the dictatorship that would characterize the remainder of his regime. He negotiated the Lateran Accords with the Vatican in February 1929. After consolidating his power within Italy, he began to concentrate on foreign affairs. He supported Francisco Franco's forces during the Spanish civil war in the mid-1930s and defied the League of Nations by conquering Ethiopia. He signed the Rome-Berlin Axis agreement with Hitler's Germany in 1936 and further solidified Italy's military ties with Germany with the "Pact of Steel" in May 1939. Italy had occupied Albania the previous month, though Mussolini was initially reluctant to enter World War II. Mussolini did not enter Italy into the war until June 1940, when he felt that Germany was already the victor. A series of military reversals damaged Mussolini's prestige at home and with his allies. He received a vote of no confidence from the Fascist grand council, which gave King Victor Emmanuel III the opportunity to force Mussolini's ouster on July 25, 1943. He was arrested by the new government and imprisoned at Campo Imperatore in the Abruzzi mountains. He was soon rescued by the Germans and installed as figurehead leader of the occupied Italian Social Republic in northern Italy. As the Allies and anti–Fascist Italian partisans advanced on his position, he fled with his mistress, Clara Petacci, and other supporters. They were captured by Italian Communist partisans led by Walter Audisio near Lake Como. Mussolini and his retinue were shot to death at Giulino di Mezzegra on April 28, 1945, and their bodies were hung and displayed in the Milan piazza.

PIETRO BADOGLIO (Prime Minister; July 25, 1943–December 10, 1944). Pietro Badoglio was born in Piedmont at Grazzano Monferrato on September 28, 1871. He attended the Turin Military Academy and graduated from the Army War College. He was commissioned as a second lieutenant and saw action in Ethiopia in 1896, barely surviving the massacre at Adowa that led to Italy's defeat. He also fought during the Libyan conflict in 1911 and 1912. He was promoted to the rank of colonel during World War I and he led an assault against the Austrians at Monte Sabotino in August 1916. Badoglio was the commanding general of the 27th Army Corps during the Italian military defeat of Caporetto in November 1917. Though Badoglio was held by some to be accountable for the defeat, he was named deputy chief of staff to General Armando Diaz, the Italian commander. He was instrumental in planning Italy's strategy for the remainder of the war. He served as chief of staff of the Italian army from 1919 until 1921. He was an initial opponent of Fascism, assuring the king of the army's loyalty in the event of a Fascist coup. After Mussolini's ascension to power, Badoglio accepted the Fascist dictatorship. He was appointed to the post of Chief of the Armed Forces General Staff in June 1925. He was promoted to the rank of marshal in 1926. Badoglio was named marquis of Sabotino and served as governor-general of Libya from 1929 until 1933. He replaced General Emilio DeBono as commander of the Italian forces in Ethiopia in November 1935 and, after the conquest of Ethiopia in May of the following year, he was named duke of Addis Ababa. Badoglio opposed Italy's involvement in the Spanish civil war and World War II, and resigned his military position in December 1940 after Italy's disastrous invasion of Greece. Badoglio was called upon to head the government on July 25, 1943, following Mussolini's ouster. He negotiated an armistice with the Allies in September 1943, but his previous association with the Fascists forced his resignation on December 10, 1944. He retired from public life and died in Grazzano Monferrato on October 31, 1956.

IVANHOE BONOMI (Prime Minister; December 10, 1944–June 20, 1945). *See earlier entry under Heads of Government.*

FERRUCIO PARRI (Prime Minister; June 20, 1945–November 24, 1945). Ferruccio Parri was born in Turin on June 19, 1890. He worked as a high school teacher before joining the Italian army during World War I. He served with distinction and received four decorations for valor. After the war he became involved in anti–Fascist activities. Parri was arrested in 1926 for his part in aiding the escape from Italy of Socialist Party leader Filippo Turati. He gave a spirited defense and was sentenced to a minimal prison sentence. Parri remained an opponent of Benito Mussolini and was often arrested during the next decade. During World War II Parri led a partisan brigade that conducted a guerrilla war in northern Italy against German occupation troops. He became known by the code names "General Maurizio" and "The Uncle" and became the leader of the anti–Nazi resistance following the ouster of Mussolini. He was captured by the Germans in 1945, but was released after a short time in a prisoner exchange. Parri founded the Action Party after the war. He was selected to lead a government as prime minister on June 20, 1945, but was forced to resign on November 24, 1945, when the rightist parties withdrew from the cabinet in protest of his plans to dismantle several large corporations. Parri later founded the Republican Party. He was appointed to the Italian senate for life as an independent leftist in 1963. Parri died in a military hospital in Rome after a long illness on December 8, 1981.

ALICIDE DE GASPERI (Prime Minister; December 10, 1945–August 17, 1953). Alicide de Gasperi was born in Pieve Tesino, Trentino, on April 3, 1881. He was educated at the University of Vienna and became the editor of the newspaper *Il Nuovo Trentino*. De Gasperi entered politics and was elected to the Austrian Parliament in 1911, where he served as an Italian Irredentist representative. He was elected to the Italian parliament in 1921, following the union of his province with Italy. His opposition to the dictatorship of Benito Mussolini resulted in the shutting down of his newspaper and his arrest in 1926. De Gasperi was released from prison after serving sixteen months of a four-year sentence. He subsequently worked in the Vatican library, where he rose to the position of secretary-general. De Gasperi was active in the Italian resistance during World War II. Following the ouster of Mussolini, de Gasperi was named minister without portfolio in Ivanhoe Bonomi's cabinet in June 1944 and was appointed foreign minister in December 1944. He subsequently was elected leader of the Christian Democratic Party. De Gasperi replaced Ferruccio Parri as Italy's prime minister on December 10, 1945. During his term of office, Italy's economy improved, and the country regained international prestige. The Christian Democratic Party was unable to capture an absolute majority in the elections in June 1953, however, and de Gasperi's government lost a vote of confidence the following month. He stepped down as prime minister on August 17, 1953. He remained leader of the Christian Democrats until his resignation in June 1954. He died of a heart attack in Sella di Valsugana, Trentino, on August 19, 1954.

Japan

Japan is a country that comprises a chain of islands off the east coast of Asia.

HEADS OF STATE

MUTSUHITO (*Meiji*) (Emperor; February 13, 1867–July 30, 1912). Mutsuhito was born in Kyoto on November 3, 1852, the son of Emperor Komei. He ascended to the throne on February 13, 1867. Shortly after his ascension the *Meiji* Restoration abolished the power of the shogunate and returned authority to the emperor. The shogunate was the military-style government that had been the dominant power in Japan since 1185. The Tokugawa family had held the shogunate since 1603. The shogunate fell in disfavor because of its inability to prevent Western encroachments on Japan following Commodore Matthew Perry's mission to the island in 1853. The emperor, with the support of feudal lords in southwestern Japan and nobles in the royal court, forced shogun Tokugawa Keiki to give up his power. The shogun resisted confiscation of his feudal holdings, but was defeated after a short battle with the imperial army. Mutsuhito took the reigning name *Meiji*, or enlightened rule. The emperor emerged from the traditional seclusion of the court to exercise executive power. Mutsuhito married Princess Haruko in February 1869. The feudal system was abolished in 1871, and the Satsuma rebellion was suppressed in 1877. He promoted a constitution in February 1889 and established the modern era of Japan. During his reign Japan built a modern army and was victorious in a war against China in 1894. The subsequent peace settlement ceded Formosa, the Pescadores Islands, and Liaotung Peninsula to the Japanese, and both countries agreed to recognize the independence of Korea. The Western powers forced the return of Liaotung Peninsula to China to maintain their influence there. Japan signed a treaty of alliance with Great Britain in 1902. Russia's incursions into Korea and Manchuria precipitated the Russo-Japanese War of 1904–1905. The Japanese navy attacked the Russian fleet at Port Arthur and destroyed the Russian Baltic Fleet during the conflict. The Russians agreed to Japan's terms for peace, recognizing Japan's supremacy over Korea and ceding their interests in Manchuria. During Mutsuhito's reign Japan became the leading military power in Asia. Mutsuhito continued to rule until his death from acute nephritis and complications from diabetes on July 30, 1912.

YOSHIHITO (Taisho) (Emperor; July 30, 1912–December 25, 1926). Yoshihito was born on August 31, 1879, the son of Emperor Mutsuhito. He was educated at the royal court and was instructed in military science. He served in both the army and the navy and was proclaimed heir apparent in 1889. Yoshihito married Princess Masako in 1900. He succeeded to the throne upon the death of his father on July 30, 1912. He was crowned on November 10, 1915, proclaiming the era of *Taisho*, or Righteousness. Yoshihito ruled Japan throughout World War I, and the country emerged from the conflict with great influence in Asia. The emperor suffered from poor health since childhood. His physical and mental health failed to such a point that the Crown Prince Hirohito was designated as regent in November 1921. Yoshihito died on December 25, 1926.

HIROHITO (Emperor; December 25, 1926–January 7, 1989). Hirohito was born in the Aoyama Palace in Tokyo on April 29, 1901. He was the son of Crown Prince Yoshihito. He was educated by tutors and at the Peers' School and developed an interest in natural history and marine biology. Hirohito was proclaimed heir apparent on September 9, 1912, when his father was crowned emperor. Hirohito became the first Japanese prince to travel abroad when he visited Europe in 1921. He was appointed prince regent in November 1921 due to his father's physical and mental illness. Hirohito married Princess Nagako Kuni in January 1924. He succeeded to the throne upon his father's death on December 25, 1926. He designated his reign as *Showa*, or Enlightened Peace. Hirohito initially supported a policy of moderation in regard to Japan's military activities. He reportedly opposed the army's actions in Manchuria in the late 1920s that culminated in the annexation of Manchuria in 1931. Hirohito ordered the suppression of a rightist revolt in February 1936. He also opposed the entry of Japan into war against the United States because he feared the risks involved in such a confrontation. He was unable to convince his ministers of his points of view, however, and ultimately supported his gov-

ernment's actions. Japan was on the verge of defeat in the summer of 1945 after atomic bombs devastated the cities of Hiroshima and Nagasaki. While the nation's leaders debated whether to surrender to the Allies or resist an invasion of the home islands, Hirohito made the decision for peace. He declared Japan's surrender in a radio address on August 15, 1945. The Allies declined to try Hirohito as a war criminal and retained him as emperor. He was forced to renounce his divinity, however, and the Japanese Constitution was changed to reflect the emperor's role as "the symbol of the state and the unity of the people." The occupation forces pressed Hirohito to become more accessible to the Japanese people. The emperor's popularity soared under the newly established constitutional monarchy in 1952. Hirohito attended the opening of the Tokyo Olympic Games in 1964. When he traveled to Europe in 1971, he became Japan's first sitting monarch to travel abroad. He visited the United States in 1975 and was received at the White House by President Gerald Ford. Hirohito's health deteriorated in September 1988. He relinquished his duties to the Crown Prince Akihito. Hirohito died at the Imperial Palace of intestinal cancer on January 7, 1989.

HEADS OF GOVERNMENT

ARITOMO YAMAGATA (Prime Minister; November 8, 1898–October 19, 1900). Aritomo Yamagata was born in Choshu on April 22, 1838. He was active in the overthrow of the shogunate in 1868. He became the leader of the Choshu militia following the inception of the *Meiji* Restoration. Yamagata traveled to Europe to study Western military methods in 1869. He was instrumental in the modernization of the Japanese army. He also became a major political

figure in Japan and was named minister of war in 1873. He was chief of staff of the imperial forces during the Satsuma rebellion in 1877. He served as home minister in 1885 and headed the government as prime minister from December 24, 1889, until May 6, 1891. The following year he served as minister of justice. He was commander of the Japanese First Army Corps during the Sino-Japanese War in 1894. He was promoted to the rank of field marshal in 1898. He returned to head the imperial government as prime minister on November 8, 1898, and served until October 19, 1900. Yamagata was chief of staff during the Russo-Japanese War in 1904–1905. He was granted the title of prince in 1907. He remained a leading advisor to the throne as one of Japan's leading elder statesmen until his death at his home in Odawara on February 1, 1922.

HIROBUMI ITO (Prime Minister; October 19, 1900–June 2, 1901). Hirobumi Ito was born in Choshu on September 2, 1842, to a Samurai family. He traveled to Europe in 1863. At that time he had to be smuggled aboard a ship as Japanese were forbidden to leave the country. He studied the European military and came to favor the opening of Japan to the West. Following the overthrow of the shogunate and the restoration of imperial powers under Emperor Mutsuhito, Ito served in the foreign ministry. He soon became governor of Hyogo Prefecture. Ito traveled to the United States to study Western currency systems in 1870 and returned to Japan to direct the tax division and national mint. He became minister of public works in 1873. He was named home minister in 1878, becoming one of Japan's leading political figures. He was the first prime minister of Japan under the new cabinet system when he took office on December 22, 1885. Ito resigned that office to head the privy council on April 30, 1888, and was instrumental in the promulgation of a constitution in 1889. He also became head of the upper house, the House of Peers, in 1890. He again was head of a government on August 8, 1892. He led the Japanese delegation to sign the Treaty of Shimonoseki with China following the Sino-Japanese War in 1895. He remained prime minister until September 18, 1896. He again headed the government from January 12, 1898, until June 30, 1898, when he resigned over the issues of imposing additional land taxes.

He formed the Friends of Constitutional Government Party in 1900 and formed a new government as prime minister on October 19, 1900, but resigned from office on June 2, 1901. Ito subsequently traveled to Russia to establish better trade relations. He returned to Japan to again head the privy council in 1903. After the Russo-Japanese War, Ito signed the Korean-Japanese Convention in 1905, which granted Japan full authority over Korea's foreign affairs. He became the first Japanese resident-general of Korea in 1906. He forced the abdication of the Korean emperor and established the country as a Japanese protectorate. He resigned in 1909 to again head the privy council. Ito was touring Manchuria when he was assassinated at a railway station in Harbin by An Chung Gun, a Korean nationalist, on October 26, 1909.

TARO KATSURA (Prime Minister; June 2, 1901–January 7, 1906). Taro Katsura was born to a Samurai family in Choshu on November 28, 1847. He fought with the imperial forces against the shogunate in 1868. In 1870 he left for Germany to study military science for a few years. He served as Japan's military attaché to Germany from 1875 until 1878. Katsura was promoted to major general in 1885. He was a general in the Third Division during the Sino-Japanese War in 1894. He was named governor general of Formosa in 1896 and served as minister of the army from 1898 until 1900. Katsura was called upon to succeed Hirobumi Ito as prime minister on June 2, 1901. His government signed the Anglo-Japanese Alliance agreement in 1902 and conducted a successful war against Russia in 1904 and 1905. The opposition Seiyukai Party gained a majority in the Diet and Katsura relinquished office to Kimmochi Saionji on January 7, 1906. He returned to head the government on July 14, 1908. Japan annexed Korea in 1910. Katsura brutally crushed the Socialist movement in Japan in 1910 and had many of the party's leaders executed on charges of plotting against the emperor. He again relinquished office to Saionji on August 30, 1911. Katsura was granted the title of prince soon after leaving office. He was again called upon to serve as prime minister on December 21, 1912, shortly after the death of Emperor Mutsuhito. His government was faced with rising discontent as riots and demonstrations took place over ever-increasing taxes to expand the military. Katsura attempted to confront the opposition Seiyukai Party by forming the Doshikai Party in 1913, but was forced to resign on February 11, 1913, as the crisis deepened. Katsura's health failed soon after he left office, and he died in Tokyo on October 10, 1913.

KIMMOCHI SAIONJI (Prime Minister; January 7, 1906–July 14, 1908). Kimmochi Saionji was born in Kyoto in October 1849. The son of a court noble, he was adopted by the Saionji family at the age of 2. He was involved in the restoration of the power of the emperor and the removal of the shogunate in the 1860s. He subsequently went to France where he studied European law until 1881. He returned to Japan to found the Meiji Law School. During the 1880s he served as Japan's minister to Austria and Germany. He returned to Japan to serve on the privy council and was vice president of the House of Peers. He was named to the cabinet in 1892 as minister of education and served until 1896 and again in 1898. He subsequently served as president of the privy council. He was an early member of the Seiyukai Party in 1900 and succeeded Hirobumi Ito as leader of the party in 1903. Over the next decade Saionji alternated the prime ministership with Taro Katsura several times. Saionji headed the government from January 7, 1906, until July 14, 1908. He again became prime minister on August 30, 1911, but his government was forced to resign on December 21, 1912, when the cabinet refused to add two additional divisions to the army.

Saionji resigned as leader of the Seiyukai Party the following year. He headed the Japanese delegation to the Paris Peace Conference after World War I in 1919 and was granted the title of prince. Saionji continued to exercise considerable influence with the emperor and the government as the last of the genro (elder statesmen). He was considered a moderate who favored good relations with Great Britain and the United States. He survived several assassination attempts by extremists following Japan's occupation of Manchuria in 1931. Saionji died at the age of ninety-one on November 24, 1940.

TARO KATSURA (Prime Minister; July 14, 1908–August 30, 1911). *See earlier entry under Heads of Government.*

KIMMOCHI SAIONJI (Prime Minister; August 30, 1911–December 21, 1912). *See earlier entry under Heads of Government.*

TARO KATSURA (Prime Minister; December 21, 1912–February 20, 1913). *See earlier entry under Heads of Government.*

GOMBEI YAMAMOTO (Prime Minister; February 20, 1913–April 16, 1914). Gombei Yamamoto was born in Satsuma Province in October 1852. He fought with the imperial forces against the shogunate in 1867. Soon after the Meiji Restoration, Yamamoto entered the Naval Training Academy. He graduated in 1874 and subsequently served aboard a German warship. He spent the next decade at sea and was promoted to captain in 1890. He was instrumental in planning Japan's naval strategy during the Sino-Japanese War in 1894 and was promoted to rear admiral the following year. He served in several cabinets as minister of the navy from 1898 until 1906. He was named to succeed Taro Katsura as prime minister on February 20, 1913. He introduced several reforms in the government before being forced to resign over a scandal involving naval officers on April 16, 1914. He also resigned from the navy and was politically inactive until September 2, 1923, when he was again called upon to serve as prime minister. His government led recovery efforts after the destruction caused by the great earthquake that devastated Japan. Yamamoto stepped down on January 7, 1924, following an assassination attempt on Prince Hirohito. He retired from politics and was inactive until his death in Tokyo on December 8, 1933.

SHIGENOBU OKUMA (Prime Minister; April 16, 1914–October 9, 1916). Shigenobu Okuma was born in Kyushu, Saga Prefecture, in 1838. He supported the *Meiji* Restoration and became a diplomatic and commercial official in Nagasaki under the new government in 1868. He subsequently served as a junior councilor in the Tokyo central government. He was instrumental in modernizing Japan's currency system in 1870 and prepared Japan's first national budget. He became minister of finance in 1881, but was forced to resign over opposition to his support for representative government. He was a founder of the Kaishinto, or Constitutional Reform Party, in 1882. He also founded Waseda University in 1882. He was named foreign minister in Hirobumi Ito's government in 1888. The following year he survived an assassination attempt when a right-wing extremist threw a bomb at his carriage. He lost a leg in the attack and temporarily retired from politics. He returned to the cabinet as foreign minister in 1896 after founding the Shimpoto Party. He also became minister of agriculture and commerce in 1897. He was named prime minister of a coalition cabinet on June 30, 1898, but the government collapsed on November 8, 1898, after only five months. He subsequently formed a party splinter group and led the Kensei Honto until 1907. He subsequently withdrew from politics to be-

come president of Waseda University. He returned to head the government on April 16, 1915, and reorganized the cabinet following a bribery scandal involving several government officials. His government resigned on October 9, 1916, and he retired from politics. He became a prince in 1918 and died in Tokyo on January 9, 1922.

MASATAKE TERAUCHI (Prime Minister; October 9, 1916–September 29, 1918). Masatake Terauchi was born in Choshu in 1852. He entered the imperial army in 1871 and was wounded in the Satsuma Rebellion in 1878, losing the use of his right arm. He was promoted to major in 1879 and continued his military studies in France in 1882. He was appointed the first inspector general of military education in 1898. Terauchi was named minister of war in 1902. He served in that position through the Russo-Japanese War in 1905 and until 1910, when he was appointed the first governor general of Korea. He ruthlessly crushed opposition to the Japanese annexation in Korea. He was called on by the emperor to head the government on October 9, 1916, after the collapse of Shigenobu Okuma's cabinet. He led a cabinet of civil bureaucrats, which caused conflicts with the major political parties. He averted a vote of no confidence in the Diet in 1917 when the emperor dissolved the house and called for new elections. He was forced to step down on September 29, 1918, when the rice riots took place, charging the government had not enacted suitable legislation to deal with wartime inflation. He subsequently served on the privy council, holding the rank of field marshal. Terauchi's health declined in the fall of 1919. He lapsed into a coma and was pronounced dead on October 20, 1919, but regained consciousness following an injection of camphor. He died two weeks later in Tokyo on November 3, 1919.

TAKASHI HARA (Prime Minister;

September 29, 1918–November 4, 1921). Takashi Hara was born at Morioka on February 9, 1856. He entered the law school at the ministry of justice in 1875 but left before obtaining his degree. He subsequently worked as a reporter before joining the foreign ministry in 1883. He served as the consul in Tientsin before being appointed chargé d'affaires in Paris in 1886. He returned to Tokyo to serve as personal secretary to Munemitsu Mutsu, the minister of agriculture and commerce, in 1890. He subsequently served as Mutsu's vice minister at the foreign office in 1895. He was named ambassador to Korea the following year, but returned to Tokyo in 1897 to become the editor of a leading Osaka newspaper. He joined Hirobumi Ito's political party Rikken Seiyukai in 1900 and was elected to the Diet. He was named to Ito's cabinet as minister of communications in 1900. He became home minister in Kimmochi Saionji's cabinet in 1906 and again in 1911. He again held that position in several other cabinets in 1912 and also from 1913 until 1914. He subsequently retired from the government to serve as president of the Seiyukai party. He was called upon to form a government on September 29, 1918, after Masatake Terauchi's cabinet was forced to resign during the rice riots. He formed Japan's first party government. He initiated moderate electoral reforms, but opposed the universal suffrage movement. He continued to head the government until November 4, 1921, when he was stabbed to death by a young right-wing fanatic at the Tokyo railway station.

YASUYA UCHIDA (Prime Minister; November 4, 1921–November 13, 1931). Yasuya Uchida was born in Kumamoto in August 1865. He graduated from Tokyo University with a degree in law. He subsequently began a career in the diplomatic corps as an attaché in Washington. He became a secretary to the minister of agriculture and commerce in 1890. He served as secretary of the lega-

tion in London in 1893 and held the same position in Peking from 1895 until 1897. He served as vice minister for foreign affairs in 1900. Uchida represented Japan as minister at Peking from 1901 until 1906 and was minister to Austria from 1907 until 1909. He was subsequently appointed ambassador to the United States, where he served until 1911. He served as ambassador to Russia during much of World War I. He was named to Takashi Hara's government as foreign minister in September 1918, and he briefly served as acting head of the government following Hara's assassination on November 4, 1921. He relinquished office on November 13, 1921, when Korekiyo Takahashi formed a government. He remained in Takahashi's cabinet as foreign minister and retained that position in Tomosaburo Kato's government until 1923. He served on the privy council from 1925 until 1929 and was president of the South Manchuria Railway in 1931. He was recalled from political retirement to serve again as foreign minister in July 1932, when his office was instrumental in Japan's recognition of the puppet government of Manchukuo in Manchuria. He stepped down in September 1933. Uchida died of pneumonia in Tokyo on March 12, 1936.

KOREKIYO TAKAHASHI (Prime Minister; November 13, 1921–June 12, 1922). Korekiyo Takahashi was born in Sendai in July 1854. He began his education in Nagasaki before emigrating to the United States in 1870. The following year he became special interpreter for Prince Iwakara, Japan's first ambassador to the United States. He returned to Japan several years later to work as a clerk in the department of education. He became the first director of the newly formed Japanese Bureau of Patents and soon entered the banking industry. He became governor of the Central Bank of Japan in 1911. Takahashi served in various cabinets as minister of finance from 1913 to 1914 and again in 1918. He was named to head the government as prime minister on November 13, 1921, following the assassination of Takashi Hara. His government collapsed on June 12, 1922, following criticism of his handling of negotiations for the naval vessels treaty between Japan, the United States, and Great Britain. He again served in the cabinet as finance minister in 1927 and 1931. Takahashi also led a short-lived government following the assassination of Tsuyoshi Inukai on May 16, 1932, until Makoto Saito formed a government on May 26, 1932. He remained in the government as finance minister until May 1934, when he stepped down for reasons of advanced age. He was asked to resume his position in November 1934 following an economic downturn. He retained office until February 26, 1936, when he was shot and hacked to death with a sword by right-wing militarists who conducted a purge of moderate Japanese statesmen and politicians as part of a failed military uprising.

TOMOSABURO KATO (Prime Minister; June 12, 1922–August 24, 1923). Tomosaburo Kato was born in Hiroshima Prefecture in 1859. He attended the Imperial Naval Academy and served in the Japanese navy. He was chief of staff during the Russo-Japanese War in 1904–1905. He subsequently served as vice minister of the navy and commander of the Kure Naval Station. He was commander and chief of the First Fleet during World War I. He was named to Shigenobu Okuma's cabinet as minister of the navy in 1915 and held that position in several succeeding governments. He represented Japan at the Washington Conference and negotiated the Naval Limitation Treaty in 1922. He was named to head the government on June 12, 1922, following the resignation of Korekiyo Takahashi. He retained office until his death in Tokyo on August 24, 1923.

GOMBEI YAMAMOTO (Prime Minister; September 2, 1923–January 7, 1924). *See earlier entry under Heads of Government.*

KEIGO KIYOURA (Prime Minister; January 7, 1924–June 5, 1924). Keigo Kiyoura was born in Kumamoto Prefecture in 1850. He was the son of a Buddhist abbot and was trained for the priesthood from an early age. He rejected a religious career at the age of eleven and was adopted by Hidetatsu Kiyoura. He joined the ministry of justice in 1876 and was instrumental in drafting Japan's legal codes. He was appointed minister of justice in Masayoshi Matsukata's government in 1898. He retained that position and also served as home minister and minister of commerce and agriculture in Taro Katsura's cabinet in 1901. He entered the privy council in 1906, becoming president of the council in 1922. He was called upon to form a government composed largely of nobles on January 7, 1924. His government was attacked by the political parties, and he was forced to resign on June 5, 1924. Kiyoura remained a leading advisor to the government as an elder statesman. He was given the title of count by Emperor Hirohito in 1928. Kiyoura died in Tokyo on November 5, 1942.

TAKAAKI KATO (Prime Minister; June 11, 1924–January 27, 1926). Takaaki Kato was born in Hattori Sakoichi on January 3, 1860. He attended the Imperial University in Tokyo to study English law and graduated in 1881. He subsequently entered into a business career with the Mitsubishi Company. He married the eldest daughter of Iwasaki Yataro, the company's founder, in 1886. Kato entered government service the following year, serving in the foreign minister's office as private secretary. He was appointed Japan's ambassador to Great Britain in 1894 and worked toward an Anglo-Japanese alliance. He stepped down from his position and returned to Japan in February 1900. He was named foreign minister in Hirobumi Ito's cabinet later in the year and was elected to the Diet in 1902. He returned to the cabinet as Kimmochi Saionji's foreign minister in January 1906, but resigned over a policy dispute two months later. He was renamed ambassador to Great Britain in 1908 and was again foreign minister in Taro Katsura's cabinet in January 1913. Kato joined Katsura's Doshikai Party soon after and became leader of the party after Katsura's death in October 1913. He again became foreign minister in April 1914 and was instrumental in Japan's decision to enter World War I. His policies were opposed by the elder statesmen, and Kato left the cabinet in 1915. He was subsequently named to the House of Peers by the emperor. He became head of the newly formed Kenseikai Party the following year. Kato formed a government as prime minister on June 11, 1924, when his party's coalition won a majority in the Diet. His government was responsible for enacting universal male suffrage in April 1925. He re-formed his cabinet in August 1925 and continued to serve as prime minister despite failing health. Kato died in Tokyo after a bout of influenza on January 27, 1926.

REIJIRO WAKATSUKI (Prime Minister; January 29, 1926–April 17, 1927). Reijiro Wakatsuki was born in Shimane Prefecture on February 5, 1866. He attended Tokyo University and joined the finance ministry upon graduation. He was named to Taro Katsura's cabinet as finance minister in 1912 and joined Katsura's Doshikai Party. He again served as finance minister in Shigenobu Okuma's government in 1914. He became home minister in Takaaki Kato's coalition cabinet in 1924. He was named prime minister on January 29, 1926, following Kato's death in office. He was forced to resign on April 17, 1927, over a conflict with the privy council concerning his government's conciliatory foreign policy. Wakatsuki served as Japan's

chief delegate to the London Naval Conference in 1930 and promoted passage of the disarmament treaty. He again became head of the government on April 13, 1931, following the shooting of Yuko Hamaguchi by right-wing extremists. He was unsuccessful in curtailing hostilities in Manchuria later in the year. He stepped down on December 11, 1931, following dissension in the cabinet over forming a coalition government. He remained a leading advisor to the government in the role of elder statesman. He survived an assassination attempt by right-wing extremists in 1933. He opposed Japan's decision to attack the United States during World War II and was a witness at the war crimes trial in 1946. Wakatsuki died at his villa near Ito after a long illness on November 21, 1949.

GIICHI TANAKA (Prime Minister; April 20, 1927–July 2, 1929). Giichi Tanaka was born in Choshu in 1864. He attended the Army Academy and graduated from the Army War College in 1892. He was sent to Russia to study military science in 1898, returning to Japan to serve on the general staff in 1902. He served under Gentaro Kodama with the Manchurian army during the Russo-Japanese War in 1904–1905. He rose to the rank of major general and, in 1911, he became director of the military affairs bureau of the army. He was an advocate of Sino-Japanese cooperation during World War I and was instrumental in negotiating the Sino-Japanese Defensive Military Agreement in 1918. He was named minister of the army in September 1923. He stepped down from active duty to accept the leadership of the Seiyukai Party in April 1925. Tanaka succeeded Reijiro Wakatsuki as prime minister on April 20, 1927. He also served in the government as foreign minister. His government was responsible for a crackdown on Communist and other leftist organizations. He gave limited support to Chiang Kai-shek's nationalist revolution in China, and sent Japanese troops to several Chinese provinces in 1928. Japanese complicity in the assassination of Manchurian warlord Chang Tso-lin and opposition to the government's signing of the Kellogg Peace Pact forced Tanaka's resignation on July 2, 1929. He died of a heart attack in Tokyo on September 29, 1929.

YUKO HAMAGUCHI (Prime Minister; July 2, 1929–April 13, 1931). Yuko Hamaguchi was born Yuko Mizoguchi in Kochi Prefecture in April 1870. He married into the wealthy Hamaguchi family in 1889 and adopted his wife's surname. He subsequently attended the University of Tokyo where he studied mathematics and law. He worked in the ministry of finance after graduation and was elected as a representative to the Diet in 1915. He became a member of the Kenseika Party and served as minister of finance in Takaaki Kato's cabinets in 1924 and 1925. He served as home minister in Reijiro Wakatsuki's government in 1926. He became leader of the Minseito party in 1927. He was asked to form a government on July 2, 1929, following the resignation of Giichi Tanaka. The Minseito party gained a majority in the elections of 1930. Hamaguchi oversaw a policy of financial austerity to improve Japan's economy. He came into conflict with the army and rival parties over his government's acceptance of the disarmament measures agreed to at the London Naval Conference in 1930. Hamaguchi was shot and seriously injured by Tomeo Sagoya, a young right-wing extremist, at the Tokyo train station on November 14, 1930. Baron Shidehara, the foreign minister, acted as head of the government while Hamaguchi recuperated. He attempted to resume his duties on March 10, 1931, but was unable to. He underwent two more surgeries and stepped down on April 13, 1931. Hamaguchi died in Tokyo of his injuries on August 25, 1931.

KIJURO SHIDEHARA (Acting Prime Minister; November 14, 1930–April 13, 1931). Kijuro Shidehara was born in Osaka on August 11, 1872. He received a law degree from Tokyo Imperial University's Law College in 1895. He worked in the ministries of agriculture and commerce before entering the diplomatic corps in 1899. Shidehara served as counselor in the Japanese embassy in Washington in 1912 and was appointed to the same position in London in 1914. He was named Japan's minister to the Netherlands later that year, serving until 1915. He subsequently returned to Japan where he became vice minister of foreign affairs. In 1919 he was appointed Japanese ambassador to the United States, where he remained until 1922. Shidehara was made a baron in 1920. He returned to the cabinet as minister of foreign affairs in 1924 and served in that capacity in six cabinets until 1931. Shidehara briefly served as acting prime minister following an assassination attempt against Prime Minister Yuko Hamaguchi on November 14, 1930. He relinquished the government to Reijiro Wakatsuki on April 13, 1931, when Hamaguchi's condition prevented him from returning to office. Shidehara continued to serve as foreign minister until December 1931, when Wakatsuki's government collapsed. Shidehara's opposition to right-wing militarist policies resulted in his exclusion from subsequent governments. Shidehara's political career was not reestablished until after World War II. He was asked by Emperor Hirohito on October 6, 1945, to form a postwar government. He administered the reconstruction programs ordered by General Douglas MacArthur under the occupation. Shidehara promoted a democratic reform package, and on April 10, 1946, Japan held its first postwar election. The election resulted in no party receiving a majority. Shidehara was unable to form a coalition cabinet and stepped down on April 22, 1946. He remained acting prime minister until

Shigeru Yoshida took over the reins of government on May 22, 1946. Shidehara became vice prime minister in the Yoshida cabinet. He was subsequently elected speaker of the Diet and remained in that position until his death of a heart attack in Tokyo on March 10, 1951.

REIJIRO WAKATSUKI (Prime Minister; April 13, 1931–December 11, 1931). *See earlier entry under Heads of Government.*

TSUYOSHI INUKAI (Prime Minister; December 13, 1931–May 15, 1932). Tsuyoshi Inukai was born in Niwase, Okayama Prefecture, in 1855. He attended Keio University and entered journalism after graduation. He became active in politics and joined the Kaishinto party in 1882. He was elected to the Diet in 1890. He briefly served as minister of education in Shigenobu Okuma's cabinet in 1898. He formed the Kokuminto Party in 1910 and was an opponent of the government of Taro Katsura. He was an advocate of universal suffrage and opposed increased military expenditures. Inukai was named minister of communications in Gombei Yamamoto's cabinet in 1923. He again headed that ministry in Takaaki Kato's coalition government in 1924. He merged his party with the Seiyukai in 1925 and announced his retirement from the cabinet and politics. His supporters refused to accept his retirement and reelected him to the Diet. He became leader of the Seiyukai Party following the death of Giinchi Tanaka in 1929. He was called upon to form a government on December 13, 1931, following the collapse of Reijiro Wakatsuki's government. His party won a majority in elections in 1932 and embarked on an effort to improve Japan's economy. His proposal to recognize Chinese sovereignty over Manchuria brought him into conflict with the military. Inukai was shot to death at his official residence in Tokyo during an uprising by rightist military officers on May 16, 1932.

KOREKIYO TAKAHASHI (Prime Minister; May 16, 1932–May 26, 1932). *See earlier entry under Heads of Government.*

MAKOTO SAITO (Prime Minister; May 26, 1932–July 4, 1934). Makoto Saito was born in Iwate Prefecture in 1858. He attended the Naval Academy and rose through the ranks of the navy. He served as vice minister of the navy during the Russo-Japanese War in 1904–1905. He became minister of the navy the following year and was promoted to admiral in 1912. He stepped down from the cabinet in April 1914 when Gombei Yamamoto's government collapsed following a bribery scandal involving naval officers. He was appointed governor general of Korea in 1919 and adopted a moderate policy there. He retained that position until 1927. Following the assassination of Tsuyoshi Inukai by rebel military officers, Saito was called upon to form a government of national unity on May 26, 1932. His government recognized the puppet state of Manchukuo in Japanese-controlled Manchuria and withdrew from the League of Nations. His government resigned on July 4, 1934, following a bribery scandal involving officials at the ministry of finance. Saito was considered a moderate in the military and was killed by right-wing militarists who conducted a purge of moderate Japanese statesmen and politicians as part of a failed military uprising on February 26, 1936.

KEISUKE OKADA (Prime Minister; July 8, 1934–March 9, 1936). Keisuke Okada was born in Fukui Prefecture in 1868. He attended the Naval Academy and Naval War College. He served in the navy during the Sino-Japanese War in 1894–1895 and in the Russo-Japanese War in 1904–1905. He became director of the Torpedo School in 1908. He was promoted to vice admiral in 1916 and placed in charge of the Sasebo Naval Arsenal. He rose to the rank of admiral in

1924 and served on the war council. He was appointed minister of the navy in Giichi Tanaka's cabinet in 1927. He served in that position until 1929 and again from 1932 until 1934. He was called upon to form a government as prime minister on July 8, 1934, following the resignation of Makoto Saito. His moderate views on the expansion of the military led to a right-wing rising that resulted in the murder of several leading Japanese political figures on February 27, 1936. Okada narrowly escaped assassination when the militants burst into his residence and killed his brother-in-law by mistake. He was initially reported to have been killed in the assault. Okada resigned soon after, and was replaced by Koki Hirota on March 9, 1936. He subsequently assumed the role of elder statesman. He opposed the government of Hideki Tojo during World War II and was instrumental in Tojo's ouster in 1944. Okada died at his home in Tokyo on October 17, 1952.

KOKI HIROTA (Prime Minister; March 9, 1936–January 23, 1937). Koki Hirota was born in Fukuoka Prefecture in 1878. He attended Tokyo University and, upon graduation, entered the diplomatic corps. He served in diplomatic positions in China, Great Britain, the United States, and the Netherlands. He served as Japan's ambassador to the Soviet Union from 1930 until 1932, where he negotiated a fishing agreement. He served as foreign minister in Makoto Saito's government from 1933 until 1934 and in Keisuke Okada's cabinet from 1934 until 1936. He was named to head the government as prime minister on March 9, 1936, following the military uprising against the Okada government. Hirota was instrumental in vastly increasing Japan's military budget and expanded the development of heavy industry. His government also signed the Anti-Comintern Pact with Germany and Italy. He was forced to step down on January 23, 1937, over a confrontation in

the Diet over the military's interference in politics. He served as foreign minister in Fumimaro Konoe's cabinet from 1937 until 1939 and supported the military's policy when hostilities broke out between Japan and China. He was a senior advisor to the government during World War II. He unsuccessfully sought a peace settlement through the offices of the Soviet ambassador as Japan faced military defeat. Hirota was arrested by the United States occupation forces after the war and tried as a Class A war criminal by the Tokyo International Military Tribunal. He was convicted of war crimes and sentenced to death on November 12, 1948. Hirota was executed at Sugamo Prison outside Tokyo on December 23, 1948.

SENJURO HAYASHI (Prime Minister; February 2, 1937–May 31, 1937). Senjuro Hayashi was born in Ishikawa Prefecture in 1876. He attended the Army War College and served in the Japanese military. Hayashi later served as head of the War College and as commanding officer of Japanese troops stationed in Korea. Hayashi sent his troops in support of the Kwantung Army in Manchuria in 1931 without authority from Tokyo. He was recognized for his initiative and was named minister of the army in Makoto Saito's government in 1934. He retained that position in Keisuke Okada's cabinet in 1935. His dismissal of supporters of former war minister Sadao Araki aggravated the conflict between Kodoha and Toseiha factions in the Japanese army. This led to a military uprising by Kodoha officers on February 26, 1935. The coup attempt was thwarted after several cabinet ministers and military officials were slain. Hayashi resigned his position and retired from the military in 1937. He was called upon to head the government on February 2, 1937, following the resignation of Koki Hirota. Opponents of his government gained an overwhelming majority in general elections soon after, and

Hayashi resigned on May 31, 1937. He died in Tokyo on February 4, 1943.

PRINCE FUMIMARO KONOE

(Prime Minister; June 4, 1937–January 5, 1939). Fumimaro Konoe was born in Tokyo to an aristocratic family in October 1891. He attended Kyoto University, graduating with a degree in law in 1917. He served as a member of the Japanese delegation to the Paris Peace Conference in 1919. Konoe was an influential member of the House of Peers from the 1920s. He served as vice president of that body in 1931 and was president from 1933 until 1937. He was an advocate of eliminating Western imperialism in Asia. He was chosen to head the government on June 4, 1937, shortly before Japan invaded China. The inability of Japan to gain a quick victory over China led to Konoe's resignation on January 5, 1939. He subsequently served as president of the privy council. He was again called upon to serve as prime minister on July 22, 1940. During his term of office the Rome-Berlin-Tokyo pact was signed, which made Japan a partner of the Axis Powers, and the Burma Road was closed to the British soon after. Relations between Japan and the United States became strained in the Pacific, and economic and military pressure from the United States jeopardized Japan's expansion. Konoe formed a new cabinet on July 18, 1941. He attempted, without success, to moderate Japan's militant policies and resigned on October 18, 1941. Konoe held no official position for the remainder of World War II, though he was instrumental in forcing the resignation of General Hideki Tojo in July 1944. Konoe was named vice prime minister in Naruhiko Higashikuni's postwar cabinet in August 1945. He was involved in revising the Japanese constitution when the occupation authorities indicted him as a war criminal. Konoe committed suicide by taking poison at his Tokyo home on December 16, 1945, rather than turn himself over for confinement and trial.

KIICHIRO HIRANUMA

(Prime Minister; January 5, 1939–August 23, 1939). Kiichiro Hiranuma was born in Okayama Prefecture in 1867. He attended Tokyo University and graduated with a degree in law in 1888. He subsequently entered the ministry of justice, where he worked in the prosecutor's office. He refused to allow the office of the prosecutor to be influenced by the political parties, which he felt were detrimental to the country. He was responsible for the conviction of 25 members of the Diet on charges of bribery from the Japan Sugar Company in 1909. He was also instrumental in forcing the resignation of Home Minister Kanetake Oura on suspected bribery charges in 1915. He served as vice minister of justice in 1923 and headed the justice ministry from September 1923 until January 1924. He was subsequently appointed to the privy council and became vice president of the council in April 1926. He held that position until becoming president of the privy council in 1936. Hiranuma was called upon to form a government as prime minister on January 5, 1939. His government debated a military alliance with Germany to oppose the Soviet Union. When Germany signed a non-aggression treaty with the Soviet Union, Hiranuma resigned on August 23, 1939. He was named home minister in the government of Fumimaro Konoe in December 1940, but he stepped down from office when Konoe resigned in October 1941. He was subsequently a senior advisor to the government and participated in discussions that led to the attack on the United States at Pearl Harbor in December 1941. Hiranuma was instrumental in the removal of General Hideki Tojo in July 1944, in hopes of gaining a negotiated peace to end the war. He was reappointed to the privy council in April 1945. He was arrested by the Allied occupation forces after the war and tried as a Class A war criminal by the International Military Tribunal in Tokyo. He was sentenced to life imprisonment at

Sugamo Prison on November 12, 1948. He suffered from poor health and advanced age and was released from prison for hospital treatment in June 1952. He died at a Tokyo hospital on August 20, 1952.

NOBUYUKI ABE (Prime Minister; August 30, 1939–January 14, 1940). Nobuyuki Abe was born in Ishikawa Prefecture in 1875. He attended the Military Academy and Army War College. He rose through the ranks of the army and served as chief of the military affairs bureau. He subsequently served as vice minister of the army until 1930, when he was named minister of state. He served as acting minister of war while Kazushige Ugaki suffered from poor health. Abe retired from active military duty with the rank of general in 1936. He was asked to form a government as prime minister on August 10, 1939, following the resignation of Kiichiro Hiranuma. Abe attempted, without success, to bring an end to the Sino-Japanese War and to maintain Japan's neutrality in the European conflict. He was unable to gain the support of the military or the major political parties and resigned on January 14, 1940. He was subsequently sent to Nanking as a special envoy to the puppet regime of Wang Ching-wei in the Japanese-occupied sections of China. He was appointed governor general of Korea in 1944. He surrendered the Japanese Seventeenth Army Group in Korea to the Allies in September 1945. Abe was listed as a war criminal by the Allied occupation forces after the war but was never indicted. He died in Tokyo on September 7, 1953.

MITSUMASA YONAI (Prime Minister; January 16, 1940–July 22, 1940). Mitsumasa Yonai was born in Iwate Prefecture on December 30, 1873. He attended the Naval Academy and rose through the ranks of the Japanese navy. He became commander in chief of the fleet in 1936 and was promoted to

admiral the following year. He was named minister of the navy in Senjuro Hayashi's government in February 1937, and retained that position in several successive cabinets. He was an opponent of Japan's alliance with the Axis Powers, favoring a pro–United States and Great Britain policy. He was named prime minister on January 16, 1940. He tried to head a moderate government in the face of growing pro–Axis sentiments in the army. His government's conflicts with the military forced his resignation on July 22, 1940. He served in several wartime cabinets as minister of the navy and was placed in charge of the dissolution of the navy following Japan's surrender at the end of World War II. Yonai died on April 20, 1948.

PRINCE FUMIMARO KONOE (Prime Minister; July 22, 1940–October 18, 1941). *See earlier entry under Heads of Government.*

HIDEKI TOJO (Prime Minister; October 18, 1941–July 18, 1944). Hideki Tojo was born in Tokyo on December 30, 1883. He was the son of Lt. Gen. Eikyo Tojo. He was educated at the Military Academy and the Army Staff College. He served as military attaché to Germany from 1919 until 1922. He taught at the Army Staff College after returning to Japan. He gained a reputation as a skilled commander and commanded the First Infantry Regiment in 1929. He was promoted to major general in 1933 and allied himself with the Toseiha faction in the army that supported advanced military technology. When the rival Kodoha faction, which was more ideologically driven, attempted a military coup in February 1936, Tojo was responsible for the arrest of coup sympathizers in Manchuria. He became chief of staff of the Kwantung army in Manchuria in 1937. He returned to Tokyo in May 1938 to serve as vice minister of the army in Fumimaro Konoe's cabinet. Tojo supported the expansion of the ongoing Sino-Japanese War. He became minister of the army in Konoe's second government in July 1940. He supported Japan's alliance with Germany and Italy. Tojo was named to head the government as prime minister following Konoe's resignation on October 18, 1941. He also retained the position of minister of the army. When his government could not reach an accommodation with the United States on Japan's plans to extend Japanese power in Asia and the Pacific, the Japanese military attacked the United States base on Pearl Harbor on December 7, 1941. Japan scored a succession of initial military victories in the Pacific, which increased Tojo's power in the government. As the war continued, the Allied counteroffensive began to drive the Japanese back. The Marianas Islands were liberated in 1944 and Saipan soon after. Tojo was held responsible for Japan's military setbacks, and a group of leading politicians and elder statesmen forced his resignation on July 18, 1944. Tojo was arrested as a Class A war criminal by the Allied occupation authorities following Japan's surrender in August 1945. He made an unsuccessful attempt to kill himself before he was imprisoned. He was indicted by the International Military Tribunal in Tokyo and convicted of war crimes on November 12, 1948. Tojo was hanged at Sugamo Prison outside of Tokyo on December 23, 1948.

KUNIAKI KOISO (Prime Minister; July 22, 1944–April 7, 1945). Kuniaki Koiso was born in Tochigi Prefecture in 1880. He attended the Army War College and entered the general staff office in 1913. He rose through the ranks of the army and headed the military affairs bureau of the army at the time of the rightist military coup attempt in March 1931. Koiso was named to Kiichiro Hiranuma's cabinet as minister of colonial affairs in 1939. He retained that position in Mitsumasa Yonai's cabinet in 1940. He was appointed governor-general of Korea

after the start of World War II. Koiso was recalled to Tokyo to head the government when Hideki Tojo was forced to step down on July 18, 1944. He attempted to regain momentum for Japan's war efforts, but increased air raids by the United States severely damaged war production. His government also tried unsuccessfully to arrange a negotiated peace through the Soviet Union. Koiso resigned on April 7, 1945, following the fall of Okinawa. He was arrested by the Allied occupation authorities following Japan's surrender and tried by the International Military Tribunal in Tokyo as a Class A war criminal. He was sentenced to life imprisonment at Sugamo Prison on November 12, 1948. Koiso died of a chest tumor at the United States Army Hospital in Tokyo on November 3, 1950.

KANTARO SUZUKI (Prime Minister; April 7, 1945–August 17, 1945). Kantaro Suzuki was born in Osaka on December 24, 1867. He attended the Naval Academy and the Naval War College. He participated in the Sino-Japanese War in 1894–1895 and the Russo-Japanese War in 1904–1905. He subsequently served as head of the Naval Academy and commander of the Kure Naval Station. Suzuki was promoted to admiral in 1923. He was appointed chief of the naval general staff in 1925. He retired from active duty in 1929 and was appointed grand chamberlain by the emperor. Suzuki was seriously injured during a right-wing military coup attempt on February 26, 1936. He was appointed president of the privy council in August 1944. He was called upon to replace Kuniaki Koiso as head of the government on April 7, 1945. Japan's military situation continued to deteriorate, and Suzuki's government tried to arrange a negotiated peace accord. The Allies refused to negotiate, and the United States destroyed the cities of Hiroshima and Nagasaki in early August 1945. The Soviet Union declared war on Japan soon after, and Suzuki's government accepted the terms of the Potsdam Declaration, surrendering unconditionally on August 14, 1945. The government resigned on August 16, 1945. Suzuki died of a liver ailment after a long illness at his home in Chiba Prefecture on April 17, 1948.

NARUHIKO HIGASHIKUNI (Prime Minister; August 17, 1945–October 9, 1945). Naruhiko Higashikuni was born in 1887. He was a member of the Japanese royal family and the uncle of Emperor Hirohito. He attended the Tokyo Military Academy and was stationed as a military attaché in Paris in 1920. His playboy reputation resulted in his recall to Japan in 1927. Higashikuni remained in the military, and in 1937 he was named chief of military aviation. Two years later he was promoted to general,

and following the Japanese attack on Pearl Harbor in December 1941, he was named to head the home defense headquarters. Following the defeat of Japan at the conclusion of World War II, Higashikuni was named by the emperor to form the first postwar cabinet on August 17, 1945. His government was unable to restore order to the country, and he resigned on October 9, 1945. Higashikuni was stripped of his royal title during the Allied occupation of Japan and became a Buddhist monk. He spent the remainder of his days away from political affairs and died at the age of 102 on January 20, 1990.

KIJURO SHIDEHARA (Prime Minister; October 9, 1945–May 22, 1946). *See earlier entry under Heads of Government.*

Latvia

Latvia is a country in northern Europe on the Baltic Sea. It proclaimed its independence from Russia on November 18, 1918. Latvia was incorporated into the Union of Soviet Socialist Republics on August 5, 1940.

HEADS OF STATE

JAÑIS ČAKSTE (President; May 1, 1920–March 14, 1927). Jañis Čakste was born on September 14, 1859. He received a degree in law from Moscow University. He served as a public prosecutor with the Courland government until 1888, when he began a private practice. He also served on the municipal council in Mitau, where he was also editor of the publication *Tevija*, (Fatherland). He was selected by the Courland government to serve in the first Russian Duma in 1906. He protested the dismissal of the Duma and was deprived of his political rights by the Russian government. He was an active member of the Latvian independence movement in exile. Čakste was elected Chairman of the People's Coun-

cil when Latvia proclaimed its independence in November 1918. Čakste was chosen as the first president of independent Latvia on May 1, 1920, and was reelected to the position in 1925. He remained in office until his death on March 14, 1927.

GUSTAV ZEMGALS (President; April 8, 1927–April 9, 1930). Gustav Zemgals was born on August 12, 1871. He was a member of the Democratic Center Party and served as Latvia's first vice president under Janis Čakste. He succeeded to the presidency on April 8, 1927, following Čakste's death. He remained in office until April 9, 1930. Zemgals died on January 7, 1939.

ALBERTS KVIESIS (President; April 9, 1930–April 11, 1936). Alberts Kviesis was born on December 2, 1881. He was a leading jurist and a member of the Farmer's Union party. He served as vice president of the Latvian Chamber of Deputies in the 1920s. He was elected president of Latvia on April 9, 1930. He retained the presidency until the election of Karlis Ulmanis on April 11, 1936. Kviesis died in Latvia during the German occupation in August 1944.

KĀRLIS ULMANIS (President; April 11, 1936–July 21, 1940). Kārlis Ulmanis was born in 1877. He was a leading agricultural expert and headed the first government of independent Latvia from November 18, 1918 until January 1919. He again served as prime minister from July 16, 1919, until he was forced to resign on June 18, 1921, when the extreme parties criticized his government's agrarian reform policies. He was a leader of the Farmer's Union Party and again headed the government from December 24, 1925, until May 6, 1926, and from March 27, 1931, until December 5, 1931. Ulmanis succeeded Adolfs Blodnieks as prime minister on March 17, 1934. He and General Janis Balodis led a coup d'état on May 15, 1934, with Ulmanis remaining as prime minister and minister of foreign affairs. The new government dismissed the Saeima (parliament), outlawed political parties, and purged Socialists from the government. Ulmanis also became Latvia's president on April 11, 1936. He remained in power until forced from office by the Soviet Union on July 21, 1940. He was deported to the Soviet Union where he died in 1942.

HEADS OF GOVERNMENT

KĀRLIS ULMANIS (Prime Minister; November 18, 1918–January 1919). *See earlier entry under Heads of State.*

PETERIS STUČKA (Prime Minister; January 1919–April 28, 1919). Peteris Stučka was born in Koknese on July 26, 1865. He graduated with a degree in law from the University of St. Petersburg in Russia in 1888. He soon became involved in revolutionary activities and was a founder of the Latvian Social Democratic Labor Party in 1904. Stučka moved to St. Petersburg in 1906 but continued to be involved in Latvian revolutionary activities. He participated in the Communist rebellion in Russia in 1917, becoming people's commissar of justice from November 1917 until March 1918. Stučka was recognized as chairman of the Soviet Government of Latvia from January 1919 to April 28, 1919. Stučka subsequently became a leading jurist in the Soviet Union. He was a professor at Moscow State University and a founder of the Institute of Soviet Law in 1931. He died in Moscow on January 25, 1932.

ANDRIEVS NIEDRA (Prime Minister; April 28, 1919–July 16, 1919). Andrievs Niedra was born in Tirza on February 8, 1871. Niedra briefly served as prime minister of Latvia from April 28, 1919, until July 16, 1919, when Kārlis Ulmanis again headed the government. Niedra died in Riga on September 25, 1942.

KĀRLIS ULMANIS (Prime Minister; July 16, 1919–June 18, 1921). *See earlier entry under Heads of State.*

ZIGFRĪDS A. MEIEROVICS (Prime Minister; June 19, 1921–January 26, 1923). Zigfrīds A. Meierovics was born in 1887. He was an economics professor and was active in the independence movement in exile in 1917. He was a member of the Farmers' Union party and became foreign minister of Latvia in

Kārlis Ulmanis' government in 1920. He was selected as Latvia's prime minister on June 19, 1921, while also continuing in his role as foreign minister in the government. He resigned on January 25, 1923. He returned to head the government on June 28, 1923, and served until January 26, 1924. He died on August 23, 1925.

JĀNIS PAUĻUKS (Prime Minister; January 27, 1923–June 27, 1923). Jānis Pauļúks was born in 1865. He served as Latvia's prime minister from January 27, 1923, until June 27, 1923. He perished during World War II in 1943.

ZIGFRĪDS A. MEIEROVICS (Prime Minister; June 28, 1923–January 26, 1924). *See earlier entry under Heads of Government.*

VOLDEMARĀS ZĀMUĒLIS (Prime Minister; January 27, 1924–December 18, 1924). Voldemarās Zāmuēlis was born on May 22, 1872. He was a lawyer and founder of the Constitutional Democratic Party. He was elected leader of the Latvian Provisional National Council in 1917. Zāmuēlis was chosen to succeed Zigfrīds Meierovics as prime minister on January 27, 1924. He resigned on December 18, 1924. He died in 1948.

HUGO CELMINŠ (Prime Minister; December 19, 1924–December 23, 1925). Hugo Celminš was born in 1877. He was a member of the Farmers' Union Party and was selected as prime minister of Latvia on December 19, 1924. He was succeeded by Kārlis Ulmanis on December 23, 1925. He returned to head the government on December 1, 1928, and served until his resignation on March 26, 1931. Celminš was deported to the Soviet Union in 1941, following the Soviet annexation of Latvia.

KĀRLIS ULMANIS (Prime Minister; December 24, 1925–May 6, 1926). *See earlier entry under Heads of State.*

ARTURS ALBERINGS (Prime Minister; May 7, 1926–December 18, 1926). Arturs Ālberings was born on December 26, 1876. He replaced Kārlis Ulmanis as prime minister on May 7, 1926, and served until December 18, 1926. He died in 1934.

MARGERS SKUJENIEKS (Prime Minister; December 19, 1926–January 24, 1928). Margers Skujenieks was born on June 23, 1886. Skujenieks served as prime minister of a government of Socialists and Democrats from December 19, 1926, with his government negotiated a trade agreement with the Soviet Union that resulted in the Democrats leaving the coalition. The cabinet resigned on December 13, 1927, and Skujenieks was replaced as prime minister by Peter Juraševskis on January 24, 1928. He returned as prime minister of a coalition government on December 6, 1931. He also served as minister of the interior until his government resigned on March 23, 1933. He died during World War II in approximately 1941.

PETER JURAŠEVSKIS (Prime Minister; January 24, 1928–November 30, 1928). Peter Juraševskis was born in 1872. He was a lawyer who served in the Russian Duma in 1906. He served as minister of justice in Kārlis Ulmanis's provisional government from 1918 until 1921. He was a member of the Democratic Center Party and was chosen to head the government on January 24, 1928, serving until November 30, 1928. He died in 1945.

HUGO CELMINŠ (Prime Minister; December 1, 1928–March 26, 1931). *See earlier entry under Heads of State.*

KĀRLIS ULMANIS (Prime Minister; March 27, 1931–December 5, 1931). *See earlier entry under Heads of State.*

MARGERS SKUJENIEKS (Prime Minister; December 6, 1931–March 23,

1933). *See earlier entry under Heads of Government.*

ADOLFS BĻODNIEKS (Prime Minister; March 24, 1933–March 16, 1934). Adolfs Bļodnieks was born in 1889. He served in the Latvian army during his nation's war of independence against Russia in 1918. He was a founder of the Latvian New Farmers and Smallholders Party and was selected as Latvia's prime minister on March 24, 1933. He headed a non-Socialist ministry of the Center and Right. He resigned on March 16, 1934, and was replaced by Kārlis Ulmanis. Bļodnieks escaped from Latvia following the country's occupation by the Soviet Union in 1940. He settled in New York City in 1951, where he served as chairman of the Committee for a Free Latvia. Bļodnieks died in New York on March 21, 1962.

KĀRLIS ULMANIS (Prime Minister; March 17, 1934–June 19, 1940). *See earlier entry under Heads of State.*

AUGUSTUS KIRCHENSTEINS (Prime Minister; June 20, 1940–August 5, 1940). Augustus Kirchenšteins was born in Mazsakica on September 28, 1872. He graduated from the Iur'ev Veterinary Institute in 1902. He became involved in revolutionary activities soon after and was forced to leave Latvia. He returned to Latvia in 1917 and he continued his political activities. He became a professor of microbiology at the Latvian University in 1923. He was chosen to head a puppet government friendly to the Soviet Union on June 20, 1940. He presided over rigged elections that resulted in Latvia's incorporation into the Union of Soviet Socialist Republics on August 5, 1940. Latvia was occupied by the German army from July 1941 until October 1944. After the Soviet Union regained control of Latvia, Kirchenšteins was named chairman of the Presidium of the Supreme Soviet of the Latvian SSR. He was succeeded by Kārlis Ozolins in 1952. He died in Riga on November 9, 1963.

Lebanon

Lebanon is a country in the Middle East. It was granted independence from a League of Nations mandate administered by the French on November 22, 1943.

HEADS OF STATE

CHARLES DABBAS (President; May 26, 1926–January 28, 1934). Charles Dabbas was born to a Greek Orthodox family in Beirut in 1885. He received a degree in law and became closely involved with the French colonial authorities. He was selected by the French to be the first president of Lebanon under the French mandate on May 26, 1926. He worked closely with Sheikh Muhammad al-Jisr, the Sunni Muslim speaker of the senate, during his term of office. Dabbas attempted to expand the government's authority and services to areas outside of Beirut. Dabbas resigned as president on January 28, 1934. He subsequently moved to Paris, where he died on August 23, 1935.

HABIB AL-SAAD (President; January 28, 1934–January 20, 1936). Habib al-Saad was born to a Maronite family in Ayn Traz in 1866. He received a degree in law from the Jesuit St. Joseph University. He was named governor of Lebanon in 1918 by the al-Sharif government. He was elected to the parliament as a deputy in 1922. He was named prime minister on August 10, 1928, remaining head of the government until May 8, 1929. Saad was appointed president of Lebanon by the French high commissioner on January 28, 1934. He remained head of state until January 20, 1936, when he relinquished power to Emile Edde. Saad died in Beirut on May 6, 1942.

EMILE EDDE (President; January 20, 1936–April 5, 1941). Emile Edde was born in Beirut in 1886. He was a leader of the nationalist forces in Lebanon before his appointment by the French to serve as president on January 20, 1936. His conciliatory relationship with the French discredited him with the pro–independence movement. He stepped down as president on April 5, 1941. He subsequently headed the national bloc, which became a leading political force under Edde's son, Raymond. Emile Edde died on September 28, 1949.

ALFRED NACCACHE (President; April 10, 1941–March 20, 1943). Alfred Naccache was born in 1886. He was educated in Jesuit schools in Lebanon and studied law in Paris. He opened a law practice in Cairo and worked as an editor for several newspapers. He was a proponent of Lebanese independence and was placed under a death warrant by the Ottoman government for his views. Naccache returned to Lebanon after World War I and worked as a lawyer and jurist. He developed close ties with the French colonial powers and was chosen as Lebanon's president on April 10, 1941, following the resignation of Emile Edde. The French forced the resignation of Naccache and his prime minister, Sami es-Solh, on March 20, 1943, when the latter became too independent. Naccache remained active in politics and was elected to the parliament from Beirut

later in the year. He served in Camille Chamoun's government as a minister in 1953. He subsequently headed the social welfare department in the government of Fuad Chehab. Naccache retired from political affairs in the early 1960s. He died in Lebanon on September 26, 1978.

AYOUB TABET (President; March 20, 1943–July 26, 1943). Ayoub Tabet was born in Bhamdun to a Maronite family in 1874. He received a degree in medicine from the Syrian Evangelical School. In 1905 Tabet went to New York to practice internal medicine. He returned to Lebanon before the start of World War I. He escaped from the Ottoman authorities and went into exile in Paris and New York. He returned to Lebanon after the war and supported the French mandate in 1918. He was subsequently elected to the Lebanese parliament. Tabet was named secretary of state after the selection of Emile Edde as president in 1936. He was selected as Lebanon's acting president on March 20, 1943, and attempted to introduce reforms in electoral laws. His policies ran afoul of the French, who forced his removal from office on July 26, 1943. Tabet died in 1947.

PIERRE TRAD (President; July 26, 1943–September 20, 1943). Pierre Trad was born to a Greek Orthodox family in Beirut in 1876. He received a degree in law from the University of Paris and began a successful practice in Beirut, where he also became involved in political affairs. He was a signer of a petition in 1913 demanding the removal of Syria and Lebanon from Ottoman control. His activities resulted in a death sentence being issued against him by the Ottoman authorities. He left Beirut but returned after World War I to form the League of Christian Sects in support of a French mandate over Lebanon. He was elected to the parliament in 1925 and was instrumental in the drafting of the French-Lebanese Treaty of 1936. He served as speaker of the parliament from 1937 until September 1939. Trad was selected by the French to serve as Lebanon's president on July 26, 1943. He stepped down on September 20, 1943, following the election of Bishara el-Khoury. Trad died in Beirut on April 5, 1948.

BISHARA KHALIL EL-KHOURY (President; September 21, 1943–September 18, 1952). Bishara Khalil el-Khoury was born in Beirut on August 1, 1890. A Maronite Christian, he graduated from the Jesuit St. Joseph University in 1909. He subsequently went to Paris to study law and received a degree in 1912. He returned to Lebanon to practice law and also entered politics. El-Khoury fled to Egypt during World War I when the Ottoman Empire reestablished control over the country. He returned after the war and presided over Lebanon's court of appeal under the French mandate. He headed the government as prime minister from May 5, 1927, until August 9, 1928, and again from May 9, 1929, until October 9, 1929. He also served as minister of the interior in the government. El-Khoury was elected president of the Senate the following year. When the constitution was abolished in 1932, el-Khoury founded the Destour (Constitutional) Party and became its leader. He fought to restore the Lebanese Constitution and to gain independence from France for the country. He was defeated in the 1936 election for the presidency by Emile Edde, the pro–French candidate. El-Khoury was elected president on September 21, 1943, but was arrested shortly after taking power for trying to eliminate Vichy French influences in the country. British troops entered the country and enforced Lebanon's independence under an agreement with the Free French. El-Khoury succeeded in forcing all foreign troops from Lebanon in 1946. He also amended the constitution to allow for a second term of office when his term came to an end in 1948. He was widely criticized for this action and was accused of allowing his family to profiteer from his position. El-Khoury was forced to resign from office on September 18, 1952, and was succeeded by Camille Chamoun. He joined critics of Chamoun's government in 1957 in the hopes that he would again be chosen as president. He was unsuccessful in that endeavor and retired from politics. He died in Beirut on January 11, 1964.

HEADS OF GOVERNMENT

AUGUSTE PASHA ADIB (Prime Minister; May 31, 1926–May 5, 1927). Auguste Pasha Adib was born in Constantinople in 1860. He was a Maronite Christian who had gained financial experience while working in Egypt. Adib headed the first government of Lebanon as prime minister and minister of finance under the French Mandate from May 31, 1926, until Bishara Khalil el-Khoury took office on May 5, 1927. He again headed the government from March 25, 1930, until March 9, 1932. Adib died in Paris on July 12, 1936.

BISHARA KHALIL EL-KHOURY (Prime Minister; May 5, 1927–August 9, 1928). *See earlier entry under Heads of State.*

HABIB AL-SAAD (Prime Minister; August 10, 1928–May 8, 1929). *See earlier entry under Heads of State.*

BISHARA KHALIL EL-KHOURY (Prime Minister; May 9, 1929–October 9, 1929). *See earlier entry under Heads of State.*

EMILE EDDE (Prime Minister; October 11, 1929–March 20, 1930). *See earlier entry under Heads of State.*

AUGUSTE PASHA ADIB (Prime Minister; March 25, 1930–March 9, 1932). *See earlier entry under Heads of Government.*

CHARLES DABBAS (Prime Minister; March 9, 1932–January 29, 1934). *See earlier entry under Heads of State.*

ABD ABDULLAH BAITHUM (Prime Minister; January 29, 1934–January 30, 1936). Abd Abdullah Baithum (Baythum) headed the Lebanese government under the presidency of Charles Dabbas from January 29, 1934, until January 30, 1936, when Ayoub Tabet assumed the office. Baithum returned to head the government as secretary of state under President Emile Edde on September 21, 1939. He was granted full executive powers by the French until his government resigned on April 4, 1941. Baithum remained a leading figure in Lebanese politics and again served in Pierre Trad's government in 1943.

AYOUB TABET (Prime Minister; January 30, 1936–January 6, 1937). *See earlier entry under Heads of State.*

KHAYR AL-DIN AL-AHDAB (Prime Minister; January 6, 1937–March 18, 1938). Khayr al-din al-Ahdab was a Sunni Muslim who was called upon to form a government in Lebanon on January 6, 1937. He received a narrow vote of confidence in the chamber and reformed his cabinet as a National Union government in March 1937. He also took the position of minister of the interior three months later, causing Bishara el-Khoury's faction to withdraw its support from the government. Ahdab's government resigned on March 18, 1938, in the face of a vote of no confidence in the chamber.

KHALED CHEHAB (Prime Minister; March 21, 1938–October 24, 1938). Khaled Chehab was born in Hasbaya in 1892. He served as prime minister and minister of justice from March 21, 1938, until October 24, 1938. He was called upon to form a government composed primarily of neutral civil servants on September 30, 1952. Chehab also served in the cabinet as minister of the interior and justice. He was given dictatorial decree-making powers to carry out election reforms, grant political rights to women, and decentralize the government. He resigned on April 28, 1953, over criticism of civil service reforms that had resulted in the dismissal of numerous government employees.

ABDULLAH AL-YAFI (Prime Minister; November 1, 1938–September 21, 1939). Abdullah Aref al-Yafi was born in Beirut in 1901. He graduated from the Jesuit St. Joseph University in 1922. He subsequently attended the Sorbonne in Paris, where he received a doctorate in law in 1926. Yafi returned to Lebanon to practice law. He also entered politics and was elected to the Lebanese parliament in 1932. He was elected to the chamber of deputies in 1938 to represent Beirut. On November 1, 1938, he became prime minister, serving until September 21, 1939. During the 1940s Yafi became involved in the quest for Arab unity. He served on the Lebanese delegation to the conference founding the Arab League in 1944. He was appointed to the cabinet as minister of justice in December 1946 and served until April 1947. Yafi was asked to form a government as prime minister on April 7, 1951. He resigned from the government on February 9, 1952, and allied himself with Camille Chamoun. Their opposition brought down the presidency of Bishara el-Khoury. Yafi was again named prime minister on August 16, 1953, after Chamoun became president. He resigned on September 17, 1954, after being attacked in parliament for failing to follow through with the domestic reforms he had promised. Chamoun asked Yafi to form another government on March 20, 1956, but Yafi resigned on November 16, 1956, because he opposed Chamoun's pro–Western stance and his failure to sever diplomatic ties with Great Britain and France during the Suez Crisis. Yafi became a leading spokesman for the opposition in the parliament, but was defeated in parliamentary elections in 1958. He became a supporter of President Gamal Abdel Nasser of Egypt and called for unification of Lebanon and Egypt into the United Arab Republic under Nasser. Yafi was a leader of the abortive revolt in the spring of 1958. He subsequently became a rival of Muslim leader Saab Salaam and was defeated in parliamentary elections in 1960 and 1964. He again served as prime minister from April 10, 1966, until December 2, 1966. Yafi was named to replace Rashid Karami as prime minister on February 8, 1968. He offered his resignation in November 1968, following student demonstrations in support of the Palestinian Liberation Organization, but he was persuaded to remain in office. He resigned on January 8, 1969, after the Lebanese army failed to prevent an Israeli raid in Beirut.

ABD ABDULLAH BAITHUM (Prime Minister; September 21, 1939–April 4, 1941). *See earlier entry under Heads of Government.*

ALFRED NACCACHE (Prime Minister; April 10, 1941–December 1, 1941). *See earlier entry under Heads of State.*

AHMAD DAOUK (Prime Minister; December 1, 1941–July 24, 1942). Ahmad Daouk was born in Beirut in 1892. He served as prime minister from December 1, 1941, until July 24, 1942. He later served as Lebanon's ambassador to France. Daouk was called to form a caretaker government on May 14, 1960. He stepped down on July 20, 1960, following parliamentary elections.

SAMI ES-SOLH (Prime Minister; July 29, 1942–March 19, 1943). Sami es-Solh was born in Acca in 1890. He was educated in Beirut, Istanbul, and Paris, where he studied law. He became active in the Arab nationalist movement and was involved in an attempted revolt against the Ottomans in 1916. After World War I he traveled to Syria and Egypt to meet with other Arab leaders. Solh returned to Lebanon in 1920, where he served as attorney general. He was subsequently appointed a criminal court judge under the French mandate. He remained in the judiciary until he entered politics in 1942 and was elected to the parliament. Solh was appointed prime minister on July 29, 1942, and served until March 19, 1943. He again formed a government as prime minister on August 22, 1945, and remained in office until May 18, 1946. He returned to power on February 11, 1952, but was forced to resign on September 9, 1952, when political opponents charged his government with corruption. Solh returned as prime minister on September 19, 1954, and remained in office until he was forced to resign on September 19, 1955. He was again asked to form a government on November 18, 1956. He won a victory in parliamentary elections in June 1957, and retained office until September 20, 1958, when he resigned with President Camille Chamoun. Lebanon was in a state of civil disorder, and Solh was criticized for supporting Chamoun's calling for American forces to put down the Arab rebellion. Fearful for his life, Solh left the country aboard a United States military plane in 1958. He remained in Turkey for two years before he returned to Lebanon. He was defeated for reelection to the parliament in 1960 but was victorious in 1964. Four years later he was again denied reelection. He died in Beirut on November 6, 1968.

PIERRE TRAD (Prime Minister; July 22, 1943–September 25, 1943). *See earlier entry under Heads of State.*

RIAD ES-SOLH (Prime Minister; August 29, 1943–July 1, 1945). Riad es-Solh was born in Saida in 1894. He was active in the Arab nationalist movement and was arrested by the Turkish authorities during World War I. He was sentenced to death, but the sentence was commuted to deportation. He returned to Lebanon after the war and fought against the French mandate. Solh was again sentenced to death by a French court-martial, but was pardoned in 1924. He continued his opposition to French rule and opposed the Franco-Lebanese treaty of November 13, 1936. He was exiled by the French government, but again returned to Lebanon to form a government as prime minister on August 29, 1943. His government amended the constitution to remove the legal right of the French to administer Lebanon under a League of Nations mandate. Solh and his cabinet were arrested by French forces in Lebanon. When widespread demonstrations against the French occurred, the British stepped in to demand that Lebanon be granted full independence. Solh remained as the first prime minister of independent Lebanon until January 1, 1945. He was again asked to form a government on December 14, 1946. An attempt was made by the Syrian National Socialist Party to overthrow the Lebanese government in 1948. The leader of the attempt, Anton Sa'adeh, was sentenced to death and executed in 1949. His supporters vowed to seek re-venge against Solh, whom they held responsible for Sa'adeh's death. An attempt was made to assassinate Solh in March 1950. He stepped down as prime minister on February 13, 1951, and paid a state visit to King Abdullah of Jordan in July 1951. He was shot to death by members of the Syrian Nationalist Socialist Party on July 16, 1951, while en route to the Amman, Jordan, airport.

ABDUL HAMID KARAMI (Prime Minister; January 1, 1945–August 10, 1945). Abdul Hamid Karami was born in Tripoli to a leading Sunni family in 1890. He was the grand mufti, or Muslim religious leader, of Lebanon. He became a leading opponent of France's occupation of Tripoli and often clashed with the French authorities. He joined the Lebanese independence movement in the early 1940s. He was named prime minister of Lebanon by President Bishara el-Khoury on January 1, 1945. He announced the formation of the Lebanese National Army in May 1945. Karami resigned on August 10, 1945, after demanding that constitutional reforms be made to prevent corruption in the government. He became the leader of the independence bloc, and later the reform bloc, in opposition to el-Khoury's government. Karami died on November 23, 1950. His son, Rashid, inherited his father's political base and later served as Lebanon's prime minister on numerous occasions.

SAMI ES-SOLH (Prime Minister; August 22, 1945–May 18, 1946). *See earlier entry under Heads of Government.*

Liberia

Liberia is a country in western Africa. Founded by former slaves from the United States, Liberia was declared a free and independent nation on July 26, 1847.

HEADS OF STATE

WILLIAM D. COLEMAN (President; November 12, 1896–January 2, 1900). William David Coleman was born in Fayette County, Kentucky, in the United States on July 18, 1842. He emigrated to Liberia with his mother in December 1853. He was educated at a mission school and became a successful farmer and merchant. He entered politics and was elected to the house of representatives, serving as speaker from 1877 until 1879. He was subsequently elected to the senate from Montserrado. He was elected vice president in May 1891 under President Joseph Cheeseman and was reelected to the position in 1893 and 1895. He succeeded to the presidency when Cheeseman died in office on November 12, 1896. Coleman was reelected to the presidency in 1897 and 1899. His government's inability to control the fighting between Gola factions in the country forced his resignation on December 10, 1899, though he retained office until the selection of his successor on January 2, 1900. He was an unsuccessful candidate for the presidency against Arthur Barclay in 1903 and 1905. Coleman died in Clay-Ashland on July 12, 1908.

GARRETSON W. GIBSON (President; January 2, 1900–January 4, 1904). Garretson Wilmot Gibson was born in Talbot County, Maryland, in the United States on May 20, 1832. He emigrated to Cape Palmas, Liberia, at the age of three. He was educated at mission schools before returning to Maryland as a theological student in 1851. He returned to Liberia and was ordained an Episcopal priest. He became rector of Trinity Church in Monrovia. He also served as president of Liberia College from 1892 until 1896. He held several positions in the government of William Coleman, serving as secretary of the interior and secretary of state. Coleman resigned from the presidency on December 10, 1899. The vice presidency was vacant and Gibson succeeded to the presidency on January 2, 1900. He was reelected the following year and continued to lead Liberia until he relinquished office to Arthur Barclay on January 4, 1904. Gibson died on April 26, 1910.

ARTHUR BARCLAY (President; January 4, 1904–January 1, 1912). Arthur Barclay was born in Bridgetown, Barbados, on July 31, 1854. He emigrated to Liberia with his father in 1865. He attended Liberia College and subsequently served as a professor of mathematics and languages there. He studied law and opened a practice in 1880. He was appointed judge in Montserrado County in 1883. He was named to the cabinet as acting secretary of state in 1892 and served as secretary of the treasury from 1896 until 1903. Barclay was elected president in 1903, taking office on January 4, 1904. His government initiated a policy of cooperation with the native tribes of Liberia. He also negotiated a loan from Great Britain in 1907, but the country had difficulty in managing its foreign debt. Barclay was reelected several times before stepping down on January 1, 1912. He remained a leading figure in Liberian politics, holding such positions as secretary of state, treasury, interior, and war in subsequent governments. He was a supporter of Marcus Garvey's plans to set up an independent African republic in 1924, but President Charles King refused to grant visas to Garvey's allies. Barclay represented Liberia at the League of Nations in 1930. He died in Monrovia on July 10, 1938.

DANIEL E. HOWARD (President; January 1, 1912–January 5, 1920). Daniel Edward Howard was born in Buchanan, Grand Bassa County, on August 4, 1861. He was educated at Liberia College and became private secretary to President Hilary Johnson in 1884. He held several civil service positions and became secretary of the True Whig Party in 1900. Howard was superintendent of Montserrado County from 1900 until 1904 and secretary of the treasury from 1904 until 1912. He was elected president of Liberia in 1911, taking office on January 1, 1912. He attempted to maintain Liberia's neutrality during World War I. A German submarine attacked Monrovia in 1917 when the government refused to close the French wireless station there. The attack prompted the government to declare its support for the Allies. Howard remained in office until January 5, 1920. He died in Monrovia on July 9, 1935.

CHARLES D. B. KING (President; January 5, 1920–December 3, 1930). Charles Dunbar Burgess King was born in Freetown, Sierra Leone, in 1875. He was educated at Liberia College. He began a career in the government, serving as attorney general from 1907 until 1912. He served in Daniel Howard's cabinet as secretary of state from 1912 until 1920. He was elected to the presidency to succeed Howard and took office on January 5, 1920. His government denied visas to Marcus Garvey's African nationalist organization in 1924. He arranged a $5 million loan from the Finance Corporation of America after granting the Firestone Concession in 1926. Allegations of slavery and forced labor in Liberia led to the formation of the

Christy Commission, which implicated many high-ranking figures in the government, including King himself. King was forced to resign from office on December 3, 1930. He retired from politics and died on September 4, 1961.

EDWIN BARCLAY (President; December 3, 1930–January 3, 1944). Edwin James Barclay was born in Brewerville, Montserrado County, on January 5, 1882. He was the nephew of Arthur Barclay, Liberia's president from 1904 to 1912. Edwin Barclay graduated from Liberia College in 1903. He served in several government positions, including attorney general, before becoming secretary of state under Charles King in 1920. He succeeded to the presidency following the resignations of King and Vice President A. N. Yancy on December 3, 1930. He completed King's term and was reelected to the presidency in 1931. The United States refused to recognize Barclay's government until 1935, when he received a large majority for an eight-year term of office. He attempted to promote economic independence for Liberia and reestablish the country's international reputation in the wake of the slavery scandal. He was successful in avoiding the mandating of Liberia under the League of Nations. Barclay succeeded in arranging that William V. S. Tubman would be his successor and stepped down from office on January 3, 1944. He retired from politics for the next decade but returned to challenge Tubman for the presidency in 1953. He was defeated in a bitter campaign and retired to his estate in Harbel where he died on November 5, 1955.

WILLIAM V. S. TUBMAN (President; January 3, 1944–July 23, 1971). William Vacanararat Shadrach Tubman was born in Harper, Liberia, on November 29, 1895. He was educated locally and received a degree in law. He began a legal practice in 1917 and served as an official of the court. Tubman entered politics in 1923 and was elected to the senate. He stepped down from the senate in 1931 following a government slavery scandal. Tubman returned to the senate in 1934 and was appointed to the Liberian Supreme Court in 1937. Tubman was the candidate of the True Whig Party in the presidential elections in 1943 and was elected on May 4, 1943. He took office on January 1, 1944. Tubman, who was known in the country as "Brother Shad," encouraged foreign investment in Liberia and received financial assistance from the United States. Tubman sponsored a constitutional amendment to allow him another term in office. He was challenged by Didwe Twe in the presidential campaign in 1951. Twe was disqualified as a candidate, and Tubman was reelected unopposed in May 1951. He received little opposition in future elections. His opponent in the 1955 elections, William Bright, received 16 votes to Tubman's nearly 260,000. Liberia prospered under Tubman, and he was recognized as an elder statesman in Africa during the 1960s. Tubman remained president until his death from complications following prostate surgery at a hospital in London on July 23, 1971.

Liechtenstein

Liechtenstein is sovereign principality in central Europe.

HEADS OF STATE

JOHANN II (Prince; November 12, 1858–February 11, 1929). Johann Marie Franz Placide von und zu Liechtenstein was born in Eisgrub, Moravia, on October 5, 1840. He succeeded his father, Prince Aloys II, as ruling prince of Liechtenstein on November 12, 1858. Liechtenstein remained a part of the German confederation until 1866, when it achieved complete independence. The country's army was abolished two years later. Johann II was a popular ruler who personally financed the construction and upkeep of roads, schools, hospitals, and public buildings in the principality. Liechtenstein remained closely allied with Austria until 1919. In 1921 the country entered the Swiss customs union, with Switzerland administering the post, telephone, and telegraph systems. Johann was sometimes known as the "phantom prince" because of his penchant of hosting lavish parties without making an appearance. He continued to rule for seventy years until his death at his castle at Schloss Feisberg, Czechoslovakia, on February 11, 1929.

FRANZ (Prince; February 11, 1929–August 25, 1938). Maria Karl August Franz von Paula was born at Castle Liechtenstein on August 28, 1853. He was the son of Prince Aloys II, who ruled Liechtenstein from 1836 until 1858. He spent most of his early life in Austria and served in the diplomatic service there. He was Austro-Hungarian ambassador to Russia from 1894 to 1898. Franz succeeded his brother, Johann II, as reigning prince of Liechtenstein on February 11, 1929. The following July he married Else von Eroes, the former Baroness Guttmann. His consort was Jewish and the union was widely attacked by the Nazis in Germany. Much pressure was put on the tiny country to unify with Germany following the Austrian *Anschluss* in March 1938. The aging monarch named his grandnephew, Franz Josef, as regent and relinquished his powers. He continued to hold the title of reigning prince until his death at his castle at Feldsberg, Czechoslovakia, on August 25, 1938.

FRANZ JOSEF II (Prince; August 25, 1938–November 13, 1989). Maria Aloys Alfred Karl Johannes Heinrich Michael Georg Ignatius Benediktus Gerhardus Majella von und zu Liechtenstein was born in Frauenthal Castle in Austria on August 16, 1906. He was a nephew of Archduke Franz Ferdinand of Austria. Franz Josef was educated in Austria and Switzerland. His great uncle, Prince Franz, named him regent on March 30, 1938, due to failing health. He succeeded his uncle to the Liechten-

stein throne as sovereign prince upon his death on August 25, 1938. He was successful in keeping Liechtenstein neutral during World War II and was able to avoid occupation by the Germans. After the war, Franz Josef refused demands to extradite Russians who had sought refuge in Liechtenstein during the war. Liechtenstein became one of the world's most prosperous nations under Franz Josef. He was also an advocate of women's suffrage and succeeded in passing a referendum on the issue in 1984. Franz Josef relinquished most of his executive power to his son, Hans Adam, in August 1984. He died after a long illness in Grabs, Switzerland, on November 13, 1989.

HEADS OF GOVERNMENT

GUSTAV SCHAEDLER (Prime Minister; June 9, 1922–August 4, 1928). Gustav Schaedler was named prime minister of Liechtenstein by Prince Johann II on June 9, 1922, following the enactment of a new constitution that provided for elections to the Landtag (parliament). Schaedler completed his six-year term on August 4, 1928, and Franz Josef Hoop was named to succeed him.

FRANZ JOSEF HOOP (Prime

Minister; August 4, 1928–July 20, 1945). Franz Josef Hoop was born in Essen on December 14, 1895. He replaced Gustav Schaedler as prime minister of Liechtenstein on August 4, 1928, and retained office until July 20, 1945. Hoop subsequently served as president of the Landtag. He became president of the national court of justice in 1953. Hoop died in Chur, Switzerland, following complications from surgery on October 19, 1959.

Lithuania

Lithuania is a country in northern Europe on the Baltic Sea. It proclaimed its independence from Russia on February 16, 1918. Lithuania was incorporated into the Union of Soviet Socialist Republics on August 3, 1940.

HEADS OF STATE

ANTANAS SMETONA (President; April 4, 1919–May 15, 1920). Antanas

Smetona was born in Uzelenis on August 10, 1874. Smetona was a leading

Lithuanian nationalist who headed the Relief Committee of Vilnius during the 1910s. He was a leader of the rightists and was chosen as the first president of independent Lithuania on April 4, 1919. He was succeeded by Aleksandras Stulginskis on May 15, 1920. He again became president on December 19, 1926, following a military coup against the government of Prime Minister Mykolas Sleževičius. He was reelected in December 1931 but was forced to resign following the establishment of a pro–Soviet puppet government on June 16, 1940. He went into exile in the United States and died in Cleveland, Ohio, on January 9, 1944.

ALEKSANDRAS STULGINSKIS (President; May 15, 1920–June 6, 1926). Aleksandras Stulginskis was born in Kutaliai on February 26, 1885. He studied agriculture in Germany in 1913. He was a founder of the Lithuanian Christian Democratic Party during the German occupation from 1915 until 1918. He served in Lithuania's first cabinet after that nation's independence in 1918 and was instrumental in drafting the 1920 constitution. Stulginskis subsequently broke with the Christian Democrats to form the Lithuanian Peasant Union. He was elected president of Lithuania by the parliament on May 15, 1920. He was reappointed to a second term in 1923 and held the position until his resignation on June 6, 1926. He subsequently retired from politics to write and farm. Stulginskis was deported to Siberia when the Russians occupied Lithuania in 1940. He was sentenced to 25 years imprisonment in 1952, but was pardoned four years later and allowed to return to Lithuania. He died in Kaunas on September 22, 1969.

KAZYS GRINIUS (President; June 6, 1926–December 19, 1926). Kazys Grinius was born in Sulemos Buda on December 17, 1866. He was an early leader of the independence movement and a journalist with the populist newspaper *Varpas* in the 1890s. Grinius served as Lithuania's prime minister from June 8, 1920, until February 2, 1922 and became president of Lithuania on June 6, 1926. He resigned following a military coup against the government of Mykolas Slezevicius and was replaced by Antanas Smetona on December 19, 1926. Grinius protested the actions of the German occupation forces during World War II and was banned from Kaunas. He remained in exile after the Soviet Union annexed Lithuania following World War II. He died in Chicago, Illinois, on June 4, 1950.

ANTANAS SMETONA (President; December 19, 1926–June 16, 1940). *See earlier entry under Heads of State.*

HEADS OF GOVERNMENT

AUGUSTINAS VOLDEMARAS (Prime Minister; November 11, 1918–December 28, 1918). Augustinas Voldemaras was born in Dysna on April 16, 1883. He was a professor at the University of Kovno. He served as head of Lithuania's first independent government from November 11, 1918, until December 28, 1918. Voldemaras was a leader of the Clerical Party and was chosen to head the government following a military coup against Prime Minister Mykolas Slezevicius on November 17, 1926. He was a virtual dictator of Lithuania, modeling his regime on the Fascist Party of Italy. Communists and other leftists were arrested under his government. He escaped an assassination attempt when a bomb was thrown at him in the streets of Kovno on May 7, 1929. He was ousted by President Antanas Smetona and Interior Minister Mutseikis while attending an assembly of the League of Nations on September 19, 1929. He was arrested in 1931 on charges of attempting to overthrow the government, but was acquitted. Members of the army attempted to restore Voldemaras to power in June 1934. He and his followers were arrested, and Voldemaras was sentenced to twelve years in prison. He was pardoned on the twentieth anniversary of Lithuania's independence in early 1938. He died in Moscow on December 16, 1942.

MYKOLAS SLEŽEVIČIUS (Prime Minister; December 28, 1918–March 12, 1919). Mykolas Sleževičius was born in Drembliai on February 21, 1882. He served as prime minister of Lithuania from December 28, 1918, until March 12, 1919. He returned to head the government from April 4, 1919, to October 7, 1919, and from June 7, 1926, until he was ousted in a military coup on November 17, 1926. While in office, he orchestrated a policy of friendship toward the Soviet Union. He and members of his government were arrested, but were released from custody soon afterward. He died in Kaunas on November 11, 1939.

PRANAS DUVYDAITIS (Prime Minister; March 12, 1919–April 4, 1919). Pranas Duvydaitis was born in Runkai on December 2, 1886. He briefly headed the Lithuanian government as prime minister from March 12, 1919, to April 4, 1919. He died during World War II in 1942.

MYKOLAS SLEŽEVIČIUS (Prime Minister; April 4, 1919–October 7, 1919). *See earlier entry under Heads of Government.*

ERNESTAS GALVANAUSKAS (Prime Minister; October 15, 1919–June 2, 1920). Ernestas Galvanauskas was born in Zizonys on November 20, 1882. He served as prime minister from October 15, 1919, until June 2, 1920. He was again called to head the government as leader of a coalition of Christian Democrats and the People's Party on February 2, 1922. He also served in the cabinet as foreign minister until his resignation on June 10, 1924. Galvanauskas remained a leading figure in Lithuanian politics, serving as finance minister during the late 1930s. He resigned and fled into exile following the Soviet annexation of Lithuania in 1940. He died in Aix-les-Bains, France, on July 24, 1967.

KAZYS GRINIUS (Prime Minister; June 8, 1920–February 2, 1922). *See earlier entry under Heads of State.*

ERNESTAS GALVANAUSKAS (Prime Minister; February 2, 1922–June 10, 1924). *See earlier entry under Heads of Government.*

ANTANAS TUMEURAS (Prime Minister; June 10, 1924–February 4, 1925). Antanas Tumeuras was born in Kurkliečiai on April 13, 1880. He served as prime minister from June 10, 1924, until February 4, 1925. He died in Bachmaning on February 8, 1946.

VYTAUTAS PETRULIS (Prime Minister; February 4, 1925–September 25, 1925). Vytautas Petrulis was chosen to head the Lithuanian government on February 4, 1925. He was forced to resign on September 25, 1925, following a miscommunication between the cabinet and the delegation at a Lithuanian-Polish conference. He died in 1942.

LEONAS BISTRAS (Prime Minister; September 25, 1925–June 7, 1926). Leonas Bistras was born in Liepnja on October 20, 1890. He was a leading member of the Christian Democratic Party. He served as prime minister of Lithuania from September 25, 1925, until June 7, 1926. He was arrested in December 1938 on charges of plotting the restoration of Augustinas Voldemaras to power. He died in 1971.

MYKOLAS SLEŽEVIČIUS (Prime Minister; June 7, 1926–November 17, 1926). *See earlier entry under Heads of Government.*

AUGUSTINAS VOLDEMARAS (Prime Minister; November 17, 1926–September 19, 1929). *See earlier entry under Heads of Government.*

JUOZAS TUBELIS (Prime Minister; September 23, 1929–March 25, 1938). Juozas Tubelis was born in Il-galankia on April 18, 1882. Tubelis was a relative of President Antanas Smetona and was named prime minister of Lithuania following the ouster of Augustinas Voldemaras on September 23, 1929. His government was forced to resign on March 25, 1938, following the shooting of a Polish soldier on the Lithuanian frontier and Poland's subsequent demand that Lithuania normalize relations with Poland. Tubelis died in Kaunas on September 30, 1939.

VLADAS MIRONAS (Prime Minister; March 25, 1938–March 27, 1939). Father Vladas Mironas was born in Kuodiškiai on June 22, 1880. He was chosen as prime minister on March 25, 1938. He resigned on March 27, 1939, and was succeeded by Jonas Černius. Mironas was deported after the Soviet Union's annexation of Lithuania in 1940.

He remained imprisoned by the Soviets and died in Vladimir Prison in 1954.

JONAS ČERNIUS (Prime Minister; March 27, 1939–November 21, 1939). Jonas Černius was born in Kupiskis on January 6, 1898. He was a general in the Lithuanian army and was chosen to succeed Father Vladas Mironas as prime minister of Lithuania on March 27, 1939. He stepped down on November 21, 1939. Černius went into exile following the Soviet annexation of Lithuania in 1940 and settled in the United States in 1948.

ANTANAS MERKYS (Prime Minister; November 21, 1939–June 17, 1940). Antanas Merkys was born in Bajorai on February 1, 1887. He was a colonel in the Lithuanian army. He became prime minister of a coalition government on November 21, 1939. He was forced to step down when the Soviet Union established a puppet government on June 17, 1940. He died in the Soviet Union in March 1955.

JUSTAS PALECKIS (Prime Minister; June 17, 1940–August 3, 1940). Justas Paleckis was a minor journalist in Lithuania when he was selected as prime minister on June 17, 1940, following the Soviet Union's demand for a friendly government. Paleckis presided over a rigged election in July 1940 that resulted in Lithuania's incorporation into the Soviet Union on August 3, 1940. Paleckis died on January 26, 1980.

Luxembourg

Luxembourg is a country in central western Europe.

HEADS OF STATE

ADOLF (Grand Duke; November 23, 1890–November 17, 1905). Adolphus William Charles Frederick Augustus was born on July 24, 1817. He succeeded his father as the Duke of Nassau in 1839.

Adolf sided with Austria in the Austro-Prussian War in 1866. He led the Nassau troops and his Duchy was annexed by Prussia after the war. He went into exile in Vienna where he remained for the next twenty-four years. Adolf became grand duke of Luxembourg when King William III of the Netherlands, who was also Luxembourg's grand duke, died in 1890. The Orange-Nassau family, with Adolf as the senior member, was granted the throne of Luxembourg when William failed to produce a male heir. Adolf arrived in Luxembourg on July 23, 1890, to ascend the throne. He proved to be an active monarch, despite his advanced age. He spent much of his time residing at his family estates in Bavaria until he was able to inhabit the Castle Berg in Colmar. He retained the throne until his death on November 17, 1905.

WILHELM IV (Grand Duke; November 17, 1905–February 25, 1912). Wilhelm Alexander was born on April 22, 1852, the son of Luxembourg's Grand Duke Adolf and Princess Adelaide of Anhalt. Wilhelm married Marie Anna, the Infanta of Portugal, in 1893. He succeeded to the throne upon the death of his father on November 17, 1905. Wilhelm reigned over Luxembourg during a period of economic prosperity. He was able to arrange legislation in the chamber of deputies that allowed female heirs to ascend to the throne of Luxembourg. Wilhelm suffered from poor health and his consort acted as regent from November 1908 until his death after a long illness on February 25, 1912.

MARIE ADELAIDE (Grand Duchess; February 25, 1912–January 15, 1919). Marie Adelaide was born on June 14, 1894, the eldest daugher of Grand Duke Wilhelm IV of Luxembourg. She succeeded to the throne upon the death of her father on February 25, 1912. She was initially a popular ruler until the start of World War I, when the German army demanded passage through Luxembourg to attack France. Though she protested the action, she made little effort to oppose the Germans, and Luxembourg was occupied during the war. Marie Adelaide was accused of harboring pro–German sentiments and of favoring a conservative government in the chamber of deputies despite Luxembourg's official policy of neutrality during the war. The leftist opposition won a majority during elections in 1915 and opposed Marie Adelaide's policies. Following Germany's defeat at the end of World War I, Marie Adelaide was forced to abdicate on January 15, 1919. She subsequently entered the Carmelite Convent as a nun. She died at Hohenburg Castle, in Bavaria, on January 24, 1924.

CHARLOTTE (Grand Duchess; January 15, 1919–November 12, 1964). Charlotte Aldegonde Elise Marie Wilhelmine was born in Colmar Berg Castle on January 23, 1896. She was the daughter of Grand Duke Wilhelm IV of Luxembourg and Princess Marie Anna of Portugal. Grand Duke Wilhelm was succeeded by Charlotte's older sister, Marie Adelaide, on February 26, 1912. However, Luxembourg was occupied by Germany during World War I, and after the war Grand Duchess Marie Adelaide was charged with supporting the Germans. She abdicated on January 15, 1919, and Charlotte ascended the throne. She remained grand duchess following a referendum that confirmed the continuation of the monarchy in September 1919. She married Prince Felix of Bourbon-Parma several months later. She ruled as a popular monarch until she was forced into exile in Paris following the German occupation of Luxembourg in May 1940. Charlotte subsequently went to Lisbon, Portugal, and remained in exile during the war. She helped to maintain the morale of her subjects through daily radio broadcasts. She was greeted by widespread rejoicing upon her return to Luxembourg in April 1945. Charlotte continued her reign over the Grand Duchy until November 12, 1964, when she abdicated in favor of her son, Jean. She continued to appear at state functions during her retirement. She died after a brief illness at Fischbach Castle on July 9, 1985.

HEADS OF GOVERNMENT

PAUL EYSCHEN (Prime Minister; September 22, 1889–October 12, 1915). Paul Eyschen was born on September 9, 1841. Eyschen became prime minister of Luxembourg on September 22, 1889, shortly before Grand Duke Adolf arrived in the country to assume the throne. Eyschen continued to serve as head of government for the next twenty-five years. He resigned from office in February 1915, over a policy dispute with Grand Duchess Marie Adelaide in regard to the German occupation. He was persuaded to resume his position soon after and continued to serve as prime minister until his death on October 12, 1915.

EMILE REUTER (Prime Minister; September 27, 1918–March 1, 1925). Emile Reuter became Luxembourg's prime minister on September 27, 1918, after the conclusion of World War I. He headed the government during the abdication of Grand Duchess Marie Adelaide and was able to stave off attempts by Belgium to annex the Grand Duchy. In a referendum in September 1919, voters voiced their desire to remain an independent country under the new monarch, Grand Duchess Charlotte. Reuter also pushed legislation to grant universal suffrage in Luxembourg in 1919. His government negotiated a treaty with Belgium in 1921 that formed a customs and monetary union. The treaty was unpopular, and his government faced further problems with postwar inflation. Reuter was forced to step down on March 1, 1925. He died in 1973.

PIERRE PROUM (Prime Minister; March 1, 1925–July 1, 1926). Pierre Proum was chosen to serve as interim prime minister of Luxembourg following the resignation of Emile Reuter on March 1, 1925. Proum stepped down on July 1, 1926, to make way for a coalition government headed by Joseph Bech.

JOSEPH BECH (Prime Minister; July 16, 1926–October 19, 1937). Joseph Bech was born in Diekirch, Luxembourg, on February 17, 1887. He received a degree in law from the University of Paris in 1912. He returned to Luxembourg and was elected to the Parliament as a member of the Social Christian Party in 1914. Bech retained office throughout the German occupation of Luxembourg during World War I. He was named to the cabinet of Prime Minister Emile Reuter in 1921 and served as minister of justice and home affairs. He was selected as prime minister of Luxembourg on July 16, 1926. Bech also served in the government as foreign minister and represented the country at the League of Nations from 1925. He retained office until October 19, 1937, when he resignd as prime minister, but he remained in the government of Pierre Dupong as foreign minister. Bech joined the government-in-exile in Paris following the German occupation of Luxembourg in May 1940. He subsequently accompanied the government to London. He returned to Luxembourg following the liberation in September 1944 and remained in the cabinet as foreign minister. Bech was instrumental in the negotiations that led to the Benelux economic agreement with Belgium, the Netherlands, and Luxembourg in 1946. He was a chief architect of the Council of Europe in 1949 and signed the North Atlantic Treaty in Washington later that year. Bech returned to office as prime minister on December 29, 1953, following the death of Dupong. He signed the Treaty of Rome, which established the European Common Market, in 1957. Bech again stepped down as prime minister on March 26, 1958. He remained foreign minister in the subsequent government of Pierre Frieden. Bech retired from politics in 1959. He died in Luxembourg on March 8, 1975.

PIERRE DUPONG (Prime Minister; November 5, 1937–December 29, 1953). Pierre Dupong was born in Luxembourg on November 1, 1885. He was educated at universities in Germany, Switzerland, and France. He received a degree in law and began a legal practice in Luxembourg in 1911. Dupong was elected to the Parliament as a member of the Social Christian Party in 1915. He was named to the government as director-general of finances and social welfare in 1926. He subsequently joined the cabinet of Prime Minister Joseph Bech as minister of labor. Dupong succeeded Bech as prime minister on November 5, 1937, when the Socialist Party refused to join Bech's coalition cabinet. Dupong escaped from Luxembourg with the royal family following the German invasion in May 1940. He led a government-in-exile in Paris and then in London until the country was liberated in September 1944. He continued to lead a national coalition government and initiated reconstruction plans for the war-damaged areas of the country. Dupong was hospitalized in December 1953 after breaking his left leg in a fall in the prime minister's office. He died of a heart attack in a Luxembourg hospital on December 22, 1953.

Mexico

Mexico is a country in the southernmost section of North America. It was granted independence from Spain on September 16, 1821.

HEADS OF STATE

PORFIRIO DÍAZ (President; December 1, 1884–May 25, 1911). Porfirio Díaz was born to a poor family in Oaxaca on September 15, 1830. He began training for the priesthood, but instead entered the army in Mexico's war with the United States in 1846. After the war, in 1849, he studied law. He supported Benito Juárez in the War of Reform from 1858 until 1861, and attained the rank of brigadier general. He fought against the French occupation and the monarchy of Emperor Maximilian. He led Mexican troops to victory against the French at Puebla in 1862 and drove the imperial army from the capital in June 1866. He subsequently retired from the military. He soon broke with Juárez and challenged him for the presidency in 1871. Díaz was defeated and led an unsuccessful revolt against Juárez. He also led a revolt against Juárez's successor, Sebastián Lerdo de Tejeda, in 1876. He was initially unsuccessful but regrouped his forces and defeated the government army at the battle of Tecoac in November 1876. Díaz became provisional president after Lerdo's resignation on December 23, 1876, and was officially elected president of Mexico on May 5, 1877. He established a political organization and successfully crushed several revolts during his term of office. He declined to run for reelection in 1880 and supported General Manuel González as his successor. Díaz relinquished office to González on December 1, 1880. The new government was criticized for rampant corruption, and Díaz broke with González. Díaz again ran for the presidency in 1884 and was victorious. He was sworn into office on December 1, 1884. Díaz soon began ruling as a dictator, suppressing and sometimes murdering his political opponents. He brought political and economic stability to Mexico and presided over the nation's agricultural and industrial growth. Díaz defeated Francisco I. Madero in the presidential election in 1910. Madero initiated a military rebellion against Díaz, who was suffering from poor health and advancing senility. The government forces proved unequal to the task of putting down the revolt and Díaz resigned on May 25, 1911. He went into exile in Paris, France, where he died on July 2, 1915.

FRANCISCO DE LA BARRA (President; May 25, 1911–November 6, 1911). Francisco Leon de la Barra was born in Queretara on June 16, 1863. He received a law degree from the National University before entering politics. He was elected a federal deputy in 1891. He entered the diplomatic corps in 1896 and served as minister to various South American countries. He was named special envoy to Belgium and the Netherlands in 1904 and became an authority on international law. He served on several international commissions over the next several years. He was Mexico's ambassador to the United States from November 1908 until April 1911, when he returned to Mexico to serve as secretary of foreign relations. When President Porfirio Díaz resigned on May 25, 1911, de la Barra became interim president. His government oversaw new elections that resulted in the election of Francisco Madero. De la Barra relinquished the presidency to Madero on November 6, 1911. He served on several special diplomatic missions overseas under Madero and returned to Mexico to again head the foreign ministry in 1913. He was elected governor of the State of Mexico later in the year, but resigned in 1914 and moved to Paris. He began a career as an international lawyer, served as president of the Permanent Court of Arbitration at The Hague, and headed various commissions after World War I. He also served as a professor of international law at the Sorbonne and at the International Academy at The Hague. De la Barra

died in Biarritz, France, on September 23, 1939.

FRANCISCO I. MADERO (President; November 6, 1911–February 18, 1913). Francisco Indalecio Madero was born to a wealthy family in Parras, Coahuila, on October 30, 1873. He studied economics in Paris from 1887 until 1892. He subsequently attended the University of California at Berkeley, where he studied agriculture. He returned to Mexico in 1893 and developed the Laguna cotton region. Madero soon became active in politics and formed the Benito Juárez Democratic Club in 1905. He was defeated for the governorship of Coahuila that year. Madero began writing a political column for the weekly newspaper *El Democrata*. He formed the National Antireelectionist Party to challenge dictator Porfirio Díaz. Madero was arrested in June 1910 on the eve of the election. He fled to San Antonio, Texas, after his release and issued a call for an armed rebellion against Díaz. The revolution began on November 10, 1910. The government was unable to suppress the rebellion and Díaz resigned on May 25, 1911. An interim government under Francisco Leon de la Barra was formed to conduct new elections. Madero was the candidate of the Constitutional Progressive Party and won the election by a wide margin. He assumed office on November 6, 1911. His government tried to introduce social legislation and political reforms that led to a rightist rebellion led by Pascual Orozco. The government forces under General Victoriano Huerta suppressed the rebellion. Followers of Emiliano Zapata also revolted against the government. They claimed Madero was going too slowly in implementing land reform and fulfilling other promises made during the revolution. A military revolt led by Felix Díaz erupted within the federal army in early 1913. General Huerta, with the approval of United States Ambassador Henry Lane Wilson, betrayed Madero and joined with the rebels. Madero was forced to resign on February 18, 1913, and was arrested. He and his vice president, José Maria Piño Suárez, were murdered while being transferred to prison on February 22, 1913.

VICTORIANO HUERTA (President; February 22, 1913–July 14, 1914). Victoriano Huerta was born in Colotán, Jalisco, on March 23, 1845. He was educated in Guadalajara and at the National Military College. He entered the army in 1876, was promoted to the rank of colonel in 1894, and led the Third Infantry Battalion. Huerta was promoted to brigadier general in 1901. He was head of public works in the state of Monterrey from 1905 to 1909. He suppressed Pascual Ortiz's Chihuahua rebellion in 1912. President Francisco Madero named Huerta military commander of all government forces during a rebellion in February 1913. Huerta betrayed Madero to the rebels and forced him and Vice president José Maria Piño Suárez to resign on February 18, 1913. Madero and Piño Suárez were murdered while in custody, and Huerta proclaimed himself president of Mexico on February 22, 1913. The United States refused to recognize the new government and Emiliano Zapata and Venustiano Carranza led separate rebellions against Huerta's government. Huerta ruled in a brutal fashion, closing the congress and ruthlessly suppressing his opponents. Huerta fled the country on July 14, 1914, as rebel armies led by Zapata, Alvaro Obregón, Pancho Villa, and Pablo Gonzalez attacked Mexico City. He went into exile in England and Spain before going to the United States to attempt to raise an army to reclaim the country. Huerta was arrested by American agents while en route by train to El Paso, Texas, on June 27, 1915. He was charged with illegally running guns across the border and fomenting rebellion. He was interned at Fort Bliss, Texas, where he died of cirrhosis of the liver on January 13, 1916.

VENUSTIANO CARRANZA (President; July 15, 1914–May 21, 1920). Venustiano Carranza was born to a wealthy family in Cuatrociénegas, Coahuila, on December 29, 1859. Carranza became active in politics in 1887 as a supporter of Bernardo Reyes. He served as a state deputy and federal senator. Carranza was defeated for the governorship of Coahuila in 1909. He supported Francisco Madero's candidacy for president against Porfirio Díaz in 1910 and took part in the subsequent revolt that ousted Díaz in May 1911. Carranza served as governor of Coahuila during Madero's presidency. After Madero's overthrow and murder in February 1913, Carranza led a revolt against General Victoriano Huerta. His revolutionary army defeated Huerta's forces and drove the dictator into exile in July 1914. Carranza became provisional president on July 15, 1914. His government was opposed by Pancho Villa and Emiliano Zapata. Alvaro Obregón, a Carranza loyalist, defeated Villa's rebels in mid-1915. Carranza was inaugurated as constitutional president in May 1917. Mexico's economy suffered during Carranza's administration and the currency collapsed. He mandated a constitutional convention in 1917 that produced a new radical constitution that supported agrarian and labor reform and anticlericalism. Carranza maintained Mexico's neutrality during World War I, rejecting an offer of an alliance with Germany by way of the Zimmerman telegram. Carranza attempted to secure Ignacio Bonnillas as his successor in the presidential election of 1920. However, the military supported Alvaro Obregón and led a coup that ousted Carranza. He fled Mexico City for Veracruz on horseback. He was ambushed and killed by troops under Rodolfo Herrera at Tlaxcalaltongo, Puebla State, on May 21, 1920.

ADOLFO DE LA HUERTA (President; June 1, 1920–December 1, 1920). Adolfo de la Huerta was born to a leading family in Guaymas, Sonora, on May 26, 1881. He studied music in Hermosillo. He became involved in politics as a member of the National Antireelectionist Party in opposition to President Porfirio Díaz in 1908. He was elected to the state legislature in 1911. He served as President Venustiano Carranza's chief clerk in 1915. He was consul general in New York City in 1918 and governor of Sonora from 1919 to 1920. He broke with Carranza in 1920 and joined the rebellion against the government. He was chosen as provisional president on June 1, 1920, after Carranza's ouster and murder. De la Huerta's government conducted elections and he relinquished office to Alvaro Obregón on December 1, 1920. He served in Obregón's cabinet as secretary of the treasury from 1920 to 1923. De la Huerta led a rebellion against Obregón in December 1923 over the president's decision to support Plutarco Elías Calles as his successor. The rebellion was suppressed, and de la Huerta was captured and sent into exile. He worked in Los Angeles as a piano teacher and voice trainer for the next dozen years. After the election of Lázáro Cardenas as president in 1934, de la Huerta was allowed to return to Mexico. He was named inspector general of Mexican consulates in the United States. He retired in 1946. De la Huerta died in Mexico City of a heart ailment on July 9, 1955.

ALVARO OBREGÓN (President; December 1, 1920–December 1, 1924). Alvaro Obregón Salido was born on a farm in Alamos, Sonora, on February 19, 1890. He entered politics and was elected mayor of Huatabampo in 1911. He supported the presidency of Francisco Madero against Pascual Orozco's rebellion in 1912. Obregón joined Venustiano Carranza's revolt against President Victoriano Huerta, after the ouster and murder of Madero in February 1913. Obregón's forces achieved victory over the government forces, and Huerta was

driven from office in July 1914. Obregón remained loyal to Carranza against Pancho Villa and Emiliano Zapata, who continued to war against the government. He inflicted serious defeats on the rebels. Obregón was instrumental in pushing through the more radical elements of the new Mexican constitution enacted in 1917. Obregón was a candidate for the presidency in 1920. Carranza attempted to arrange the election of Ignacio Bonnillas as his successor, and Obregón joined in a rebellion against the government. Carranza was ousted and murdered in May 1920, and Obregón was subsequently elected president. He took office on December 1, 1920. His government implemented numerous social and economic reforms. He crushed a rebellion led by Adolfo de la Huerta in late 1923. He supported the election of Plutarco Elías Calles as his successor and left office on December 1, 1924. Obregón again ran for the presidency in 1928. He was reelected in a violent and bitter campaign. Obregón returned to Mexico City to attend a victory celebration. During dinner on July 17, 1928, he was shot to death by José de Leon Toral, a Roman Catholic seminary student who opposed Obregón's anticlerical policies.

PLUTARCO ELÍAS CALLES (President; December 1, 1924–December 1, 1928). Plutarco Elías Calles was born in Guaymas, Sonora, on September 25, 1877. He worked as a schoolteacher before joining the revolutionary movement against President Porfirio Díaz. He served in the revolutionary army as a colonel in 1913 and was promoted to general two years later. He was governor of Sonora from 1915 to 1916 and again from 1917 to 1919. He was named secretary of industry, commerce, and labor in Venustiano Carranza's cabinet in 1919. He supported Alvaro Obregón's candidacy for president in 1920 and served in his government as minister of the interior. Obregón supported Calles candidacy for president in 1924, and Calles took office on December 1, 1924, after crushing a revolt led by Adolfo de la Huerta. Calles continued Obregón's policies of agrarian reform and radical anticlericalism. Obregón was assassinated after winning reelection to succeed Calles in 1928. Calles allowed the congress to select an interim president and stepped down on December 1, 1928. He remained a leading force in the government and led federal troops against a rebellion in opposition to President Emilio Portes Gil in March 1929. Calles served as minister of war in 1932. He reluctantly supported the election of Lázáro Cardenas as president in 1934. Calles broke with Cardenas two years later and was arrested and deported to the United States in April 1936. He remained in California until he was allowed to return to Mexico by Cardenas' successor, Manuel Avila Camacho, in 1941. Calles died at a Mexico City hospital on October 19, 1945.

EMILIO PORTES GIL (President; December 1, 1928–December 21, 1929). Emilio Portes Gil was born in Ciudad Victoria, Tamaulipas, on October 3, 1890. He was educated as a lawyer in Mexico City. Portes Gil supported Alvaro Obregón's rebellion against Venustiano Carranza in 1920. Portes Gil served as governor of Tamaulipas after Obregón became president. He also served as a member of the federal congress and was again governor of Tamaulipas from 1925 until 1928. Portes Gil was selected by congress to serve as interim president when Obregón was assassinated before taking office for a second term. Portes Gil took office on December 1, 1928. His government survived a revolt by General José Gonzalo Escobar the following year. He stepped down on December 21, 1929, after Pascual Ortiz Rubio was elected to the presidency. Portes Gil served as leader of the National Revolutionary Party until 1931, when elements in the party forced his resignation. He was named minister to France and also served as Mexico's representative to the

League of Nations from 1931 to 1932. He returned to Mexico to serve as attorney general until 1934, when he was named foreign minister. Portes Gil retired from politics in 1936, but remained active as a lawyer and sponsor of cultural and artistic events. He died in Mexico City from cardiac arrest on December 10, 1978.

PASCUAL ORTIZ RUBIO (President; December 21, 1929–September 2, 1932). Pascual Ortiz Rubio was born in Morelia, Michoacan, on March 10, 1877. He received an engineering degree from the National College of Mines in 1902. He returned to Morelia, where he became active in local politics. He supported Francisco Madero's revolt against Porfirio Díaz in 1910. Ortiz Rubio was elected to the chamber of deputies in 1912. He was arrested and imprisoned for several months after Victoriano Huerta's ouster of Madero in 1913. Ortiz Rubio joined Venustiano Carranza's rebellion against Huerta after his release. He worked in Carranza's government for several years before becoming governor of Michoacan in 1917. He supported Alvaro Obregón's revolt against Carranza in 1920 and served in Obregón's government as secretary of public works from 1920 until 1921. He was appointed ambassador to Germany in 1923 and subsequently served as ambassador to Brazil. He returned to Mexico in 1929 to become the National Revolutionary Party's candidate for president. He was elected and took office on December 21, 1929. Shortly after his formal inauguration on February 5, 1930, Ortiz Rubio was shot in the jaw by an assassin. He was seriously injured, but subsequently recovered. His government instituted a series of land reform measures. He was also responsible for the construction of numerous schools and roads throughout the country. Ortiz Rubio resigned from the presidency on September 2, 1932, in protest of former president Plutarco Elías Calles' strong influence on the government. He retired from politics and went to California for several years. After his return to Mexico he worked as an engineer. Ortiz Rubio died in Mexico City on November 4, 1963.

ABELARDO RODRÍGUEZ LUJAN (President; September 4, 1932–November 30, 1934).

Abelardo Rodríguez Lujan was born in Guaymas, Sonora, on May 12, 1889. He joined the constitutionalist army during the revolution in 1913. He saw action in the revolution in 1914 and was active in the campaign against Pancho Villa in 1915. He rose through the ranks of the army and became governor and military commander of Baja California del Norte in 1923. He was promoted to the rank of division general in 1928. Rodríguez retired from the army in 1930. He was appointed undersecretary of war the following year and was named minister of industry, commerce, and labor in January 1932. He was appointed minister of war and the navy the following August. Rodríguez was chosen by the Mexican congress to serve as provisional president following the resignation of Pascual Ortiz Rubio and took office on September 4, 1932. He worked closely with former president Plutarco Elías Calles during his term of office, which ended on November 30, 1934, after the election of Lázaro Cardenas. Rodríguez returned to active duty in the military to serve as commander of the Mexican Gulf Zone at the start of World War II. He also headed the office of coordination of promotion and production during the war. Rodríguez was governor of Sonora from 1943 until his retirement in 1949. He settled at a ranch near Ensenada, in Lower California. Rodriguez died of an abdominal disorder in a LaJolla, California, hospital on February 13, 1967.

LÁZÁRO CARDENAS (President; November 30, 1934–December 1, 1940).

Lázáro Cardenas del Rio was born in Jiquilpan, Michoacan, on May 21, 1895. He joined the revolutionary army under Guillermo Garcia Aragon in Apatzingan in 1913. He led troops against rival insurgents Emiliano Zapata and Pancho Villa and was promoted to the rank of brigadier general. Cardenas became governor of Michoacan in 1920. He was given command of the armies in Michoacan and Oaxaca with the rank of major general in 1928. He was named minister of the interior in 1931 and was appointed minister of war and the navy in 1933. Cardenas was the presidential candidate of the National Revolutionary Party in 1934. He was victorious and was sworn into office on November 30, 1934. He was a strong supporter of the labor movement, and the government seized many industries and transformed them into cooperatives for the workers. His policies caused a break with former president Plutarco Elías Calles, whom Cardenas forced into exile in 1936. Cardenas nationalized the oil industry in March 1938 and instituted vast land reform measures. He completed his term of office on December 1, 1940, and retired to Patzcuaro. He remained a leading figure in the state of Michoacan and an effective speaker on leftist causes. He was awarded the Stalin Peace Prize by the Soviet Union in 1955. He also served as director of the Rio Balsas Commission, which constructed hydroelectric dams in Michoacan. Cardenas continued to serve on government commissions until his death in Mexico City on October 19, 1970.

MANUEL AVILA CAMACHO (President; December 1, 1940–December 1, 1946).

Manuel Avila Camacho was born in Teziutlan, Puebla, on April 24, 1897. He studied accounting to become a bookkeeper before he joined the Mexican Revolution in 1914 to fight in the successful revolt against Victoriano Huerta. He fought against the Cristero Rebellion in 1923 and served under Lázáro Cardenas. Avila gained recognition for his ability to arbitrate military disputes. He continued to serve in the

military and was named first undersecretary of war in 1933. He was promoted
to secretary of war in 1938 and was given
the rank of general of a division later in
the year. Avila was nominated for the
presidency in November 1939 and was
elected the following July. He succeeded
Cardenas to office on December 1, 1940.
Avila moved the government away from
the leftist positions of his predecessor to
a more moderate level. He also advocated close ties to the United States and
pushed through a declaration of war
against the Axis Powers during World
War II. He completed his term of office
on December 1, 1946, and retired from
the political scene. He died of a heart
ailment at his ranch near Mexico City
on October 13, 1955.

Monaco

*Monaco is a small independent principality on the Mediterranean coast
of southeastern France. It has been independent from France since 1861.*

HEADS OF STATE

ALBERT (Prince; September 10,
1889–June 26, 1922). Albert Honoré
Charles was born in Paris on November
13, 1848. He was the son of Prince
Charles III of the House of Goyon de
Matignon-Grimaldi. Albert joined the
Spanish navy at an early age and developed a love for the sea. He succeeded to
the throne of Monaco upon his father's
death on September 10, 1889. He ruled
as an absolute monarch until January
1911, when he promoted a constitution
establishing parliamentary government.
Albert was renowned as a leading scientist and oceanographer. He established
the Museum of Oceanography in
Monaco in 1910. He died in a Paris hospital following abdominal surgery on
June 26, 1922.

LOUIS II (Prince; June 26, 1922–
May 9, 1949). Louis Honoré Charles Antoine de Grimaldi was born in Baden-
Baden, Germany, on July 12, 1870. He
was the only son of Prince Albert, the
ruler of Monaco. Louis attended the St.
Cyr Military Academy in France and
joined the French army in 1883. He
served in the French Foreign Legion in
Africa, and during World War I he was
a cavalry commander in the French
army. He distinguished himself in action
and was promoted to the rank of
brigadier general. Louis succeeded his
father as Monaco's head of state on June
26, 1922. Louis preferred to live in
France and spent relatively little time in
the nation he ruled. He fell ill in May
1949 and relinquished his duties to his
grandson and successor, Prince Rainier,
on May 4, 1949. He died in Monaco on
May 9, 1949.

Mongolia

Mongolia is a country in central Asia between China and Russia. It gained independence from China on March 13, 1921. The constitutional monarchy, headed by the Living Buddha, lasted only until his death in 1924. It was followed by the creation of the Mongolian People's Republic under the auspices of the Soviet Union. Mongolia was recognized as an independent nation by China on January 5, 1946.

HEADS OF STATE

THE JAVZANDAMBA KHUTAGT (Bogd Khan; November 18, 1911–May, 1924). The Eighth Javzandamba Khutagt, or Living Buddah, was born in Tibet in 1870. He was revered as a leader of the Buddhists, following the Dalai Lama and Panchen Lama in the Buddhist pantheon. Russia abolished Mongolia's relationship with China and granted the region limited autonomy and, on November 18, 1911, the Living Buddah was proclaimed the Bogd Gegeen Ezan Khan of Mongolia. China reasserted its influence over Mongolia following the fall of the Russian tsar in 1917. In October 1919 the Chinese government demanded the end of the autonomous system in Mongolia. The Living Buddha was allowed to maintain his status as religious leader but all treaties between Mongolia and Russia were annulled and the Mongolian army was disbanded. White Russian troops led by Baron Roman von Ungern-Sternberg invaded Mongolia in October 1920 and captured Urga in February 1921. The Living Buddah was returned to the throne under the White Russians. The invaders were defeated and expelled by a Mongolian nationalist army and Soviet Army troops led by Suhe Baator in June 1921. A constitutional monarchy, headed by the Living Buddah, was proclaimed and lasted until the latter's death in Urga in May 1924.

HEADS OF GOVERNMENT

NAMNANSUREN, THE SAIN NOYON KHAN (Prime Minister; Autumn 1912–1919). Namnansuren, the Sain Noyon Khan, was a leading hereditary ruler of Outer Mongolia. He was named prime minister of the autonomous government of Mongolia in the autumn of 1912. He signed the Russo-Mongolia Treaty in November 1912, ending Mongolia's long-standing association with China. He continued to head the government until his death by poisoning in 1919.

SHANZAV BADAMDORG (Prime Minister; July 1919–November 17, 1919). Shanzav Badamdorf was born a commoner. He served in the autonomous government and was a supporter of the conservative lamas. He was installed as prime minister by the Chinese in July 1919. His government was forced to accept China's demands to end Mongolia's autonomy on November 17, 1919.

CHAGDARJAV (Prime Minister; March 31, 1921–July 1921). Chagdarjav was a wealthy Mongolian lama who joined the revolutionary movement. He was a member of the Mongolian delegation that sought help from Russia seeking help in 1920. He was an ally of Bodo and headed the provisional government from March 31, 1921, until July 1921. He subsequently went to organize activities in Northwest Mongolia. He was arrested and executed with Bodo in September 1922.

DOGSOMYN BODO (Prime Minister; July 1921–June 1922). Dogsomyn Bodo was born in 1885. He was a lama and served in the autonomous government. He also worked as an instructor of translators at the Russian consulate in Urga and became a leading Mongolian journalist. Bodo was selected as prime minister of the people's government in July 1921. Bodo was forced to resign from the government in June 1922. He was subsequently arrested and charged with conspiring against the government. He was executed in September 1922.

THE JALKHANZ KHUTAGT DAMDINBAZAR (Prime Minister; June 1922–1923). The Jalkhanz Khutagt Damdinbazar was a leading Buddhist religious figure in Mongolia and a close associate of the Bogd Khan. He was chosen to head the government following the ouster of Bodo in June 1922. He introduced some democratic reforms in the government before his death in 1923.

NEUTANDR (Prime Minister; 1923). Neutandr was an associate of the Jalkhanz Khutagt Damdinbazar. He headed an interim government in 1923 following the death of the Jalkhanz. He was replaced soon after by Danzan. Neutandr was arrested and executed with Danzan in August 1924.

DANZAN (Prime Minister; 1923–August 1924). Danzan Khorloo was born in 1873. He was a leading revolutionary figure in Mongolia, who served as commander-in-chief of the army and secretary of the central committee. He was named minister of finance in Bodo's gov-

ernment in 1921 and was called to head the government as prime minister in 1923. He was a capitalist and nationalist who favored trade with China and supported limiting the scope of the revolution. Danzan was purged and executed in August 1924.

BALINGIIN TSERENDORJI (Prime Minister; 1924–1928). Balingiin Tserendorji was born in 1868. He was active in the Mongolian government during the autonomous period. He served as deputy head of the foreign ministry in 1911 and subsequently held the posts of vice minister and minister. He briefly served as acting premier of the autonomous government in 1916. He was vice minister of the interior during Baron Roman von Ungern-Sternberg's occupation in the spring of 1921. Tserendorji became prime minister and foreign minister of the people's government in 1923. He continued to head the government until his death in 1928.

ANANDYN AMOR (Prime Minister; 1928–1932). Anandyn Amor was born in 1886. He served in the Mongolian foreign ministry during Mongolia's period of autonomy. He served in several governments as foreign minister and deputy premier during the 1920s. Amor was prime minister from 1928 until 1932 and again headed the government from 1936 until 1938, also holding the position of foreign minister. Amor was accused of counterrevolutionary activities by Choibalsan in 1939. He was purged from the government and liquidated.

P. GENDUNG (Prime Minister; 1932–March 1936). P. Gendung was a leading figure in Mongolia's revolutionary movement. He replaced Anandyn Amor as prime minister and foreign minister in 1932. His government implemented the "New Turn" policy. He negotiated the Treaty of Friendship with the Soviet Union in March 1936, but then he was expelled from the presidium of the central committee and removed from office that same month. Gendung was charged with conspiring with General Demid in counterrevolutionary and pro-Japanese activities. He was purged and executed in 1937.

ANANDYN AMOR (Prime Minister; 1936-1938). *See earlier entry under Heads of Government.*

KHORLOGHIYUIN CHOIBAL-SAN (Prime Minister; 1939–January 26, 1952). Khorloghiyuin Choibalsan was born in Tsetsenkhan Aimak on February 8, 1895. He was educated locally and in Irkutsk. He became a leader of a pro-Communist revolutionary group that opposed the Chinese occupation of Mongolia in October 1919. The Chinese were forced from the capital by a White Russian force in October 1920, and Choibalsan continued to fight for independence. He merged his organization with Suhe Baator's nationalist forces later in 1920 and formed the Mongolian People's Party. The nationalists were assisted by Soviet troops in defeating the White Russians, and a nationalist government was formed in July 1921. Dogsomyn Bodo headed the new government and Choibalsan remained the leader of the Mongolian military. The Living Buddha, Mongolia's religious leader, died in May 1924, and the government allowed no further incarnations to be proclaimed. Choibalsan served as commander-in-chief of the Mongolian army from 1924 until 1928. He was chairman of the Presidium of the Lesser People's Hural from 1928 until 1930, when he was named minister of foreign affairs following the Japanese invasion of Manchuria. He and Premier Gendung negotiated a military alliance between Mongolia and the Soviet Union in November 1934. Gendung was executed as a Japanese spy the following month, and Choibalsan became first deputy premier. He was given the rank of marshal in 1936 and became Mongolia's prime minister in 1939. He signed a Soviet-Mongolian mutual assistance treaty in 1939, and Soviet troops assisted Mongolia in its fight against the Japanese during World War II. The Allies acknowledged Mongolia as part of the Soviet sphere of influence in a secret agreement at Yalta in February 1945. A plebiscite was held the following October confirming independence, and China recognized the Mongolian People's Republic on January 5, 1946. Choibalsan remained prime minister and commander-in-chief until his death in Moscow on January 26, 1952, following surgery for kidney cancer.

Montenegro

Montenegro was a principality in southeastern Europe, which had effectively maintained independence from the Ottoman Empire since the fourteenth century. It became a part of Yugoslavia after World War I on December 1, 1918.

HEADS OF STATE

NICHOLAS I (Prince; August 14, 1860–August 28, 1910; King, August 28, 1910–December 1, 1918). Nicholas I Petrovic was born in Njegosh on October 7, 1841. He was the son of Micko Petrovich-Njegosh and the nephew of Prince Danilo of Montenegro. Nicholas was educated in Trieste and Paris. He succeeded to the throne of Montenegro as prince following the assassination of Danilo on August 13, 1860. He married Milena, daughter of Petar Vukotich, later in the year. He distinguished himself in the wars against the Turks in 1861, 1875, and 1876. He captured Bar and Ulcinj during the last campaign, and Montenegro was recognized as a sovereign state by the Congress of Berlin in 1878. He was an advocate of a Yugoslav state encompassing Montenegro and Serbia, which was ruled by his son-in-law, Peter Karageorgevich. Nicholas was forced to approve a constitution for Montenegro in 1905. He proclaimed himself king on August 28, 1910. He again fought against the Turks in the Balkan Wars of 1912 and 1913. He sided with Serbia against Austria-Hungary in the early years of World War I. He sought a separate peace with Austria-Hungary in January 1916 and fled into exile in Italy. Serbia subsequently occupied Montenegro, and Nicholas was deposed by the Congress of Podgoritsa on November 26, 1918. Montenegro became a part of the newly formed kingdom of the Serbs, Croats, and Slovenes on December 1, 1918. Nicholas remained in exile in Italy and France. He died in Antibes, France, on March 2, 1921.

Morocco

Morocco is a country in northwestern Africa. It was granted independence from France on March 2, 1956.

HEADS OF STATE

'ABD AL-'AZIZ (Sultan; June 7, 1894–August 21, 1908). 'Abd al-'Aziz ibn al-Hassani ibn Muhammad al-Hasani al-'Alawi was born on February 18, 1881, the son of Sultan Hassan I of Morocco. He succeeded his father as sultan on June 7, 1894, though the early years of his reign were dominated by the regent, Grand Vizier Ahmad ibn Musa. He began to rule directly after Ahmad's death during a cholera epidemic in 1900. 'Abd al-'Aziz attempted to institute reforms in the administration of the government, incorporating European administrative methods. His tax reforms reduced state revenue, which resulted in European control of much of Morocco's public finances. His policies alienated many of the Moroccan political elite. A rebellion sprang up in the Taza region led by Bu Hamara, who was defeated in his attempt to capture Fez, the capital. The Sultan's brother, Abd al-Hafid, led a revolt in Marrakech against the regime in 1907 and defeated forces loyal to 'Abd al-'Aziz on August 19, 1908. 'Abd al-'Aziz abdicated his position on August 21, 1908, and retired to Tangiers. He died there on June 10, 1943.

ABD AL-HAFID (Sultan; August 21, 1908–August 18, 1912). Abd al-Hafid was born in Fez, Morocco, in 1875. He was the brother of Sultan Abd al-Aziz, who named Abd al-Hafid caliph of Marrakech. He was also a noted poet, historian, and soldier. Dissatisfaction with 'Abd al-'Aziz's westernization of Morocco led Hafid to begin a revolt against his brother. Hafid defeated 'Aziz's troops in battle on August 19, 1908, and Hafid assumed the title of sultan two days later. He was recognized by the European powers the following year. Morocco was often a focal point for European intrigues. The arrival of a German warship in Agadir in 1911 nearly led to a European war. Hafid accepted the assistance of the French to put down a rebellion in 1912. That same year he signed the Treaty of Fez with France, which established a protectorate over Morocco. He subsequently abdicated the throne on August 18, 1912, and went into exile in Spain. He settled in France in the mid-1920s and died at his villa in Enghien-les-Bains, France, on April 4, 1937.

YUSEF (Sultan; August 18, 1912–November 18, 1927). Yusef was born in Meknes in 1882, the son of Sultan Hassan I. He was proclaimed sultan following the abdication of his brother, Abd al-Hafid, on August 18, 1912. He pledged loyalty to France and began a policy of modernization in the country. Yusef abandoned the capital in Fez to reside in Rabat in the French Zone. The French protected his government against several uprisings, the most serious being led by Rift leader Abdelkrim. The Rifts had begun their rebellion in the Spanish-influenced area of Morocco, but threatened to spill over into the French Zone. Spanish and French troops struck the Rifts in August 1925 and forced Abdelkrim's surrender the following year. Yusef retained the throne until his sudden death due to uremia at the Imperial Palace in Fez on November 18, 1927.

MOHAMMED V (Sultan; November 18, 1927–August 20, 1953). Sidi Mohammed ben Youssef was born in Fez on August 10, 1909. He was the youngest of three sons of Sultan Yusef of Morocco. His father died on November 18, 1927, and Mohammed was chosen by the Council of Ulemas (Muslim wise men) to succeed to the throne. Mohammed was considered by the French to be more controllable than his older brothers. He ruled under the regency of the grand vizier, Muhammad el-Muqri, until 1930. He continued to cooperate with the French colonial authorities. Mohammed suffered from poor health and underwent major surgery in December 1937. He initially gave his support to the Vichy regime during World War II, but later sided with the Allies after American troops landed in Casablanca in November 1942. Mohammed became involved in the Moroccan independence movement after the war. He demanded that the French end the protectorate over Morocco. Mohammed was deposed by the pro-French pasha of Marrakech, Hadj Thami el Mezouari el Glaoui, on August 20, 1953. He was sent into exile by the French and was replaced on the throne by his uncle, Sidi Mohammed ben Moulay Arafa. Mohammed was sent to Corsica, where he remained until being removed to Madagascar in April 1954. The exiled sultan became a rallying point for the independence movement. Riots and demonstrations took place throughout Morocco, and the French were forced to restore Mohammed to the throne on November 6, 1955. The French also agreed to grant independence to Morocco on March 2, 1956. The sultan adopted the title of King Mohammed V on August 11, 1957. Mohammed dismissed the cabinet of Prime Minister Abdullah Ibrahim on May 20, 1960, and led his own cabinet. Mohammed died suddenly in Rabat on February 26, 1961, following a minor operation to remove a growth in his throat.

HEADS OF GOVERNMENT

MUHAMMAD EL-MUQRI (Grand Vizier; August 19, 1917–November 1955). Muhammad el-Muqri was born in Fez in 1841. He entered the service of Sultan Hassan I in the 1880s. He remained in the government of Hassan's successor,

Sultan 'Abd al-'Aziz and El-Muqri served as Morocco's representative at the Conference of Algeciras in 1906. He was subsequently appointed minister of finance. He was named grand vizier in the court of Sultan 'Abd al-'Aziz in 1908. El-Muqri was named minister of finance in 1909 following the succession of Sultan Abd al-Hafid and was again named grand vizier in 1911. He stepped down from office in 1913, but was recalled as grand vizier by Sultan Yusef in 1917. He retained office throughout the reign of Sultan Yusef and continued during the

reign of Sultan Mohammed V. El-Muqri served as a mediator between the sultanate and the French resident-general. He was retained by the French after the ouster of Sultan Mohammed in August 1953. He served on the Regency Council following the abdication of Sultan Moulay Arafa in October 1955. Mohammed returned to the throne the following month, and El-Muqri withdrew from politics prior to Morocco's independence. He died in Rabat at the age of 116 on September 9, 1957.

Nepal

Nepal is a country in the Himalayan mountain range in central Asia and is located between India and China.

HEADS OF STATE

PRITHVI (King; May 17, 1881–December 11, 1911). Prithvi Bir Bickrum Shah was born in 1875, the son of Crown Prince Trialokya Vikram. His father died in 1878, and Prithvi succeeded to the throne at the age of six, following the death of his grandfather, Surendra Vikram, on May 17, 1881. He ruled under the regency of the Queen Mother. Nepal was largely controlled by the powerful Rana family that held the hereditary prime ministership. Prithvi was married to two illegitimate daughters of Prime Minister Bir Shumshere Rana, though they bore him no sons. His only son, Tribhuvan, was born in 1906 to a Punjabi princess. Prithvi remained a virtual prisoner in the palace under the Rana leadership. He died, allegedly of slow poisoning, on December 11, 1911.

TRIBHUVAN (King; December 11, 1911–March 13, 1955). Tribhuvan Bir Bikram Shah Dev was born in 1906. He was the only son of King Prithvi. Trib-

huvan ascended to the throne on December 11, 1911, at the age of five, following the death of his father. The Nepal monarchy continued to be controlled by the Rana family, the hereditary prime ministers of Nepal. The Rana family wanted Nepal to join forces with the British in World War I, but the Queen Mother and the army wished to remain neutral. To force the monarchy to accept their position, Prime Minister Chandra Shumshere Rana put a loaded gun to the head of the Queen Mother and ordered King Tribhuvan to address the military on his behalf. The military's loyalty to the monarch resulted in Nepal's alliance with Britain during the war. The young king was kept a virtual prisoner of the Rana family and was coerced into serving as spokesman for their plans, which included the suppression of all liberal and democratic movements in the country. As King Tribhuvan reached adulthood, he chafed under the restraints the Ranas placed on him. The Praja Panchayat movement, formed in 1936, was one of several movements designed to restore power to the monarchy and end the rule of the Ranas. The movements were brutally suppressed, and many of the members were imprisoned or executed. The king's life was reportedly threatened by the Ranas in 1940. Tribhuvan was saved by the influence of the British, who recognized his importance in controlling the military, which was assisting the Allies during World War II. By 1946 opposition to the Ranas had grown to the extent that the Nepali Congress Party was formed. King Tribhuvan was in sympathy with the democratic movements, and in November 1950 he escaped from the palace with most of his family and took refuge in the Indian embassy. He was subsequently granted asylum in India. Prime Minister Mohan Shumshere Rana attempted to install Tribhuvan's young grandson, Jagendra, on the throne, but was thwarted by the refusal of other nations to recognize the new monarch. Early in 1951 the Ranas accepted democratic reforms, and Tribhuvan returned to Nepal and was restored to the throne as a constitutional monarch on February 18, 1951. Tribhuvan suffered from heart disease and went to Zurich, Switzerland, for treatment in 1954. He died in Zurich of a heart attack on March 13, 1955.

HEADS OF GOVERNMENT

BIR SHUMSHERE JUNG BAHADUR RANA (Prime Minister; November 22, 1885–March 5, 1901). Bir Shumshere Jung Bahadur Rana was born in 1852. He was the brother of Jung Bahadur Rana, the initiator of the powerful Rana family's claim to the hereditary prime ministership in 1848. Jung Bahadur died in February 1877, and was succeeded by another brother, Rannoddip. Bir Shumshere arranged the murder of Rannoddip and succeeded him to office on November 22, 1885. Bir Shumshere revised the rolls of succession, favoring his brothers and sons, and executed other members of the Rana family to protect his position. He survived a conspiracy led by his brother, Khadga Shumshere Rana, in 1893. Bir Shumshere held complete control of the Nepal government during his rule, with the minor King Prithvi on the throne. He negotiated a treaty with the British that kept Nepal from becoming a part of the British Empire. Bir Shumshere greatly increased the wealth and property of the Rana family during his rule by his exploitation of the country. He retained power until his death on March 5, 1901.

DEV SHUMSHERE JUNG BAHADUR RANA (Prime Minister; March 5, 1901–June 26, 1901). Dev Shumshere Jung Bahadur Rana was born in 1862. He served as an army commander during the rule of his brother, Prime Minister Bir Shumshere Rana. He succeeded his brother to the hereditary prime ministership of Nepal upon Bir Shumshere's death on March 5, 1901. He began to institute various reforms throughout the country, and considered drafting a new constitution. Other members of the Rana family feared that Dev Shumshere would restore power to the monarchy and force the Ranas from power. The prime minister's brother, Chandra Shumshere, ousted Dev Shumshere from office on June 26, 1901. Dev Shumshere subsequently went into exile and died on February 20, 1914.

CHANDRA SHUMSHERE JUNG BAHADUR RANA (Prime Minister; June 26, 1901–June 22, 1929). Chandra Shumshere Jung Bahadur Rana was born in 1863. He was an army commander during the rule of his brother, Prime Minister Bir Shumshere Rana. Another brother, Dev Shumshere Rana, succeeded to the hereditary prime ministership in March 1901. Chandra Shumshere feared the reforms Dev Shumshere was considering and so deposed him from office on June 26, 1901. Like his predecessors, Chandra Shumshere's government retained complete power in the country. King Prithvi died in 1911, allegedly poisoned by members of the Rana family. His infant son, Tribhuvan, succeeded to the throne, further ensuring the power of the Rana family. A reformist movement sprang up in Nepal during Chandra Shumshere's rule, but the government used repressive measures to crush it. Chandra Shumshere did institute some reforms, such as improving medical care, liberating slaves, and improving the training of the army and the police. The Rana family forced the king to agree to Nepal joining the British war effort during World War I in 1914. He attempted to change the laws of succession to allow his eldest son, Mohan Shumshere, to succeed him to office. This was made difficult by the Dharma Pact, which he had signed in 1913, mandating exile to anyone trying to deprive his brothers of the prime ministership. Chandra poisoned one brother, Fateh Shumshere, to obtain the document, which found its way into the hands of another brother, Juddha Shumshere, who refused to give it to Chandra. The government negotiated a treaty of friendship with Great Britain in 1923 that recognized Nepal's complete independence. Chandra was succeeded in office by his brother, Bhim Shumshere, on June 22, 1929. He died in November 1929.

BHIM SHUMSHERE JUNG BAHADUR RANA (Prime Minister; June 22, 1929–September 1, 1932). Bhim Shumshere Jung Bahadur Rana was born in 1869. He served as a commander in Nepal's army during the administrations of his brothers, Bir Shumshere and Chandra Shumshere. He succeeded Chan-

dra Shumshere to the hereditary prime ministership on June 22, 1929. He continued his predecessors pro–British policies and suppression of reformist elements in the country. He continued to hold office until his death on September 1, 1932.

JUDDHA SHUMSHERE JUNG BAHADUR RANA (Prime Minister; September 1, 1932–November 28, 1945). Juddha Shumshere Jung Bahadur Rana was born in April 1875. He was the son of General Dhir Shumshere Rana. He succeeded to the hereditary prime ministership of Nepal on September 1, 1932, following the death of his elder brother Bhim Shumshere Rana. Two years later Nepal was devastated by a major earthquake, which set back his efforts to modernize the country. Juddha was able to effect numerous social reforms and made advancements in the education and transportation systems of Nepal. During World War II he was a firm ally of Great Britain and increased the number of Gurkha battalions that fought alongside the Allied powers. He also opened Nepal's first foreign embassy in London in 1941 and made efforts to industrialize Nepal. Juddha retired from office on November 28, 1945, because he feared the returning Gurkha soldiers would bring home with them democratic ideas that would threaten the rule of the Rana family. He was succeeded by his brother, Padma Shumshere Rana. Juddha retired to West Nepal, renounced worldly life, and dedicated the remainder of his life to religious contemplation. He died in Dehra Dun, Nepal, on November 23, 1952.

PADMA SHUMSHERE JUNG BAHADUR RANA (Prime Minister; November 28, 1945–February 9, 1948). Padma Shumshere Jung Bahadur Rana was born in 1882. He served as commander-in-chief of the Nepal army and succeeded to the hereditary office of prime minister following the retirement of his brother, Juddha Shumshere Rana, on November 28, 1945. Padma Shumshere began an effort to liberalize Nepal and approved a new constitution in 1948 that gave limited rights to the people. The constitution was never implemented, however, and he resigned on February 9, 1948. He died of a heart attack near Calcutta, India, on April 11, 1961.

Netherlands

The Netherlands is a country in western Europe.

HEADS OF STATE

WILHELMINA (Queen; November 23, 1890–September 4, 1948). Wilhelmina Helena Pauline Maria was born in The Hague on August 31, 1880. She was the daughter of William III and Emma of the Netherlands. She succeeded to the throne following the death of her father on November 23, 1890. Wilhelmina ruled under the regency of her mother until September 6, 1898, when she came of age. She married Prince Hendrik in February 1901. Wilhelmina supported the neutrality of the Netherlands during World War I and left the Netherlands following the Nazi invasion of her country in May 1940. She stayed in London during World War II, where she remained a symbol of opposition to the German occupation. She returned to the Netherlands following the defeat of the Axis Powers in 1945. Wilhelmina abdicated the throne in favor of her daughter, Juliana, on September 4, 1948. She spent her retirement years involved in gardening and writing her memoirs, which were published in 1959. She died of heart disease in Apeldoorn on November 28, 1962.

HEADS OF GOVERNMENT

NICOLAS PIERSON (Prime Minister; July 27, 1897–August 1, 1901). Nicolas Gerard Pierson was born in Amsterdam on February 7, 1839. He was largely self-educated and became a leading Dutch banker. He became president of the Netherlands Bank in 1885. He was also a noted economist and was named to the cabinet as minister of finance in 1892. He worked toward revising the tax system before his resignation in 1894. He was a member of the left wing of the Liberal Party and became prime minister on July 27, 1897. During his term of office he introduced compulsory education, reorganized the army, and improved the public health service. He continued to head the government until August 1, 1901, when Abraham Kuyper became prime minister. Pierson died in Heemstede on December 24, 1909.

ABRAHAM KUYPER (Prime Minister; August 1, 1901–August 16, 1905). Abraham Kuyper was born in Maassluis on October 29, 1837. He was educated at Leiden and became pastor of the Dutch Reformed Church in Beesd in 1863. He went to Amsterdam in 1870 and formed the Anti-Revolutionary Party six years later. His party's platform was to restore Christian tenets to the affairs of government. He was also a leading writer of religious and political works. He became head of the government on August 1, 1901. He sponsored an act of parliament to crush a railway strike, which drew the ire of the Socialists. He remained premier until June 30, 1905, when his conservative coalition was defeated. Kuyper subsequently entered the Dutch senate. He supported Dutch neutrality during World War I despite his personal sympathy for Germany. Kuyper remained a leading political figure in the Netherlands until his death in The Hague on November 8, 1920.

JOHAN DE MEESTER (Prime Minister; August 16, 1905–December 21, 1907). Johan de Meester was born in Hardewijk on December 16, 1851. He formed a coalition government of Liberals and Socialists on August 16, 1905. He worked to improve the army and abolished the system of paid substitution to avoid induction into the army. A controversy concerning military matters brought down his government on December 21, 1907, when the Anti-Revolutionary Party regained power. De Meester died in The Hague on December 27, 1919.

THEODORUS HEEMSKERK (Prime Minister; February 11, 1908–June 27, 1913). Theodorus Heemskerk was born in Amsterdam on July 20, 1852. He was a leader of the Anti-Revolutionary Party and became head of the government on February 11, 1908. He stepped down on June 27, 1913. Heemskerk died in Utrecht on June 12, 1932.

PIETER WILLEM CORT VAN DER LINDEN (Prime Minister; August 29, 1913–July 13, 1918). Pieter Willem Adriaan Cort van der Linden was born in The Hague in 1846. He became prime minister on August 29, 1913. His government initiated a revision of the constitution. He headed the Dutch government throughout World War I and advocated a policy of neutrality. He left office on July 13, 1918. Cort van der Linden died in The Hague on July 15, 1935.

CHARLES RUYS DE BEEREN-BROUCK (Prime Minister; September 9, 1918–June 29, 1925). Charles Joséph Maria Ruys de Beerenbrouck was born in Roermond on December 1, 1873. He was from a noble Catholic family. He was minister of justice in 1907. He was called upon to head the government on September 9, 1918, and remained prime minister until June 29, 1925. He returned to office on August 10, 1929, and served until May 26, 1933. Ruys de Beerenbrouck died in Utrecht on April 17, 1936.

HENDRIK COLIJN (Prime Minister; July 30, 1925–November 12, 1925). Hendrikus Colijn was born in Haarlemmermeer on June 22, 1869. He entered the Dutch army in 1892 and saw action in the Dutch East Indies. He was elected to parliament in 1909 and was named to the cabinet as minister of war in 1911. He reorganized the army before his retirement in 1913 to become director of Batavia Oil Company. He went to London in 1919 to serve as a director of Royal Dutch Shell until 1922. He became the leader of the Calvinist Anti-Revolutionary Party and briefly headed the government as prime minister from July 30, 1925, to November 12, 1925. He returned to office as prime minister on May 26, 1933. He was an outspoken critic of Germany's Nazi government. Colijn left office on July 25, 1939. He supported the Allied cause during the early days of World War II. He was taken into custody soon after the German invasion of the Netherlands in May 1940. He was subsequently imprisoned and died during the occupation of a heart ailment in Illmenau, Thuringia, on September 18, 1944.

DIRK JAN DE GEER (Prime Minister; March 8, 1926–July 1, 1929). Dirk Jan de Geer was born in Groningen on

December 14, 1870. He was educated at the University of Utrecht, where he received a degree in law in 1895. He entered politics in 1901 and became a town councilor in Rotterdam. He was elected to the chamber of deputies as a member of the Christian Historical Party in 1907. He was named to the cabinet as minister of finance in 1921 and served until 1923. He was minister of the interior in Hendrik Colijn's government in 1925. He formed a coalition government as prime minister on March 8, 1926, four months after Colijn had resigned the office. Premier-designates Johan de Visser and Joséph Limburg had been unable to form a cabinet. De Geer also served as minister of finance until stepping down from office on July 1, 1929. He was named minister of state in 1933. De Greer formed a coalition government on August 1, 1939. He was prime minister at the time of the German invasion of the Netherlands in May 1940. He accompanied the government to London. He proposed a peace settlement that was strongly opposed by Queen Wilhelmina, and so De Geer stepped down on September 4, 1940. He was sent on a mission to the Dutch East Indies, but instead, he defected from the government-in-exile and returned to occupied Holland. After the liberation he was charged with having "shaken the determination of the Dutch people to continue the war." He was fined and sentenced to a year imprisonment in May 1947, but the sentence was suspended because of his advanced age. De Geer died in Soest on November 28, 1960.

CHARLES RUYS DE BEEREN-BROUCK (Prime Minister; August 10, 1929–May 26, 1933). *See earlier entry under Heads of Government.*

HENDRIK COLIJN (Prime Minister; May 26, 1933–July 25, 1939). *See earlier entry under Heads of Government.*

DIRK JAN DE GEER (Prime Minister; August 1, 1939–September 4, 1940). *See earlier entry under Heads of Government.*

PIETER S. GERBRANDY (Prime Minister; September 4, 1940–June 25, 1945). Pieter Sjoerds Gerbrandy was born in Goengamieden on April 13, 1885. He was educated at the Zetten Gymnasium and the Amsterdam Free University, where he received a degree in law. He subsequently served as a law professor at the University from 1930 to 1939. Gerbrandy was named minister of justice in 1939 and accompanied the Dutch government-in-exile in London following the German occupation of the Netherlands in 1940. He succeeded Dirk Jan de Geer as prime minister of the Dutch government-in-exile on September 4, 1940. He also retained his position as minister of justice and served as minister of the colonies until 1942. Gerbrandy was minister of coordination and warfare from 1942 to 1945. His government returned to the Netherlands following the liberation of the country. He and his cabinet announced their resignations in February 1945, and he was replaced as prime minister by Willem Schermerhorn on June 25, 1945. Gerbrandy went on to serve in the Dutch parliament. He was named an honorary minister of state in 1955. Gerbrandy died in The Hague on September 7, 1961.

WILLEM SCHERMERHORN (Prime Minister; June 25, 1945–July 2, 1946. Willem Schermerhorn was born in Akersloot on December 17, 1894. Educated as a civil engineer, he was the founder of the Dutch Institute of Geodesy and served as its director until 1931. He surveyed New Guinea at the request of the Dutch government in 1936 and assisted the Chinese government of Chiang Kai-shek as a cartographical advisor in 1937. Schermerhorn was an advisor to the Dutch ministry of public works and was the leader of the Dutch Anti-Fascist League prior to World War II. He was arrested by the Germans during the oc- cupation of the Netherlands. When he was released in 1943, he became the leader of the Dutch Resistance. Scher- merhorn was a founder of the Labor Party after the liberation of the Nether- lands and was selected to head an in- terim coalition government as prime minister on June 25, 1945. He retained the position until general elections could be held and stepped down on July 2,

1946. He subsequently served as presi- dent of a government commission on the Dutch East Indies from 1946 until 1947. Schermerhorn entered parliament in 1948 and was elected to the senate in 1951. He also accepted a position as pro- fessor of geodesy at the Delft Technical University in 1951. He retired from pol- itics in 1963 and left his teaching posi- tion the following year. Schermerhorn died in Akersloot on March 10, 1977.

New Zealand

New Zealand is an island country in the Pacific Ocean. It was granted dominion status by Great Britain on September 26, 1907.

HEADS OF STATE

EARL OF LIVERPOOL (Gover- nor-General; June 28, 1917–July 7, 1920). Arthur William de Brito Saville Fol- jambe, the second Earl of Liverpool, was born on May 27, 1870, the son of Lord Hawkesbury. He was educated at Eton and Sandhurst and had a distinguished military career. He served as aide-de- camp to Earl Cadogan, Lord Lieutenant of Ireland, from 1898 to 1900. He saw action in South Africa in 1901 and 1902. He served as state steward and lord chamberlain to Lord Aberdeen in Ire- land from 1906 until 1908. He succeeded to the title of second Earl of Liverpool in 1907. He retired from the army with the rank of lieutenant colonel. Lord Liv- erpool went to New Zealand as governor and commander-in-chief in 1912. He be- came the first governor-general of the dominion of New Zealand on June 28, 1917. He retired from his post on July 7, 1920. Lord Liverpool died at his home, Canwick Hall, near Lincoln, England, on May 15, 1941.

VISCOUNT JELLICOE (Gover- nor-General; September 27, 1920–No-

vember 26, 1924). John Rusworth Jelli- coe was born in Southampton, England, on December 5, 1859. He was educated at Rottingdean and entered the British navy. He served as a lieutenant in the Egyptian War in 1881. He was promoted to commander in June 1891 and to cap- tain in January 1897. He was badly wounded in Peitsang, China, during the Boxer Rebellion in 1898. He served as commander-in-chief to the First Sea Lord, Lord Fisher, from February 1905 until August 1907. He was promoted to rear admiral in February 1907 and be- came controller of the navy the follow- ing year. He commanded the Atlantic Fleet as vice admiral from December 1910 until he was appointed commander- in-chief of the Grand Fleet in August 1914 and became First Sea Lord in No- vember 1916, a position he held until De- cember 1917. He was granted the title Viscount Jellicoe of Scarpa in 1919 and was promoted to admiral of the fleet in April of that year. He was appointed governor-general of New Zealand on September 27, 1920. He remained in New Zealand until his term ended on

November 26, 1924. He returned to England and retired from the navy at the end of the year. Lord Jellicoe served as president of the British Legion from 1928 until 1932. He also authored several books about the navy. He died in London on November 20, 1935.

SIR CHARLES FERGUSSON (Governor-General; December 13, 1924–February 8, 1930). Charles Fergusson was born in Edinburgh, Scotland, on January 17, 1865. He was educated at Eton and Sandhurst and entered the Grenadier Guard in 1883. He served with distinction under Lord Kitchener in the Sudan campaigns in the late 1890s. He became adjutant general of the Egyptian army in 1901. Fergusson succeeded to the title of Seventh Baronet of Kilkerran in 1907 when his father was killed in an earthquake in Jamaica. He was promoted to major general in 1908 and served as inspector of infantry from 1908 until 1912. Fergusson commanded troops in France during World War I and served as military governor of Cologne from December 1918 until August 1919. He was promoted to general in July 1921 and retired from the military the following year. He was an unsuccessful candidate for parliament in 1923. Fergusson was appointed governor-general of New Zealand the following year and took office on December 13, 1924. He was active in promoting the social and industrial development of New Zealand. He completed his term on February 8, 1930, and returned to Great Britain. Fergusson died at his home in Ayshire on January 20, 1951.

VISCOUNT BLEDISLOE (Governor-General; March 19, 1930–March 15, 1935). Charles Bathurst was born in Lydney House, Gloucestershire, on September 21, 1867. He was educated at Eton and University College, Oxford. He continued his education at the Royal Agricultural College. He was elected to the House of Commons in 1910 as a Unionist. He established himself as a leading agricultural authority. He represented the food controller in the House of Commons in 1916 and became chairman of the royal commission on the sugar supply. He was created Baron Bledisloe of Lydney in 1917. He held various other agricultural appointments over the next several years. Lord Bledisloe took office as governor-general of New Zealand on March 19, 1930. He continued his interest in agricultural matters while there. He completed his term on March 15, 1935, and was created a viscount upon his return to England. Lord Bledisloe served as chairman of a royal commission to South Africa in 1938. He served as president of the Royal Agricultural Society of England in 1946. Lord Bledisloe died at his home at Lydney, Gloucestershire, on July 3, 1958.

VISCOUNT GALWAY (Governor-General; April 12, 1935–February 3, 1941). George Vere Arundell Monckton-Arundell was born on May 24, 1882. He was educated at Eton and Christ Church, Oxford. He entered the military and served with the Sherwood Rangers Yeomanry from 1900 until 1904, and then with the 1st Life Guards. He served with distinction during World War I. He was promoted to lieutenant colonel in 1919 and commanded the First Life Guards from 1925 until 1929, when he retired from the military. He succeeded his father to the titles of 8th Viscount Galway, Baron Killard, and Baron Monckton. He was appointed governor-general of New Zealand and took office on April 12, 1935. He was a popular figure with the people and the government of New Zealand and his term was extended for over a year in 1940 at the start of World War II. He remained in New Zealand until February 3, 1941, and then returned to England. He died at his home in Nottinghamshire on March 27, 1943.

SIR CYRIL L. N. NEWALL (Governor-General; February 22, 1941–April

19, 1946). Cyril Louis Norton Newall was born in England on February 15, 1886. He joined the British army and served in India before the start of World War I. He became a pilot in 1911 and served in the Royal Flying Corps in France during the war. Newall became an early member of the Royal Air Force. He was named chief of the air staff in 1937 and was instrumental in preparing Britain's defenses against Germany during World War II. Newall remained leader of the air command until October 1940, when he was appointed governor-general of New Zealand. He assumed the position on February 22, 1941, and assisted the British war effort. After Newall completed his term on April 19, 1946, he returned to England, where he was granted the title of Baron Newall of Clifton-upon-Dunsmoor. He died in London on November 30, 1963.

HEADS OF GOVERNMENT

RICHARD JOHN SEDDON (Prime Minister; April 27, 1893–June 10, 1906). Richard John Seddon was born in Eccleston, Lancashire, on June 22, 1845. He emigrated to Australia in 1863 and went to New Zealand three years later. He worked in the gold mines there and opened a general store. He also entered politics and was elected to parliament in 1879. He was named to John Ballance's Liberal government as minister of mines and public works in December 1890. He succeeded to the office of prime minister when Ballance died in office in April 1893. His government introduced much social legislation, including old-age pensions and industrial reforms. New Zealand annexed the Cook Islands in 1901. The Liberals under Seddon were victorious in elections in December 1905. Seddon died suddenly while at sea on a return visit from Sydney, Australia, on June 10, 1906.

SIR JOSEPH G. WARD (Prime Minister; June 1906–July 1912). Sir Joséph George Ward was born in Melbourne in 1856. He began working at the age of 13 as a telegraph boy and was soon working for the department of railways. After beginning a successful mercantile business, he entered politics in the late 1880s. He was elected to the New Zealand parliament as a Liberal in 1887, and entered the cabinet as postmaster-general in 1891. He was also named colonial treasurer in 1893. Ward became prime minister after Richard Seddon's death in June 1906, and held that office until his resignation in July 1912. He was named minister of finance and postmaster-general in the National cabinet in 1915. He was defeated for reelection to Parliament in 1919, but was returned to office in 1925. He became the leader of the National Party in 1928, taking office as prime minister on December 10, 1928. He stepped down due to poor health on May 15, 1930, and died on July 8, 1930.

WILLIAM F. MASSEY (Prime Minister; July 10, 1912–May 10, 1925). William Ferguson Massey was born in Limavady, County Derry, Ireland, on March 26, 1856. He joined his family in New Zealand in 1870 and became a successful farmer. He entered politics and was elected to the Parliament from Waitemata in 1894. He became leader of the opposition Conservative Party in 1903. The Conservatives took control of the government in 1912, and Massey formed a cabinet on July 10, 1912. He also headed the ministries of finance, railways, and agriculture. Massey actively supported the British effort during World War I. He attended several meetings of the war cabinet during the conflict and represented New Zealand at the Paris Peace Conference after the war.

He continued to lead New Zealand's government in the postwar era until his death in Wellington on May 10, 1925.

SIR FRANCIS H. D. BELL (Prime Minister; May 14, 1925–May 30, 1925). Francis Henry Dillon Bell was born in Nelson on March 31, 1851. He received a degree in law from St. John's College, Cambridge, and then began a law practice in Wellington and became crown solicitor there in 1885. He served as mayor of Wellington in 1892, 1893, and 1897. He was elected to the legislative council in 1912 and was named to the government as governor of marine in 1921. He served until 1922. He briefly served as prime minister of New Zealand from May 14, 1925, to May 30, 1925, following William Massey's death. He stepped down when Joséph Coates formed a government on May 30, 1925. Bell served as minister of external affairs in Coates's government from 1925 to 1926. He served as a member of the executive council without portfolio from 1926 until 1928. Bell died on March 13, 1936.

JOSÉPH G. COATES (Prime Minister; May 30, 1925–December 10, 1928). Joséph Gordon Coates was born in Matakohe, North Auckland, on February 3, 1878. He was educated locally and entered politics when he was elected to the Otameatea County Council. Coates was elected to the parliament from Kaipara in 1911. He commanded the 1st Auckland Infantry in combat in France during World War I. He returned to New Zealand after the war and was named minister of justice in 1919. He was also given the post of minister of public works and, in 1921, was named minister of native affairs. He remained in the cabinet as minister of railways in 1923. He was selected to become prime minister on May 30, 1925, following the death of William Massey. He led the government until December 10, 1928, when the Parliament gave him a vote of no confidence. He led the opposition for the next

three years. He returned to the cabinet as minister of public works, employment, and transportation in a coalition cabinet in 1931. He served as minister of finance, customs, and transport from 1933 until 1935. He became a member of the war cabinet in 1940 and minister of the armed forces and war coordination in June 1942. Coates died at his office in Wellington on May 27, 1943.

SIR JOSEPH G. WARD (Prime Minister; December 10, 1928–May 15, 1930). *See earlier entry under Heads of Government.*

GEORGE W. FORBES (Prime Minister; May 28, 1930–December 6, 1935). George William Forbes was born in Lyttleton on March 12, 1869. He was elected to the New Zealand Parliament from Hurunui in 1908 and became the chief whip of the Liberal Party in 1912. He formed the National Party in 1925 and merged the new party with other former Liberals in the United Party in 1928. He served in several cabinets as minister of lands and agriculture and also as minister of finance. He was leader of the United Party when he became prime minister as head of a coalition government on May 28, 1930. He also served in the government as minister for external affairs. He was active in the promotion of trade in the British Empire and represented New Zealand at the World Economic Conference in 1932. His party was defeated in elections in 1935, and Forbes stepped down on December 6, 1935. He led the opposition until 1936. Forbes continued to serve in Parliament until his retirement in 1943. He died in Wellington on May 18, 1947.

MICHAEL JOSÉPH SAVAGE (Prime Minister; December 6, 1935–March 26, 1940). Michael Joséph Savage was born in Benalla, Victoria, Australia, on March 7, 1872. He went to New Zealand in 1907 where he worked as a miner and became active in the trade union movement. He entered politics and was elected to the Parliament as a Labor Party member from Auckland West in 1919. He succeeded Henry Holland as leader of the Labor Party in 1933. Savage became New Zealand's first head of a Labor government when being elected prime minister on December 6, 1935. He also headed the ministries of external affairs and native affairs. His government promoted such social welfare measures as national medical aid and housing and established the forty-hour work week. His government was returned to power in the 1938 elections. Savage continued to head the government until his death in Wellington on March 26, 1940.

PETER FRASER (Prime Minister; April 1, 1940–December 12, 1949). Peter Fraser was born in Fearn, Rosshire, Scotland, on August 28, 1884. Though his father was a member of the local Liberal Party, Fraser joined the Independent Labor Party when he moved to London in 1908. Fraser relocated to New Zealand in 1910 and took a job as a longshoreman in Auckland. He became president of the Auckland General Laborers' Union and served as editor of the Maoriland *Worker*, a Socialist national newspaper. He was imprisoned for several months during World War I for his opposition to conscription. Fraser was elected to the house of representatives in 1918, and the following year he was also elected as a member of the Wellington city council. He remained on the council until 1923 and served again from 1933 until 1936. He was selected as deputy leader of the Labor Party in 1934 and was appointed to the cabinet in the Labor government from 1935 until 1940 as minister of education, health, and marine. In 1939 Fraser advanced to deputy prime minister, and he became acting prime minster in August due to the ill health of Michael Joséph Savage. He became party leader and prime minister after Savage's death the following year on March 26, 1940. He led the New Zealand government throughout World War II and threw the weight of New Zealand's forces solidly behind the Allied cause. He also continued to advocate the social security and welfare legislation enacted by his predecessor. Following the war, Fraser was an active participant in the formation of the United Nations and served as chairman of the committee that drafted the trusteeship chapter of the United Nations charter. Fraser remained as head of the government until the Labor Party's defeat in the elections of 1949, which forced him to step down as prime minister on December 12, 1949. He remained as leader of the opposition until his death in Wellington from heart failure on December 12, 1950.

Nicaragua

Nicaragua is a country in Central America. It was granted independence from Spain on September 28, 1821.

HEADS OF STATE

JOSÉ SANTOS ZELAYA (President; February 1, 1894–December 16, 1909). José Santos Zelaya was born on October 31, 1853. He was the son of a wealthy coffee planter. He was educated in France and England before returning to Nicaragua. He served in the army and was promoted to the rank of general. Zelaya supported Conservative General Francisco Gutierrez's revolt against the government of Roberto Sacasa in June 1893. Zelaya led a Liberal rebellion against Gutierrez's successor, Salvador Machado, and became president on February 1, 1894. Zelaya introduced numerous reforms to the country and was successful in establishing industries in Nicaragua. He ruled as a dictator, using a modernized army to put down numerous rebellions during his term of office. He was a supporter of a Central American union between Nicaragua, El Salvador, and Honduras. Zelaya came into conflict with the United States when he stymied an agreement to build a canal through Nicaragua rather than Panama. Nicaragua defeated Honduras in a border war in 1906. Zelaya's dispute with the United States over the possibility of another European-sponsored canal being constructed in Nicaragua led the United States to support a rebellion against Zelaya. He was ousted in an uprising led by General Juan José Estrada on December 16, 1909. Zelaya went into exile in the United States and died after a long illness in New York City on May 17, 1919.

JOSÉ MADRIZ (President; December 16, 1909–August 20, 1910). José Madriz was born in León. He was educated as a lawyer and served as a judge on the Central American Court of Justice. He was named to succeed José Santos Zelaya as president when Zelaya was forced from office on December 16, 1909. General Juan José Estrada continued his rebellion against Madriz's government and ousted him from office on August 20, 1910. Madriz fled to Amapala Island, in Honduras before settling into exile in Mexico. He died in Mexico City on May 15, 1911.

JOSÉ DOLORES ESTRADA (President; August 20, 1910–August 29, 1910). José Dolores Estrada was the brother of General Juan José Estrada. His brother led the rebellion that ousted

the government of José Madriz on August 20, 1910. José Estrada briefly served as interim president from August 20, 1910, until Juan Estrada assumed power on August 29, 1910.

JUAN JOSÉ ESTRADA (President; August 29, 1910–May 8, 1911). Juan José Estrada was born in 1871. He served in the Nicaraguan army and attained the rank of general. Estrada served as governor of the department of Mosquitia under President José Santos Zelaya. Estrada was a leader of the revolt that forced Zelaya from office in 1909. He continued the rebellion against Zelaya's successor, driving him from office in August 1910. Estrada's brother, José Dolores Estrada, briefly assumed office until Juan Estrada became provisional president on August 29, 1910. He was elected to the presidency the following December, though his administration was largely controlled by his minister of war, General Luis Mena. Estrada clashed with Mena in 1911 and was forced to resign on May 8, 1911. He went into exile in the United States and lived in Brooklyn. He eventually returned to Nicaragua and served as governor of the Bluefields District from 1928 until 1929. He subsequently retired from public life and died in Managua following abdominal surgery on July 11, 1947.

ADOLFO DÍAZ (President; May 8, 1911–December 31, 1916). Adolfo Díaz was born in Costa Rica on July 15, 1877. He worked as a clerk for the Bluefields District Mining Company before entering politics. He supported Juan Estrada's rebellion against José Santos Zelaya in 1909. Díaz became Estrada's vice president in 1911 after Zelaya's ouster. Estrada resigned on May 8, 1911, and Díaz succeeded to the presidency. He developed close financial and political ties with the United States. General Luis Mena led a revolt against the government in July 1912, and Díaz requested support from the United States for his regime. United

States marines were dispatched to crush the rebellion. Diáz was reelected president in January 1913. He completed his term of office on December 31, 1916, and was replaced by Emiliano Chamorro. Chamorro reclaimed the presidency in a coup after losing the election in 1926. The United States refused to recognize his government, and the Nicaraguan senate designated Diáz president on October 30, 1926. He received the support of the United States and retained office until January 1, 1929. Diáz went into exile in Costa Rica during the presidency of Anastasio Somoza García. He died in San José on January 27, 1964.

EMILIANO CHAMORRO VARGAS (President; January 1, 1917–December 31, 1920). Emiliano Chamorro Vargas was born on May 11, 1871. He began his career as a revolutionary when he led an uprising against President José Santos Zelaya in 1893. The rebellion was unsuccessful, and he took part in over a dozen other revolts against Zelaya. Chamorro participated in Juan José Estrada's successful coup against Zelaya in 1909. Chamorro subsequently served as chairman of the constituent assembly and leader of the Conservative Party. Chamorro defeated General Luis Mena's revolt against President Adolfo Diáz in 1912 and was named minister to the United States, where he negotiated the Bryan-Chamorro Treaty in 1914, which gave the United States an option to build a canal through Nicaragua. Chamorro returned to Nicaragua in 1916 to contest the presidency. He was elected and took office on January 1, 1917. He attempted to improve the economy and pay off foreign creditors. Chamorro was succeeded by his uncle, Diego Manuel Chamorro, on December 31, 1920. Emiliano Chamorro was defeated in the presidential election of 1923 by Carlos Solórzano. He led a revolt against Solórzano, ousting him and claiming the presidency on January 17, 1926. The United States refused to recognize his presidency, and he was pres-

sured to relinquish the office to Adolfo Diáz on October 30, 1926. Chamorro subsequently served as minister to several European countries. He was an opponent of the regime of Anastasio Somoza and made several attempts to overthrow the government. He reached an accommodation with Somoza in 1950 that granted the Conservative Party a set number of seats in the congress. His acceptance of Somoza's terms cost him the support of many of the more radical members of the Conservative Party. Chamorro died on February 26, 1966.

DIEGO MANUEL CHAMORRO (President; January 1, 1921–October 12, 1923). Diego Manuel Chamorro was born in 1861. He was the son of Dr. Pedro J. Chamorro, who had been Nicaragua's president from 1875 until 1879. The younger Chamorro entered politics and became mayor of Granada in 1882. He was named to the cabinet as minister of foreign affairs in 1911 and became minister of public instruction in 1913. He served as Nicaragua's minister to the United States from May 1918 until 1920, when he was elected Nicaragua's president. He took office on January 1, 1921, succeeding his nephew Emiliano Chamorro. Diego Chamorro died in office in San Juan on October 12, 1923.

BARTOLO MARTÍNEZ (President; October 12, 1923–January 1, 1925). Bartolomo Martínez served as vice president under Diego Manuel Chamorro. He succeeded to the presidency on October 12, 1923, following the death of Diego Chamorro. Martínez was unsuccessful in the subsequent election and relinquished office to Carlos Solórzano on January 1, 1925. He remained in Solórzano's government as minister of the interior. He fled into exile in El Salvador after Solórzano's ouster in 1926 but returned to Nicaragua the following year. Martínez died of a heart attack at his home in Matagalpa on January 30, 1936.

CARLOS SOLÓRZANO (President; January 1, 1925–January 14, 1926). Carlos Solórzano was born in 1860. He was the Conservative Party's candidate for president in 1924. He was victorious and took office on January 1, 1925, but a revolt led by Emiliano Chamorro forced him from office on January 14, 1926. Solórzano went into exile in the United States. He settled in San Francisco, where he remained until 1935. He then went to San José, Costa Rica, where he died of a heart attack on April 30, 1936.

EMILIANO CHAMORRO VARGAS (President; January 17, 1926–October 30, 1926). *See earlier entry under Heads of State.*

ADOLFO DIÁZ (President; October 30, 1926–January 1, 1929). *See earlier entry under Heads of State.*

JOSÉ MARIA MONCADA (President; January 1, 1929–January 1, 1933). José Maria Moncada was born in 1871. He served in the Nicaraguan military, rising to the rank of general. He was a leading member of the Liberal Party and led a revolt against Emiliano Chamorro's revolutionary government in 1926. Moncada was elected president in an election supervised by the United States and took office on January 1, 1929. He was instrumental in the construction of several major rail lines and nationalized the National Bank. It was during his administration that a major earthquake devastated Managua in 1931. Moncada completed his term on January 1, 1933. He remained active in politics, serving as president of the senate. He was secretary of state in Anastasio Somoza's cabinet when he died of a heart attack in Managua on February 23, 1945.

JUAN BAUTISTA SACASA (President; January 1, 1933–May 31, 1936). Juan Bautista Sacasa was born on December 21, 1874. Sacasa received a medical degree and served as dean of the University of León's School of Medicine. He became president of the Public Health Counsel. He was a leading member of the Liberal Party and served as Carlos Solórzano's vice president in 1925. The government was ousted in a coup led by Emiliano Chamorro. He and General José Maria Moncada staged the subsequent Liberal revolt against Chamorro. Moncada was elected president in 1929, and Sacasa served as minister to the United States during that administration. Sacasa was elected president in 1932 and took office on January 1, 1933. Guerrilla leader Augusto César Sandino continued to rebel against the government. The United States created the Nicaraguan National Guard under the command of Anastasio Somoza García. Sandino was assassinated by Somoza's troops while Sacasa was attempting to negotiate a peace settlement. Sacasa was forced from office by Somoza on May 31, 1936. He went into exile in the United States and died at his home in Los Angeles on April 17, 1946.

CARLOS BRENES JARQUÍN (President; June 9, 1936–December 31, 1936). Carlos A. Brenes Jarquín was born in Masaya in 1886. He studied medicine in California and San Salvador and was a practicing physician before he entered politics. He became a leading member of the Liberal Party and was elected to the Nicaraguan senate. He was chosen by the congress to serve as president on June 9, 1936, following the resignation of Juan Bautista Sacasa. Brenes Jarquín was granted dictatorial powers to overhaul Nicaragua's financial situation and to balance the budget. He relinquished office to military strongman Anastasio Somoza García on December 31, 1936, following Somoza's election to the presidency. He died of heart disease in Managua on January 2, 1942.

ANASTASIO SOMOZA GARCÍA (President; January 1, 1937–May 1, 1947). Anastasio Somoza García was born in

San Marcos on February 1, 1896. He was educated in Nicaragua and at Pierce Commercial College in Philadelphia, Pennsylvania. He worked with the Paige Motor Company before returning to Nicaragua. Somoza joined the Liberal Party and gained influence by serving as an interpreter during the intervention of United States marines in Nicaragua in 1927. Liberal Party candidate José M. Moncada was elected president in November 1928, and Somoza was appointed governor of León. He also achieved prominence in the Civil Guard, where he rose to the rank of general. Juan B. Sacasa, the uncle of Somoza's wife, was elected president in 1932, and Somoza was named minister of war. The Nicaraguan army and United States marines continued to battle insurgents led by César Sandino. Sandino accepted an armistice with the Nicaraguan government and attended a dinner meeting with President Sacasa on February 21, 1934, under a promise of safe conduct. However, he was arrested by officers of Somoza's national guard following the meeting, and was summarily executed. Somoza became the leading figure in the Nicaraguan government and ousted Sacasa in 1936. He installed Carlos Brenes Jarquín as interim president. Somoza was unopposed for the presidency in elections in December 1936 and was sworn into office on January 1, 1937, and

was reelected president in 1942. He declined to be a candidate in the presidential election in 1947 and relinquished office to his handpicked successor, Leonardo Arguello, on May 1, 1947. Arguello attempted to govern without consulting Somoza and was ousted by a military coup later in the month. Somoza installed Victor Román y Reyes as president in August 1947. Somoza was again elected president by congress on May 7, 1950, following the death of Román y Reyes. He was reelected in government-controlled elections in May 1951. During Somoza's reign the economic situation of Nicaragua greatly improved due to the president's rigid control over the country. Somoza's personal wealth and that of his family also greatly increased. Nicaragua engaged in a brief border war with Costa Rica in January 1955. Somoza challenged Costa Rican president José Figueres Ferrer to a duel before the Organization of American States negotiated an end to the fighting. Somoza was shot four times and seriously wounded in León on September 21, 1956. His assailant, Rigoberto Lopez Perez, was immediately slain by Somoza's bodyguards. Somoza was taken to a hospital in the Panama Canal Zone, where he underwent surgery. He died of his wounds on September 29, 1956, and was succeeded in the presidency by his son, Luis.

Norway

Norway is a country in the western Scandinavian peninsula in northern Europe. It was granted independence from Sweden on October 26, 1905.

HEADS OF STATE

OSCAR II (King; September 18, 1872–November 18, 1905). *See earlier entry under Sweden: Heads of State.*

HAAKON VII (King; November 18, 1905–September 21, 1957). Haakon was born Christian Frederick Charles George

Waldemar Axel in Charlottenlund, Denmark, on August 3, 1872. He was the second son of the future King Frederick VIII of Denmark and was known as Prince Carl. He entered the Danish navy in 1886. Prince Carl married Princess Maud, the daughter of the future King Edward VII of Great Britain, in July 1896. He was asked to become king of the newly independent country of Norway following the dissolution of the Swedish-Norwegian union in 1905. He agreed to assume the throne provided a referendum was held in which the Norwegian people would approve his selection. They did so by a large majority, and Prince Carl was crowned King Haakon VII of Norway on November 18, 1905. He supported Norway's neutrality during World War I. King Haakon attempted to ensure Norway's neutrality and independence during World War II, but Germany invaded Norway in April 1940, and the king fled with the royal family to avoid capture. He went to Great Britain, where he remained in exile during the war. He returned to Oslo in June 1945, following the liberation. Haakon celebrated the golden anniversary of his rule in 1955. He died in Oslo from a respiratory ailment on September 21, 1957.

HEADS OF GOVERNMENT

JOHANNES WILHELM CHRISTIAN STEEN (Prime Minister; February 12, 1898–April 21, 1902). Johannes Wilhelm Christian Steen was born in Kristiania on June 14, 1834. He was a grammar school headmaster and an advocate of reform in rural education. He was elected to the Storting (parliament) in 1859 as a member of the Radical Left Party. He was a leading ally of Johan Sverdrup. Steen was selected to head the government as prime minister on February 12, 1892. His government resigned on April 22, 1893, when King Oscar II refused to allow the formation of a Norwegian consular service separate from Sweden. He again headed the government from February 12, 1898, to April 21, 1902. Steen died in Voss on April 1, 1906.

OTTO ALBERT BLEHR (Prime Minister; April 21, 1902–October 21, 1903). Otto Albert Blehr was born in Stange on February 17, 1847. He was a leading lawyer and a member of the Liberal Party. He was instrumental in the establishment of parliamentary government in Norway in 1884. He formed a government as prime minister on April 21, 1902, and advocated Norway's separation from Sweden. He was defeated in elections in 1903 and stepped down on October 21, 1903. He withdrew from politics until 1917, when he was named to the cabinet as minister of finance. Blehr was again called upon to head the government on June 22, 1921. His government enacted the prohibition of alcohol. The import of strong wines was allowed in order to maintain Norway's fish trade with Portugal and Spain. His government was defeated by a large margin in 1923, and he stepped down on March 2, 1923. He subsequently served as a member of Norway's delegation to the League of Nations. Blehr died on July 17, 1927.

GEORG FRANCIS HAGERUP (Prime Minister; October 21, 1903–March 2, 1905). Georg Francis Hagerup was born in 1853. He was a leading law professor and legal scholar. A member of the Conservative Party, he served as minister of justice under Emil Stang from 1893. He succeeded Stang as prime minister on October 14, 1895. He headed a coalition government, while also holding the justice ministership, until February 12, 1898. Hagerup again served as prime minister from October 21, 1903, until his resignation over a domestic issue on March 2, 1905. He subsequently served as a delegate to the Hague Conference in 1907 and led the first Norwegian delegation to the League of Nations in 1920. Hagerup died on February 8, 1921.

CHRISTIAN MICHELSEN (Prime Minister; March 2, 1905–October 28, 1907). Peter Christian Hersleb Michelsen was born in Bergen on March 15, 1857. He was a leading lawyer and was later involved in the shipping business. He was elected to the Storting in 1891 as a member of the Radical Left. He stepped down from politics after three years to resume his business career. He returned to the Storting in 1903 as the leader of a Liberal splinter group of the Radical Left. He joined Georg Hagerup's Liberal-Conservative coalition government as a member of the state council later in the year and subsequently served as minister of finance. He succeeded Hagerup as prime minister on March 2, 1905. His government was responsible for the final separation of Norway from Sweden, as Norway proclaimed its independence in November 1905. Michelsen remained prime minister during the early years of the reign of King Haakon VII. He resigned on October 28, 1907, and returned to business. He served as the first chairman of the Norwegian Association of Shipping the following year. He remained a major figure in Norwegian politics until his death on June 29, 1925.

JORGEN G. LOVLAND (Prime Minister; October 28, 1907–March 13, 1908). Jorgen Gunnerson Lovland was born in Lauvland on February 3, 1857. He was a teacher and leading nationalist. He served in the Storting from the early 1880s, where he was an opponent of the government of Johan Sverdrup. He served in the first government of independent Norway in 1905 as resident

minister to Stockholm and foreign minister. He succeeded Christian Michelsen as prime minister on October 28, 1907. His government fell after a negative vote in the Storting, and he stepped down on March 13, 1908. He remained a leading political figure in Norway and served as president of the Storting from 1913 until 1915. He subsequently served as minister of church and education from 1915 until 1920. Lovland died in Kristiania on August 21, 1922.

GUNNAR KNUDSEN (Prime Minister; March 19, 1908–January 21, 1910). Gunnar Knudsen was born in Stokke on September 19, 1848. He was a leading shipowner and business executive. He was elected to the Storting in 1891 as a member of the Liberal Party. He served as minister of finance under Christian Michelsen from March until October 1905. He subsequently became an opponent of the Michelsen government. He led a minority government from March 19, 1908, until January 21, 1910. He returned to power to head the government on January 29, 1913. His government instituted numerous reforms in workers rights and health care and granted full voting rights to women. He remained prime minister throughout World War I and maintained Norway's neutrality during the conflict. The Liberal Party suffered a major setback in the 1918 elections, though Knudsen continued to govern until his resignation on June 21, 1920, over an issue of government spending. He subsequently retired from politics and died on December 1, 1928.

WOLLERT KONOW (Prime Minister; February 1, 1910–January 11, 1912). Wollert Konow was born in Bergen in 1845. He was a leading landowner and represented Sondre Bergenhus in the Storting until 1885, when his support for a government grant for controversial satiric novelist Alexander Kielland cost him his reelection. He briefly returned to the Storting from 1898 until 1900. He was reelected in 1909 and was called upon to head the government on February 1, 1910. He headed a cabinet composed primarily of members of the Liberal Left until he was forced to step down on January 11, 1912. Konow died in 1924.

JENS C. M. BRATLIE (Prime Minister; February 19, 1912–January 24, 1913). Jens Christian Meinich Bratlie was born in Nordreland on January 17, 1856. He was a leading army officer and held many posts in the ministry of defense. He became head of the services enrollment in 1898. He became leader of the Conservative Party in 1911 and formed a government as prime minister on February 19, 1912. The Conservatives were defeated in subsequent elections and Bratlie stepped down on January 24, 1913. He continued to lead the Conservative Party until 1919 and remained director of the services enrollment until his retirement in 1919. Bratlie died in 1939.

GUNNAR KNUDSEN (Prime Minister; January 29, 1913–June 21, 1920). *See earlier entry under Heads of Government.*

OTTO BAHR HALVORSEN (Prime Minister; June 21, 1920–June 22, 1921). Otto Bahr Halvorsen was born in Kristiania on May 28, 1872. He was a leading lawyer before he entered politics. He was elected to the Storting in 1913 and became leader of the Conservative Party in 1919. He also served as the president of the Storting in 1919. Halvorsen was called upon to form a government as prime minister on June 21, 1920. He was unable to negotiate a suitable trade agreement with Portugal and Spain after Norway's enactment of prohibition of alcoholic beverages and his government collapsed on June 22, 1921. He again formed a government on March 5, 1923, and remained prime minister until his death in Kristiania on May 23, 1923.

OTTO ALBERT BLEHR (Prime Minister; June 22, 1921–March 2, 1923). *See earlier entry under Heads of Government.*

OTTO BAHR HALVORSEN (Prime Minister; March 5, 1923–May 23, 1923). *See earlier entry under Heads of Government.*

ABRAHAM BERGE (Prime Minister; May 30, 1923–July 7, 1924). Abraham Teodor Berge was born in Bergen on August 20, 1851. He entered politics and served as minister of finance under Christian Michelsen from 1906 until 1907. He was a founder of the Moderate Liberal Party in 1909. Berge again served as finance minister under Wollert Konow from 1910 until 1912 and again under Otto Halvorsen in 1923. He was selected to serve as prime minister on May 30, 1923, following Halvorsen's death. Berge retained office until July 7, 1924. He was subsequently under investigation on charges of obtaining an improper government loan for a major Oslo bank during his administration. He was acquitted of charges in 1927 and died in 1936.

JOHAN L. MOWINCKEL (Prime Minister; July 7, 1924–February 28, 1926). Johan Ludwig Mowinckel was born to a wealthy family in Bergen on October 22, 1870. He was educated at the University of Oslo and in Germany, Great Britain, and France before entering the shipping business. He entered local politics and was elected to the Bergen town council in 1899. He became Bergen's mayor in 1902. He was elected to the Storting as a member of the Liberal Party in 1907 and served as president of the Storting from 1913 until 1921, when he was named to the cabinet as minister of trade. He became foreign minister the following year. He was called upon to head the government as prime minister on July 7, 1924, retaining office until February 28, 1926, when he resigned over a financial issue. Mowinckel was a member of the Nobel Prize Commission from 1925 to 1936. He again headed the government from February 13, 1928, until May 8, 1931, when the cabinet's inability to solve economic difficulties brought on by the worldwide depression forced his resignation. He again served as prime minister from March 2, 1933, until March 15, 1935. Mowinckel served in Johan Nygaardsvold's Labor government as a representative of the Liberal Party after the German invasion of Norway in April 1940. He stepped down from the government in 1942 to head the Consultative Commission of the Norwegian Shipping and Trade Mission in New York. He died at his home in New York on September 30, 1943.

IVAR LYKKE (Prime Minister; March 4, 1926–January 27, 1928). Ivar Lykke was born in Trondheim on January 9, 1872. He was a leading merchant before entering the Storting as a Conservative. He formed a government on March 4, 1926. The harsh economic policies instituted by his government led to the Conservative Party's failure in the 1927 elections. Lykke stepped down on January 27, 1928. He was chairman of a trade delegation to Great Britain in 1932. He remained a leading Conservative member of the Storting and participated in negotiations with the Germans in the summer of 1940. He died in December 1949.

CHRISTOPHER HORNSRUD (Prime Minister; January 27, 1928–February 8, 1928). Christopher Anderson Hornsrud was born in Ovre Eiker on November 15, 1859. He was a small farmer and joined the newly formed Labor Party in the 1890s. He served as chairman of the party from 1903 until 1906 and led the party in the Storting from 1921. He served as a representative of the Labor Party on the Provisioning Commission during World War I. He led a short-lived Labor government from January 27, 1928, until February 8, 1928, when a financial crisis brought down the government. He remained active in politics and later joined the Social Democratic Party. Hornsrud died in Oslo at the age of 101 on December 13, 1960.

JOHAN L. MOWINCKEL (Prime Minister; February 13, 1928–May 8, 1931). *See earlier entry under Heads of Government.*

PEDER KOLSTAD (Prime Minister; May 12, 1931–March 5, 1932). Peder Kolstad was born in 1878. He began heading an agricultural school in 1912 and was elected to the Storting as an Agrarian in 1922. He led the first Agrarian government when he was elected prime minister on May 12, 1931, and also served in the cabinet as minister of finance. Kolstad's health began to fail later in the year. He suffered from kidney trouble and died in office of a blood clot on March 5, 1932.

JENS HUNDSEID (Prime Minister; May 12, 1932–January 25, 1933). Jens Hundseid was born in 1883. He was a farmer and a principal at an agricultural school. He was elected to the Storting as a member of the Agrarian Party in 1924, and he led the party in the Storting from 1931 until he became prime minister on May 12, 1932, following the death of Peder Kolstad. He led the government until January 25, 1933. He became a county governor in 1935. Despite a personal dislike for Vidkun Quisling, Hundseid joined Quisling's National Unification Party (Nasjonal Samling) during the German Occupation. After the liberation of Norway, Hundseid was tried and convicted of treason as a collaborationist and sentenced to ten years imprisonment. He died in 1965.

JOHAN L. MOWINCKEL (Prime Minister; March 2, 1933–March 15, 1935). *See earlier entry under Heads of Government.*

JOHAN NYGAARDSVOLD (Prime Minister; March 20, 1935–November 1, 1945). Johan Nygaardsvold was born in Hommelvik on September 6, 1879. In the early 1900s Nygaardsvold went to the United States and worked on the railroads. He returned to Norway in 1907 and became involved in politics. He joined the Labor Party and was elected to the Storting in 1916. Nygaardsvold became speaker in 1928 and later in the year was appointed minister of agriculture in the Labor cabinet, which lasted eighteen days. He again served as speaker of the Storting in 1934 and 1935. Nygaardsvold was chosen as prime minister on March 16, 1935. Following the German invasion of Norway in April 1940, Nygaardsvold escaped to London where he headed the Norwegian government-in-exile. He remained prime minister until after the liberation and retired on June 25, 1945. Following the war, Nygaardsvold's government was held partially responsible for Norway's inadequate defense preparations during the war. Nygaardsvold died in Trondheim on March 13, 1952.

VIDKUN QUISLING (Minister President; February 1, 1942–May 1945). Vidkun Abraham Lauritz Jonsson Quisling was born in Fyresdal, Telemark, on July 18, 1887. He attended the Military Academy in 1911 and served in the Norwegian army as a junior member of the general staff. He served as military attache in Russia and Finland from 1918 until 1921, when he abandoned his military career. He was a relief commissioner in the Soviet Union from 1922 until 1926. He remained in the Soviet Union to represent Great Britain's interests, until 1929, when he returned to Norway. He subsequently entered politics and gained a reputation for his extreme rightist positions. He served as minister of defense in the Agrarian cabinets from May 1931 until the government collapsed in January 1933. He subsequently broke with the Agrarians to form the National

Unification Party (Nasjonal Samling) in May 1933. His party was unsuccessful at the polls, and Quisling moved toward Fascism. Despite a lack of popularity within Norway, he gained the support of Adolf Hitler's Nazi regime in Germany in 1939. Germany invaded Norway on April 9, 1940, and Quisling unilaterally declared himself head of the government when the legitimate Labor government left the capital. His so-called government received no support within the country and he was forced to step down after six days. Because of his support of the occupation forces, the name of Quisling became synonymous with traitor. The occupation government was headed by German Reichskommissar Joséf Terboven. Quisling's party was the only one allowed to exist during the occupation. He was named to the position of minister president by Terboven on February 1, 1942. His government attempted to nazify churches and schools and sent many Jews to death in concentration camps. He was reviled by his fellow countrymen and was arrested following Norway's liberation in May 1945. He was tried for military and civilian treason, illegally changing the constitution, illegal confiscation, theft, and murder. He was convicted and executed by a firing squad on October 24, 1945.

EINAR GERHARDSEN (Prime Minister; November 1, 1945–November 13, 1951). Einar Henry Gerhardsen was born in Oslo on May 10, 1897. He began working in construction in the Oslo office of roads in 1914. Becoming active in the trade union movement, he served as chairman of the Road Repairer's Union in 1919. He became secretary of Oslo's Labor Party in 1925 and was elected to the Oslo town council in 1932. Gerhardsen became secretary of the Norwegian Labor Party in 1935 and was elected mayor of Oslo in 1940. He was dismissed from office following the German invasion in April 1940. He worked with the Resistance during the German occupation and was arrested by the Gestapo in September 1941. Gerhardsen was imprisoned in Sachsenhausen concentration camp in Germany until 1944. He was subsequently imprisoned at Gestapo headquarters in Oslo until the liberation of Norway in May 1945. He was returned to office as mayor of Oslo and became leader of the Labor Party. Gerhardsen formed a coalition government as prime minister on June 22, 1945. He presided over the reconstruction of postwar Norway and implemented numerous social welfare programs in the country. He also approved Norway's entry into the North Atlantic Treaty Organization (NATO) in 1949. Gerhardsen resigned from office on November 13, 1951, and was replaced as prime minister

by Oscar Torp. He resumed office on January 22, 1955, as head of a Labor government. Gerhardsen was forced to step down on August 28, 1963, following a vote of no confidence over the government's alleged mismanagement of the Spitsbergen mines. He returned to office on September 23, 1963, and replaced a short-lived Conservative coalition government led by John Lyng. The Labor Party was defeated in parliamentary elections in September 1965, and Gerhardsen stepped down from office on October 12, 1965. He remained a leading figure in the Labor party until his retirement from the Storting in 1972. Gerhardsen died from a heart condition at a nursing home in Lilleborg at the age of 90 on September 19, 1987.

Oman, Sultanate of

Oman is a country in the southeastern Arabian peninsula. It was recognized as an independent sultanate by Great Britain on December 20, 1951.

HEADS OF STATE

FAISAL IBN TURKI (Sultan; 1888–1913). Faisal ibn Turki Al Bu Sa'id was born in 1864, the son of Sultan Turki. He succeeded his father to the Sultanate in 1888. His reign was marred by tribal conflicts in central Oman. The British largely dominated affairs in Muscat during his rule. He retained the throne until his death on October 5, 1913.

TAIMUR IBN FAISAL (Sultan; 1913–1932). Taimur ibn Faisal Al Bu Sa'id was born in Muscat on June 4, 1888, the son of Sultan Faisal. He was educated in Baghdad and India. He succeeded his father to the sultanate in 1913. Tribes in central Oman rebelled shortly after Taimur took the throne and an imam was elected in Oman. The latter

was murdered in 1920, and Taimur was forced to sign the Treaty of Sib, providing for internal tribal autonomy for the new imam. Taimur abdicated in favor of his son, Sa'id ibn Taimur, on February 28, 1932. He died in 1965.

SA'ID IBN TAIMUR (Sultan; February 28, 1932–July 23, 1970). Sa'id ibn Taimur Al Bu Sa'id was born on April 13, 1910. He was the son of Taimur ibn Faisal, the sultan of Muscat. He was educated in Iraq and India. He succeeded his father as sultan of Muscat following Taimur's abdication on February 28, 1932. Sa'id also held sovereignty of the provinces of Oman and Dhofar. He continued to rule Muscat and Oman under a treaty of friendship with Great Britain.

The sultanate was recognized as an independent state on December 20, 1951. Sultan Sa'id refused to use his country's income from oil concessions for the benefit of his subjects. He faced a separatist revolt from the imam of Oman in 1955 and crushed the rebellion with the assistance of the British. He survived another rebellion by the imam in July 1957 that was supported by the Saudi Arabian and Egyptian governments. The western province of Dhofar went into revolt in 1965, and the sultan survived an assassination attempt the following year. The revolt in Dhofar continued with the support of Communist China and leftist Arab nationalists. The sultan's son, Qabus ibn Sa'id, ousted his father in a coup on July 23, 1970. Sa'id was slightly injured in the coup and was sent into exile in Great Britain. He lived on a pension at the Dorchester Hotel in London until his death of a heart attack on October 19, 1972.

Orange Free State

The Orange Free State was a self-governing province of South Africa that existed as an independent republic from 1884 until 1902, when the British reannexed the area after the Boer War. It obtained self-government in 1907 and became a province of the Union of South Africa in 1910.

HEADS OF STATE

MARTHINUS STEYN (Head of State; February 22, 1896–March 31, 1902). Marthinus Theunis Steyn was born in Winburg, Orange Free State, on October 2, 1857. He was educated at Grey College, Bloemfontein, and Deventer in Holland, where he graduated in 1879. He became a lawyer in Bloemfontein and was a judge on the Orange Free State bench from 1889. He defeated J. G. Fraser for the presidency by a large margin and took office as president of the Orange Free State on February 22, 1896. He allied the Orange Free State with Paul Kruger's Transvaal in 1897 and joined in Transvaal's war against Great Britain in September 1899. The British were successful in the conflict and occupied Pretoria on June 5, 1900. The Boers continued to wage a guerrilla war against the British until the signing of the Treaty of Vereenignin on May 31, 1902. Steyn opposed the terms of the treaty. Suffering from poor health at the war's end, he went to Europe to recuperate. He returned to Orange River Colony in 1905 and was an opponent of Louis Botha's policy of conciliation. He was a member of the national congress in 1908 that led to the formation of the Union of South Africa two years later. Steyn died in Bloemfontein while addressing a women's congress on November 28, 1916.

Panama

*Panama is a country in southern Central America. It was granted in-
dependence from Colombia on November 3, 1903.*

HEADS OF STATE

MANUEL AMADOR GUER-
RERO (President; January 15, 1904–
January 15, 1908). Manuel Amador
Guerrero was born in Turbaco, Colombia, on June 30, 1833. He studied medicine in 1855 and became a physician. He
served as chief physician to the Panama
Railroad in 1868. He gained the support
of the railroad officials and French engineer Philippe Jean Bunau-Varilla for an
independent Panama. He agreed to the
Hay-Bunau-Varilla Treaty in 1903,
which gave the United States a dominant interest in Panamanian affairs.
Amador Guerrero was chosen by a national convention to become Panama's
first president, taking office on January
15, 1904. He attempted to improve sanitation conditions in Panama and implemented numerous public works programs. During his administration a drive
was initiated to eliminate malaria and
yellow fever. Amador Guerrero completed his term of office on January 15,
1908. He died on May 2, 1909.

JOSÉ DOMINGO DE OBALDÍA
(President; January 15, 1908–March 1,
1910). José Domingo de Obaldía was
born in the Department of Panama,
Colombia, in 1845. He became active in
politics and was elected to the Colombian senate in 1893. He was a supporter
of the independence of Panama and the
construction of the Panama Canal. He
served as governor of the Department of
Panama at the time the country declared
its independence in November 1903. He
accepted Panamanian citizenship and
was a supporter of President Manuel
Amador Guerrero. He was appointed
minister to the United States by Amador

Guerrero in 1904. He was elected to succeed Amador Guerrero as president, taking office on January 15, 1908. Obaldía
died in office of heart disease on March
1, 1910.

CARLOS ANTONIO MEN-
DOZA (President; March 1, 1910–October 1, 1910). Carlos Antonio Mendoza
was born in 1856. He was the author of
the Panamanian declaration of independence in 1903. He was elected second
vice president of Panama under President José Domingo de Obaldía in 1908.
He succeeded to the first vice presidency
upon the death of J. A. Arango in May
1909. Mendoza became acting president
on March 1, 1910, following the death of
President Obaldía. He stepped down on
October 1, 1910, after the selection of
Pablo Arosemena as president. He remained a leader of the Liberal Party and
supported Belisario Porras' candidacy for
president in 1912. He subsequently broke
with Porras in 1915. Mendoza died in
Panama of a heart attack on February 13,
1916.

PABLO AROSEMENA (President;
October 1, 1910–October 1, 1912). Pablo
Arosemena was born on September 24,
1836. He was a leading proponent of
Panamanian independence. He briefly
served as president of the Sovereign
State of Panama in 1875, but was ousted
by the Colombian army. He was elected
second vice president of Colombia in
1886. He again briefly served as president when Panama declared its independence in 1885, and he was again
ousted when Colombia reclaimed the
country. He was elected president of the

national constituent assembly of an independent Panama in 1904. He was appointed to the presidency by the national assembly on October 1, 1910, to complete the unexpired term of President José Domingo de Obaldía, who had died in office. He completed the term and stepped down on October 1, 1912. Arosemena died on August 29, 1920.

FELIX BELISARIO PORRAS (President; October 1, 1912–October 1, 1916). Felix Belisario Porras was born in Las Tablas on November 28, 1856. He was educated as a lawyer and became active in politics in Colombia. He served as consul in Brussels in 1881. He was a supporter of the Liberal revolution to establish Panama's independence in 1901. He opposed the treaty that established an independent Panama in 1903, fearing the United States would exercise too much control over the country. He was stripped of his citizenship from 1905 until 1906 over his opposition to the treaty. He was elected to the national assembly and served as president of the Panama municipal council from 1908 until 1910. He served on the Panama supreme court and was named minister to Brazil in 1910. He served as minister to Costa Rica and the United States in 1911. He was subsequently elected to the presidency, taking office on October 1, 1912. He did much to modernize Panama, establishing the national bank and the national archives. He also initiated the drafting of Panama's legal codes. The Panama Canal was completed during his first administration and was opened in August 1914. Porras completed his term and stepped down on October 1, 1916. He was subsequently named minister to the United States. When his successor, Ramon Valdes, died in office in June 1918, Porras was chosen by the national assembly to complete the unexpired term; he took office on October 1, 1918. Porras briefly stepped down on January 30, 1920, to run for another term of office. He was reelected and resumed

office on October 1, 1920. His presidency withstood an unsuccessful coup attempt in February 1921, after a short war against Costa Rica over a boundary dispute. Porras completed his term and relinquished office to Rodolfo Chiari on October 1, 1924. Porras served as minister to France and Great Britain from 1925 until 1926. He was minister to Italy in 1933 and minister to France and Great Britain from 1933 until 1935. He was defeated in another campaign for the presidency in 1936. Porras died on August 28, 1942.

RAMÓN VALDES (President; October 1, 1916–June 3, 1918). Ramón Maximiliano Valdes served as Panama's minister to the United States in 1912. He subsequently served as minister of justice and was first vice president under Belisario Porras. He was elected to succeed Porras to the presidency and took office on October 1, 1916. Valdes supported the war effort of the United States during World War I and expelled Germany's consul in 1917. Valdes died in office of a heart attack on June 3, 1918.

CIRO LUIS URRIOLA (President; June 3, 1918–October 1, 1918). Ciro Luis Urriola served as president of the national assembly and first vice president under Ramón Valdes. He succeeded to the presidency when Valdes died in office on June 3, 1918. Former president Belisario Porras was chosen by the national assembly to complete Valdes' unexpired term, and Urriola relinquished office on October 1, 1918. He died in Panama on June 27, 1922.

FELIX BELISARIO PORRAS (President; October 1, 1918–January 30, 1920). *See earlier entry under Heads of State.*

ERNESTO LEFEVRE (President January 30, 1920–October 1, 1920). Ernesto Tisdal Lefevre served in several governments as minister of posts and telegraphs and as foreign minister. He served as first vice president from 1918 when Felix Belisario Porras was chosen to succeed President Ramón Valdes, who had died in office, until 1920. Porras stepped down from office to run in the new election, and Lefevre succeeded to the presidency on January 30, 1920. He presided over the elections and stepped down when Porras resumed office on October 1, 1920. Lefevre died in Panama City after surgery on December 25, 1922.

FELIX BELISARIO PORRAS (President; October 1, 1920–October 1, 1924). *See earlier entry under Heads of State.*

RODOLFO CHIARI (President; October 1, 1924–October 1, 1928). Rodolfo E. Chiari was born in Aguadulce on November 15, 1870. He was educated in Panama and became a successful sugar planter. He became active in politics following Panama's independence and was elected to the national assembly in 1904. He served as treasurer of Panama City from 1905 until 1906 and was deputy secretary of the treasury in 1908. Chiari was manager of the national bank from 1909 until 1914. He became a leading figure in the Liberal Party and served as secretary of government and justice in 1914. He was defeated for the presidency by Ramón Valdes in 1916, and again served as secretary of government and justice in the subsequent government. He was elected first vice president in 1922 under Belisario Porras. Chiari was elected to succeed Porras and took office on October 1, 1924. He was successful in putting down a revolt by Cuna Indians in San Blas in 1925. He was also faced with a tenants strike in Panama City. He called upon American troops in the Canal Zone to assist in putting down the strike. Chiari also negotiated a new treaty with the United States, but the treaty was never ratified by the national assembly due to objections to terms of the agreement that committed Panama to the United States during times of war. Chiari completed his term and stepped down on October 1, 1928. He remained a leading figure in Panamanian politics. He went to the United States to seek medical treatment in 1936. He died in Los Angeles on August 16, 1937.

FLORENCIO HARMODIO AROSEMENA (President; October 1, 1928–January 2, 1931). Florencio Harmodio Arosemena was born in Panama City on September 17, 1873. He was educated in Switzerland and Germany and received a degree in civil engineering from the University of Munich in 1895. He worked as an engineer in Panama and throughout Central America. He received the Liberal Party nomination for president in 1928. He defeated Jorge E. Boyd in the election and assumed office on October 1, 1928. He attempted to reduce Panama's budget through economic policies. The economic depression in 1929 led to criticism against his administration. He was overthrown by an armed rebellion on January 2, 1931. Arosemena was charged with fraud over the construction of a railroad during his administration. He was exonerated in 1932. His brother, Juan Demóstenes Arosemena, served as Panama's president from 1936 until 1939. Florencio Arosemena died after a long illness in a New York City hospital on August 30, 1945.

HARMODIO ARIAS (President; January 2, 1931–January 16, 1931). Harmodio Arias Madrid was born on July 3, 1886. He was educated at the London School of Economics and received a degree in law and political science from Cambridge University in 1911. He became active in politics after his return to Panama in 1912. He represented Panama at the League of Nations in 1920 and was a member of the Permanent Court of Arbitration at The Hague. He served as minister to Argentina in 1921 and briefly as minister to the United States in 1931.

He was a leader of the rebellion that ousted President Florencio Harmodio Arosemena on January 2, 1931. He served as provisional president until January 16, 1931, when he relinquished the office to Ricardo Alfaro in order to become a candidate in a new election. He was victorious and resumed office on October 1, 1932. Arias attempted to eliminate corruption in the government. He founded the University of Panama in 1935 and negotiated a new agreement with the United States in 1936 that disallowed the United States the right to intervene in Panama's domestic affairs. Arias completed his term and left office on October 1, 1936. His brother, Arnulfo Arias, served as president of Panama on several occasions. Harmodio Arias was the publisher of *The Pan American*, a leading Panamanian newspaper. He died of a heart ailment on December 23, 1962, while returning to Panama aboard a plane after seeking medical treatment at a Boston, Massachusetts, hospital.

RICARDO J. ALFARO (President; January 16, 1931–October 1, 1932). Ricardo Joaquín Alfaro was born on August 20, 1882. He was a leading Panamanian diplomat and historian. He was named minister to the United States in 1922. He was recalled to Panama to serve as interim president on January 16, 1931, following the ouster of President Florencio Harmodio Arosemena. He presided over new elections and relinquished office to Harmodio Arias on October 1, 1932. He resumed his position as minister to the United States the following year. He negotiated the Hull-Alfaro Treaty in 1936 before returning to Panama. He was a candidate for president in 1940, but was defeated by Arnulfo Arias in an election marked by violence. He briefly served as foreign minister under President Enrique Adolfo Jiménez in 1946. Alfaro served as a member of the International Court of Justice in The Hague from 1959 until 1964. He died in Panama after undergoing intestinal surgery on February 23, 1971.

HARMODIO ARIAS (President; October 1, 1932–October 1, 1936). *See earlier entry under Heads of State.*

JUAN DEMÓSTENES AROSEMENA (President; October 1, 1936–December 16, 1939). Juan Demóstenes Arosemena was born on June 24, 1879. He was named chief justice of the Supreme Court in 1912 and governor of Colon Province in 1922. Arosemena served as foreign minister during the administration of his brother, Florencio Arosemena, from 1928 until 1931. He also served as foreign minister in President Harmodio Arias's subsequent administration following the ouster of his brother. Juan Arosemena received Arias' support in the 1936 presidential election as the candidate of the National Revolutionary Party. He defeated Domingo Diáz in a close race and took office on October 1, 1936. He remained in office until his death while visiting the town of Penomone on December 16, 1939.

AGUSTO S. BOYD (President; December 18, 1939–October 1, 1940). Agusto Samuel Boyd was born in 1879. He was educated in San Francisco and received a medical degree at Columbia University in 1899. He returned to Panama as a surgeon. He entered politics and became president of the municipal council of Panama in 1906. He also served as a member of the national assembly. He was elected first vice president of Panama in 1936. He also served as Panama's minister to the United States. He returned to Panama to succeed to the presidency on December 18, 1939, following the death of President Juan Arosemena. He completed Arosemena's term and stepped down on October 1, 1940, following the election of Arnulfo Arias. Boyd remained active in Panamanian politics. He died in Panama City after a long illness on June 17, 1957.

ARNULFO ARIAS (President; October 1, 1940–October 9, 1941). Arnulfo Arias Madrid was born in Penomone on August 15, 1901. He was educated in the United States and received a degree in medicine from Harvard University in 1924. He subsequently worked at Boston City Hospital before returning to Panama in 1925. Arias continued to practice medicine and also became involved in politics. He was a leader of the coup that ousted President Florencio Harmodio Arosemena in January 1931 and installed Ricardo J. Alfaro as president. Arias was shot in an assassination attempt later in the year, but recovered from his injuries. He was appointed to direct the department of health and implemented numerous reforms in Panama's public welfare system. He was instrumental in the election of his brother, Harmodio Arias, to the presidency in 1932. Arnulfo Arias served in his brother's government as secretary of agriculture and public works until August 1934, when he was sent to Italy as an envoy. He returned to Panama the following year to form the National Revolutionary Party. The government banned all opposition parties and secured the election of Juan Demóstenes Arosemena as president in 1936. Arias returned to Italy as ambassador. He also represented Panama in France and Sweden and served as a delegate to the League of Nations. He returned to Panama near the start of World War II in 1939. Arias was a victorious candidate for the presidency in 1940 and took office on October 1, 1940. He instituted Panama's social security system and promoted a new constitution in January 1941. The constitution granted women the right to vote and extended the term of the president from four to six years. Arias' government was accused of supporting the Axis Powers during the war, and Arias was ousted in a coup when he left the country on October 9, 1941. He remained in exile until 1945, but was again a candidate for president in 1948.

He received a slight majority of the popular vote, but his opponent was declared the victor. A military coup the following year resulted in the election results being reversed, and Arias was again installed as president on November 25, 1949. He ruled in a dictatorial fashion, dissolving the national assembly and ruling by decree. He was ousted in a coup led by the national guard on May 10, 1951. Arias was stripped of his political rights until 1960. He was an unsuccessful candidate for the presidency in 1964, but was again victorious in 1968. He took office on October 1, 1968, but was ousted by a military coup eleven days later, on October 12, 1968. Arias went into exile in Miami, Florida, where he was a vocal critic of the military regime of Brigadier General Omar Torrijos. He returned to Panama in June 1978 and was the candidate for the Authentic Panamanian Party in the presidential election in 1984. He was defeated, though his supporters accused the government of electoral fraud. Arias went back into exile in Miami, where he remained a critic of the government of General Manuel Noriega. Arias died of a heart attack at his home in Miami on August 10, 1988.

ERNESTO JAEN GUARDIA (President; October 9, 1941). Ernesto Jaen Guardia was born in 1895. He served as vice president under Arnulfo Arias in 1940, and when Arias was ousted from office by the national assembly on October 9, 1941, Jaen Guardia briefly served as interim president until the cabinet chose Ricardo de la Guardia to serve as president later in the day. Jaen Guardia remained active in Panamanian politics. He was foreign minister in the late 1940s. Jaen Guardia died on April 18, 1961.

RICARDO DE LA GUARDIA (President; October 9, 1941–June 15, 1945). Ricardo Adolfo de la Guardia was born in Panama City on June 14, 1899. He was educated locally and entered government service in 1919. He returned to private business in 1930. De la Guardia was appointed governor of the Province of Panama by President Juan Demóstenes Arosemena in 1936. He again left the government in 1938 to become superintendent of the Santo Tomas Hospital. He returned to the government to serve as minister of justice in the cabinet of President Arnulfo Arias in October 1940. Arias was ousted from office when he left the country without the permission of the cabinet on October 9, 1941. Vice President Ernest Jaen Guardia served as interim president before de la Guardia was elected president by the new cabinet later in the day. De la Guardia eliminated pro-Nazi members of the government and established closer relations with the United States. He also banned gambling in Panama, established price ceilings on food products, and instituted other social reforms in the country. De la Guardia suspended the constitution in 1945 so he could remain in office despite calls for his resignation. The Panamanian congress ousted him on June 15, 1945, and replaced him with Enrique Adolfo Jiménez. De la Guardia remained active in Panamanian politics. He was arrested on charges of insulting the president in 1951, following Arnulfo Arias's return power. He was beaten and briefly imprisoned, though his sentence was later dismissed. De la Guardia died in Panama City after a long illness on December 29, 1969.

ENRIQUE ADOLFO JIMÉNEZ (President; June 15, 1945–October 1, 1948). Enrique Adolfo Jiménez was born in 1888. He was a prominent Panamanian politician who had served as president of the national assembly, minister of finance, ambassador to the United States, and vice president on two occasions. He was elected provisional president by Panama's constitutional congress on June 15, 1945, following the ouster of Ricardo de la Guardia. Jiménez presided over elections held in 1948. Domingo Díaz Arosemena was declared the victor over Arnulfo Arias, although Arias received a majority of the votes. Arias' supporters protested against the results, and Jiménez declared a state of siege in July 1948. The national assembly voted to dismiss Jiménez on July 12, 1948. He defied the ouster and remained in office with the support of Colonel José Remon, the national police chief. Jiménez relinquished office to Díaz Arosemena on October 1, 1948. He remained a leading political figure in Panama and served as ambassador to the United States in the late 1950s and early 1960s.

Paraguay

Paraguay is a country in central South America. It was granted independence from Spain on May 14, 1811.

HEADS OF STATE

EMILIO ACEVAL (President; November 25, 1898–January 9, 1902). Emilio Aceval was born in 1854. He was a leader of the Colorado Party and became president of Paraguay on November 25, 1898. He was forced from office in a revolt on January 9, 1902. Aceval died in 1931.

HECTOR CARVALLO (President; January 9, 1902–November 25, 1902). Hector Carvallo became provisional president of Paraguay following the revolt that ousted Emilio Aceval on January 9, 1902. He was replaced by Juan Escuarra on November 25, 1902.

JUAN ESCUARRA (President; November 25, 1902–December 19, 1904). Juan Antonio Escuarra was a leader of the faction of the Colorado Party that ousted President Emilio Aceval in January 1902. Escuarra became president of Paraguay on November 25, 1902. In August 1904 the Liberal Party staged a revolt, led by General Benigno Ferreira from Argentina, against his administration. After months of fighting, Escuarra was forced from office on December 19, 1904, and signed the Pact of Pilcomayo aboard an Argentine gunboat. The Pact gave power to the Liberals. Escuarra was sent into exile.

JUAN BAUTISTA GAONA (President; December 19, 1904–December 9, 1905). Juan Bautista Gaona was born in 1846. He was a leader of the Liberal Party and instrumental in the revolution that forced the ouster of President Juan Escuarra on December 19, 1904. Gaona replaced Escuarra as Paraguay's president. He was replaced by Cecilio Báez on December 9, 1905. Gaona was elected vice president under Manual Gondra in 1910, but was forced from office in a military revolt in January 1911. Gaona died in Asuncion on May 19, 1932.

CECILIO BÁEZ (President; December 9, 1905–November 25, 1906). Cecilio Báez was born on February 1, 1862. He was a doctor of law and a prominent opponent of President Francisco Solano López in the mid–1860s. He was a founder of the Liberal Party in 1887 and later served as the party's leader. He was elected to the Paraguayan congress in 1895. Báez was appointed provisional president of Paraguay on December 9, 1905. He stepped down on November 25, 1906. He was instrumental in educational reform during his brief tenure. He

remained a leading figure in Paraguay's government, serving as minister to Mexico, the United States, and Great Britain. Báez was rector of the National University during the 1920s and 1930s. He was minister of foreign affairs in 1938 and 1939 and represented Paraguay at the signing of the peace treaty ending the Chaco War in July 1938. Báez died in Asunción on June 11, 1941.

BENIGNO FERREIRA (President; November 25, 1906–July 2, 1908). Benigno Ferreira was born in Limpio on February 18, 1840. He received a degree in law from the University of Buenos Aires in Argentina. He was a leading opponent of the regimes of Carlos Antonio López and his son, Francisco Solano López, and fought with the Argentine army in the War of the Triple Alliance in 1864. He served as minister of the interior in the cabinet of Salvador Jovellanos in the early 1870s and was subsequently vice president of the Liberal Party. Ferreira went into exile in Argentina in the 1880s and remained there until the Liberal revolution in 1904. He was called upon to serve as Paraguay's president on November 25, 1906, but was forced to step down on July 2, 1908, following a revolt against his government. He returned to exile in Argentina and died in Buenos Aires on November 24, 1920.

EMILIANO GONZALEZ NAVERO (President; July 2, 1908–November 25, 1910). Emiliano Gonzalez Navero was born in Caraguatay in 1861. He was a leading member of the Liberal Party and was instrumental in the planning of the revolution in August 1904 that brought the Liberals to power. He was a prominent member of several Liberal governments and served as president of Paraguay's Supreme Court. He was vice president under Benigno Ferreira and succeeded to the presidency when Ferreira was forced to step down on July 2, 1908. Gonzalez completed Ferreira's term of office and stepped down on November 25, 1910. He was again called upon to be provisional president and served from March 15, 1912, to August 15, 1912. He remained a leading jurist and statesman. Gonzalez Navero died on October 18, 1934.

MANUEL E. GONDRA (President; November 25, 1910–January 17, 1911). Manuel E. Gondra was born on January 1, 1871. He was educated at the National College and began a career in politics in 1902. He served as minister to Brazil from 1905 until 1908. He was elected president of Paraguay on November 25, 1910. He was unable to bring order to the political chaos in Paraguay and was forced to resign when his minister of war, Albino Jara, seized power on January 17, 1911. Gondra remained a leading political figure. He served as minister of war and as Paraguay's minister in Washington over the next decade and was again sworn in as president on August 15, 1920. Continuing political unrest again forced Gondra's resignation on November 7, 1921. Gondra continued to remain active in political affairs and was the sponsor of the Treaty to Avoid or Prevent Conflicts between the American States, which was signed at the Fifth International Conference of American States at Santiago, Chile, in 1923. Gondra died on March 8, 1927.

ALBINO JARA (President; January 17, 1911–July 5, 1911). Albino Jara was born in 1878. He was a colonel in the Paraguayan army. He served as minister of war in 1908 and was a leader of the revolt that ousted President Benigno Ferreira that year. He forced Manuel Gondra's resignation from the presidency on January 17, 1911, and became provisional president. A revolt by Gondra loyalists forced Jara's resignation from office on July 5, 1911. Jara died in May 1912.

LIBERATO MARCIAL ROJAS (President; July 5, 1911–March 1, 1912).

Liberato Marcial Rojas was born in 1870. A leading Paraguayan journalist and politician, he was chosen as president of Paraguay on July 5, 1911. Civil unrest widened during his administration, and he was forced to resign on March 1, 1912. Rojas subsequently went into exile and died in Montevideo, Uruguay, in 1922.

PEDRO PEÑA (President; March 1, 1912–March 15, 1912). Pedro Peña was born in 1867. He briefly served as Paraguay's president from March 1, 1912, until March 15, 1912, during a period of serious civil unrest. Peña was a compromise candidate of the various Liberal factions and left office when Emiliano Gonzalez Navero was chosen as president. Peña died in Asuncion on July 29, 1943.

EMILIANO GONZALEZ NAVERO (President; March 15, 1912–August 15, 1912). *See earlier entry under Heads of State.*

EDUARDO SCHAERER (President; August 15, 1912–August 15, 1916). Eduardo Schaerer was born in Caazapá on December 2, 1873. He was educated at the National College and became a leading figure in the Liberal Party after the revolution of 1904. Schaerer was also a successful business leader and served as mayor of Asunción. He also served in the cabinet as minister of the interior. Schaerer was chosen as Paraguay's president on August 15, 1912. His administration was instrumental in the modernization of Asunción's transportation system. He maintained Paraguay's neutrality during World War I. He completed his term of office on August 15, 1916. Schaerer remained a leading political figure in Paraguay, later serving as president of the senate. He continued to sponsor the Liberal Party financially until his death on November 12, 1941.

MANUEL FRANCO (President; August 15, 1916–June 5, 1919). Manuel

Franco was born in 1871. He was a leading member of the Liberal Party who served in Paraguay's senate and in the cabinet as minister of justice. Franco was also a supreme court justice and president of the Liberal Party. He was chosen as Paraguay's president on August 15, 1916. He was responsible for electoral reforms and implemented the secret ballot voting system. Franco retained office until his death on June 5, 1919.

JOSÉ P. MONTERO (President; June 5, 1919–August 15, 1920). José P. Montero served as vice president under Manuel Franco. He succeeded to the presidency on June 5, 1919, following Franco's death in office. He retained the presidency until Manuel Gondra's election on August 15, 1920.

MANUEL E. GONDRA (President; August 15, 1920–November 7, 1921). *See earlier entry under Heads of State.*

EUSEBIO AYALA (President; November 7, 1921–April 11, 1923). Eusebio Ayala was born in an Andean province of Paraguay on August 15, 1874. He was educated in Germany and earned a degree in law. He returned to Paraguay to teach philosophy, sociology, and political law at the National University. He became a leading member of the Liberal Party and served in President Manuel Gondra's cabinet. He replaced Gondra as provisional president on November 7, 1921, when Gondra was forced to resign. He stepped down on April 11, 1923, after the constitutional government was reestablished. Ayala subsequently served as Paraguay's minister to the United States. He was elected president in 1932. Shortly after taking office on August 15, 1932, Ayala led Paraguay into war with neighboring Bolivia in a border dispute over the Gran Chaco region. Paraguay was successful in the Chaco War but popular discontent over the peace settlement led to a military rebellion led by war hero Colonel Rafael Franco. Ayala

was ousted on February 17, 1936, and was placed in protective custody. He was released and sent into exile six months later. Ayala died in Buenos Aires, Argentina, on June 4, 1942.

ELIGIO AYALA (President; April 11, 1923–March 17, 1924). Eligio Ayala was born in Mbuyapey in 1880. He received a doctorate in law from the National College in 1908. He became active in the Liberal Party and served as a member of Paraguay's congress. Ayala spent much of the 1910s in Europe, returning to Paraguay after the end of World War I. He was again elected to the congress and was named minister of finance in the administration of President Manuel Gondra. He was selected as provisional president of Paraguay on April 11, 1923. He stepped down on March 17, 1924, to run for the presidency and was elected. He resumed office on August 15, 1924. Ayala was instrumental in economic reforms in Paraguay. He balanced the national budget and paid off a large portion of the country's international debt. Ayala attempted to negotiate a solution to the border dispute with Bolivia. He completed his term of office and stepped down on August 15, 1928. He served as minister of finance in the government of his successor, José P. Guggiari, until he was killed over a romantic entanglement on October 24, 1930.

LUIS A. RIART (President; March 17, 1924–August 15, 1924). Luis A. Riart was born in 1891. He was a leading member of the Liberal Party and served as vice president under Eligio Ayala in 1923. He became interim president of Paraguay on March 17, 1924, following the resignation of Ayala. He stepped down on August 15, 1924, following an election that returned Ayala to the presidency. He remained a member of Ayala's government as minister of war and the navy and minister of finance. He returned to the government with Ayala in

1932 and served as foreign minister. He was instrumental in negotiating the peace treaty that ended the Chaco War. Ayala was ousted in a military coup in February 1936 and Riart was arrested and sent into exile. He was allowed to return to Paraguay soon afterward and was named minister to Brazil. Riart remained active in politics and was a leading supporter of José Félix Estigarribia's presidential candidacy in 1939. He served as Estigarribia's vice president until 1940. Riart died in Asunción on October 2, 1953.

ELIGIO AYALA (President; August 15, 1924–August 15, 1928). *See earlier entry under Heads of State.*

JOSÉ PATRICIO GUGGIARI (President; August 15, 1928–October 26, 1931). José Patricio Guggiari was born in Asuncion on March 17, 1884. He received a degree in law from the National University in 1910. He was an early member of the Liberal Party and was elected to the chamber of deputies in 1912. He became president of the chamber six years later and was named to President Manuel Gondra's cabinet as minister of the interior in 1920. He defeated Eduardo Fleitas for the presidency and was sworn in on August 15, 1928. Paraguay's relationship with neighboring Bolivia continued to deteriorate over a border dispute during Guggiari's term of office. Civil unrest over his government's response to Bolivia's incursions onto Paraguayan territory resulted in tragedy when student protestors were fired upon by police in front of the National Palace in October 1931. Guggiari resigned from the presidency several days after that on October 26, 1931. He was forced into exile in 1947 and died in Buenos Aires after a long illness on October 29, 1957.

EMILIANO GONZALEZ NAVERO (President; October 26, 1931–January 28, 1932). *See earlier entry under Heads of State.*

JOSÉ PATRICIO GUGGIARI (President; January 28, 1932–August 15, 1932). *See earlier entry under Heads of State.*

EUSEBIO AYALA (President; August 15, 1932–February 17, 1936). *See earlier entry under Heads of State.*

RAFAEL FRANCO (President; February 18, 1936–August 15, 1937). Rafael Franco was born in 1897. He served in Paraguay's army, and in 1928 he led an attack on a Bolivian-held fort in the Chaco region. He was removed from command for this action, which he had initiated without orders. The border dispute with Bolivia evolved into an open war in 1932, and Franco was recalled to duty as a colonel. He served with distinction during the Chaco War. After the conclusion of the war, Franco plotted against the Liberal government of Eusebio Ayala. He organized the military coup that ousted Ayala and was installed as provisional president on February 18, 1936. He began to initiate social legislation, such as land reform and giving labor unions the right to strike. Franco was ousted in another military coup led by officers loyal to the Liberal Party on August 15, 1937. He went into exile, where he formed the Febrerista Party. Franco was allowed to return to Paraguay in 1946 and participated in a coalition government under President Higinio Moriñigo. Growing civil unrest led to a collapse of the coalition, and Franco joined in the subsequent civil war in 1947. Franco's forces were defeated at the siege of Asunción in August 1947, and he again fled into exile. He remained in exile until 1964, when President Alfredo Stroessner granted Franco's Febristas permission to contest elections. The party had little influence in the 1967 elections, and Franco entered into semi-retirement. He died in Asunción in 1973.

FELIX PAIVA (President; August 15, 1937–August 15, 1939). Felix Paiva was born in 1877. He was a member of the Liberal Party and participated in the revolution against Juan Escuarra's government in August 1904. He served in several cabinets before accepting the position of dean of the National University Law School. Paiva was chosen as provisional president on August 15, 1937, following the ouster of the Febrerista government of Rafael Franco. Paiva stepped down on August 15, 1939, following the selection of José Estigarribia as president. Paiva died in 1965.

JOSÉ FÉLIX ESTIGARRIBIA (President; August 15, 1939–September 7, 1940). José Félix Estigarribia was born in Caraguatay on February 21, 1888. He was educated at the National College in Asunción. Estigarribia joined the army in 1911 and received further training in Chile over the next two years. He also received training in France from 1922 until 1927. He was named chief of the general staff upon his return. He commanded Paraguay's forces during the Chaco War against Bolivia from 1932 until 1935. After the ouster of the Liberal government of Eusebio Ayala in 1936, Estigarribia accepted a teaching position at the Montevideo War College in Uruguay. He was appointed ambassador to the United States in 1938. The following year he was selected as the Liberal Party's presidential nominee. He took office on August 15, 1939, and began attempts to pass social welfare legislation. He dissolved congress in 1940 when it refused to pass his programs. He ruled as a dictator while creating a new constitution. Soon after the constitution was enacted, Estigarribia was killed in an airplane crash outside of Asunción on September 5, 1940.

HIGINIO MORIÑIGO (President; September 7, 1940–June 3, 1948).

Higinio Moriñigo was born in Paraguari on January 11, 1897. He attended military college and entered the army in 1922. He saw action during the Chaco War against Bolivia from 1932 until 1935. Moriñigo was promoted to general and named to the cabinet of General José Félix Estigarribia as minister of war in May 1940. When President Estigarribia was killed in an airplane crash on September 7, 1940, General Moriñigo was chosen as interim president by the cabinet. Moriñigo proclaimed a dictatorship on November 30, 1940, and dissolved all opposition parties. He was elected to the presidency unopposed in February 1943. He led Paraguay during World War II and promoted a policy of neutrality. Moriñigo led a primarily military government until June 1946. He then dismissed Colonel Benitez Vera, the rightist leader of the army. He crushed a brief revolt by Vera's supporters and appointed a civilian cabinet from members of the Colorado and Febrerista parties. The leftist Febrerista Party resigned from the government and went into revolt against Moriñigo in January 1947. The rebellion was led by former president Rafael Franco, who established a rebel government in northern Paraguay. The rebellion was crushed by the loyalist military in August 1947. Moriñigo proceeded to hold national elections in February 1948 and supported the candidacy of Juan Natalicio Gonzalez. Gonzalez was elected unopposed, and his supporters, who feared that Moriñigo might retain power, forced the president's resignation on June 3, 1948. He went into exile in Argentina. Moriñigo reentered Paraguay briefly in 1956 and then returned to Argentina. He remained politically inactive and died in 1985.

Peru

Peru is a country on the western coast of South America. It was granted independence from Spain on July 28, 1821.

HEADS OF STATE

EDUARDO DE ROMAÑA (President; September 8, 1899–September 8, 1903). Eduardo de Romaña was born in Arequipa on March 19, 1847. He was educated at the seminary at San Jeronimo. He entered the Peruvian army and served as commandant general of the national guard in 1879. He was elected to the senate in 1898 and became president of Peru on September 8, 1899. He completed his term of office on September 8, 1903. Romaña died in 1912.

MANUEL CANDAMO (President; September 8, 1903–May 7, 1904). Manuel Candamo was born in 1842, the son of a wealthy Peruvian merchant. He became active in politics and joined the Civilista Party. He served as mayor of Lima and was president of the Lima Chamber of Commerce in 1902. He was a candidate for president in 1903, running as a moderate between the rival factions of the Democratic and Civilista parties. Candamo was the one candidate trusted by all factions and so was victorious in the election. He took office on September 8, 1903. He fell ill soon after his election and died in office on May 7, 1904.

SERAPIO CALDERON (President; May 7, 1904–September 24, 1904). Serapio Calderon was born in 1843. He served as acting president of Peru following the death of Manuel Candamo on May 7, 1904. He relinquished office on September 24, 1904, following the election of José Pardo. Calderon died in 1922.

JOSÉ PARDO Y BARREDA (President; September 24, 1904–September 24, 1908). José Pardo y Barreda was born in Lima on February 24, 1864. He was the son of Manuel Pardo y Lavalle, Peru's president from 1872 to 1876. The younger Pardo studied literature and political science at San Marcos University. He graduated with a degree in law in 1887. He practiced law for a period before entering Peru's diplomatic corps. He served in Manuel Candamo's government as foreign minister from September 1903 until he was chosen as the Civilista Party's presidential candidate following Candamo's death. He was elected to the presidency and took office on September 24, 1904. His government was instrumental in negotiating treaties to settle Peru's border disputes with its neighbors. He was also instrumental in improving the country's educational system, constructing major rail lines, and reorganizing the military. He completed his term and relinquished office to Augusto Leguía on September 24, 1908. Pardo spent the next five years in Europe, and returned to Lima only at the outset of World War I. He became president of San Marcos University in 1914. He was again chosen as a presidential candidate the following year, running with the support of the Civilista, Liberal, and Constitutionalist parties. He was elected with a vast majority and took office on August 18, 1915. Peru was in the midst of an economic crisis, and Pardo was able to reduce the country's foreign debt through currency reform. Despite raising the minimum wage and other reforms, his second administration was beset by labor and student strikes. Augusto Leguía was the victor in the presidential elections in 1919 and ousted Pardo on July 4, 1919, six weeks before his scheduled inauguration. Pardo was briefly arrested, but was soon freed and allowed to leave the country. He and his family lived in exile in France until 1940. He subsequently returned to Lima, where he died on August 4, 1947.

AUGUSTO BERNARDINO LEGUÍA (President; September 24, 1908–September 24, 1912). Augusto Bernardino Leguía y Salcedo was born in Lambayeque on February 19, 1863. He was educated at the English school in Valparaiso, Chile. He became a successful businessman, establishing the British Sugar Company in 1896 and the South American Insurance Company in 1900. He was named minister of finance in Manuel Candamo's government in 1903 and retained that position in José Pardo's subsequent government. He was the Civilista Party's presidential nominee in the election in 1908. He succeeded Pardo to the presidency on September 24, 1908. Leguía narrowly survived a coup attempt in 1909, vowing to die rather than give up his office. He initiated various reforms during his first term, improving Peru's educational system and founding a national bank. He was defeated for reelection in 1912 by Guillermo Billinghurst, who took office on September 24, 1912. The new government ordered Leguía's arrest, and he retaliated with an attack on the home of his successor. He was seized and imprisoned before being allowed to go into exile in London. He returned to Peru in 1918 and again ran for the presidency, this time as an independent. He won the election, but seized power in a coup with the support of the army on July 5, 1919, six weeks prior to his inauguration. This was done to preempt opposition from his political opponents in congress. He promulgated a new constitution in 1920. Leguía ruled in an increasingly dictatorial manner. He was reelected in a manipulated contest in 1924. He sought to encourage economic and industrial growth in Peru, but he incurred a huge national debt by accepting loans from the United States. He bypassed elections in 1929 and had himself reinaugurated instead. He survived an assassination attempt in the spring of 1930. Peru's growing economic crisis, spurred by the worldwide economic depression, caused widespread discontent against his regime. An army uprising in Arequipqa forced his resignation on August 25, 1930. He was arrested by the subsequent government of Colonel Luís M. Sánchez Cerro. He was initially imprisoned on the island of San Lorenzo before being transferred to a prison in Lima. With his health failing due to a bout of bronchial pneumonia, he was taken to the Naval General Hospital in November 1931. His condition deteriorated, and Leguía died of a heart attack on February 6, 1932.

GUILLERMO BILLINGHURST (President; September 24, 1912–April 25, 1914). Guillermo Enrique Billinghurst was born to a wealthy family in Arica in 1851. He served in the Peruvian army in the War of the Pacific against Chile from 1879 until 1883. He became a close associate of Nicolas de Pierola. He used his wealth to finance Pierola's military uprising against the government of General Andres Caceres in 1895. Following Pierola's victory, Billinghurst served as first vice president and president of the senate. Billinghurst lost the support of Pierola and was defeated in the presidential election in 1899. He subsequently became a leader of the Democratic Party and served as mayor of Lima in 1909 and 1910. He was elected president of Peru and took office on September 24, 1912. His attempts to enact legislation to benefit workers met with opposition from the Civilistas in the legislature. His attempts to bypass the congress resulted in a military coup led by General Oscar Benavides on April 25, 1914. Billinghurst went into exile in Iqique, Chile, and died there on January 28, 1915.

ROBERTO LEGUA (President; April 25, 1914–May 15, 1914). Roberto Legua was born in 1866. He was a leading political figure in Peru, serving as president of the senate and speaker of the chamber of deputies. He served as vice president under Guillermo Billinghurst from 1912 on. When Billinghurst was ousted in a military coup, Legua briefly served as interim president until the military junta under Oscar Benavides assumed power on May 15, 1914. He died in Lima on March 19, 1931.

OSCAR R. BENAVIDES (President; May 15, 1914–August 18, 1915). Oscar Raimundo Benavides was born in Lima on May 18, 1876. He attended the Chorrillos Military Academy and graduated as a second lieutenant in the 1890s. He completed further studies at San Marcos University in 1905 and received advanced military training in France from 1906 until 1912. He returned to Peru to accept the position of chief of staff of the army in 1913. He opposed President Guillermo Billinghurst's attempts to gain greater executive power and was dismissed in 1914. Benavides led a military coup against the government in April 1914. He became leader of the ruling military junta on May 15, 1914, and subsequently ruled as provisional president. He returned the country to constitutional rule the following year and stepped down on August 18, 1915, when José Pardo was selected as president. Benavides resumed his military service and was named minister to Italy in 1918. He returned to Peru in 1921, but his opposition to President Augusto Leguía resulted in his banishment to Guayaquil. He returned to Lima in 1930 when Colonel Luis Sanchez Cerro ousted Leguía. Sánchez Cerro feared Benavides' popularity in the army and sent him to Spain as Peru's ambassador. He also served as ambassador to Great Britain before being recalled to Peru in 1932 to assist in Peru's military conflict with Colombia. Sánchez Cerro was as-sassinated on April 30, 1933, and Benavides was chosen by the congress to assume the presidency. He proscribed the Peruvian Aprista Party and when the 1936 presidential election was won by Luis Antonio Eguiguren, the Aprista-backed candidate, Benavides nullified the results. He extended his term of office and disbanded the legislature. He was instrumental in securing the election of Manuel Prado as his successor and stepped down from office on December 8, 1939. He was subsequently promoted to field marshal and served as Peru's ambassador to Spain from 1940 until 1943 and to Argentina, where he remained until 1944. He returned to Peru to assist in the formation of the National Democratic Front. He died in Lima on July 2, 1946.

JOSÉ PARDO Y BARREDA (President; August 18, 1915–July 4, 1919). *See earlier entry under Heads of State.*

AUGUSTO BERNARDINO LEGUÍA (President; July 5, 1919–August 25, 1930). *See earlier entry under Heads of State.*

MANUEL MARIA PONCE (President; August 25, 1930–August 27, 1930). Manuel Maria Ponce was born in Arequipa in 1874. He attended the Military Academy and served in the Peruvian army. He was promoted to the rank of colonel in 1916 and to general in 1929. He was a leader of the military coup that ousted President Augusto Leguía in August 1930. He briefly headed the ruling military junta from August 25, 1930, until August 27, 1930, when Luis Sanchez Cerro assumed the leadership. Ponce died in Lima in 1966.

LUÍS SÁNCHEZ CERRO (President; August 27, 1930–March 1, 1931). Luís Manuel Sánchez Cerro was born in Piura in 1889. He graduated from the Chorrillos Military Academy in 1910. He participated in the military uprising that ousted President Guillermo Billinghurst in 1914. He participated in an unsuccessful attempt to overthrow President Augusto Leguía in 1922. He was imprisoned for his part in the revolt but subsequently was released and promoted to lieutenant colonel by Leguía. He led another military coup against Leguía and ousted the president on August 25, 1930. He headed the ruling military junta from August 27, 1930, until opposition from the armed forces forced his resignation on March 1, 1931. He founded the revolutionary Union Party and successfully ran in the presidential election in October 1931, defeating Victor Raul Haya de la Torre's Aprista Party. Sánchez Cerro assumed office on December 8, 1931, and embarked on a ruthless campaign to crush the opposition Aprista Party. Many of its members were arrested or deported. Sánchez Cerro put down several rebellions and survived an assassination attempt in 1932. He was shot to death by Abelardo Hurtado De Mendoza, an Aprista member, in Lima on April 30, 1933.

RICARDO LEONICIO ELIAS (President; March 1, 1931–March 5, 1931). Ricardo Leonicio Elias was born in 1874. He received a degree in law from the University of San Marcos in 1899. He entered the judiciary and became a supreme court justice in 1923. He was president of the Supreme Court at the time of the military coup that ousted President Luís Sánchez Cerro. He briefly served as interim president from March 1, 1931, until March 5, 1931. Elias died in Lima in 1951.

GUSTAVO JIMÉNEZ (President; March 5, 1931–March 11, 1931). Gustavo A. Jiménez was born in 1886. He attended the Military School in Chorrillos and served in the Peruvian army. He was a leader of the military coup that ousted President Luís Sánchez Cerro in March 1931. Jiménez headed the ruling military junta from March 5, 1931, until

March 11, 1931. He died in Paijan on March 14, 1933.

DAVID SAMANEZ OCAMPO (President; March 11, 1931–December 8, 1931). David Samanez Ocampo was born in Huambo in 1866. He entered politics and was elected to the chamber of deputies from Antabamba. He participated in the rebellion against President Augusto B. Leguía in 1909. He was a supporter of President Guillermo Billinghurst, who was ousted in 1914. Samanez Ocampo remained a leading figure in the Liberal Party until his retirement from politics in the 1920s. He was chosen to head a caretaker government on March 11, 1931, following Luís Sánchez Cerro's resignation as head of a military junta. Samanez Ocampo's government oversaw the elections in October 1931 that resulted in a victory for Sánchez Cerro. Samanez Ocampo relinquished office to Sánchez Cerro on December 8, 1931. He resumed his retirement and died in 1947.

LUÍS SÁNCHEZ CERRO (President; December 8, 1931–April 30, 1933). *See earlier entry under Heads of State.*

OSCAR R. BENAVIDES (President; April 30, 1933–December 8, 1939). *See earlier entry under Heads of State.*

MANUEL PRADO Y UGARTECHE (President; December 8, 1939–July 28, 1945). Manuel Prado y Ugarteche was born in Lima on April 21, 1889. He was the son of General Mariano Ignacio Prado, who served as Peru's president from 1865 until 1868 and from 1876 until 1879. The younger Prado was educated at the University of San Marcos, where he received a degree in engineering. He subsequently entered the Peruvian army and saw action in the cavalry during Peru's brief border conflict with Ecuador in 1910. Prado also continued his studies at the University of San Marcos and became a faculty member in the department of mathematics in 1912. He entered politics and was elected to the chamber of deputies in 1919. He was a leading opponent of the regime of Augusto B. Leguía and was forced into exile in Europe in 1923. Prado returned to Peru in 1932 following the ouster of Leguía. He became president of the Central Reserve Bank of Peru in 1934. Prado was chosen as the handpicked successor of President Oscar Benavides in 1939. He was the only candidate in the subsequent election and took office on December 3, 1939. He encouraged close relations with the United States and entered Peru into World War II on the side of the Allies. Prado increased industrialization in the country and successfully negotiated a settlement to a long-standing border dispute with Ecuador in 1942. He completed his term of office on July 28, 1945, and relinquished the presidency to José Luís Bustamente y Rivero. Prado was the candidate of the National Coalition Party in the presidential election in 1956 and returned to office with the support of the leftist American Popular Revolutionary Alliance (APRA). He took office on July 28, 1956. He allowed the return of Aprista leader Victor Haya de la Torre from exile in July 1957. Prado became one of the first South American leaders to break diplomatic relations with Fidel Castro's Cuba. He maintained close relations with the United States and ended censorship restrictions on the Peruvian press. Prado was ousted in a military coup on July 19, 1962, following a presidential election that resulted in a victory for Haya de la Torre. Prado was sent into exile in Paris, where he died of a heart attack on August 14, 1967.

JOSÉ BUSTAMENTE Y RIVERO (President; July 28, 1945–October 28, 1948). José Luís Bustamente y Rivero was born in Arequipa on January 15, 1894. He was educated in Peru and received a degree in law. He was active in the revolt that ousted the dictatorship of Augusto Leguía in 1930. Bustamente served in the government as minister of education in 1931 and subsequently joined the faculty of the University of San Augustin in Arequipa as a professor of civil law. He left the university to enter the foreign ministry in 1934. He served as Peru's ambassador to various South American countries, including Bolivia, Paraguay, and Uruguay. Bustamente was elected president in 1945 and took office on July 28, 1945. His government was challenged by the leftist American Popular Revolutionary Alliance (APRA) which controlled a majority in the Peruvian congress. Bustamente declared a state of emergency in October 1948 and ruled by decree. The Aprista Party attempted a left-wing revolt on October 3, 1948, but the rebellion was crushed by the army the following day. The president was subsequently ousted in a rightist coup led by his minister of war, Manuel Odria, on October 28, 1948. Bustamente returned to private life to practice law. He also became the dean of the Lima Law College. He was appointed to the International Court of Justice in The Hague in 1961 and served as its president from 1967 until 1970. Bustamente also served as a mediator in the war between El Salvador and Honduras in 1977. He was hospitalized with heart problems in 1988 and died in a Lima hospital at the age of 94 on January 11, 1989.

The Philippines

The Philippines is an archipelago off the coast of southeastern Asia. It was granted independence from the United States on July 4, 1946.

HEADS OF STATE

MANUEL QUEZÓN (President; November 15, 1935–August 1, 1944). Manuel Luís Quezón y Molina was born in Baler, Tayabas Province, on August 19, 1878. He was active in Emilio Aguinaldo's rebellion from 1899 until 1902 but subsequently gave his allegiance to the territorial administration. He served in the Philippine assembly from 1907 until 1909 and was named resident-commissioner to the United States in 1909. He returned to the Philippines to serve as president of the senate in 1916, where he remained until 1935. He was a leading nationalist and was instrumental in the passage of the Philippine Commonwealth and Independence Act in 1934. He was elected the Philippine Commonwealth's first president, taking office on November 15, 1935. He instituted numerous social reforms in the country and was successful in encouraging of commerce and industry. He was renominated by the Nacionalista Party in 1941 and was reelected to the presidency by a wide margin over Popular Front Party candidate Juan Sumulong. Quezón went to the United States following the Japanese invasion of the Philippines in January 1942. He served as a member of the Pacific War Council and continued to head the government in exile. Quezón died of tuberculosis at Saranac Lake, New York, on August 1, 1944.

SERGIO OSMEÑA (President; August 1, 1944–May 28, 1946). Sergio Osmeña was born in Cebu on September 9, 1878. He received a degree in law from the University of the Philippines. He entered politics and was elected governor of Cebu Province. In 1906 he was elected to the House of Representatives. Osmeña was a leader of the independence movement and head of the Nacionalista Party. He was elected speaker of the house in 1907 and was elected to the senate in 1922. He attended the independence conference in the United States in 1931. Osmeña was elected vice president under Manuel Quezón after the establishment of the Philippine Commonwealth and took office in November 1935. He went to the United States following the Japanese occupation of the Philippines in 1942 and returned with the American troops in October 1944. President Quezón died in office on August 1, 1944, and Osmeña succeeded him as president. He ran for reelection in 1946, but was defeated by Manuel Roxas y Acuna. He relinquished office to Roxas on May 28, 1946. Osmeña died at his home in Cebu from heart and kidney ailments on October 19, 1961.

Poland

Poland is a country in eastern Europe. Portions of Poland were claimed by Russia, Austria, and Prussia prior to World War I. Poland was reconstituted as an independent nation in 1918, but was occupied by German troops early in World War II, and after the war came under the sphere of influence of the Soviet Union.

HEADS OF STATE

JÓZEF PIŁSUDSKI (President; November 22, 1918–December 11, 1922). Józef Piłsudski was born in Zulów, Wilno Province, on December 5, 1867. He became involved in revolutionary activities against Poland's Russian rulers at an early age. He was arrested and banished to Siberia in 1887. He joined the Polish Socialist Party after his return to Wilno in 1892 and became leader of the party two years later. He was again arrested in February 1900, but effected an escape the following year. He went to Kraków, in Austrian-controlled Poland, where he continued his revolutionary activities against the Russians. He began to form an underground Polish army in Lwow in 1908. Piłsudski's Polish troops fought with the Austro-Hungarians against the Russians during World War I. The Central Powers proclaimed an independent Polish state on November 5, 1916. This action was reinforced by the revolution in Russia in March 1917. Germany refused to commit itself to Poland's independence, and Piłsudski objected to Germany's demands that the Polish army come under control of the Central Powers. He was arrested by the Germans and imprisoned in Magdeburg. He was released after Germany's defeat in the war and returned to Poland on November 10, 1918. He was proclaimed independent Poland's first president on November 22, 1918. He led the Polish army in a war against the Soviet Red Army and regained much of Poland's eastern territory, but failed in an invasion of the Ukraine. Piłsudski retired after the adoption of a new constitution and relinquished the presidency to Gabriel Narutowicz, the newly elected president, on December 11, 1922. Narutowicz was assassinated several days later, and Piłsudski agreed to serve as chief of the general staff under his successor, Stanislaw Wojciechowski. Piłsudski retired to Sulejowek on May 29, 1923, after the formation of a right-wing government under Wincenty Witos. Piłsudski was recalled to Warsaw by President Wojciechowski in mid-1925 when the government proved unable to bring political and economic stability to the country. Piłsudski led troops on Warsaw in May 1926, and after several days of fighting, he forced the creation of a new government. He was chosen by the national assembly to replace Wojciechowski as president, but instead allowed his ally, Ignacy Mościcki, to assume the presidency. Piłsudski took the position of minister of war and inspector-general of the army. He also served as prime minister from October 2, 1926, until June 25, 1928, and from August 30, 1930, until November 28, 1930. He ruled Poland as a virtual dictator from September 1930, when he ordered the arrest of leading opponents of the government. Piłsudski's health began to fail during the 1930s. He remained minister of war and leader of the country until he died of liver cancer in Warsaw on May 12, 1935.

GABRIEL NARUTOWICZ (President; December 11, 1922–December 16, 1922). Gabriel Narutowicz was born in

Teleze, Lithuania, on March 3, 1865. He was educated in St. Petersburg and Zurich, where he trained as an engineer. He subsequently worked as a professor at Zurich University. Narutowicz was named to the government as minister of public works in June 1920. He subsequently served as foreign minister in Julian Nowak's government in 1922. He was supported by the parties of the Left in the presidential election in 1922 and was elected to the presidency after a bitter campaign against the nationalists. He succeeded Józef Piłsudski to the office on December 11, 1922. Several days later Narutowicz was shot three times in the back by Niewadomski, a deranged artist, while attending an exhibition of paintings at the Palace of Fine Arts on December 16, 1922.

STANISŁAW WOJCIECHOWSKI (President; December 20, 1922–May 15, 1926). Stanisław Wojciechowski was born in Kalisz on March 15, 1869. He was educated at Warsaw University. Wojciechowski for his nationalist activities. He went to Paris after his release. While in exile he met with Jozef Piłsudski and was a founder of the Polish Socialist Party. Wojciechowski returned to Poland in 1905 and remained active in the Socialist movement. He was instrumental in the formation of the Polish army in 1917. He became minister of the interior in the first government of the Polish Republic in January 1919. He remained in the cabinet until June 1920. He was elected to the presidency following the assassination of Gabriel Narutowicz, and took office on December 20, 1922. He continued to serve as president until May 15, 1926, when Jozef Piłsudski and his supporters marched on Warsaw and brought down the government. Wojciechowski retired from politics to study the cooperative movements. He died in Golabki, near Warsaw, on April 9, 1953.

IGNACY MOŚCICKI (President; June 1, 1926–September 30, 1939). Ignacy

Mościcki was born in Mierzanow on December 1, 1867. He studied chemistry at the Polytechnic School of Riga. He became involved in nationalist activities and in 1892 fled to London to avoid arrest. He continued his education there. Mościcki accepted a teaching position at the University of Freiburg in Switzerland in 1897. He returned to Poland and joined the faculty of the Polytechnic School at Lwow as a professor of electrochemistry. He became a leading scientist and developed a method of manufacturing synthetic nitric acid. He held several hundred patents for inventions related to electrochemistry. Mościcki became president of Poland with the support of Marshal Józef Piłsudski on June 1, 1926. He was reelected in May 1933. He gained greater authority in the government after the death of Marshal Piłsudski in 1935. Poland was threatened by Germany in 1939, and Mościcki vowed to defend his country's borders. When the Germans invaded Poland in September in 1939, Mościcki and the government were forced to flee to Romania, and he was interned in Bicaz. He resigned from the presidency on September 30, 1939, and was replaced by Władysław Raczkiewicz. Mościcki was permitted to leave Romania for Switzerland in December 1939, and there he resumed his scientific work. He remained in exile until his death after a long illness at his farm in Versoix on October 1, 1946.

WŁADYSŁAW RACZKIEWICZ (President; September 30, 1939–July 22, 1944). Władysław Raczkiewicz was born on January 16, 1885. He was educated at St. Petersburg and Dorpat, where he became involved with the Polish nationalist movement. He received a degree in law and practiced in Minsk. Raczkiewicz served in the Russian army during World War I. He entered the newly formed Polish army after the Russian revolution in 1917. Raczkiewicz served in the government of the Polish Republic as minister of the interior in 1921 and from 1925 until 1926. He also served as governor of Wilno in 1926. He subsequently served as marshal of the Polish senate. Raczkiewicz was again minister of the interior in a coalition cabinet in 1935. He was governor of Pomorze at the time of the German invasion in 1939 and escaped to Paris. He was chosen as president of the Polish government-in-exile on September 30, 1939. He appointed General Władysław Sikorski as premier and minister of war. The government remained in Angers, near Paris, until the fall of France. They subsequently relocated to London. Raczkiewicz opposed the establishment of a Polish provisional government sponsored by the Soviet Union in Lublin on December 31, 1944. He continued to assert that his was the legitimate government of Poland despite Allied recognition of the Lublin regime. Raczkiewicz died at Ruthin Castle, Denbighshire, North Wales, on June 6, 1947, after a long illness.

BOLESŁAW BIERUT (President; December 31, 1944–November 22, 1952). Bolesław Bierut was born Bolesław Krasnodebski in Laczna on April 18, 1892. He was educated locally and joined the trade union movement as a young man. He became a Communist during World War I and worked as a party organizer after the war. Bierut was imprisoned for six months in 1922 for editing a leftist newspaper. He left Poland in 1928 to work with the Comintern in Vienna. In 1932 he returned to Poland and was again arrested. He escaped several years later and fled to the Soviet Union. Bierut accompanied Soviet troops in the invasion of Poland in 1939 and organized the purge of non-Communists throughout the country. He used several aliases during his revolutionary activities, including Bienkowski and Rutkowski, before he adopted the name Bierut. He again fled to Moscow following the German occupation of Poland, but was sent back to Poland in 1942 to establish an underground Communist government. Bierut organized the Polish Workers' Party the following year. He became acting president of the provisional government of Poland in Lublin on December 31, 1944. A government of National Unity, including members of the democratic Polish government-in-exile, was proclaimed on June 28, 1945. The new government established close relations with the Soviet Union. Parliamentary elections were held in January 1947 that resulted in a major victory for the Communists. Bierut was elected president of Poland on February 5, 1947. He stepped down as president to become Poland's premier on November 20, 1952. He served as head of the government until March 19, 1954. Bierut remained first secretary of the Communist party and the leading political figure in the country until his death. He suffered a heart attack while attending the 20th Congress of the Soviet Communist Party in Moscow in February 1956 and died in a Moscow hospital on March 12, 1956.

HEADS OF GOVERNMENT

JAN KUCHARZEWSKI (Prime Minister; November 20, 1917–February 27, 1918). Jan Kucharzewski was born in Wysokie Mazowieckie on May 27, 1876. He studied law at the University of Warsaw. He was on the faculty of the Free University of Warsaw. He was chosen to serve as prime minister of the Polish provisional government on November 20, 1917, during the occupation of Poland by the Central Powers in World War I. Kucharzewski resigned on February 27, 1918, when it was learned that Austria planned the annexation of East Galicia and Bukovina. Kucharzewski again briefly headed the provisional government from September 6, 1918, until October 9, 1918. He served as Poland's delegate to the Permanent Court of International Justice at The Hague from 1923 until 1930. He authored numerous historical and biographical books during his career. He was allowed to leave Poland during the German occupation in 1940. He went to Italy and Portugal before settling in the United States. He was the founder of the Polish Institute of Arts and Sciences in America in 1942. Kucharzewski remained in exile after the formation of Poland's Communist government after the war. He died in a New York City hospital on July 4, 1952.

ANTONI PONIKOWSKI (Prime Minister; February 27, 1918–April 3, 1918). Antoni Ponikowski was born in Siedlce on May 29, 1878. He was rector of Warsaw University. He served as minister of education and public worship in Poland's first provisional government from November 1917 until he was called to head the provisional government as prime minister from February 27, 1918, to April 3, 1918. He remained in the government as minister of education until November 1918. He again headed the government from September 19, 1921, until March 1, 1922. He died in 1949.

JAN KANTZ STECZKOWSKI (Prime Minister; April 4, 1918–September 6, 1918). Jan Kantz Steczkowski was born in 1863. He was a leading Polish financier and economist. He served as prime minister and minister of finance in the provisional Polish government from April 4, 1918, until September 6, 1918. He remained minister of finance in several successive governments. Steczkowski died in Kraków on September 4, 1929.

JAN KUCHARZEWSKI (Prime Minister; September 6, 1918–October 9, 1918). *See earlier entry under Heads of Government.*

JÓZEF ŚWIERZYŃSKI (Prime Minister; October 22, 1918–November 5, 1918). Józef Świerzyński was born in 1868. He briefly headed the provisional Polish government from October 22, 1918, to November 5, 1918.

WŁADYSŁAW WRÓBLEWSKI (Prime Minister; November 5, 1918–November 11, 1918). Władysław Wróblewski was born in Kraków on March 21, 1875. He briefly served as prime minister of the provisional government from November 5, 1918, until November 11, 1918. He was a general in the Polish army and a supporter of Józef Piłsudski. Wróblewski was named commander of the Fifth Army Corps in Kraków when Piłsudski reclaimed the government in 1926. Wróblewski headed the main auditing office in the finance department from 1927, until his resignation in October 1930.

IGNAZ DASZYŃSKI (Prime Minister; November 14, 1918–November 18, 1918). Ignaz Daszyński was born in Zbaraz on October 26, 1866. He was educated at universities in Kraków, Zurich, and Paris. He formed the Polish Socialist Party in 1897 and was elected to the Austrian parliament. He was editor of *Napzrod*, the Socialist newspaper in Kraków. He became prime minister of the first independent Polish government on November 14, 1918, but stepped down several days later on November 18, 1918. He served as vice premier in a coalition government under Wincenty Witos in 1920. Daszyński was the marshal of the Seym (parliament) in the mid–1920s. He attempted to mediate between Marshal Józef Piłsudski and the parties of the Left. He became an opponent of Piłsudski's dictatorship in the late 1920s. Daszyński died in Byastra on October 31, 1936.

JEDRZEI MORACZEWSKI (Prime Minister; November 18, 1918–January 16, 1919). Jedrzei Moraczewski was born in Trzemeszno on January 13, 1870. He was appointed by Marshal Józef Piłsudski to form a government on November 18, 1918, following the dissolution of the regency council. His government was not recognized by the Allies, and he relinquished office to Ignaz Paderewski on January 18, 1919. Moraczewski was a leading Socialist and labor leader. He formed the Union of Trade Unions in support of the government in 1931. Moraczewski died in Sulejówek on August 5, 1944.

IGNAZ JAN PADEREWSKI (Prime Minister; January 18, 1919–December 14, 1919). Ignaz Jan Paderewski was born in Kurylopka on November 6, 1860. He began studying music at the Conservatoire of Warsaw at the age of twelve. He became a professor there six years later. He began teaching music in Strasbourg in 1883. Paderewski made public performances in Vienna, Paris, and London in 1887, and began a tour of the United States in 1891. He gained acclaim as a piano virtuoso for his renditions of works by Chopin, Bach, Beethoven, and Schumann. He settled in Switzerland in 1898 and composed the opera *Manru* in 1901. Paderewski was a prominent supporter of Polish nationalism and commissioned a statue in 1910 honoring the 500th anniversary of Poland's victory at the Battle of Grunwald. Paderewski served on the Polish National Committee during World War I and represented the committee in the United States. He convinced President Woodrow Wilson to include the issue of Polish independence in his peace proposal in 1917. Paderewski returned to Poland in December 1918. He convinced Józef Piłsudski, the provisional president, to form a national government, and Paderewski became prime minister and foreign minister on January 18, 1919. As head of the government he signed the Treaty of Versaille. Paderewski, who aspired to the presidency, soon came into conflict with Piłsudski. He resigned from office on December 14, 1919, and returned to Switzerland. Paderewski resumed his concert career in 1921 and never returned to Poland. After the Polish occupation by Germany, Paderewski was asked by General Władysław Sikorski, prime minister of the government-in-exile in London, to become chairman of the Polish National Council in October 1939, but Paderewski went to the United States after the fall of France in 1940. He died in New York City on June 29, 1941.

LEOPOLD SKULSKI (Prime Minister; December 14, 1919–June 9, 1920). Leopold Skulski was born in Zamość on November 15, 1878. He was named prime minister on December 14, 1919. His government's proposal of land reform brought down his government on June 9, 1920. He died in 1942 during the German occupation.

WŁADYSŁAW GRABSKI (Prime Minister; June 24, 1920–July 23, 1920). Władysław Grabski was born in Borowe on July 7, 1874. He served in the Russian Dumas from 1906 to 1912. He became a leader of the National Democratic Party following the creation of the Polish Republic in 1918. He served as prime minister and minister of finance from June 24, 1920, until July 23, 1920, and again from September 21, 1923, to November 13, 1925. He retired from politics to serve as president of the Warsaw Agricultural College in December 1925. Grabski died in Warsaw after a long illness on March 1, 1938.

WINCENTY WITOS (Prime Minister; July 23, 1920–September 19, 1921). Wincenty Witos was born in Wierzchosławice on January 22, 1874. He was a founder of the Peasant Party and served in the Sejm as a deputy from 1919. He was prime minister from July 23, 1920, to September 19, 1921, and again from May 27, 1923, to December 11, 1923. He was again prime minister from May 10, 1926, to May 15, 1926, when Józef Piłsudski forced him from office.

He was an opponent of Piłsudski's dictatorship and was imprisoned in Brest fortress in 1930. Witos was exiled to Czechoslovakia in 1933. He was imprisoned by the Germans in 1939 after the start of World War II. Witos was released following the liberation of Poland. He refused to join forces with the Communists after the war. He died on October 31, 1945.

ANTONI PONIKOWSKI (Prime Minister; September 19, 1921–March 1, 1922). *See earlier entry under Heads of Government.*

ARTUR ŚLIWIŃSKI (Prime Minister; June 28, 1922–July 7, 1922). Artur Śliwiński was born in Ruszki on August 17, 1877. He was a close associate of Marshal Józef Piłsudski. He briefly served as prime minister from June 28, 1922, until July 7, 1922. He declined Piłsudski's offer to become president following the marshal's coup in 1926. Śliwiński died in Warsaw on January 16, 1953.

WOJCIECH KORFANTY (Prime Minister; July 14, 1922–July 29, 1922). Wojciech Korfanty was born in Sadzawka on April 20, 1873. He served as a minister without portfolio in Jedrzei Moraczewski's government from November 1918 until January 1919. He briefly headed the government as prime minister from July 14, 1922, until July 29, 1922. Korfanty died in Warsaw on August 17, 1939.

JULIAN NOWAK (Prime Minister; July 31, 1922–December 14, 1922). Julian Ignacy Nowak was born in Okocim on March 10, 1865. He was the rector of Kraków University when he was named prime minister by Józef Piłsudski on July 31, 1922. He was an economic expert, and he attempted to establish cordial relations with Germany and Russia. He stepped down from office on December 14, 1922. He subsequently served as professor of bacteriology at the University of

Kraków. He died in Kraków on November 7, 1946.

WŁADYSŁAW SIKORSKI (Prime Minister; December 16, 1922–May 27, 1923). Władysław Sikorski was born in Tuszowo, in Galicia, on May 20, 1881. He was educated at the University Technical College at Lwow, where he received a degree in civil engineering. Sikorski became involved in the Polish independence movement and was instrumental in the formation of the Polish army in 1917. He commanded an army corps during the Polish-Ukraine War in 1919 and during the Polish-Russian War in 1920. He served as chief of the general staff in 1921. He became prime minister on December 16, 1922, following the assassination of President Gabriel Narutowicz. He stepped down on May 27, 1923. Sikorski served as minister of war from 1924 until 1925. He retired from the army in 1928 in opposition to Józef Piłsudski's dictatorship. He went to Paris for a decade, returning to Poland in 1938. He went back to Paris following the German occupation of Poland in 1939. He became premier and minister of war in the Polish government-in-exile on September 30, 1939. He also became commander-in-chief of all Polish forces in November 1939. Sikorski established his headquarters in London after the fall of France. He was killed off the coast of Gibraltar when the plane he was traveling in crashed into the sea on July 3, 1943.

WINCENTY WITOS (Prime Minister; May 27, 1923–December 11, 1923). *See earlier entry under Heads of Government.*

WŁADYSŁAW GRABSKI (Prime Minister; September 21, 1923–November 13, 1925). *See earlier entry under Heads of Government.*

ALEKSANDER, COUNT SRZYŃ-SKI (Prime Minister; November 20,

1925–April 21, 1926). Aleksander, Count Srzyński, was born in Ruszki on August 17, 1877. He served as foreign minister in Artur Śliwiński's government in 1922. He also served as foreign minister under Władysław Sikorski from December 1922 until May 1923. He headed the government as prime minister from November 20, 1925, until April 21, 1926. Count Srzyński died in Ostrowo on September 25, 1931.

WINCENTY WITOS (Prime Minister; May 10, 1926–May 15, 1926). *See earlier entry under Heads of Government.*

KAZIMIERZ BARTEL (Prime Minister; May 15, 1926–October 2, 1926). Kazimierz Bartel was born in Lwow on March 3, 1882. He was a math professor at Lwow Polytechnic. He served as minister of railways from 1919 to 1920. He was elected to the Sejm in 1922 and founded the Labor Party in 1924. He was named by Marshal Józef Piłsudski to serve as prime minister on May 15, 1926, but served only until October 2 of that year. He subsequently served as deputy premier under Piłsudski until June 25, 1928, when Piłsudski stepped down for reasons of health, and Bartel again assumed the prime ministership. He stepped down on April 13, 1929. He was persuaded to head the government again on December 21, 1929, and retained office until March 15, 1930. Bartel was executed in Lwow by the Germans on July 26, 1941, during the occupation of Poland.

JÓZEF PIŁSUDSKI (Prime Minister; October 2, 1926–June 25, 1928). *See earlier entry under Heads of State.*

KAZIMIERZ BARTEL (Prime Minister; June 25, 1928–April 13, 1929). *See earlier entry under Heads of Government.*

KAZIMIERZ ŚWITALSKI (Prime Minister; April 13, 1929–December 21, 1929). Kazimierz Świtalski (Swietoslawski) was born in Sanok on March 4, 1886. He worked with the Polish independence movement and was a close advisor to Marshal Józef Piłsudski. He served as director of the president's civil chancellery after Piłsudski's coup in 1926. Świtalski was appointed minister of education in June 1928. He briefly served as prime minister from April 13, 1929, until December 21, 1929. Świtalski died in Warsaw on December 28, 1962.

KAZIMIERZ BARTEL (Prime Minister; December 21, 1929–March 15, 1930). *See earlier entry under Heads of Government.*

VALERIAN SŁAWEK (Prime Minister; March 29, 1930–August 23, 1930). Valerian Sławek was born on November 2, 1879. He was a close associate of Marshal Józef Piłsudski. He served as prime minister from March 29, 1930, until August 23, 1930, and from December 5, 1930, until May 26, 1931. Sławek again headed the government from March 28, 1935, until October 12, 1935. He died in Warsaw on April 3, 1939.

JÓZEF PIŁSUDSKI (Prime Minister; August 30, 1930–November 28, 1930). *See earlier entry under Heads of State.*

VALERIAN SŁAWEK (Prime Minister; December 5, 1930–May 26, 1931). *See earlier entry under Heads of Government.*

ALEKSANDR PRYSTOR (Prime Minister; May 27, 1931–May 9, 1933). Aleksandr Prystor was born in Vilnius on January 2, 1874. He served in the Polish army and was promoted to colonel in 1926. He served as minister of labor from April 1929 until March 1930. He served as prime minister from May 27, 1931, until May 9, 1933. He died in the Soviet Union in 1941.

JANUSZ JĘDRZEJEWICZ (Prime Minister; May 10, 1933–May 13, 1934). Janusz Jędrzejewicz was born in Spiczynce on June 21, 1885. He joined the Polish army in 1917. He retired from the army in 1924 and subsequently served as director of the Warsaw Teachers' Training College until 1926. Jędrzejewicz was elected to the Sejm in 1928. He served in the cabinet as minister of education from May 1931 until May 10, 1933, when he headed the government as prime minister. He held that position until May 13, 1934. He died in 1951.

LEON KOZŁOWSKI (Prime Minister; May 13, 1934–March 28, 1935). Leon Kozłowski was born in Rebieszyce in 1892. He was a leading Polish archaeologist. He served as minister of land reform from 1930 until 1932. He headed the government as prime minister from May 13, 1934, until March 28, 1935. He died in Berlin in May 1944.

VALERIAN SŁAWEK (Prime Minister; March 28, 1935–October 12, 1935). *See earlier entry under Heads of Government.*

MARJAN ZYNDRAM-KOŚCIA-TOWSKI (Prime Minister; October 12, 1935–May 15, 1936). Marjan Zyndram-Kościatowski was born in Ponedele on March 16, 1892. He was a founder of the League of Active Struggle in St. Petersburg in support of Polish independence in 1914. He was appointed minister of the interior in June 1934. He headed the government as prime minister from October 12, 1935, until May 15, 1936. He died in 1946.

FELICJAN SŁAWOJ-SKŁAD-KOWSKI (Prime Minister; May 16, 1936–September 30, 1939). Felicjan Sławoj-Składkowski was born in Gabin on June 9, 1885. He fought with Marshal Józef Piłsudski's Polish army against the Germans during World War I. He headed the Polish army's health depart-

ment from 1922 until 1926 and briefly served as governor of Warsaw. He was promoted to the rank of general and served as minister of the interior after Piłsudski's coup in 1926. He served as minister of the interior in several successive governments from June 1930 until May 1933. Sławoj-Składkowski became premier and minister of the interior on May 16, 1936. He condemned anti-Semitic acts in Poland. He fled to Romania after the German invasion of Poland in September 1939. He was replaced as prime minister on September 30, 1939, and remained interned in Romania for eighteen months. He subsequently went to the Middle East, where he remained until the end of the war. He then settled in England. He died at his home in London on August 31, 1962.

WŁADYSŁAW SIKORSKI (Prime Minister; September 30, 1939–July 4, 1943). *See earlier entry under Heads of Government.*

STANISŁAW MIKOŁAJZYK (Prime Minister; July 4, 1943–November 24, 1944). Stanisław Mikołajzyk was born in Holsterhausen on July 18, 1901. He was a leader of the Peasant Party. He became prime minister of the Polish government-in-exile in London on July 4, 1943, following the death of Władysław Sikorski. He stepped down on November 24, 1944, and joined the provisional government in Lublin as deputy prime minister in charge of agriculture. He fled Poland in October 1947 under the Communist regime. He went into exile in the United States and died in Chevy Chase, Maryland, on December 13, 1966.

TOMASZ ARCIZSEWSKI (Prime Minister; November 30, 1944–July 6, 1945). Tomasz Arciszewski was born in Sierzchow on November 4, 1877. He joined the Polish Socialist Society in 1893. Arciszewski went to London in 1899. He was arrested by the Russians upon his return to Poland in 1901. He was an early advocate of Polish independence. He served in the cabinet after the establishment of the Polish Republic in 1918. He was elected to the Sejm in 1919. Arcizsewski fought with the Polish underground against the Germans during World War II. He escaped to London in August 1944. He succeeded Stanisław Mikołajzyk as prime minister of the Polish government-in-exile in London on November 30, 1944. The Soviet Union installed a rival provisional government in Lublin in December 1944. Arcizsewski condemned the Yalta agreement that ceded eastern Poland to the Soviet Union. The Allies withdrew recognition of Arcizsewski's government on July 6, 1945, in favor of the Communist-dominated Lublin government. Arcizsewski remained a leader of the Polish exile community, serving as a director of the State for Polish Exiles. He collapsed in a London subway and died in a hospital on November 20, 1955.

EDWARD OSÚBKA-MORAW-SKI (Prime Minister; June 28, 1945–

February 7, 1947). Edward Osúbka-Morawski was born in Blizyn on October 5, 1909. He was an early member of the Polish Socialist Party and was imprisoned for antigovernment activity in 1934. He remained a leading Socialist organizer after his release and edited the underground Socialist newspaper *Robotnik*. Osúbka-Morawski participated in the defense of Warsaw during World War II and was president of the Political Committee for National Liberation during the war. He was named premier of the provisional government on June 28, 1945. He retained office until February 7, 1947, when the Communist party took control of the government. Osúbka-Morawski remained in the government as minister of public administration until January 1949. He was then named director of the State Holiday Resorts Corporation. Osúbka-Morawski was granted membership in the Communist Party in 1956. He was dropped from the ballot in January of the following year and withdrew from political affairs. He died on January 9, 1997.

Portugal

Portugal is a country on the Iberian Peninsula in southwest Europe.

HEADS OF STATE

CARLOS I (King; October 19, 1889–February 1, 1908). Carlos was born in Lisbon on September 23, 1863. He was the son of King Luís of Portugal and Princess Pia of Savoy. He received an education at court and became a talented artist and sailor. Carlos married Marie Amelie of Orleans, the daughter of the Comte de Paris, in 1886. He succeeded to the throne upon his father's death on October 19, 1889. His reign was soon beset by both international and domes-

tic crises. The long-standing alliance between Portugal and Great Britain was threatened in 1890 over a border dispute in the Zambezi region of Africa. The conflict was settled the following year at the Anglo-Portuguese Convention. Portugal's economic condition deteriorated under mounting debts and oppressive taxes. Corruption in the government and the inability of the government to secure additional loans brought about calls for the establishment of a republic. Carlos declared a tobacco monopoly for the government in 1906, and discontent spread to the armed forces. Carlos dissolved the parliament in May 1907 and granted dictatorial powers to Premier João Franco. Rioting took place throughout the country amid renewed calls for the abolishment of the monarchy. Another revolt broke out in late January 1908, and the royal family returned to Lisbon from Vila Vicosa. Upon their arrival in Lisbon on February 1, 1908, two radical Republican gunmen shot Carlos and the Crown Prince Louis Philippe to death in the royal carriage.

MANUEL II (King; February 1, 1908–October 5, 1910). Manuel Marie Philippe Charles Amelio Louis Michael Raphael Gabriel Gozague Xavier Francois d'Assise Eugene de Braganza was born in Lisbon on November 15, 1889. He was the second son of King Carlos of Portugal and held the title of Duke of Beja. He succeeded to the throne on February 1, 1908, when his father and elder brother were shot to death by Republican radicals. Manuel was slightly injured in the attack. His reign was short-lived, as Republican sentiments were on the rise throughout Portugal. The revolution began in the autumn of 1910. He fled the Necessidades Palace in Lisbon for the Northern Provinces but was seized by the insurgents and banished to Gibraltar. He went into exile in London on October 5, 1910. Manuel married Princess Augusta Victoria of Hohenzollern in 1913. He discouraged royalist sentiments to restore him to the throne. He spent the remainder of his life in exile in Twickenham, England, where he became a leading private collector of rare Portuguese books. Manuel died at his estates in Twickenham of a throat disorder on July 2, 1932.

THEÓPHILO BRAGA (President; October 5, 1910–August 24, 1911). Joaquim Theóphilo Fernandes Braga was born in Ponta Delgada, in the Azores, on February 24, 1843. He was educated at the University of Coimbra, and became a leading scholar of history, literature, and philosophy. He authored numerous major works on Portuguese literature and history. He served as a professor at the Lisbon Higher School before becoming involved in the Republican movement in 1910. The subsequent revolution overthrew the monarchy and Braga became provisional president and head of the government on October 5, 1910. He relinquished the office of president to Manoel d'Arriaga on August 24, 1911, following elections. He again briefly served as interim president from May 28, 1915, until October 5, 1915. Braga subsequently retired from politics to resume his academic studies. He died in Lisbon on January 29, 1919.

MANOEL D'ARRIAGA (President; August 24, 1911–May 29, 1915). Manoel José d'Arriaga Brun da Silveira e Peyrelongue was born in Horta, in the Azores, in 1839. He was educated at the University of Coimbra and graduated with a degree in law in 1866. He was sympathetic to the Republican cause and served in parliament from 1882 to 1884 and from 1890 to 1892. D'Arriaga supported the abolition of the monarchy in 1910 and became the first elected president of the Portuguese Republic on August 24, 1911. He completed his term of office on May 29, 1915. D'Arriaga died in Lisbon on March 6, 1917.

THEÓPHILO BRAGA (President; May 28, 1915–October 5, 1915). *See earlier entry under Heads of State.*

BERNARDINO MACHADO GUIMARÃES (President; October 5, 1915–December 8, 1917). Bernardino Machado Guimarães was born in Rio de Janeiro, Brazil, on March 28, 1851. He was educated in Portugal and graduated from the University of Coimbra in 1876. He became a professor at the university soon after. Machado was elected to the chamber of peers in 1890. He served in the government as minister of public works in 1893. He became active in the republican movement in 1902 and resigned from the university following a student strike in 1907. He served in the newly formed government of the Portuguese Republic as foreign minister from 1910 until 1911. He was elected to the constituent assembly in 1911 and was named Portugal's ambassador to Brazil the following year. Machado headed the government as premier from February 8, 1914, until December 7, 1914, during which time he committed Portugal to Great Britain's side during World War I. Machado was elected president of Portugal and took office on October 5, 1915. Sidónio Paes led a rebellion against the government, and Machado was ousted from office on December 8, 1917. He remained involved in politics and again headed the government as premier from February 24, 1921, until May 24, 1921. Machado was again elected president and took office on December 11, 1925. He was ousted by a revolution on June 1, 1926. Machado was sent into exile in France. He was allowed to return to Portugal in 1940 and died in Oporto on April 29, 1944.

SIDÓNIO CARDOSO DE SILVA PAES (President; December 8, 1917– December 14, 1918). Sidónio Cardoso de Silva Paes was born in Caminha in the Minho district in 1872. He received a doctorate in mathematics from the University of Coimbra. He became active in politics and joined the moderate republican Unionist Party. Paes served in the cabinet as minister of public works and finance in 1911. He served as Portugal's minister to Berlin from 1912 until March 1916. Paes was a major in the army reserve and led the military coup in December 1917 that ousted the government of Afonso Da Costa. Paes assumed power as head of state and government on December 8, 1917, and called his regime "the New Republic." He was

elected president in the spring of 1918, and was officially installed in office on May 10, 1918. He continued Portugal's pro-Allies policy during World War II. Opposition to his government mounted in the summer of 1918. A counterrevolutionary movement led by the Democrats was suppressed in October 1918. There was an unsuccessful attempt to assassinate Paes on December 6, 1918. Paes was shot to death by José Julio da Costa, a Democratic fanatic, at Rossio railway station in Lisbon on December 14, 1918.

JOÃO DE CANTO E CASTRO SILVA ANTUNES (President; December 16, 1918–October 5, 1919). João de Canto e Castro Silva Antunes was born in 1862. He served in the Portuguese navy and attained the rank of rear admiral. He served in Sidónio Paes's cabinet as minister of the marine. Canto e Castro was chosen by the cabinet to head an interim government on December 16, 1918, following the assassination of Paes. He stepped down on October 5, 1919, when Antonio José de Almeida's was elected to the presidency. Canto e Castro died on March 14, 1934.

ANTONIO JOSÉ DE ALMEIDA (President; October 5, 1919–October 5, 1923). Antonio José de Almeida was born in 1866. He received a medical degree from the University of Coimbra in 1895. He participated in the unsuccessful Republican uprising in 1891. He spent the next ten years practicing medicine in the Portuguese colony of Sao Tome. He returned to Portugal in 1901 and was elected to parliament in 1906. He served as minister of home affairs in the provisional government following the establishment of the republic in 1910. He was the leader of the Evolutionist Party. Almeida became premier of a coalition government on November 30, 1915, and also served in the cabinet as minister of the colonies. He remained in office until December 8, 1917. He was subsequently elected president of Portugal and took office on October 5, 1919. Almeida completed his full term on October 5, 1923, relinquishing office to Manoel Teixeira Gomes. He died on October 30, 1929.

MANOEL TEIXEIRA GOMES (President; October 5, 1923–December 10, 1925). Manoel Teixeira Gomes was born in 1862. He was a leading businessman and writer before being named Portugal's ambassador to Great Britain in 1911. He remained in London until 1923, when he was urged by his friend, Afonso Da Costa, to run for the presidency. A liberal Republican, Teixeira Gomes was chosen by congress on October 5, 1923, to replace Antonio José de Almeida as president. He resigned from office on December 10, 1925, for reasons of health. He subsequently retired to Bougie, Algeria, where he died on October 18, 1941.

BERNARDINO MACHADO GUIMARÃES (President; December 11, 1925–June 1, 1926). *See earlier entry under Heads of State.*

ANTÓNIO ÓSCAR DE FRAGOSO CARMONA (President; November 29, 1926–April 18, 1951). António Óscar de Fragoso Carmona was born in Lisbon on November 24, 1869. He joined the Portuguese military and was a full general when he first became involved in politics. He served as a member of the cabinet from November to December 1923. Carmona led a coup d'état on May 28, 1926, and led a military junta composed of himself, General Manuel de Oliveira Gomes da Costa, and Commander José Mendes Cabecadas. Carmona ousted the other two members of the junta, and on July 9, 1926, he became premier of Portugal. He also assumed the presidency on November 26, 1926. He was confirmed as president by a plebiscite in March 1928 and relinquished the post of premier on November 12, 1928. When António de Oliveira Salazar was named premier in 1932, Carmona remained as head of state, but held little power. He was reelected as president in 1935, 1942, and 1949. He was promoted to the rank of first marshal of Portugal on May 28, 1947. Carmona remained in office until his death in Lisbon from influenza on April 18, 1951.

HEADS OF GOVERNMENT

JOSÉ LUCIANO DE CASTRO (Premier; February 5, 1897–June 21, 1900). José Luciano de Castro was born on December 14, 1835. He was elected to the chamber of deputies in 1854 and was named minister of justice in 1869. He served as minister of the interior in Anselmo José Braamcamp's cabinet in 1879. He became the leader of the Progressist Party after the death of Braamcamp in December 1885. He was named to head the government as premier on February 16, 1886. He remained in office when Carlos I took the throne in October 1889. He was forced to resign on January 14, 1890, over a conflict between Portugal and Great Britain over interests in East Africa. He again held office from February 5, 1897, until June 21, 1900, and from October 20, 1904, until failing health and an internal party dispute over the government's tobacco monopoly led to the fall of his government on March 20, 1906. He died on March 9, 1914.

ERNST RUDOLF HINTZE-RIBEIRO (Premier; June 21, 1900–October 20, 1904). Ernst Rudolf Hintze-Ribeiro was born on November 7, 1849.

He was the leader of the Regenerators, Portugal's conservative party. He headed the government as premier from February 22, 1893 until February 5, 1897. He again headed the government from June 21, 1900, until October 20, 1904. He again served as premier from March 20, 1906, until May 17, 1906, when King Carlos appointed João Franco to head the government. He continued to lead the Regenerators until he died suddenly in Lisbon while attending a funeral on August 1, 1907.

JOSÉ LUCIANO DE CASTRO (Premier; October 20, 1904–March 20, 1906). *See earlier entry under Heads of Government.*

ERNST RUDOLF HINTZE-RIBEIRO (Premier; March 20, 1906–May 17, 1906). *See earlier entry under Heads of Government.*

JOÃO FRANCO (Premier; May 17, 1906–February 4, 1908). João Franco Castello Franco was born on February 14, 1855. Franco served in Ernst Hintze-Ribeiro's Regenerator government from 1893 until 1897. He left the Regenerator Party in 1901 and formed the Centro Regenerador Liberal Party in 1903. His party supported decentralized administration and reform of the national finances. He was called upon by King Carlos I to form a coalition government with the Progressists on May 17, 1906. He attempted to crush the Republicans and closed down the party newspapers. The Progressists left the cabinet, and Franco closed the Cortes in May 1907. He subsequently governed by decree. Franco's dictatorship led to increased calls for the establishment of a republic. Rioting and civil unrest took place throughout the country. King Carlos I was assassinated by radical Republicans on February 1, 1908. Franco resigned several days later on February 4, 1908. He feared for his life and went into exile in Spain. Franco subsequently returned to

Portugal and was arrested by the government following the fall of the monarchy in October 1910. He was acquitted of charges of exceeding his powers while he held office and retired from public life. Franco died in Lisbon on April 4, 1929.

FRANCISCO JOAQUIM FERREIRA DO AMARAL (Premier; February 4, 1908–December 19, 1908). Francisco Joaquim Ferreira do Amaral was born on June 11, 1844. He served in the Portuguese navy and was promoted to the rank of admiral. He was chosen by King Manuel II to head the government on February 4, 1908. He led a coalition government of Regenerators and Progressists until his resignation on December 19, 1908. Ferreira do Amaral died on August 11, 1923.

ARTURO ALBERTO DE CAMPOS HENRIQUES (Premier; December 19, 1908–March 30, 1909). Arturo Alberto de Campos Henriques was born on April 28, 1853. He was a leader of the conservative faction of the Regenerator Party and was chosen to head a coalition government of Regenerators and Progressists on December 19, 1908. His government collapsed on March 30, 1909, because of a financial issue. Campos Henriques died on November 7, 1922.

SEBASTIAO TELLEZ (Premier; April 2, 1909–May 13, 1909). Sebastiao Tellez was a former minister of war. He was called upon by King Manuel II to form a government composed of Progressists and dissident Regenerators on April 2, 1909. The Progressists withdrew, and the government collapsed on May 13, 1909.

VENCESLAU DE SOMA PERREIRA DE LIMA (Premier; May 13, 1909–December 22, 1909). Venceslau de Soma Perreira de Lima was born in 1858. He was a leader of the Progressist Party and served in the cabinet as minister of foreign affairs in 1909. He was chosen to head the government on May 13, 1909. He also served in the cabinet as minister of the interior until his government resigned on December 22, 1909. De Lima died in Lisbon on January 29, 1920.

FRANCISCO ANTONIO DA VEIGA BEIRAO (Premier; December 22, 1909–June 26, 1910). Francisco Antonio da Veiga Beirao was born on July 24, 1841. He was called upon to head the government on December 22, 1909. He stepped down on June 26, 1910, when Regenerator leader Antonio Teixeira de Sousa formed a government. He died on November 11, 1916.

ANTONIO TEIXEIRA DE SOUSA (Premier; June 26, 1910–October 4, 1910). Antonio Teixeira de Sousa was born on May 5, 1857. He was the leader of the Regenerators and was called upon to form a government on June 26, 1910. He introduced anticlerical legislation in the hopes of appeasing the Republicans. Strikes and civil disorders against the government spread throughout the country and culminated in a revolution that overthrew the monarchy on October 4, 1910. Teixeira was forced from office when a provisional government under Theóphilo Braga was formed. He died on June 5, 1917.

THEÓPHILO BRAGA (Premier; October 5, 1910–September 2, 1911). *See earlier entry under Heads of State.*

JOÃO PINHEIRO CHAGAS (Premier; September 2, 1911–November 12, 1911). João Pinheiro Chagas was born on September 1, 1863. He was educated in Portugal and became a journalist. He became involved with the Republican movement and was a leader of an unsuccessful revolt against the monarchy in Oporto in January 1891. He was exiled to a convict plantation in Portuguese Africa, where he remained until the establishment of the republic in 1910. He served

the new government as minister to Paris. He returned to Lisbon to head the government as premier from September 2, 1911, until November 12, 1911. He remained a leading member of the government serving as minister of the interior and, again, as minister to Paris. Chagas was a supporter of Portugal's alliance with Great Britain during World War I. He was named again to head the government on May 14, 1915. He was shot three times and seriously wounded by João de Freitas, a member of the Portuguese senate, on May 19, 1915. The seriousness of his wounds, which included the loss of his right eye, prevented him from forming a government. However, he recovered sufficiently to serve as a member of the Portuguese delegation to the Versailles Peace Conference in 1919. Chagas died in Lisbon on May 28, 1925.

AUGUSTO DE VASCONCELLOS (Premier; November 12, 1911–June 4, 1912). Augusto de Vasconcellos was born on September 24, 1867. He headed the government as premier from November 12, 1911, until June 4, 1912. He remained a leading political figure in Portugal, often serving in the cabinet as foreign minister. He was Portugal's delegate to the League of Nations from 1923 to 1937. Vasconcellos subsequently retired from politics and died in Lisbon on September 27, 1951.

DUARTE LEITE (Premier; June 16, 1912–January 9, 1913). Duarte Leite was born on August 11, 1864. He headed the government as premier from June 16, 1912, until January 9, 1913. He remained a leading member of the government, serving as minister of finance and ambassador to Brazil. He was a leading opponent of the dictatorship of Antonio Salazar during the 1930s and 1940s. He died in an Oporto nursing home after a long illness on September 29, 1950.

AFONSO DA COSTA (Premier; January 9, 1913–February 8, 1914). Afonso

Da Costa was born on March 6, 1871. He was a law professor at Coimbra University when he became involved in the movement to overthrow the monarchy and establish a republic. Following the abdication of King Manuel II, Costa served as minister of justice in the provisional government of Theóphilo Braga from 1910 until 1911. Costa headed the government from January 9, 1913, until February 8, 1914. He was instrumental in Portugal's entry into World War I on the side of the Allies. He again headed the government from November 30, 1915, until March 16, 1916. He returned to serve as premier on April 15, 1917. Costa's government was ousted in a military coup led by Sidónio Paes on December 8, 1917. He was arrested and imprisoned for four months by the new government before he was allowed to go into exile in Paris. He gained a reputation as a leading international lawyer, often speaking before the League of Nations. He declined several invitations to return to Portugal to head the government. Costa was an opponent of the military dictatorship that took power in May 1926. He continued to reside in Paris, where he died on May 11, 1937.

BERNARDINO MACHADO GUIMARÃES (Premier; February 8, 1914–December 7, 1914). *See earlier entry under Heads of State.*

VICTOR HUGO DE AZEVEDO COUTINHO (Premier; December 7, 1914–January 28, 1915). Victor Hugo de Azevedo Coutinho was born on November 12, 1871. Azevedo Coutinho was a leading Democrat and former president of the chamber of deputies. He was called upon to head the government on December 7, 1914, and to preside over the elections the following year. His government was accused of a lack of impartiality in the coming elections, and civil disorders resulted. The president refused to declare a state of emergency to allow the government to move against the dissi-

dents. Azevedo Coutinho was ousted in a military coup on January 28, 1915. He subsequently served as Portuguese high commissioner in Mozambique from 1923 until 1926. Azevedo Coutinho died in Lisbon on June 27, 1955.

JOAQUIM PEREIRA PIMENTA DE CASTRO (Premier; January 28, 1915–May 14, 1915). Joaquim Pereira Pimenta de Castro was born on September 5, 1846. He served in the Portuguese army and attained the rank of general. He briefly served as minister of war in João Pinheiro Chagas's cabinet in 1911. He was dismissed when the Democrats accused him of not acting quickly enough against rebel monarchists. He was the senior general in the army when the military ousted the government of Victor Hugo de Azevedo Coutinho on January 28, 1915. Pimenta de Castro, who was considered nonpolitical, was chosen to head the new military government. The Democrats opposed the government and were outraged when Pimenta de Castro agreed to recognize monarchist parties in the election. The government was ousted by an armed uprising organized by the Democrats on May 14, 1915. Pimenta de Castro died on May 14, 1918.

JOÃO PINHEIRO CHAGAS (Premier; May 14, 1915–May 19, 1915). *See earlier entry under Heads of Government.*

JOSÉ DE CASTRO (Premier; May 19, 1915–November 30, 1915). José de Castro was born on April 7, 1868. He was a leading Democrat and was chosen to form a government on May 19, 1915, when injuries received in an assassination attempt prevented João Chagas from taking office. Dr. Castro continued to serve as premier until Afonso Da Costa became head of the government on November 30, 1915. He died on June 30, 1929.

AFONSO DA COSTA (Premier;

November 30, 1915–March 16, 1916). *See earlier entry under Heads of Government.*

ANTÓNIO JOSÉ DE ALMEIDA (Premier; March 16, 1916–April 15, 1917). *See earlier entry under Heads of State.*

AFONSO DA COSTA (Premier; April 15, 1917–December 8, 1917). *See earlier entry under Heads of Government.*

SIDÓNIO CARDOSO DE SILVA PAES (Premier; December 8, 1917–December 14, 1918). *See earlier entry under Heads of State.*

JOÃO TAMAGNINI BARBASA (Premier; December 23, 1918–January 25, 1919). João Tamagnini Barbasa was born on December 30, 1883. He served in the army and attained the rank of brigadier general. He was one of Portugal's leading generals serving in France during World War I. He was a Presidentialist and served as minister of finance in Sidónio Paes's government. He was chosen by President João de Canto e Castro to head the government as premier on December 23, 1918, following the assassination of Paes. His cabinet fell on January 25, 1919, because of his refusal to allow Democrats to join the government. He was a target of the assassins who murdered Granjo and several members of his cabinet in October 1921, but Barbasa escaped with his life. Barbasa was a defender of military officers involved in a failed coup attempt in July 1925. He later served as administrator of the Lisbon Tramway Company. Barbasa died on December 15, 1948.

JOSÉ RELVAS (Premier; January 25, 1919–March 31, 1919). José Relvas was born on March 5, 1858. Relvas was a political independent and leading Portuguese landowner. He participated in the first provisional government of the newly established Portuguese Republic in 1910. He was chosen to form a Republican coalition government on January 25, 1919. A monarchist rebellion was put down soon after he assumed office. He stepped down on March 31, 1919. Relvas died on October 31, 1929.

DOMINGOS LEITE PEREIRA (Premier; March 31, 1919–July 1, 1919). Domingos Leite Pereira was born in Braga on September 19, 1882. He was a leader of the Liberal Party and served in several cabinets as foreign minister and minister of the interior. He was named to head the government on March 31, 1919, serving until July 1, 1919. He again headed the government from January 21, 1920, until March 5, 1920, when a railroad strike led to his government's resignation. He died on October 28, 1956.

ALFREDO ERNESTO DE SÁ CARDOSO (Premier; July 1, 1919–January 10, 1920). Alfredo Ernesto de Sá Cardoso was born on June 6, 1864. He was called upon to head the government on July 1, 1919, but his government resigned on January 10, 1920. He died on April 23, 1950.

DOMINGOS LEITE PEREIRA (Premier; January 21, 1920–March 5, 1920). *See earlier entry under Heads of Government.*

ANTÓNIO MARIA BAPTISTA (Premier; March 9, 1920–June 6, 1920). António Maria Baptista was born on January 5, 1866. He served in the Portuguese army and was promoted to the rank of colonel. He was chosen to head the government on March 9, 1920. Baptista headed the government until his sudden death on June 6, 1920.

JOSÉ RAMOS PRETO (Premier; June 6, 1920–June 26, 1920). José Ramos Preto served as minister of justice in the government of António Maria Baptista. He was chosen to succeed to the premiership when Baptista died in office on June 6, 1920, but he resigned from office on June 26, 1920.

ANTÓNIO MARIA DA SILVA
(Premier; June 26, 1920–July 9, 1920). António Maria da Silva was born in 1872. He was a leader in the movement to abolish the monarchy and establish a republic in 1910. He headed the Democratic right and was called upon to form a government on June 26, 1920. He was replaced as premier by António Granjo on July 9, 1920. He again headed the government from February 5, 1922, until November 15, 1923. He returned to office as premier on June 20, 1925, until August 1, 1925. Da Silva was again named premier on December 17, 1925. His government was ousted during a military rising by Marshal Manuel de Oliveira Gomes da Costa on May 29, 1926. Da Silva went into exile in Paris where he remained until 1928. He was subsequently allowed to return to Portugal. He was arrested and briefly detained on several occasions for plotting against the military government. Da Silva died in Lisbon on October 14, 1950.

ANTÓNIO GRANJO
(Premier; July 17, 1920–November 16, 1920). António Granjo was born in 1881. Granjo was called upon to head the government on July 17, 1920. He initiated reforms in the colonial administration and introduced a measure calling for the amnesty of monarchist rebels still imprisoned from a rebellion the previous year. He stepped down on November 16, 1920, when the Republicans opposed his amnesty measure. He served in the cabinet as minister of commerce before again being called upon to head the government on August 28, 1921. Granjo and several members of his cabinet were murdered by a group of rebels the night of October 19, 1921. Granjo was dragged from the home of his finance minister, Francisco Cunha Leal, taken to the arsenal, and shot to death.

ÁLVARO DE CASTRO
(Premier; November 20, 1920–November 27, 1920). Álvaro de Castro was born on September 9, 1878. De Castro served in various cabinets before being called upon to head the government on November 20, 1920. He stepped down a week later on November 27, 1920. He also headed the government from December 18, 1923, until July 6, 1924. He was accused of being involved in plots against the government in 1926 and went into exile in Paris. He returned to Portugal shortly before his death in Coimbra on June 29, 1928.

ABEL HIPOLITO
(Premier; November 27, 1920–November 29, 1920). Abel Hipolito was born in 1860. He served in the Portuguese army and was promoted to the rank of general. He was briefly called upon to head the government as premier from November 27, 1920, until November 29, 1920. He died on October 12, 1929.

LIBERATO PINTO
(Premier; November 29, 1920–February 12, 1921). Liberato Damiao Ribeiro Pinto was born on September 29, 1880. He was a colonel in the Portuguese army and served as chief of staff of the National Republican Guard. He was a leading conservative and was called upon to form a government on November 29, 1920. He initiated several administrative reforms during his few months in office. He stepped down on February 12, 1921, when a printers' strike led to civil disorders. Pinto subsequently retired from politics. He died on September 4, 1949.

BERNARDINO MACHADO GUIMARÃES
(Premier; February 24, 1921–May 24, 1921). *See earlier entry under Heads of State.*

TOMÉ DE BARROS QUEIROS
(Premier; May 24, 1921–August 28, 1921). Tomé de Barros Queiros was a former Unionist. He was called upon to head a Liberal government on May 24, 1921. His government was mandated to hold elections. Barros Queiros resigned

on August 28, 1921, over resistance to his legislation for financial and economic reform. He was a target of the assassins who murdered António Granjo and several members of his cabinet in October 1921, but Barros Queiros escaped with his life. He died in 1926.

ANTÓNIO GRANJO (Premier; August 28, 1921–October 19, 1921). *See earlier entry under Heads of Government.*

MANUEL MARIA COELHO (Premier; October 20, 1921–November 4, 1921). Manuel Maria Coelho was born on March 6, 1857. He was a Republican who became premier following a coup by the National Republican Guard against the government of António Granjo on October 19, 1921, when Granjo and several members of his cabinet were assassinated. Coelho's government was held responsible for the murders, and he was forced to step down on November 4, 1921. Coelho was arrested in 1922 for his part in the uprising and spent several years in exile. He died on January 10, 1943.

CARLOS MAIA PINTO (Premier; November 4, 1921–December 20, 1921). Carlos Maia Pinto was a Republican called upon to form a coalition government when Manuel Maria Coelho's military cabinet collapsed on November 4, 1921. Maia Pinto resigned on December 20, 1921.

FRANCISCO PINTO DA CUNHA LEAL (Premier; December 20, 1921– February 5, 1922). Francisco Pinto da Cunha Leal was born on August 23, 1888. He was a leading nationalist and served as minister of finance in António Granjo's government from August 1921 until Granjo was ousted and murdered during a military coup the following October. Cunha Leal was also injured during the assassination attempt. He was called upon to head the government on December 20, 1921. He stepped down on February 5, 1922, after elections were held. He returned to the government as António Ginestral Machado's minister of finance in November 1923. He subsequently split with Álvaro de Castro and formed a splinter group of the Nationalist Party. Cunha Leal was a defender of military officers involved in a failed coup attempt in July 1925. He was an outspoken opponent of the dictatorship of António Salazar in the 1930s and the leader of the Organization for Social Democratic Action. Cunha Leal died in Lisbon on April 26, 1970.

ANTÓNIO MARIA DA SILVA (Premier; February 5, 1922–November 15, 1923). *See earlier entry under Heads of Government.*

ANTÓNIO GINESTRAL MACHADO (Premier; November 15, 1923– December 18, 1923). António Ginestral Machado was named to lead Nationalist government on November 15, 1923. He resigned on December 18, 1923, when he failed to persuade President Manoel Teixeira Gomes to dissolve the chamber of deputies and hold new elections.

ALVARO DE CASTRO (Premier; December 18, 1923–July 6, 1924). *See earlier entry under Heads of Government.*

ALFREDO RODRIGUES GASPAR (Premier; July 6, 1924–November 19, 1924). Alfredo Rodrigues Gaspar was born in 1865. He was called upon to lead a Democratic cabinet on July 6, 1924. Divisions in the party made governing difficult, and Rodrigues Gaspar resigned on November 19, 1924. He died on December 1, 1938.

JOSÉ DOMINGOS DOS SANTOS (Premier; November 21, 1924–February 15, 1925). José Domingos dos Santos was born on August 15, 1885. He was a successful lawyer and the leader of a splinter group of Democrats called the Democratic Leftists. He was called upon to head a government on November 21, 1924. He introduced social welfare legislation. His government received a vote of no confidence from the congress, and he resigned on February 15, 1925. He went into exile in Paris following the establishment of the military dictatorship in 1926. Domingos dos Santos worked with the French Resistance during World War II. He returned to Portugal in the early 1950s, where he was an active opponent against the government of António Salazar. Domingos dos Santos died at his home in Matosinhhos on August 15, 1958.

VITORINO MAXIMO DE CARVALHO GUIMARÃES (Premier; February 15, 1925–June 30, 1925). Vitorino Maximo de Carvalho Guimarães was born on November 13, 1876. He was a leader of the movement to establish the Portuguese Republic in 1910. He served in various cabinets as minister of finance, commerce, and war. He was a leader of the Democratic Party and formed a coalition government on February 15, 1925. His government survived a military revolt in April 1925. He stepped down on June 30, 1925. He died at his home in Lisbon on October 18, 1957.

ANTÓNIO MARIA DA SILVA (Premier; June 20, 1925–August 1, 1925). *See earlier entry under Heads of Government.*

DOMINGOS LEITE PEREIRA (Premier; August 7, 1925–December 17, 1925). *See earlier entry under Heads of Government.*

ANTÓNIO MARIA DA SILVA (Premier; December 17, 1925–May 29, 1926). *See earlier entry under Heads of Government.*

JOSÉ MENDES CABECADAS (Premier; May 30, 1926–June 20, 1926). José Mendes Cabecadas was born on August 19, 1883. He served in the Por-

tuguese navy and was a leader of the Republican movement that overthrew the monarchy in 1910. A navy commander, he was the leader of an unsuccessful military rising in July 1925. He and many of his supporters were subsequently court-martialed, but were acquitted by a military court. He participated in the coup that ousted the government in May 1926 and took office as head of the military government on May 30, 1926. He was replaced by his fellow junta leader, Manuel Gomes da Costa, on June 20, 1926. Cabecadas returned to the navy, where he was promoted to the rank of admiral. He was a critic of António Salazar's dictatorship for the next several decades. He was a founder of the Organization for Social Democratic Action in 1963. Cabecadas died of heart disease in Lisbon on June 11, 1965.

MANUEL DE OLIVEIRA GOMES DA COSTA (Premier; June 20, 1926–July 9, 1926). Manuel de Oliveira Gomes da Costa was born in Lisbon on January 14, 1863. He served in the Portuguese army and was stationed in India as a staff officer in 1893. He also took part in several campaigns in Africa and was placed in command of Portuguese operations in East Africa in 1899. He led the First Portuguese Division during World War I. He was a leader, with António Carmona, of the military uprising that ousted the government in May 1926. He initially served as minister of war before replacing José Cabecadas as head of the military government on June 20, 1926. Gomes was ousted by General Carmona on July 9, 1926, and banished to the Azores. He returned to Portugal in 1927 and organized the National Union. He was again arrested by the government and sent into exile in Rome. He was subsequently allowed to return to Portugal and died there on December 17, 1929.

ANTÓNIO ÓSCAR DE FRAGOSO CARMONA (Premier; July 9,

1926–November 12, 1928). *See earlier entry under Heads of State.*

JOSÉ VICENTE DE FREITAS

(Premier; November 12, 1928–July 5, 1929). José Vicente de Freitas was born on January 22, 1869. He served in the Portuguese army and attained the rank of general. He was selected by the military junta under António Óscar de Fragoso Carmona to head the government from November 12, 1928, until July 5, 1929. De Freitas died in Lisbon on September 6, 1952.

ANTÓNIO IVENS FERRAZ (Premier; July 9, 1929–January 10, 1930). António Ivens Ferraz was born on December 1, 1870. He was a general in the Portuguese army. He served as premier under António Carmona's military junta from July 9, 1929, until January 10, 1930. Ivens Ferraz subsequently served as president of the Portuguese Red Cross. He died in Lisbon on January 16, 1933.

DOMINGOS DE COSTA OLIVEIRA (Premier; January 21, 1930–June 20, 1932). Domingos de Costa Oliveira was born on June 30, 1873. He served as minister of justice before being called upon to head the government on January 21, 1930. Oliveira was replaced as premier by his finance minister, António Salazar, on June 20, 1932. He died on December 25, 1957.

ANTÓNIO DE OLIVEIRA SALAZAR (Premier; July 5, 1932–September 27, 1968). António de Oliveira Salazar was born to a peasant family in the village of Santa Comba Dao on April 28, 1889. He was educated at the Jesuit seminary in Vieseu and intended to become a priest, but he decided instead to pursue a career in education, and in 1910 he entered the University of Coimbra. Salazar graduated in 1914 and joined the teaching staff. He continued his education as well and received a doctorate in law in 1918. He entered politics in 1921 as a founder of the Portuguese Catholic Centre party and was elected to the Cortes (parliament). Salazar returned to his teaching career shortly thereafter because he believed that his influence in Parliament was limited. He was called back into government service following the military coup led by General Manuel de Oliveira Gomes da Costa and General António Oscar de Fragoso Carmona in May 1926. Salazar was appointed minister of finance to solve the serious economic difficulties Portugal was facing, but resigned after two days when his demands for autonomy for his position were refused by the government leaders. When General Carmona ousted General Gomes da Costa in November 1926, Salazar was again named minister of finance with full authority to deal with Portugal's economy. He instituted harsh taxation measures and slashed the government's budget. His austerity measures succeeded in producing a balanced budget for the nation after his first year in office. Salazar was also named colonial minister in 1930 and was appointed premier by President Carmona on July 5, 1932. The following year he drafted a new constitution for the nation, which resulted in his being the virtual dictator of Portugal. He also became foreign minister in 1936 and sided with Generalissimo Francisco Franco's rebellion against the Republican government in Spain. Portugal remained neutral during World War II, but Salazar did allow the use of the Azores for Allied air and naval bases. Salazar relinquished the finance ministry in 1940, and stepped down as foreign minister in 1947. After the conclusion of World War II, Salazar took some steps to democratize Portugal and permitted opposition candidates to stand for office in the election in November 1945. When the opposition coalition, the Movimento Unidade Democratica, gained support, Salazar outlawed the party in 1948. He was offered the presidency when Carmona died in office on April 18, 1951, but turned down the office and remained premier instead. Salazar's party was challenged by Lt. Gen. Humberto Delgado in the presidential elections in 1958. Salazar's candidate, Admiral Americo Tomas, defeated the challenger decisively, but Delgado, who subsequently went into exile, remained a major critic of the regime until his bludgeoned corpse was discovered in Spain in 1965. In the early 1960s Portugal was faced with insurrections in its colonial empire when nationalist movements in Angola, Mozambique, Cape Verde, Portuguese Guinea, Macao, and Timor demanded independence. Salazar's policy in dealing with the insurrections was to crush them with military force. This was successful in the short run, but was financially expensive and cost Portugal much in the way of soldiers and negative world opinion. Salazar's rule faced several abortive revolts during the 1960s, but they scarcely threatened his power. He suffered a major stroke in early September 1968. As his condition worsened, he was replaced as premier by Marcello Caetano on September 27, 1968, but was not told of his removal because his doctors feared the shock might kill him. Salazar lived for the next 20 months believing that he still controlled the country. He died in Lisbon on July 27, 1970.

Romania

Romania is a country in southeastern Europe. It received independence from the Ottoman Empire in 1878.

HEADS OF STATE

CAROL I (Prince; May 22, 1866–March 26, 1881; King, March 26, 1881–October 10, 1914). Carol I was born Karl Eitel Friedrich de Hohenzollern in Sigmaringen, Germany, on April 20, 1839. He was the son of Prince Carol Anton of Hohenzollern-Sigmaringen. He received a military education in Munster and Berlin and served in the Prussian Royal Guard. He saw action during the war between Russia and Denmark in 1864. Romanian political leader Ion C. Brătianu called Carol to Romania in 1866 after the abdication of Prince Alexandru John Cuza. A plebiscite and parliamentary action established Carol as prince of Romania on May 22, 1866, despite the opposition of the Great Powers. Carol married Elizabeth von Wied in 1869. His wife was an acclaimed poet under her pseudonym Carmen Sylva. A financial scandal involving a railroad scheme caused public discontent with his rule. He was also attacked by supporters of France during the Franco-Prussian War. Carol offered to abdicate, but his offer was withdrawn when his supporters were victorious in the general election in May 1871. Carol continued his attempts to modernize the country and the army along the lines of the Prussian model. He also worked toward Romanian independence, which was proclaimed during the Russo-Turkish War on May 21, 1877. Romania soon joined the Russians in the battle against the Ottoman Empire, with Carol commanding the western army. The Treaty of San Stefano and the Congress of Berlin granted recognition of Romania's independence in 1878. Carol was crowned as Romania's first king on May 22, 1881, after Romania was proclaimed a kingdom. He worked with Prime Minister Ion C. Brătianu to enhance the country's defenses and secretly entered the Triple Alliance in 1883. Carol accepted Romanian neutrality in the early part of World War I, despite alliances with the Central Powers. Carol died soon after of heart failure at the Castle of Pelesh in Sinaia on October 10, 1914.

FERDINAND (King; October 11, 1914–July 20, 1927). Ferdinand I was born Viktor Albert Meinrad of Hohenzollern in Sigmaringen, Germany, on August 24, 1865. He was the second son of Leopold of Hohenzollern and the nephew of King Carol of Romania. Carol had no sons and Ferdinand was proclaimed heir presumptive of Romania on March 18, 1889. He soon entered the Romanian army under the guidance of his uncle. Ferdinand married Princess Marie, the daughter of the Duke of Edinburgh and granddaughter of Queen Victoria, in December 1892. He became a general in the army. He commanded the Romanian army in 1913 against the Bulgarians in the Second Balkan War. The following year he succeeded to the throne upon the death of Carol on October 11, 1914. He maintained Romania's neutrality during the early years of World War I. Romania entered the war on the side of the Entente Powers in 1916, but the country was forced to negotiate a peace treaty with the Central Powers when they occupied much of the country two years later. The royal family and the government withdrew to Moldavia and established the capital in Iasi. Ferdinand refused to accept the harsh terms of the Treaty of Bucharest, and Romania reentered the war in November 1918. The subsequent peace treaty granted Romania's claims to the territories of Transylvania, Bessarabia, Bucovina, and the Banat. Ferdinand was crowned king of Greater Romania on October 15, 1922. The king promoted agrarian reform and universal suffrage and sponsored a new constitution in 1923. Ferdinand maintained a close rela-

tionship with Ion I. C. Brătianu , who served as his prime minister during much of his reign. He had a difficult relationship with his eldest son, Crown Prince Carol, and several scandals resulted in Carol's renunciation of his rights to the throne in December 1925. Ferdinand's infant grandson, Prince Michael, was designated heir to the throne with Ferdinand's second son, Nicholas, as regent. The king's health soon began to fail. He succumbed to a lengthy bout with cancer at Sinaia Palace outside of Bucharest on July 20, 1927.

MICHAEL (King; July 20, 1927–June 8, 1930). Michael was born on October 25, 1921. He was the son of Carol II of Romania and Princess Helene of Greece. Michael was named heir apparent by his grandfather, King Ferdinand of Romania, in 1925 when his father was disinherited. He succeeded to the throne under a regency council upon King Ferdinand's death on July 20, 1927. The council was headed by his uncle, Prince Nicholas, and included the Patriarch Miron Christea and Supreme Court President George Buzdugan. Carol returned from exile in 1930 and was proclaimed king on June 8, 1930. When King Carol was forced to abdicate on September 6, 1940, Michael was reinstated as king. Michael led the coup that ousted Ion Antonescu, the pro-Nazi dictator, in 1944. He was forced to abdicate on December 30, 1947, following the Communist takeover of Romania. He went into exile in Great Britain and subsequently went to Switzerland in 1956, where he worked as a test pilot. Michael later worked as a stockbroker and also for an electronics company. Following the overthrow of the Communist government of Nicolae Ceausescu, Michael returned to Romania in December 1990 but was subsequently deported. Michael was invited by the Eastern Orthodox Primate of Suceava to celebrate Easter in Romania, and he visited the country on April 26, 1992.

CAROL II (King; June 8, 1930–September 6, 1940). Carol II was born in Sinaia on October 16, 1893, the son of Romania's future King Ferdinand. Carol was sent to serve in the Prussian army in Potsdam in 1914 to learn military discipline. He returned to Romania at the outbreak of World War I to enter the Romanian army. His military career was inauspicious, and he drew criticism from his superiors. He deserted the army in September 1918 during the German occupation of Romania, renounced his rights to the throne in order to enter into a morganatic marriage with a Romanian commoner, Zizi Lambrino. The royal family strongly disapproved of the union, and the Romanian Supreme Court annulled the marriage in March 1919. Carol was subsequently sent abroad. He returned to Romania in 1921 and was soon wed to Princess Helene of Greece. A son, Michael, was born later in the year. The marriage was troubled from the start, and Carol soon began an affair with Helen Wolff, who was better known as Magda Lupescu. Carol deserted his wife and child and went into exile in Paris with his mistress in 1925, again renouncing his rights to the throne. King Ferdinand died in June 1927, and Carol's young son succeeded to the throne. The subsequent death of Romanian Premier Ion Brătianu, a vocal critic of Carol, and popular discontent with the regency council under his younger brother, Prince Nicholas, led the National Peasant government under Iulio Maniu to invite Carol to return to the country. He was offered a position on the regency council, but rejected the offer to claim the throne. Several days later the regency council was abolished and Carol was proclaimed king on June 8, 1930. Carol's reign was turbulent, as he became increasingly involved in political affairs. He undermined existing political parties and created splinter groups to confound his opponents. Allegations of corruption and incompetence in the court led to an increase in his unpopularity. His continued relationship with Magda Lupescu also added to his problems. Carol promoted a new constitution in February 1938 that created a personal dictatorship in response to the growing power of the Iron Guard. Romania was beset by territorial demands from the Germans and the Soviets in the early years of World War II. Carol was forced to abdicate in favor of his son, Michael, on September 6, 1940, and went into exile in Spain. He was interned by the Spanish government for several months before escaping to Portugal. He subsequently continued his exile in Cuba, Mexico, and Brazil, where he finally married Magda Lupescu in July 1947. The couple returned to Portugal, where he remained until his death from a heart attack in Estoril on April 4, 1953.

MICHAEL (King; September 6, 1940–December 30, 1947). *See earlier entry under Heads of State.*

HEADS OF GOVERNMENT

GHEORGHE G. CANTACUZINO (Prime Minister; April 23, 1899–July 17, 1900). Gheorghe Gregory Cantacuzino was born in Bucharest in 1837. He was a man of immense wealth, who succeeded Lastar Catargiu as leader of the Conservative Party in 1899. He was named to head the government as prime minister on April 23, 1899, after Dimitrie Sturdza resigned from office during an economic crisis in Romania. Cantacuzino's proposal of a large tax increase was unpopular, and he resigned on July 17, 1900. He returned to office on January 5, 1905. He retained office until March 24, 1907, when a peasant insurrection forced his government's resignation. He remained a leading political figure and was elected president of the senate in 1913. He died on April 5, 1913.

PETRE CARP (Prime Minister; July 20, 1900–February 26, 1901). Petre P. Carp was born in Iasi on July 11, 1837. He was educated in Berlin and Bonn and served on the state council in 1865. He was instrumental in forcing the abdication of Prince Alexander John Cuza in February 1866. He served on the governing regency council until Carol I assumed the throne in May 1866. He was also a founder of the Junimea Literary Society. Carp was elected to parliament in 1867 and served in several governments. He was selected to head the government on July 20, 1900, and served until July 17, 1902. He remained a prominent political figure and was again called upon to head the government on January 11, 1911. He stepped down on April 10, 1912. He was an advocate of Romania's entry into World War I on the side of the Central Powers. Carp died on June 22, 1919.

DIMITRIE A. STURDZA (Prime Minister; February 27, 1901–January 5, 1905). Dimitrie A. Sturdza was born in Miclauseni on March 22, 1833. He served in Ion C. Brătianu's cabinet as foreign minister during the 1880s. Sturdza became the leader of the National Liberal Party in 1893. He orchestrated demonstrations against the Conservative government and forced the resignation of Lascar Catargiu. Sturdza formed a government as prime minister on October 15, 1895, serving until December 2, 1896, and again from April 12, 1897, until April 23, 1899. Sturdza replaced Petre Carp as prime minister on February 27, 1901. He remained head of the government for five years until Gheorghe Cantacuzino succeeded him on January 5, 1905. When a peasant's revolt forced Cantacuzino's resignation, Sturdza was again called upon to head the government on March 26, 1907. The Liberals joined with the Conservatives to brutally

put down the revolt. Sturdza remained head of the government until January 1, 1909, when he stepped down for reasons of health. He died on October 21, 1914.

GHEORGHE G. CANTACU-ZINO (Prime Minister; January 5, 1905–March 24, 1907). *See earlier entry under Heads of Government.*

DIMITRIE A. STURDZA (Prime Minister; March 26, 1907–January 1, 1909). *See earlier entry under Heads of Government.*

ION I. C. BRĂTIANU (Prime Minister; January 1, 1909–December 23, 1909). Ion I. C. Brătianu was born in Florica on September 11, 1864. He was the eldest son of Ion C. Brătianu, who served as Romania's prime minister from 1881 until 1888. He was educated in Bucharest and Paris and received a degree in civil engineering. He briefly worked as an engineer before entering politics after his father's death in 1891. Brătianu joined the Liberal Party and was elected to parliament in 1895. He was named to Dimitrie Sturdza's government as minister of public works in 1896. He became foreign minister in 1901 and minister of the interior in 1907. He succeeded Sturdza as prime minister and leader of the Liberal Party on January 1, 1909, serving until December 23, 1909. He again headed the government from January 1910 until January 10, 1911. Brătianu became very wealthy with his involvement in finance and industry. He returned to power on January 16, 1914, and headed the government during World War I. Though an ally of France, Brătianu maintained Romania's neutrality for the first two years of the war. Romania joined the war against the Central Powers in August 1916. Southern Romania was occupied after a series of military defeats and Brătianu resigned on January 29, 1918, rather than sign the Treaty of Bucharest with the Central Powers. He was recalled to office on December

14, 1918, after the collapse of Germany. As leader of the Romanian delegation during the peace conference, he pressed for major concessions for his country. He also instigated Romania's intervention in Hungary to oust the Communist regime of Bela Kun in 1919. Romania was granted the additional territory of Bessarabia and Transylvania in the treaty that ended World War I, and Brătianu stepped down from office on September 27, 1919. He returned to power on January 19, 1922, and led a virtual dictatorship for the next five years. He promoted a new constitution in 1923 and helped engineer Prince Carol's renunciation of his rights to the throne. He stepped down on March 27, 1926, but returned to office on June 22, 1927. After the death of King Ferdinand, Brătianu was largely in control of the regency council during the minority of King Michael. He continued to lead the government until his death at his palace in Bucharest on November 24, 1927. He succumbed to a blood infection after surgery on his throat glands.

MIHAI PHEREKYDE (Prime Minister; December 23, 1909–January 1910). Mihai Pherekyde was born in Bucharest in 1841. He was a leading member of the National Liberal Party. He headed an interim cabinet from December 23, 1909, until January 1910, when Ion Brătianu returned to head the government. Pherekyde died on January 28, 1924.

ION I. C. BRĂTIANU (Prime Minister; January 1910–January 10, 1911). *See earlier entry under Heads of Government.*

PETRE CARP (Prime Minister; January 11, 1911–April 10, 1912). *See earlier entry under Heads of Government.*

TITU MAIORESCU (Prime Minister; April 10, 1912–January 16, 1914). Titu Maiorescu was born in Ciaiova on March 1, 1840. He was educated in Vienna,

Berlin, and Paris. He returned to Romania to serve as a professor of logic and philosophy at the University of Iasi in 1863. He was a founding member of the Junimea Literary Society the following year and was elected to the Romanian Academic Society in 1867. He remained in Iasi until 1871, when he entered politics. He served in parliament and participated in several governments. He was also a professor at the University of Bucharest from 1884 until 1909, and was a leading literary critic. He was named to the cabinet as foreign minister in 1911 and was selected as Romania's prime minister on April 10, 1912. He headed a coalition government during the Second Balkan War and presided over the Bucharest Conference. He remained prime minister until January 16, 1914. Maiorescu died on July 1, 1917.

ION I. C. BRĂTIANU (Prime Minister; January 16, 1914–January 29, 1918). *See earlier entry under Heads of Government.*

ALEXANDRU AVERESCU (Prime Minister; February 9, 1918–March 14, 1918). Alexandru Averescu was born in Bessarabia on March 9, 1859. He served in the army during the war for independence in 1877 and was promoted to the rank of sergeant. He was commandant of the Superior War College from 1894 until 1895 and served as Romania's military attaché to Berlin from 1895 until 1898. He attained the rank of general in 1906 and was named minister of war the following year. He was instrumental in putting down the Peasant Revolt of 1907. He was chief of the Romanian general staff from 1911 to 1913 and planned Romania's actions during the Second Balkan War against the Bulgarians. He remained a military leader during Romania's involvement in World War I. He entered politics after the conclusion of the war and was a founder of the People's Party. He succeeded Ion Brătianu as prime minister on February 9, 1918, and took over peace negotiations with the Central Powers. He refused to sign the treaty demanded by the Central Powers and resigned on March 14, 1918. He again headed the government from March 16, 1920, until December 17, 1921. He was again called upon to serve as prime minister on March 30, 1926, when the Liberal Party under Brătianu lost support in the parliament. He was forced to resign at the instigation of King Ferdinand on June 5, 1927. He remained a leading political figure and served as a minister and royal counselor to King Carol II until his death on October 3, 1938.

ALEXANDRU MARGHILOMAN (Prime Minister; March 19, 1918–November 10, 1918). Alexandru Marghiloman was born in Buzeu on February 8, 1854. He served in Teodore G. Rosetti's government as minister of justice in 1889. He was a close advisor to King Carol I until the monarch's death in 1914. He also remained on close terms with his successor, King Ferdinand. Marghiloman was a supporter of Germany and the Central Powers during World War I. He was called upon to head Romania's government on March 19, 1918, and signed the Treaty of Bucharest with the Central Powers in May of that year. The peace settlement was responsible for major economic problems for the country. His government was forced to resign on November 10, 1918, when the Central Powers were near defeat. Marghiloman subsequently had little influence in government and died at his villa in Buzeu on May 10, 1925.

CONSTANTIN COANDĂ (Prime Minister; November 10, 1918–November 29, 1918). Constantin Coandă was a general in the Romanian army. He replaced Alexandru Marghiloman as prime minister on November 10, 1918, when the defeat of the Central Powers was assured. His government repealed most of the legislation passed under Marghiloman

and Romania re-entered the war against Germany. He stepped down in favor of Ion Brătianu when King Ferdinand and the government returned to Bucharest on November 29, 1918, after the occupation forces had evacuated. He died in 1932.

ION I. C. BRĂTIANU (Prime Minister; December 14, 1918–September 27, 1919). *See earlier entry under Heads of Government.*

ARTHUR VAITOIANU (Prime Minister; September 27, 1919–December 2, 1919). Arthur Vaitoianu replaced Ion I. C. Brătianu as prime minister on September 27, 1919. He stepped down on December 2, 1919, when Alexandru Vaida-Voevod assumed the premiership. Vaitoianu remained a leading political figure in Romania, serving in various cabinets. He was named minister without portfolio in 1938.

ALEXANDRU VAIDA-VOEVOD (Prime Minister; December 2, 1919–March 13, 1920). Alexandru Vaida-Voevod was born on February 27, 1873, in Olpret, Transylvania, which was then part of the Austro-Hungarian Empire. He received a medical degree from the University of Vienna. He became active in politics in the 1890s and joined the central committee of the Romanian National Party of Transylvania in 1896. He was elected to the Hungarian chamber of deputies in 1906 and served until 1907 and again from 1910 until 1918. He lived in Vienna and Switzerland during much of World War I. He was an advocate of the self-determination of Romanians in Transylvania and represented his constituency at the Peace Conference in 1919. He worked with other members of the Romanian delegation to ensure Transylvania's incorporation into Romania. Vaida-Voevod became a leader of the National Peasants Party and was called upon to head a coalition government on December 2, 1919. He was forced to step down on March 13, 1920, when the conservative People's Party reclaimed the government. Vaida-Voevod remained active in politics, serving as minister of the interior during the 1920s. He returned to head the government briefly from June 4, 1932, until October 17, 1932. He formed another cabinet on January 14, 1933, and his government was forced to deal with the Communist-inspired railway strike in Grivita the following month. He stepped down on November 12, 1933. He became associated with nationalist and fascist elements in the country and led the right wing of the National Peasants Party to form the Romanian Front in March 1935. He joined Octavian Goga's rightist government in December 1937 and remained in Miron Cristea's subsequent cabinet. He became president of the National Renaissance Front in 1940. Vaida-Voevod and other rightist leaders were arrested and imprisoned by the Communist authorities after World War II. He died in prison on March 19, 1950.

ALEXANDRU AVERESCU (Prime Minister; March 16, 1920–December 17, 1921). *See earlier entry under Heads of Government.*

TAKE IONESCU (Prime Minister; December 17, 1921–January 19, 1922). Take Ionescu was born on October 13, 1858. He was a leading Romanian journalist and lawyer. He became president of the Conservative Democratic Party when it was formed in February 1908. He was a leader of the peasant uprising in 1911. Ionescu was a supporter of the Allied cause during World War I, and his efforts were instrumental in Romania entering the war on the side of the Entente Powers in 1916. Ionescu was selected as president of the council of Romanian National Unity in October 1918 and was a principal negotiator for Romania at the Paris Peace Conference. He was also instrumental in the formation of the Little Entente in 1921. Ionescu became foreign minister in Alexandru

Averescu's government in March 1920. He succeeded Averescu as prime minister on December 17, 1921. He stepped down on January 19, 1922. Ionescu died on June 21, 1922.

ION I. C. BRĂTIANU (Prime Minister; January 19, 1922–March 27, 1926). *See earlier entry under Heads of Government.*

ALEXANDRU AVERESCU (Prime Minister; March 30, 1926–June 5, 1927). *See earlier entry under Heads of Government.*

BARBU ȘTIRBEI (Prime Minister; June 7, 1927–June 22, 1927). Prince Barbu Știrbei was born in 1873. He was a descendant of the Fanarlot Greeks of Constantinople and was one of the wealthiest men in Romania. Știrbei was the brother-in-law and partner of Ion Brătianu. He was a close confidant of Queen Marie and held a leading position at the court. He was selected by Brătianu to succeed Alexandru Averescu as prime minister on June 7, 1927. He stepped down several weeks later on June 22, 1927, when Brătianu reclaimed the premiership. Știrbei's political influence was curtailed when Carol II assumed the throne of Romania in 1930. Știrbei was called upon to negotiate Romania's armistice with the Allies in 1944. He was asked to form a government by King Michael in March 1945, but his selection as prime minister was vetoed by the Soviet Union, and Petru Groza assumed the premiership. Știrbei died of jaundice in a Bucharest sanatorium the following year on March 24, 1946.

ION I. C. BRĂTIANU (Prime Minister; June 22, 1927–November 24, 1927). *See earlier entry under Heads of Government.*

VINTILA I. C. BRĂTIANU (Prime Minister; November 24, 1927–November 3, 1928). Vintila I. C. Brătianu was born on September 28, 1867. He was the son of former Romanian premier Ion C. Brătianu and the younger brother of Premier Ion I. C. Brătianu. He served in his brother's cabinet on several occasions as minister of finance during the 1920s. Brătianu succeeded his brother as prime minister and head of the Liberal Party upon the latter's death on November 24, 1927. He headed the government until the Liberal Party was forced from power by Iulio Maniu's Peasant National Party on November 3, 1928. He exercised little political influence after his fall from power. He died suddenly at his estate in Micaesti after a stroke of apoplexy on December 22, 1930.

IULIO MANIU (Prime Minister; November 11, 1928–June 7, 1930). Iulio Maniu was born on January 8, 1873. He was a leading lawyer in Transylvania and a prominent member of the Romanian nationalist movement there. He served in the Hungarian chamber of deputies from 1906 until 1910. He was instrumental in the process that led to Transylvania's incorporation into Romania after World War I. Maniu led the Romanian National Party of Transylvania, which became the National Peasant Party in 1926. He was called upon to form a government as prime minister on November 11, 1928, and his party was victorious in Romania's first free election the following month. His government instituted economic and political reforms, including the abolishment of censorship and martial law. He was instrumental in the return of King Carol II from exile in June 1930. Maniu resigned from office on June 7, 1930, when Carol reneged on his promise to break off his relationship with his Jewish mistress Magda Lupescu. He was called upon to return to office two days later on June 9, 1930, and continued to head the government until October 6, 1930. He again served as prime minister from October 17, 1932, until January 3, 1933. He was a critic of the corruption in King Carol II's court and a proponent of democratic principles. Maniu supported the Allied cause during World War II and was a leading opponent of the regime of Marshal Ion Antonescu. He was instrumental in planning the coup against Antonescu in August 1944. Maniu was a leader of the anti-Communist opposition after the war. He was arrested for treason against the Communist regime and sentenced to life imprisonment in November 1947. He reportedly died in Sighet prison in 1952.

GHEORGHE G. MIRONESCU (Prime Minister; June 7, 1930–June 9, 1930). Gheorghe G. Mironescu was born in 1874. He was a leading member of the National Peasant Party and joined Iulio Maniu's government in November 1928. He briefly succeeded Maniu as prime minister from June 7 until June 9, 1930. He again replaced Maniu as head of the government on October 10, 1930, serving until April 4, 1931. He died in 1949.

IULIO MANIU (Prime Minister; June 9, 1930–October 6, 1930). *See earlier entry under Heads of Government.*

GHEORGHE G. MIRONESCU (Prime Minister; October 10, 1930–April 4, 1931). *See earlier entry under Heads of Government.*

NIKOLAI IORGA (Prime Minister; April 19, 1931–May 31, 1932). Nikolai Iorga was born in Botosani on June 17, 1871. He was educated at the University of Iasi and continued his education in Paris, Berlin, and Leipzig. He returned to Romania to join the faculty of the University of Bucharest as a history professor in 1894. He was an internationally renowned historian of the Romanian people and authored numerous scholarly works. Iorga was also active politically, cofounding the Democratic Nationalist Party in 1910. He served in the chamber of deputies during the 1920s and was called upon to serve as prime minister on April 19, 1931. He relinquished the position to Alexandru Vaida-Voevod on May 31, 1932. He was a supporter of King Carol II and served as minister without portfolio in the government during the 1930s. He was instrumental in the arrest and trial of Iron Guard leader Corneliu Zelea Codreanu in 1938. Iorga and many other prominent members of the Romanian regime were assassinated by the Iron Guard on November 28, 1940.

ALEXANDRU VAIDA-VOEVOD (Prime Minister; June 4, 1932–October 17, 1932). *See earlier entry under Heads of Government.*

IULIO MANIU (Prime Minister; October 17, 1932–January 3, 1933). *See earlier entry under Heads of Government.*

ALEXANDRU VAIDA-VOEVOD (Prime Minister; January 14, 1933–November 12, 1933). *See earlier entry under Heads of Government.*

ION DUCA (Prime Minister; November 14, 1933–December 30, 1933). Ion Gheorghe Duca was born in Bucharest on December 20, 1879. He was educated at the University of Bucharest and the University of Paris. He began his political career with his election to the chamber of deputies as a member of the National Liberal Party in 1907. He entered the government in 1914 as minister of education, and served throughout World War I. He was named foreign minister in 1922 and was a strong supporter of the Polish alliance and the Little Entente. He remained foreign minister until 1926. He succeeded Vintila Brătianu as leader of the National Liberal Party in December 1930. Duca was named to head the government as prime minister by King Carol II on November 14, 1933. His government moved to outlaw the Fascist Iron Guard movement in anticipation of elections in December 1933, which the Liberal Party won hand-ily. Duca was shot to death soon afterward by Radu Constantinescu, an Iron Guard sympathizer. The prime minister was shot four times in the head while waiting on a platform at the Sinaia train station after a meeting with King Carol II on December 30, 1933.

CONSTANTIN ANGELESCU (Prime Minister; December 30, 1933–January 3, 1934). Constantin Angelescu was born in 1869. He was a leading physician and medical writer in Romania before entering politics. He served in several governments and was appointed Romania's first minister to the United States in January 1918, but he resigned several months after his appointment. He remained a leading member of the Liberal Party in Romania and had close personal and political ties to Ion Brătianu. Angelescu served as minister of the interior in 1930, and narrowly escaped assassination when a student shot him five times. He was called upon by King Carol II to succeed assassinated Prime Minister Ion Duca on December 30, 1933. The new government was opposed by Foreign Minister Nicolas Titulescu, and Angelescu was forced to resign on January 3, 1934, after only a few days in office. Angelescu subsequently exercised little political influence. He died in Bucharest on September 4, 1948.

GHEORGHE TĂTĂRESCU (Prime Minister; January 10, 1934–December 28, 1937). Gheorghe Tătărescu was born in Targu Jiu in 1886, the son of an army general. He studied law in Paris. He entered politics as a member of the Liberal Party and was appointed undersecretary of state in 1923. He subsequently became secretary general of the Liberal Party. Tătărescu was appointed to the cabinet as minister of industry and commerce in 1933. He was asked by King Carol II to form a government as prime minister on January 10, 1934. Romania's economic condition improved during his tenure, though his support of the Iron Guard brought him into conflict with the king. He was asked to resign on December 28, 1937. He was subsequently appointed Romania's ambassador to France. He was recalled to head a new government on November 24, 1939, but was criticized for allowing the Soviet Union to take control of the territories of Bessarabia and Northern Bucovina in June 1940. He resigned on July 4, 1940. He held little influence under the regime of Marshal Ion Antonescu, but served as leader of a small splinter group of the National Liberal Party. He served in Petru Groza's Communist government as vice premier and foreign minister from March 1945 until his dismissal in November 1947. Tătărescu was subsequently arrested by the Communist regime and spent the next several years in detention or under house arrest. He was released in October 1955. Tătărescu died on March 28, 1957.

OCTAVIAN GOGA (Prime Minister; December 29, 1937–February 10, 1938). Octavian Goga was born in the village of Rasinari, Transylvania, on April 1, 1881. He was the son of a clergyman and was educated in Budapest and at the University of Berlin. He returned to Transylvania to begin a literary career and founded the literary review *Luceafurul* in 1902. He also became a leading poet and translator of Hungarian verse. His works were collected in the volumes *Ne cheama pamantul* and *Cantec fara tara*. He joined the Romanian army shortly before World War I and served as an advisor to the Romanian delegation at the peace conference in Paris after the war. Goga remained active in politics, serving as minister of the interior in Alexandru Averescu's cabinet in 1926. He founded the rightist National Agrarian Party after a split with Averescu's People's Party in 1927. Goga's party was united with Alexander Cuza's National Christian Defense to form the National Christian Party in the mid-1930s. Goga was called upon by King Carol II to head the government on December 29, 1937.

His government was sympathetic to Nazi Germany and passed harsh anti-Semitic legislation that drew international criticism. Goga was dismissed from office when King Carol II formed a royal dictatorship on February 10, 1938. After suffering a paralytic stroke, he died of pneumonia in Bucharest on May 7, 1938.

MIRON CRISTEA (Prime Minister; February 10, 1938–March 6, 1939). Miron Cristea was born Ilie Cristea in Toplitza, Transylvania, in 1867. He studied theology in Sibiu and continued his education at the University of Budapest, where he received a doctorate in philosophy. He subsequently entered the hierarchy of the Romanian Orthodox Church and became bishop of Carensebes in 1910. He was selected as archbishop of Ungro-Vlahiei in 1920 and became the first patriarch of the Romanian Orthodox Church on February 25, 1925. He served as a member of the regency council during the minority of King Michael following the death of King Ferdinand in July 1927. The council ruled Romania until King Carol II claimed the throne in June 1930. Cristea was called upon to become prime minister on February 10, 1938, when King Carol II dismissed the government of Octavian Goga to establish the royal dictatorship. The following month imprisoned Iron Guard leader Corneliu Zelea Codreanu and many of his supporters were killed, purportedly while trying to escape. Cristea was in poor health during his tenure. He went to Cannes, France, for his health in February 1938. He died there of bronchial pneumonia and heart disease on March 6, 1939.

ARMAND CĂLINEȘCU (Prime Minister; March 7, 1939–September 21, 1939). Armand Călinescu was born in Pitesti on May 22, 1893. He received a degree in law from the University of Bucharest. He became active in politics as a member of the Peasant Party and was elected to the parliament in 1926. He served in several governmental positions in the late 1920s and early 1930s. He became a close advisor to King Carol II and served in Octavian Goga's cabinet as minister of the interior from December 1937 until February 1938. He was an opponent of Corneliu Zelea Codreanu's Fascist Iron Guard, or the Legion of the Archangel Michael, and was instrumental in arranging the arrest and subsequent execution of Codreanu and many of his followers. He was also instrumental in the establishment of the king's royal dictatorship and was a strong supporter of Romanian neutrality during World War II. He remained minister of the interior in Miron Cristea's government in February 1938 and also assumed the post of vice premier, handling many executive duties as Cristea's health failed. Călinescu was named to succeed Cristea as prime minister following the latter's death on March 6, 1939. His tenure was cut short when he was shot to death by Iron Guardists in retaliation for the execution of Codreanu. He was ambushed while driving through the streets of Bucharest from his office to his home on September 21, 1939.

CONSTANTIN ARGETOIANU (Prime Minister; September 28, 1939–November 23, 1939). Constantin Argetoianu was born in 1871. He was a leading political figure in Romania and served as head of the delegation that led to Romania's withdrawal from World War I in the spring of 1918. Argetoianu served in the Romanian parliament and was a member of several cabinets. He was a leader of the People's Party and, later, the National Liberal Party. He founded the Agrarian Party in 1932. Argetoianu and Prime Minister Nikolae Iorga led the "Government of National Unity" from April 1931 until June 1932. Argetoianu was named prime minister by King Carol II on September 28, 1939, following the assassination of Armand Calinescu. He remained head of the government until November 23, 1939. Argetoianu was arrested by the Communist regime that took power after World War II. He died in prison in 1952.

GHEORGHE TĂTĂRESCU (Prime Minister; November 24, 1939–July 4, 1940). *See earlier entry under Heads of Government.*

ION GIGURTU (Prime Minister; July 4, 1940–September 2, 1940). Ion Gigurtu was born in 1886. He was a leading reactionary and was called upon to form a government as prime minister on July 4, 1940. His cabinet included representatives of many fascist groups. Repressive measures were taken against democratic forces, with opponents of fascism sent to concentration camps. The government was forced by Germany to sign the Vienna Fascist Diktat in August 1940, with Northern Transylvania being turned over to Hungary. This agreement resulted in numerous demonstrations against the government. Gigurtu resigned on September 2, 1940, to make way for the dictatorship of Ion Antonescu. Gigurtu was arrested as a war criminal in October 1944.

ION ANTONESCU (Prime Minister; September 2, 1940–August 23, 1944). Ion Antonescu was born in Pitesti on June 14, 1882. He was educated in military schools in Craiova and Iasi. He served in the Romanian army as a second lieutenant during the 1907 Peasant Revolt. He subsequently attended the Romanian War College and served with distinction during the Second Balkan War and World War I. Antonescu served as military attaché to several European capitals from 1922 until 1927. He was named chief of the general staff in 1933, but resigned the following year over waste and corruption in the army. He was ordered by King Carol II to serve in Octavian Goga's government in December 1937, but resigned the following March in opposition to the king's use of the military to suppress the Iron Guard. Antonescu's conflict with King Carol led to his arrest and confinement in a monastery following the Soviet invasion of Bessarabia in July 1940. Antonescu was released from confinement on September 4, 1940, following Romania's loss of Transylvania due to German and Italian pressure. He formed a coalition government as prime minister with Iron Guard leader Horia Sima. King Carol II was forced to abdicate in favor of his son, Michael, several days later. Antonescu ousted Sima from the government in January 1941 and suppressed the Iron Guard. The following June Romania joined with Germany in an attack on the Soviet Union to recover the territories of Bessarabia and northern Bucovina. As Germany's fortunes waned during World War II, King Michael led a royal coup against the government, ousting Antonescu and ordering his arrest on August 23, 1944. Antonescu and other members of his government were turned over to the Soviet Union. They were held in Moscow until they were returned to Romania in May 1946 to stand trial. Antonescu, Deputy Premier Michael Antonescu, Deputy Interior Minister General Constantine Vasiliu, and other leading figures in the government were tried and convicted of war crimes. They were sentenced to death and executed by a firing squad at Fort Jilava on June 1, 1946.

CONSTANTIN   SĂNĂTESCU (Prime Minister; August 23, 1944–December 2, 1944). Constantin Sănătescu was born in 1885. He served in the Romanian army during World War I and subsequently attended the Superior War College in Bucharest. He became a colonel in the late 1920s. He served as Romanian military attache in London from 1928 to 1930. He was promoted to general in 1935 and served as head of Romania's delegation to Moscow in 1940. He became King Michael's leading military advisor in 1943 and was instru-

mental in the coup that ousted Marshal Ion Antonescu's government on August 23, 1944. He headed the subsequent government until November 4, 1944, when pressure from the Soviets forced him to re-form the cabinet, eliminating members of the Peasant and Socialist parties. Continued pressure forced Sănătescu's resignation on December 2, 1944. He served as chief of the general staff until June 21, 1945. He subsequently retired from the army to write his memoirs and died in Bucharest after a brief illness on November 8, 1947.

NICOLAI RĂDESCU (Prime Minister; December 6, 1944–February 28, 1945). Nicolai Rădescu was born in 1874. During World War I he served with distinction in the Romanian army. He became a colonel in the mid-1920s and served as military attaché in London from 1926 to 1928. He was an opponent of the regime of Marshal Ion Antonescu during World War II. His criticism of Antonescu and Manfred von Killinger, the German ambassador to Romania, resulted in his arrest in 1942. He was held in a concentration camp for the next two years. Antonescu was ousted in a royal coup led by King Michael on August 23, 1944. Rădescu, now a general, was installed as chief of staff of the army in October 1944. He was named to head the government as prime minister on December 6, 1944, after the Soviet Union forced the resignation of Constantin Sănătescu's government. He attempted to resist Communist control of Romania and was widely criticized by Moscow. He survived an assassination attempt on February 24, 1945. He was ousted from the government several days later on February 28, 1945, by order of the Soviet Deputy Foreign Minister Andrei Y. Vishinsky. Rădescu took refuge in the British embassy in Bucharest, where he remained until June 1946. He then escaped from government surveillance to make his way to Cyprus. He subsequently went to Portugal before settling in the United States in 1947. He became the first president of the Romanian National Committee, an anti–Communist government-in-exile, from 1948 until 1950. He also headed the League of Free Romanians. Radescu died in New York City after a long illness on May 16, 1953.

PETRE GROZA (Prime Minister; March 6, 1945–December 30, 1947). Petre Groza was born in Bacia, Transylvania, on December 6, 1884. He attended the Universities of Budapest, Berlin, and Leipzig and received a degree in law. He returned to Deva and opened a legal practice. Groza served on the grand council of Transylvania from 1918 until 1919, when he was elected to the Romanian chamber of deputies as a member of the Progressive Peasants' Party. He served in the cabinet of Alexandru Averescu as minister for Transylvania from 1920 until 1921 and as minister of

public works and communications from 1926 until 1927. He then retired from politics until 1933, when he founded the Ploughmen's Front. Groza reemerged to prominence on March 6, 1945, when the Soviet Union forced King Michael to name him as prime minister to succeed General Nicolai Radescu. Groza forced King Michael's abdication in December 1947 and declared Romania a people's republic. Communist party leader Gheorghe Gheorghiu-Dej remained the most powerful figure in the country and replaced Groza as prime minister on June 2, 1952. Groza was named to the position of chairman of the presidium of the grand national assembly and thus served as Romania's head of state. He was renamed to the chairmanship in March 1957. Groza suffered from poor health in 1957 and was hospitalized for a stomach operation. He died in Bucharest on January 7, 1958.

Russia

Russia is a country that stretches from eastern Europe across northern Asia to the Pacific Ocean.

HEADS OF STATE

NICHOLAS II (Czar; November 1, 1894–March 12, 1917). Nikolai Aleksandrovich was born on May 18, 1868, in Tsarskoe Selo. He was the eldest son of the future Czar Alexander III and his consort Maria Fedorovna, Princess Dagmar of Denmark. Nicholas' father ascended to the throne as Czar of Russia following the assassination of Alexander II in March 1881. Nicholas was educated by tutors, particularly General G. D. Danilovich, who trained him in military matters. He succeeded his father as Czar following Alexander III's death on November 1, 1894, and he was coronated as Nicholas II on May 26, 1895. He married

Alix, the daughter of German Grand Duke Louis IV of Hesse–Darmstadt on November 26, 1894. His wife was a strong-willed woman who had vast influence upon the Czar despite her unpopularity with the royal court and the populace. The couple had four daughters before the birth of their son, the Czarevich Aleksei, in 1904. Nicholas ruled Russia as an autocrat whose absolute power over the country was granted by God. He distrusted his ministers and was unyielding in his view that the government would exercise no powers not derived from the throne. He continued his father's policy of Russification, which resulted in increasing dissatisfaction among the non-Russian ethnic people of the empire. Nicholas tried to expand Russia's sphere of influence in Asia in the early 1900s. His policy toward Korea sparked the Russo-Japanese War of 1904, which ultimately resulted in the defeat of Russia's Baltic Fleet in May 1905. The subsequent peace settlement forced Russia to abandon all claims to Korea, though it was allowed to maintain influence in northern Manchuria. The cost of the war in lives and money sparked a worker's rebellion, with thousands of workers marching in St. Petersburg on January 22, 1905. Government troops fired into a crowd of peaceful demonstrators, killing and wounding hundreds. Riots and strikes took place throughout Russia, culminating in a general strike in October 1905. Nicholas then agreed to allow the establishment of an elected legislature, the Duma. The Duma attempted to institute numerous political reforms, but the Czar refused to consider them. Nicholas and his prime minister, Pyotr Stolypin, dismissed the Duma in July 1906, setting the stage for the election of the second Duma. This legislature was even more reform-minded than the first, which made agreement between it and the Czar's government impossible. The second Duma was dissolved in June 1907, and Nicholas subsequently reneged on many of the political reforms of 1905. Though two more Dumas were subsequently selected, Nicholas continued to rule Russia as an absolute monarch with the able assistance of Stolypin until the latter's murder in 1911. International tensions were on the rise throughout Europe, and Russia entered World War I against Germany and the Austro-Hungarian Empire as an ally of Great Britain and France. The Russian army was ill-prepared for the battle ahead and suffered numerous casualties during the invasion of East Prussia in August 1914. Nicholas took personal command of the Russian armies in September 1915, leaving the country largely in the hands of the Czarina. She had allied herself with Grigori Y. Rasputin, a self-styled holy man. Rasputin was considered a malign influence on the royal court and government, whose authority was derived largely from his ability to control the bleeding of the young, hemophiliac Czarevich Aleksei. The Czarina's German background also led to distrust and allegations of treason against her and her advisor. Members of the royal court took matters into their own hands and orchestrated the brutal murder of Rasputin at the end of December 1916. With Nicholas still absent from the capital, rioting broke out in Petrograd in March 1917. The Czar sent troops to restore order, but the government resigned and calls for Nicholas's abdication increased. Amidst widespread civil unrest, the Czar agreed to renounce the throne on March 15, 1917, in favor of his brother, the Grand Duke Michael, who declined the crown. Nicholas was initially held at Tsarskoe Selo, before being taken with his family to Tobolsk, in Western Siberia. They were held prisoner for over a year by the Bolsheviks. The royal family was removed to Ekaterinburg in the Urals in April 1918. The approach of the White Russian army on Ekaterinburg led to an order by the Bolshevik leadership to prevent the rescue of Nicholas. The local captors executed the Czar, his wife, and their five children and other members of the royal court during the night of July 29, 1918. The bodies were burned, and the remains were unceremoniously dumped into an abandoned mineshaft.

LEV B. KAMENEV (Chairman of the Presidium of the Supreme Soviet; November 7, 1917–November 1917). Lev Borisovich Kamenev was born in Tylis on July 22, 1883. He joined the Social Democratic Party in 1901 and was soon engaged in revolutionary activities. He left Russia in 1908 and became a close associate of Lenin. He returned to St. Petersburg in 1914 to direct Bolshevik activities in Russia. He was arrested the following year and banished to Siberia. He returned to St. Petersburg at the outbreak of the revolution in March 1917 and was the principal Bolshevik leader in the country until the return of Lenin. Kamenev soon broke with Lenin over the issue of joining with other Socialist parties to form a coalition government. He was elected to the politburo in October 1917 and briefly served as chairman of the Presidium of the Supreme Soviet in November 1917. He joined with Joséf Stalin and Grigori E. Zinoviev in opposition to Leon Trotsky in 1923. He subsequently broke with Stalin and was removed from his party positions in 1926. He served as Soviet ambassador to Italy the following year. His opposition to Stalin's regime led to his ouster from the Communist Party and his arrest in 1935. He and several of his allies were tried and convicted of treason during the Stalin purge trials, and Kamenev was executed on August 24, 1936.

YAKOV SVERDLOV (Chairman of the Presidium of the Supreme Soviet; November, 1917–March 16, 1919). Yakov Mikhailovich Sverdlov was born in Nizhny Novgorod on June 3, 1885. He joined the Social Democratic Party in 1901 and was soon involved in revolutionary activities. He was a leading supporter of Lenin and was active in the Urals during the 1905 revolution. He was arrested several times over the next few years and spent several years in exile in Siberia. Sverdlov was selected to serve on the central committee of the party in 1912. He was again arrested the following year and was banished to Turuhan

Province in the Arctic circle. He was released at the outbreak of the revolution in March 1917 and was sent to Ekaterinburg to head the Bolshevik movement in the Urals. Sverdlov was elected chairman of the All-Russian Central Executive Committee in November 1917, becoming Russia's head of state. He was instrumental in the drafting of the Soviet constitution and served as a delegate to the Communist International in early 1919. He died in Moscow on March 16, 1919.

MIKHAIL KALININ (Chairman of the Presidium of the Supreme Soviet; March 1919–February 25, 1946). Mikhail Ivanovich Kalinin was born in Vershanaya, in the province of Tver, on November 7, 1875. He worked in a munitions factory and became involved with revolutionary organizations in the 1890s. He was arrested on numerous occasions for antigovernment activities and was exiled to Siberia in 1916. Kalinin escaped the following year to take part in the October Revolution. He was appointed chairman of the Petrograd Soviet in 1918 and was elected to the central committee of the Communist Party the following year. Kalinin became the Soviet Union's president in March 1919 when he succeeded Yakov Sverdlov as chairman of the Presidium of the Supreme Soviet. He was a popular figure among the Russian peasants and was awarded the Order of Lenin in 1935. He survived the Stalinist purges in the late 1930s and retained the presidency until he retired for reasons of health on February 25, 1946. He died in Moscow on June 3, 1946.

HEADS OF GOVERNMENT

IVAN N. DURNOVO (Prime Minister; 1895–May 29, 1903). Ivan Nikolaevich Durnovo was born in Chernigov Province on March 1, 1834. He was ed-

ucated at the Mikhail Artillery School before entering government service. He served as governor of Chernigov Province from 1863 to 1870. He subsequently served as governor of Ekaterinoslav Province until 1882. He then entered the department of internal affairs and served as deputy minister until 1889, when he became interior minister. He implemented policies designed to reduce the power of local representative governments, or zemstvos, and made it more difficult for peasants to participate in voting. Durnovo was named chairman of the committee of ministers in 1895. He retained that position until his death on a train between Königsberg and Marienburg on May 29, 1903.

COUNT SERGEI WITTE (Prime Minister; August 29, 1903–April 24, 1906). Sergei Yulyevich Witte was born in Tiflis, Georgia, on July 29, 1849, to a noble family. He studied mathematics at the Novorossiysky University in Odessa. He began his career in government in the railways administration. He advanced through the ranks of the administration in Odessa and became minister of transport and communications in February 1892. He was also named minister of finance in August of that year. Witte began the institution of various reforms designed to assist in Russia's economic development. He began the remodeling of the State Bank to increase the flow of capital to industry. He also reformed Russia's currency policy to make the ruble convertible and gained financial support from other European countries to assist Russia's industrial development. Witte also oversaw a vast increase in the building of Russian railways, including the Trans-Siberian line. His relationship with agrarian interests was strained due to his support of increased industrialization, and he also lost favor with the Czar. Nicholas dismissed him as finance minister on August 29, 1903, relegating him to the largely ceremonial position of chairman of the council of ministers. Although Witte had opposed the Czar's policies in Asia that led to the Russo-Japanese War in 1904, he was called upon to head the Russian peace delegation in

1905. He negotiated a largely favorable settlement when the Japanese signed the Portsmouth Peace Treaty in 1906. He was also instrumental in persuading the Czar to issue a proclamation ensuring political reforms following the general strike in October 1905. Witte became prime minister of the new system of government that followed. He helped to improve Russia's badly damaged economy by negotiating a series of loans from European banks. As a moderate conservative, his efforts brought him little popularity as he remained largely distrusted by both the Left and the Right. He was forced to resign the premiership on April 24, 1906. He subsequently served on the council of state, where he opposed the policies of his successors, Ivan Goremykin and Pyotr Stolypin. Witte had very little influence in subsequent years. He was an outspoken critic of Russia's involvement in World War I in 1914. Witte died an embittered man in St. Petersburg on March 13, 1915.

IVAN L. GOREMYKIN (Prime Minister; April 24, 1906–July 8, 1906). Ivan Longinovich Goremykin was born to a prominent family in the province of Novgorod on October 27, 1839. He graduated from the Imperial Law School and entered government service in 1860. He served in the first department of the senate, where he remained for four years. He then began a decade-long period of service in Poland, where he was named commissioner of peasant affairs. He was named vice governor of Plotsk in 1866 and of Keletsk in 1869. He returned to St. Petersburg in 1873, where he entered the ministry of interior as a member of the provisional committee for peasant affairs. He was named director-general of the first department of the senate in 1882, where he continued to be involved in peasant affairs. He was appointed assistant minister of justice in 1891, and was named a senator three years later. He replaced Ivan Durnovo as minister of interior in October 1895. He came into conflict with Sergei Witte who, in October 1899, forced Goremykin's retirement. He subsequently served on the state council but exercised little influence over the next six years. He was called upon by Czar Nicholas II to head a conference on peasant landownership in early 1905. He also consulted with the Czar to formulate a response to the Russian general strike in October 1905 and again conflicted with Witte. The Czar dismissed Witte as chairman of the council of ministers in April 1906, and Goremykin was named to replace him upon the opening of the newly created State Duma on April 24, 1906. He served as a loyal supporter of the Czar, downplaying the Duma's influence on the government. He gained a reputation for senility due in part to his penchant for pretending to doze off while chairing meetings of the Duma. Goremykin was dismissed by the Czar in favor of Pyotr Stolypin on July 8, 1906. He held no major position in subsequent governments until February 11, 1914, when he was again called upon by Nicholas II to replace Vladimir Kokovtsev as chairman of the council of ministers. Goremykin put forth little substantive legislation for the Duma to consider, and was a largely insignificant figure in matters leading to Russia's entry into World War I. He continued to support the Czar in the face of growing unrest throughout the country. His increasing inability to effectively serve as a buffer between the government and the Duma led to his dismissal on February 2, 1916, and he retired from politics. Goremykin was forced to flee to the Caucasus following the Bolshevik Revolution in 1917. He, his wife, and his brother-in-law were killed by robbers at their country house in Sotchy, on the Black Sea, on December 11, 1917.

PYOTR A. STOLYPIN (Prime Minister; July 23, 1906–September 18, 1911). Pyotr Arkadyevich Stolypin was born in Dresden, Saxony, on April 14, 1862, the son of a Russian general. He was educated in St. Petersburg and entered government in the ministry of domains. He was placed in charge of the royal estates at Kovno in 1888. He was appointed governor of Grodno in 1902 and governor of Saratof the following year. He gained the notice of Czar Nicholas II, who named Stolypin minister of the interior in May 1906. He was appointed premier two months later on July 23, 1906. Stolypin was instrumental in the dismissal of the first Duma, Russia's legislative body, and subsequently ruled by executive decree. He instituted a series of reforms to enhance the welfare of the peasantry. He also began a policy of ruthless suppression against alleged terrorists and rebels, thousands of whom were executed by "Stolypin's necktie," which became synonymous with the hangman's noose. He survived an attempt on his life on August 25, 1906, when a bomb exploded during a party at his summer residence, seriously injuring many of his guests and two of his children. Stolypin dismissed the second Duma in June 1907, several months after it was convened, because of the Duma's refusal to ratify his agrarian reforms. It also refused to authorize the prosecution of members of the body on charges of conspiracy against the government. Stolypin again ruled by executive decree and altered the constitution by imperial decree to limit the franchise for future elections. The third Duma was dominated by the moderate right party, the Octobrists, who obliged Stolypin in passing agrarian reform programs. He also instituted a harsh policy of Russification in the Grand Duchy of Finland. Stolypin and the Czar bypassed the Duma by suspending the body so as to impose the extension of the zemstovo, or local council, system in the western regions, including Polish territory, in March 1911. He gained the enmity of most of Russia's political factions because of his disregard for constitutional niceties. Stolypin was shot twice and critically wounded by Socialist revolutionary terrorist Dmitry Bogrov while attending a performance at the Kiev opera on September 14, 1911. He died three days later in a Kiev hospital on September 17, 1911.

VLADIMIR KOKOVTSEV (Prime Minister; September 23, 1911–February 11, 1914). Vladimir Nikolaevich Kokovtsev was born to a prominent family in Gorna, Yaroslav Province, on April 6, 1853. He graduated with a gold medal from the Imperial Alexander Lyceum in 1873 and began his career in the Russian bureaucracy as a clerk in the ministry of justice. He advanced through the ranks in the ministry and, in 1876, he began working under State Secretary Konstantin Grot on the matter of prison reform. He was appointed by Grot to serve as assistant head of the central administration of prisons in 1879. He remained in that position for the next 11 years, during which time he sought to institute prison reforms. Kokovtsev began working with the imperial chancellery in 1890 and was promoted to the position of assistant imperial secretary. He transferred to the ministry of finance in 1896 as secretary of the department of economy under Finance Minister Sergey Witte. He gained a reputation as a fiscal conservative and assisted Witte in the reorganization of the Russian monetary system. He returned to the imperial chancellery as imperial secretary in 1902 and remained there for two years. He was named to succeed E. D. Pleske as minister of finance in February 1904. He was involved in the negotiations of loans to finance Russia's war against Japan, which were complicated by the outbreak of the 1905 revolution. He was replaced as minister of finance in October 1905 following Witte's appointment to head the government. Kokovtsev subsequently served as Czar Nicholas II's secretary before returning to the finance ministry following Witte's resignation in April 1906. He developed a close relationship with Prime Minister Pyotr Stolypin,

under whom he sought to balance the budget and pay off Russia's loans. Kokovtsev succeeded to the premiership several days after Stolypin's assassination on September 17, 1911. He also retained the position of finance minister in the new government. His use of funds from the state liquor monopoly to help balance the budget drew heavy criticism from powerful temperance groups in Russia, which had the support of the Czar. Kokovtsev's criticism of the growing power of Rasputin in the court also brought him into conflict with the royal family. Increasing civil unrest in the country cost him further support, and he was dismissed from office on February 11, 1914. He was subsequently named to the council of state, where he remained until the February Revolution of 1917. He was briefly held prisoner by the Bolsheviks before fleeing with his family to France later in the year. He became a leader of the anti-Bolshevik exiles in Paris, authoring numerous articles on Russian affairs. He also served as director of the International Bank of Paris. Kokovtsev died in Paris on January 29, 1943.

IVAN L. GOREMYKIN (Prime Minister; February 11, 1914–February 2, 1916). *See earlier entry under Heads of Government.*

BORIS STÜRMER (Prime Minister; February 2, 1916–November 23, 1916). Boris Vladimirovich Stürmer was born on July 28, 1848. He was educated at St. Petersburg University, where he studied law before entering the ministry of justice. Stürmer became closely aligned with the royal court and held subsequent governorships in Nizhnii Novgorod and Yaroslavi. He was named to the internal affairs ministry in 1902 and was appointed to the state council two years later. Stürmer became closely associated with the Czarina Alexandra and her advisor, Grigori Rasputin. He used his close relationship with Rasputin to get appointed chairman of the council of ministers on February 2, 1916. He also claimed the position of minister of the interior, where he promoted the wishes of Rasputin and the Czarina. He was perceived as an incompetent and corrupt administrator whose term of office led to increasing criticism of the government and the monarchy. Stürmer was also an outspoken opponent of Russia's entry into World War I as an ally of Britain and France. He was also named foreign minister in July 1916, and his continued view that Russia was fighting on the wrong side in the war led to widespread belief that he was a German sympathizer. Continued criticism of his administration led to his dismissal by Czar Nicholas II on November 23, 1916. Stürmer was arrested by the Bolsheviks following the February Revolution of 1917, and he was interned in the Peter and Paul Fortress. He died in prison of uremia on August 20, 1917.

ALEKSANDR TREPOV (Prime Minister; November 23, 1916–January 9, 1917). Aleksandr Fyodorovich Trepov was born in 1862, the younger brother of Dmitrii and Vladimir Trepov. He was a graduate of the Imperial Corps des Pages and became active in politics in 1899 while working in the ministry of the interior. He served in the Pereiaslavi District as marshal of nobility from 1892 until 1895. He was named assistant state secretary for the state council in 1899 and was appointed to the senate in 1906. Trepov served as a member of the committee which created the Duma in 1905. He subsequently began a study tour of European governments that resulted in his becoming a leading opponent of a constitutional monarchy. He was appointed to the state council by Czar Nicholas II in 1914, and became a member of the rightist faction. The Czar appointed Trepov to the cabinet as minister of ways and communications in October 1915. He became a leading critic of the influence of Rasputin in the royal court

and was named to replace Boris Stürmer as chairman of the council of ministers on November 23, 1916. He unsuccessfully sought to engineer the ouster of Interior Minister Aleksandr Protopopov and other protegés of Rasputin and the Czarina from the government. He offered his resignation to the Czar several times before it was accepted on January 9, 1917. His efforts against Protopopov earned him the leadership of the rightist faction on the state council, where he urged cooperation between the government and the Duma. Following the Russian revolution in February 1917, Trepov was involved with promonarchist groups that attempted to aid the royal family. His activities brought him into conflict with the Bolsheviks, and Trepov fled the country with the assistance of the German embassy in July 1918. He went into exile in England and France and died in Nice, France, on November 10, 1928.

NIKOLAI GOLITSYN (Prime Minister; January 9, 1917–March 15, 1917). Nikolai Dmitrievich Golitsyn was born in Poreche'e, Moscow Oblast, on March 31, 1850. He was educated at the Imperial Alexander Lyceum and began his governmental career in the ministry of the interior in 1871. He remained with the ministry for the next fourteen years. He was then named to a succession of provincial governorships, to Arhangel'sk in 1885, to Kaluga in 1893, and to Tver in 1897. He was appointed to the Senate in 1903. Golitsyn also became involved with the raising of funds for charitable organizations four years later, serving as minister of the Russian Red Cross. He was named chairman of the Committee to Bring Aid to Russian Prisoners of War during World War I. Golitsyn was also appointed to the council of state in 1915 and served as a member of the rightist faction. Considered a loyal supporter of the Czar and the Czarina with little personal ambition, he was chosen to replace Aleksandr Trepov as the last prime minister of Imperial Russia on

January 9, 1917. He attempted to decline the appointment, but acceded at the insistence of Nicholas II. As the country edged toward insurrection, Golitsyn tried to orchestrate the ouster of the unpopular interior minister, A. D. Protopopov. He was initially unsuccessful, but as conditions deteriorated, he persuaded the minister to step down on February 27, 1917. This did little to appease the political climate, which now called for the dissolution of the monarchy. Golitsyn attempted to save the monarchy by persuading Nicholas's brother, the Grand Duke Michael, to claim the throne. He was unable to persuade the Grand Duke to accept and also met with failure in attempting to persuade the Czar to appoint a new government composed of more popular figures. The government collapsed on February 28, 1917, and the Czar was forced to abdicate the following month. Golitsyn and other members of the government were placed in protective custody by the Duma. When the Bolsheviks took power, Golitsyn was put under virtual house arrest, where he remained until his death in Leningrad on July 3, 1925.

PRINCE GEORGI LVOV (Prime Minister; March 15, 1917–July 20, 1917). Prince Georgi Yevgenyevich Lvov was born to an aristocratic family in Popovka, Tula Province, on October 21, 1861. His father was the composer of the Russian national anthem. Lvov graduated from the University of Moscow with a degree in law. He entered the civil service, where he remained until 1893. He then returned to his home province of Tula, where he served on the zemstvo, or local council. He worked for reforms for the welfare of the peasantry and established schools and hospitals. He helped to organize relief work in Asia during the Russo-Japanese War in 1904 and 1905 and to assist with sanitary and feeding stations for the Russian army. Lvov was a founding member of the newly formed Constitutional Democrat, or Kadet, Party in 1905, and was elected to the first Duma the following year. He was elected mayor of Moscow in 1913, but the government refused to recognize his election. Lvov became chairman of the Pan-Russian Union of Zemstvos at the start of World War I in 1914. He gained widespread admiration for his relief efforts during the war. Lvov was selected as prime minister of the first provisional government on March 15, 1917, following the collapse of the imperial government. He also served as minister of the interior in the short-lived government composed primarily of liberals. The Bolsheviks continued to agitate against the government, and a major demonstration forced Lvov to resign on July 20, 1917. He was replaced by Alexander Kerensky, who remained prime minister until the Bolsheviks took control of Russia in November 1917. Lvov was arrested by the Bolsheviks but escaped from custody. He went into exile and eventually settled in Paris. Lvov continued his involvement in relief work, serving as Chairman of the Association of Russian Zemstvos Outside Russia. He remained an active fund-raiser for his fellow Russian expatriates until his death from heart disease at his suburban Paris apartment on March 8, 1925.

ALEXANDER I. KERENSKY (Prime Minister; July 21, 1917–November 8, 1917). Alexander Fyodorovich Kerensky was born in Simbirsk, Russia, on May 2, 1881. He attended the University of St. Petersburg and graduated with a degree in law in 1904. He became involved with the revolutionary movement while at the university. He opened a law practice in Saratov and became a leading defender of political prisoners. He was elected to the fourth Duma in 1912 as a member of the Trudoviki, or Labour, Party from Volsk. Kerensky was a supporter of Russia's war efforts against Germany during World War I but grew increasingly disenchanted with the imperial government's conduct of the war.

He was named deputy chairman of the St. Petersburg Soviet of Workers' Deputies following the dissolution of the monarchy in March 1917, and served in Prince Lvov's first provisional government as minister of justice. He became minister of war and the navy in May 1917. He organized a new offensive in the war effort that proved unsuccessful the following month. Kerensky became prime minister in the provisional government when Lvov was forced to step down on July 21, 1917. His initial popularity diminished in September 1917 when he dismissed General Lavr G. Kornilov, who was plotting a rightist military coup, and personally replaced him as commander-in-chief. He also alienated the leftists by his refusal to implement radical social and economic policies. Kerensky was forced from power following the Bolshevik's October Revolution in 1917, giving way to the establishment of Lenin's Bolshevik government on November 8, 1917. Kerensky escaped to the front, but was unable to raise an army to return him to power. He remained in hiding in Russia until May 1918, when he emigrated to London. He eventually settled in Paris, where he served as a publisher of the left-wing newspaper *Dri* (The Days), and wrote books about the revolution. He moved to the United States in 1940 and continued to write and lecture at universities. He lived as a house guest in New York City during most of his stay in the United States. Kerensky was hospitalized in New York in April 1970 after suffering a fall. He died of heart disease on June 11, 1970.

LENIN (Chairman of the Council of People's Commissars; November 8, 1917–January 2, 1924). Lenin was born Vladimir Ilyich Ulyanov in Simbirsk on April 22, 1870, to a cultured and educated family. His eldest brother, Aleksandr, was hanged for conspiracy in a plot to assassinate Czar Alexander III in 1887. Lenin entered Kazan University later in the year to study law, but was ex-

pelled soon after for participating in revolutionary activities. He spent a year in exile in the village of Kokushkino, where he read political literature and met with other exiled rebels. He returned to Kazan in 1888 and became a Marxist the following year. Lenin passed law exams in late 1891 and opened a practice in Samara. He moved to St. Petersburg in August 1893, where he worked as a public defender. He continued his revolutionary activities and was sent to Western Europe in 1895 to meet with Russian exiles. He returned to Russia later in the year to form the Union for the Struggle for Liberation for the Working Class, an umbrella group for Marxists. He was arrested in June 1895 and imprisoned for over a year. He was subsequently exiled to Siberia for three years. He was joined there by his fiancée, Nadezhda Krupskaya, whom he soon married. He left Russia after his exile in January 1900, adopting the name Lenin the following year to disguise his revolutionary activities. He was cofounder of the Marxist newspaper *Iskra* (The Spark). He called the second congress of Marxists in London in 1903. Lenin felt that a centralized party was needed to guide the proletariat in revolution. His views caused a schism at the congress. Lenin's supporters narrowly won and became known as the Bolsheviks (members of the majority). The leading rival group, led by L. Martov, were the Mensheviks (members of the minority). Lenin was in Switzerland when the revolution of January 1905 broke out in Russia. The split between Lenin and the Mensheviks widened over Lenin's view that the peasants, not the bourgeois, were the natural allies of the proletariat in the revolution. The failure of the 1905 revolution brought the two factions closer together. Lenin convened a Bolshevik Party congress in Prague in 1912, where the Mensheviks were officially ousted from the party. Lenin was an outspoken opponent of Russia's participation in World War I. He felt the masses were being sent to give up their lives in an imperialistic war. Lenin went into exile in Switzerland with other antiwar revolutionaries. As Russia reached the brink of revolution, Lenin remained out of the country. When the revolution succeeded in deposing the czar in March 1917, Lenin, with the assistance of Germany, returned to Russia. He immediately began an attack on the provisional government and called on the Bolsheviks to establish a Marxist state. Lenin's view increased in popularity as the war dragged on. He went to Finland where he was forced into hiding by Alexander Kerensky's government. He returned to Russia on October 20, 1917, and convinced the Bolsheviks that they should try to seize power. Lenin's assistant, Leon Trotsky, helped him plan the takeover. The Bolshevik-led Red Guards, a worker's militia, deposed Kerensky's provisional government on November 8, 1917, and proclaimed the Soviet state. The Allied Powers refused to recognize the new regime, and Lenin's government entered into negotiations with Germany and her allies for peace. A treaty was signed at Brest-Litovsk in March 1918 that imposed harsh conditions on the Russians. The treaty, plus Lenin's decision to repudiate foreign loans to the czarist government, led the Allied powers to support a counterrevolutionary movement against the Soviet government. Lenin was shot twice by disgruntled revolutionary Fanya Kaplan in an assassination attempt on August 30, 1918. He initially recovered from his injuries, but was plagued by poor health for the remainder of his life. His government held off the anti-Soviet, or White, forces during the civil war that raged for the next two years. Lenin secured his government's position by 1921, with himself as the preeminent leader. The economy was in shambles, which led to some dissension in the country. Lenin resorted to harsh measures, including show trials and summary executions, to combat criticism of his regime. Lenin allowed Joséf Stalin

to play a key role in government affairs and named him general secretary of the party in April 1922. Lenin's health began to fail in the spring of 1922. Doctors removed a bullet from his neck that had been there since the assassination attempt four years earlier. His health further deteriorated, and he suffered from periods of semiparalysis. During a period of recovery in June 1922, Lenin began the formation of the Union of Soviet Socialist Republics. During his periods of incapacitation, he expressed concerns about the possibility of such forceful figures as Stalin and Leon Trotsky gaining control and perverting the ideals of the Soviet state. Lenin suffered a major stroke on March 10, 1923, which caused him to lose the power of speech. He remained seriously ill until his death in Gorky on January 21, 1924.

ALEKSEI I. RYKOV (Chairman of the Council of People's Commissars; February 2, 1924–December 19, 1930). Aleksei Ivanovich Rykov was born in Saratov on February 13, 1881. He joined the Social Democratic Workers' Party in 1899 and became an active revolutionary soon after. He was arrested and deported several times but each time was able to escape and return to Russia. He supported Lenin in his break with the Mensheviks in 1904 and was active in the revolution the following year. He spent several years abroad before returning to Russia in 1911. He was again arrested and banished to Siberia in 1913. He was released at the start of the revolution in March 1916. Rykov supported a conciliatory policy with other Socialist factions in the formation of a coalition government. After the revolution in November 1917, Rykov served in Lenin's first government as people's commissar of the interior. He served as chairman of the supreme council of national economy from 1918 until 1921 when he was appointed deputy chairman of the council of people's commissars from 1921. He succeeded Lenin as chairman on February 2, 1924. He initially supported Joséf Stalin against party rival Leon Trotsky, but soon broke with Stalin to become a leader of the "Right Opposition." Stalin emerged from the conflict victorious and Rykov was replaced as chairman of the people's commissars on December 19, 1930. He subsequently served as people's commissar for communications until his dismissal from the government in 1936. Rykov was expelled from the party in 1937 and arrested for treason the following year. He was convicted with Nikolai Bukharin and others during one of Stalin's purge trials. He was sentenced to be executed and was shot to death in Moscow on March 14, 1938.

VYACHESLAV M. MOLOTOV

(Prime Minister; December 19, 1930–May 27, 1941). Vyacheslav Mikhailovich Molotov was born in Kukarka, Vyatka Province, on March 9, 1890. He became active in the Bolshevik movement in 1906. He was arrested in 1909 and spent the next two years in exile in the Vologda region. He went to St. Petersburg in 1911 and helped found the party newspaper *Pravda* the following year. He was again arrested in 1915 and banished to Manzurka, but escaped the following year. He held several party positions after the 1917 revolution and became a member of the central committee in 1921. He was selected to full membership in the politburo in 1926. He was a close ally of Joséf Stalin and was named to replace Aleksei Rykov as chairman of the people's commissars on December 19, 1930. Molotov also was foreign minister in May 1939. He was instrumental in the negotiation of the nonaggression pact with Germany the following August. Molotov stepped down as prime minister on May 27, 1941, when Stalin assumed the position. Molotov remained in the government as foreign minister and was Stalin's first deputy prime minister. He was a leading spokesman for the government following the German invasion of the Soviet Union during World War II. He con-

ducted negotiations that allied the Soviet Union with the United States and Great Britain and participated in the conferences in Tehran, Yalta, and Potsdam. He stepped down as foreign minister in March 1949, but returned to hold that position after Stalin's death in March 1953. He lost a power struggle with Nikita Khrushchev and was replaced as foreign minister in June 1956. He headed the ministry of state control until June 1957 when Khrushchev removed him from all important government and party offices. He was subsequently named ambassador to Mongolia and served as delegate to the International Atomic Energy Agency in Vienna in 1960 and 1961. Molotov was expelled from the Communist Party in the early 1960s and retired to his home near Moscow. He lived in relative obscurity and engaged in no political activity. Molotov was readmitted to the party in 1984. He died in Moscow after a long illness on November 8, 1986.

JOSÉF STALIN

(Prime Minister; May 27, 1941–March 5, 1953). Joséf Stalin was born Josif Vissarionovitch Dzhugashvili in the village of Gori in Georgia on December 21, 1879. He was educated at the Orthodox Church Seminary in Tiflis, where he became active in the revolutionary movement in 1897. He joined the Russian Social-Democratic Workers' Party in Tiflis in 1898 and was expelled from the seminary for his revolutionary activities the following year. Stalin was active as a strike organizer in the early 1900s. He was forced to go underground in November 1901 and was arrested in the spring of 1902. He was exiled to Siberia, but escaped after a short time. Stalin subsequently supported Lenin and the Bolsheviks against the Mensheviks in the schism that developed in the Social Democratic Party in 1903. He attended several international Socialist conferences and was elected to the Baku Party committee in 1907. He was again arrested and deported in

November 1908. Stalin again escaped but was rearrested in March 1910. He was released in June 1911 and moved to St. Petersburg, where he helped to establish the party newspaper *Pravda*. He traveled abroad from 1912 until 1913 and spent some time with Lenin. Stalin was again arrested on his return to Russia in February 1913. He remained imprisoned until the revolution in February 1917. He returned to Petrograd, where he assumed the editorship of *Pravda*. Stalin became a member of the politburo in May 1917 and was active in the October Revolution that resulted in the Communists taking control of the government. He served as people's commissar of nationalities from 1917 until 1923 and also served as a member of the revolutionary war council from 1920 until 1923. He was also selected as general secretary of the central committee of the Communist Party in April 1922. When Lenin died in January 1924, Stalin became part of a ruling triumvirate with Grigori E. Zinoviev and Lev B. Kamenev and thus prevented his chief rival, Leon Trotsky, from taking power. Stalin broke with Zinoviev and Kamenev in April 1925 and joined with Nikolai I. Bukharin, Alexei Rykov, Mikhail P. Tomsky, and the right wing of the party. He succeeded in expelling Trotsky, Zinoviev, and Kamenev from the party in 1928 and then successfully turned against Bukharin and his supporters. After gaining total control of the government, Stalin embarked on a program to industrialize the Soviet Union. Opposition to his policies was ruthlessly suppressed, and he succeeded in relocating millions of Russian peas-ants to industrial centers to be trained as factory workers. In 1936 Stalin began the first of the major purge trials to eliminate political opponents in the party and the military. During the next several years, Zinoviev, Kamenev, Bukharin, Rykov, and many others were tried for treason and executed. Trotsky, who was living in exile in Mexico, was tried and sentenced to death in absentia and was assassinated in 1940. Stalin was also concerned with the growing threat posed by Germany under the leadership of Adolf Hitler. After failing to convince the Western powers to enter into an alliance with the Soviets against Germany, Stalin entered into a nonaggression agreement with Hitler in August 1939, shortly before the start of World War II. Stalin also took the office of premier on May 6, 1941, shortly before Hitler violated the peace pact and attacked the Soviet Union on June 22, 1941. Stalin assumed control of the Soviet military during the war years, and the Soviet army successfully halted Germany's attempt to conquer the country. Stalin participated in the Allied conferences in Tehran and Yalta and, at the Potsdam Conference in July 1945, agreed to enter the war against Japan. After the conclusion of the war, Stalin extended the Soviet sphere of influence throughout Eastern Europe, as most of the countries in that region adopted, or were forced to adopt, Soviet-dominated Communist governments. He remained the dominant figure in the Soviet Union and the Communist world until he suffered a brain hemorrhage on March 1, 1953. He died in Moscow on March 5, 1953.

Saudia Arabia

Saudi Arabia is a country that occupies most of the Arabian peninsula in southwestern Asia. It was created by royal decree when the kingdoms of Hejaz and Najd were unified as the Kingdom of Saudia Arabia on September 18, 1932.

HEADS OF STATE

HUSAIN IBN ALI (King of the Hejaz; May 5, 1916–October 6, 1924). Husain ibn Ali was born in 1852, the son of Ali ibn Mohammed. He was called to Constantinople by Ottoman Sultan Abdul Hamid II in 1893. He remained there until 1908, when the Sultan granted Husain the position of emir of Mecca. He came into conflict with the subsequent Young Turk government in Istanbul and opposed the extension of the Hejaz railway to Mecca in 1913. Husain soon became involved in the Arab nationalist movement and entered into negotiations with the British near the start of World War I. Husain began the Arab Revolt in June 1916. He proclaimed himself king of Arabia but officially was recognized only as king of the Hejaz. After the war he refused to accept the terms of the 1919 Treaty of Versailles because he felt the British had reneged on promises they had made to him. He soon came into conflict with Ibn Saud of the Nejd. He further added to the conflict when he proclaimed himself caliph in 1924. Ibn Saud and his Wahabi followers launched an attack on the Hejaz at At Ta'if. Husain was forced to abdicate in favor of his son, Ali, on October 6, 1924, and went to Aqaba. Ali was ousted the following year when Ibn Saud claimed the Hejaz. The British arranged Husain's exile in Cyprus soon after, where he remained until 1930. He subsequently went to Transjordan, where his son, Abdullah, was king. Another son, Faisal, became king of Iraq. Husain died at the royal palace in Amman, Transjordan, on June 4, 1931.

ALI IBN HUSAIN (King of the Hejaz; October 6, 1924–December 19, 1925). Ali ibn Husain was born in 1882, the eldest son of Husain ibn Ali. He fought with his brothers against the Ottoman Empire during the Arab Revolt in 1916. He was a close advisor to his father and succeeded him as king of the Hejaz upon his abdication on October 6, 1924. Ibn Saud continued his attack on the Hejaz and Ali was forced to abdicate on December 19, 1925. He went into exile in Baghdad, Iraq, where he died of a stroke at the royal palace of his nephew, King Ghazi, on February 14, 1935.

IBN SAUD (King; September 18, 1932–November 9, 1953). Ibn Saud was born 'Abdul-ul'Aziz ibn 'Abd-ul-Rahman ibn Reisal al Saud on October 21, 1882 in Riyadh. He was the son of Emir Abdur Rahman and the grandson of Emir Faisal, who ruled the Nejd from 1834 until 1867. Ibn Saud accompanied his family into exile in 1891 when Ibn Rashid claimed Riyadh. Abdur Rahman was defeated in an attempt to depose Ibn Rashid in 1900 and relinquished his rights of succession to his son the following year. Ibn Saud recaptured Riyadh in January 1902 and proclaimed himself king of the Nejd. He withstood an attack from the Turks in 1904. Ibn Saud supported the British against the Turks during World War I and signed a treaty of friendship with Great Britain in 1915. He engaged in a successful military action against Ibn Rashid following the war and added Rashid's territory to his own. He also engaged in a rivalry with Hashemite King Husain, the grand sherif of Mecca. War broke out between Ibn Saud and Husain in 1924, and Ibn Saud captured the Hejaz and Mecca and forced Husain's abdication in October 1924. Ibn Saud was recognized as king of the Hejaz, Nejd, and their dependencies by Great Britain in May 1927. Ibn Saud put down several revolts in the early 1930s and renamed his kingdom Saudi Arabia in September 1932. He granted oil concessions to an American oil company in 1933, which eventually brought vast

riches to his country. He defeated Yemen in a battle over a territorial dispute in 1934, though he allowed Imam Yahya of Yemen to remain on the throne. Ibn Saud maintained close relations with Great Britain during World War II, but Saudi Arabia remained officially neutral. When Ibn Saud's health and eyesight began to fail in the early 1950s, he relinquished many of his duties to his son Saud. Ibn Saud died in Riyadh after a long illness on November 9, 1953.

Saxony

The kingdom of Saxony was a member of the German empire from 1871 until the collapse of Germany at the end of World War I in November 1918. Saxony no longer exists as an independent country but is part of Germany.

HEADS OF STATE

ALBERT (King; October 29, 1873– June 19, 1902). Albert was born in Dresden on April 23, 1828. His father was Prince John, who succeeded to the throne of Saxony in 1854. Albert served in the artillery corps as a lieutenant in 1843. He attended Bonn University from 1847 until 1848 and fought against the Danes as a captain in the battles of 1849. He married Caroline, the granddaughter of King Gustavus IV of Sweden, in 1853. He attained the rank of general of the infantry in 1857 and became a member of the Saxon parliament's upper chamber in 1862. He led the Saxon army against the Prussians when Saxony was invaded during the Seven Weeks' War in 1866. He subsequently agreed to Saxony's entry into the North German federation. He was commander of the federation's Twelfth Army Corps during the Franco-German War of 1870 and 1871. He led Prussian and Saxon troops into Paris as commander of the 4th Army during the

war and was involved in the battle of Sedan. He served as commander of the occupation forces in France from March until June 1871. He was subsequently named inspector general of the German army by the emperor. He succeeded his father to the throne on October 28, 1873. He instituted administrative and fiscal reforms early in his reign and nationalized the railways in 1876. He was a popular ruler, despite being a Catholic in a predominantly Protestant country. He retained the throne until his death in Schloss Sibyllenort, Silesia, on June 19, 1902.

GEORGE (King; June 19, 1902–October 15, 1904). George was born in Pillnitz on August 8, 1832. He was the youngest son of Prince John of Saxony and Queen Amelie. His father succeeded to the throne of Saxony in 1854. He studied history and law at the University of Bonn. He married the Infanta Maria of Portugal in 1859. He entered the military and was appointed to command the First Brigade of Cavalry in 1863. He saw action in Saxony's war against Prussia in 1866 and commanded an infantry corps against the French during the Franco-Prussian War in 1870. He subsequently commanded the Twelfth Army Corps for the next thirty years. He succeeded his brother, King Albert, to the throne of Saxony on June 19, 1902. His reign was brief, as George died only two years later, on October 15, 1904.

FREDERICK AUGUSTUS III (King; October 15, 1904–November 2, 1918). Frederick Augustus was born in Dresden on May 25, 1865. He was the eldest son of Prince George of Saxony. He entered the army as a lieutenant at the age of twelve. He studied law and political science at the universities of Strasbourg and Leipzig. He married the Archduchess Louise of Austria-Tuscany in 1891. Louise abandoned her husband and children and eloped with her children's French tutor in 1903. Frederick Augustus became commanding general of the Twelfth Army Corps upon his father's ascension to the throne in June 1902. He succeeded his father to the throne on October 15, 1904. He was an extremely popular monarch. During his reign the Social Democrats held a majority of seats in the Reichstag. Saxony contributed to the German war effort during World War I. Frederick Augustus abdicated on November 2, 1918, after Germany's collapse near the end of the war. He retired to Sybillenort Castle in Silesia, where he died of a stroke on February 18, 1932.

Serbia

Serbia was a country in the Balkan area of Southeastern Europe. It was an autonomous principality of the Ottoman empire from 1830 until it gained its independence in 1878. Serbia became part of the kingdom of the Serbs, Croats and Slovenes on December 1, 1918. The name was changed to Yugoslavia in 1929.

HEADS OF STATE

ALEXANDER (King; March 6, 1889–June 11, 1903). Alexander Obrenovich was born in Belgrade on August 14, 1876. He was the only child of Milan Obrenovich and his consort Natalie. Alexander succeeded to the throne of Serbia after the abdication of his father on March 6, 1889. He ruled under a regency council until April 13, 1893, when he staged a royal coup and took personal control of the country. The following year Alexander abolished the liberal constitution that had been in effect since the abdication of his father, and restored the more conservative constitution of 1869. Alexander appointed his father commander-in-chief of the armed forces in 1898. Two years later Alexander announced his engagement to Draga Masin, a widow who had served as his mother's lady-in-waiting. His government resigned in protest of this relationship, and Alexander had difficulty forming another one. He was married on August 5, 1900. The following year he tried to regain the confidence of his subjects by granting a more liberal constitution. He suspended the constitution in 1903 in order to gain greater control of the government and to dismiss political figures he differed with. His actions led to revolt against his reign. Conspirators attacked the palace early in the morning on June 11, 1903. They forced their way into the king's chamber and shot him and Queen Draga to death. Their bodies were then hacked by swords and thrown over the balcony to the courtyard below.

PETER (King; June 15, 1903–December 1, 1918). *See entry under Yugoslavia: Heads of State*

HEADS OF GOVERNMENT

VLADAN DJORDEVIĆ (Prime Minister; October 19, 1897–July 27, 1900). Vladan Djordević was born in Belgrade on December 3, 1855. He was a leading scholar and founded the literary journal *Otadzbina* in 1875. Djordević served as Serbia's envoy to Greece in 1891. He was appointed prime minister by King Alexander on October 19, 1897 and his government was largely controlled by King Alexander. The army was placed under the command of former King Milan and political opposition inside of Serbia was curtailed. Alexander's engagement to his mistress, Draga Masin, caused widespread consternation throughout the country and Djordević's cabinet resigned on July 27, 1900, in protest. He died on August 31, 1930.

ALEKSA JOVANOVIĆ (Prime Minister; July 27, 1900–April 2, 1901). Aleksa Jovanović was born in Cuprija on August 31, 1846. He was a minor jurist when he was called upon to form a cabinet on July 27, 1900. Most of Serbia's more distinguished political figures refused to participate in the government in opposition to King Alexander's wedding plans to his mistress, Draga Masin. Jovanović was dismissed on April 2, 1901. He died in Belgrade on May 6, 1920.

MIHAJLO VUJIĆ (Prime Minister; April 2, 1901–October 18, 1902). Mihajlo Vujić was born in Belgrade on November 7, 1853. He was a distinguished scholar and a professor at the Great School. He was a member of the Radical Party and served as finance minister in 1889. He was named to Aleksa Jovanović's government in February 1901 and replaced Jovanović as prime minister on April 2, 1901. He headed a Radical and Progressive cabinet and promulgated a new constitution. His government fell because of a stalemate in parliament in May 1902, but he remained prime minister when Nikola Pašić was unable to form a government. Vujić was dismissed by King Alexander on October 18, 1902, over his government's inability to arrange a visit to Russia for the king. He died in Susak on March 14, 1913.

PERA VELIMIROVIĆ (Prime Minister; October 18, 1902–November 18, 1902). Pera Velimirović was born in Sikol on January 28, 1848. He was a member of the Radical Party and was called upon to form a government on October 18, 1902. He received no support from the Radicals in the parliament and so resigned on November 18, 1902. He was again named to head the government on July 20, 1908. He also served as foreign minister. His government was faced with the crisis of Austria-Hungary's annexation of Bosnia-Herzegovina. He stepped down on February 24, 1909. Velimirović died in Belgrade on January 6, 1922.

DIMITRIJE CINCAR-MARKOVIĆ (Prime Minister; November 18, 1902–June 11, 1903). Dimitrije Cincar-Marković was born in Sabac on September 9, 1849. He was a general in the Serbian army. He was named prime minister by King Alexander on November 18, 1902. He was supported by the parties of the right and his government served as a vehicle for Alexander's personal rule of the country. Cincar-Marković was killed during the revolt on June 11, 1903, when rebels assassinated the king.

JOVAN AVAKUMOVIĆ (Prime Minister; June 11, 1903–February 11, 1904). Jovan Avakumović was born in Belgrade on December 29, 1841. He was educated in Germany and France. He was a lawyer and a leader of the Liberal Party from the 1880s. He headed a Liberal government from August 22, 1892, until April 13, 1893, when he was ousted by King Alexander in a royal coup. He was involved in the conspiracy that ousted and killed the king. He was named to head the government on June 11, 1903, following Alexander's death. His government restored the constitution of 1901. He presided over the selection of Peter Karageorgevich as Serbia's new king, and then his government resigned on February 11, 1904. Avakumović died on August 3, 1928.

SAVA GRUJIĆ (Prime Minister; February 11, 1904–December 10, 1904). Sava Grujić was born in Kolar on December 7, 1840. He served in the Serbian military and became minister of war in Jovan Ristić's cabinet in 1876. He was named to head the government by King Milan on December 29, 1887. He was subsequently promoted to the rank of general. Grujić led a Radical cabinet until April 1888. He continued to head the government following Milan's abdication in March 1889. He stepped down in February 1891, when Nikola Pašić formed a government. He resumed office the following year. Grujić resigned on October 20, 1893, when King Alexander invited Milan to return to Serbia. King Peter appointed Grujić prime minister in September 1903. His government fell over a parliamentary dispute about a loan from German and French financiers on December 10, 1904. Grujić died in Belgrade on November 3, 1913.

NIKOLA PAŠIĆ (Prime Minister; December 10, 1904–May 25, 1905). *See entry under Yugoslavia: Heads of Government.*

LJUBOMIR STOJANOVIĆ (Prime Minister; May 28, 1905–March 7, 1906). Ljubomir Stojanović was born in Uzice on August 31, 1861. He was an Independent Radical and served as minister of education in Jovan Avakumovic's cabinet following the murder of King Alexander in June 1903. He was appointed to head the government on May 28, 1905. A customs agreement between Serbia and Bulgaria brought about a suspension of trade negotiations with Austria-Hungary. Stojanović resigned on March 7, 1906. He died on June 16, 1930.

SAVA GRUJIĆ (Prime Minister; March 7, 1906–April 28, 1906). *See earlier entry under Heads of Government.*

NIKOLA PAŠIĆ (Prime Minister; April 28, 1906–June 23, 1908). *See entry under Yugoslavia: Heads of Government.*

PERA VELIMIROVIĆ (Prime Minister; July 20, 1908–February 24, 1909). *See earlier entry under Heads of Government.*

STOJAN NOVAKOVIĆ (Prime Minister; February 24, 1909–October 13, 1909). Stojan Novaković was born in Sabac on November 13, 1842. He was educated in Serbia and was a scholar in literature as well as a philologist. He was a professor at the Great School and head of the National Library and Museum during the 1870s. He served as minister of education in 1873 and in 1883. He was named minister of the interior in Milutin Garašanin's government in 1884. He was the first president of the Serbian Literary Cooperative in 1892. He headed a Progressive government from July 7, 1895, until his cabinet resigned over a dispute with King Alexander on December 27, 1896. He subsequently served as Serbia's envoy to Istanbul. He was again called upon to head the government on February 24, 1909, but stepped down on October 13, 1909. He died in Nish on February 18, 1915.

NIKOLA PAŠIĆ (Prime Minister; October 13, 1909–June 26, 1911). *See entry under Yugoslavia: Heads of Government.*

MILOVAN MILOVANOVIĆ (Prime Minister; July 8, 1911–July 1, 1912). Milovan Milovanović was born in Belgrade on March 1, 1863. He was named to Aleksa Jovanović's cabinet in February 1901 and was the author of the new constitution. He was Serbia's envoy to Rome in 1906. He was named to head the foreign ministry in 1908. He became prime minister on July 8, 1911. He worked toward an alliance with Bulgaria to offset Austria-Hungary's power in the Balkans. Milovanović died in office in Belgrade on July 1, 1912.

MARKO TRIFKOVIĆ (Prime Minister; July 2, 1912–September 8, 1912). Marko Trifković was born in Belgrade on September 18, 1864. He was a leading Serbian politician and close ally to Nikola Pašić. He served in various Pašić governments, and briefly served as Serbia's prime minister from July 2, 1912, until September 8, 1912. He was named minister of the interior in November 1918. Trifković served as president of the national assembly in 1927. He suffered a stroke in 1929 and died in Belgrade on July 26, 1930.

NIKOLA PAŠIĆ (Prime Minister; September 12, 1912–November 30, 1918). *See entry under Yugoslavia: Heads of Government.*

Slovakia

Slovakia was a country in central Europe. It became independent from Czechoslovakia under German protection on March 14, 1939. The country was reabsorbed by Czechoslovakia in April 1945 following its defeat in World War II.

HEADS OF STATE

JOSEF TISO (President; October 26, 1939–May 8, 1945). Josef Tiso was born in Velká Bytča on October 13, 1887, while Slovakia was still a part of Hungary. Tiso was ordained a priest in 1910. He became a leading member of the Slovak People's Party after World War I. He joined the Czechoslovak government in January 1927 but withdrew from the cabinet two years later. He succeeded Andrej Hlinka as leader of the Slovak People's Party after the latter's death in August 1938. Tiso became premier of an autonomous Slovakia within Czechoslovakia on October 6, 1938. Slovakia declared itself independent following the German division of Czechoslovakia on March 14, 1939, and Tiso was elected the country's first president on October 26, 1939. Tiso's government was closely allied with Nazi Germany and declared war on the Soviet Union and the United States during World War II. The Soviet and Czech armies drove out the Germans and captured Bratislava in April 1945. Tiso surrendered Slovakia to the Allies on May 8, 1945, and was captured while in hiding in Austria. He was tried for treason in a Czechoslovak court in April 1947, and sentenced to death. Despite international pressure for a reprieve, he was hanged in Bratislava on April 18, 1947.

HEADS OF GOVERNMENT

VOJTĚCH BALU TUKA (Prime Minister; November 2, 1939–September 5, 1944). Vojtěch Balu Tuka was born in 1880 in Slovakia of Hungarian parents. He was a professor at the Hungarian Law Academy in Bratislava. Slovak Populist Party leader Andrej Hlinka named Tuka editor of the party's newspaper *Slovak* in 1922. Tuka organized the paramilitary group Rodobrana, or Home Defense, the following year. He was elected to the chamber of deputies in 1925. Tuka was arrested and charged with treason in January 1929. He was found guilty and sentenced to fifteen years in prison. He was granted amnesty by President Eduard Benes in June 1937. He was named prime minister of the newly independent Slovakia by President Josef Tiso on November 2, 1939. He also was named foreign minister in July 1940. Tuka was an admirer of Adolf Hitler and led the country into a close alliance with Nazi Germany during World War II. He

came into conflict with President Josef Tiso, but was able to remain head of the government with German support until September 5, 1944. Slovakia was conquered in April 1945, and Tuka was arrested. He suffered a stroke while imprisoned. Tuka was tried and convicted of war crimes and sentenced to death as a collaborator on August 11, 1946. He was executed in Prague on August 20, 1946.

ŠTEFAN TISO (Prime Minister; September 5, 1944–May 8, 1945). Štefan Tiso was a cousin of Slovakian President Josef Tiso. He headed the puppet government of Slovakia under the German occupation forces from September 5, 1944, until Slovakia surrendered to the Allies on May 8, 1945. Tiso was arrested as a war criminal. He was tried and convicted of collaborating with the enemy and was sentenced to thirty years imprisonment in November 1947.

South Africa, The Union of

The Union of South Africa is a country in southern Africa formed by the unification of the British colonies of Transvaal, Orange Free State, Cape of Good Hope, and Natal on May 31, 1910.

HEADS OF STATE

LORD GLADSTONE (Governor-General; May 31, 1910–February 12, 1914). Herbert John Gladstone was born in London on January 7, 1854. He was the youngest son of British Prime Minister William E. Gladstone. The younger Gladstone was educated at Eton and University College, Oxford. He was a history professor at Keble College from 1877 until 1880. He subsequently entered politics and was elected to the House of

Commons for Leeds in 1880. He served as his father's private secretary from 1880 until 1881. He was made a privy councilor in 1894 and served as chief whip of the Liberal Party from 1899 until 1906. Gladstone served as home secretary from 1908 until 1910. He was raised to the peerage as Viscount Gladstone in March 1910, and was appointed the first governor-general of the Union of South Africa, taking office on May 31, 1910. He had a good working relationship with South African Prime Minister Louis Botha. He completed his term of office on February 12, 1914, and returned to England where he served on the War Refugees Committee as treasurer during World War I. Lord Gladstone withdrew from politics in 1924. He died after a long illness at his home in Dane End, Hertfordshire, on March 6, 1930.

LORD BUXTON (Governor-General; September 8, 1914–November 20, 1920). Sydney Charles Buxton was born in Newtimber Place, Sussex, England, on October 15, 1853. He was educated at Clifton and Trinity College, Cambridge. He was defeated for a seat in the House of Commons in 1880, but secured election as a Liberal in 1883. He was rejected by the voters two years later, but returned to Parliament in 1886. He served on the Royal Education Committee from 1886 until 1889. He was undersecretary of state for the colonies from 1892 until 1895. Buxton was named to the cabinet as postmaster-general in Sir Henry Campbell-Bannerman's government in 1905 and served until 1907. He was president of the board of trade from 1910 until 1914 when he was appointed governor-general of the Union of South Africa. He took office on September 8, 1914. He was also raised to the peerage as Viscount Buxton that year. Lord Buxton worked closely with South African Prime Minister Louis Botha to ensure South Africa's loyalty to Great Britain during World War I. He remained in South Africa throughout the war and his term was extended for a year before he stepped down from office on November 20, 1920. Lord Buxton returned to England and served as president of the African Society from 1921 until 1933. He died at his home, Newtimber Place, Sussex, after a long illness on October 15, 1934.

ARTHUR, PRINCE OF CONNAUGHT (Governor-General; No-vember 20, 1920–December 7, 1923). Arthur Frederick Patrick Albert was born in Windsor Castle on January 13, 1883. He was the only son of Prince Arthur William Patrick Albert, Duke of Connaught, and a grandson of Queen Victoria. Prince Arthur was educated at Eton and Sandhurst and served in the Seventh Hussars during the Boer War in South Africa in 1901. He was named to the privy council in 1910. He served in the Scots Greys throughout World War I. Prince Arthur retired from the military as a lieutenant colonel in 1919. He was appointed governor-general of the Union of South Africa and took office on November 20, 1920. During his term of office, Southern Rhodesia rejected incorporation into the Union. Prince Arthur's term was extended for one year before he stepped down on December 7, 1923. He returned to England and was appointed a personal aide to King George V in 1927. Prince Arthur died of throat cancer at his home in Belgrave Square, London, on September 12, 1938.

EARL OF ATHLONE (Governor-General; January 21, 1924–January 26, 1931). *See entry under Canada: Heads of State.*

EARL OF CLARENDON (Governor-General; January 26, 1931–April 5, 1937). George Herbert Hyde Villiers was born on June 7, 1877. He succeeded to the title as the Sixth Earl of Clarendon upon the death of his father in 1914. He became lord-in-waiting to King George V in 1921 and became chief whip of the Conservative Party in the House of Lords in the late 1920s. Lord Clarendon served as chairman of the board of the newly established British Broadcasting Corporation in May 1927. He was appointed governor-general of the Union of South Africa and took office on January 26, 1931. He completed his term on April 5, 1937, and returned to England. In April 1938 he was appointed Lord Chamberlain by King George VI. The

Lord Chamberlain was the custodian of the King's palaces and was responsible for the moral tone of theatrical productions performed in England. Lord Clarendon remained in that position until after the death of King George VI, stepping down on October 10, 1952. He was subsequently appointed permanent lord-in-waiting by Queen Elizabeth II. Lord Clarendon died at his home in London on December 13, 1955.

SIR PATRICK DUNCAN (Governor-General; April 5, 1937–August 28, 1943). Sir Patrick Duncan was born in Fortrie, Banffshire, Scotland, on December 21, 1870. He was educated at the University of Edinburgh and Balliol College, Oxford. He received a degree in law and entered the British colonial service in 1894. He was sent to South Africa where he became colonial secretary for the Transvaal in December 1903. He returned to England after Transvaal was granted self-government in 1907. Duncan returned to South Africa the following year to practice law in Johannesburg. He became a leader of the Progressive Party and was an advocate of a union of the South African colonies. He was elected to Parliament as a Unionist in 1910. He was defeated in the elections of 1920 but returned to the Parliament the following year. He served in Jan Christian Smuts's cabinet as minister of the interior, public health and education from 1921 until 1924. He remained in the Parliament and was instrumental in the formation of the United Party in 1933. He served in the cabinet as minister of mines and industry from 1933 until 1936.

Duncan became the first South African citizen to be appointed governor-general of the Union, assuming office on April 5, 1937. World War II broke out in 1939, and the parliament rejected Prime Minister James Hertzog's position of neutrality in the conflict. Duncan rejected a call for new elections and asked Smuts to form a government that supported the British war effort. Duncan was appointed to a second term in February 1942. His health soon began to fail, and he underwent surgery. He recovered sufficiently to resume his duties in May 1943. Duncan suffered a relapse and died in Pretoria on July 17, 1943.

NICOLAS JACOBUS DE WET (Governor-General; August 23, 1943–December 31, 1945). Nicolas Jacobus De Wet was born in Aliwal North on September 11, 1873. He was educated at Victoria College and Cambridge University and returned to South Africa to practice law. He was elected to the Transvaal legislative assembly in 1907 and served until 1910. De Wet was appointed to Louis Botha's government as minister of justice in 1913. He left the government in 1924. He had been elected to the senate from Transvaal in 1921, and he remained in the Upper House until 1929. De Wet was appointed to the court of appeals in 1932 and became chief justice of South Africa in 1939. He became acting governor-general of South Africa on August 23, 1943, following the death of Sir Patrick Duncan. He retained that position until December 31, 1945. De Wet died in Hatfield on March 16, 1960.

HEADS OF GOVERNMENT

LOUIS BOTHA (Prime Minister; May 31, 1910–August 27, 1919). Louis Botha was born in Greytown, Natal, on September 27, 1862. He went with his family to the Orange Free State in 1869.

He was instrumental in the formation of the New Republic in 1884. The New Republic was incorporated into the South African Republic in 1888. Botha was elected to the South African parliament, or Volksraad, in 1897, where he was a critic of the government of President Paul Kruger. Botha became an active participant in the Boer War against the British from 1899. He was appointed commandant-general of the Transvaal in March 1900 following the death of General Piet Joubert. After the British capture of Pretoria, Botha continued to lead his forces in a guerrilla war against the British. The Boer's military position continued to decline, and Botha urged the acceptance of a peace settlement at Vereeniging in May 1902. Botha subsequently became active in South African politics after the war and was named chairman of the Het Volk, or The People, Party. Botha became prime minister of the Transvaal when self-government was granted in 1907. He sought to improve relations between the Boers and British and supported the formation of the Union of South Africa, which incorporated the colonies of Orange Free State, Transvaal, the Cape of Good Hope, and Natal. He became the first prime minister of the Union on May 31, 1910. Botha supported the British war effort against Germany from the start of World War I in 1914. His pro–British policies led to a rebellion by Afrikaaners. His government put down the revolt in February 1915, and Botha commanded the forces that captured German South-West Africa in July 1915. He headed the South African delegation to the Paris Peace Conference after the war and signed the Treaty of Versailles in 1919. Botha's health was failing as he returned to South Africa, and he died of influenza in Pretoria on August 28, 1919.

JAN CHRISTIAN SMUTS (Prime Minister; August 31, 1919–June 18, 1924). Jan Christian Smuts was born in Cape Province on May 24, 1870. He worked on his family's farm and later entered Victoria College in Stellenbosch. In 1891 he attended Cambridge University in Great Britain on a scholarship. Smuts studied law and returned to South Africa in 1895.

He initially supported Cecil Rhodes' government in Cape Town before becoming disillusioned with Rhodes following the Jameson Raid. He went to Johannesburg, where he joined the Transvaal government. He was named state attorney in 1898 and worked closely with Paul Kruger in an attempt to prevent a war between the Dutch and British in South Africa. When the Boer War began, Smuts was a leader in the resistance to the British. He took government funds from the banks in Pretoria before the British captured the city and used the money to finance a guerrilla war against the British. His group fought until the end of the war in 1902 and then took part in the peace negotiations. Following the war, Smuts was a founder of the Het Volk Party. When the Liberal Party came to power in Britain, Smuts assisted in negotiations that returned self-rule to South Africa. The Het Volk Party was successful in the 1907 elections, and Smuts became colonial secretary and minister of education in the government led by Louis Botha. Smuts was forced to make a series of unpopular decisions, including the arrest of Mohandas Gandhi. He also broke a miners' strike in Johannesburg by imposing martial law and calling in the troops. Smuts was also a leading supporter of South Africa's entry into World War I on the side of the British. He was forced to put down a brief rebellion in October 1914 by Boer veterans who opposed working with the British. After entering the war, South Africa successfully fought against the Germans in South-West Africa, and Smuts was named commander-in-chief of the forces in East Africa. After leading successful campaigns against the Germans in Tanganyika, he attended the Imperial War Congress in London in March 1917. He remained in London as part of the British war cabinet and took part in the peace conference following the war. Smuts returned to South Africa to become prime minister on August 31, 1919, following the death of Botha. Smuts was faced with another violent miners' strike in 1922, and he was unsuccessful in convincing Southern Rhodesia to join the Union of South Africa later in the year. The opposition Nationalist Party joined with the Labor Party and defeated Smuts' South African Party in the election of 1924. He was succeeded by J. B. M. Hertzog as prime minister on June 18, 1924. While out of office, Smuts wrote *Holism and Evolution*, a philosophical work published in 1926. Following the depression of 1929, economic difficulties forced a coalition between Hertzog's Nationalists and Smuts's South African Party in 1933. Smuts joined the cabinet as deputy prime minister. The coalition lasted until the onset of World War II. Smuts advocated South Africa's entry into the war on the side of the British, while Hertzog supported neutrality. The issue was settled in the House of Assembly in favor of Smuts's position, and he became prime minister on September 3, 1939. Smuts also served as commander-in-chief of the South African armed forces, and he often visited sectors where South African troops served. Following Germany's defeat, Smuts took part in the peace negotiations and assisted in the drafting of the United Nations charter in 1945. Smuts was less successful in dealing with domestic problems. The government had relaxed the enforcement of segregation policies during the war. The new Nationalist Party under Daniel Malan advocated apartheid policies to support white supremacy in South Africa. The Nationalists narrowly defeated Smuts in the elections of 1948. Smuts relinquished the office of prime minister to Malan on June 3, 1948, and became leader of the opposition. He died at his home in Irene, near Pretoria, on September 11, 1950.

JAMES B. M. HERTZOG (Prime Minister; June 18, 1924–September 6, 1939). James Barry Munnik Hertzog was born in Wellington, Cape Colony, on April 3, 1866. He accompanied his family to the Orange Free State in 1879. Hertzog was educated at Victoria College and Amsterdam University, where he received a degree in law. He practiced law in Pretoria from 1892 until 1895, when he became a judge on the Orange Free State's high court. He fought against the British during the Boer War from 1899 until 1902. He remained a critic of the British colonial government and formed the Orangia Unie Party. He served in Abraham Fischer's cabinet when the Orange Free State was granted self-rule in 1907. After the formation of the Union of South Africa in 1910, Hertzog was named to Louis Botha's cabinet as minister of justice. Hertzog's fiery oratory jeopardized Botha's conciliatory policy toward the British, and Hertzog was dropped from the cabinet after two years. He founded the Afrikaaner National Party in 1914 and opposed the government's decision to enter World War I on the side of the British. Hertzog's party allied with the Labor Party to form a government on June 18, 1924. Hertzog continued to try and secure the independence of the Union of South Africa. Afrikaans was made the official language of the Union, and a new national flag was created. His government passed a measure that protected white laborers from competition from African and Indian workers. Hertzog was forced to form a coalition government with Jan Christian Smuts's South African Party in 1934, with Hertzog remaining as prime minister and Smuts serving as deputy prime minister. Hertzog's government continued its policies of segregation of African natives. He supported a policy of neutrality at the outset of World War II. The parliament rejected his position, and Hertzog resigned on September 6, 1939. He briefly joined Daniel Malan's reunited Nationalist Party and was an outspoken critic of Smuts's pro–British policy during the war. He resigned from parliament and retired from politics in November 1940. Hertzog underwent abdominal surgery in 1942. He died after a long illness at his son's home in Pretoria on November 21, 1942.

JAN CHRISTIAN SMUTS (Prime Minister; September 6, 1939–June 3, 1948). *See earlier entry under Heads of Government.*

Spain

Spain is a country on the Iberian Peninsula in southwest Europe.

HEADS OF STATE

ALFONSO XIII (King; May 17, 1886–April 14, 1931). Alfonso de Bourbon of Hapsburg was born in Madrid, on May 17, 1886. He was the posthumous son of King Alfonso XII and Maria Cristina and was proclaimed king under his mother's regency immediately upon birth. He was proclaimed of age in 1902 upon his sixteenth birthday, but allowed his mother to continue to rule in his stead until 1906. Alfonso was married to Victoria Eugenie of Battenburg on May 31, 1906. He and his bride survived an assassination attempt when a bomb was thrown at the bridal coach following the wedding ceremony. During much of his reign the leadership of the Spanish government rotated between the Liberal and Conservative parties, and Alfonso became increasingly involved in political affairs. He maintained Spain's neutrality during World War I. Alfonso began to exercise more direct political power in the postwar period and was held personally responsible for the Spanish military disaster in Morocco in 1921. His reign was saved by a military coup led by General Miguel Primo de Rivera in September 1923. Alfonso associated himself closely with Primo de Rivera's dictatorship. When the dictatorship ended in January 1930, Alfonso's reign was placed in serious jeopardy. A new government under General Damaso Berenguer tried to preserve the monarchy by reestablishing a constitutional regime. General elections were held that gave an overwhelming victory to the Republican parties, who called for Alfonso's abdication. He refused to abdicate, but he went into exile to spare the country a civil war on April 14, 1931. In November 1931 Alfonso was tried in absentia by the Cortes and found guilty of high treason. His properties were confiscated, and he was banished from Spain for life. He was sympathetic to the insurgents under Generalissimo Francisco Franco during the Spanish Civil War. Franco restored Alfonso's property and citizenship in April 1939, though he made no attempt to restore the monarchy at that time. Alfonso formally abdicated on January 15, 1941, in favor of his third son, Don Juan. Suffering from poor health, Alfonso died in Rome on February 28, 1941.

NICETO ALCALÁ ZAMORA Y TORRES (President; April 14, 1931–April 7, 1936). Niceto Alcalá Zamora y Torres was born in Priego, Cordoba, on July 6, 1877. He entered politics and was elected to the Spanish parliament, or Cortes, in 1905. He was named to the cabinet as minister of works in 1917 and was minister of war in 1922. He joined the Republicans in 1930 and was imprisoned for instigating a military uprising in La Jara that year. He became head of the revolutionary committee in April 1931 and demanded the abdication of King Alfonso XIII. Alcalá Zamora became prime minister of the provisional government and acting president on April 14, 1931, after the departure of the king. He stepped down on October 14, 1931, when the Cortes passed anticlerical legislation to seize church property. He was elected the first president of the second Spanish republic on December 11, 1931. He attempted to serve as a moderating influence on rightist and leftist elements in the government. He found himself under attack from both sides and was deposed by the Cortes on April 7, 1935, after the Popular Front victory several months earlier. Alcalá Zamora went into exile in France before settling in Buenos Aires, Argentina. He died there on February 17, 1949.

DIEGO MARTÍNEZ BARRIO
(President; April 7, 1935–May 10, 1936). Diego Martínez Barrio was born in Seville on November 25, 1883. He worked as a printer before he entered politics as a member of the Radical Party. He was a supporter of the establishment of the Spanish republic in 1931. He served as minister of communications in the provisional government and subsequently served as minister of the interior. He broke with the Radicals and formed the Republican Union in 1933. Martínez Barrio succeeded Alejandro Lerroux as prime minister on October 9, 1933. He relinquished the government to Lerroux on December 16, 1933. He was president of the Cortes in 1936 and briefly served as acting president following the ouster of Niceto Alcalá Zamora on April 7, 1936. He stepped down when Manuel Azana was confirmed as president on May 10, 1936. Martínez Barrio again briefly headed the government as prime minister on July 19, 1936, when the army revolted against the Popular Front government. He attempted to avert a civil war, and when he failed, he relinquished power to Jose Giral. He went to Valencia and Alicante in the hopes of persuading those cities to support the government. He continued to preside over the Cortes until February 1939, when Generalissimo Francisco Franco's forces were victorious. He went into exile in France. Martínez Barrio was named president of the republic in-exile in August 1945 and remained a leading critic of the Franco regime. He died suddenly in Paris on January 1, 1962.

MANUEL AZAÑA Y DIAZ
(President; May 11, 1936–February 5, 1939). Manuel Azaña y Diaz was born in Alcalá de los Henares, in Castile, on January 10, 1880. He was educated at the Colegio Maria Cristina in Escorial and in Paris, where he studied law. He became a prominent journalist and playwright and served as general secretary of the Madrid Atenco, a literary society, from 1913 to 1920. Azaña was a member of the revolutionary committee that established the Spanish republic in 1931. He served in Niceto Alcalá Zamora's government as minister of war and conducted a purge of the army. He succeeded Alcalá Zamora as prime minister when the latter resigned on October 14, 1931. His government implemented constitutional reforms, suppressed the Jesuit religious order, and seized church property for distribution to the poor. Azaña resigned on September 8, 1933. He was arrested in October 1934 for his support of the uprising by Socialists and Catalans. He was acquitted of the charges and was elected to the Cortes. He replaced Alcalá Zamora as president of the republic on May 10, 1936. Several months later, Generalissimo Francisco Franco began a military uprising against the republic. Azaña's government fled Madrid in November 1936 as Franco's army advanced. The government went to Barcelona, but as the Republican forces continued to be pushed back, Azaña fled to Paris. He lived in the Spanish embassy where he conducted a government-in-exile. He resigned on February 5, 1939, when France and Great Britain recognized Franco's government. Azaña died in Montauban, Southern France, on November 4, 1940.

MIGUEL CABANELLAS Y FER-RER (President; July 24, 1936–October 1, 1936). Miguel Cabanellas y Ferrer was born in Cartagena on January 1, 1862. He attended the General Military Academy and served in the cavalry in Cuba and Morocco after his graduation in 1889. He was an opponent of the dictatorship of General Miguel Primo de Rivera and, following Primo de Rivera's ouster, Cabanellas was named military commander of Morocco in 1931. He was appointed director-general of the Civil Guard the following year. He was elected to the Cortes in 1933 as a deputy from Jaen. He also headed the Fifth Division in Saragossa, and under pressure he joined the military rebellion against the Popular Front government in 1936. He was distrusted by his fellow officers, who suspected him of Republican sentiments. He became head of the ruling military junta on July 24, 1936. He was replaced as head of the junta by Generalissimo Francisco Franco on October 1, 1936. He had little influence in Franco's government but was given the honorary title of inspector general of the army. Cabanellas died in Malaga of natural causes on May 14, 1938.

FRANCISCO FRANCO Y BAHA-MONDE (President; October 1, 1936–October 30, 1975). Francisco Paulino Hermenegildo Teodulo Franco y Bahamonde was born in El Ferrol, Galicia, on December 4, 1892. He graduated from the military academy in Toledo in 1910. He entered the Spanish military and was stationed in Morocco the following year. Franco was wounded in action in 1916 and returned to Spain for three years. He was then assigned to the Spanish foreign legion in Morocco and served as deputy commander from 1920 until 1923, when he was promoted to commander of the legion with the rank of lieutenant colonel. He was active in the military campaign against Abd-el-Krim, the leader of the Rifs. Franco departed Morocco in 1926 with the rank of brigadier

general. He subsequently returned to Spain as the director of the military academy at Saragossa. The academy was abolished with the advent of the Spanish republic and the ouster of the monarchy in 1931. Franco was sent to the Baleric Islands, where he remained until 1934, when the government recalled him to put down a miners strike. His ruthlessness in dealing with the revolt earned him the nickname "the Butcher." He made contact with other military commanders opposed to the republican government before he was sent into virtual exile in the Canary Islands. Franco returned to Spain to attend the funeral of José Calvo Sotelo, an assassinated rightist leader, in July 1936. He then joined with a military revolt that the assassination had precipitated and took command of rebel troops in North Africa. He assumed control of all the rebel forces following the death of General José Sanjurjo in a plane crash in July 1936. Franco was proclaimed generalissimo of the army and leader of the nationalist government in October 1936. The bloody civil war raged on for the next three years, with Italy and Germany supporting the nationalist cause and the Soviet Union backing the republican government. Franco led the assault that captured Barcelona in January 1938, and the war ended with the fall of Madrid in March 1939. Franco was officially recognized as head of the ruling military junta on October 1, 1936, and became president of Spain on August 9, 1939. He was initially supportive of the Axis Powers during World War II but backed away from his earlier endorsement of Hitler and Mussolini as the Allies advanced through Europe and proclaimed Spanish neutrality. After the conclusion of the war, Franco's Spain was viewed with distrust and hostility by the victorious Allies. Spain was refused membership in the United Nations, and many Western nations, including the United States, withdrew their diplomatic representatives from Madrid. Franco began a quest to restore respectability abroad for his regime. Western governments restored diplomatic relations in late 1950, largely as a result of the Cold War. The United States approved a large loan to Spain in 1950 and was granted the use of Spanish air and naval bases in an agreement signed in September 1953. Spain was admitted to the United Nations in 1955. Franco continued to rule Spain in an authoritarian manner that was often criticized at home and abroad. Spain prospered economically during the 1950s and 1960s, and Franco allowed some liberal reforms to be carried out. His government was faced with a revolt from a militant nationalist organization that demanded autonomy for the Basque region of Spain. Student groups and labor unions also became active in the movement to grant the Spanish people greater freedom. Franco continued to hold on firmly to power, and in his later years gave serious consideration to his succes-

sor. In July 1969 he announced his decision to restore the monarchy and named Prince Juan Carlos de Bourbon, the grandson of Spain's last king, Alfonso XIII, as heir. Despite the assassination by Basque separatists of his premier, Admiral Luis Carrero Blanco, in a bombing on December 20, 1973, Franco continued to liberalize Spain's political system. He became seriously ill in July 1974 when he suffered from a severe hemorrhage. Franco allowed Prince Juan Carlos to take the powers of government until he had sufficiently recovered in September 1974. Franco's health again failed on October 21, 1975, when he was stricken by severe heart disease. His health continued to deteriorate from various ailments, and Prince Juan Carlos again became acting chief of state on October 30, 1975. Franco succumbed to his illnesses at La Paz Hospital in Madrid on November 20, 1975.

HEADS OF GOVERNMENT

FRANCISCO SILVELA (Prime Minister; March 5, 1899–October 23, 1900). Francisco Silvela y Le Vielleuze was born in Madrid on December 15, 1843. He was elected to the constituent assembly as a conservative in 1868. He served a leading role in Antonio Cánovas del Castillo's Conservative government in 1874. He subsequently broke with Canovas during the regency of Queen Maria Cristina. Cánovas was forced to step down in 1892 when Silvela's group split from the party. Canovas returned to power with a majority in 1895, but was assassinated two years later. Silvela was selected to serve as prime minister on March 5, 1899, after Spain's unsuccessful war against the United States. He implemented severe financial measures to improve Spain's economic position. The unpopularity of these measures led to his resignation on October 23, 1900. He re-

turned to head the government on December 6, 1902. His term was short-lived, and Silvela stepped down and retired from politics on July 20, 1903. He died on May 29, 1905.

MARCELO DE AZCÁRRAGA (Prime Minister; October 23, 1900–February 25, 1901). Marcelo de Azcárraga y Palmero was born in Manila, the Philippines, on September 4, 1832. He entered the military as a second lieutenant in the Spanish Cavalry in 1850. He was promoted to lieutenant in 1854 and captain in 1856. The following year he was sent to Cuba with the rank of commandant. He served in Mexico as chief of staff of the Spanish expeditionary forces in 1861. In Spain de Azcarraga held the position of assistant secretary of state on several occasions during the reign of King Alfonso XII. He was promoted to lieutenant general in 1877. He was instrumental in quashing a Carlist insurrection in Valencia in 1887. He was named to Antonio Cánovas' cabinet as minister of war in 1890 and served until 1892. He again held that position when Cánovas returned to power in 1895. He briefly headed the government from August 8, 1897, until September 29, 1897, following the assassination of Cánovas. He remained a leading military and political figure in Spain. He served as minister of war in Francisco Silvela's cabinet from 1899 until he replaced Silvela as prime minister on October 23, 1900. He stepped down as head of the government on February 25, 1901. De Azcárraga died in Madrid on May 30, 1915.

PRÁXADES MATEO SAGASTA

(Prime Minister; February 26, 1901–December 6, 1902). Práxades Mateo Sagasta was born in Torrecilla de Cameros, in Old Castile, in 1827. He attended the Government College in Madrid, where he studied civil engineering. He worked as an engineer of roads and bridges in Zamora before his election to the Cortes in 1854 as a member of the Progressive Party. He opposed the coup of Don Leopold O'Donnell in 1856 and briefly went into exile. He was defeated for reelection to the Cortes upon his return. He then moved to Madrid where he worked as a journalist. Sagasta returned to the Cortes but again went into exile in France for his part in a revolt against O'Donnell in 1866. He returned to Spain in 1868 and was a leader of the rebellion against Queen Isabella that resulted in her ouster. He served in the subsequent government as minister of the interior during the reign of Amadeo. He remained out of the government for several years before the coup of 1874, when he again served in the cabinet. After the restoration of the monarchy under King Alfonso XII in December 1874, Sagasta became leader of the liberal opposition. He served several terms as prime minister, governing from February 8, 1881

until 1883, from 1885 until July 5, 1890, and from December 11, 1892 until March 23, 1895. Spain was often beset with civil disorder from labor strikes and riots during his terms of office. Despite his liberal leanings, he was unable to implement any meaningful reforms. His leading rival during most of this period was the leader of the Conservative Party, Antonio Cánovas del Castillo, who was assassinated by an anarchist on August 8, 1897. Sagasta returned to office on October 4, 1897, and led the government during the disastrous Spanish-American War. He stepped down on March 1, 1899. He again served as prime minister from February 26, 1901, until December 6, 1902. Sagasta died the following year in Madrid on January 5, 1903.

FRANCISCO SILVELA

(Prime Minister; December 6, 1902–July 20, 1903). *See earlier entry under Heads of Government.*

RAIMUNDO FERNÁNDEZ VILLAVERDE

(Prime Minister; July 20, 1903–December 4, 1903). Raimundo Fernández Villaverde was born in Palma on January 20, 1848. He was a leading member of the Conservative Party and served in Francisco Silvela's cabinet as minister of finance in 1899 and 1900. He instituted severe austerity measures, reformed the tax system, and reduced spending after Spain's war with the United States. Villaverde succeeded Silvela as prime minister on July 20, 1903, serving until December 4, 1903. He again headed the government from January 27, 1905, to June 23, 1905. He died on July 15, 1905.

ANTONIO MAURA

(Prime Minister; December 4, 1903–December 14, 1904). Antonio Maura y Montaner was born in Palma on May 2, 1853. He studied law at Madrid University, and subsequently began a law practice. He was elected to the Cortes from Palma in 1881 as a member of the Liberal Party. He served as minister of the colonies from 1892 until 1894 and was briefly minister of justice in 1895. He abandoned the Liberals to become leader of the Monarchist Conservative Party in 1901. He served in Francisco Silvela's government as minister of the interior from December 1902 until October 1903. He was called upon to serve as prime minister on December 4, 1903, heading the government until December 14, 1904. He again became prime minister on January 25, 1907. He instituted a program of political, economic, and educational reforms known as "revolution from above." Spain's war against Rif tribesmen in Morocco inspired an uprising by Socialists in Barcelona in 1909. Maura brutally crushed the revolt but was forced to step down from office on October 20, 1909. He survived an assassination attempt in 1910, when he was shot by radical Manuel Posada. He resigned from the leadership of the Conservative Party in 1913. Maura favored Germany and the Central Powers during World War I. He was called upon to form a coalition government on March 22, 1918, serving until November 6, 1918. He again became prime minister after the collapse of Count de Romanones's government on April 14, 1919. He stepped down two months later, on July 20, 1919. Maura returned to head the government on August 14, 1921, after the military disaster at Anual in Morocco. The Moroccan crisis brought the military into conflict with the government, and Maura was forced to step down on March 8, 1922. Maura opposed Miguel Primo de Rivera's military coup in 1923. He died suddenly at his son's estate in Torrelodones, near Madrid, on December 14, 1925.

MARCELO DE AZCÁRRAGA (Prime Minister; December 15, 1904–January 26, 1905). *See earlier entry under Heads of Government.*

RAIMUNDO FERNÁNDEZ VILLAVERDE (Prime Minister; January 27, 1905–June 23, 1905). *See earlier entry under Heads of Government.*

EUGENIO MONTERO RÍOS (Prime Minister; June 23, 1905–December 1, 1905). Eugenio Montero Ríos was born in Santiago de Compostela on November 13, 1832. He was a leading Spanish legal scholar and political figure. He was first elected to the Chamber of Deputies in 1869. He often served in the ministry of justice, first as undersecretary and later as minister. He served as president of the Spanish Supreme Court in 1888. Montero Ríos was called upon to head the Spanish delegation to the peace commission in Paris that negotiated a settlement to the Spanish-American War in 1898. The treaty provided for the independence of Cuba and Spain's leading of the Philippines to the United States. Montero Ríos remained a leading figure in the government and was responsible for the drafting of the Spanish criminal code. He headed the government as prime minister from June 23, 1905, until December 1. 1905. He continued to serve in the Spanish parliament and subsequent governments until his death in Madrid on May 12, 1914.

SEGUSMUNDO MORET Y PRENDERGAST (Prime Minister; December 1, 1905–July 6, 1906). Segusmundo Moret y Prendergast was born in Cadiz on July 2, 1838. He was elected to the Cortes as a Liberal in 1863. He was also known as a leading economist and served in the cabinet as minister of the interior and minister of finance in 1870 and 1871. He subsequently served as Spain's ambassador to London. He returned to the Cortes in 1879 and was named foreign minister in 1885. He again became minister of the interior later in the year, and served until 1888. He held various other cabinet positions and was again foreign minister in 1893 and 1894. Moret was also leader of the Liberal Party and was called upon to head the government as prime minister on December 1, 1905. He stepped down as prime minister on July 6, 1906. He again briefly headed the government for several days from November 30, 1906, until December 4, 1906. Moret, as leader of the opposition, attacked the Conservative government of Antonio Maura for its harsh repression of the uprising in Barcelona in July 1909 and the subsequent execution of anarchist theorist Francisco Ferrer. Maura's government stepped down, and Moret headed a new cabinet in October 20, 1909. He was forced to step down due to dissension in his cabinet on February 8, 1910, and was replaced by another Liberal government headed by José Canalejas y Mendes. Moret died on January 28, 1913.

JOSÉ LÓPEZ DOMÍNGUEZ (Prime Minister; July 6, 1906–November 27, 1906). José López Domínguez was born in Marbella on November 29, 1829. López Domínguez joined the Spanish army at an early age and fought in the revolution in 1854. He subsequently served as a Spanish military attaché in the Crimean and Franco-Italian Wars. He was active in the conflict in Morocco in 1859 and fought with the military revolt in 1867. He led the forces that captured Cartagena and put down the Federalist insurrection in January 1874. He entered politics after the restoration of the monarchy in 1874 and was a founder of the Party of the Dynastic Left in 1883. López Domínguez rose to the rank of captain-general in 1895. He was called upon to head the government as prime minister on July 6, 1906. His anticlerical policies divided the Liberal Party, and he stepped down from office on November 27, 1906. López Domínguez died on October 17, 1911.

SEGUSMUNDO MORET Y PRENDERGAST (Prime Minister; November 30, 1906–December 4, 1906). *See earlier entry under Heads of Government.*

MARQUIS VEGA DE ARMIJO (Prime Minister; December 4, 1906–January 24, 1907). Antonio Aguilar y Correa, Marquis de la Vega de Armijo was born in Madrid on June 30, 1824. He was called upon by King Alfonso XIII to form a government on December 4, 1906, when Segusmundo Moret was forced to resign over divisions in the Liberal Party. Vega's government was faced with numerous crises, notably legislation that would govern religious associations. Threats of demonstrations by clerical and anticlerical groups and divisions on the issue within the Liberal Party itself forced Vega's resignation on January 24, 1907. He died on June 13, 1908.

ANTONIO MAURA (Prime Minister; January 25, 1907–October 20, 1909). *See earlier entry under Heads of Government.*

SEGUSMUNDO MORET Y PRENDERGAST (Prime Minister; October 20, 1909–February 8, 1910). *See earlier entry under Heads of Government.*

JOSÉ CANALEJAS Y MÉNDES (Prime Minister; February 8, 1910–November 12, 1912). José Canalejas y Méndes was born to a wealthy family in El Ferrol on July 31, 1854. He graduated from the Madrid University in 1872. He subsequently worked as a university professor and lawyer. He entered politics in 1881 and was elected to the Cortes from Soria. Two years later he was named to the prime minister's cabinet as an undersecretary. He joined the cabinet as minister of public works and justice in 1888 and served as minister of finance in 1894. He stepped down from Praxades Mateo Sagasta's cabinet in 1902, feeling the government was not going far enough in settling the question of religious orders. He served as president of the Chamber of Deputies in 1906. Canalejas, a leftist member of the Liberal Party, succeeded Segismundo Moret as prime minister on February 8, 1910.

His administration instituted a number of reforms that gave Protestants greater religious liberties. His policies caused problems between Spain and the Vatican, resulting in a break in diplomatic relations for several years. Canalejas was successful in reducing tensions in Morocco by negotiating a treaty with France in 1912 that further reduced Spanish territory in North Africa. His government was faced with a railway strike in mid-1912. He responded by compelling the workers to return to their jobs by conscripting them into the military. He also attempted to decentralize the Spanish government to give more power to the provinces. Canalejas was shot to death by Manuel Pardinas, a young anarchist, while entering the ministry of the interior for a conference on November 12, 1912.

COUNT DE ROMANONES (Prime Minister; November 12, 1912–November 15, 1912). Álvaro de Figueroa y Torres, Count de Romanones, was born in Madrid on August 1, 1863. He studied law at the University of Madrid. He entered politics as a member of the Liberal Party and became president of the Chamber of Deputies in 1911. He was named prime minister on November 12, 1912, following the assassination of José Canalejas. His ministry lasted three days, and he was replaced by the Marquis de Alhucemas on November 15, 1912. As the leader of the opposition, he supported the government's policy of neutrality at the outbreak of World War I in 1914, and maintained the policy after again becoming prime minister on December 9, 1915. Count Romanones's government fell on April 19, 1917, and he subsequently resigned from the Liberal Party. He served as minister of justice in Antonio Maura's coalition cabinet in March 1918. He became foreign minister the following November and again formed a government as prime minister on December 5, 1918. He was ousted by a military junta on April 14, 1919. He

served as speaker of the senate during the dictatorship of Miguel Primo de Rivera from 1923 until 1930. Following Primo de Rivera's ouster, he became minister of state in 1931. He opposed the abdication of King Alfonso XIII and was arrested by the republicans following the start of the Spanish Civil War in 1936. He was allowed to go into exile in France. He returned to Spain after the victory of Francisco Franco's nationalist forces but remained politically inactive. He died in Madrid on September 11, 1950.

MANUEL GARCÍA PRIETO, MARQUIS DE ALHUCEMAS (Prime Minister; November 15, 1912–October 27, 1913). Manuel García Prieto was born in Astorga, Leon Province, on November 5, 1859. He entered politics and was elected to the Cortes in 1887. He held various government positions before being named to the cabinet as minister of the interior in 1905. He became minister of justice the following year. Prieto assumed the title of Marquis of Alhucemas. He served as minister of state in 1912 at the time of Prime Minister José Canalejas' assassination. He became prime minister on November 15, 1912, serving until October 27, 1913. He subsequently left the Liberal Party to form the Democratic Party. He again headed the government from April 19, 1917, until June 11, 1917, and from November 3, 1917, until March 22, 1918, during World War I. He again briefly served as prime minister from November 9, 1918, until December 4, 1918. He returned to head the government on December 5, 1922. His government was ousted by the military coup that installed Miguel Primo de Rivera as dictator on September 15, 1923. Prieto returned to the government in February 1931 as minister of justice. The monarchy was abolished later in the year, and the Marquis retired from politics to practice law. He died in San Sebastian on September 15, 1938.

EDUARDO DATO Y IRADIER (Prime Minister; October 27, 1913–December 6, 1915). Eduardo Dato y Iradier was born in Corunna on August 12, 1856. He studied law before entering politics. Dato became secretary of state for the interior in 1892 and was named to the cabinet as minister of the interior in 1899. During his ministry he instituted labor reforms. He returned to the cabinet as minister of justice in 1903. Dato was elected mayor of Madrid in 1907 and also served as speaker of the House of Representatives. He was a member of the moderate wing of the Conservative Party. Dato replaced Antonio Maura as leader of the party in 1913. He was named to head the government as prime minister on October 27, 1913. Despite his sympathies for the Allied cause, Dato maintained Spain's neutrality in the early days of World War I. He stepped down from office on December 6, 1915. He again briefly headed the government from June 9, 1917, until October 27, 1917, when Spain was beset by labor strikes and civil unrest. He used harsh measures to suppress the workers' movement. Dato served as secretary of state for foreign affairs in 1918. He returned to head the government on May 5, 1920, and attempted to bridge the rift in the Conservative Party. Dato continued to serve as prime minister until he was shot to death by two anarchists while driving near his home in Madrid on March 8, 1921.

COUNT DE ROMANONES (Prime Minister; December 9, 1915–April 19, 1917). *See earlier entry under Heads of Government.*

MANUEL GARCÍA PRIETO, MARQUIS DE ALHUCEMAS (Prime Minister; April 19, 1917–June 9, 1917). *See earlier entry under Heads of Government.*

EDUARDO DATO Y IRADIER (Prime Minister; June 9, 1917–October 27, 1917). *See earlier entry under Heads of Government.*

MANUEL GARCÍA PRIETO, MARQUIS DE ALHUCEMAS (Prime Minister; November 3, 1917–March 22, 1918). *See earlier entry under Heads of Government.*

ANTONIO MAURA (Prime Minister; March 22, 1918–November 6, 1918). *See earlier entry under Heads of Government.*

MANUEL GARCÍA PRIETO, MARQUIS DE ALHUCEMAS (Prime Minister; November 9, 1918–December 5, 1918). *See earlier entry under Heads of Government.*

COUNT DE ROMANONES (Prime Minister; December 5, 1918–April 14, 1919). *See earlier entry under Heads of Government.*

ANTONIO MAURA (Prime Minister; April 14, 1919–July 20, 1919). *See earlier entry under Heads of Government.*

JOAQUIN SÁNCHEZ DE TOCA (Prime Minister; July 20, 1919–December 12, 1919). Joaquin Sánchez de Toca was born in Madrid on September 24, 1852. He was a prominent political figure in Spain, serving as minister of justice before becoming president of the cortez in 1915. He was called upon to form a government in October 1917, but was unsuccessful. He subsequently served as a confidential advisor to King Alfonso XIII. Toca was named prime minister on July 20, 1919, following the resignation of Antonio Maura. His government was short-lived, and he stepped down on December 12, 1919. Toca died on July 13, 1942.

MANUEL ALLENDÉ SALAZAR (Prime Minister; December 12, 1919–April 30, 1920). Manuel Allendé Salazar was born in 1856. He was educated as an agricultural engineer. Allendé Salazar became mayor of Madrid in the late 1890s and was named to the cabinet as minister of finance in 1901. The following year he became minister of education and served as minister of agriculture in 1904. Allendé Salazar served as foreign minister from 1907 until 1909. He led a Conservative government as prime minister from December 12, 1919, until April 30, 1920. He returned to head the government on March 13, 1921, following the assassination of Eduardo Dato. He stepped down several months later on August 14, 1921, when Liberals in the Cortes attacked the government's handling of the deteriorating situation in Morocco. Allendé Salazar died on March 13, 1923.

EDUARDO DATO Y IRADIER (Prime Minister; May 5, 1920–March 8, 1921). *See earlier entry under Heads of Government.*

GABINO BUGALLAL ARAUGO (Acting Prime Minister; March 8, 1921–March 13, 1921). Count Gabino Bugallal Araugo was a leading Spanish political figure and served in numerous governments from 1913 on, holding the ministries of finance, justice, and interior. He also served as speaker of the Chamber of Deputies. Bugallal briefly served as acting premier from March 8, 1921, until March 13, 1921, following the assassination of Prime Minister Eduardo Dato. Bugallal became president of the Rightist Conservatives in 1930. He was a critic of the dictatorship of Miguel Primo de Rivera. He returned to the government as minister of the economy in Juan Bautista Aznar's cabinet, which resigned following the abdication of King Alfonso XIII in April 1931. Bulgallal died in Paris on May 31, 1932.

MANUEL ALLENDÉ SALAZAR (Prime Minister; March 13, 1921–August 14, 1921). *See earlier entry under Heads of Government.*

ANTONIO MAURA (Prime Minister; August 14, 1921–March 8, 1922). *See earlier entry under Heads of Government.*

JOSÉ SÁNCHEZ GUERRA (Prime Minister; March 8, 1922–December 5, 1922). José Sánchez Guerra y Martínez was born in Cordova on June 30, 1859. He studied law at the University of Madrid. He subsequently worked as a journalist before his election to the Chamber of Deputies in 1886. He was appointed governor of Madrid in 1902. He served in Antonio Maura's cabinets as minister of the interior in 1903 and as minister of public works in 1908 and 1909. He was again minister of the interior in Eduardo Dato's cabinets from 1913 until 1915 and again in 1917. He was elected speaker of the Chamber of Deputies in 1919. Sanchez Guerra became leader of the Conservative Party after the assassination of Dato in 1921. He formed a government on March 8, 1922. He attempted to quell the growing strength of the military juntas. He was forced from office by Miguel Primo de Rivera on December 5, 1922. He went into exile in Paris where he remained an outspoken opponent of Primo de Rivera. He returned to Spain in January 1929 to lead an unsuccessful rebellion against the dictator. He was arrested and imprisoned but was later acquitted of charges. Primo de Rivera's dictatorship fell in January 1930. Guerra left the Conservative Party to join the Constitutionalists. He advocated a revision of the constitution and pressed for King Alfonso to renounce his legal prerogatives. Guerra was asked to form a coalition cabinet in February 1931, but was unable to succeed. The revolution ousted the monarch several months later. Guerra was reelected to the Chamber of Deputies in July 1931. He died in Madrid on January 26, 1935.

MANUEL GARCÍA PRIETO, MARQUIS DE ALHUCEMAS (Prime Minister; December 5, 1922–

September 13, 1923). *See earlier entry under Heads of Government.*

MIGUEL PRIMO DE RIVERA
(Prime Minister; September 15, 1923–January 28, 1930). Miguel Primo de Rivera y Oraneja was born in Jerez de la Frontera on January 8, 1870. He attended the General Military Academy in Madrid and saw action in Cuba, Morocco, and the Philippines from 1893 until 1898. He was promoted to colonel in 1908 and was named military governor of Cadiz in 1915. He was forced to resign two years later. Primo de Rivera was promoted to lieutenant general in 1919 and served as captain general of Valencia. He was sent to Barcelona in 1922 to bring stability to Catalonia. Spain's government was in disarray in the early 1920s, and the monarchy was in jeopardy following a military disaster in Morocco. Primo de Rivera, who had inherited the title Marques de Estella from his uncle, staged a military coup on September 13, 1923, and suspended the constitution. He established a provisional military directorate with himself as leader with the support of King Alfonso XIII. Martial law was officially lifted in May 1925, and Primo de Rivera continued to head the government as prime minister. Primo de Rivera brought political and economic stability to Spain under his rule. Spain regained its prestige in North Africa with a successful military attack on Moroccan Rif leader Abd-el-Krim in 1925. The Spanish zone of Morocco was pacified over the next two years. The dictatorship survived a military rebellion in June 1926 as well as several other uprisings during that year. Civil discontent against Primo de Rivera's rule intensified in 1929, and the dictator's relationship with the king became strained. When the army indicated that it no longer supported the dictatorship, Primo de Rivera resigned on January 28, 1930, and retired to France. He died suddenly of an embolism brought on by a diabetic condition in his Paris hotel room on March 16, 1930.

DÁMASO BERENGUER
(Prime Minister; January 28, 1930–February 14, 1931). Dámaso Berenguer y Fusté was born in Cuba on August 4, 1873. He was educated at a military school for orphans in Spain. He and his two brothers all advanced through the ranks of the army to become generals. Berenguer served as Spain's high commissioner in Spanish Morocco in the early 1920s. He was named by King Alfonso XIII to head the king's military household in 1926. Berenguer was called upon to head the government after the resignation of General Miguel Primo de Rivera on January 28, 1930. The new government tried to reestablish constitutional rule after six years of Primo de Rivera's dictatorship. The government faced numerous strikes and civil unrest as the economy suffered. There were increased calls for the removal of the monarchy and the establishment of a republic. Berenguer's government resigned on February 14, 1931, and he was replaced by Admiral Juan Bautista Aznar. Berenguer remained in the cabinet as minister of war. Three months later Alfonso was forced to vacate the throne, and the Spanish republic was proclaimed. Berenguer was arrested soon after on charges of having ordered the execution of leaders of an unsuccessful republican revolt in Jaca in 1930. He was defended by General Francisco Franco and was absolved by the Supreme Court in 1935. Berenguer died on May 19, 1953.

JUAN BAUTISTA AZNAR
(Prime Minister; February 18, 1931–April 14, 1931). Juan Bautista Aznar-Cabañas was born in 1860. He was an admiral in the Spanish navy when he was chosen by King Alfonso XIII to head the government on February 18, 1931. The monarchy was under siege by republican sentiments and Alfonso was forced to leave the country on April 14, 1931. Aznar relinquished power to the provisional government under Niceto Alcalá Zamora. He died on May 19, 1933.

NICETO ALCALÁ ZAMORA Y TORRES (Prime Minister; April 14, 1931–October 14, 1931). *See earlier entry under Heads of State.*

MANUEL AZAÑA Y DIAZ (Prime Minister; October 14, 1931–September 8, 1933). *See earlier entry under Heads of State.*

ALEJANDRO LERROUX Y GARCÍA (Prime Minister; September 12, 1933–October 3, 1933). Alejandro Lerroux y García was born in Posadas, Cordova Province, on February 26, 1866. He began working as a journalist at the Madrid newspaper *El Pais* in 1885. He later became a successful businessman before studying law and entering politics. He was elected to the Cortes in 1919, retaining office until the dictatorship of Miguel Primo de Rivera abolished the elected government. He went underground during Primo de Rivera's rule, escaping to France. He returned to Spain after the removal of the dictatorship and became a leading voice for the abolishment of the monarchy. The Spanish Republic was established in April 1931. Lerroux became prime minister on September 12, 1933, but was forced to step down on October 3, 1933. He again became prime minister on March 3, 1934. Lerroux re-formed his government on March 3, 1934, and served until April 25, 1934. He was renamed to head the government on October 4, 1934. He re-formed the government on April 3, 1935 and again on May 7, 1935. He relinquished office to Joaquín Chapaprieta on October 20, 1935. He served as foreign minister in Chapaprieta's government in 1935. Lerroux went into exile in Portugal when the Spanish Civil War broke out the following year. He spent the next eleven years in exile until Generalissimo Francisco Franco allowed him to return to Spain in 1947. He died in Madrid on June 27, 1949.

DIEGO MARTÍNEZ BARRIO (Prime Minister; October 9, 1933–December 16, 1933). *See earlier entry under Heads of State.*

ALEJANDRO LERROUX Y GARCÍA (Prime Minister; December 16, 1933–April 25, 1934). *See earlier entry under Heads of Government.*

RICARDO SAMPER IBAÑEZ (Prime Minister; April 28, 1934–October 1, 1934). Ricardo Samper Ibañez was born on August 25, 1881. He served in Alejandro Lerroux's government and succeeded Lerroux as prime minister on April 28, 1934. He stepped down on October 1, 1934, and Lerroux resumed power. Samper supported the Republic during the Spanish Civil War. He attempted to go into exile in France in August 1936 but was arrested when he tried to board a French steamer in Valencia. He was imprisoned by the opponents of the republic and died in 1938.

ALEJANDRO LERROUX Y GARCÍA (Prime Minister; October 4, 1934–October 20, 1935). *See earlier entry under Heads of Government.*

JOAQUÍN CHAPAPRIETA Y TERRAGOSA (Prime Minister; October 25, 1935–December 9, 1935). Joaquín Chapaprieta y Terragosa was born on October 26, 1871. He was a leading Spanish financier who became finance minister in Alejandro Lerroux's government in 1934. A political independent, he succeeded Lerroux as prime minister on October 25, 1935. His government fell on December 9, 1935, because of a conflict over the budget. He continued to serve in Manuel Portela Valladares' cabinet as minister of finance until 1936. Chapaprieta died in Madrid on October 15, 1951.

MANUEL PORTELA VAL-LADARES (Prime Minister; December 31, 1935–February 19, 1936). Manuel Portela Valladares was born in 1868. He was a leading historian and served as governor of Barcelona in the early 1920s. He was named to the cabinet in 1923, and remained a leading political figure throughout the next decade. He was the leader of the Centre Party and became prime minister on December 31, 1935. He presided over the elections that resulted in a victory for the Popular Front. Portela Valladares stepped down on February 19, 1936, when Manuel Azaña assumed office. He went into exile during the Spanish Civil War. He died in exile in Bandol, France, on May 2, 1958.

MANUEL AZAÑA Y DIAZ (Prime Minister; February 19, 1936–May 11, 1936). *See earlier entry under Heads of State.*

SANTIAGO CASARES QUIROGA (Prime Minister; May 13, 1936–July 19, 1936). Santiago Casares Quiroga was born in La Coruña in 1884. He was a member of the Galician Autonomy Party. He entered Niceto Alcalá Zamora's first republican government as minister of the marine in 1931. He was called to head a leftist cabinet on May 12, 1936. He attempted to urge Socialists and Communists to exercise moderation following their electoral victory. He was unsuccessful in his attempt, and Generalissimo Francisco Franco began a military rebellion on July 19, 1936. Casares resigned from the government. He went into exile in Paris as Franco's nationalist forces took control of the country during the subsequent civil war. He escaped to London at the time of the German occupation during World War II. He returned to Paris after the liberation. His daughter, Maria Casares, became a leading stage and screen star in France. Casares died in Paris on February 17, 1950.

DIEGO MARTÍNEZ BARRIO (Prime Minister; July 19, 1936). *See earlier entry under Heads of State.*

JOSÉ GIRAL Y PEREYRA (Prime Minister; July 19, 1936–September 4, 1936). José Giral y Pereyra was born in Santiago de Cuba on October 22, 1879. He was a chemistry professor before entering politics as a member of the Republican Left. He was a close ally of President Manuel Azaña and served in the government as minister of the navy from 1931 until 1933 and again in 1936. After the start of the nationalist uprising, Giral was called upon to form a government on July 19, 1936. His government supplied arms to the workers in Madrid to form a militia to fight the nationalists. He attempted without success to secure aid from the French in the conflict. Giral was thought too moderate by the Socialists, and he was replaced by Francisco Largo Caballero on September 4, 1936. He served in the cabinet as minister without portfolio, but exercised little power in the government. He was named foreign minister in Juan Negrín's government in May 1937. He attempted to gain support for the republicans from the Soviet Union and other countries opposed to the nationalists. As it became increasingly apparent that the government forces were losing the war, Giral was instrumental in securing safe passage into exile for republican refugees. He continued to serve in the government until he himself was forced to flee into exile in late March 1939. He subsequently headed the Spanish republican government-in-exile until he resigned the position in January 1947. Giral died in Mexico City on December 23, 1962.

FRANCISCO LARGO CABALLERO (Prime Minister; September 4, 1936–May 15, 1937). Francisco Largo Caballero was born in Madrid on October 15, 1869. He worked as a stonemason and was active in the trade union movement at an early age. He joined the Socialist Party in 1894. Largo Caballero was the founder and president of the Union General de Trabajadores, which served as his political base. He was arrested for his part in the revolutionary general strike in August 1917. He was sentenced to life imprisonment, but his election to the Cortes the following year effected his release. He was instrumental in the movement that forced the abdication of King Alfonso XIII and established the republic in 1931. He became minister of labor and later headed the ministry of transportation. He became disillusioned with the republican government's inability to implement social reform and was a leader of the uprising by militant Socialists against the government in October 1934. He was arrested when the rebellion failed and spent over a year in prison before being tried and acquitted. Largo Caballero's refusal to allow the Socialists to collaborate with the republican government was a factor in the right-wing military uprising that started the Spanish Civil War in 1936. Electoral victories by the parties of the Left resulted in Largo Caballero being named prime minister on September 4, 1937. He also served as minister of war in a cabinet that included Communists and Anarch-Syndicalists. A leftist uprising in Barcelona in May 1937 resulted in the Communists leaving the coalition, and Largo Caballero was forced to resign on May 15, 1937. He fled into exile in France as Generalissimo Francisco Franco's nationalists took control of the country in 1939. He was arrested during the German occupation of France and spent much of World War II in Dachau concentration camp. He survived the war and returned to Paris after the liberation. Largo Caballero died in a Paris hospital after a brief illness on March 23, 1946.

JUAN NEGRIN LÓPEZ (Prime Minister; May 18, 1937–March 5, 1939). Juan Negrín López was born in the Canary Islands in 1889. He received a medical degree in Germany. He was a professor of physiology at the University of Madrid Medical School when the Spanish Civil War began in July 1936. Negrín was a moderate Socialist and was appointed to Francisco Largo Caballero's cabinet as minister of finance. Negrín became prime minister on May 18, 1937, following Largo Caballero's resignation. He also became minister of defense in April 1938. Nationalist forces under Generalissimo Francisco Franco advanced against the government over the next few years and President Manuel Azaña resigned and fled to France in February 1939. Negrín continued to lead the government against the rebels, relying heavily on Communists and the Soviet Union. Colonel Segismundo Casado, fearing a Communist coup, led a military rising against Negrín's government on March 5, 1939. Negrín fled into exile in France. He settled in London in 1940. He attempted to maintain a government-in-exile until his government officially resigned in Mexico City in 1945. He retired from politics to author his memoirs. He later returned to Paris, where he died on November 12, 1956.

JOSÉ MIAJA (Head of Government; March 5, 1939–March 29, 1939). José Miaja Menant was born in Asturias in 1878. He graduated from the Spanish Military Academy and served in the army in Spanish Morocco. He served with distinction and was promoted to the rank of colonel. He was one of the few military officers to support the establishment of the Spanish republic in 1931. He was promoted to the rank of general before the outbreak of the Civil War in 1936. He commanded the republican forces in Madrid and briefly served as minister of war. He was subsequently sent to Albaceto, and he captured that town from the rebels. He commanded forces in Valencia before returning to Madrid in November 1936. General Miaja headed the defense council during the siege of Madrid. He was acknowledged as military and civil leader of the republicans after the ouster of Juan Negrín's government on March 5, 1939. As food, fuel, and ammunition supplies dwindled, the defenders were forced to capitulate, and Generalissimo Francisco

Franco's forces marched into Madrid on March 28, 1939. Miaja fled into exile in Mexico. He died in Mexico City of a heart attack on January 13, 1958.

FRANCISCO FRANCO Y BAHA-MONDE (Prime Minister; April 1, 1939–June 9, 1973). *See earlier entry under Heads of State.*

Sweden

Sweden is a country on the eastern Scandinavian peninsula in northern Europe.

HEADS OF STATE

OSCAR II (King; September 18, 1872–December 8, 1907). Oscar Fredrik was born in Stockholm on January 21, 1829. He was the third son of Oscar I, Sweden's king from 1844 until 1859. Oscar was the duke of Ostergotland as a prince. He was educated at the University of Uppsala and entered the navy as a young man. He married Princess Sophia of Nassau in June 1857. Oscar succeeded to the throne of Sweden and Norway upon the death of his brother, King Karl XV, on September 18, 1872. As king, Oscar attempted to restore the influence of the monarchy. Sweden underwent an industrial revolution during his reign and prospered economically. The king supported the strengthening of the Swedish military in the 1890s. Growing tension between Sweden and Norway led to sentiments for a dissolution of the union between the two countries. Oscar attempted to maintain the union but declined to use military force when Norway dissolved the union in October 1905. Oscar abdicated from the throne of Norway officially on November 18, 1905. He died at the royal palace in Stockholm on December 8, 1907.

GUSTAV V ADOLF (King; December 8, 1907–October 29, 1950). Oscar Gustav Adolf was born in the royal palace of Drottningham, near Stockholm, on June 16, 1858. He was the son of Oscar II, who became king of Sweden in 1872. He was educated at the University of Uppsala in Sweden and served in the Swedish army. Gustav was made a general in the Swedish and Norwegian armies in 1898. He served as regent for his father while King Oscar was ill in the early 1900s. Norway voted to secede from Sweden in 1905. King Oscar died two years later on December 8, 1907, and his son succeeded to the throne as King Gustav V Adolf. The king was instrumental in maintaining Swedish neutrality during World War I. He also succeeded in keeping Sweden out of World War II when he allowed the German army to cross through the country in 1941. Gustav suffered from a chronic bronchial condition during the late 1940s. He died in Stockholm after a brief illness at the age of 92 on October 29, 1950.

HEADS OF GOVERNMENT

ERIK GUSTAV BOSTROM (Prime Minister; July 10, 1891–September 12, 1900). Erik Gustav Bostrom was born in Stockholm on February 11, 1842. He was educated at Uppsala University. He was elected to the Riksdag (parliament) in 1876. Bostrom was a founder of the New Ruralist Party in 1888. He became prime minister on July 10, 1891. Bostrom supported protectionist trade policies and worked toward strengthening the military. He stepped down on September 12, 1900, for reasons of health. Bostrom resumed office two years later, on July 5, 1902, and attempted to maintain the union of Sweden and Norway. He stepped down on April 13, 1905, when it became apparent that the union would be dissolved. He died in Stockholm on February 21, 1907.

FREDRIK WILHELM VON OTTER (Prime Minister; September 12, 1900–June 28, 1902). Fredrik Wilhelm von Otter was born on April 11, 1833. He headed the government as prime minister from September 12, 1900, until his government fell on June 28, 1902, over its inability to solve the issue of universal suffrage. Von Otter died on March 9, 1910.

ERIK GUSTAV BOSTROM (Prime Minister; July 5, 1902–April 13, 1905). *See earlier entry under Heads of Government.*

JOHAN OLOF RAMSTEDT (Prime Minister; April 13, 1905–August 2, 1905). Johan Olof Ramstedt was born in 1852. He was a Swedish civil servant. Ramstedt was chosen to head the government on April 13, 1905, after the resignation of Erik Bostrom. Norway unilaterally dissolved the union between Sweden and Norway on June 7, 1905. Ramstedt stepped down to allow the formation of a new government by Christ-ian Lundeberg on August 2, 1905. Ramstedt died in 1925.

CHRISTIAN LUNDEBERG (Prime Minister; August 2, 1905–October 20, 1905). Christian Lundeberg was born on July 14, 1842. He was a leader of the parties of the right in the upper chamber of the Riksdag. He was chosen to head the government on August 2, 1905, to formulate a response to Norway's dissolution of the union with Sweden. His government was mandated to present terms to Norway in regard to the dissolution. The agreement was accepted by Norway in October 1905, and a military conflict was avoided. Lundeberg stepped down on October 20, 1905. He died on November 10, 1911.

KARL ALBERT STAAF (Prime Minister; November 7, 1905–May 29, 1906). Karl Albert Staaf was born on January 21, 1860. He was a leader of the Liberal Party. He served in Christian Lundeberg's coalition cabinet in August 1905. He formed a Liberal cabinet on November 7, 1905, also serving as minister of justice. He resigned on May 29, 1906, when his government's plan for voting rights failed in the Riksdag. Staaf again became prime minister on October 7, 1911. His government resigned on February 10, 1914, over a dispute between King Gustav and the cabinet regarding the king's right to make political speeches without prior approval of the government. Staaf died in Stockholm on October 4, 1915.

ARVID A. LINDMAN (Prime Minister; May 29, 1906–September 30, 1911). Salomon Arvid Achates Lindman was born on September 19, 1862. He served in the navy from 1882 until 1892, when he began a business career. He was also elected to the provincial assembly in 1892. Lindman was elected to the upper chamber of the Riksdag in 1905. He served as minister of the navy under Christian Lundeberg from August until October 1905. Lindman formed a moderate Conservative government on May 29, 1906. His government was forced to resign on September 30, 1911, when his party was defeated in elections. He subsequently became leader of the Conservative Party in the lower chamber of the Riksdag. He served as foreign minister in Karl Swartz's government from March until October 1917. Lindman again formed a government as prime minister on October 2, 1928. He stepped down on June 2, 1930. He remained leader of the Conservative Party until his death in an airplane crash near London en route to Amsterdam on December 8, 1936.

KARL ALBERT STAAF (Prime Minister; October 7, 1911–February 10, 1914). *See earlier entry under Heads of Government.*

KNUT HJALMAR HAMMARSK-JOLD (Prime Minister; February 16, 1914–March 13, 1917). Knut Hjalmar Hammarskjold was born in Vaderum on February 4, 1862. He graduated from the University of Uppsala in 1880. He began teaching at the university in 1886. Hammarskjold served as minister of justice from 1901 until 1902 and was minister of education in 1905. He served as Sweden's ambassador to Denmark from 1905 until 1907. Hammarskjold formed a Conservative government as prime minister on February 16, 1914. He also served in the government as minister of war. He led Sweden during World War I, supporting a policy of neutrality. His government's insistence on building up the military for self-defense and an ongoing food shortage forced his government's resignation on March 13, 1917. He subsequently served as governor of Uppsala Province until his retirement in 1930. He was also a leading jurist and served as chief justice of the superior court, representing Sweden at the Permanent Court of In-

ternational Justice at The Hague. His son, Dag Hammarskjold, served as secretary general of the United Nations from 1953 until his death in an airplane crash in 1961. The elder Hammarskjold died in Stockholm after a long illness on October 23, 1953.

KARL JOHAN GUSTAV SWARTZ (Prime Minister; March 30, 1917–October 19, 1917). Karl Johan Gustav Swartz was born on June 9, 1858. He was named to head a moderate Conservative government on March 30, 1917. He stepped down on October 19, 1917, after elections were held. Swartz died on November 6, 1926.

NILS EDEN (Prime Minister; October 19, 1917–March 20, 1920). Nils Eden was born in Pitea on August 25, 1871. He received a doctorate of science from the University of Uppsala in 1899. He became a professor at the university in 1903. Eden was elected to the Riksdag in 1909. He was a leader of the Liberal Party, and he formed a coalition government with the Social Democrats on October 19, 1917. His government carried out a number of democratic reforms before he was replaced by Karl Branting on March 20, 1920. His party split in 1923, and he retired from the Riksdag the following year. Eden died in Stockholm on June 16, 1945.

KARL HJALMAR BRANTING (Prime Minister; March 20, 1920–September 1, 1920). Karl Hjalmar Branting was born in Stockholm on November 23, 1860. He was educated at the University of Uppsala, where he studied mathematics and astronomy. He was a founder of the Social Democratic Party in Sweden in 1889. He served as editor of the party's newspaper, *Social-Demokraten.* He was elected to the Riksdag in 1896. He was instrumental in ensuring that the dissolution of the union between Sweden and Norway was peaceful in 1905. He became leader of the Social Democrats in 1907. He briefly served as finance minister in 1917 and 1918. Branting was a strong proponent of Sweden's neutrality during World War I. He represented Sweden at the Paris Peace Conference and at the League of Nations. He became Sweden's first Socialist prime minister on March 20, 1920. He stepped down on September 1, 1920, following elections. He was the recipient of the Nobel Prize for Peace in 1921. Branting formed another government on October 13, 1921. He remained prime minister until April 19, 1923. He again headed the government from October 14, 1924, until poor health forced him to resign on January 24, 1925. He died in Stockholm on February 24, 1925.

LOUIS DE GEER (Prime Minister; September 2, 1920–February 23, 1921). Louis de Geer was born on November 27, 1854. He was the son of the eminent statesman Louis Gerhard de Geer, who was Sweden's prime minister from 1876 to 1880. The younger de Geer formed a nonparty cabinet on September 2, 1920. His government stepped down on February 23, 1921. He died on February 25, 1935.

OSKAR FREDRICK VON SYDOW (Prime Minister; February 23, 1921–October 13, 1921). Oskar Fredrick von Sydow was born on July 12, 1873. He was educated at Uppsala University. Von Sydow became governor of Thenberg in 1911. He served as minister of the interior in Knut Hammarskjold's government from 1914 to 1917. He headed a Liberal government from February 23, 1921, until October 13, 1921, when election results granted the Social Democrats a victory. He subsequently returned to the position of governor of Thenberg. He died in Stockholm on August 19, 1936.

KARL HJALMAR BRANTING (Prime Minister; October 13, 1921–April 19, 1923). *See earlier entry under Heads of Government.*

ERNST TRYGGER (Prime Minister; April 19, 1923–October 14, 1924). Ernst Trygger was born on October 20, 1857. He earned a doctorate of law at the University of Uppsala in 1885. He subsequently served as a professor at the university. Trygger was elected to the upper chamber of the Riksdag in 1897. He served in Sweden's supreme court from 1905 until 1907. He was a leader of the right wing of the Conservative Party. He served as prime minister from April 19, 1923, until October 14, 1924. Trygger was foreign minister in Arvid Lindman's government from 1928 until 1930. He remained in the Riksdag as leader of the Conservative opposition until 1937. He died in Stockholm on September 24, 1943.

KARL HJALMAR BRANTING (Prime Minister; October 14, 1924–January 24, 1925). *See earlier entry under Heads of Government.*

RICKARD JOHANNES SANDLER (Prime Minister; January 24, 1925–June 6, 1926). Rickard Johannes Sandler was born on January 29, 1884. He was a leader in the Social Democratic Party and served in Hjalmar Branting's government from 1921 until 1923. He became minister of finance in Branting's government in October 1924. He succeeded Branting as prime minister when the latter resigned for reasons of health on January 24, 1925. His government fell on June 6, 1926. Sandler served as minister of foreign affairs from 1932 until 1939. He died in Stockholm on November 12, 1964.

KARL GUSTAV EKMAN (Prime Minister; June 7, 1926–September 26, 1928). Karl Gustav Ekman was born in Vastmanland on October 5, 1872. He became active in the temperance movement in the late 1880s and was named its national director in 1899. He also served on the staff of several local newspapers during the 1890s. He was defeated for a seat in the Riksdag in 1897. Ekman held several provincial positions and was elected to the first chamber of the Riksdag in 1911. He formed the Liberal People's Party in 1923. Ekman became Sweden's prime minister on June 7, 1926. His government sponsored an education reform program and established a labor court. He stepped down on September 26, 1928. Ekman returned to head the government on June 7, 1930. His government was faced with social unrest during the worldwide economic crisis. Ekman was forced to resign on August 6, 1932, when it was revealed that he had accepted financial gifts from the match magnate, Ivar Kreuger. Ekman subsequently retired from politics. He died in Stockholm on June 15, 1945.

ARVID A. LINDMAN (Prime Minister; October 2, 1928–June 2, 1930). *See earlier entry under Heads of Government.*

KARL GUSTAV EKMAN (Prime Minister; June 7, 1930–August 6, 1932). *See earlier entry under Heads of Government.*

FELIX TEODOR HAMRIN (Prime Minister; August 6, 1932–September 24, 1932). Felix Teodor Hamrin was born in Monteras on January 14, 1875. He was a leading businessman and was elected to the Riksdag in 1911. He was a leader of the Liberal Party before joining Karl Ekman's Liberal People's Party in 1923. He served as minister of commerce in Ekman's government from 1926 to 1928 and was finance minister from 1930 to 1932. He became prime minister on August 6, 1932, following Ekman's resignation. He also succeeded Ekman as leader of the Liberal People's Party. He was unsuccessful in forming a coalition government following elections and stepped down on September 24, 1932. He remained active in politics, serving as governor of Jonkoping. He died in Stockholm on November 27, 1937.

PER ALBIN HANSSON (Prime Minister; September 24, 1932–June 11, 1936). Per Albin Hansson was born in Scania Province on October 28, 1885. He joined the Social Democratic Party at an early age and worked for the party's newspaper. He was elected to the lower chamber of the Swedish parliament in 1918. Hansson was named to the cabinet of Prime Minister Hjalmar Branting as minister of war and national defense in 1920. He was an antimilitarist, and his views led to his resignation in 1926. He was named to the Swedish government's Public Debt Commission in 1929. Hansson was selected to lead the Social Democratic Party in 1936 and became prime minister on September 23, 1936. He advocated Swedish neutrality during World War II and formed a coalition cabinet in December 1939. His party received an absolute majority in general elections in 1940, though he continued to lead an all-party wartime coalition government. Hansson dismissed the government after the war and formed a Social Democratic cabinet in July 1945. He remained prime minister of Sweden until he died from a stroke while he was riding a tram through Stockholm on October 5, 1946.

AXEL A. PEHRSSON-BRAMSTORP (Prime Minister; June 11, 1936–September 23, 1936). Axel A. Pehrsson-Bramstorp was born on August 19, 1883. He was elected to the Riksdag in 1918 and served until 1921. He again served in the Riksdag from 1929 to 1932 and from 1934 to 1936. He was leader of the Peasant Party and formed a union with the Liberal People's Party and the Farmers Party when he succeeded Socialist Prime Minister Per Albin Hansson as head of the government on June 11, 1936. The Social Democrats were victorious in subsequent elections, and Pehrsson-Bramstorp's government stepped down on September 23, 1936. He subsequently served in the cabinet as minister of agriculture until his retirement in 1945.

Pehrsson-Bramstorp died in Trelleborg in southern Sweden, on February 19, 1954.

PER ALBIN HANSSON (Prime Minister; September 23, 1936–October 6, 1946). *See earlier entry under Heads of Government.*

Switzerland

Switzerland is a country in central Europe.

HEADS OF STATE

WALTER HAUSER (President of the Federal Council; January 1, 1900–January 1, 1901). Walter Hauser was born in Wadenswil on May 1, 1837. He was a member of the Radical Party and was named to the Swiss Federal Council in December 1888. He was head of the military department in 1889 and 1890. He subsequently headed the finance department. Hauser was president of the council in 1892 and 1900. He remained a leading member of the Swiss government until his death on October 22, 1902.

ERNEST BRENNER (President of the Federal Council; January 1, 1901–January 1, 1902). Ernest Brenner was born in Basel on December 9, 1856. He was elected to the Swiss Federal Council in 1897. He served as chief of the federal department of justice and police. Brenner headed the Federal Council in 1901 and 1908. He also served in the government as foreign minister. He remained a member of the council until his death on March 11, 1911.

JOSEPH ZEMP (President of the Federal Council; January 1, 1902–January 1, 1903). Joseph Zemp was born in Entlebuch on November 3, 1834. He was elected to the Federal Council as a member of the Catholic Conservative Party in December 1891. He served as president of the council in 1895 and 1902. He retired from the council in June 1908 and

died several months later on December 8, 1908.

ADOLF DEUCHER (President of the Federal Council; January 1, 1903–January 1, 1904). Adolf Deucher was born in Stechborn on February 15, 1831. He was elected to the Federal Council in April 1883. Deucher headed the Federal Council in 1886, 1897, 1903, and 1909. He remained a leading member of the council until his death on July 10, 1912.

ROBERT COMTESSE (President of the Federal Council; January 1, 1904–January 1, 1905). Robert Comtesse was born in La Sagne on August 14, 1847. He elected to represent Neuchatel on the Federal Council in 1899 and served as chief of the finance department. Comtesse headed the Federal Council in 1904 and 1910. He remained a member of the council until his death in La Tour de Peilz on November 17, 1922.

MARC-EMILE RUCHET (President of the Federal Council; January 1, 1905–January 1, 1906). Marc-Emile Ruchet was born in Saint Saphorin, on September 14, 1853. He was educated as a lawyer and entered the federal government in 1899. He served as president of the Federal Council in 1905. He subsequently headed the ministry of the interior. Ruchet again headed the government as president of the Federal Council in 1911. He died the following year in Bern on July 13, 1912.

LUDWIG FORRER (President of the Federal Council; January 1, 1906–January 1, 1907). Ludwig Forrer was born in Islikon on February 9, 1845. He was educated as a lawyer and served as attorney general in Zurich. He served on the Swiss Federal Council and became president in 1892. He retired from politics in 1900 to become director of the Central Office for International Railway Transport. He returned to the Federal Council in 1902. He again headed the council in 1906 and 1912. He retired from politics to resume his position with the railway council in 1917. Forrer died in Bern on September 28, 1921.

EDUARD MÜLLER (President of the Federal Council; January 1, 1907–January 1, 1908). Eduard Müller was born in Dresden on November 12, 1848. He was elected to the Federal Council as a member of the Radical Party in 1895. Müller headed the Federal Council in 1899, 1907, and 1913. He remained a leading member of the council until his death on November 9, 1919.

ERNST BRENNER (President of the Federal Council; January 1, 1908–January 1, 1909). *See earlier entry under Heads of State.*

ADOLF DEUCHER (President of the Federal Council; January 1, 1909–January 1, 1910). *See earlier entry under Heads of State.*

ROBERT COMTESSE (President of the Federal Council; January 1, 1910–January 1, 1911). *See earlier entry under Heads of State.*

MARC-EMILE RUCHET (President of the Federal Council; January 1, 1911–January 1, 1912). *See earlier entry under Heads of State.*

LUDWIG FORRER (President of the Federal Council; January 1, 1912–January 1, 1913). *See earlier entry under Heads of State.*

EDUARD MÜLLER (President of the Federal Council; January 1, 1913–January 1, 1914). *See earlier entry under Heads of State.*

ARTHUR HOFFMAN (President of the Federal Council; January 1, 1914–January 1, 1915). Arthur Hoffman was born in St. Gall on June 18, 1857. He was a member of the Radical Party and was elected to the Federal Council in 1911. He became head of the council in 1914. He retired from the government in 1917. Hoffman died on July 23, 1927.

GIUSEPPE MOTTA (President of the Federal Council; January 1, 1915–January 1, 1916). Giuseppe Motta was born in Airolo on December 29, 1871. He received a degree in law from Heidelberg University. He entered politics and was elected to the council of state, where he served as leader of the Conservative-Catholic party from 1895. He was elected to the national council in 1899 and to the Swiss Federal Council in 1911. He headed the federal finance department throughout World War I from 1914 until 1918 and also headed the Federal Council in 1915. He became foreign minister in 1920 and represented Switzerland at the League of Nations. Motta again headed the Federal Council in 1920, 1927, 1932, and 1937. He remained a leading figure in Swiss politics until his death in Bern on January 23, 1940.

CAMILLE DECOPPET (President of the Federal Council; January 1, 1916–January 1, 1917). Camille Decoppet was born in Suzevaz on June 4, 1862. He was educated as a lawyer and opened a practice in 1888. He was elected to the Federal Council the following year. He served as director of the Swiss war department during World War I and headed the Swiss Federal Council in 1916. He became director of the International Postal Bureau in Switzerland in 1919. Decoppet died in Bern on January 14, 1925.

EDMUND SCHULTHESS (President of the Federal Council; January 1, 1917–January 1, 1918). Edmund Schulthess was born in Villnachern on March 2, 1868. Schulthess received a degree in law from Bern University. He was elected to the parliament in 1905 and served as a Radical member of the Federal Council in July 1912. He headed the council in 1917 and 1921. He was subsequently director of the department of national economy. Schulthess again served as president of the Federal Council in 1928 and 1933. He retired from the government in 1935. Schulthess died in Bern on April 22, 1944.

FELIX-LOUIS CALONDER (President of the Federal Council; January 1, 1918–January 1, 1919). Felix-Louis Calonder was born in Schuls on December 7, 1863. He was a lawyer in Char and entered politics as a federal legislator in 1899. He became a leader of the Radical Party and was elected to the Federal Council in June 1913. He headed the council in 1918. Calonder retired from the government in February 1920. He died in Char on June 14, 1952.

GUSTAVE ADOR (President of the Federal Council; January 1, 1919–January 1, 1920). Gustave Ador was born in Geneva on December 23, 1845. He entered politics and was recognized as an authority on financial matters. He was elected to the Swiss parliament as a Liberal-Conservative in 1879. He became a national councilor in 1891. Ador became president of the International Committee of the Red Cross in 1910. He was elected to the Swiss Federal Council in 1917 and served as minister of foreign affairs. He headed the council in 1919. He represented Switzerland at the League of Nations, serving as honorary president of the assembly in 1921. He remained at the League of Nations until 1924. Ador died in Cologny on March 31, 1928.

GIUSEPPE MOTTA (President of the Federal Council; January 1, 1920–January 1, 1921). *See earlier entry under Heads of State.*

EDMUND SCHULTHESS (President of the Federal Council; January 1, 1921–January 1, 1922). *See earlier entry under Heads of State.*

ROBERT HAAB (President of the Federal Council; January 1, 1922–January 1, 1923). Robert Haab was born in Wadenswil on August 8, 1865. He was educated as a lawyer at the Universities of Zurich, Strasbourg, and Leipzig. He served as a member of the administrative council of the Southwest Railway of Switzerland from 1894 until 1911. He briefly served as Switzerland's diplomatic representative in Germany in 1917. He returned to Switzerland at the end of the year and was elected to the Swiss Federal Council. He headed the postal and railroad departments and led the Federal Council in 1922. Haab again headed the federal council in 1929 and retired from the council after completing his term. He died in Zurich on October 15, 1939.

KARL SCHEURER (President of the Federal Council; January 1, 1923–January 1, 1924). Karl Scheurer was born in Sumiswald on September 27, 1872. He was a member of the Radical Party and was elected to the Swiss Federal Council in 1919. He headed the council in 1923. Scheurer also served as director of the military department. He remained a member of the council until his death in Bern on November 14, 1929.

ERNEST CHUARD (President of the Federal Council; January 1, 1924–January 1, 1925). Ernest Chuard was born in Corcelles on July 31, 1857. He was a member of the Radical Party and was elected to the Swiss Federal Council in 1919. He headed the department of home affairs in the early 1920s and served as president of the council in 1924. He retired from the council in December 1928. Chuard died in Lausanne on November 9, 1942.

JEAN-MARIE MUSY (President of the Federal Council; January 1, 1925–January 1, 1926). Jean-Marie Musy was born in Albeuve on April 10, 1876. He was a leader of the Catholic Conservative Party and was elected to the Swiss Federal Council in 1919. He headed the department of finance in the early 1920s. He was president of the Federal Council in 1925 and again in 1930. He retired from the government in 1940. Musy died in Albeuve on April 19, 1952.

HEINRICH HÄBERLIN (President of the Federal Council; January 1, 1926–January 1, 1927). Heinrich Häberlin was born in Weinfelden on September 6, 1868. He was educated in Zurich, Leipzig and Berlin. He was elected to the national council in 1904, serving as its president in 1919. He was elected to the Federal Council in 1920. He headed the department of justice and police in the early 1920s and was president of the council in 1926 and 1931. He retired from the government in 1934. Häberlin died in Thurgau on February 26, 1947.

GIUSEPPE MOTTA (President of the Federal Council; January 1, 1927–January 1, 1928). *See earlier entry under Heads of State.*

EDMUND SCHULTHESS (President of the Federal Council; January 1, 1928–January 1, 1929). *See earlier entry under Heads of State.*

ROBERT HAAB (President of the Federal Council; January 1, 1929–January 1, 1930). *See earlier entry under Heads of State.*

JEAN-MARIE MUSY (President of the Federal Council; January 1, 1930–January 1, 1931). *See earlier entry under Heads of State.*

HEINRICH HÄBERLIN (President of the Federal Council; January 1, 1931–January 1, 1932). *See earlier entry under Heads of State.*

GIUSEPPE MOTTA (President of the Federal Council; January 1, 1932–January 1, 1933). *See earlier entry under Heads of State.*

EDMUND SCHULTHESS (President of the Federal Council; January 1, 1933–January 1, 1934). *See earlier entry under Heads of State.*

MARCEL PILET-GOLAZ (President of the Federal Council; January 1, 1934–January 1, 1935). Marcel-Edouard-Ernest Pilet-Golaz was born in Cossonay on December 31, 1889. He was educated in Lausanne, Leipzig, and Paris and earned a degree in law. He was elected to the Vaud grand council in 1921, to the National Council in 1925, and to the Federal Council in 1928. He was also director of the department of posts and railways. Pilet-Golaz headed the Federal Council in 1934 and 1940. He retired from the council in 1944. Pilet-Golaz died in Paris on April 11, 1958.

RUDOLF MINGER (President of the Federal Council; January 1, 1935–January 1, 1936). Rudolf Minger was born in Bern on November 13, 1881. He became active in the Swiss Peasants' Union and was elected to the parliament in 1919. He became a member of the Swiss Federal Council in December 1929, and served as director of the military department. Minger served as president of the council in 1935. He retired from the government in 1940. Minger died in Schupfen on August 23, 1955.

ALBERT MEYER (President of the Federal Council; January 1, 1936–January 1, 1937). Albert Meyer was born in Fällanden on March 13, 1870. He was educated in Zurich, Leipzig, and Berlin. He became a journalist and served as editor of the newspaper *Neue Zurcher Zeitung* before entering politics. He was elected to the Swiss Federal Council in 1929. He headed the interior department until 1934, when he became head of the finance department. Meyer was president of the council in 1936 and retired from politics in 1938. Meyer died in Zurich on October 22, 1953.

GIUSEPPE MOTTA (President of the Federal Council; January 1, 1937–January 1, 1938). *See earlier entry under Heads of State.*

JOHANNES BAUMANN (President of the Federal Council; January 1, 1938–January 1, 1939). Johannes Baumann was born in Herisau on November 27, 1874. He was elected to the Swiss Federal Council in March 1934 and headed the council in 1938. Baumann retired from the government in 1940. He died on September 8, 1953.

PHILIPP ETTER (President of the Federal Council; January 1, 1939–January 1, 1940). Philipp Etter was born in Menzingen on December 21, 1891. He studied law in Zurich. He served as examining judge in the canton of Zug from 1917 to 1922. Etter was elected to the district council in 1923 and served in the education and military departments. He also served as mayor of Zug from 1930 to 1934. He was elected to the council of state and served as head of the department of the interior from 1934 to 1959. Etter first served as president of the Swiss Federal Council in 1939. He was reelected in 1942 and for a third time on December 12, 1946, when he defeated the Socialist candidate Ernst Nobs by a wide margin. His final term as president came in 1953. He retired from the Fed-

eral Council in 1959 and died in Bern on December 23, 1977.

MARCEL PILET-GOLAZ (President of the Federal Council; January 1, 1940–January 1, 1941). *See earlier entry under Heads of State.*

ERNST WETTER (President of the Federal Council; January 1, 1941–January 1, 1942). Ernst Wetter was born in Winterthur on August 27, 1877. He was a professor at the Zurich Commercial School from 1914 to 1920. He served in the federal ministry of public economy in Bern until 1924. He was elected to the canton council as a Radical Democrat in 1929 and served on the Swiss national council from 1929 to 1938. He was subsequently elected to the Federal Council. He served as president of the council in 1941. Wetter remained on the council until 1943. He died on October 8, 1963.

PHILIPP ETTER (President of the Federal Council; January 1, 1942–January 1, 1943). *See earlier entry under Heads of State.*

ENRICO CELIO (President of the Federal Council; January 1, 1943–January 1, 1944). Enrico Celio was born in Ambri on June 19, 1889. He studied law and subsequently became a member of the Tessin Canton government. He was elected to the Swiss Federal Council in 1940. Celio served as director of the department of transport, communications, and energy. He also served as president of the Swiss Federal Council in 1943 and 1948. Celio left the Federal Council in 1950 and was appointed minister plenipotentiary to Rome, where he served until 1956. He died on February 23, 1980.

WALTER STAMPFLI (President of the Federal Council; January 1, 1944–January 1, 1945). Walter Stampfli was born in Buren, Soleure Canton, on December 3, 1884. He received a doctorate in economics and law from Zurich University in 1908. He was the editor of the *Oltner Tagblat* until 1918 and subsequently became a director of the Von Roll iron works. He entered the Soleure Canton government, becoming president in 1922. He was elected to the national council in 1931 and became a federal councilor in 1940. He served as minister of public economy during most of World War II. Stampfli headed the Federal Council in 1944. He retired from the government in 1947. Stampfli died on October 11, 1965.

EDUARD VON STEIGER (President of the Federal Council; January 1, 1945–January 1, 1946). Eduard von Steiger was born in Langnau on July 2, 1881. He was elected to the Swiss Federal Council in December 1940 and was named head of the department of justice in 1941. He served as president of the Federal Council in 1945 and 1951. Von Steiger retired from the government in December 1951. He died in Bern on February 10, 1962.

Syria

Syria is a country in the Middle East. It was granted independence from a League of Nations mandate administered by France on April 17, 1946.

HEADS OF STATE

FAISAL I (King; March 1920–July 26, 1920). *See entry under* Iraq: Heads of State.

MUHAMMAD 'ALI AL-'ABID (President; June 11, 1932–December 21, 1936). Muhammad 'Ali al-'Abid was born in 1868. His father was Ahmad Izzat Pasha, who was a leading advisor to Ottoman Sultan Abdul Hamid. Muhammad 'Ali was raised in Istanbul and educated in Paris. He joined the Ottoman ministry of foreign affairs in 1905 and was named minister to Washington in 1908. He went into exile in Paris with his family following the Young Turk Revolt in July 1908. He returned to Damascus in 1919. Muhammad 'Ali was elected the first president of the Syrian Republic on June 11, 1932. He served under the French mandate until December 21, 1936. Muhammad 'Ali died on October 22, 1939.

HASHIM AL-ATASSI (President; December 21, 1936–July 7, 1939). Hashim al-Atassi was born in 1875. He attended Istanbul University and was elected to the Syrian General Congress in 1919. He was leader of the first Syrian government when nationalists proclaimed the nation's independence in March 1920, but France was given control of Syria under a League of Nations mandate the following month. Atassi was elected president of the constituent assembly in 1928, after France allowed the restoration of some political rights in Syria. The assembly was dissolved two years later. Atassi led a delegation to Paris to negotiate a treaty with the French government. He returned to Syria to become president on December 21, 1936. He resigned from office on July 7, 1939, and retired from politics after France failed to honor the treaty. Atassi returned to the government on August 15, 1949, when he was appointed prime minister following a military coup led by Sami Hinnawi. He became president of the nation when a second coup led by Abid es-Shishakli ousted Hinnawi on December 19, 1949. Shishakli led another coup against Prime Minister Maruf ed Dawalibi in November 1951, and Atassi resigned as president on December 2, 1951. He was again named president on February 25, 1954, following the ouster of Shishakli. Atassi ordered the restoration of a democratic government and stepped down on September 6, 1955, following the election of Shukri el-Kuwatli. Atassi retired from politics and returned to his home in Homs. He died there on December 5, 1960.

TAJ-ED DIN-EL-HASSANI (President; September 14, 1941–January 18, 1943). Taj-ed din-el-Hassani was born in Damascus in 1886. He began teaching at the Sultaniyya School in Damascus in 1912. He began publishing the *al-Sharq* newspaper in 1916 and was named a member of the council of state during the rule of King Faisal. He subsequently served as a judge in Damascus. He was named prime minister under the French mandate on December 29, 1925 and held office until January 6, 1926. He was again called upon to form a government on February 15, 1928, and served until November 19, 1931. He returned to head the government on March 17, 1934 and stepped down on February 24, 1936. He subsequently went to France, where he remained until he was named to the presidency on September 14, 1941. He retained office until his death on January 18, 1943.

JAMIL AL-ULSHI (Acting President; January 21, 1943–March 25, 1943). Jamil al-Ulshi was born in 1883. He was educated at the Istanbul Military College and served in the Syrian government in the fall of 1920. He also served in the cabinet as minister of finance from 1928 to 1930 and from 1934 to 1936. He was a close ally to Taj-ed din-el-Hassani and was named prime minister on January 18, 1943. He became acting president on January 10, 1943, following Hassani's death. He was replaced by 'Ata al-Aiyubi on March 25, 1943.

'ATA AL-AIYUBI (Acting President; March 25, 1943–July 17, 1943). 'Ata al-Aiyubi was born in Damascus in 1877. He was educated in Istanbul and entered the Syrian government as a minister in 1922. He served until 1924, and again in 1925. He returned to the government in 1934. He was named prime minister on February 24, 1936, and served until December 21, 1936. Al-Aiyubi was appointed by the French high commissioner to serve as prime minister and acting president on March 25, 1943, to prepare for new elections. Shukri el-Kuwatli was victorious in the election, and al-Aiyubi relinquished the presidency on July 17, 1943. He stepped down as head of the government the following month.

SHUKRI EL-KUWATLI (President; July 17, 1943–March 30, 1949). Shukri el Kuwatli was born in Damascus in 1891. He was educated in Damascus and Istanbul, where he studied political science. He became involved in the Arab nationalist movement and was a leader in the *Al Arabiya al Fatat*. Kuwatli was imprisoned by the Turks for his nationalist activities during World War I. He participated in the regime of Emir Faisal in Damascus after the war and remained in the country when Faisal was expelled by the French in 1920. He was a leading opponent of the French occupation and participated in the Druze revolt in 1925. Kuwatli was forced to flee to Egypt and was sentenced to death in absentia. He was pardoned and returned to Syria in 1931. He became the leader of the Istiqlalists, a radical group in the National Bloc Party. Kuwatli served on the Syrian delegation that negotiated the Franco-Syrian Treaty of Friendship and Alliance in Paris in 1936. The National Bloc was victorious in subsequent elections, and Kuwatli was named minister of finance and defense in Jamil Mardam's government. He resigned from the government two years later to protest the concessions granted to the French by Mardam. He continued his fight for full independence for Syria during World War II, and he again fled the country when British and Free French forces invaded in 1941. Kuwatli returned the following year and was allowed by the French authorities to participate in elections. He was elected president and took office on July 17, 1943. He continued to press for the withdrawal of the French from Syria. Syria faced mounting civil disorder as the French refused to liberate the country. The French responded with a military attack on Damascus and other Syrian towns in May 1945. Kuwatli requested that the British government intervene, and the fighting stopped when British troops entered the country and confined the French troops to their barracks. The following year the question of Syrian and Lebanese independence was put before the United Nations, and the two countries were granted control of their own lands. Kuwatli ran for reelection in April 1948, despite a constitutional prohibition of a second term. His actions prompted a wave of popular discontent, and he was forced from office on March 30, 1949, in a military coup led by Husni Zaim. Kuwatli was held prisoner for several months before he was allowed to leave the country for Switzerland. He went into exile in Egypt in 1949, where he remained for the next five years. Syria underwent several more military coups before Kuwatli was invited to return to the country in August 1954. He again ran for the presidency and was victorious. He took office on September 6, 1955. Kuwatli led a pro-Egyptian government and tried to establish closer ties with the Soviet Union. In 1957 he advocated a union with Egypt. Kuwatli and President Gamal Abd-el Nasser of Egypt announced the union of their two countries as the United Arab Republic on February 1, 1958. Kuwatli stepped down from office, leaving Nasser as president of the unified government. Kuwatli was awarded the honorary title of "First Arab Citizen," but broke with Nasser in 1959. Kuwatli again went into exile and settled in Beirut, Lebanon. He died there of a heart attack on June 30, 1967.

HEADS OF GOVERNMENT

RIDA PASHA AL-RIKABI (Prime Minister; October 1918–April 1920). Rida Pasha al-Rikabi was born in 1860. He served as military governor of Syria in 1918 and was chief of the council of state under King Faisal. He went to Transjordan after Faisal's ouster in July 1920. He became Amir Abdullah's chief advisor in March 1922. He returned to Syria in 1923 and led the monarchist faction in the 1931 elections. He was defeated in the elections and had little future influence on Syrian politics.

HASHIM AL-ATASSI (Prime Minister; May 3, 1920–June 1920). *See earlier entry under Heads of State.*

ALA AD-DIN AR-RUBI (Prime Minister; July 26, 1920–August 20, 1920). Ala ad-Din ar-Rubi briefly served as head of the Syrian government following the ouster of King Feisal on July 26, 1920. He stepped down the following month. Ar-Rubi died on August 21, 1926.

SUBHI BEY BARAKAT (Prime Minister; January 1, 1925–December 21, 1925). Subhi Barakat was born in Antioch in 1889. He was a leader of the nationalist revolt in Antioch until his surrender to the French in June 1920. He was elected to the federal council in July 1922 with French support. He led the Syrian Union Party and was opposed by the nationalists. He headed the Syrian government from January 1, 1925, until his resignation on December 21, 1925. He subsequently became an agent of an international oil company. He was narrowly defeated by Muhammad 'Ali al-'Abid for the Syrian presidency and subsequently served as speaker of the chamber of deputies.

TAJ-ED DIN-EL-HASSANI (Prime Minister; December 29, 1925–January 6, 1926). *See earlier entry under Heads of State.*

DAMAD AHMAD NAMI (Prime Minister; April 27, 1926–February 9, 1928). Damad Ahmad Nami was born in Beirut in 1880 to a prominent family. He was the son-in-law of the Ottoman sultan, Abdul Hamid. He became Syria's prime minister on April 27, 1926, forming a cabinet that included several nationalist leaders. He re-formed the government in June 1926 with a cabinet of moderates. Damad Ahmad made several attempts to have himself made king of Syria. He was forced to resign on February 2, 1928, when the French high commissioner decided that his government lacked the confidence to preside over elections.

TAJ-ED DIN-EL-HASSANI (Prime Minister; February 15, 1928–November 19, 1931). *See earlier entry under Heads of State.*

HAQQI AL-AZM (Prime Minister; June 15, 1932–March 17, 1934). Haqqi al-Azm was born in Damascus in 1864. He came from a leading Sunni Muslim family and was educated in Istanbul. He moved to Cairo in 1912 where he formed the nationalist Ottoman Party of Administrative Decentralization. He worked with the Arab nationalist movement during World War I. He was appointed by the French to serve as the first governor of Damascus in 1920. He was widely criticized by Syrian nationalists because of his cordial relationship with the French colonial authorities. Azm was

named prime minister of Syria on June 15, 1932. He also served as minister of the interior. He led the government until he was dismissed by the French high commissioner, Comte Damien de Martel, on March 17, 1934.

TAJ-ED DIN-EL-HASSANI (Prime Minister; March 17, 1934–February 24, 1936). *See earlier entry under Heads of State.*

'ATA AL-AIYUBI (Prime Minister; February 24, 1936–December 21, 1936). *See earlier entry under Heads of State.*

JAMIL MARDAM (Prime Minister; December 21, 1936–February 18, 1939). Jamil Mardam was born in Damascus in 1888. He was educated in Paris, where he founded the Arab nationalist organization *al-Fatat* in 1911. He served in the Syrian delegation to the Paris Peace Conference in 1919. Mardam was a leader of the Druze revolt against the French in Syria in 1925. He subsequently was a founder of the National Bloc. He was part of the Syrian diplomatic team that negotiated a treaty with France in 1936. He became prime minister on December 21, 1936, and served until February 18, 1939, when he resigned over France's failure to implement the treaty. He was again named prime minister on December 28, 1946. Mardam's government was forced to resign on December 1, 1948, following public criticism of his economic and financial policies. Mardam retired from politics the following year. He died in Cairo on March 28, 1960.

LUTFI AL-HAFFAR (Prime Minister; February 23, 1939–March 13, 1939). Lutfi al-Haffar was born in Damascus in 1891. He was given a Sunni Muslim education and became active in the nationalist movement at an early age. He was a founder of the Arab Renaissance Society and was exiled by the French in 1927. He was one of the founders of the National Bloc and served in various governments as minister of finance, education, and the interior. He was named prime minister on February 23, 1939, but was forced to step down on March 13, 1939. Haffar fled to Iraq the following year under suspicion of murder of an opposition politician. He later returned to Syria and was elected to the parliament. He served as minister of the interior from 1943 to 1946. He was also a founder of the National Party in 1947, and briefly served as its president.

NASUHI AL-BUKHARI (Prime Minister; April 6, 1939–May 14, 1939). Nasuhi al-Bukhari was born in 1881. He was educated in Istanbul and served in the military. He became a leading politician in Syria under the French mandate, serving as a minister from 1920 to 1922 and from 1926 to 1928. He briefly formed a government as prime minister from April 6, 1939, until May 14, 1939. He was elected to the chamber of deputies in 1943, and served in the cabinet as minister of education and defense.

BAHIJ AL-KHATIB (Prime Minister; July 9, 1939–April 3, 1941). Bahij al-Khatib served as interim governor of Jabal in 1937 while presiding over elections. He became head of the Syrian government on July 9, 1939. He was instrumental in discrediting nationalist leader Jamil Mardam. He survived an assassination attempt by the nationalists and stepped down from office on April 3, 1941.

KHALID EL-AZAM (Prime Minister; April 3, 1941–September 1941). Khalid el-Azam was born to a wealthy family in Damascus in 1895. He entered politics as an independent and served as prime minister under the Vichy regime from April 3, 1941, until September 1941. He was again named prime minister on December 16, 1948. Azam retained office until he was ousted in the coup led by Husni Zaim on March 30, 1949. He was again asked to form a government on

December 28, 1949, following the coup led by Abid es-Shishakli. He resigned in May 1950 but was reappointed on March 27, 1951. Azam was again forced to step down on August 9, 1951, following a strike by government employees in opposition to his labor policies. He served as deputy prime minister, minister of defense, and minister of finance from 1955 to 1957. During this period he advocated closer relations with the Soviet Union. He was politically inactive during Syria's unification with Egypt as part of the United Arab Republic from 1958 to 1961. He was again named prime minister on September 13, 1962. He retained office until March 8, 1963, when he was ousted in a Ba'athist coup. Azam sought asylum in the Turkish embassy until he was allowed to leave the country. He went into exile in Lebanon. He died in Beirut on February 18, 1965, from complications of acute diabetes.

HASAN AL-HAKIM (Prime Minister; September 20, 1941–April 18, 1942). Hasan al-Hakim was born in 1888. He became a leading figure in the Syrian nationalist movement during the French mandate. He was an independent member of the Syrian parliament. He was named to serve as prime minister and finance minister by President Taj-ed Din-el-Hassani on September 20, 1941. Hakim resigned on April 18, 1942. He was again asked to form a cabinet by President Hashim al-Atassi on August 9, 1951. He also headed the ministry of finance in the government. He resigned on November 10, 1951, following a dispute with Foreign Minister Faidi al-Atassi over Hakim's support for the Middle East Defense Plan and the United States Mutual Aid Program.

HUSNI EL-BARAZI (Prime Minister; April 19, 1942–January 10, 1943). Husni el-Barazi was born in Hama in 1893. He was educated in Istanbul and became a leading political figure in Syria in the 1920s. He served in Damad Ahmad

Nami's government as minister of the interior in 1926. He was subsequently arrested and deported by the French for nationalist activities. He was pardoned in an amnesty in March 1928 and joined the National Bloc. He was subsequently elected to the constituent assembly from Hama. He broke with the National Bloc in the early 1930s and again served in the government as a minister from 1934 to 1936. He was called upon to replace Hasan al-Hakim as prime minister on September 20, 1941. A growing financial crisis in Syria and estranged relations with the president, Taj-ed Din-el-Hassani, forced Barazi's resignation on January 10, 1943. Barazi's brother, Muhsin al-Barazi, served as prime minister several times in the 1940s until his execution by military coup leaders in August 1949.

JAMIL AL-ULSHI (Prime Minister; January 10, 1943–March 25, 1943). *See earlier entry under Heads of State.*

'ATA AL-AIYUBI (Prime Minister; March 25, 1943–August 20, 1943). *See earlier entry under Heads of State.*

SAADULLA EL-JABRI (Prime Minister; August 20, 1943–October 14, 1944). Saadulla el-Jabri was born in Aleppo in 1893. He became active in nationalist politics during the Ottoman era, participating in Ibrahim Hananu's revolt. He remained a leading nationalist figure under the French mandate. Jabri was a founder of the Red Hand nationalist movement in 1922. He was arrested by the French for his role in the 1925 revolt and spent the next two years in exile. He returned to Syria in 1928 and became an early leader of the National Bloc in 1932. He served in Jamil Mardam's government from 1936 until 1938. He became prime minister of Syria's first independent elected government on August 20, 1943. He retained office until October 14, 1944. Jabri was again named prime minister on October 2, 1945, and served until December 28, 1946, when he resigned for reasons of health. He died in Aleppo on June 19, 1947.

FARIS AL-KHOURI (Prime Minister; October 14, 1944–August 23, 1945). Faris al-Khouri was born in Kfeir, near Hasbaya, in 1879. He attended the American University in Beirut and received a degree in law in 1897. He became a lawyer in Damascus in 1908 and was elected to the Ottoman parliament in 1914. Khouri was arrested and charged with treason the following year, but was acquitted of the charges. He began a career teaching law at the Syrian University in 1919. He served as minister of finance in the government of Faisal, who was proclaimed king of Syria in 1920. Khouri took part in the Druze revolt in 1925 and was banished to Lebanon by the French government. He returned in 1926 and was appointed minister of education. He became a leader of the National Bloc in 1928 and was elected to the Syrian parliament in 1936. Khouri became speaker of the parliament in 1938 and retained his position until parliament was dissolved in 1939. He served as foreign minister in 1941 before he returned to the parliament as speaker in 1943. Khouri was named prime minister on October 14, 1944. He retained office until October 2, 1945, when he resumed the office of speaker of the parliament. Khouri was appointed Syria's chief delegate to the United Nations in 1947 and served as president of the United Nations Security Council the following year. He returned to Syria to again serve as prime minister on October 29, 1954. He resigned on February 25, 1955. Khouri died in Damascus after a long illness on January 2, 1962.

SAADULLA EL-JABRI (Prime Minister; October 1, 1945–December 21, 1946). *See early entry under Heads of Government.*

Thailand

Thailand (Siam) is a country in Southeast Asia.

HEADS OF STATE

CHULA-LONGKORN (King; October 19, 1868–October 23, 1910). Somdet-Phra-Chula-Longkorn-Chula-Chom-Kiao (Rama V) was born in Bangkok on September 22, 1853. He was one of 84 sons of King Mongkut Pra Chom Klao. He succeeded to the throne upon his father's death on October 19, 1868. He ruled under the regency of Chao Phya Sri Suriyawongse until reaching his majority in 1873. During the early years of his reign Chula-longkorn traveled throughout Asia to study other systems of government. He also introduced elements of Western culture into the country and the royal court. He established the Siamese navy of twenty ships, commanded by a Danish officer. He introduced other social and political reforms created a new governmental system of ministries in 1892, and abolished slavery in 1905. He settled a territorial dispute with France in 1906 and improved the quality of education and health care in the country. He remained a popular monarch until his death of uremic poisoning in Bangkok on October 23, 1910.

VAJIRAVUDH (King; October 23, 1910–November 26, 1925). Chowfa Maha Vajiravudh (Rama VI) was born on January 1, 1881, the son of King Chula-longkorn. He was proclaimed crown prince in January 1895. He was educated at Oxford University and the Sandhurst Military Academy in Great Britain. He succeeded his father to the throne on October 23, 1910. Vajiravudh created the Siamese nationalist volunteer military organization known as the Wild Tiger Corps. He continued to bring Western influences to Siam. He also worked to improve the educational system and founded Chula-longkorn University. He was successful in revising Siam's treaties with Japan and Western nations to guarantee judicial and economic autonomy for Siam. Vajiravudh was also interested in drama and translated Shakespeare's *Romeo and Juliet* and *The Merchant of Venice* into Siamese. He remained Siam's monarch until he died of complications from abdominal surgery on November 26, 1925.

PRAJADHIPOK (King; November 26, 1925–March 2, 1934). Somdech Chao Fa Prajadhipok (Rama VII) was born on November 8, 1893. He was the youngest son of King Chula-longkorn. Prajadhipok was born to the title of Prince of Sukhodaya. He was educated in Bangkok and France and received military training in Great Britain. He succeeded to the throne upon the death of his brother, King Vajiravudh, on November 26, 1925, becoming the seventh monarch in the ruling Chakkri dynasty. His reliance on the advice of conservative senior princes and continuing economic difficulties in Siam led to public discontent with his reign. A group of high ranking civil and military officials forced Prajadhipok to end the absolute monarchy and accept constitutional rule in 1932. He found it increasingly difficult to deal with the new junta and abdicated the throne on March 2, 1934. He went into exile in England and died of a heart attack at his home at Virginia Water, Surrey, on May 30, 1941.

ANANDA MAHIDOL (King; March 2, 1934–June 9, 1946). Ananda Mahidol (Rama VIII) was born in Germany on September 20, 1925. He was the son of Prince Mahidol of Songkhim. He was sent to Switzerland for his education following the death of his father in 1928. Mahidol assumed the throne of Siam under a regency council on March 2, 1935, following the abdication of his uncle, King Prajadhipok. He continued his studies at the University of Lausanne in Switzerland. He came of age in Sep-

tember 1945 and returned to Siam the following December to prepare for his coronation. He was found dead in his bed at the royal palace from a gunshot wound to the head on June 9, 1946. It was initially announced that the king had been the victim of an accident, though later investigations indicated the likelihood of murder or suicide.

HEADS OF GOVERNMENT

MANOPAKORN NATTIHADA (Prime Minister; June 27, 1932–June 20, 1933). Manopakorn Nattihada was born in 1884. He was educated in England, where he studied law. He served as chief justice of the Supreme Court of Appeals during the reign of King Prajadhipok. Manopakorn was chosen to be the first prime minister of Siam following the 1932 revolution. He took office on June 27, 1932. He was forced to step down on June 20, 1933, following a disagreement with the coup leaders and the national assembly. He went into exile in Penang, where he died in 1948.

PHAHON PHON PHAYUHA (Prime Minister; June 21, 1933–December 21, 1938). Phahon Phon Phayuha (Phahonyothin) was born in 1889. He was educated in Siam, Germany, and Denmark. He returned to Siam and served with distinction in the army. He and Luang Pibul Songgram were the leaders of the revolution in 1932 that established Siam as a constitutional monarchy. He was selected as prime minister on June 21, 1933. Siam held its first national election in 1933 and Phahon's government survived a coup attempt by Prince Bowaradet in October 1933. The government was unable to reach an accommodation with King Prajadhipok, and forced his abdication in 1934. Phahon stepped down from office on December 21, 1938. He died in 1958.

LUANG PIBUL SONGGRAM (Prime Minister; December 21, 1938–August 2, 1944). Luang Pibul Songgram (Phibunsongkhram) was born near Bangkok on July 14, 1897. He attended military school in Bangkok and joined the Siamese army. He continued his training in France and was promoted to lieutenant in 1926. Pibul was active in the coup in June 1932 that made Siam a constitutional monarchy. He served as field commander during a military coup attempt by Prince Bowaradet in October 1933. Pibul was named minister of defense in September 1934 in the government of Phahon Phon Phayuha. He replaced Phahon as prime minister on December 21, 1938. The following year the country's name was officially changed from Siam to Thailand. Pibul entered into a treaty with Japan during World War II and declared war on the Allies. He was forced from office on August 2, 1944. He returned to prominence following the death of King Ananda Mahidol in June 1946. Prime Minister Pridi Phanomyong was accused of complicity in the king's death, and Pibul was a leader of the coup that overthrew his government. He again became prime minister on April 9, 1948. His government faced opposition from Pridi's supporters and survived several coup attempts in the early 1950s. Thailand entered the South East Asia Treaty Organization (SEATO) in 1955. Pibul remained in office following a general election in February 1957. His government was charged with electoral fraud, and he was ousted in a military coup led by Field Marshal Sarit Thanarat on September 16, 1957. Pibul went into exile in the United States and Japan. He went to India in 1960 to become a Buddhist monk. He died of a heart attack at his home in Tokyo on June 11, 1964.

KHUANG APHAIWONG (Prime Minister; August 2, 1944–August 18, 1945). Khuang Aphaiwong was born in 1902. He was educated in Paris, where he studied engineering. He returned to Siam and entered government service. Khuang worked in the telegraph department, where he rose to the position of director-general. He participated in the coup in 1932 that established Siam as a constitutional monarchy. He subsequently served in Phahon Phon Phayuha's cabinet. Khuang remained in the government of Luang Pibul Songgram. He was a leader of the Democratic party and served in the house of representatives as vice president in 1943 and 1944. He replaced Pibul as prime minister on August 2, 1944. Khuang was forced to resign on August 18, 1945, because of his association with the Japanese during World War II. He was again selected as prime minister on January 30, 1946, but his government collapsed on March 18, 1946. He was again named prime minister on November 10, 1947, following a military coup. The Democratic Party won a slight majority in the elections in January 1948, and Khuang remained head of the government. He was forced by the military to resign on April 7, 1948. He remained involved in the Democratic Party and served as leader of the opposition from 1955 until he withdrew from politics in the 1960s to work with an insurance company. He died of cancer in Bangkok on March 15, 1968.

THAWI BUNYAKET (Prime Minister; August 18, 1945–September 1, 1945). Thawi Bunyaket was a prominent Thai political figure when he was chosen to serve as prime minister in a caretaker cabinet on August 18, 1945, following the resignation of Khuang Aphaiwong. The government was largely controlled by the regent, Pridi Phanomyong, who voided Thailand's declaration of war against the Allies. Thawi also served in the cabinet as foreign minister and minister of agriculture, welfare, and public instruction. He remained in office until Seni Pramoj was selected as prime minister on September 1, 1945.

SENI PRAMOJ (Prime Minister; September 1, 1945–January 31, 1946). Seni Pramoj was born in Nakhon Sawan Province on May 26, 1905. He received a degree in law from Oxford University. He served as Thailand's ambassador to the United States in 1941. Seni refused to deliver Thailand's declaration of war to American officials in 1941 and joined the Free Thai movement to oppose the Japanese. When World War II was concluded, Seni became prime minister on September 1, 1945, and served until January 31, 1946. He helped arrange a satisfactory peace settlement with the Allied Powers. Seni resumed his law practice and remained active in politics. He became the leader of the Democratic Party in 1968 and was elected to parliament the following year. He formed a government as prime minister on February 21, 1975. Seni resigned on March 6, 1975, after failing to win a vote of confidence in the parliament. He was again appointed to the office of prime minister to succeed his younger brother, Kukrit Pramoj, on April 20, 1976. He also served in the government as minister of the interior. Seni was criticized for allowing the return of exiled former prime minister Thanon Kittakachorn in September 1976. Seni was ousted by a military coup led by Admiral Sangad

Chaloryu on October 6, 1976. He served on the committee to draft a new Thai constitution from 1978 until 1979. He subsequently retired from active politics.

Seni died in a Bangkok hospital of kidney failure and complications of heart disease and emphysema on July 28, 1997.

Tibet

Tibet is a country in central Asia. It proclaimed its independence from China in January 1913. Tibet was invaded and occupied by the Chinese Communists in October 1950 and renamed Xizang.

HEADS OF STATE

THUPTEN GYATSO (Dalai Lama; 1876–December 17, 1933). Ngawang Lopsang Thupten Gyatso was born to a peasant family in the village of Per-Ho-Dee in Tak-Po Province on June 26, 1876. He was brought to Lhasa at the age of two and was confirmed as the thirteenth reincarnation of the Dalai Lama by the main Buddhist monasteries in Lhasa and the state oracle. It was believed that the Dalai Lama was the incarnation of Bodhisattva Chen-re-zi, the patron god of Tibet, a man who had won the right to Nirvana but agreed to continued rebirth to assist his fellow man. The reborn Dalai Lama had vast religious and secular power in Tibet and was venerated by most Buddhists. He was trained in Lhasa during his minority while a regent ruled in his stead. When the Dalai Lama reached the age of eighteen, the regent and prime minister plotted to retain power by poisoning him. The plot was exposed, and they were imprisoned. The Dalai Lama assumed power in 1895 and began challenging China's control of Tibet. He also opposed efforts to open British trade routes in Tibet. His emissaries entered into negotiations to gain Russia's support for Tibet's autonomy. Britain opposed such a treaty and sent troops to Tibet in March 1904. The Dalai Lama was forced to flee to Outer Mongolia the following

September. Britain effectively established a protectorate over Tibet in the Dalai Lama's absence. He continued to work for Tibet's independence. He made a state visit to the dowager empress of China in September 1908, but remained committed to eliminating Chinese suzerainty over Tibet. He returned to Lhasa in December 1909, but advancing Chinese troops forced him to flee in February 1910. The Chinese imperial government officially deposed the Dalai Lama on February 25, 1910. The Panchen Lama was invited to become ruler of Tibet, but he refused to accept the appointment. The Dalai Lama subsequently went to India and sought British aide against the Chinese. China underwent a nationalist revolution in 1911, and the Dalai Lama attempted to return to Tibet. He was unable to reenter Lhasa until January 1913 when the Chinese forces finally left the city. The Dalai Lama proclaimed Tibet's independence from China in January 1913. The Simla Convention in April 1914 divided Tibet into two regions, Inner Tibet and Outer Tibet, with the latter gaining full autonomy. Tibet and Great Britain agreed to the arrangement, though Peking rejected the treaty. China initiated an unsuccessful military attack on Tibet in late 1917. Friction developed between the Dalai Lama and the Panchen Lama, and the latter fled Tibet in November 1923 and went to Peking two years later. The Dalai Lama began to seek a more moderate policy toward China in the late 1920s, but Tibetan and Chinese forces again clashed in the early 1930s. The Dalai Lama continued to exercise spiritual and political control over Tibet until his death on December 17, 1933. Ra-dreng Hutukhto, the leader of the Ra-dreng lamasery, became regent until the next reincarnation could be located.

TENZIN GYATSO (Dalai Lama; February 22, 1940–Present). Tenzin Gyatso was born in Amdo, Tsinghai Province, on June 7, 1935. He was proclaimed the fourteenth Dalai Lama on February 22, 1940. The regent Ra-dreng Hutukhto

ruled in his name and resigned in 1941. Ra-dreng died on May 8, 1947. Taktra Rimpoche served as regent from 1941 until the Dalai Lama assumed full power on November 17, 1950. The Communist Chinese had invaded Tibet the previous month and the Dalai Lama attempted to preserve as much autonomy for Tibet as possible. He was forced to flee into exile in India in March 1959 when a nationalist uprising was crushed by the Chinese. The Dalai Lama spent his years in exile as a spokesman for Tibetan independence. He made numerous tours throughout the world to gain support for his position. He also remained the preeminent figure in the Buddhist religion. He was awarded the Nobel Peace Prize in 1989.

Tonga

Tonga is a country consisting of a group of islands in the South Pacific Ocean. A constitutional monarchy since 1862, the country became a protectorate of Great Britain in 1900. It was granted independence on June 4, 1970.

HEADS OF STATE

GEORGE TUPOU II (King; February 1893–April 5, 1918). George Tupou II was born in 1874. He succeeded his great-grandfather to the throne of the Tonga, or Friendly, Islands in February 1893. Tonga was claimed as a British Protectorate in 1900. George remained ruler until his death from heart failure on April 5, 1918.

SALOTE TUPOU III (Queen; April 5, 1918–December 18, 1965). Salote Tupou was born in Nukualofa on March 13, 1900. She was the oldest daughter of

King George II of Tonga and succeeded him to the throne upon his death on April 5, 1918. She was a well-loved leader who established free educational facilities and health care for her people. Her husband, Prince Tungi, served as her prime minister from 1923 until his death in 1941. Salote Tupou made a public visit to Great Britain in 1953 for the coronation of Queen Elizabeth II. She was hospitalized in Auckland, New Zealand, in November 1965 for treatment for cancer and diabetes. Her condition worsened, and she died on December 15, 1965.

Transvaal

The Transvaal was a self-governing province of South Africa that existed as an independent republic from 1884 until 1902. After the Boer War, Transvaal and the Orange Free State became crown colonies of Great Britain. In 1910 they were joined through the South Africa Act with Natal and Cape of Good Hope as provinces of the Union of South Africa.

HEADS OF STATE

PAUL KRUGER (Head of State; May 8, 1883–May 31, 1902). Stephanus Johannes Paulus Kruger was born in Bulhoek, near Colesberg, on October 10, 1825. He left Cape Colony with his family in 1835 and settled in the Transvaal in 1841. He was active in the civil war to unify the Transvaal from 1861 to 1864 and subsequently became commandant-general. He served on the executive council of Transvaal where he became an opponent of the government of T. F. Burers. Kruger, who was known as "Oom Paul," led the Reactionary Party. The British occupied the Transvaal in April 1877, and Kruger soon became involved with the growing independence movement. He advised the Boers not to side with the Zulu tribesmen against the British in 1878. The Boers soon took up arms against the British and scored a victory at Majuba in 1881. Kruger was elected president of the Transvaal Republic and took office on May 8, 1883. He defeated General P. J. Joubert in re-election bids in 1888, 1893, and 1898. Kruger allied Transvaal with the Orange Free State in treaties in 1889 and 1897. He opposed the colonial policies of British Colonial Secretary Joseph Chamberlain, fearing they would deprive Transvaal of its independence. He declared war on Great Britain in October 1899 and attacked Cape Colony and Natal. British troops occupied Pretoria on June 5, 1900, and Kruger fled to Europe. Kruger made unsuccessful attempts to persuade the European powers to intervene in the conflict. The Boers continued to fight a guerrilla war against the British until the signing of the Treaty of Vereenignin on May 31, 1902. Kruger settled in Holland and died in Clarens, Switzerland, on July 14, 1904.

Tunisia

Tunisia is a country on the northern coast of Africa. A protectorate of France since 1881, Tunisia was granted independence on March 20, 1956.

HEADS OF STATE

ALI III (Bey; October 28, 1882–June 11, 1902). Ali III was born in 1817. Bey Mohammed Sadoq signed the Treaty of Bardo with France in May 1881, granting the French vast influence over the Tunisian government. Ali succeeded Mohammed as bey on October 28, 1882. The following year another concession at La Marsa granted the French full authority over Tunisia. Ali remained the figurehead sovereign of Tunisia, with the French resident-general controlling the government. Ali reigned until his death on June 11, 1902.

MUHAMMAD IV (Bey; June 11, 1902–May 11, 1906). Muhammad IV succeeded Ali III as bey of Tunisia on June 11, 1902. He reigned under the French colonial authority until his death on May 11, 1906.

MUHAMMAD V (Bey; May 11, 1906–July 10, 1922). Mohammed Nassef Pasha became bey of Tunisia on May 11, 1906, and reigned as Muhammad V. The following year young Tunisian students began agitating for greater control over the government. The nationalists formed Tunisia's first political party, the Destour, in 1920. Muhammad V remained bey until his death on July 10, 1922.

MUHAMMAD VI (Bey; July 10, 1922–February 11, 1929). Sidi Muhammad Ben-el-Habib was born on August 13, 1858. He succeeded his cousin, Muhammad V, as bey on July 10, 1922. Nationalists continued to agitate against the French colonial authorities during his reign. The leader of the Destour Party were either exiled or went underground in the mid-1920s. Muhammad VI reigned until his death on February 11, 1929.

AHMAD II (Bey; February 11, 1929–July 19, 1942). Sidi Ahmed Bey succeeded his cousin, Sidi Muhammad Ben-el-Habib, as bey of Tunisia upon the latter's death on February 11, 1929. Boycotts and demonstrations against French colonial authorities continued during his reign, culminating in violent rioting in Monastir in 1933. The new

French resident-general, Marcel Peyrouton, banned the Neo-Destour Party and jailed most of its leaders in 1934. Several hundred Tunisian nationalists were killed when the French fired on a demonstration in April 1937. Ahmad continued to reign under the Vichy French in the early 1940s. He died on July 19, 1942.

MUHAMMAD VII (Bey; July 19, 1942–May 14, 1943). Sidi Mohammed al-Moncef was born on March 4, 1881. He was the son of Mohammed Nassef Pasha, who ruled Tunisia as Muhammad V from 1906 until 1922. He succeeded Ahmad II to the throne on July 19, 1942. He formed a national ministry in December 1942, granting Tunisians more control of the government under the Vichy regime. After the Allies landed in Algeria during World War II, he was deposed on May 14, 1943, on the grounds that he had cooperated with the Vichy government. He was sent into exile in Paris after the war and died there on September 1, 1948.

MUHAMMAD VIII EL-AMIN (Bey; May 15, 1943–July 25, 1957). Muhammad el-Amin was born on September 4, 1881. He was a descendant of Hussein Bey, who had been the first bey of Tunisia in 1705. Muhammad el-Amin was placed on the throne of Tunisia by the French on May 15, 1943. He served as bey of Tunisia under the French colonial government. Tunisia was granted independence on March 20, 1956, and the bey was relegated to the status of a figurehead when Habib Ben Ali Bourguiba became prime minister the following month. The bey was deposed by the national assembly, and Tunisia was proclaimed a republic on July 25, 1957. Muhammad el-Amin was placed under house arrest until 1960. He died in his small apartment in Tunis on October 1, 1962.

Turkey

Turkey is a country in Asia Minor. It was formally proclaimed a republic in October 1923.

HEADS OF STATE

ABDUL HAMID II (Sultan; August 31, 1876–April 27, 1909). Abdul Hamid II was born in Constantinople on September 21, 1842. He was the son of Sultan Abdul Mejid I, who ruled the Ottoman Empire from July 1839 until his death on June 25, 1861. Abdul Hamid II succeeded to the throne following the deposition of his brother Murad V on the grounds of insanity on August 31, 1876. He proclaimed the Ottoman Empire's first constitution the following December. Abdul Hamid suspended the constitution in February 1878 and ruled as an absolute monarch for the next three decades. During the 1880s Abdul Hamid moved Turkey closer to Germany in international affairs. A rising in Armenia in 1895 resulted in the massacre of numerous Armenians in Constantinople and Armenia to the consternation of other European powers. Turkey engaged in a brief and successful war against Greece in 1897 over Crete. Abdul Hamid's government also championed Pan-Islamic causes, but this did little to quell rising unrest throughout the empire and demands for political reforms. The Sultan's increasing paranoia led to long periods of seclusion. A group of reformers known as the Young Turks led a military revolt against Abdul Hamid's government in 1908, and the Sultan was forced to restore the constitution on July 24, 1908. The Young Turks were briefly forced from power by a counterrevolution in April 1909. The Young Turks rallied when their army from Salonika restored them to power, and Abdul Hamid was deposed on April 27, 1909. He was succeeded by his brother, who ruled as Mehmet V. Abdul Hamid was confined at Salonika. He was returned to Constantinople in 1912 and died in confinement at Beylerbeyi Palace on February 10, 1918.

MEHMET V (Sultan; April 27, 1909–July 2, 1918). Mehmet V Reshid was born on November 3, 1844. He was the son of Sultan Abdul Mejid I. He succeeded his brother, Abdul Hamid II, to the throne of Turkey when the latter was deposed on April 27, 1909. Mehmet V exercised little power during his reign, with most authority coming from the Committee of Union and Progress (CUP), which had led the constitutional revolution the year before. Mehmet V remained sultan during World War I but had little influence on policy. He died in Yildiz on July 2, 1918, shortly before the Allied occupation.

MEHMET VI (Sultan; July 3, 1918–November 17, 1922). Mehmet VI Vahided-Din was born on January 14, 1861, the son of Sultan Abdul Mejid I. He succeeded to the throne following the death of his brother, Mehmet V, on July 2, 1918. He opposed Mustafa Kemal Ataturk's nationalist movement, and sided with the Allied forces occupying Constantinople after World War I. The Grand National Assembly in Ankara abolished the sultanate on November 16, 1922, and Mehmet VI went into exile in Italy aboard a British destroyer. He died in San Remo, Italy, on May 16, 1926.

ABDUL-MEJID II (Caliph; November 17, 1922–March 3, 1924). Abdul-Mejid II was born in Constantinople on May 30, 1868. He was a son of Sultan

Abdul-Aziz, who ruled the Ottoman Empire from June 1861 until his deposition in May 1876. He was confined to the palace for the first forty years of his life. He was proclaimed crown prince when Mehmet VI assumed the sultanate. He was stripped of the title following the deposition of Mehmet VI in 1922 and the overthrow of the sultanate. Abdul-Mejid II was chosen as the Ottoman empire's caliph on November 17, 1922. The caliphate was abolished on March 3, 1924, several months after the proclamation of Turkey as a republic. Abdul-Mejid and other members of the royal family were forced into exile. He died in Paris on August 23, 1944.

MUSTAFA KEMAL ATATURK (President; October 29, 1923–November 10, 1938). Mustafa Kemal Ataturk was born in Salonika in 1881. He was named Mustafa and was the son of a Turkish militia officer. He was educated in a secular school at the insistence of his father, who died when Mustafa was seven. He received the secondary name Kemal while in school. He was accepted in the military school in Monastir in 1895 and continued his education at the War College and the General Staff College, from which he graduated in 1905. While still in school, Mustafa Kemal became involved in the movement against Sultan Abdul Hamid II. He joined the antigovernment Committee of Union and Progress (CUP) in 1907. The "Young Turk" revolution, led by Enver Pasha and others, took place in July of the following year and forced reforms and a representative government on the sultan. A counterrevolution was put down by the army in April 1909 and the sultan was forced to abdicate. Mustafa Kemal felt that the army should withdraw from political affairs. His views, and his rising popularity among military officers, brought him into conflict with the CUP, which consistently denied him a promotion. Mustafa Kemal went into active duty when the Italians invaded the Ot-

toman province of Libya in late 1911. Health problems forced him to leave the front for treatment in Vienna, Austria. He was there when the First Balkan War broke out in October 1912. Mustafa Kemal was placed in charge of the Turkish defense at Gallipoli. The Turkish defeat there resulted in the loss of much of Turkey's territory in Europe, some of which was restored following the Second Balkan War in July 1913. Despite his opposition to Enver's ties with Germany, Mustafa Kemal sought an active role when the Ottoman Empire entered World War I on the side of the Central Powers. He was credited with halting the Allies' advance at Gallipoli and was proclaimed the "Savior of Constantinople." His successes earned him the rank of colonel in June 1915. The following year he was assigned to the Russian front, where he achieved the rank of general and the title of pasha. Mustafa Kemal was named to a command in Syria after the Russian Revolution in March 1917. He was dismayed by the state of the army there and returned to Constantinople without permission, which resulted in a nine-month suspension. He was sent back to Syria in the closing days of World War I. The Turkish army was disbanded after the defeat of the Ottoman Empire, and the Allies began claiming Turkish territory. Mustafa Kemal vowed to oppose the Allied presence on Turkish soil. He was sent by the sultan to Anatolia to restore order after militants attacked non-Muslims and threatened Allied positions. On May 19, 1919, Mustafa Kemal ignored the orders of the sultan to tell a cheering crowd that he would lead the fight for Ottoman independence. He ignored a recall by the sultan and resigned from the army. Mustafa Kemal, with the backing of General Kazim Karebekir, called a congress in Erzurum that called for the establishment of inviolate borders for the six eastern Turkish provinces. A sympathetic government was established in Constantinople, though Mustafa Kemal remained in Ankara. The Allied occupation forces, with the support of the sultan, moved against the nationalists in March 1920 and arrested many of the movement's leaders. A new Grand National Assembly was elected the following month and Mustafa Kemal was chosen as its president. He refused to accept the Treaty of Sevres, signed by the sultan in August 1920, which greatly reduced the size of the Ottoman Empire. Mustafa Kemal began a military campaign to force Greek troops from southern Turkey and to recapture Armenia, which had been granted independence by the Allies. The nationalists received support from the Bolshevik government in the Soviet Union, and France and Italy agreed to withdraw their troops from the area. Armenia was quickly overwhelmed, and the Turkish army drove the Greeks back the following year. The Grand National Assembly voted to abolish the sultanate in November 1922. The Allies subsequently negotiated the Treaty of Lansanne with the nationalists, establishing Turkey's European borders. The Turkish republic, with its capital in Ankara, was proclaimed on October 29, 1923, with Mustafa Kemal as its first president. He put down several revolts during the early years of the republic. Mustafa Kemal began a program of modernization and Westernization in the country. The wearing of the fez headdress was banned, and the emancipation of women was begun. Western judicial systems were implemented to replace Islamic law, and the Latin alphabet was instituted to replace Arabic script. Mustafa Kemal also modernized the Turkish army and navy. Titles were abolished and surnames adopted in 1934, with Mustafa Kemal taking the name Ataturk, meaning "Father of the Turks." He ruled in an autocratic fashion, allowing little dissent against the government, which was generally popular. Ataturk's health began to fail in the late 1930s, and he was diagnosed with cirrhosis of the liver. He died at his residence at Colmabahce Palace in Istanbul on November 10, 1938.

ISMET INONU (President; November 11, 1938–May 14, 1950). Ismet Inonu was born in Inonu on September 25, 1884. He was educated at the Constantinople Military Academy and entered the Turkish army as a captain upon his graduation in 1906. He was active in the revolutionary movement of Young Turks that ousted Sultan Abdul Hamid II in 1909. Inonu remained in the army and served in Yemen as chief of the general staff in 1912, and participated in the Balkan war against Greece, Bulgaria, and Serbia. Inonu commanded Turkish troops in alliance with Germany during World War I. He rose to the rank of major general and became a leading advisor to Turkish nationalist leader Mustafa Kemal Ataturk. He again commanded troops against the Greeks in the early 1920s while trying to establish Turkey's borders. Inonu joined the cabinet as minister of foreign affairs in 1922, and on November 30, 1923, he became Turkey's first prime minister following the proclamation of the Turkish republic. He remained prime minister until November 21, 1924, and again headed the government from March 4, 1925, to October 25, 1937. He worked closely with President Ataturk to reform and modernize Turkey. His relationship with Ataturk became strained, and he stepped down as prime minister in October, 1937. Ataturk died the following year, and on November 11, 1938, Inonu was chosen by the Grand National Assembly to serve as Turkey's president. He ruled in an authoritarian manner and rigidly controlled the political opposition and the press. Turkey remained neutral until the final months of World War II, when it declared war on the Axis Powers. Inonu allowed the formation of opposition parties after the war, and he was defeated by the Democratic Party in Turkey's first two-party election in 1950. He relinquished office to Celal Bayar on May 22,

1950, and became the leader of the Opposition in the Turkish parliament. The Turkish military ousted the Democratic Party government in 1961, and Inonu was asked to form a coalition government as prime minister on November 10, 1961. He maintained close relations with the United States and was a strong supporter of the North Atlantic Treaty Organization (NATO). His government survived coup attempts in January 1962 and in May 1963. Inonu's coalition collapsed on several occasions, but he was able to form new cabinets. His government was forced to resign on February 13, 1965, following the National Assembly's rejection of the budget. Inonu led the Republican People's Party in opposition to the Justice Party government of Suleyman Demirel. Inonu was replaced as leader of the party by Bulent Ecevit in 1972 and was given the ceremonial position of party chairman. He died of a heart attack at his home in Ankara on December 25, 1973.

HEADS OF GOVERNMENT

HALIL RIFAT PASA (Grand Vizier; November 7, 1895–November 9, 1901). Halil Rifat Pasa was born in 1830. He served as a provincial governor and was minister of the interior from 1893 until 1895. He was subsequently named grand vizier on November 7, 1895. He served until November 9, 1901, and died in 1903.

MEHMET SAIT PASA (Grand Vizier; November 18, 1901–January 14, 1903). Mehmet Sait Pasa was born in 1838. He served as chief secretary to Sultan Abdul Hamid II from 1876 until 1878. He was appointed grand vizier for the first of many times on October 18, 1879, serving until June 9, 1880. He also served from September 12, 1880, until May 2, 1882; July 12, 1882 until November 30, 1882; and again from December 3, 1882, until September 25, 1885, when he was dismissed over Bulgaria's annexation of East Rumelia. He returned for several months in 1895. He faithfully carried out the sultan's wishes and instituted the modernization of the civil service system. He was called upon to serve as grand vizier again on November 18, 1901, and retired on January 14, 1903. He returned to the government under the Committee for Union and Progress, serving as grand vizier from September 30, 1911, to July 16, 1912, after which he retired. He died in 1914.

MEHMET FERIT PASA (Grand Vizier; January 14, 1903–July 22, 1908). Mehmet Ferit Pasa was born in Jannina in 1852. He was educated in Albania and was a close advisor to Islamic movement leader Gazi Osman Pasa. He served on the council of state from the 1890s and was named grand vizier on January 14, 1903. He retained office for five years and stepped down on July 22, 1908. He died in San Remo on December 9, 1914.

MEHMET KÂMIL PASA (Grand Vizier; August 5, 1908–February 14, 1909). Mehmet Kâmil Pasa was born in Cyprus in 1832. He served in the Egyptian civil service and worked in the Ottoman bureaucracy from 1860 until 1879. He subsequently served as governor of Lebanon, where he drew the attention of the sultan. He was named grand vizier on September 25, 1885, and worked to stabilize the Ottoman Empire's economy. He served until September 4, 1891. He was named grand vizier again on October 2, 1895, but was forced to resign on November 7, 1895, over a conflict with the sultan concerning his attempts to interfere in the government. Kâmil was exiled to Izmir as governor. He returned to serve as grand vizier under the Committee for Union and Progress on August 5, 1908. He stepped down on February 14, 1909. Kâmil died in 1913.

HÜSEYIN HILMI PASA (Grand Vizier; February 14, 1909–April 13, 1909). Hüseyin Hilmi Pasa was born in Lesbos in 1855. As a provincial administrator, he worked to settle the Macedonian problems in 1900. He was a supporter of the Committee of Union and Progress, and served as minister of the interior in 1908 and 1909. He served as grand vizier from February 14, 1909, until April 13, 1909, during the counterrevolution. He served as minister of justice in 1912 and was the Ottoman Empire's ambassador to Austria-Hungary during World War I. He died in Vienna in 1921.

AHMET TEVFIK PASA (Grand Vizier; April 14, 1909–May 5, 1909). Ahmet Tevfik Pasa was born in Constantinople on February 11, 1845. He was a professional soldier and diplomat. He served as minister of foreign affairs from 1895 until 1908. He was named grand vizier on April 14, 1909, and served until May 5, 1909. He returned to head the government from November 11, 1918, until March 3, 1919 and again from October 21, 1920, until November 4, 1922, after the Grand National Assembly had abolished the sultanate. He died in Istanbul in 1936.

HÜSEYIN HILMI PASA (Grand Vizier; May 5, 1909–December 28, 1909). *See earlier entry under Heads of Government.*

IBRAHIM HAKKI PASA (Grand Vizier; January 12, 1910–September 29, 1911). Ibrahim Hakki Pasa was born in Constantinople on April 12, 1863. He was a leading expert in administrative law and served as minister of education from 1908 until 1909. He subsequently served as ambassador to Rome before

being named grand vizier on January 12, 1910. He stepped down on September 29, 1911. He was named ambassador to Germany in 1916 and served until his death in Berlin on July 30, 1918.

MEHMET SAIT PASA (Grand Vizier; September 30, 1911–July 16, 1912). *See earlier entry under Heads of Government.*

AHMET MUHTAR PASA (Grand Vizier; July 22, 1912–October 29, 1912). Gazi Ahmet Muhtar Pasa was born in Bursa on November 1, 1839. He was a hero in the Russo-Turkish War in 1878, halting the Russian's advance on the Eastern front. He served as the Ottoman Empire's high commissioner to Egypt from 1895 until 1906. He was an advocate of modernization and reform in the Ottoman Empire and allied himself with the Committee of Union and Progress. He was chosen as grand vizier on July 22, 1912. The outbreak of the First Balkan War forced Ahmet Muhtar's resignation on October 29, 1912. He died in Constantinople on January 21, 1918.

MEHMET KÂMIL PASA (Grand Vizier; October 29, 1912–January 23, 1913). *See earlier entry under Heads of Government.*

MAHMUD SEVKET PASA (Grand Vizier; January 23, 1913–June 11, 1913). Mahmud Sevket was born in 1858, in Baghdad, and was educated in Constantinople. He subsequently served in the Turkish army. He was stationed in Germany for nine years and was promoted to the rank of general in 1901. He supported the Young Turk Revolution in 1908 and, as inspector general and commander of the Third Army, he suppressed a counterrevolution the following year. Following the abdication of Sultan Abdul Hamid II, Sevket became minister of war. Following an insurrection by members of the Committee of Union and Progress (CUP) and the subsequent resignation of

Kamil Pasa as grand vizier, Sevket assumed that office on January 23, 1913. He was assassinated by opponents of the CUP on June 11, 1913.

SAIT HALIM PASA (Grand Vizier; June 12, 1913–February 3, 1917). Sait Halim Pasa was born in Cairo in 1863. Sait Halim was an Egyptian prince who became active in Ottoman politics in the early 1900s. He was elected to the parliament, where he became affiliated with the Committee of Union and Progress. He was chosen as grand vizier on June 12, 1913, following the assassination of Mahmud Sevket. He was largely a figurehead during his term of office, with the real power residing with the CUP leadership. He was involved in the negotiations with Germany that resulted in an alliance with the Ottoman Empire during World War I. He resigned in protest over the conduct of war policy on February 3, 1917. Sait Halim was arrested by the Allies following the occupation of Constantinople in 1918. He died in Rome on December 7, 1921.

MEHMET TALÂT PASA (Grand Vizier; February 4, 1917–October 8, 1918). Mehmet Talât Pasa was born in Edirne in July 1874. He was a leader of the Committee for Union and Progress during the revolution in 1909, and became minister of the interior in the subsequent government. He served as minister of the interior and grand vizier from February 4, 1917 until October 8, 1918. Talât was considered responsible for the Turkish policy of genocide against Armenians, in which more than 500,000 were reported massacred. He went into exile following Turkey's defeat by the Allies in 1918. Talât was shot and killed in Berlin by an Armenian, Saro Melikian, on March 15, 1921.

AHMET IZZET PASA (Grand Vizier; October 14, 1918–November 8, 1918). Ahmet Izzet Pasa was born in Naslic in 1864. He was a professional soldier and served as second scribe to Sultan Abdul Hamid II in 1893. He commanded the Ottoman forces on the Caucasus front during World War I. He briefly served as grand vizier from October 14, 1918, until November 8, 1918. During that time he signed the armistice with the British to officially end the Ottoman Empire's participation in World War I. Izzet served under Ataturk as minister of war in the early years of the Turkish Republic. He died in Istanbul on March 31, 1937.

AHMET TEVFIK PASA (Grand Vizier; November 11, 1918–March 3, 1919). *See earlier entry under Heads of Government.*

DAMAT MEHMET FERIT PASA (Grand Vizier; March 4, 1919–October 1, 1919). Damat Mehmet Ferit Pasa was born in Constantinople in 1853. He was married to Mediha Sultan, the daughter of Sultan Abdul Mecit I. He was a professional diplomat and served in the Chamber of Notables in 1908. He was appointed grand vizier on March 4, 1919, and opposed the nationalists. He was forced to step down on October 1, 1919. Ferit died in Nice, France, on October 6, 1923.

ALI RIZA PASA (Grand Vizier; October 2, 1919–March 3, 1920). Ali Riza Pasa was born in Constantinople in 1859. He was a military officer who served as minister of war during the Young Turk period. He was named grand vizier on October 2, 1919, serving until March 3, 1920. He died in Istanbul on October 31, 1932.

SALIH HULUSI PASA (Grand Vizier; March 8, 1920–April 2, 1920). Salih Hulusi Kezrak Salih Pasa was born in Constantinople in 1864. He was a military officer who served as minister of the navy and public works during the Young Turk period. He represented the government in the Amasya conference with Ataturk in 1919. He served as grand vizier from March 8, 1920, until April 2, 1920. He subsequently served as minister of the navy until 1922, when he joined the nationalists. He died on October 24, 1939.

DAMAT MEHMET FERIT PASA
(Grand Vizier; April 5, 1920–October 17, 1920). *See earlier entry under Heads of Government.*

AHMET TEVFIK PASA (Grand Vizier; October 21, 1920–November 4, 1922). *See earlier entry under Heads of Government.*

MUSTAFA KEMAL ATATURK
(Prime Minister; May 3, 1920–January 24, 1921). *See earlier entry under Heads of State.*

FEVZI CAKMAK (Prime Minister; January 24, 1921–July 9, 1922). Fevzi Cakmak was born in Constantinople on January 12, 1876. He was educated at the military college and entered the army as a lieutenant in 1895. He rose through the ranks, serving as a lieutenant colonel and chief of staff of the Kosova Army Corps in 1910. He served as chief of staff of the western army during the Italo-Turkish war in 1911 and commanded a division during the Balkan Wars from 1912 until 1914. During World War I Cakmak was instrumental in the defense of the Dardanelles, and he led Turkish troops against the Greeks after the war. He served as minister of war in the imperial government in 1920 and was named minister of national defense after Mustafa Kemal took control of the revolutionary government in 1921. He headed the prime minister's council from January 24, 1921, until July 9, 1922. He was subsequently promoted to general and served as chief of staff. He was a leading candidate to succeed to the presidency after Ataturk's death in 1938, but withdrew his candidacy. He remained chief of staff until 1944. He was elected to the Grand National Assembly in 1946 and contested the presidency later in the year. He was defeated by Ismet Inonu. Cakmak became honorary leader of the newly formed Nation's Party in 1948. He died in Istanbul after a lengthy illness on April 10, 1950.

RAUF ORBAY (Prime Minister; July 12, 1922–August 13, 1923). Huseyin Rauf Orbay was born in Constantinople in 1881. He served with distinction in the Ottoman navy during World War I. He was named minister of the navy near the end of the war and signed the armistice in 1918. He was initially a supporter of Mustafa Kemal Ataturk, but later opposed Ataturk's modernization policies in the Grand National Assembly. Orbay was chosen as prime minister on July 12, 1922. He stepped down on August 13, 1923, when Ataturk was elected president. He resigned from the assembly the following year when the caliphate was abolished. He subsequently formed the Progressive Republican Party in opposition to Ataturk. Orbay was exiled by Ataturk and died in 1964.

FETHI OKYAR (Prime Minister; August 14, 1923–October 27, 1923). Ali Fethi Okyar was born in Prilep, Macedonia, in 1880. He fought with the Ottoman army in the Tripolitanian war and served as minister of the interior in 1917. He entered the Grand National Assembly in 1920 and served as minister of the interior and prime minister from August 14, 1923, until October 27, 1923, and again from November 21, 1924, until March 2, 1925. He served as Turkey's ambassador to Paris from 1925 until 1930. He founded the Free Republican Party in 1930, when he was named ambassador to Great Britain. Okyar also served as minister of justice. He died on May 7, 1943.

ISMET INONU (Prime Minister; November 30, 1923–November 21, 1924). *See earlier entry under Heads of State.*

FETHI OKYAR (Prime Minister; November 21, 1924–March 2, 1925). *See earlier entry under Heads of Government.*

ISMET INONU (March 4, 1925–October 25, 1937). *See earlier entry under Heads of State.*

CELAL BAYAR (Prime Minister; October 25, 1937–January 25, 1939). Mahmut Celal Bayar was born in Umurbey on May 15, 1884. He was educated locally and worked as a bank clerk in Bursa. He joined the Young Turks movement in 1907 and participated in the rebellion that deposed Sultan Abdul Hamid II in 1909. Bayar served as a deputy in the Grand National Assembly after World War I and was named to the cabinet as minister of the economy in 1921. He was named minister of reconstruction in 1922. He left the government to reenter the banking industry in 1924. Bayar returned to the government as minister of national economy in 1932 and instituted programs to improve Turkey's economy. He was named to replace Ismet Inonu as prime minister on October 25, 1937. He retained office following Inonu's election to the presidency after Ataturk's death in November 1938. Bayar resigned on January 25, 1939, and was replaced by Refik Saydam. He remained in the Grand National Assembly until 1945, when he resigned to form the Democratic Party with Adnan Menderes. He was reelected to the Grand National Assembly the following year and served as leader of the opposition. The Democratic Party was victorious in elections in 1950, and Bayar replaced Inonu as president on May 22, 1950. He pursued an economic policy that encouraged private industry, and he was reelected in 1954 and 1957. The growing authoritarian nature of the Democratic Party government led to student riots in April 1960. The military led a coup that ousted Bayar and Prime Minister Adnan Menderes on May 27, 1960. Bayar and other leaders of the Democratic Party were arrested by the new regime. Menderes was hanged, but Bayar's sentence was commuted to life imprisonment due to his advanced age. He was released in a general amnesty in 1964, and his political rights were restored in 1974. Bayar died in a hospital in Istanbul at the age of 102 on August 21, 1986.

REFIK SAYDAM (Prime Minister; January 26, 1939–July 8, 1942). Refik Saydam was born Salahaddin Refik Bey in 1881. He headed the public health administration in Samsun, where he met Mustafa Kemal Ataturk. He became Ataturk's personal physician and was named minister of health after the formation of Ataturk's revolutionary government in 1920. He did much to improve health care in Turkey, founding numerous hospitals and clinics throughout the country. He resigned from the government in 1937, but returned to the cabinet as minister of the interior in November 1938. Saydam was appointed prime minister on January 26, 1939, after Ismet Inonu's election as Ataturk's successor to the presidency. He signed the Anglo-French-Turkish agreement later in the year. Saydam continued to head the government until his death in an Istanbul hotel while vacationing on July 8, 1942.

FIKRI TUZER (Acting Prime Minister; July 8, 1942–July 10, 1942). Fikri Tuzer served as minister of the interior in Refik Saydam's government. He became acting prime minister upon Saydam's death on July 8, 1942, but stepped down two days later on July 10, 1942, when President Ismet Inonu appointed Sukru Saracoglu to head the government.

SUKRU SARACOGLU (Prime Minister; July 10, 1942–August 7, 1946).

Sukru Saracoglu was born in Odemis in 1887. He was educated locally and attended the University of Lausanne, where he received a degree in law. He joined Mustafa Kemal Ataturk's nationalist movement and was elected to the Ottoman parliament in 1919. Saracoglu participated in the establishment of the Turkish republic in 1923 and served as a member of Ataturk's Republican People's Party in the Grand National Assembly. He was appointed to the cabinet as minister of finance in 1927 and was a close advisor to President Ataturk and Prime Minister Ismet Inonu. He left the cabinet in 1930 to serve as Turkey's economic emissary to the United States and France. Saracoglu returned to Turkey to serve as minister of justice in 1932. He was named foreign minister in 1938 and negotiated treaties with Great Britain and France to preserve Turkey's neutrality during World War II. He was selected as prime minister on July 10, 1942, following the death of Refik Saydam. Saracoglu remained foreign minister in the new government. He served as head of the government when Turkey declared war on the Axis Powers in February 1945. Saracoglu was replaced by Recep Peker as prime minister on August 7, 1946. He became president of the Republican People's Party in 1947 and was elected president of the Grand National Assembly in 1948. Saracoglu was defeated for reelection to the assembly when the Democratic Party came to power in the general elections in 1950. He retired from politics and died at his home in Istanbul on December 27, 1953.

Ukraine

The Ukraine declared itself an autonomous republic on June 23, 1917. The region was occupied variously by German, Polish, White Russian, and Soviet troops over the next several years. It was annexed as a state in the Union of Soviet Socialist Republics in December 1922. Following the breakup of the Soviet Union, Ukraine gained its independence in 1991.

HEADS OF STATE

MYHAILO HRUSHEVSKY (President; June 23, 1917–April 24, 1918). Myhailo Hrushevsky was born in 1866. He became a professor of the history of southeastern Europe at Lwow University in 1890. He began writing his ten-volume *History of the Ukraine-Rus* in 1898. He returned to Kiev in 1905. Hrushevsky was elected leader of the Rada (central committee) of the Ukraine in April 1917 after the Russian revolution began. The Ukraine was proclaimed an autonomous republic on June 23, 1917, with Hrushevsky as president. The Communist forces captured Kiev in February 1918 and the government fled to Zhitomir. The Austrian and German forces staged a coup on April 24, 1918, and Hrushevsky was replaced as president by Pavilo Skoropadsky. He died in 1934.

PAVILO SKOROPADSKY (President; April 24, 1918–December 14, 1918). Pavilo Petrovich Skoropadsky was born in Weissbaden on May 15, 1873. He graduated from the Corps of Pages in 1893 and served in the czar's mounted guard. He commanded the First Guards Cavalry Division during World War I.

He became head of the newly formed Ukrainian military units in October 1917 after the Russian Revolution. Skoropadsky was installed as hetman, or head of state, of the Ukraine by the Germans on April 24, 1918. His government collapsed on December 14, 1918, after the Central Powers were defeated in World War I. He fled to Germany, where he was an outspoken opponent of the Soviet Union's Communist regime. Skoropadsky died in Murnau on April 26, 1945.

VOLODYMIR VINNICHENKO (President; December 14, 1918–February 1919). Volodymir Kirillovich Vinnichenko was born in Kherson Province on July 26, 1880. He was educated at the University of Kiev and joined the Revolutionary Ukrainian Party in 1901. The organization became known as the Ukrainian Social Democratic Labor Party, and Vinnichenko served on the central committee in 1907. He subsequently lived abroad for seven years, returning to the Ukraine in 1914. He was an organizer of the Radu, or central committee, when the Ukraine proclaimed its autonomy in June 1917. He was named premier of an independent Ukraine on July 16, 1917. His government was ousted by the German and Austrian armies on April 24, 1918. He returned to serve as chairman of the central committee on December 14, 1918, after the collapse of the Central Powers in World War I. Vinnichenko was supplanted as Ukraine's leader by General Simon Petlyura in February 1919. He went into exile until the summer of 1920, when he returned to briefly serve on the Soviet-dominated Council of People's Commissars as vice chairman. He broke with the Communists

and again went into exile at the end of the year. He settled in Paris, where he wrote and lectured until his death in 1951.

SIMON PETLYURA (President; February 1919–May 25, 1926). Simon Petlyura was born in Poltava on May 17, 1879. He was a founder of the Ukrainian Social Democratic Workers' Party in 1905. He was editor of the Socialist newspaper *Slovo* in Kiev until 1909 and published the Moscow weekly *Ukrainskaya Zhizn* from 1912 until 1914. He served in the Russian army during World War I. After the Russian revolution in March 1917, Petlyura became a member of the Ukrainian central council. He served as minister of war after the formation of an autonomous Ukrainian government in June 1917. He was forced from the government when the Germans occupied the Ukraine in April 1918. He returned to power as commander-in-chief of the Ukrainian army in November 1918. He was recognized as head of state the following February. The Soviet and White Russian armies contested Petlyura's forces in the Ukraine over the next several years. Petlyura turned to Poland for assistance. A treaty with Polish leader Jozef Piłsudski in April 1920 led to the Russo-Polish War. The Soviets forced Petlyura and the Polish from the Ukraine, and Petlyura formed a government-in-exile in Warsaw. He soon moved to Paris where he continued to head the exile government. Petlyura was shot to death on May 25, 1926, in the streets of Paris by Shalom Schwarzbard, a Jewish student who held Petlyura responsible for the persecution of Ukrainian Jews.

United Kingdom

Great Britain is in northwestern Europe on the British Isles.

HEADS OF STATE

VICTORIA (Queen; June 20, 1837–January 22, 1901). Alexandrina Victoria was born at Kensington Palace, London, on May 24, 1819. She was the only child of Edward, Duke of Kent, the fourth son of King George III, and Princess Mary Louisa Victoria of Saxe-Coburg-Gotha. Her father died the year after her birth. She had an unhappy childhood and grew up isolated from much of her family because of the desire of her mother's advisor, Sir John Conroy, to manipulate the future queen. She ascended to the throne on June 20, 1837, following the death of her uncle, William IV, who had produced no surviving heir. Once on the throne she largely rid herself of the influence of her mother and Conroy. Victoria had a close relationship with Whig Prime Minister Lord Melbourne. When he resigned in 1939 Conservative leader Sir Robert Peel suggested that Victoria dismiss the Whig ladies in her court. She refused and "the bedchamber crisis" resulted in Melbourne resuming office for two more years. Victoria married her first cousin, Prince Albert of Saxe-Coburg-Gotha, on February 10, 1840. Prince Albert encouraged Victoria to make her views known to the government on matters of importance and was instrumental in repairing her relationship with Peel. Victoria was partially responsible for the resignation of Lord Palmerston as foreign secretary in 1851 over her opposition to his policy of encouraging democracy in Europe. Victoria and Albert produced nine children before his death on December 14, 1861. Victoria spent the next forty years of her life in mourning after Albert's passing. The prudish and straightlaced manner associated with the Victorian Age is more rightly attributed to the influence of that time of mourning. Her primary companion and confidant during this period was a Scottish servant, John Brown. Her virtual seclusion in the 1860s resulted in a decrease in her popularity and republican sentiment caused some concern about the future of the monarchy. She regained some of her standing with her support of Benjamin Disraeli's imperialist policies. Victoria became empress of India in 1876. She was bitterly opposed to the policies of Liberal leader William E. Gladstone, whom she also disliked personally. She consulted often with the government and made her opinions known without hesitation. Her influence decreased during the later years of her reign as growing party strength largely eliminated the need of the monarch as a mediator. She retained great popularity with her subjects as evidenced by the sentiment shown her on her golden and diamond jubilees in 1887 and 1897. She continued to reign until her death after a short illness on January 22, 1901.

EDWARD VII (King; January 22, 1901–May 5, 1910). Edward VII was born Albert Edward in London on November 9, 1841. He was the eldest son of Queen Victoria and Prince Albert of Saxe-Coburg-Gotha. He was created Prince of Wales and Earl of Chester on December 4, 1841. He was educated at Edinburgh University and Christ Church, Oxford. In the late 1850s he embarked on a tour to such countries as Spain, Portugal, Canada, and the United States. Edward's association with an actress he met in June 1861 caused serious problems with the royal family. His relationship with his mother, Queen Victoria, never fully recovered from the affair. Edward married Princess Alexandra, the daughter of King Christian IX of Denmark, in March 1863. The couple had five children that survived to maturity. Edward had entered the House of Lords in February 1863, after which he did much of the royal family's work of attending public functions. He became seriously ill with typhoid in 1871 but recovered the following year. Edward was a familiar figure in the sporting and social world throughout Europe, with particular interests in yachting and racing. He eventually succeeded to the throne upon the death of his mother on January 22, 1901. He was crowned in August 1902. His outgoing nature was a marked contrast to the many years of seclusion Queen Victoria had spent since becoming a widow. Edward was a popular monarch in Britain and abroad, though his relationship with his nephew, Kaiser Wilhelm II of Germany, was somewhat strained. Edward reigned for nearly a decade before his death of heart failure following bronchitis and bronchial pneumonia in London on May 6, 1910.

GEORGE V (King; May 5, 1910–January 20, 1936). George Frederick Ernest Albert was born in London on June 3, 1865. He was the second son of the future King Edward VII and Queen Alexandra. He attended the Royal Naval College and served as an officer in the English navy. His hopes for a career in the active ranks of the navy were abandoned following the death of his older brother, the Duke of Clarence, on June 14, 1892. George became the heir presumptive to the throne and was created Duke of York, Earl of Inverness, and Baron Killarney the following May. He married his brother's fiancee, Princess Mary of Teck, in July 1893. George was created Duke of Cornwall and Prince of Wales following his father's ascension to the throne on January 22, 1901. King Edward VII died on June 22, 1911, and the

prince ascended the throne as George V. He was a popular monarch and made a personal attempt to maintain peace in Europe prior to the start of World War I. His attempts were unsuccessful, and he made several visits to the front during the conflict. England was beset by economic problems and industrial strife in the 1920s. He personally selected Stanley Baldwin to head a Conservative government following the resignation of Arthur Bonar Law in May 1923. The king became seriously ill in November 1928 and made a slow recovery. The worldwide economic crisis resulted in a collapse of the pound in 1931. The king called for the formation of a national coalition cabinet under Ramsay MacDonald to handle the nation's economic problems in August of 1931. George's health continued to fail during his Silver Jubilee celebration in May 1935. He contracted a bronchial condition and succumbed to his illness at Sandringham, Norfolk, on January 20, 1936.

EDWARD VIII (King; January 20, 1936–December 11, 1936). Edward Albert Christian George Andrew Patrick David was born in Richmond, Surrey, England, on June 23, 1894. He was the eldest child of the future King George V and Queen Mary. He was educated at the Royal Naval College, Dartmouth, and Oxford. He became heir apparent after the ascension of his father in May 1910 and was invested as Prince of Wales in 1911. Edward served as a staff officer in the army's Grenadier Guards during World War I. After the war Edward represented England abroad on a number of goodwill tours. He began to take a great interest in matters of state following his father's illness in 1928. The prince had a reputation of a playboy during the 1920s. He became acquainted with Mrs. Wallis Warfield Simpson in 1930. The two fell in love, and she obtained a divorce from her husband, Ernest Simpson, in October 1936. The prince had ascended the throne as Edward VIII upon the death of his father on January 20, 1936. The royal family and the Church of England bitterly opposed the relationship between the king and Mrs. Simpson. Prime Minister Stanley Baldwin insisted to the king that the nation would not accept a divorced American in the palace. Edward was faced with the choice of abandoning his romance with Mrs. Simpson or renouncing the throne. He made his choice and submitted his abdication on December 10, 1936. The following day in a radio address he said "I have found it impossible to carry on the heavy burden of responsibility and to discharge the duties of king as I would wish to do without the help and support of the woman I love." He was succeeded by his brother, who took the throne as George VI. Edward was granted the title of Duke of Windsor soon after his abdication. He wed Mrs. Simpson in Chateau de Cande, France, on June 3, 1937. The royal family refused to extend the rank of royal highness to the new duchess, severely damaging relations between the duke and his family. The duke and duchess resided in France for the next several years. They went to Madrid after the fall of France during World War II. The duke was the object of several overtures by the Nazis to return him to the throne as a pawn against Britain during the war. The British government offered him the governorship of the Bahamas in 1940, and he remained there throughout the war. He returned to Paris in 1945. He made several visits to London over the next two decades, attending the funeral of his brother in 1952 and his mother's funeral the following year. The couple was not invited to participate in an official royal function until 1967. The Duke's health began to deteriorate in 1971, and he died at his home in Paris on May 27, 1972, after a lengthy illness. The Duchess died fourteen years later on April 24, 1986, and was buried by his side at Frogmore on the grounds of Windsor Castle.

GEORGE VI (King; December 11, 1936–February 6, 1952). Albert Frederick Arthur George was born in York Cottage at Sandringham in Norfolk on December 14, 1895. He was the second son of George V, who became king of England in May 1911. He was known as Prince Albert before he ascended to the throne. He attended the Royal Naval College and Dartmouth. Prince Albert served in the navy and saw action during the early years of World War I, but poor health forced an end to his naval career in August 1917. He recovered after surgery for an ulcer and subsequently entered the Royal Air Force. He was created Duke of York, Earl of Inverness, and Baron Killarney on June 3, 1920. He married the Lady Elizabeth Bowes-Lyon in April 1923. The duke and duchess performed their public duties at home and abroad. King George V died on January 20, 1936, and he was succeeded by his eldest son, King Edward VIII. When Edward abdicated the throne to marry Wallis Simpson on December 11, 1936, the Duke of York ascended the throne. He was crowned King George VI on May 12, 1937, in Westminster Abbey. The following year the new king paid a state visit to France, and in 1939 he became the first British monarch to visit the United States. Britain entered World War II shortly after the king's return home. The king helped to maintain the morale of the British people during the war years through radio broadcasts and personal tours of areas that had been damaged by German bombs. He also paid visits to British troops engaged in the fighting. Following the war, the king worked with the Labour government in implementing social reforms for the country. India gained independence from Britain in 1947, and George VI relinquished the title of emperor of India. The king toured South Africa and Rhodesia in 1947, but was forced to cancel a trip to Australia the following year due to poor health. He successfully underwent surgery in March 1949. His health again declined in 1951, and he was diagnosed as having lung cancer. He again had surgery in September 1951. George VI seemed to be recovering from his illness when he died suddenly of a heart attack in Sandringham on February 6, 1952.

HEADS OF GOVERNMENT

ROBERT ARTHUR TALBOT GASCOYNE-CECIL, MARQUESS OF SALISBURY (Prime Minister; July 2, 1895–July 12, 1902). Robert Arthur Talbot Gascoyne-Cecil was born in Hatfield, Hertfordshire, on February 3, 1830. He was the son of the 2nd Marquess of Salisbury. Robert Cecil briefly attended Christ Church, Oxford, but poor health cut short his education. He subsequently spent two years at sea, traveling to Australia and New Zealand. His health improved, and he returned to England and entered politics. He was elected to the House of Commons in 1853 as a Conservative from Stamford. He briefly served in the cabinet as secretary of state for India from July 1866 until March 1867. He inherited his father's titles and estates in 1868, becoming the Third Marquess of Salisbury. He again was named to the position of secretary of state for India in Benjamin Disraeli's cabinet in February 1874. He was a close ally of the prime minister and was named foreign minister in April 1878. Salisbury became leader of the Conservative opposition in the House of Lords after Disraeli's death in 1881. After William Gladstone's Liberal government fell because of a fiscal issue, Salisbury led the government as prime minister from June 24, 1885, until February 6, 1886, when the Liberals again took power. His opposition to Gladstone's position on home rule for Ireland returned Salisbury to office on August 3, 1886. He continued to lead the government until August 18, 1892, when Gladstone again replaced him. Salisbury returned by the post of prime minister on July 2, 1895, also serving as foreign minister for most of his term. His government sought to improve relations between Britain and the United States. Great Britain also engaged in the South African war against the Boers from 1899 until 1902. Salisbury reconstructed his cabinet after the elections of 1900. He remained in office until failing health forced his retirement on July 12, 1902. He died at Hatfield House, Hertfordshire, on August 22, 1903.

ARTHUR JAMES BALFOUR (Prime Minister; July 12, 1902–December 5, 1905). Arthur James Balfour was born in Whittinghame, East Lothian, Scotland, on July 25, 1848. He was the eldest son of James Maitland Balfour and a member of a prominent British family. He was educated at Eton and Trinity College, Cambridge, where he studied philosophy. He was elected to Parliament from Hertford in 1874 as a Conservative. He briefly associated with Lord Randolph Churchill's Independent Party in opposition to William E. Gladstone's policies in 1880. Balfour's uncle, Robert Cecil, Third Marquess of Salisbury, became prime minister in 1885, and Balfour served in his government as president of the local government board. The following year he was named secretary for Scotland and chief secretary for Ireland. He was an opponent of home rule for Ireland and used severe methods in putting down uprisings. Balfour became leader of the House of Commons in 1891. He led the opposition to Gladstone's Liberal government from 1892 until 1894. He returned to the cabinet under Lord Salisbury as first lord of the treasury in 1895. He became a leading figure in the government as Lord Salisbury's health declined. Balfour succeeded his uncle as prime minister on July 12, 1902. He was responsible for the passage of the Education Act which modernized Britain's school system. He completed negotiations for a treaty with France in 1904 that recognized Britain's supremacy over Egypt. Disagreement within the Conservative Party over the issue of tariffs and free trade brought about Balfour's resignation on December 5, 1905. He continued to lead the party in the House of Commons until 1911. Balfour joined H. H. Asquith's wartime government as first lord of the admiralty, succeeding Winston Churchill, in May 1915. He was named foreign minister in David Lloyd George's government in December 1916. The following year he wrote the Balfour Declaration, which pledged Britain's support for Zionism and a Jewish homeland in Palestine. He stepped down from the foreign ministry in 1919 after attending the Paris Peace Conference that ended World War I. He was subsequently served as lord president of the council until 1922. He was created Earl of Balfour and Viscount Traprain of Whittinghame in 1922. Balfour returned to the government, again serving as lord president of the council under Stanley Baldwin from 1925 until 1929. He died in Woking, Surrey, on March 19, 1930.

SIR HENRY CAMPBELL-BANNERMAN (Prime Minister; December 5, 1905–April 8, 1908). Henry Campbell-Bannerman was born Henry Campbell in Glasgow, Scotland, on September 7, 1836. He was educated at Glasgow University and Trinity College, Cambridge, where he graduated in 1858. He subsequently worked in his father's drapery business. Campbell entered Parliament from Stirling Burghs as a Liberal in 1868. He inherited the estate of his uncle in 1872 and assumed the Bannerman surname. His political career progressed, as he served as financial secretary to the war office from 1871 to 1874,

and again from 1880 to 1882. He was named secretary of the admiralty in 1882 and chief secretary for Ireland in 1884. He served in William E. Gladstone's cabinet as war secretary in 1886 and again from 1892 to 1895. Campbell-Bannerman was instrumental in arranging the resignation of the Duke of Cambridge as commander-in-chief of the armed forces in June 1895. Campbell-Bannerman was subsequently asked to resign under charges of negligence, which ultimately brought about the resignation of Lord Rosebery's government. Campbell-Bannerman was elected leader of the Liberal opposition in the House of Commons following the resignation of Sir William Harcourt in February 1899. He was a vocal opponent of the government's policy that led to the Boer War. Campbell-Bannerman was called upon by King Edward VII to form a government after the resignation of Arthur James Balfour on December 4, 1905. The Liberal Party received a large majority in general elections the following month, though much of Campbell-Bannerman's legislation was vetoed by the House of Lords. He was able to secure the passage for the 1906 Trade Disputes Act, which granted labor unions greater freedom to strike. He also allowed self-government for Transvaal and the Orange River Colony in South Africa. Campbell-Bannerman suffered a heart attack in November 1907. His health continued to fail and he resigned from the House of Commons after an attack of influenza in February 1908. He resigned as prime minister on April 8, 1908, and died in London on April 22, 1908.

HERBERT HENRY ASQUITH, EARL OF OXFORD (Prime Minister; April 8, 1908–December 7, 1916). Herbert Henry Asquith was born in Morley, Yorkshire, on September 12, 1852. He was educated at the City of London School and received a scholarship from Balliol College, Oxford, in 1870. He subsequently studied law at Lincoln's Inn and was called to the bar in 1876. He soon became a successful lawyer, and in 1886 he was elected to Parliament from East Fife as a Liberal. He became home secretary under William E. Gladstone in 1892 and was a supporter of the Second Home Rule Bill. He joined his party in opposition in 1895, and in 1901 he formed the Liberal League with Sir Edward Grey and Lord Rosebery in opposition to Liberal Party leader Sir Henry Campbell-Bannerman's policy on British imperialism in general and South Africa in particular. The Liberals were returned to power in 1905, and Asquith put aside his differences with Campbell-Bannerman to join his cabinet as chancellor of the exchequer. Poor health forced Campbell-Bannerman's resignation as prime minister in April 1908, and Asquith succeeded him to office. His government's policies of reform were often the subject of vetoes in the House of Lords and Asquith advocated limiting the power of the upper house. After several successful elections, he was able to pass the Parliament Bill, which ended the veto powers of the House of Lords in August 1911. The next several years saw increased conflict over Ireland between Home Rulers and Unionists that almost led to a civil war in 1914. After England's entry into World War I, Asquith formed a coalition cabinet in May 1915, but dissension in the cabinet, combined with a lack of success in the war against Germany and the Easter Rising in Ireland in 1916, led to Asquith's resignation on December 7, 1916. He was replaced by David Lloyd George but remained leader of the Liberal Party. He lost his seat in the House of Commons in 1918, but was returned two years later from Paisley. He was again unsuccessful in his bid for reelection in 1924. Asquith accepted peerage in 1925 and entered the House of Lords as Earl of Oxford and Asquith. Continuing differences with Lloyd George led to Asquith's resignation as Liberal Party leader in 1926. He died in Sutton, Courtenay, Berkshire, on February 15, 1928.

DAVID LLOYD GEORGE (Prime Minister; December 7, 1916–October 23, 1922). David Lloyd George was born in Manchester on January 17, 1863. His father died when Lloyd George was an infant, and he and his mother were taken in by his uncle in Llanystrumdwy, Wales. In his early teens he began working as a solicitor for a firm in Portmadoc. Lloyd George entered politics as a Liberal and was narrowly elected to the House of Commons in a by-election in 1890. He became a leading figure in the radical wing of the party while the Liberals were in opposition. He was an outspoken opponent of the Boer War and a critic of Arthur Balfour's Education Act in 1902. He was also known as a leading spokesman for Welsh nationalism. Lloyd George was named president of the board of trade in Sir Henry Campbell-Bannerman's government in December 1905. He succeeded Henry Herbert Asquith as chancellor of the exchequer when Asquith replaced Campbell-Bannerman as prime minister in April 1908. Lloyd George was the architect of the modern welfare state with his proposal in 1911 of the National Insurance Act to provide health and unemployment benefits to British citizens. He was initially opposed to Britain's involvement in World War I, but soon accepted his country's intervention on the side of France. He supported increased production of munitions in the early months of the war, becoming minister of munitions in 1915. In this position he was credited with greatly improving Britain's military position by his tireless efforts. He replaced Earl Kitchner at the war office for five months when Kitchner drowned in June 1916. Lloyd George became dissatisfied with Prime Minister Asquith's leadership as the war progressed, and he and other critics forced Asquith's resignation on December 5, 1916. Lloyd George was selected to head the government on December 7, 1916. He reconstituted the war cabinet and began a vigorous effort to halt the submarine menace to British shipping by using the convoy system. He also instituted food rationing and increased agricultural production to deal with food shortages in 1918. After the armistice in November 1918, Lloyd George continued to govern as head of a coalition cabinet that included Conservatives. He led the British delegation to the peace talks, attempting to act as a conciliator between France's Georges Clemenceau and Woodrow Wilson. He was also faced with a growing problem in Ireland, where civil war raged. Lloyd George entered into negotiations with Arthur Griffith and Michael Collins that resulted in the Irish treaty in December 1921. Dissatisfaction with the government's policy in Ireland and Turkey brought the coalition cabinet to an end on October 23, 1922. Lloyd George's coalition Liberals ran poorly in the general elections. He returned to lead the Liberal Parliamentary Party, but was viewed with some distrust by the party membership. He stepped down as party leader in 1931. He spent most of the next decade writing such works as *War Memoirs* (1933–36) and *The Truth about the Peace Treaties* (1938). He was an outspoken critic of Neville Chamberlain's policy of appeasement toward Adolf Hitler's Germany in 1939. Lloyd George was invited to join Winston Churchill's war cabinet in 1940, but he declined for reasons of health. He was elevated to the peerage as Earl Lloyd George of Dwyfor in January 1945, but never took his seat in the House of Lords. He suffered from influenza in February of 1945 and died at his home in Llanystrumdwy, near Criccieth, in Caernarvonshire, North Wales, on March 26, 1945.

ARTHUR BONAR LAW (Prime Minister; October 23, 1922–May 22, 1923). Arthur Bonar Law was born in New Brunswick, Canada, on September 16, 1858. He was sent to Glasgow, Scotland, to attend high school, and after completing his education, he became a successful iron merchant. He subsequently became involved in politics, and was elected to Parliament from the Blackfriars Division of Glasgow in 1900 as a Conservative. He became parliamentary secretary of the board of trade in 1902, remaining there until he lost his seat in Parliament in 1906. He soon returned as a member from Culwich and was a leading proponent of the party's policy of protective tariffs. Law was chosen as a compromise candidate to succeed Arthur James Balfour as leader of the Conservative Party in November 1911. He led the opposition until the outbreak of World War I. Law then joined H. H. Asquith's coalition cabinet as colonial secretary in 1915 and was chancellor of the exchequer in David Lloyd George's wartime government in December 1916. He also led the House of Commons and became chancellor for the office of lord privy seal in January 1919. He retired from his positions due to poor health in March 1921. Despite continuing illness, Law returned to Parliament in 1922. He criticized the formation of a new coalition government under Lloyd George, who resigned as prime minister. Law formed a Conservative government on October 23, 1922. During his brief term of office his government broke off diplomatic relations with France in January 1923 over that country's occupation of the Ruhr region. He also opposed his chancellor of the exchequer, Stanley Baldwin, on the issue of the settlement of the British war debt with the United States. Law's health continued to deteriorate from inoperable throat cancer, and he stepped down from office on May 20, 1923. He died in London on October 30, 1923.

STANLEY BALDWIN (Prime Minister; May 22, 1923–January 22, 1924). Stanley Baldwin was born in Bewdley, Worcestershire, on August 3, 1867. He was the son of Alfred Baldwin, a leading industrialist and chairman of the Great Western Railway. The younger Baldwin was educated at Trinity College, Oxford, before working in his father's industries. He entered politics and was elected to the House of Commons as a Conservative in 1908. Baldwin was named financial secretary of the treasury in 1917 and became president of the board of trade in 1921. He was named to Arthur Bonar Law's cabinet as minister of the exchequer in October 1922. He headed the British delegation to settle the issue of war debt with the United States in January 1923. Baldwin was called upon to form a government on May 22, 1923, when poor health forced Bonar Law's retirement. His government was faced with a growing unemployment problem. Baldwin attempted to gain a mandate to repeal Bonar Law's fair trade policy, but the mandate was rejected and Baldwin's government stepped down on January 22, 1924. He returned to head a new Conservative government following the collapse of Ramsay MacDonald's Labour cabinet on November 4, 1924. Baldwin's government reacted harshly to a coal miner's strike in May 1926, refusing to negotiate until the strike was ended. He promoted the passage of the Trade Disputes Act in 1927, which limited the rights of unions. A continuing unemployment problem led to the Conservatives' defeat in elections later in the year and Baldwin stepped down on June 8, 1929. He sat in opposition until 1931, when he was named lord president of the council in MacDonald's coalition government. He returned to head the government on June 7, 1935. He belatedly began to strengthen the military in the face of a growing threat from Nazi Germany and Italy's invasion of Ethiopia. He faced strong criticism for his government's decision with France to accept the Italian action in Ethiopia in December 1935. A major domestic crisis arose in 1936 when the new king, Edward VIII, announced his intention to marry American divorcée Wallis Warfield Simpson. Fearing a public backlash against the monarchy, Baldwin was successful in arranging Edward's abdication in December 1936. He stepped down

from office on May 28, 1937, and retired from politics. He was subsequently granted the title of 1st Earl Baldwin of Bewdley, Viscount Corvedale of Corvedale. Baldwin died at Astley Hall, Worcestershire, on December 14, 1947.

JAMES RAMSAY MacDONALD (Prime Minister; January 22, 1924–November 4, 1924). James Ramsay MacDonald was born in Lossiemouth, Moray, Scotland, on October 12, 1866. The son of an unmarried servant, he was educated at the village school where he worked as a pupil-teacher for six years. He went to Bristol in 1885, where he became involved with left-wing politics. He joined the Fabian Society and was a founder of the Socialist Union. MacDonald joined the newly formed Independent Labour Party in 1893 and was defeated for a seat in the House of Commons two years later. He again ran for Parliament unsuccessfully in 1900. He was elected first secretary of the Labour representation committee the same year and was instrumental in drafting the party's constitution. He was elected to the House of Commons in 1906 and succeeded Keir Hardie as the party's parliamentary leader in 1911. His opposition to England's declaration of war on Germany in 1914 forced his resignation. Though he supported the subsequent war effort, his popularity diminished and he lost his seat in Parliament in 1918. He again suffered defeat in 1921 before returning to Parliament the following year. He was subsequently selected to lead the Labour opposition. After the defeat of Prime Minister Stanley Baldwin in a vote of no confidence, MacDonald, with the support of Liberal Party leader H. H. Asquith, became head of the government on January 22, 1924. He also served in the government as foreign minister. MacDonald's government recognized the Communist regime in the Soviet Union. He also arranged a settlement with the Irish Free State that alleviated the dispute over the six northern counties in Ireland in return for Britain canceling its debts. The Conservatives regained a majority in the Parliament later in the year, and MacDonald resigned on November 4, 1924. The Labour Party received a majority of seats in the 1929 elections and MacDonald returned as prime minister on June 8, 1929. His government's inability to cope with the ongoing worldwide economic depression led to the government's resignation on August 24, 1931. MacDonald remained prime minister as head of a coalition government with Conservative and Liberal support. Conservative leader Stanley Baldwin exercised much influence on the government. MacDonald stepped down as prime minister on June 7, 1935, and was succeeded by Baldwin. He accepted Baldwin's former position as lord president of the council, where he remained until May 1937. MacDonald died of heart failure on November 9, 1937, while traveling aboard the ocean liner *Reina del Pacífico* en route to South America.

STANLEY BALDWIN (Prime Minister; November 4, 1924–June 8, 1929). *See earlier entry under Heads of Government.*

JAMES RAMSAY MacDONALD (Prime Minister; June 8, 1929–June 7, 1935). *See earlier entry under Heads of Government.*

STANLEY BALDWIN (Prime Minister; June 7, 1935–May 28, 1937). *See earlier entry under Heads of Government.*

NEVILLE CHAMBERLAIN (Prime Minister; May 28, 1937–May 11, 1940). Arthur Neville Chamberlain was born in Birmingham, Warwickshire, England, on March 18, 1869. He was the son of British statesman Joseph Chamberlain. As a young man, he managed his father's sisal plantation in the Bahamas for nearly seven years. He returned to Birmingham in 1897, where he became a successful businessman, heading Elliott's

Metal Company and the Birmingham Small Arms Company. He also became involved in local politics and was elected to the Birmingham town council in 1911. Chamberlain was elected lord mayor of Birmingham four years later. He accepted the position of director general of national services in David Lloyd George's government in January 1917. He resigned later in the year because he did not have the political power to implement his programs. Chamberlain was elected to Parliament in December 1918 as a Conservative. He was appointed to Arthur Bonar Law's cabinet in 1922 as postmaster general, and also became paymaster general of the armed services in 1923. He was named minister of health later in the year. He was appointed chancellor of the exchequer in Stanley Baldwin's cabinet in 1923. The Baldwin government fell later in the year, but when Baldwin reformed a government in 1924, Chamberlain returned to his position of minister of health and retained that position until 1929. He returned to the cabinet as minister of health in Ramsay MacDonald's government in 1931. He was again named chancellor of the exchequer later in the year. He retained that position for the next six years until he succeeded Baldwin as prime minister on May 28, 1937. Chamberlain was instrumental in advancing England's policy of appeasement with the Axis Powers. He entered into negotiations with Benito Mussolini's government in Italy despite that country's continued aggression in Ethiopia. He met three times with Adolf Hitler in September 1938 in regard to Germany's demands that Czechoslovakia cede the Sudetenland to Germany. He and Premier Edouard Daladier of France agreed to the Munich Agreement on September 30, 1938, which granted Hitler most of his demands. Chamberlain returned to England proclaiming the agreement assured "peace in our time." However, Europe's hopes for peace were dashed when Germany seized the rest of Czechoslovakia in March 1939. Chamberlain denounced Hitler's breach of the Munich Agreement and declared England's commitment to protect Poland, Romania, and Greece from German aggression. Germany invaded Poland on September 1, 1939, and two days later, Great Britain declared war on Germany. Britain's inability to protect Norway from the advancing Nazis in April 1940 cost Chamberlain the support of Parliament. He resigned on May 11, 1940. He remained in Winston Churchill's wartime government as lord president of the council until poor health and several intestinal operations forced his retirement on October 1, 1940. Chamberlain died at his home in Heckfield, near Reading, Hampshire, on November 9, 1940.

SIR WINSTON CHURCHILL

(Prime Minister; May 11, 1940–July 26, 1945). Winston Leonard Spencer Churchill was born at Blenheim Palace near Woodstock in Oxfordshire on November 30, 1874. He was the son of Lord Randolph Churchill, the former Conservative Party leader. He attended the military academy at Sandhurst, where he graduated eighth in his class. In 1895 he was appointed to the Fourth Hussars as a sublieutenant. Churchill served in several expeditionary forces and wrote several histories. He returned to England in 1898 and ran unsuccessfully for a seat in Parliament. He went to South Africa as a journalist during the Boer War, and in November 1899 he was taken prisoner by Louis Botha, the future South African prime minister. Churchill escaped and wrote several books on his South African experiences. He returned to England, and in 1900 he was elected to a seat in the House of Commons as a Conservative. He joined the Liberal Party in 1904, and two years later he was named undersecretary for the colonies. Churchill was appointed president of the board of trade in the government of Herbert Henry Asquith in 1908 and served until 1910. He was subsequently named home secretary until 1911, when he became first

lord of the admiralty. He was replaced in 1915 because of criticism of his handling of the Gallipoli disaster. Churchill left government to join the British military during World War I, but was recalled by Prime Minister David Lloyd George to serve as minister of munitions in July 1916. He continued to serve in the postwar cabinet as secretary of state for war and the air from 1918 to 1921 and secretary of state for the colonies from 1921 to 1922. He lost his seat in Parliament in the 1922 elections and was defeated in several attempts to return to Parliament before he was elected to a seat in the fall of 1924. He rejoined the Conservative Party and was subsequently named chancellor of the exchequer in the cabinet of Stanley Baldwin. He continued his writings following the Labour Party victory in 1929. Churchill soon broke with Baldwin and was excluded from a cabinet position when Baldwin again became prime minister in 1935. Churchill was a leading advocate of British rearmament prior to World War II. He was also a critic of the appeasement policies of Baldwin's successor, Neville Chamberlain. When Great Britain declared war on Germany on September 3, 1939, Churchill was named first lord of the admiralty. Chamberlain resigned as prime minister following the German invasion of Belgium in May of 1940. When Churchill was asked to form a government as prime minister on May 10, 1940, he formed a coalition war cabinet and also served as minister of defense. He was given a unanimous vote of confidence by the House of Commons following a rousing speech on May 13, 1940. He led his country during World War II with courage and determination. The Allied forces defeated Germany in 1945, and Churchill was faced with political problems at home in England. The Labour Party defeated the Conservatives in the elections on July 25, 1945, and Churchill was replaced as prime minister by Clement Attlee. Churchill led the opposition until 1951, when the Conservatives were returned to power. Churchill again became prime minister on October 26, 1951, and also served as first lord of the treasury. He was awarded the Nobel Prize for Literature in 1953 for his historical writings, and he was also knighted that year. Churchill retired as head of the government on April 6, 1955, but remained in the House of Commons until 1964. He was made an honorary citizen of the United States by an act of Congress on April 9, 1963. Churchill died of a stroke in London on January 25, 1965.

United States of America

The United States of American consists of fifty states. Forty-eight states lie in central North America between the Atlantic and Pacific Oceans, while Alaska is located in the northwest corner of North America and Hawaii is located in the central Pacific Ocean. The United States declared its independence from Great Britain on July 4, 1776.

HEADS OF STATE

WILLIAM McKINLEY (President; March 4, 1897–September 14, 1901). William McKinley was born in Niles, Ohio, on January 29, 1843. He taught school until the advent of the Civil War, when he entered the army as a private in the 23rd Ohio volunteer regiment. He became aide-de-camp to Colonel Rutherford B. Hayes. McKinley served with distinction and was promoted to the rank of major upon his discharge in 1865. He studied law after the war and opened a practice in Canton, Ohio, in 1867. He became prosecuting attorney in Stark County in 1869. McKinley married Ida Saxton in 1871. He was elected to the United States Congress as a Republican representative from Ohio's 17th district in 1876. He was defeated for the position of Speaker of the House in 1889, but was appointed chairman of the ways and means committee. He supported protective tariffs, but the enactment of the McKinley Tariff of 1890 led to a Democratic majority in Congress following the next elections. McKinley retired from Congress and was elected governor of Ohio in 1891. He was reelected in 1893 and received the Republican nomination for the presidency in 1896. Garret A. Hobart of New Jersey was chosen as his running mate. He defeated Democratic nominee William Jennings Bryan by a wide margin and took office on March 4, 1897. The United States battleship *Maine* was sunk by a mine in Havana harbor in Cuba on February 15, 1898. The press publicized the incident as the result of Spanish intrigue. The slogan "Remember the *Maine!*" became the call for American intervention in Cuba. The Congress adopted a resolution on April 20, 1898, demanding Spain's withdrawal from Cuba, and Commodore George Dewey attacked and destroyed the Spanish fleet in Manila the following month. The Spanish forces were routed during the Spanish-American War, which ended with a peace protocol on August 12, 1898. The subsequent peace agreement granted independence to Cuba and forced Spain to cede Puerto Rico, Guam, and the Philippines to the United States. Filipino insurgents under the leadership of Emilio Aquinaldo transferred their hostilities from the Spanish rulers to the new American occupation forces. The guerrillas continued their battle for independence until Aquinaldo's capture the following year. McKinley was renominated without opposition at the 1900 Republican convention. New York Governor Theodore Roosevelt was chosen as his running mate, replacing Hobart, who had died the previous November. McKinley again defeated William Jennings Bryan by a large margin. His second term was cut short when anarchist Leon Czolgosz shot McKinley at the Temple of Music at the Pan-American exposition in Buffalo, New York, on September 6, 1901. The assassin had a gun in his hand with a handkerchief wrapped around it. As he drew near McKinley, as if to shake his hand, Czolgosz fired two shots into the president before being wrestled to the ground. McKinley's wounds were not immediately considered serious, but his condition soon worsened. He died on September 14, 1901.

THEODORE ROOSEVELT (President; September 14, 1901–March 4, 1909). Theodore Roosevelt was born in New York City on October 27, 1858. He graduated from Harvard University in 1880 and married Alice Hathaway Lee soon after. He served as a member of the New York state assembly from 1882 until 1884. Roosevelt was defeated for mayor of New York City in 1886. Roosevelt, who had been widowed in 1884, married Edith Kermit Carow in 1886. He served as a member of the U.S. Civil Service Commission in 1889 and was president of the New York Police Board in 1895. He was named assistant secretary of the navy in William McKinley's administration in 1897. Roosevelt organized the First United States Volunteer Cavalry, known as the Rough Riders, to fight in the Spanish American War. As a lieutenant colonel, he led the charge up Kettle Hill, which flanked the Spanish position on San Juan Hill in Santiago, Cuba. He was elected governor of New York in 1898. He was so vigorous in his battle against political corruption that

Republican leaders in New York supported his nomination for vice-president to remove him from the state. He received the Republican nomination for president under McKinley in 1900. The ticket was victorious, and Roosevelt became vice president in March 1901. He succeeded to the presidency on September 14, 1901, following the assassination of McKinley. He actively fought corruption in politics and promoted the use of antitrust laws to keep businesses in check. Roosevelt was reelected in 1904, defeating the Democratic nominee, Alton B. Parker. His mediation of a peace settlement of the Russo-Japanese War in 1905 resulted in his being awarded the Nobel Peace Prize in 1906. Roosevelt was instrumental in gaining the Republican nomination for William Howard Taft in 1908 and relinquished office to the victorious Taft on March 4, 1909. He later felt that Taft had betrayed his policies and challenged him for the Republican nomination in 1912. When Taft won the contest, Roosevelt ran for the presidency as an independent on the Progressive "Bull Moose" ticket. Roosevelt was shot and wounded by John N. Schrank before addressing a crowd in Milwaukee, Wisconsin, on October 14, 1912, in the midst of his presidential campaign. But Roosevelt proceeded to give his speech to the crowd before seeking medical attention. He recovered from his wounds and went on to place second, ahead of Taft, in the November elections. However, this split the Republican vote, and the election went to the Democratic candidates, Woodrow Wilson. Roosevelt was a critic of the American policy of neutrality in the early years of World War I and supported intervention on the side of the British. Roosevelt died in his sleep at Sagamore Hill, Oyster Bay, New York, on January 6, 1919.

WILLIAM HOWARD TAFT (President; March 4, 1909–March 4, 1913). William Howard Taft was born in

Cincinnati, Ohio, on September 15, 1857. He attended Yale University and graduated from the Cincinnati Law School in 1880. He became an assistant prosecuting attorney in 1881 and an assistant county solicitor in 1885. Taft married Helen Herron in 1886. He became a judge on the superior court in 1887 and was named solicitor general of the United States in 1890. He was appointed to the federal circuit court in 1892. Taft served as the first civil governor of the Philippines from 1901 until 1904, when he was named to Theodore Roosevelt's cabinet as secretary of war. He briefly served as provisional governor of Cuba in 1906. He was supported by Roosevelt to succeed him to the presidency and won the Republican nomination in 1908. He defeated the Democratic nominee, William Jennings Bryan, and took office on March 4, 1909. He continued the antitrust efforts of his predecessor and dissolved Standard Oil and the tobacco trusts. He signed constitutional amendments to create an income tax and allow the direct election of senators. He lost the support of Roosevelt over his tariff policies and was challenged in the next election by the former president, who ran as an independent. The result split the Republican vote, and Taft was defeated by Democrat Woodrow Wilson. He relinquished office to Wilson on March 4, 1913. He subsequently served as a professor of constitutional law at Yale University. He was named chief justice of the Supreme Court in 1921. He led the court until illness forced his retirement in early 1930. He died of heart disease in Washington, D.C., on March 8, 1930.

WOODROW WILSON (President; March 4, 1913–March 4, 1921). Thomas Woodrow Wilson was born in Stanunto, Virginia, on December 28, 1856. He graduated from Princeton University in 1879 and received a degree in law from the University of Virginia in 1881. He married Ellen Louise Axson in 1885. He practiced law briefly in Atlanta

before becoming a law professor. He taught at Bryn Mawr, Wesleyan, and Princeton universities and was president of Princeton from 1902 to 1910. He was subsequently elected governor of New Jersey. He gained the Democratic nomination for the presidency in 1912 and defeated incumbent President William Howard Taft and former President Theodore Roosevelt in a three-man race. Wilson was sworn into office on March 4, 1913. Wilson's wife died in 1914, and he married Edith Bolling Galt the following year. He initially maintained the United States' neutrality during World War I. He was narrowly reelected president in 1916, defeating Republican nominee Charles E. Hughes with the slogan "He kept us out of war." Wilson's inability to mediate a peace during the conflict as well as sinkings of American ships by the Germans led to the United States' entry into the war on April 6, 1917. He proposed a peace settlement, known as the "Fourteen Points" in January 1918, which was accepted by the Germans the following November. He was a key figure at the Paris peace conference where he worked to form the League of Nations to prevent further wars. The League was accepted by the European powers, but Wilson was unable to persuade the U.S. Senate to accept his proposal. Wilson suffered a stroke in October 1919, and his wife largely handled his affairs while he recovered. He was awarded the Nobel Peace Prize in 1919 for his formulation of the League of Nations. He completed his term of office on March 4, 1921. He lived in retirement in Washington, D.C., until his death in his sleep several years later on February 3, 1924.

WARREN G. HARDING (President; March 4, 1921–August 3, 1923). Warren Gamaliel Harding was born near Corsica, Morrow County, Ohio, on November 2, 1865. He studied law at Ohio Central College. He married Florence Kling De Wolfe in 1891, entered politics, and was elected to the Ohio state senate in 1900. He served as lieutenant governor of Ohio from 1904 until 1906. Harding was defeated in an election for governor in 1910. He was elected to the Senate as a Republican from Ohio in 1915. He was a proponent of antistrike legislation and opposed the formation of the League of Nations while in the Senate. He gained the Republican nomination for the presidency in 1920 and defeated James M. Cox by a wide margin in the election with a pledge of "return to normalcy." His government convened the Washington Conference in 1921 as an international forum to reduce naval power and ease tension in the Far East. Harding's administration was troubled by the Teapot Dome scandal, when members of his administration, including Interior Secretary Albert Fall, were accused of profiting from the U.S. naval oil reserves. Though Harding was not implicated in the scandal, his health suffered from the revelations. He developed bronchopneumonia in San Francisco while returning from a trip to Alaska. He died there of an embolism on August 3, 1923.

CALVIN COOLIDGE (President; August 2, 1923–March 4, 1929). John Calvin Coolidge was born in Plymouth, Vermont, on July 4, 1872. He graduated from Amherst College in 1895 and became a lawyer. He married Grace Anna Goodhue in 1905. Coolidge entered politics and became mayor of Northampton, Massachusetts. He served in the state legislature and was lieutenant governor before his election as governor of Massachusetts in 1919. He achieved national prominence for calling out the national guard to halt a police strike in Boston in September 1919. He gained the Republican nomination for the vice presidency under Warren Harding in 1920. The Republican ticket was victorious, and Coolidge served as vice president until Harding's death in office on August 3, 1923, when he succeeded to the

presidency. Coolidge won reelection by a large margin in 1924 over John W. Davis. He was a supporter of industry and business and, as an isolationist, he continued to oppose the United States' entry into the League of Nations. He managed to reduce the national debt during his term of office by $2 billion. Coolidge declined to seek renomination in 1928, and stepped down from office on March 4, 1929. Coolidge was found dead in his bedroom in Northampton of a coronary thrombosis on January 5, 1933.

HERBERT C. HOOVER (President; March 4, 1929–March 4, 1933). Herbert Clark Hoover was born in West Branch, Iowa, on August 10, 1874. Hoover was raised in Oklahoma and Oregon. He received a degree in geology and engineering from Stanford University in 1891 and worked as a mining engineer throughout the world. He married Lou Henry in 1899. He was chief engineer at the imperial mines in China during the Boxer Rebellion in 1900 and directed food relief programs during the uprising. He headed the American Relief Committee in London at the start of World War I in 1914 and served as U.S. commissioner for relief in Belgium from 1915 until 1919. He also served as United States food administrator from 1917 until 1919 and was American relief administrator from 1918 until 1923. He was named to Warren G. Harding's cabinet as secretary of commerce and retained that position under Calvin Coolidge until 1928. He received the Republican nomination to succeed Coolidge as president in 1928 and defeated the Democratic nominee Alfred E. Smith. Hoover was sworn into office on March 4, 1929. Shortly after his election the United States was plunged into the Great Depression. He attempted to utilize government assistance programs to help the unemployed, but refused direct federal aid. Hoover was decisively defeated for reelection by Franklin D. Roosevelt in 1932 and stepped down from office on

March 4, 1933. He was appointed coordinator of the European food program by President Harry Truman in 1947. He also served as chairman of the Commission for Reorganization of the Executive Branch from 1947 until 1949 and again from 1953 until 1955. Hoover died in New York City at the age of ninety-one on October 20, 1964.

FRANKLIN D. ROOSEVELT
(President; March 4, 1933–April 12, 1945). Franklin Delano Roosevelt was born near Hyde Park, New York, on January 30, 1882. He graduated from Harvard in 1903 and studied law at Columbia University Law School. He married Anna Eleanor Roosevelt, a distant cousin, in March 1905. He was elected to the New York state senate in 1910. He was appointed assistant secretary of the navy by President Woodrow Wilson in 1913. Roosevelt was the unsuccessful Democratic nominee for vice president under James Cox in 1920. He returned to New York to work as a lawyer. Roosevelt was stricken with polio in 1921 and became unable to walk without the assistance of leg braces and a cane. He was elected governor of New York in 1928 and was reelected two years later. He received the Democratic nomination for president in 1932 and defeated incumbent President Herbert Hoover by a wide margin in the election. Roosevelt survived an assassination attempt on February 15, 1933, when Giuseppe Zangara fired at his motorcade at Miami Bayfront Park in Florida. Roosevelt was uninjured in the attack but Chicago Mayor Anton J. Cermak, who was traveling in Roosevelt's car, was shot and killed. Roosevelt was sworn into office on March 4, 1933. He proclaimed his administration the New Deal and sought to halt the hardship caused by the economic depression of 1929. He used government funding for numerous relief and public works programs. He also pushed for legislation to provide federal insurance for banks to prevent a recurrence of

the problems. Congress blocked some of Roosevelt's effort, and the Supreme Court overruled some of his New Deal programs. In 1935 Roosevelt signed the Social Security Act. He defeated Republican nominee Alf Landon in his reelection bid in 1936 and became the first United States president to win a third term in office by defeating Wendell Willkie in 1940. Roosevelt was sympathetic to the Allied cause during the early years of World War II and initiated the lend-lease program, but maintained the United States' neutrality. The United States was attacked by Japan at Pearl Harbor, Hawaii, on December 7, 1941, and as a result was drawn into the conflict. Roosevelt participated at Allied wartime conferences at Casablanca, Quebec, and Cairo, and also met with Soviet leader Joseph Stalin at Tehran and Yalta. Roosevelt was reelected to an unprecedented fourth term as president, defeating Thomas E. Dewey in 1944. Roosevelt's health began to fail soon after, and he died suddenly of a stroke in Warm Springs, Georgia, on April 12, 1945.

HARRY S TRUMAN
(President; April 12, 1945–January 20, 1953). Harry S Truman was born in Lamar, Missouri, on May 8, 1884. He attended high school in Independence, Missouri, and joined the Missouri National Guard. He saw active duty in France during World War I. Truman returned to Missouri following the war and married Bess Wallace in 1919. He opened a haberdashery in Kansas City, but the business went under in 1921. Truman entered politics in 1922 and was elected a county court judge. Truman remained on the county court and became presiding judge in 1926. He was elected to the United States Senate from Missouri in 1934 and reelected in 1940. Truman served as chairman of the special Senate committee that investigated graft and waste in government in 1941. His work on this committee led to a more prominent position in the

Democratic Party. He was selected by President Franklin D. Roosevelt to be his running mate in the 1944 elections. The Roosevelt-Truman ticket was successful, and Truman took office as vice president early in 1945. He succeeded to the presidency following the death of President Roosevelt on April 12, 1945. Truman was faced with bringing World War II to a successful conclusion. He authorized the dropping of the atomic bomb on the Japanese cities of Hiroshima and Nagasaki in August 1945, which forced the Japanese to surrender. He established the Truman Doctrine in 1947, which provided support to Greece, Turkey, and other countries threatened by Communism. Truman also established the Marshall Plan in 1947, which provided for the economic recovery of postwar Europe. In the presidential elections of 1948, Truman and his running mate, Alben Barkley, defeated the Republican nominee Thomas Dewey in an upset victory. During Truman's second term, the United States assisted in the creation of the United Nations and joined the North Atlantic Treaty Organization (NATO) in 1949. Truman was the

target of an unsuccessful assassination attempt by Puerto Rican nationalists in November 1950. The United States committed troops to Korea in June 1950 following the invasion of South Korea by the North Korean army. In the early 1950s the Cold War continued to escalate, and the government was subjected to loyalty programs and paranoia about Communism. Senator Joseph McCarthy, a militant anticommunist vigorously attacked liberal activists and others and in the process destroyed many lives and jobs. President Truman declined to seek the presidential nomination in 1952. The Democratic nominee, Adlai E. Stevenson, was defeated by General Dwight D. Eisenhower in the November elections, and Truman stepped down from office on January 20, 1953. He retired to Independence, Missouri, where he worked to establish the Truman Library, which was dedicated in 1957. He also remained an active campaigner for Democratic candidates. Truman fell ill in early December 1972. He was taken to a hospital in Kansas City, where he remained until his death from heart failure on December 26, 1972.

Uruguay

Uruguay is a country on the southeastern coast of South America. It was granted independence from Brazil on August 25, 1828.

HEADS OF STATE

JUAN LINDOLFO CUESTAS (President; August 25, 1897–March 1, 1903). Juan Lindolfo Cuestas was born on January 6, 1837. He was a leading political figure and was allied with the Colorado Party. He became president of the senate in 1895. He became provisional president of Uruguay on August 25, 1897, following the assassination of Juan Idarte Borda. He reached an agreement

with Aparicio Saravia's Blanco Party, ending a period of revolution. He attempted to steer a moderate course to gain the support of the rival Colorado and Blanco parties. Cuestas assumed dictatorial powers in February 1898 and dissolved the assembly. His government survived several coup attempts and Cuestas was elected to the presidency in 1899. He retained office until March 1,

1903, when José Batlle y Ordóñez was elected to the presidency. Cuestas subsequently went to Europe and died in Paris on June 21, 1905.

JOSÉ BATLLE Y ORDÓÑEZ

(President; March 1, 1903–March 1, 1907). José Batlle y Ordóñez was born on May 21, 1856. He was the son of Lorenzo Batlle y Grau, who served as president of Uruguay from 1868 until 1872. José Batlle was an opponent of the dictatorships of Lorenzo Latorre and Maximo Santos. He was involved in the unsuccessful revolution against Santos in 1886. He founded the Colorado Party's newspaper *El Día* in 1886. Batlle was appointed political chief of the department of Mines in 1887. He was elected to the chamber of deputies in 1893 and to the senate in 1896. He supported the government of Juan Cuestas in 1897 and became president of the senate, serving until 1901. Batlle was elected president to succeed Cuestas and took office on March 1, 1903. Blanco Party leader Aparicio Saravia led a rebellion soon after his election, and the government defeated the Blancos in September 1904 when Saravia was killed in battle. Batlle sponsored the establishment of secondary schools throughout the country and instituted numerous public works programs. He completed his term of office on March 1, 1907, and departed for Europe. He returned to Uruguay in 1911 and was again elected to the presidency. He took office on March 1, 1911. During his second term he established several national banks and attempted to institute numerous political and economic reforms. He caused a split in the Colorado Party over his proposal to establish a collective head of the executive branch modeled on the Swiss system of government. Batlle completed his term on March 1, 1915. He remained a leading figure in Uruguayan politics and served as president of the National Council of Administration in 1926. Batlle died on October 20, 1929.

CLAUDIO WILLIMAN (President; March 1, 1907–March 1, 1911). Claudio Williman was born on September 2, 1863. He received a degree in law and became a professor at the University of the Republic. He served as a member of the Montevideo municipal council from 1899 to 1901. He became rector of the university in 1902. Williman was also minister of government in José Batlle y Ordóñez's cabinet from 1903 until 1907. He was the Colorado Party's candidate for president in 1907. He was elected to succeed Batlle and took office on March 1, 1907. He led a conservative administration that exercised strict control over public spending. He also dismantled most labor organizations and put down a Blanco uprising in January 1911. He completed his term of office on March 1, 1911, and relinquished office to Batlle following his reelection. Williman died on February 9, 1934.

JOSÉ BATLLE Y ORDÓÑEZ

(President; March 1, 1911–March 1, 1915). *See earlier entry under Heads of State.*

FELICIANO VIERA (President; March 1, 1915–March 1, 1919). Feliciano Viera was born on November 8, 1872. He was a leader in the Colorado Party and a supporter of José Batlle y Ordóñez. He succeeded Batlle as president on March 1, 1915. Viera halted many of his predecessor's social reforms. He succeeded in passing Batlle's constitutional changes that established a nine-man council of state as Uruguay's executive branch. Viera completed his term of office on March 1, 1919. He died in November 13, 1927.

BALTASAR BRUM (President; March 1, 1919–March 1, 1923). Baltasar Brum was born on June 18, 1883. He began a career in politics and became minister of public education in 1913. He served as foreign minister under José Batlle y Ordóñez from 1914 until 1915. He was elected president of Uruguay under the new collegial executive branch and took office on March 1, 1919. He supported such social reforms as minimum wage laws, social security, and child labor laws. He completed his term of office on March 1, 1923. Brum remained a leading political figure, serving as president of the National Council of Administration from 1929 until 1931. When President Gabriel Terra assumed dictatorial powers in 1933, Brum publicly committed suicide on March 31, 1933, in protest against Terra's actions.

JOSÉ SERRATO (President; March 1, 1923–March 1, 1927). José Serrato was born in Montevideo on September 30, 1868. He was educated as a civil engineer and worked as a mathematics professor at the university before entering politics in 1897. He was elected to the Uruguayan congress in 1899 and was subsequently appointed to the senate. He served in several governments as minister of public works and became finance minister in 1904. He was the Colorado Party's nominee for president in 1922. He was elected to the presidency and took office on March 1, 1923. He completed his term of office on March 1, 1927. Serrato remained a leading political figure in Uruguay. He served as foreign minister from 1943 until 1944. He also served as chairman of the Uruguayan delegation to the United Nations in 1945. Serrato died in Montevideo at the age of 91 after a brief illness on September 7, 1960.

JUAN CAMPISTEGUY (President; March 1, 1927–March 1, 1931). Juan Campisteguy was born in Montevideo on September 7, 1859. He was involved in the rebellion against the dictatorship of Maximo Santos in 1886. He became an editor of José Batlle y Ordóñez's newspaper, *El Día*, in 1886. Campisteguy was elected to the house of representatives in 1891 and served as minister of finance from 1897 to 1898. He served in Batlle's cabinet as minister of government from

1903 until 1904. Campisteguy served in the senate from 1905 until 1911. He broke with Batlle over the issue of reforming the executive branch, and he became a founder of the Riveristas, the conservative wing of the Colorado Party. He served as a member of the chamber of deputies from 1920 until 1923 and was a member of the National Council of Administration from 1921 until 1927. He was subsequently elected to the presidency, taking office on March 1, 1927. Campisteguy completed his term of office on March 1, 1934, and retired from politics. He died in Montevideo on September 4, 1937.

GABRIEL TERRA (President; March 1, 1931–June 19, 1938). Gabriel Terra was born in 1873. He was a lawyer and teacher before he entered politics. He served in Claudio Williman's cabinet from 1907 until 1911 and in Baltasar Brum's government from 1919 until 1921. Terra also served as Uruguay's minister to Italy. He served on the National Council of Administration before his election to the presidency. He took office on March 1, 1931. Terra joined with Luis Alberto de Herrera, the opposition Blanco Party leader, to stage a coup on March 13, 1933, that eliminated the National Council of Administration. A new constitution was promoted that grant full executive power to the president. Terra ruled as a dictator for the remainder of his term. He relinquished office to his brother-in-law, Alfredo Baldomir, on June 19, 1938. Terra died on September 15, 1942.

ALFREDO BALDOMIR (President; June 19, 1938–March 1, 1943). Alfredo Baldomir was born in Montevideo on August 27, 1884. He entered the army in 1900. He became head of the Uruguay general staff's engineering section in 1917. He became a professor at the National Military School in 1923. Baldomir served as chief of police in Montevideo from 1931 to 1934. He was the brother-in-law of dictator Gabriel Terra and served in his government as minister of defense from 1935 to 1936. Baldomir was elected to succeed Terra as president, taking office on June 19, 1938. Baldomir supported the United States' war efforts during World War II. This met with opposition from pro–Axis Luis Alberto de Herrera, leader of the Blanco Party. The Blancos had been guaranteed control of half the seats in the senate in an arrangement with Terra. Baldomir dissolved the parliament and removed the Blancos from the cabinet. He restored a democratic system of congressional selection. He completed his term on March 1, 1943. He remained a leader of the Colorado Party until his death in Montevideo on February 25, 1948.

JUAN JOSÉ AMÉZAGA (President; March 1, 1943–March 1, 1947). Juan José de Amézaga was born on January 28, 1881. He was educated as a lawyer and served in the government as minister of agriculture and as Uruguay's delegate to the League of Nations. He was a member of the democratic faction of the Colorado Party and defeated Dr. Luis Alberto de Herrera for the presidency of Uruguay in November 1942. Amézaga took office on March 1, 1943. He survived a right-wing plot against the government in July 1946. Amézaga completed his term of office and stepped down on March 1, 1947. He retired from politics and died after a long illness in Montevideo on August 21, 1956.

Vatican City

Vatican City State is located within the city of Rome, Italy. It was granted recognition as an independent country by the Lateran Treaty with Italy in February 1929 and is ruled by the Supreme Pontiff, or Pope, of the Roman Catholic Church.

HEADS OF STATE

LEO XII (Pope; February 20, 1878–July 20, 1903). Vincenzo Gioacchino Pecci was born in Carpiento Romano on March 2, 1810. He was educated in Rome at the Academy of Noble Ecclesiastics and was ordained a priest in 1837. He subsequently entered the diplomatic corps of the papal states, rising to the position of papal nuncio in Belgium in 1843. He was created an archbishop soon after. He returned to the papal states to serve as bishop of Perugia in 1846 and was created a cardinal in 1853. His theological works and administrative efficiency brought him to the notice of the church hierarchy. He was appointed to the office of camerlengo, or chief administrative officer of the church, in 1877. Pope Pius IX died in February 1878, and Cardinal Pecci was elected pope by the college of cardinals on February 20, 1878. He took the name Leo XII. He continued to assert the temporal authority of the church, though he was more conciliatory toward civil governments than his predecessor. He was an opponent of freemasonry and secular liberalism. He was a strong supporter of the organization of Catholic laity and a proponent of dialogue with non–Catholics. Leo XII died in Rome on July 20, 1903.

PIUS X (Pope; August 4, 1903–August 20, 1914). Giuseppe Melchiorre Sarto was born in Rise, Venetia, then part of the Austrian Empire, on June 2,

1835. He was ordained a priest in 1858 and worked as a parish priest in Venetia. He was created a bishop in 1884 and became a cardinal in 1897. He also served as patriarch of Venice. Cardinal Sarto was elected to succeed Leo XII as pope on August 4, 1903. He took the name Pius X. He was more conservative on social issues than his predecessor, and he urged the censorship of modernist teachings. He also condemned the Catholic political movements in various countries and condemned France's anticlericalism that resulted in legislation separating church and state in 1905. Pius X reorganized the administration of the church and oversaw the publication of a new canon law in 1907. He died in Rome on August 20, 1914, and was canonized a saint on May 29, 1954.

BENEDICT XV (Pope; September 3, 1914–January 22, 1922). Giacomo Della Chiesa was born in Pegli, Sardinia, on November 21, 1954. He was educated at the University of Genoa and was ordained a priest in 1878. He entered the papal diplomatic corps and became secretary to the papal embassy in Spain in 1882. He became an assistant to Cardinal Rampolla, the papal secretary of state, in 1887. He was appointed archbishop of Bologna in 1907 and created a cardinal in May 1914. He was elected to succeed Pius X as pope on September 3, 1914, taking the name Benedict XV. He observed strict neutrality during World War I and attempted without success to mediate a solution to the conflict. Relations between the Vatican and France improved during Benedict's papacy and the British government was granted diplomatic representation at the Vatican. Benedict died in Rome on January 22, 1922.

PIUS XI (Pope; February 6, 1922–February 10, 1939). Ambrosio Damiano Achille Ratti was born in Desio, Lombardy, on May 31, 1857. He was educated at the College of San Carlo in Milan and

Lombard College in Rome. He was ordained a priest in December 1879 and became professor of theology at the College of San Carlo in 1882. He took a position at the Vatican library in 1888, becoming prefect of the library in 1907. He served as papal nuncio in Poland in 1919 and was created a cardinal and named archbishop of Milan in February 1921. He was elected to succeed Benedict XV as pope on February 6, 1922. He chose the name Pius XI and the motto "the peace of Christ in the Kingdom of Christ." Pius signed the Lateran Treaty with Benito Mussolini's Fascist government in Italy in February 1929. The treaty gave Italian recognition to the independence of Vatican City and the Vatican acceptance of the kingdom of Italy and the renunciation by Italy of all claims to the papal states. Pius denounced the extreme anticlericalism in Mexico in 1932 and protested the actions of the Nazi government in Germany in the mid–1930s. He supported a vast increase in overseas missionary work and reunited the Syro-Melankarese Christians of India to the church. Pius XI died in Rome on February 10, 1939.

PIUS XII (Pope; March 2, 1939–October 9, 1958). Pius XII was born Eugenio Maria Giuseppe Giovanni Pacelli in Rome on March 2, 1876. He studied for the priesthood at home and was ordained in 1899. Two years later he joined the Vatican secretariat of state, where he remained until 1917. He was subsequently named the titular archbishop of Sardis and was appointed nuncio to Berlin in 1918. He was created a cardinal in 1929 and returned to the Vatican the following year. He resumed his duties with the secretariat of state and was elected pope on March 2, 1939, succeeding Pius XI. An opponent of Naziism, he was criticized as being too weak in his opposition to Hitler, though he was successful in his attempts to protect the lives of many Jews residing in Italy during World War II. Pius XII organized Catholic Action after the war in opposition to Communism and excommunicated Catholic Communists in 1949. Though considered an autocrat, he liberalized church laws and paved the way for the reforms of the Second Vatican Council under his successor, John XXIII. Pius XII was gravely ill in the winter of 1954, though he recovered to continue his duties. He died at Castel Gandolfo, the papal summer palace near Rome, on October 9, 1958, after suffering several strokes.

Venezuela

Venezuela is a country on the northern coast of South America. It was granted independence from Spain on July 5, 1821.

HEADS OF STATE

CIPRIANO CASTRO (President; October 21, 1899–December 10, 1908). Cipriano Castro was born in Capucho, Tachila, on October 12, 1858. He became active in politics as a supporter of José Manuel Hernandez in the mid-1880s. He was elected to the chamber of deputies in 1890. He was forced into exile in 1892 when Joaquín Crespo seized power in Venezuela. He returned to Venezuela in 1899 and joined with Juan Vicente Gomez to lead a revolt against the government of Ignacio Andrade. The campaign against the government forces lasted from May until October 21, 1899, when Castro took power as provisional president. Castro's allies soon turned against him because of his intransient attitude. Castro crushed a rebellion led by Jose Manuel Hernandez shortly after taking power. A major rebellion broke out in 1902 led by General Manuel Antonio Matos, which lasted for nearly a year. Castro also antagonized the European powers over Venezuela's outstanding debts, and Great Britain, Germany, and Italy established a blockade of Venezuelan ports. The United States ended the blockade, and the dispute was settled by the Permanent Court of Arbitration in the Hague. Castro suffered from poor health in 1908 and went to Germany for medical treatment.

Soon after he left the country, Vice President Juan Vicente Gómez seized power on December 20, 1908. Castro remained in exile and settled in San Juan, Puerto Rico, where he died of a hemorrhage of the stomach on December 5, 1924.

JUAN VICENTE GÓMEZ (President; December 20, 1908–April 19, 1914). Juan Vicente Gómez was born in Tachira on July 24, 1857. He became active in politics in 1892 as a supporter of Cipriano Castro. He was forced into exile in Colombia with Castro soon after. He served in Castro's insurgent army when he returned to Venezuela in 1899. When Castro's forces were victorious, Gómez became his leading advisor. He became vice president under Castro in February 1901 and was placed in command of the army in 1902. He put down several revolts against the regime over the next several years. Gómez was named acting president when Castro went to Europe for medical treatment in 1908, and Gómez seized power on December 20, 1908. Gómez's government was recognized by the United States and Europe, and developed close ties with foreign investors. It granted large concessions to foreign oil companies to exploit Venezuela's oil resources. Gómez's regime, which was sometimes ruthless, brought prosperity and political stability to the country. Gómez allowed Victoriano Márques Bustillos to become provisional president on April 19, 1914. Gómez resumed the presidency on May 3, 1915. Gómez stepped down on April 22, 1929, and arranged for Juan Bautista Perez to succeed him. Perez was forced to resign by the congress, and Gómez again assumed the presidency on June 13, 1931. He retained office until his death on December 17, 1935.

VICTORIANO MÁRQUES BUSTILLOS (President; April 19, 1914–May 3, 1915). Victoriano Márques Bustillos was born in 1858. He was the editor of the newspaper *El Trujillano* from 1877 until 1897. He was elected to congress in 1890 and became associated with Cipriano Castro and Juan Vicente Gómez. He served as secretary to the governor of Trujillo from 1902 to 1904 and was deputy to the state assembly from 1904 to 1906. He was elected to the federal senate in 1910 and served as governor of the federal district from 1911 to 1912. He served in Gómez's cabinet as minister of war from 1913 to 1914. He was selected by Gómez to serve as provisional president from April 19, 1914, until May 3, 1915, while Gómez remained at his home in Maracay. He remained a leading advisor to Gómez and briefly served as first secretary to President Eleazar López Contreras following Gómez's death in 1935. Marques Bustillos died in 1941.

JUAN VICENTE GÓMEZ (President; May 3, 1915–April 22, 1929). *See earlier entry under Heads of State.*

JUAN BAUTISTA PEREZ (President; August 22, 1929–June 13, 1931). Juan Bautista Perez was born on December 21, 1869. He was educated as a lawyer and entered the Venezuelan judiciary. He served as president of the supreme court in 1929. When President Juan Vicente Gómez declined to return

to the capital following his reelection on August 22, 1929, Perez assumed the presidency, though Gómez largely controlled the government from his home in Maracay. The congress forced Perez's resignation on June 13, 1931, and reelected Gómez. Perez was subsequently named ambassador to Spain, a post he held until 1933. Perez was expelled from Venezuela by President Eleazar López Contreras after Gómez's death in 1935. He returned to the country in 1939 and retired from active politics. Much of Perez's property was seized by the military junta that took control in 1945. Perez died in 1952.

JUAN VICENTE GÓMEZ (President; June 13, 1931–December 17, 1935). *See earlier entry under Heads of State.*

ELEAZAR LÓPEZ CONTRERAS (President; December 18, 1935–May 5, 1941). Eleazar López Contreras was born in Queniquea, Tachira, on May 5, 1883. He joined Cipriano Castro's rebel army in 1899 and remained in the army after Castro gained control of Venezuela. He was promoted to the rank of colonel before retiring in 1908. He was recalled to active duty in 1913 and was given command of the Caracas infantry the following year. He was named to Juan Vicente Gómez's cabinet as minister of war in 1914. He was a loyal supporter of Gómez and was also named commander-in-chief in 1930. López succeeded to the presidency on December 18, 1935, following Gómez's death. He initially allowed some political reforms, but sent numerous opposition leaders into exile after crushing an oil strike in February 1937. He exercised greater control over the economy and created the central bank of Venezuela and the industrial bank. López stepped down on May 5, 1941, after having assured the selection of Isaias Medina Angarita as his successor. Lopez planned to return to power after Medina's term ended in 1945, but a military coup ousted Medina on October 18,

1945. López was sent into exile, where he remained until 1948. He returned to Venezuela but was not remained politically active. López died in Caracas on January 2, 1973.

ISAIAS MEDINA ANGARITA
(President; May 5, 1941–October 18, 1945). Isaias Medina Angarita was born in San Cristobal on July 6, 1897. He attended the Venezuelan Military Academy and joined the army in 1914. He was promoted to captain in 1917 and became a teacher at the military school two years later. Medina returned to active duty in 1927 with the rank of lieutenant colonel. He subsequently served again as a teacher at the Venezuelan Military Academy. He was promoted to colonel in 1935 and was named chief of staff of the Venezuelan army. Medina subsequently was appointed minister of war and the navy in the government of President Eleazar López Contreras. He attained the rank of general in 1940. Medina resigned from the cabinet in 1941 to campaign for the presidency. He was elected by the Venezuelan congress and took office on May 5, 1941. He maintained close relations with the United States and severed diplomatic relations with the Axis Powers during World War II. Medina also sought to ensure civil rights for Venezuelans and to maintain democratic principles. Venezuela's economic stability was jeopardized by difficulties in the industrial and agricultural industries. Medina was ousted in a military coup led by Romulo Betancourt on October 18, 1945. He was sent into exile in the United States in December 1945 and lived in New York for the next seven years. He was invited to return to Venezuela shortly after he suffered a stroke in 1952. Medina died at his home in La Florida on September 15, 1953, after a long illness.

ROMULO BETANCOURT (President; October 18, 1945–February 15, 1948). Romulo Betancourt was born in Gautire, near Caracas, on February 22, 1908. He was educated at the Central University in Caracas, where he formed a leftist student movement. Betancourt was briefly imprisoned in 1928 for his opposition to President Juan Vicente Gómez. He led a rebellion against Gómez in April 1928 and fled to Colombia when the rebellion failed. He remained an outspoken opponent of Gómez and supported several abortive rebellions against the dictatorship while in exile in various Latin American countries. Betancourt returned to Venezuela after Gómez's death in 1936 and founded the leftist newspaper *Orve*. He was again ordered into exile by President Eleazar López Contreras the following year, but remained in hiding in Venezuela. He was captured in 1939 and sent into exile in Chile and Argentina. Betancourt was allowed to return to Venezuela in 1941 and founded the Democratic Action Party. The party's nominee, Romulo Gallegos Freire, was defeated by General Isaias Medina Angarita in the presidential election in 1941. Betancourt founded another opposition newspaper, *El Pais*, in 1943. He participated in a coup against Medina Angarita on October 18, 1945. Medina Angarita was ousted, and Betancourt became provisional president as head of the seven-man revolutionary junta. Betancourt promised to allow free elections in 1948, and the Democratic Action Party nominee, Romulo Gallegos, was elected president. Betancourt relinquished office to him on February 15, 1948. Gallegos was ousted in a military coup led by former junta member Marcos Perez Jimenez in November 1948. Betancourt was again sent into exile to the United States. He remained out of Venezuela for nine years, while he traveled to Cuba, Costa Rica, and Puerto Rico. Betancourt was invited to return to Venezuela following Perez Jimenez's ouster in January 1958. He reorganized the Democratic Action Party and was the party's nominee in elections the following December. Betancourt was vic-

torious and took office on February 13, 1959. He pushed for an agrarian reform program and increased industrial development in the country. He survived an army revolt in April 1960 and an assassination attempt in June 1960, when a bomb exploded near his car. Betancourt completed his term of office on December 1, 1963, and relinquished the presidency to his long-time associate, Raul Leoni. Betancourt traveled throughout Europe after leaving office. He settled in Switzerland, where he remained until 1972. He returned to Venezuela and again became active in Venezuelan political affairs and served as the elder statesman of his party and the democracy movement. Betancourt moved to New York City in the early 1980s to work on his memoirs. He died there of complications from a stroke on September 28, 1981.

Vietnam

Vietnam is a nation in Southeast Asia that became a French protectorate in the nineteenth century. The Emperor of Annam reigned in the north and central sections of Vietnam, but was largely under the control of the French until 1954 when the country gained independence. However, the country was divided into Chinese-backed, Communist North Vietnam and Western-oriented South Vietnam.

HEADS OF STATE

THANH-THAI (Emperor; January 31, 1889–September 3, 1907). Thanh-Thai was born in 1878. He was the son of Emperor Duc-Duc, who reigned briefly in July 1883 before he was deposed by the French. Thanh-Thai became the tenth emperor in the Nguyen Dynasty when the French installed him on the throne at the age of ten on January 31, 1889. Thanh-Thai opposed France's acquisition of the ports of Tourane and Haiphong and the city of Hanoi during his reign. He became involved in conspiracies against the colonial power and was forced to abdicate on September 3, 1907, when the French learned of his actions. He was deported to Reunion Island off the African coast in 1915. He returned to Saigon in 1947. He lived there as a private citizen until his death on March 20, 1954.

DUY-TAN (Emperor; September 3, 1907–May 1916). Duy-Tan was born in 1899. He was the fifth son of Emperor Thanh-Thai. He was placed on the throne of Annam after his father was deposed by the French on September 3, 1907. He became a critic of the French colonial authorities at an early age. Colonial oppression of his subjects led him to become involved with Vietnamese nationalists in 1916. The French became aware of a planned military rebellion and Duy-Tan was deposed in May 1916. He was deported to Reunion Island off the African coast. Duy-Tan remained there until World War II. He joined the Allied forces with the rank of major and was lost in a plane crash in 1945.

KHAI-DINH (Emperor; May 1916–November 6, 1925). Khai-Dinh was the son of Emperor Dong-Khanh, who reigned from 1885 until 1889. He was chosen by the French to succeed to the throne in May 1916 when Emperor Duy-Tan was deposed for conspiring against the colonial authorities. Khai-Dinh was a weak ruler who was often manipulated by the French. He became the first emperor of Annam to leave his country when he made a state visit to Paris in 1922. Khai-Dinh remained on the throne until his death in Saigon on November 6, 1925.

BAO DAI (Emperor; November 6, 1925–August 28, 1945). Bao Dai was born Nguyen Vinh Thuy in Hue on October 22, 1913. He was the son of Khai-Dinh, who reigned as emperor from 1916 to 1925. Bao Dai was educated in Paris. He ascended the throne upon the death of his father on November 6, 1925, but did not return to Vietnam from France until two months later to begin his reign. A regency council was established to rule until he came of age, and Bao Dai returned to France to continue his education. He returned to Vietnam to take the throne of the French protectorate in September 1932. He ruled under the French colonial government until 1940, when the Japanese invaded Indochina. The French were expelled in March 1945, and Bao Dai accepted limited independence from the Japanese. Japan was defeated the following August, and Bao Dai was forced by the Viet Minh to abdicate on August 25, 1945. He cooperated briefly with Ho Chi Minh, the president of the newly established Democratic Republic of Vietnam (North Vietnam). He went into exile in Hong Kong in July 1946. The French attempted to reestablish colonial authority in Indochina and engaged in a war with the Viet Minh. The French entered into negotiations with Bao Dai, and the autonomous Associated State of Vietnam was established in March 1949. Bao Dai became the chief of government and took office in Saigon on June 14, 1949. The French continued to battle Ho Chi Minh's troops until suffering a major defeat at Dien Bien Phu in July 1954. A treaty was agreed to in Geneva that established two separate countries divided by the seventeenth parallel. Bao Dai remained head of state of South Vietnam. His premier, Ngo Dinh Diem, sponsored a referendum in 1955 to determine the form of government for Vietnam. The plebiscite overwhelmingly endorsed a republic, and Ngo Dinh Diem was selected as president on October 26, 1955. Bao Dai remained in exile in France and was not involved in Vietnamese political affairs. He lived in a modest apartment in Paris until his death in a military hospital there on July 31, 1997.

Yugoslavia

Yugoslavia was a federation of states in southeastern Europe, consisting of Serbia, Montenegro, Croatia, Bosnia-Hercegovina, Macedonia, and Slovenia. It was proclaimed the kingdom of the Serbs, Croats, and Slovenes on December 1, 1918, following World War I. Its name was changed to Yugoslavia in 1929.

HEADS OF STATE

PETER I (King; December 1, 1918–August 16, 1921). Peter Karageorgevich was born in Belgrade on July 11, 1844, the third son of Prince Alexander Kara-georgevich. He was educated in Switzerland and France and joined the French Foreign Legion as Lieutenant Kara in 1867. He served with distinction in the

Franco-Prussian War in 1871 and made a daring escape after being captured by the Germans. Several years later he fought against the Turks in Herzegovina. He subsequently settled in Montenegro and married Zorka, the eldest daughter of Prince Nicholas in July 1883. He moved to Geneva after the death of his wife in 1890. The Obrenovich dynasty in Serbia became extinct with the assassination of King Alexander in 1903, and Peter was elected king of Serbia on June 15, 1903. He returned to Belgrade and was crowned on September 21, 1904. He reigned as a constitutional monarch and attempted to bring stability to Serbia's political situation. His failing health and advanced age led to his appointment of his son and heir, Prince Alexander, as regent in June 1914, near the start of World War I. He retreated with the Serbian army to Albania as the country was overrun by the combined German-Autro-Hungarian-Bulgarian coalition during the war. He returned to Belgrade after the liberation at the end of the war and was proclaimed king of the newly formed Kingdom of the Serbs, Croats, and Slovenes on December 1, 1918. Peter died at Topchider, near Belgrade, on August 16, 1921.

ALEXANDER (King; August 16, 1921–October 9, 1934). Alexander was born in Cetinje on December 16, 1888. He was the second son of Peter Karageorgevích and Zorka. He spent much of his youth in exile in Geneva with his father. He was sent to St. Petersburg in 1899. His father gained the throne of Serbia in 1903. Alexander returned to Serbia in 1909 and became heir to the throne when his brother, George, renounced his right of succession in March 1909. Alexander commanded the Serbian army during the first Balkan War of 1912 and distinguished himself in the battle of Kumanovo. He also served with honor during the second Balkan War. Alexander was named regent of Serbia on June 24, 1914, due to the poor health of his

father. He also served as commander-in-chief of the armed forces. He remained at army headquarters during World War I and returned to Belgrade in October 1918. Alexander remained regent of the newly formed kingdom of the Serbs, Croats, and Slovenes on December 1, 1918. The constituent assembly passed a new constitution in June 1921, and Alexander narrowly escaped an assassination attempt after swearing allegiance to that constitution. He succeeded as king upon the death of his father on August 16, 1921. He married Marie, daughter of Ferdinand I of Rumania, on June 8, 1922. They had three children: Peter in 1923, Tomislav in 1928, and Andrei in 1929. Political conflict between the Serbs and Croats escalated in the kingdom following the murder of two Croatian politicians on the floor of the Skupstina (parliament) in June 1928. Alexander felt compelled to abolish the constitution in January 1929 and assumed full powers to keep the country from splitting apart. He changed the name of the kingdom to Yugoslavia on October 3, 1929, and promoted a new constitution in September 1931. Yugoslavia's relationship with its neighbors Italy and Hungary was strained during the early 1930s. Alexander survived another assassination attempt in 1933. He was murdered in Marseilles, France, by Vlada Cherzozensky, a Croatian terrorist, on October 9, 1934.

PAUL (Regent; October 9, 1934–March 27, 1941). Paul Karageorgevích was born in St. Petersburg, Russia, on April 15, 1893. He was the son of Prince Arsen Karageorge and the younger brother of King Peter I of Serbia. He was educated at Christ Church, Oxford, in England. He was named senior regent for his nephew King Peter II of Yugoslavia, following the assassination of his cousin, King Alexander, on October 9, 1934. The other members of the regency council included the minister of education, Radenko Stankovic, and Ivan Perovic, the governor of Croatia. Paul advocated a conciliatory policy with Adolf Hitler's Nazi Germany. King Peter ousted the regency on March 27, 1941, shortly before the German invasion of Yugoslavia. Paul fled the country and was interned in Kenya by the British until the end of World War II. He remained in exile after the war in Florence, Italy. He died in Paris on September 14, 1976.

PETER II (King; October 9, 1934–November 29, 1945). Peter Karageorgevích was born on September 6, 1923. He was the oldest son of King Alexander and Queen Marie of Yugoslavia. He succeeded his father as king of Yugoslavia following Alexander's assassination in France on October 9, 1934. King Peter II was eleven years old at the time of his ascension to the throne and ruled under a regency council headed by his cousin, Prince Paul. Peter came of age in 1941 and ruled briefly, leading a revolt against the pro-German Prince Paul before being ousted by the German occupation forces. He went into exile in Great Britain and headed a Yugoslav government-in-exile. During the war he flew combat missions with the Royal Air Force. He also supported the Yugoslavian resistance forces led by General Draga Mikhailovich during World War II. A rival resistance force was led by Communist partisan Marshal Tito. Tito's forces captured General Mikhailovich and executed him. Marshal Tito set up a Communist government after the liberation from the Germans, and King Peter was formally deposed on November 29, 1945. Peter remained in exile and was employed by a public relations firm in New York in the 1950s. He worked for the Sterling Savings and Loan Association of California, where he became chairman of their international advisory board in 1967. He died in Los Angeles from complications from pneumonia on November 3, 1970.

HEADS OF GOVERNMENT

NIKOLA PAŠIĆ (Prime Minister; December 1, 1918–December 19, 1918). Nikola Pašić was born on January 1, 1846. He was educated in Switzerland and became involved in Serbian politics at an early age. He was a founder of the Radical Party in 1881 and was a leading advocate of Serbian independence from Turkish and Austro-Hungarian rule. Pašić was arrested and sentenced to death for his participation in an insurrection. He escaped from prison and went into exile in Bulgaria, where he was instrumental in forcing the abdication of King Milan. Pašić served as prime minister several times following the ascension to the throne of King Alexander in 1889, heading the government from February 1891 until August 22, 1892. He was appointed Serbia's minister to St. Petersburg in 1893. He returned to serve as prime minister on December 10, 1904, the year after the assassination of King Alexander. He retained that position until May 25, 1905, and was again named to head the government on April 28, 1906. He served until June 23, 1908, and again from October 13, 1909, until June 26, 1911. During that period he attempted to strengthen the Serbian army and stabilize the dynasty by forcing Prince George to renounce his right of succession in favor of his brother Alexander. Pašić was again named prime minister on September 12, 1912. He was a supporter of the Balkan League and continued to head the government during World War I until November 30, 1918. He was instrumental in the formation of the Kingdom of the Serbs, Croats, and Slovenes, and was named prime minister of the new kingdom on January 2, 1921.

He stepped down on July 27, 1924, but reclaimed the office on November 6, 1924. He remained leader of the government until April 5, 1926. Pašić died on December 10, 1926.

STOYAN PROTIĆ (Prime Minister; December 29, 1918–August 2, 1919). Stoyan Protić was born in Kruševac on January 28, 1857. He was first elected to the Serbian parliament in 1897. He also served as editor of the Liberal-Radical journal *Dnevnik*. He was a critic of the policies of King Milan and was imprisoned several times for his opposition to the King. He served in the Serbian cabinet as minister of the interior in 1903. He served as minister of finance from 1909 until 1911. He was one of the authors of the Pact of Corfu, which ultimately created Yugoslavia. He served in the Serbian government-in-exile in Corfu as finance minister during World War I. He served as head of the newly formed Yugoslav government from December 29, 1918, until August 2, 1919. He again headed the government from February 19, 1920, until May 16, 1920. He subsequently served as minister of the interior in Milan Vesnić's government until 1921. Protić died on October 28, 1923.

LJUBOMIR DAVIDOVIĆ (Prime Minister; August 2, 1919–February 19, 1920). Ljuba Davidović was born in Vlasko Polje in 1863. He was a teacher of natural science before entering Serbian politics. He joined the Serbian Radical Party and was elected to the chamber of deputies in 1901. He left the Radicals to form an independence radical party the following year. Davidović was named to the cabinet as minister of education in 1904. He was elected president of the Skupstina (parliament) the following year. He soon returned to the cabinet to head the education ministry and continued to hold that position for most of the next thirteen years. Davidović was a founder and president of the new Democratic Party in 1919. He formed a coalition government with the Socialists on August 2, 1919, heading the government until February 19, 1920. He again headed a coalition government as prime minister from July 27, 1924, until October 15, 1924. He was largely out of power during King Alexander's reign from 1929 to 1934. He was a leader of the Democratic Party's opposition to the government of Milan Stojadinovic in the elections of 1935 and 1938. Davidović died in Belgrade on February 19, 1940.

STOYAN PROTIĆ (Prime Minister; February 19, 1920–May 16, 1920). *See earlier entry under Heads of Government.*

MILAN VESNIĆ (Prime Minister; May 16, 1920–January 2, 1921). Milan R. Vesnić (Milenko Vesnitch) was born in Dunišić on February 25, 1862. He was named Serbia's minister to Rome in 1901, and became minister to France in 1904. Vesnic was a member of the Serbian delegation to the Balkan Peace Conference in London after the First Balkan War. He was minister of finance in the Serbian government during World War I and served on various diplomatic delegations during the conflict. He was a signatory of the Treaty of Versailles for the newly formed state of Yugoslavia. Vesnic subsequently served as foreign minister and headed the government as prime minister from May 16, 1920, until January 2, 1921. He was then again named minister to France and died in Paris on May 15, 1921.

NIKOLA PAŠIĆ (Prime Minister; January 2, 1921–July 27, 1924). *See earlier entry under Heads of Government.*

LJUBOMIR DAVIDOVIĆ (Prime Minister; July 27, 1924–October 15, 1924. *See earlier entry under Heads of Government.*

NIKOLA PAŠIĆ (Prime Minister; November 6, 1924–April 5, 1926). *See earlier entry under Heads of Government.*

NIKOLA UZONOVIĆ (Prime Minister; April 8, 1926–February 8, 1928). Nikola T. Uzonović (Ouzounovitch) was born in Nish in 1873. He began his political career as a county magistrate before being elected to the Serbian parliament in 1907. He also served as mayor of Nish and was an officer during World War I. He remained in the parliament after the formation of the Kingdom of the Serbs, Croats, and Slovenes in 1921. He was a leader of the Serb Radical Party in 1921. Uzonović was chosen to head the government on April 8, 1926. He headed several successive ministries before stepping down on February 8, 1928. He again served as prime minister from January 27, 1934, until December 19, 1934. Uzonović died in Belgrade on September 20, 1954.

VELJA VUKITCHEVICH (Prime Minister; February 28, 1928–July 28, 1928). Velja Vukitchevich was born on July 23, 1871. He became a leading political figure in Yugoslavia as chairman of the Radical Party. Vukitchevich formed a government as prime minister on February 28, 1928. During his term hostilities between the Serbs and the Croats continued to increase. In June 1928 Stefan Radic, the founder and leader of the Croatian Peasant Party, was assassinated in parliament with two other Croatian deputies. This action forced Vukitchevich to resign on July 28, 1928. He subsequently retired from public life and died in Belgrade on November 27, 1930.

ANTON KOROSEC (Prime Minister; July 28, 1928–January 6, 1929). Anton Korosec was born in Videm, Slovenia, on May 12, 1872. He was a Catholic priest and an early leader of the Slovene People's Party. He served in the Austrian parliament as a deputy from 1906 until 1918. He participated in several governments after the establishment of the Kingdom of Serbs, Croats, and Slovenes in 1918. He also served as chairman of the Zagreb Popular Vece. He be-

came prime minister on July 28, 1928, and was a supporter of autonomy for Slovenia. He stepped down from office on January 6, 1929. Korosec served as minister of the interior in Milan Stojadinovic's government from 1935 until 1938. He subsequently retired from politics and died in Belgrade on December 14, 1940.

PETAR ŽIVKOVITCH (Prime Minister; January 7, 1929–April 4, 1932). Petar Zivkovitch was born in Negotin, Serbia, on January 23, 1879. He attended the Belgrade Military Academy, graduating in 1899. He was involved in the conspiracy that resulted in the assassination of King Alexander Obrenovich in 1903. He rose through the ranks of the army, becoming a general in 1928. He was a close ally of King Alexander of Yugoslavia, serving as commander of the Royal Guard. He was named prime minister on January 7, 1929. He stepped down on April 4, 1932. He returned to the government as minister of war after the assassination of Alexander in 1934. He was dismissed from the cabinet in March 1936 and barely escaped an assassination attempt the following year. He subsequently headed the Yugoslav National Party. Živkovitch escaped the country after the German invasion in 1941. He went to Capetown, South Africa, and was named commander-in-chief of Yugoslav forces in exile. He resigned that position in December 1943. He was an opponent of the Communist government formed by Marshal Tito after the war. Živkovitch was tried and sentenced to death in absentia. He remained in exile and died in Paris on February 3, 1947.

VOYISLAV MARINKOVITCH (Prime Minister; April 4, 1932–July 1932). Voyislav Marinkovitch was born in Belgrade on May 1, 1876. He was educated in Belgrade and at the Sorbonne in Paris, where he studied law. He returned to Belgrade in 1900 and entered the ministry of finance. He was elected to the Serbian parliament, or Skupstina, in 1906. Marinkovitch was appointed Serbia's chief financial delegate at the Paris Conference after the Second Balkan War in 1913. He was named to Nikola Pašić's cabinet in 1914 and was instrumental in the drafting of the Corfu declaration. He returned to the government following the establishment of the Kingdom of the Serbs, Croats, and Slovenes, again serving under Pašić as minister of the interior in 1922. He was appointed foreign minister in July 1924. He was again named foreign minister in Velja Vukitchevich's government in February 1928, retaining the post for the next five years. He served as president of the Council of the League of Nations in Geneva in 1930. He also became prime minister in succession to General Petar Živkovitch on April 4, 1932. Marinkovitch stepped down several months later in July 1932. He returned to the cabinet as minister without portfolio following the assassination of King Alexander in October 1934. He retired from politics shortly before his death on September 18, 1935.

MILAN SRŠKIĆ (Prime Minister; July 1932–January 25, 1934). Milan Srškić was born in 1880. He was a leading Centralist who was chosen to head the government after the resignation of Prime Minister Voyislav Marinkovitch in July 1932. His cabinet resigned on November 3, 1932, but resumed office after several days with little change. He stepped down on January 25, 1934. Srškić was named to Nikola Uzonović's cabinet as minister without portfolio after the assassination of King Alexander in 1934. He resigned with the rest of the cabinet near the end of the year. He died in 1937.

NIKOLA UZONOVIĆ (Prime Minister; January 27, 1934–December 19, 1934). *See earlier entry under Heads of Government.*

BOGOLJUB JEVTIC (Prime Minister; December 31, 1934–June 23, 1935). Bogoljub Jevtic was born on December 24, 1886. He served as foreign minister at the time of the assassination of King Alexander in October 1934. The Regent, Prince Paul, called upon Jevtić to form a government as prime minister on December 31, 1934. He dissolved parliament and called for new elections. His coalition government collapsed when Milan Stojadinović and his supporters resigned from the government. Jevtić stepped down on June 23, 1935. He died in Paris on June 7, 1960.

MILAN STOJADINOVIĆ (Prime Minister; June 23, 1935–February 4, 1939). Milan Stojadinović was born in Chacak on August 4, 1888. He graduated from the University of Belgrade in 1910. He entered politics and served as finance minister from 1922 to 1926 and from 1934 to 1935. He was named prime minister on June 23, 1935, and headed the Yugoslav Radical Union. He headed an unpopular Fascist government until February 4, 1939. Stojadinović remained in Yugoslavia until March 1941. He was turned over to the British and was interned in Mauritius for the remainder of the war. Stojadinović went to Argentina after World War II. He lived there in exile until his death in Buenos Aires on October 24, 1961.

DRAGIŠHA CVETKOVIĆ (Prime Minister; February 4, 1939–March 27, 1941). Dragišha Cvetković (Tsvetković) was born in Nis on January 15, 1893. He became a lawyer and served in the government as minister of religion in 1928. He was an opponent of the dictatorship of King Alexander. He was elected to the parliament in 1935 after Alexander's assassination and became minister of social policy and public health. He became head of the government on February 4, 1941. He signed the Berlin Pact in 1941, which bound Yugoslavia with Nazi Germany. He was ousted in a coup on March

27, 1941, and was replaced by Dušan Simović. Cvetković left Yugoslavia in 1943. He remained in exile after the war and died in Paris on February 18, 1969.

DUŠAN T. SIMOVIĆ (Prime Minister; March 27, 1941–January 11, 1942). Dušan T. Simović was born in Kragujevac on November 9, 1882. He graduated from the Belgrade Military Academy in 1905. He saw action in the Balkan Wars of 1912 and 1913 and during World War I. He was promoted to brigadier general in 1925. He became chief of the Yugoslavian army general staff at the start of World War II in 1939. He subsequently served as chief of the royal air staff. He became prime minister following the coup d'état that abolished the regency of Prince Paul on March 27, 1941. The Simović government fled when Yugoslavia was occupied by the Nazis in April 1941. He remained prime minister of the Yugoslav government-in-exile until January 11, 1942. He returned to Yugoslavia after the liberation in 1945. He retired to Belgrade, where he died on August 26, 1962.

SLOBODAN JOVANOVIĆ (Prime Minister; January 11, 1942–June 17, 1943). Slobodan Jovanović was born in Novi Sad on November 21, 1869. He received a degree in law in Geneva in 1890. He served as professor at the University of Belgrade from 1897 until 1941. He was called upon to serve as Dušan Simović's deputy prime minister from March until April 1941. Jovanović became head of the Yugoslav government-in-exile in London on January 11, 1942. He retained that position until June 17, 1943. He was an opponent of Marshal Tito's Communist regime after the liberation of Yugoslavia. He was tried in absentia in July 1946 and sentenced to sixteen years imprisonment. Jovanović remained in exile in London as leader of an exile group. He died in there on December 12, 1958.

MILOŠH TRIFUNOVIĆ (Prime Minister; June 17, 1943–August 10, 1943). Milošh Trifunović was born in 1871. He was a leader of the Radical Party in the Yugoslav parliament and served as a minister in several governments. He joined the National Coalition government after the ouster of the pro–Fascist government in 1941. He fled with the government after the Nazi occupation several weeks later. He became prime minister of the Yugoslav government-in-exile in London on June 17, 1943. He resigned on August 10, 1943, over conflicts between the Croats and the Serbs in the government. He returned to Yugoslavia after the liberation. Trifunović was arrested by Tito's Communist government in 1947 on charges of spying for the United States. He was sentenced to eight years imprisonment but was released after eighteen months. He subsequently lived in retirement in Belgrade, where he died on February 21, 1957.

MILAN PURITIĆ (Prime Minister; August 10, 1943–June 1, 1944). Milan Puritić was born in 1891. He fled Yugoslavia after the German occupation in 1941 and served in the government-in-exile. He succeeded Milošh Trifunović as prime minister of the exiled government on August 10, 1943. He stepped down on June 1, 1944. He remained in exile after the war and the establishment of a Communist state under Marshal Tito. Puritić was tried in absentia in Belgrade in July 1946 and sentenced to 16 years imprisonment.

IVAN SUBAŠIĆ (Prime Minister; June 1, 1944–March 6, 1945). Ivan Subašić was born in Vukova Gorica, Karlovac, on May 27, 1892. He was educated as a lawyer and was a leader of the Croatian Peasant Party. He served as Croatia's ban, or governor, from 1939 until 1941. He emigrated to Yugoslavia in April 1941. He served as prime minister in the Yugoslav government-in-exile from June 1, 1944, until March 6, 1945.

He served as foreign minister in Marshal Tito's provisional government from March until November 1945. Subašić subsequently retired from politics. He died in Zagreb on March 22, 1955.

TITO (Prime Minister; March 6, 1945–June 29, 1963). Josip Broz was born in Kumrovec, Croatia, on May 7, 1892. He served in the Austro-Hungarian army during World War I. He was captured by the Russians in March 1915 and became a Communist three years later. He returned to Croatia (which was then part of the new Kingdom of Serbs, Croats, and Slovenes) and was active in the Communist party there. He was arrested in 1928 and sentenced to five years in prison. When he was released, he went to Moscow to meet with the Comintern. During the 1930s he adopted the name Tito as a cover for his Communist activities. He was active as a recruiter for the Republican cause during the Spanish Civil War in 1936. Tito became secretary-general of the Yugoslav Communist party the following year. After the German occupation of Yugoslavia in April 1941, Tito became the leader of the Partisan Resistance. His forces were suc-cessful in driving the Germans out of large portions of Yugoslavia, and his successes were recognized by the Allied forces. Tito entered Belgrade on October 20, 1944, and began the transformation of Yugoslavia into a Communist state. He was recognized as prime minister on March 6, 1945. Tito broke with the Soviet Communists and Joseph Stalin in 1948 following an attempt by the Soviets to oust him. This began a feud between Tito and Stalin that lasted until the Soviet dictator's death in 1953. Tito sponsored a new constitution in 1953 that gave more power to an executive presidency. He was elected president on January 13, 1953. Tito was also a leader of the nonaligned nations movement and served as host to the first conference in 1961. He remained prime minister until June 29, 1963, when he relinquished the position. Tito remained the predominant force in Yugoslavian politics throughout his life. He was named president for life in 1974. Tito became seriously ill in January 1980 when his left leg was amputated because of a blood vessel blockage. He remained hospitalized in Ljubljana until his death from heart failure on May 4, 1980.

Zanzibar

Zanzibar is an island in the Indian Ocean. It was granted independence from Great Britain on December 9, 1963.

HEADS OF STATE

HAMOUD IBN MOHAMMED (Sultan; August 27, 1896–July 18, 1902). Hamoud ibn Mohammed ibn Said was born in 1853. He was a cousin of Hamad ibn Thuwaini, who died in August 1896. Another cousin, Said Khalid, seized power by force, though his rule was not recognized by the British consular powers. Great Britain sent warships to bom-bard the palace and depose him and Said Khalid fled into exile in German East Africa. Hamoud was proclaimed sultan on August 27, 1896. The following year Hamoud issued a degree outlawing slavery in Zanzibar. He ruled under British authority until his death on July 18, 1902.

ALI IBN HAMOUD (Sultan; July 20, 1902–December 9, 1911). Ali ibn Hamoud was born on June 7, 1884. He was the son of Hamoud ibn Mohammed and he succeeded to the sultanate on July 20, 1902, following his father's death. Sultan Ali suffered from poor health and abdicated on December 9, 1911. He died in 1918.

KHALIFAH IBN HARUB (Sultan; December 9, 1911–October 9, 1960). Seyyid Khalifah ibn Harub ibn Thuwaini ibn Said was born in Muscat, Arabia, on August 26, 1877. He ascended to the throne of Zanzibar following the abdication of Sultan Ali ibn Hamoud on December 9, 1911. He ruled as a constitutional monarch and was a loyal ally of Great Britain. Khalifah supported the Allies during World War I and called upon all Muslims in East Africa to do likewise. He remained loyal to Great Britain during World War II. He attended the coronation of Queen Elizabeth II in London in 1952. The British colonial authorities allowed the organization of political parties in 1955, and a growing independence movement developed in the late 1950s. Sultan Khalifah remained Zanzibar's monarch until his death in the royal palace on October 9, 1960.

Index